THEMES IN ROMAN SOCIETY AND CULTURE

An Introduction to Ancient Rome

Edited by Matt Gibbs | Milorad Nikolic | Pauline Ripat

OXFORD

UNIVERSITY PRESS

OXFORD
UNIVERSITY PRESS

Oxford University Press is a department of the University of Oxford.
It furthers the University's objective of excellence in research, scholarship,
and education by publishing worldwide. Oxford is a registered trade mark of
Oxford University Press in the UK and in certain other countries.

Published in Canada by
Oxford University Press
8 Sampson Mews, Suite 204,
Don Mills, Ontario M3C 0H5 Canada

www.oupcanada.com

Library and Archives Canada Cataloguing in Publication

Themes in Roman society and culture : an introduction to ancient Rome / edited by Matt Gibbs,
Milorad Nikolic, and Pauline Ripat.

Includes bibliographical references and index.
ISBN 978-0-19-544519-0

1. Rome—Civilization. 2. Rome—History. I. Gibbs, Matt, 1976–
II. Nikolic, Milorad, 1968– III. Ripat, Pauline, 1973–

DG77.T54 2013   937'.63   C2013-900339-8

Oxford University Press is committed to our environment.
Wherever possible, our books are printed on paper which comes from responsible sources.

Printed and bound in Canada

7 8 9 — 19 18 17

Contents

Preface and Acknowledgements x

Contributors xii

A Note to the Reader xv

Introduction xxiii

1   The Development of Roman Social History   1
Pauline Ripat

Introduction   2
The Development of Social History   3
Social History and the Classics   4
    Traditional Approaches to Roman History before the 1960s   4
    New Approaches to Ancient History   7
    Social History and the Classics: Debates and Problems   11
Social History and This Volume   15
Summary   18
Questions for Review and Discussion   19
Suggested Reading   20
Notes   21

2   A Summary of Roman History   23
Matt Gibbs, Milorad Nikolic, and Andrew Sherwood

Introduction   24
Early Rome: Legends and Kings   25
The Early Republic (508–287 BCE)   26
The Middle Republic (287–133 BCE)   27
The Late Republic (133–31 BCE)   28
Augustus   33
The Julio-Claudians (14–68 CE)   34
The Flavians (69–96 CE)   36
From Nerva to the Antonines (96–192 CE)   38
The Severans (193–235 CE)   40
"Military Anarchy," or "Crisis of the Third Century" (235–284 CE),
    and Tetrarchy (293–311 CE)   42

Summary   43
Questions for Review and Discussion   43
Suggested Reading   44
Notes   45

3   Class and Status   46
Pauline Ripat

Introduction   47
Terms   49
   Class   49
   Status   50
Class and Status: Changes over Time   52
Mobility   57
Did Class and Status Matter?   59
The Persistence of Hierarchy   65
Summary   67
Questions for Review and Discussion   67
Suggested Reading   68
Notes   69

4   Roman Slavery   72
Leslie Shumka

Introduction   72
Definitions   74
Sources of Slaves   77
Slave Experience and Resistance   82
The Success of Slavery at Rome   88
Summary   90
Questions for Review and Discussion   91
Suggested Reading   91
Notes   92

5   The Roman Household   94
Alison Jeppesen-Wigelsworth

Introduction   95
Terms, Concepts, and the Shape of the Roman Family   96
Household Members and Relationships   98
   Wives and Marriage   98
   Parents and Children   103
   Slaves and Freedpersons   107

The Physical House   109
Summary   112
Questions for Review and Discussion   113
Suggested Reading   113
Notes   114

6   Education in the Roman World   117
Fanny Dolansky

Introduction   118
"Letters are a good start to life."   120
    The First Elements: Early Education at Home and School   120
    Beyond the Basics: *Grammaticē*, Rhetoric, and Vocational Training   124
"A proper education is the source and root of all goodness."   130
Summary   134
Questions for Review and Discussion   135
Suggested Reading   135
Notes   136

7   Latin Literature   139
Luke Roman

Introduction   140
Defining *Literature*   140
Chronology   144
Greece and Rome   146
Literature and the Roman Elite   153
Tradition, Intertextuality, and Decline   158
Summary   160
Questions for Review and Discussion   161
Suggested Reading   161
Notes   163

8   Roman Sexuality and Gender   164
Kelly Olson

Introduction   164
Literary Sources   165
Prudery and Expurgation   167
Terminology   169
Gender Identity versus Sexual Orientation   171
The Phallus   173
Female Sexuality   174

Sexual Scenes   177
   Private Houses   177
   Public Places   178
Oral Sex   179
Same-Sex Couplings   179
Passive-Sexual Labels as Abuse   181
Pederasty   182
Female Homosexuality   183
Sexuality and the Law: *Stuprum* and Rape   184
Summary   186
Questions for Review and Discussion   186
Suggested Reading   187
Notes   188

9   Religion at Rome   189
Andreas Bendlin

Introduction   191
Practice, Belief, and Divinity: Some Salient Features of Religion at Rome   191
Civic Religion   197
From Roman Religion to Religion at Rome   203
Summary   213
Questions for Review and Discussion   214
Suggested Reading   214
Notes   215

10   Roman Government in the Republic and Early Empire   217
John Vanderspoel

Introduction   218
The Voting Assemblies   219
   The "Servian Constitution"   219
   The Tribal Assembly   221
   The Plebeian Assembly   223
   The Curial Assembly   224
The Senate and Senators   225
The Elected Officials of the State   227
   Annually Elected Magistrates   228
   Other Elected Officials   234
   Dictator   236
   Priesthoods   236
The People in the Late Republic and Early Empire   236

The Imperial Period and Beyond   237
Summary   239
Questions for Review and Discussion   239
Suggested Reading   239
Note   240

11   Crime, Law, and Order   241
Benjamin Kelly

Introduction   242
"Crime" in the Roman World   243
Courts, Justice, and Terror   248
Roman "Policing Officials"   250
Self-Help   255
Summary   258
Questions for Review and Discussion   259
Suggested Reading   259
Notes   260

12   Entertainment in the Roman World   263
Michael Carter

Introduction   264
Public Entertainment   265
    Ludi   266
    Munera   272
The Political Importance of Entertainment Spectacles   279
Summary   283
Questions for Review and Discussion   283
Suggested Reading   284
Notes   284

13   The Roman Army   285
Conor Whately

Introduction   286
The Composition of the Roman Army   287
    The Legions   287
    The Auxiliaries   289
    The Praetorian Guard   292
Professionalization and the Roman Army   294
Warfare   296

Preparing for War   296
Battle, Bravado, and Discipline   298
War: The Aftermath   299
The Army and Society   300
The Army and Civilians: Policing and the Abuse of Authority   300
The Army and Civilians: Women and Families   301
The Army as Distinct Society   303
Summary   304
Questions for Review and Discussion   304
Suggested Reading   304
Notes   305

14   Foreign Relations: War and Conquest   307
Greg Fisher

Introduction   307
Foreign Relations and Expansion to the End of the Second Punic War: Concepts
    and Themes   309
Roman Expansion in the Second Century BCE: Greed and Fear?   313
The End of the Republic: The Consequences of Conquest   315
Pax Romana: New Enemies   318
The Third Century CE: A Changing Order   321
From Diocletian to Theodosius: Unity and Division   323
Summary   325
Questions for Review and Discussion   326
Suggested Reading   327
Notes   328

15   The Economy   329
Matt Gibbs

Introduction   331
Evidence and Theory   331
Demography   333
Land and Property   334
Moneylending and Interest Rates   338
Taxation   340
Production and Trade   344
Summary   349
Questions for Review and Discussion   350
Suggested Reading   350
Notes   352

16   Roman Technology and Engineering   355
Milorad Nikolic

Introduction   356
Terminology and Transfer of Knowledge   357
Technology Assimilated   361
Streets and Bridges   361
Water Transport   363
Concrete   366
Water Supply   368
Instruments   370
Sources of Energy   371
The People behind the Works   373
Summary   374
Questions for Review and Discussion   375
Suggested Reading   375
Notes   377

17   Art and Architecture   378
Beth Munro

Introduction   378
Defining *Romanness*   380
Augustan Rome: Image of an Empire   385
Imperial Dynasties and Dominance   390
Responses to Economic and Social Change   395
Summary   399
Questions for Review and Discussion   400
Suggested Reading   400
Notes   401

Conclusion   402

Epilogue   Roman Themes in Modern Society and Popular Culture   404

Appendix   Resources for Students   412

Glossary   418

Works Cited   435

Index   450

Preface and Acknowledgements

A common desire to provide students of Roman society with readings well suited to the introductory level inspired the conception of this volume. A communal effort by academics from classics departments across Canada and beyond has ensured its realization. We would like to thank all the contributors for their generosity in lending their time and expertise to this project. Their participation demonstrates the true value that they place on student training and the perpetuation of Roman studies. We would also like to thank Peter Chambers, our developmental editor at Oxford University Press, for his excellent advice (of which we availed ourselves often) and insight through this process; his guidance and good humour helped us clear innumerable hurdles that would have otherwise been insurmountable. We extend our special thanks as well to Janna Green, our copy editor; her meticulous reading and helpful suggestions have fostered clarity, consistency, and completeness. Along with our publisher, we are indebted to the following reviewers, who provided invaluable comments and critiques: Daniel Hutter, University of Waterloo; Adam Kemezis, University of Alberta; Philip Kiernan, University of British Columbia, David Meban, Campion College, University of Regina; Lionel J. Sanders, Concordia University; Lisa Trentin, Wilfrid Laurier University; and the three anonymous reviewers. Thanks also go to members of the Classics Students Association at the University of Winnipeg for their willingness to act as a focus group regarding the shape of the volume, thereby helping us to move from quandary to action.

Matt Gibbs would like to thank Georgy Kantor, who read several sections of this volume and provided valuable feedback and support; David Hollander for so willingly sharing his research; and his fellow editors for not only their wisdom and experience but also their amiability, geniality, and (in particular) infinite patience. He would like to offer special thanks to Chinta, Livia, and Madeleine (who was born during the final edit of Chapter 8), who gamely endured this project's intrusion into their lives.

Milorad Nikolic would like to thank John Peter Oleson and John Humphrey for their excellent advice, enduring support, and valuable feedback, as well as his co-editors for their energy, insight, patience, and good humour.

Pauline Ripat would like to thank Sinclair Bell, Mark Golden, and Lea Stirling for their help and advice; her appreciation also goes to her co-editors for sharing this experience. She thanks her husband, Darren, for being a frequent technical consultant, sometimes single parent, and consistently supportive partner, and Nicholas and Alex for allowing this project to be part of their family for such a long time.

Finally, the editors and contributors acknowledge a debt of special gratitude to those teachers, professors, supervisors, and mentors who first inspired or nurtured their fascination with Roman society and who, by being role models, taught them how to teach. It is to them that this volume is dedicated.

Dedication

———•◆•———

The editors and contributors dedicate this volume to the following people, with thanks:

Colin Adams, Elizabeth Archibald, Lawrence Bliquez, Alan Bowman, Keith Bradley, Peter Burnell, David Campbell, Hubert Cancik, Edward Champlin, Patricia Clark, Janet DeLaine, Ruth Edwards-Thomas, Michele George, Mark Golden, Alain Gowing, Evan Haley, John Humphrey, Bernard Kavanagh, Andrew Lintott, Iain McDougall, Anthony Marshall, John Peter Oleson, David Page, Ronald Payne, the late Simon Price, Hanne Sigismund Nielsen, William Slater, A.M. Stone, Robert Thom, Jackie Tinson, Michael Walbank, Kathryn Welch, and Haijo Westra.

Contributors

Andreas Bendlin is an associate professor at the University of Toronto, where he teaches classics and Roman history. His research and publications focus on religion at Rome and in the Roman empire, Roman cultural and social history, and the history of scholarship. Recent publications address topics such as Graeco-Roman divination, religious pluralism in the ancient world, and associations in the Roman world. A monograph on religious pluralism in ancient Rome in the late Republic and early Empire is forthcoming.

Michael Carter is an associate professor in the Department of Classics at Brock University. His primary research interest relates to the social and cultural significance of mass public entertainment spectacles, such as gladiatorial contests and similar (Roman) shows. He is especially interested in the impact that the Greek adoption and adaptation of such thoroughly Roman spectacles had on Greek society and identity, and he has published several articles on the topic in journals such as *Phoenix, Zeitschrift für Papyrologie und Epigraphik*, and *Greek, Roman and Byzantine Studies*.

Fanny Dolansky is an associate professor in the Department of Classics at Brock University, where she teaches Latin language and literature, Roman history, and Roman religion. Her research focuses mainly on the history of the Roman family, particularly domestic religious rites. She has published articles on the Parentalia (*Phoenix*, 2011) and Matronalia festivals (*Classical World*, 2011); book chapters on the *toga virilis* ceremony (2008) and Saturnalia festival (2011); and has a study on children's dolls forthcoming in *Classical Antiquity*. She is currently completing a sourcebook on the ancient city of Rome for Continuum Press (with Stacie Raucci of Union College) and working on a book manuscript on Roman domestic religion.

Greg Fisher is an associate professor in the Department of History and the Department of Greek and Roman Studies at Carleton University. He is an expert on the Middle East in late antiquity, and his current research focuses on the political and cultural relationships between states and inhabitants of frontier regions across the late antique world. He is the author of *Between Empires: Arabs, Romans and Sasanians in Late Antiquity* (Oxford University Press, 2011) and the novel *The Iranian Conspiracy* (FastPencil, Inc., 2011), as well as the editor of *Arabs and the Empires Before Islam* (Oxford University Press, 2015).

Matt Gibbs is an assistant professor in the Department of Classics at the University of Winnipeg. His current research concerns professional associations, taxation, and the economy of Ptolemaic and Roman Egypt, as well as the Roman empire generally. He also has research interests in the political history of the late Roman Republic and early Roman Empire. He has published on professional associations and the economy of Ptolemaic and Roman Egypt and the Roman empire.

Alison Jeppesen-Wigelsworth is an instructor and learning designer at Red Deer College and the editor of *Cloelia: The Newsletter of the Women's Classical Caucus*. Her research focuses on the family, with particular emphasis on Roman marriage and the portrayal of Roman women in inscriptions. She has published in *Latomus* and *Arethusa* and is currently completing a manuscript exploring the changing depiction of Roman wives in funerary epitaphs.

Benjamin Kelly is an associate professor in the Department of History at York University. His research interests include crime, policing, and the courts in the Roman world. He is the author of *Petitions, Litigation, and Social Control in Roman Egypt* (Oxford University Press, 2011).

Beth Munro is a lecturer at the University of Edinburgh. Until recently, she was a postdoctoral fellow in Roman archaeology at the University of Manitoba. She has also lectured in Roman art and architecture at the University of Winnipeg and tutored at The Queen's College and Hertford College at the University of Oxford and at Roehampton University. She is the finds supervisor on the Dorchester-on-Thames archaeological project. Her research interests include the architecture and decoration of villas and the recycling of stone, glass, and metals in the imperial and late antique periods. She has published numerous articles on recycling at villas and on the relationship between marble statuary and lime kilns.

Milorad Nikolic is an assistant professor in the Department of Classics at Memorial University. He is trained as both a mechanical engineer and a classicist. His research interests are ancient technology and engineering (more precisely, water supply systems), ancient technical literature, Greek and Roman art and architecture, and the northern Roman frontier. He has published on Greek and Roman technical vocabulary.

Kelly Olson is an associate professor in the Department of Classical Studies at Western University. Her research focuses on Roman society, sexuality, and appearance. She is the author of several articles and book chapters on female clothing in Roman antiquity, published in *Mouseion*, *The American Journal of Ancient History*, *Fashion Theory*, and *Classical World*. Her book *Dress and the Roman Woman: Self-Presentation and Society* was published by Routledge in 2008. She is presently working on a monograph entitled *Men, Appearance, and Sexuality in Roman Antiquity*.

Pauline Ripat is an associate professor in the Department of Classics at the University of Winnipeg. Her research interests include Roman magic and divination, particularly as they pertain to social relations and communication. She is the author of several book chapters and journal articles published in *Greece and Rome*, *Phoenix*, and *Classical Philology*.

Luke Roman is an associate professor of classics at Memorial University. His research interests include Roman poetry of the late Republic and early Empire, representations of writing and the material book, the relation between Roman literature and concepts of monumentality, and Renaissance Latin poetry. He has published articles on the epigrammatist Martial and other Latin poets and is completing a book on the rhetoric of poetic autonomy in ancient Rome.

Andrew Sherwood is an associate professor of classics at the University of Guelph. His research interests have led to land and underwater archaeological fieldwork in Italy, Greece, Turkey, Israel, Jordan, and Romania. His publications encompass studies of Latin and Greek epigraphy, Greek and Roman technology, and the excavations of Caesarea Martima, Israel, and Humayma, Jordan.

Leslie Shumka is an assistant professor of classics at Mount Allison University. Her research interests include gender and status in Roman antiquity, women in the Roman economy, and funerary archaeology.

John Vanderspoel is a professor of Roman history in the Department of Greek and Roman Studies at the University of Calgary, where he has taught since 1985. Although he focuses on the later Roman Empire, he has researched and written extensively on many aspects and periods of the Roman world. He has published *Themistius and the Imperial Court* (University of Michigan Press, 1995) and was a co-editor of *The Cambridge Dictionary of Classical Civilization* (Cambridge University Press, 2008). He has written numerous articles that have appeared in a variety of academic journals and is a founding editor of *The Ancient History Bulletin*, for which he currently serves as online editor.

Conor Whately is an assistant professor in the Department of Classics at the University of Winnipeg. His current research interests include ancient historiography and empire (particularly frontiers, imperialism, and warfare) in the Roman world. He has contributed several entries to the *Encyclopedia of Ancient History* (Wiley-Blackwell, 2012), the *Encyclopedia of the Roman Army* (Wiley-Blackwell, 2012), and the Late Antique Archaeology volume *War in Late Antiquity*. He is currently working on two monographs: a cultural and historiographical study of military narratives in Procopius's *Wars* and an examination of the Roman armed forces in Moesia from 27 BCE to 337 CE.

A Note to the Reader

The translations of ancient sources in this volume use the following common epigraphic, papyrological, and textual conventions:

- Parentheses ( ) enclose clarifications, supplements, or comments made by the modern author or editor or expansions of abbreviations that appear in the original text. They may also indicate parenthetical statements made by the original author.
- Brackets [ ] enclose damaged or mutilated text; they may also enclose words that have been restored with certainty.
- An ellipsis in brackets [. . .] indicates missing letters or words where restoration is impossible.
- Angled brackets < > enclose words omitted by the original author or scribe but added by the modern editor or translator.
- Ellipses . . . indicate that part of the ancient source has been omitted by the modern author.

The reader should note that brackets are used in quotations of modern scholarship to indicate that a clarification has been made by someone other than the original author.

References to ancient sources generally follow the abbreviations used in *The Oxford Classical Dictionary*[1] and the *Checklist of Editions of Greek Latin, Demotic and Coptic Papyri, Ostraca and Tablets*, which are explained in the following list.[2] Various print and electronic translations of these and other ancient works are widely available. In the event that only one work of a given author is extant, it is the convention to refer to that work by the author's name (or abbreviation of the author's name) only.

AE	*L'Année épigraphique*
Amm. Marc.	Ammianus Marcellinus
App.	Appian
B Civ.	*Bella civilia*
Mac.	Μακεδονική
Pun.	Λιβυκή
Apul.	Apuleius
Flor.	*Florida*
Met.	*Metamorphoses*
Archil.	Archilochus

Aristid.	Aelius Aristides
Or.	*Orationes*
Arr.	Arrian
Epict. diss.	*Epicteti dissertationes*
Artem.	Artemidorus Daldianus
Asc.	Asconius
Mil.	*Pro Milone*
Auct. ad Her.	*Auctor ad Herennium*
BGU	*Berliner Griechische Urkunden*
BJ	*Bonner Jahrbücher*
BL	Preisigke, F., et al. 1922–. *Berichtigungsliste der griechischen Papyrusurkunden aus Ägypten*. Berlin-Leipzig.
Caes.	Caesar
BGall.	*Bellum Gallicum*
Cass. Dio	Cassius Dio
Catull.	Catullus
CFA	Scheid, J. 1998. *Commentarii Fratrum Arvalium qui supersunt: Les copies épigraphiques des protocols annuels de la confrérie arvale (21 av.–304 ap. J.-C.)*. Collection Roma antica 4. Rome.
Chrest.Mitt.	*Grundzüge und Chrestomathie der Papyruskunde*, II Bd. *Juristischer Teil*, II Hälfte *Chrestomathie.*
Cic.	Cicero
Amic.	*De amicitia*
Att.	*Epistulae ad Atticum*
Brut.	*Brutus* or *De Claris Oratoribus*
Cael.	*Pro Caelio*
De or.	*De oratore*
Div.	*De divinatione*
Dom.	*De domo sua*
Fam.	*Epistulae ad familiares*
Fin.	*De finibus*
Flac.	*Pro Flacco*
Har. Resp.	*De haruspicum responso*
Leg.	*De legibus*
Leg. Man.	*Pro lege Manilia* or *De imperio Cn.*

Mil.	*Pro Milone*
Nat. D.	*De natura deorum*
Off.	*De officiis*
Orat.	*Orator ad M. Brutum*
Phil.	*Orationes Philippicae*
Q Fr.	*Epistulae ad Quintum fratrem*
Rep.	*De republica*
Rosc. Am.	*Pro Sexto Roscio Amerino*
Sen.	*De senectute*
Sest.	*Pro Sestio*
Tusc.	*Tusculanae disputationes*
Vat.	*In Vatinium*
Verr.	*In Verrem*
CIL	*Corpus Inscriptionum Latinarum*
CISem.	*Corpus Inscriptionum Semiticarum*
Cod.	Codex
Cod. Theod.	*Codex Theodosianus*
Columella	
Rust.	*De re rustica*
Dig.	*Digesta*
Dio Chrys.	Dio Chrysostomus
Or.	*Orationes*
Dion. Hal.	Dionysius of Halicarnassus
Ant. Rom.	*Antiquitates Romanae*
Comp.	*De compositione verborum*
Euseb.	Eusebius
Hist. eccl.	*Historia ecclesiastica*
Eutr.	Eutropius
Festus	
Gloss. Lat.	*Glossaria Latina*
Frontin.	Frontinus
Aq.	*De aquae ductu urbis Romae*
Str.	*Strategemata*
Gai.	Gaius
Inst.	*Institutiones*

Gell.	Aulus Gellius
NA	*Noctes Atticae*
Hdn.	Herodianus
Heron	
Pneum.	*Pneumatica*
Hor.	Horace
Carm.	*Carmina* or *Odes*
Epist.	*Epistulae*
Sat.	*Satirae* or *Sermones*
HRRel.	Peter, H. 1967. *Historicorum romanorum reliquiae.* Stuttgart, Germany.
IGRom	*Inscriptiones Graecae ad res Romanas pertinentes*
ILS	*Inscriptiones Latinae Selectae*
Inscr. Ital.	*Inscriptiones Italiae*
IPOstie-A	Hylander, H. 1952. *Inscriptions du port d'Ostie.* Lund.
ISIS	Helttula A. 2007. *Le iscrizioni sepolcrali latine nell'Isola sacra.* Rome.
Jer.	Jerome
Ep.	*Epistulae*
Joseph	Josephus
BJ	*Bellum Judaicum*
Just.	Justinus
Epit.	*Epitome* (of Trogus)
Juv.	Juvenal
Lactant.	Lactantius
De mort. pers.	*De mortibus persecutorum*
Livy, *Epit.*	*Epitomae*
Per.	*Periochae*
Luc.	Lucan
Lucian	
Alex.	*Alexander*
Nav.	*Navigium*
Somn.	*Somnium*
Lucr.	Lucretius
MAMA	*Monumenta Asiae Minoris Antiquae*
Mart.	Martial

Nep.	Nepos
Att.	*Atticus*
Nic. Dam.	Nicolaus Damascenus
OGI	*Orientis Graeci Inscriptiones Selectae*
Oros.	Orosius
Ov.	Ovid
Am.	*Amores*
Ars am.	*Ars amatoria*
Fast.	*Fasti*
Met.	*Metamorphoses*
Tr.	*Tristia*
P.Amh.	*Amherst Papyri*
P.Athen.	*Papyri Societatis Archaeologicae Atheniensis*
Paus.	Pausanias
P.Bour.	*Les Papyrus Bouriant*
P.Brem.	*Die Bremer Papyri*
P.Colon.	*Kölner Papyri*
Pers.	Persius
Petron.	Petronius
Sat.	*Satyrica*
P.Euphrates	Documents d'archives romains inédits du Moyen Euphrates
P.Fay.	*Fayum Towns and their Papyri*
P.Gen.	*Les Papyrus de Genève*
P.Graux.	*Papyrus Graux*
Philo	Philo Judaeus
Leg.	*Legatio ad Gaium*
Plaut.	Plautus
Rud.	*Rudens*
Plin.	Pliny the Elder
HN	*Naturalis historia*
Plin.	Pliny the Younger
Ep.	*Epistulae*
Pan.	*Panegyricus*
P.Lond.	*Greek Papyri in the British Museum*
Plut.	Plutarch

Caes.	Caesar
Cat. Mai.	Cato Maior
Cat. Min.	Cato Minor
Cic.	Cicero
Crass.	Crassus
Flam.	Flamininus
Mar.	Marius
Mor.	Moralia
Pomp.	Pompeius
Pyrrh.	Pyrrhus
Rom.	Romulus
P.Mich.	Michigan Papyri
P.Mon. Epiph.	The Monastery of Epiphanius at Thebes
Polyb.	Polybius
P.Oxy.	The Oxyrhynchus Papyri
P.Petaus	Das Archiv des Petaus
Prop.	Propertius
P.Ryl.	Catalogue of the Greek Papyri in the John Rylands Library, Manchester
PSI	Papiri Greci e Latini, Pubblicazioni della Società italiana per la ricerca dei papiri greci e latini in Egitto
P.Tebt.	The Tebtunis Papyri
P.Thmouis	Le Papyrus Thmouis 1, colonnes 68—160
P.Turner	Papyri Greek and Egyptian Edited by Various Hands in Honour of Eric Gardner Turner on the Occasion of his Seventieth Birthday
P.Vind.Bosw.	Einige Wiener Papyri
Quint.	Quintilian
Inst.	Institutio oratoria
RG	Monumentum Ancyranum
RMD	Roxan, M., and P. Holder, eds. Roman Military Diplomas. 5 vols.
Sall.	Sallust
Cat.	Bellum Catilinae or De Catilinae coniuratione
SB	Sammelbuch griechischen Urkunden aus Ägypten
SEG	Supplementum epigraphicum Graecum

Sel.Pap. II	Hunt, A.S., and C.C. Cary, trans. 1934. *Select Papyri Volume II: Public Documents.* The Loeb Classical Library 282. Cambridge, MA: Harvard University Press.
Sen.	Seneca the Younger
Brev. Vit.	*De brevitate vitae*
Clem.	*De clementia*
Constant.	*De constantia sapientis*
Ep.	*Epistulae*
Helv.	*Ad Helviam*
QNat.	*Quaestiones naturales*
SHA	Scriptores Historiae Augustae
Gall.	*Gallienus*
Hadr.	*Hadrian*
Marc.	*Marcus*
Sev.	*Severus*
Tyr. Trig.	*Tyranni Triginta*
Sor.	Soranus
Gyn.	*Gynaeceia*
Stud.Pal.	*Studien zur Palaeographie und Papyruskunde*
Suet.	Suetonius
Aug.	*Divus Augustus*
Calig.	*Caligula*
Claud.	*Divus Claudius*
Dom.	*Domitianus*
Galb.	*Galba*
Gram.	*De grammaticis*
Iul.	*Divus Iulius*
Ner.	*Nero*
Tib.	*Tiberius*
Tit.	*Divus Titus*
Vesp.	*Divus Vespasianus*
Tac.	Tacitus
Agr.	*Agricola*

Ann.	*Annales*
Dial.	*Dialogus de oratoribus*
Hist.	*Historiae*
Tert.	Tertullian
Apol.	*Apologeticus*
Thuc.	Thucydides
Tib.	Tibullus
T. Vindol.	*Vindolanda: the Latin Writing Tablets*
Val. Max.	Valerius Maximus
Varro	
Ling.	*De lingua Latina*
Rust.	*De re rustica*
Vegetius	
Mil.	*De re militari*
Vitr.	Vitruvius
De arch.	*De architectura*
Xen.	Xenophon
Oec.	*Oeconomicus*

Notes

1   Hornblower, Spawforth, and Eidinow (2012).
2   Oates et al. (2011). This list, which provides full bibliographic and other useful information for papyri, ostraca, and related materials (such as the Vindolanda Tablets), is
available online at http://library.duke.edu/rubenstein/scriptorium/papyrus/texts/clist.
html.

Introduction

This volume aims to introduce students to fundamental aspects of Roman society—its composition, institutions, structures, and cultural products—particularly in the period 200 BCE to 200 CE. While there are several excellent introductions to Roman history (some of which include a discussion of cultural issues), this book differs from them by approaching Roman society thematically rather than chronologically. In other words, we do not ask how Rome expanded from a city to an empire but what Roman society looked like. How was it organized, and what practices, ideas, and social institutions supported these structures? The chapters of this volume, each of which has been written by an active researcher and instructor in the field, address these questions with reference to specific elements of Roman society. Our objective is to provide a sense of the relevant evidence and an assessment of the current state of scholarship, thereby forming a basis for further study of Roman life or history.

Content of This Book

By taking a thematic approach, we have given priority to seminal concepts with the broadest relevance in the chosen time period. This method means that chapters do not have to be read in order; however, thought has been put into their arrangement. Chapter 1 offers a sketch of the development of social historical research in the discipline, while Chapter 2's brief history of Roman political life supplies a broad chronological framework for the subsequent chapters' discussion. Chapters 3 to 5 introduce the human elements of Roman society (class and status, slavery, and the household) and their relationships to each other. Chapters 6 to 8 examine the intellectual life that reflected and perpetuated Roman social values (education and literature) and the social construction of self and others (gender and sexuality). Chapter 9 not only considers religion but also acts as a bridge between the previous chapters' focus on the human components of society and the next three chapters' discussion regarding the social structures and institutions (government, law and order, and entertainment) that governed them, supported social cohesion, and provided an opportunity for the expression of collective values. Rome's relations with others is the subject of chapters 13 and 14; Chapter 15 looks at economic dynamics. The final two chapters focus on the physical products of Roman society, technology and engineering and art and architecture, respectively. Although not given individual chapters, topics such as philosophy, the environment, and Christianity are included where relevant.

The emphasis on themes also creates some overlap between chapters. A critical aspect of the study of Roman society is that social structures, institutions, and relationships did not exist in isolation. In fact, Roman society is best comprehended as the connections between topics, which often elucidate or provide context for others. For example, investigations into the importance of slavery in the Roman world must take into account the household and the economy. Meanwhile, neither of these subjects can be understood without consideration of the presence of slaves. Further associations can be made between the domestic sphere, social roles, and gender and sexuality. The expansion of the empire also involves various overlapping topics, including the military, technological knowledge, taxation, and justice. Marginal notes throughout the text draw attention to such links.

Each chapter of this book includes review questions to help solidify knowledge and develop awareness of the problems surrounding past studies. Annotated suggested reading lists provide sources for further research, as does the text's appendix. The book also features a conclusion, which brings together the themes discussed, and an epilogue, which demonstrates how Roman history continues to influence modern society. Key terms are bolded at their first appearance in each chapter and defined in the glossary.

Another area worth noting is the treatment of the terms *Roman society*, *Republic*, and *Empire*. *Roman society* may seem rather narrowly defined in this volume, given that most of the discussion focuses primarily upon the city of Rome, urban life, men, and citizens (at the expense of provincial communities, rural existence, women, children, non-citizens, and people from other areas). This uneven treatment is both typical of introductory volumes and regrettable. It is typical because more attention must be given to the better documented parts of Roman society in order to study the more elusive elements. It is regrettable because such a lopsided discussion creates a skewed impression of Roman society. The truth of the matter is that the population of the Roman empire was one of astonishing variety, and male citizens living in the city of Rome were only a very small percentage of it. Discussion has been expanded to acknowledge this fact wherever possible.

An important convention of this volume is the use of *Republic* and *Empire* to refer to the chronological span of the political systems (Rome under the leadership of the senate in the Republic; Rome under the leadership of the emperor in the Empire) and *empire* to refer to the geographical expanse over which Rome had extended political control. One may speak, therefore, of the empire under the Republic (the physical territory under Roman rule during the time of the Republic) or of the empire under the Empire (the physical territory under Roman rule when emperors held power). The term *Monarchy* is also used to denote the political system, not the monarch and his or her family.

Categories of Ancient Sources

Research into classical antiquity involves the study of primary sources (ancient evidence in its many forms) and secondary sources (modern scholars' arguments and opinions about aspects of ancient life or history, based on their interpretation of primary sources and the work of their contemporaries).[1] Examples of both types are provided in the appendix. Because familiarity with the ancient evidence is critical to studying antiquity, this section introduces the types of primary sources available for inquiries into ancient Roman society and discusses their advantages and disadvantages.

There are six broad categories of ancient evidence: literary, archaeological, iconographic (or art historical), numismatic, epigraphic, and papyrological. Though countless examples could demonstrate the benefits and limitations of each kind of evidence, it is useful to address both factors in the context of one famous, fixed location: Pompeii and its surroundings. Pompeii, a port city on the Bay of Naples, looms large in the imagination of scholars and tourists alike. Covered in a deep layer of volcanic debris following the eruption of Mount Vesuvius in 79 CE, it is popularly referred to as a "time capsule" of Roman antiquity and a city "frozen in time." Such descriptions suggest that one need only visit the excavated site to gain a comprehensive understanding of Roman society. But quite apart from the question of how representative of Roman life Pompeii is (Can it be said to be representative of anything but Pompeian life, given the heterogeneous nature of the Roman empire?), careful consideration of the site and the evidence we have from or about it demonstrates that we know much less than we might have thought.

Let us begin with literary evidence, the writings of ancient authors.[2] These authors were almost exclusively wealthy men who were also the intellectual and political elite of their communities. Their writings are categorized as either poetry or prose, but these genres have many subheadings. Poetic works range from long works of epic poetry to brief lines of epigram. Dramatic forms also fall under the heading of poetry because both tragedy and comedy were composed in verse form. Prose works include history, biography, oratory (speeches), letters, and philosophical treatises. Each literary genre was employed for specific purposes and deployed within specific contexts, considerations that must be taken into account when using literary works as evidence.

For example, in a famous letter addressed to the historian Tacitus, Pliny the Younger (*Ep.* 6.16) describes the death of his uncle, Pliny the Elder, during the volcanic explosion that buried Pompeii.[3] Pliny the Younger writes that he and his uncle were residing at Misenum, across the Bay of Naples, when the eruption occurred. The Elder decided to take a closer look (he was in charge of the fleet located at Misenum) and investigate the eruption for scientific purposes, but the Younger chose to stay behind. When word arrived that a friend was trapped in her villa on the Bay of Naples and was begging for his help, the Elder's voyage of discovery immediately changed to a rescue mission. Sailing conditions, however, did not permit him to reach her villa. Crying "Fortune favours the brave!" he sailed on to the abode of another friend further along the coast at Stabiae, where he and his crew were eventually marooned. Pliny the Younger tells Tacitus (and the readers of his carefully edited collection of letters) that his uncle maintained good humour and even had a bath, dinner, and a good night's sleep before expiring on the beach the next day, where he had gone (using two slaves as crutches) to see if sailing conditions had improved.

Perhaps Pliny the Younger's narrative is true to the events as they occurred. But we would be justified in questioning the absolute truthfulness of the details about his uncle's bravery, in part because the reports he received were second-hand at best and in part because the portrait was being submitted for inclusion in a work of history (or at least in his own corpus of letters edited for publication). He writes to Tacitus, "I realize that his death will be granted undying fame if it is celebrated by you." This realization was surely followed by another: posterity, his uncle's reputation, and his own dutifulness to his uncle's memory all demanded a good, brave death. Perhaps his uncle had co-operated by providing one, Pliny's informants had assisted by shaping their reports to provide one, or Pliny the Younger massaged the reports into something suitable by including some details and neglecting others.

Literary sources also tend to fail to tell the whole story in another way. Pliny's description perhaps justifiably focuses on his uncle's actions to the exclusion of most others'. But his off-hand reference to the slaves who had assisted his uncle to the beach is a sudden reminder that, while Pliny the Elder and his friends were keeping stiff upper lips throughout the eruption, their slaves were preparing their baths, dinner, and beds. We had not imagined them there before because Pliny the Younger had seen no need to mention them. Literary sources generally reflect the priorities of their well-to-do male authors and, consequently, the social value that these same people placed on different elements of society. In other words, those deemed most important receive the most literary attention (wealthy adult males, their thoughts, and their actions receive the lion's share) and those deemed less important receive less. When the latter are mentioned, they are often described in a prejudicial light.

Literary genre and authorial agenda or bias must therefore be considered when interpreting literary evidence. But there is yet another difficulty inherent in the use of literary sources as historical evidence. Most of the ancient literature that we have is thanks to the manuscript tradition, the work of monks copying selected texts. But the copying process often introduced errors into the texts, meaning that we do not have precisely what the ancient authors wrote. For example, Pliny's letter includes the date of Mount Vesuvius's eruption. Different manuscripts, however, state different dates: it might have been 24 August or 23 November. The difference seems extreme in English, but in Latin the dates look and sound much more similar—*nonum kal. Septembres* and *nonum kal. Decembres*, respectively. The mistake was an easy one for a copyist to make, but it has left us unsure of when the famous eruption actually occurred.[4]

The next category of evidence is archaeological, the physical remains of the ancient Roman world.[5] These are various and include everything from the buildings of the Roman Forum to animal bones in the towns of a far-flung province. Although the practice of archaeology is subject to a number of practical limitations—it is expensive, funding is often scarce, and it is impossible to dig everywhere—archaeological evidence has the potential to tell us much about the lives of larger ancient society because, unlike literary sources, material remains are not exclusively the work of ancient wealthy adult males. This is not to suggest, however, that the lives of all elements of society are equally represented in the physical record. Slaves, for example, were a ubiquitous element of the ancient population but may be as elusive in the physical remains of Roman houses as they are in our literary sources. The design of Roman houses suggests that slaves hid in plain sight. Slave quarters are difficult to identify and perhaps did not exist; slaves might have slept where they could or where they were needed.[6] As this example suggests, the physical evidence is not always straightforward: it is not necessarily obvious what an object or area is or how it is significant.

What is more, the agenda of the one excavating (or funding the excavation) can dictate what is and what is not preserved, and personal expectation of "how things must have been" or other forces can affect interpretation. The site of Pompeii presents an extreme example of excavation undertaken to serve the agendas of those funding the digging, as the area was first treated as a mine of decorative art and sculpture to sate the aesthetic desires of the aristocracy and then to support the political programs of leaders such as Mussolini.[7] In short, all finds were not treated equally. Those deemed less spectacular or less useful were disposed of and, it must be suspected, not even recorded in many cases. Even more recently, political pressure has given way to the influence of popular culture on the selection and interpretation of finds.[8] Estelle Lazer describes the impact of romanticizing fiction (for example, *The Last Days of Pompeii* by Edward Bulwer-Lytton) on the interpretation of human remains at Pompeii and nearby Herculaneum. The popularity of such tales has sometimes inspired scholars to create personas ("the soldier," "the pretty lady," and so on) for some remains by relying on flimsy evidence or, in some cases, by overlooking evidence.[9] Archaeological evidence emerges in response to choices made by the excavators regarding what to look for, and the interpretation of physical remains is as susceptible to the attitudes of the archaeologist as the interpretation of literary sources is to the attitudes of the historian.

The physical record also includes iconographic evidence (for example, wall paintings, sculptures, and mosaics). These sorts of cultural artifacts can tell us much about Roman aesthetics, self-presentation, and identity. They also sometimes give us tantalizing images of historical events or social or religious life. For example, a relief panel on the familial altar (the *lararium*) in the so-called House of Caecilius Iucundus is thought to depict the Pompeian Forum during the earthquake of 62 CE, while daily life in the Forum (when not rocked by earthquakes) is shown in wall paintings from the Estate of Julia Felix.[10] A wall painting from Herculaneum (now in the Naples Museum) shows a ceremony in honour of the Egyptian goddess Isis (a deity popular in Italy since the second century BCE), complete with priests sporting requisite Egyptian robes and bald heads. This scene exemplifies some of the difficulties involved in the interpretation of iconographical evidence. Is this a depiction of "real" Isis worship? If so, is it a depiction of how Isis worship was undertaken in Egypt or only in southern Italy in the first century CE? This question is justified by the observation that "Egyptomania" took hold in Italy following Egypt's annexation as a province in 30 BCE, with the result that idyllic scenes of Egypt began to appear as domestic decorative motifs. The Egyptians themselves, however, might be depicted as pygmies who were sometimes even engaging in acts of bestiality. In short, paintings of Egypt were often (or always?) of the "Egypt" of Roman imagination rather than the Egypt of reality.[11] Can we therefore trust depictions of other vignettes to act as "photographs" and, if so, of what time and place?

The problem becomes more immediate when we consider how artistic evidence has been used to describe aspects of ancient life that carry moral baggage in our society, such as sex and prostitution. Roman "orgies" have long been a staple of popular depictions of Roman behaviour. It does appear that the Romans (who did not live in the long shadow cast by the prudishness of the Victorian period) did not place the same taboo on sex as a subject for artistic representation that we do: images of sexual acts and sexual organs appear frequently in both public and private locations in Pompeii. However, the ubiquity of body parts (entwined and otherwise) drawn on Pompeian walls has previously led many scholars to conclude that the city housed dozens of brothels: where sex was represented, sex must have been sold. But this logic also leads to the unlikely theory that a small interior room of the opulent House of the Vettii, which featured a painting of a couple having sex, must have been a brothel. Artistic evidence might indicate that the Romans had different attitudes towards sex than we do, but it alone cannot point to locations of the sex trade.[12]

Numismatics (coins or objects that could be used as such) is yet another form of material evidence.[13] Coins often present the opportunity to address quite specific questions or to illuminate specific issues. For example, coins could be (and still are) minted with symbols that were ideologically significant to the community or its ruling authorities. Coin hoards, the savings of individuals who hid them and never returned to collect them, can perhaps say something about the liquidity of individual wealth and the justified anxiety of individuals in uncertain times. Even so, the discovery of coins on dead Pompeians should surely not be taken as an indication of the kind of cash that individuals would normally carry around but rather as all the cash that they had on hand and with which to escape.[14]

Attention to the find spot of coins often yields valuable information for the interpretation of other kinds of evidence. A coin's mint date will provide a *terminus post quem* ("date after which") the layer in which it is found must exist. Indeed, the discovery of a coin that probably dates to September 79 CE in the ash of Pompeii means that Mount Vesuvius could not have erupted in August of that year, thereby possibly answering the question of the season, if not the precise date, of the event.[15]

Epigraphic evidence (words or symbols carved, scratched, written, or painted on stone, wood, plaster, pottery, or metal) is plentiful (and, unlike the body of literary sources, enjoys constant new finds) and can present unique information.[16] Consider, for example, the vast number of so-called *programmata*, statements of support for local political candidates, that were painted on Pompeii's walls or the graffiti that conveyed rather more personal content (for example, "Chios, I hope your piles again become sore, so that they smart more than they smarted before").[17] Although epigraphic evidence presents as straightforward—if it is literally "written in stone," how could interpretation be in question?—complications nonetheless exist. Formulaic expressions find their way into commemorations, making any attempt to discern the "true feelings" of the commemorator difficult. Most inscriptional evidence dates to the second century CE (a phenomenon referred to as the "epigraphic habit"), while other time frames are not as well represented. Reading epigraphic remains is also challenging: stone is hard to carve, and so abbreviations are common. Because inscriptions are rarely found intact, informed guesses must be made about what letters or words are missing.

Even when the basic meaning of an inscription is known, its actual significance often is not. Consider the inscription with which the amphitheatre at Pompeii was dedicated in the years immediately following the city's conversion into a Roman colony: "Gaius Quinctius Valgus and Marcus Porcius, for the honour of the colony, saw to the construction of amphitheatre at their own expense and gave the area to the colonists in perpetuity."[18] But who are the colonists? Are they exclusively the general Sulla's veterans, who had been grafted onto the existing community as colonists? Or are they everyone who lived in Pompeii, including the original inhabitants? Is this dedication an example of an inclusive or exclusive act on the part of the Roman newcomers? The inscription could be understood either way.

The physical context of an inscription is also both critical and potentially problematic for understanding the inscription's significance and for appreciating the insight it can lend to the interpretation of other evidence. For example, a series of *programmata* proclaiming support for one Gaius Julius Polybius in proximity to a house has been interpreted to mean that the house belonged to Polybius (and the human remains found inside to him and to his family); however, exterior street-facing house walls appear to have been public domain as far as graffiti artists and political slogan painters were concerned. Thus, there is no reason to attach home ownership to a name painted on a wall.[19] Similarly, the presence of graffiti conveying statements of sexual conquests on the walls of bars or inns was once interpreted to mean that all bars and inns doubled as brothels. But on this logic, public toilets in our own society could be identified as brothels by future scholars.[20] The location of inscriptions is an important consideration for both what they can and cannot tell us about ancient society.

Finally, we come to papyrological evidence, which comprises writings on papyrus, an ancient form of paper. However, other substances, such as potsherds (ostraca), are sometimes gathered under the same heading when they have been used as paper would be.[21] Papyrus is a form of evidence almost entirely exclusive to Egypt,[22] where dry conditions encouraged the survival of otherwise friable material. A notable exception is the collection of papyri from the library in the so-called Villa of the Papyri (at Herculaneum, close to Pompeii), which has survived because it was carbonized by the eruption of Vesuvius.[23] Some of these charred rolls have been unfurled painstakingly (and at great expense) to reveal the philosophical works of Philodemus, apparently a favourite of the villa's owner.

The variety of information contained by the papyrological evidence from Egypt, in particular, is immense: copies of works of literature, personal letters, petitions to the authorities, legal documents, inventory lists, census documents, and astrological charts are but a few examples of what the desert sands have yielded. Difficulties nonetheless present themselves here too. Bad handwriting competes with wormholes and other deteriorating factors as issues that impede easy comprehension of the papyrological material. The fact that much of what we have, including prized fragments of lost literature, has come from ancient garbage heaps might make us wonder about their perceived value in antiquity, as does the repurposing of inscribed papyrus as material for making mummy masks (which must be destroyed for the paper to be read). Furthermore, papyrological finds do not uniformly represent all areas or centuries of Greek and Roman Egypt. There is also the question of how much the information gleaned from papyri represents areas outside of Egypt. This is not because Egypt was an aberration among the Roman provinces but because each Roman province was to some extent unique.

In sum, very little of what once existed in the Roman world survives for us to use as evidence for historical investigations and very little of what survives is without obstacles. Attention must always be paid not only to the content but also to the context of any piece of evidence. The more types of evidence that can be gathered to consider any issue or question, the better. In an ideal world, we would never impose our own expectations of "how it must have been" upon our interpretations or propose conclusions that exceed the evidence upon which they are based. These goals are worthy but very difficult to meet; often the best that any student of Roman society can do is to pursue informed and tempered conclusions rather than the holy grail of incontrovertible pronouncements. Although little can be said with certainty about Roman society, much can be suggested and put forth for academic debate. Indeed, many come to study Roman society out of a fascination with the "facts" of ancient life, but it is the pursuit of the unknowns that are often more captivating and rewarding.

Notes

1   Technically, the term *primary source* should refer to a source that is contemporary with the events or situations for which it provides evidence. Based on this definition, not all evidence from antiquity would qualify as primary in every situation, since many authors describe events that occurred before their time. However, it is common practice to refer to all ancient sources as primary sources and to use the term *secondary sources* to refer to modern discussions of ancient evidence.

2   For the use of literary evidence in the writing of Roman history, see Potter (1999).

3   Quotes from this letter are taken from Cooley and Cooley (2004: 32–4 [C9]).

4   Lazer (2009: 79–80) discusses this and new numismatic evidence that might conclusively date the eruption to the fall rather than the summer.

5   See Biers (1992).

6   George (2007: 539).

7   See Cooley (2003: 65–96).

8   Pressure from commercial funding bodies also exists. See Lazer (2009: 28–9) for a discussion of *National Geographic* and the interpretation of the skeletal remains from the eruption of Vesuvius.

9   Ibid.: 5–35.

10   See Cooley and Cooley (2004: 30 [C3]) and Beard (2008: Plate 7), respectively.

11   See Versluys (2002).

12   See Beard (2008: 236–7, 331–2).

13   See Howgego (1995) for a more in-depth consideration of numismatic evidence.

14   Beard (2008: 1–4).

15   See Lazer (2009: 80).

16   For a broad introduction to epigraphy and its uses, see Bodel (2001).

17   *CIL* 4.1829, translated in Cooley and Cooley (2004: 78 [D91]).

18   *CIL* 10.852, slightly adapted from Cooley and Cooley (2004: 21 [B10]).

19   See Lazer (2009: 32–5).

20   DeFelice (2007: 481).

21   See Bagnall (1995).

22   Papyri and similar forms of evidence have also been found in other parts of North Africa and the Near East. The wooden tablets from Vindolanda, a Roman fort situated 1.5 kilometres south of Hadrian's Wall, are also noteworthy because they contain a variety of information, from expense accounts to personal letters, relating to members of the Roman garrison (see Bowman 1998 for a general introduction).

23   See Zarmakoupi (2010).

1

The Development of Roman Social History

Pauline Ripat

Inquiries into the ancient past are often directed by modern concerns: the issues that interest us now are the issues that interest us in Roman society. But while the present can help us ask the questions, it should not give us the answers. It is difficult to avoid imposing our own social bias on our conclusions, however, and the fact that we often do so unconsciously is one of the major reasons that the last word is rarely had on any historical subject.

To demonstrate this point, consider how W. Warde Fowler (fellow and lecturer at Lincoln College, University of Oxford) described Roman women in 1909.[1] Fowler's willingness to entertain the subject of women in Roman history was unusual for classicists at the time, but it was not surprising given contemporary events: women were making modern history in Britain in the early twentieth century. Thought by some to be the direct result of too much education, the "new woman" (a phrase coined in 1894) was very much in the public consciousness. This type of woman agitated for greater economic and political equality with men, sometimes criticized the institution of marriage (equality in marriage was difficult to achieve), and was, in many cases, a suffragette. (British women—more specifically, "respectable," married women over the age of 30—would finally gain the right to vote in 1917.)[2]

But according to Fowler, the new woman was not new at all. She was known to the Romans, and the results were horrid: "There was a 'new woman' even then, who had ceased to be satisfied with the austere life of the family . . . and was ready to break out into recklessness even in matters which were the concern of the State." Certainly, he continues, the "typical [Roman] matron would assuredly never dream of playing a part in history," and so history has respectfully forgotten most of them. In contrast, "the woman whose memory survives is apt to be the woman who . . . forces herself into notice by violating the traditions of womanhood." Such were the "loud and vicious ladies" who were the new women of Roman antiquity.

Unsurprisingly, we learn that the Roman new woman also despised marriage, realizing that her unseemly ambitions were incompatible with such a respectable institution. Undeterred by lack of evidence, Fowler speculates that the Roman new woman "would probably marry, play fast and loose with the married state, neglect her children if she had any, and after one or two divorces, die or disappear." Just one dire result of this developing breed was that divorce became "so common as to be almost inevitable." A foreboding message lies beneath his discussion: beware, new women of the twentieth century and unlucky men who know them—those who forget history are doomed to repeat it.

The trouble with this argument is that Fowler was not describing history but expressing his own fears and prejudices about his female contemporaries. We learn much about Fowler and something about the attitudes towards women in early twentieth-century Britain but nothing much about Roman women. Numerous scholars since have investigated the lives of Roman women, with results that have been more illuminating than Fowler's. However, as this chapter will show, although Fowler's conclusions are outdated, he and those who have superseded him share with all historians a common starting point: historical studies are informed by contemporary concerns and interests.

Introduction

Interest in ancient society at large—that is, interest in the experiences and interactions of all members of ancient society, not just of wealthy male citizens—did not characterize the field of classics until relatively recently. This chapter will examine the development of this interest as a field of historical research within classics in general, and within Roman studies in particular, during the second half of the twentieth century. To this end, it discusses the sources of information and methodologies that historians employ in their attempts to gain a better understanding of Roman society and considers the problems they encounter.

This chapter has several objectives. By contrasting the characteristics of Roman history as it was written prior to the mid-twentieth century with those of social historical inquiries, it highlights the significant conceptual shifts that Roman social history brought (and still brings) to the intellectual table. This recognition underscores the vitality of the modern pursuit of Roman history: far from being an unchanging narrative composed primarily of names and dates, Roman history is dynamic, elastic, and keenly attuned to the social and intellectual context of those who study it. This is not to say, however, that history written with a more traditional political focus has no place in the present. On the contrary, this chapter demonstrates the mutually productive debates in which political and social historical inquiries have engaged and identifies how they illuminate each other. Finally, the chapter also clarifies why the chapters of this volume deal with the subjects they do.

Social history as discussed in the following pages includes what might be called cultural studies. The former could be defined as an interest in how members of all segments of a society experienced all facets of life. Socio-historical investigations into ancient Rome might therefore focus on issues such as the rate of manumission of slaves or life expectancy among the ancient population and the effects upon familial relationships. The sources used are often non-literary, such as tombstone inscriptions, and anthropological or sociological theories and cross-cultural comparisons are sometimes invoked as investigative tools. The field of cultural studies, on the other hand, often looks at how different elements of Roman society presented themselves and were perceived by others and so frequently deals with issues of identity and power exerted through, for example, the use of stereotypes. Literary or social theory is often employed to clarify whose agenda is at work, why, and to what effect in any given source's presentation of society, its members, or their actions. But clear lines between social history and cultural studies are absent. The two areas have common interests and are often pursued in tandem. They will therefore be treated as a single field in this text.[3]

————•◆•————

The Development of Social History

Though earlier movements can be detected, the birth of social history is often placed in Strasbourg, France, in 1929, with the inception of the journal *Annales d'histoire économique et sociale*, edited by Marc Bloch and Lucien Febvre. Around this publication developed the so-called Annales School, a strain of historical inquiry that rejected traditional preferences for political history. Instead, the school focused on social and cultural developments over the long term (the *longue durée*) and, within these developments, the role of those who did not belong to the ruling elite. Such inquiries welcomed the instructive value of other fields of study, such as anthropology, geography, and psychology (disciplines that focused on individuals, society, and culture more comprehensively than merely on members of the elite and their activities).[4]

In the following decades, interest in the aims and approaches associated with the Annales School grew. This was particularly true among historians not only in France but also in the United States, spurred on not least of all by the social changes of the mid-twentieth century. Traditional values and established social structures were being questioned through, for example, the civil rights movement, the women's movement (sometimes called second wave feminism), and widespread student protests. Greater social, economic, and political equality were being sought by elements of society that had not previously enjoyed it. Alongside these contemporary social changes, new interest in those who had not traditionally commanded social, economic, and political power in historical societies developed.

Social History and the Classics

Historians of ancient Greece and Rome were comparatively slow to adopt social history. It was not until the 1960s and 1970s, when social history was already firmly established as a viable field of study in other areas, that classicists really started to engage with it in great numbers. In the early twentieth century, they had instead been occupied by an enthusiasm for prosopography, the study of the relationships between members of the ruling elite, as the key to understanding politics and government.[5] Today, when the pro-creative power of social networks is widely recognized, prosopography initially sounds like a sort of social history. But as Michael Peachin notes, the study of relationships was just a means to an end (the fuller explication of political history) while the "social element remained to a great extent under-argued."[6]

Before the 1960s, however, there were a handful of attempts to approach Roman history with aims or methods that resonated with those of the Annales School. These works sought to add flesh to ancient society beyond the activities of the political elite: Samuel Dill's *Roman Society from Nero to Marcus Aurelius* (1904), W. Warde Fowler's *Social Life at Rome in the Age of Cicero* (1909), and Jérôme Carcopino's *Daily Life in Ancient Rome* (1939) are notable in this regard. But these studies were closer in outlook and approach, if not focus, to more traditional works of ancient history (the characteristics of which are described below) than to those arising from the developing field of social history.

In contrast to Dill, Fowler, and Carcopino, some classical scholars, such as Michael Rostovtzeff and Moses Finley, aimed to approach ancient history with interests adopted from other disciplines and to answer questions by invoking new methodologies or kinds of evidence that had rarely been employed by historians of ancient Greece or Rome. Their works therefore represent both significant departures from the way ancient history had usually been conducted and important steps in the development of ancient social history. Before discussing these scholars' contributions, however, it is worth considering the traditional characteristics of ancient history more carefully.

Traditional Approaches to Roman History before the 1960s

Two characteristics of ancient history up to the mid-twentieth century deserve particular attention. First, priority was given to literary evidence, which was inevitably authored by ancient males of the social, economic, and political elite. This focus sent historical investigations down the well-trodden paths of political history because literary sources can answer only certain questions.[7] Second, an attitude of uncritical admiration for these same authors and their thoughts prevailed. Classics was originally mainly the study of philology ("word loving"), and the study of Greece and Rome through literature was supposed to be an edifying—indeed, humanizing—experience.[8] The words of the Greeks and the Romans were felt to confer different benefits upon the modern student of their cultures and histories, however. This perspective can be seen, for example, in H.D.F. Kitto's *The Greeks* (1951) and R.H. Barrow's *The Romans* (1949).

The Greeks were to be admired primarily for their literary ingenuity and their philosophy. Kitto explains: "That which distils, preserves and then enlarges the experience of a people is Literature . . . "Epic" poetry, history and drama; philosophy in all its branches, from metaphysics to economics; mathematics and many of the natural—all these begin with the Greeks."[9] For the Romans, it was law and orderliness that deserved veneration, as Barrow makes clear: "The greatest achievement of the Romans, whether we consider it on its own intrinsic merits or in its influence on the history of the world, is without doubt their law."[10]

Despite the different rewards gained from studying the Greeks and the Romans, contemplation of what were often called "the achievements" of each was equally a sort of self-exploration. Western civilization began with the Greeks and continued with the Romans (as the Greeks' successors), and the modern societies of Western Europe and North America were the intellectual inheritors and political progeny of both. Logic consequently dictated that if we are like the ancients, then they were like us. More specifically, some of them (the leading politicians and intellectuals of antiquity) were like some of us (the leading politicians and intellectuals of the modern West). Empathy suppressed criticism and instead inspired conclusions that drew the ancients and moderns ever closer together in the imagination.

Again, we can look to Kitto and Barrow for examples. Kitto addresses the position of women in ancient Athenian society, an uncomfortable topic for the modern admirer of the glory that was Greece. Literary evidence, which included such things as Pericles's famous statement that women should not be spoken of in praise or in criticism (Thuc. 2.45.2), suggested to some scholars that "the Athenian treated his women with considerable indifference, for which 'contempt' may not be too harsh a substitute."[11] Even though Kitto's writing displays a condescending attitude towards women of his own time (his discussion begins: "Most men are interested in women, and most women in themselves. Let us therefore consider the position of women in Athens"[12]), Kitto felt sure that the impression of Athenian disdain must be incorrect: "What is wrong is the picture it gives of the Athenian man." This statement shows that Kitto's focus lies not with Athenian women but with Athenian men. He reasons: "The Athenian had his faults, but pre-eminent among his better qualities were lively intelligence, sociability, humanity, and curiosity. To say that he habitually treated one-half of his own race with indifference, even contempt, does not, to my mind, make sense."[13] Rather than invoking ancient evidence that contradicts the impression of the contemptuous Athenian male, Kitto furnishes support for his position by raising the spectre of William Gladstone, a leading British statesman of the nineteenth century: "Take Pericles' dictum . . . Suppose Gladstone had said, 'I do not care to hear a lady's name bandied about in general talk, whether for praise or dispraise': would that imply disdain, or an old-fashioned deference and courtesy?"[14] It is safe to say that both Pericles and Kitto (and Gladstone, had he expressed such a statement) were products of their time, but few historians would now say that the similarity of their times is great enough to carry the weight of proof Kitto attempts to impose.

Barrow, for his part, is faced with an even bigger hurdle to unbridled admiration for the Romans: for all their imperial grandeur and good government, the Romans made heavy use of the practice of slavery, the human by-product of imperial expansion. As David Mattingly has recently observed, modern historians, particularly those from countries with imperial pasts or presents, have habitually put a positive spin on imperialism.[15] Barrow exemplifies this tendency. He manages to rehabilitate the Romans by arguing that imperial conquest and the consequent enslavement of formerly free people were really conferred benefits rather than imposed injustices, provided that the imperial power was a civilized one: "Indeed, slavery comes nearest to its justification in the early Roman Empire: for a man from a 'backward' race might be brought within the pale of civilization, educated and trained in a craft or profession, and turned into a useful member of society."[16] Furthermore, Barrow argues that, while slaves reaped the many benefits of slavery, their masters carried the burden. He tells us that the slaves had "often enviable" positions that featured "opportunities without responsibilities." They benefited from the civilizing influence of kindly masters, public opinion that ensured legislation against misuse, and the almost certainty that they would be freed. Meanwhile, Romans jeopardized their moral and economic growth so that others (that is, slaves) might experience the "compulsory initiation into a higher culture" for their own good and thereby flourish.[17]

Until the mid-twentieth century, the refurbishment of the less admirable habits of the Greeks and Romans into something more palatable to modern tastes was made easier by the other tendency that marked ancient history: trust that the words of the elite men who authored literature and law described the truth. Historians certainly recognized the limited potential of such sources to provide much evidence for the lives of anyone but elite males,[18] and they were also aware that some ancient authors might be prone to exaggeration or other distortions when describing other elements of society. But this awareness was limited. Descriptions of women in the works of Carcopino (1939) and Fowler (1909) provide good examples. When discussing the poet Juvenal's negative presentation of Roman women with intellectual pretensions in his sixth *Satire*, Carcopino clearly recognizes Juvenal's biases with the following remark: "If Juvenal were alive today he would be pretty sure to shower abuse on women drivers and pilots."

But Carcopino soon becomes less cautious about taking the poet's perspectives as an untarnished mirror of reality. He goes on to consider Juvenal's verses about women at banquets, which include descriptions of women gorging themselves with food and wine to the point of vomiting. Carcopino observes that "it is bad enough that satire should be able to draw such types and expect readers to recognise them." To be fair, it could be true that some women behaved as Juvenal says, but Carcopino's obvious disapproval points to the weakening of his objectivity. The last vestiges of Carcopino's skepticism about Juvenal's truthfulness vanish when he considers the portrayal of women engaging in the lewdest displays of adultery: "It is evident that the independence which women at this time enjoyed frequently degenerated into licence, and that the looseness of their morals tended to dissolve family ties."[19]

It was not only the negative that was swallowed wholesale: similar trust was invested in positive accounts of female behaviour. Fowler, for example, considers the so-called *laudatio Turiae* (the "praise of Turia"), an inscription in which a husband eulogized his dead wife, whose life was (in Fowler's admiring summation) "spent in unselfish devotion to her husband's interests."[20] In Turia, Fowler finds a pleasant contrast to the Roman "new woman" (see this chapter's opening discussion) and states with approval: "No one can study this inscription without becoming convinced that it tells an unvarnished tale of truth—that here was really a rare and precious woman . . . And we feel that there is one human being, and one only, of whom she is always thinking, to whom she has given her whole heart—[her] husband."[21]

Carcopino and Fowler share with each other, and with most historians of the time, the same unstated assumption that ancient sources do not misrepresent the truth. Why would ancient authors, who were educated and upright men, be untruthful? But interpreting and understanding ancient sources is not as simple as assuming that dead men do or do not lie. As social and cultural historians have since demonstrated, ancient evidence of all types must be approached with sensitivity to the social position and aims of its creator(s) and with careful attention to its context.[22] The number of factors that might influence the impression of society left by any source is vast, but the most basic application of the considerations of author, aim, and context shifts Juvenal's presentation of women's conduct from the realm of unfiltered reality to the territory of stereotype (as one might expect in satire) and that of the *laudatio Turiae* from "the unvarnished truth" to a utopia of idealized behaviour (as one might expect in a eulogy). Neither a stereotype nor an ideal tells us much about women's usual activity or actual experience, though they might say something about the social expectations against which their behaviour might be judged.

New Approaches to Ancient History

As discussed above, literary sources can provide only certain types of answers, and limited answers mean limited questions. New questions require new ways of answering them. The works discussed in this section are notable for the questions they asked, the methods they employed to suggest answers (even if many of these answers have since been overturned), and their use of various types of evidence. They also demonstrate that it is possible to admire the work of a historian while disagreeing with his or her conclusions.[23]

Classical history is a relatively conservative field: established, traditionally trained classicists have often dismissed novel approaches as misdirected (see, for example, Box 1.1). It is therefore unsurprising that two historians who managed to gain a foothold with new focuses and methodologies in the first half of the twentieth century both had rather unusual backgrounds and experience and were sufficiently confident to hold their own against their critics. The first is Michael Rostovtzeff, a White Russian who fled the Bolsheviks in 1918 to land first at Oxford and then at Yale. In 1926 he published *The Social and Economic History of the Roman Empire*.[24] This work, hefty in both physical weight and scholarship, sought to describe the history of Rome in light of the evolving relationship of social groups as impacted by economic considerations. The study was unique in its approach and its failure to take the prosopographical perspective so fashionable at the time (which had its critics too: the eminent Arnaldo Momigliano observed that Rostovtzeff "was lucky in being born early enough to escape the present ridiculous adoration of so-called prosopography").[25]

Roman imperial society, in Rostovtzeff's formulation, developed two significant populations: the unsophisticated rural population, who were great in numbers; and the less numerous culturally sophisticated urban merchants, towards whom the rural population was hostile. It has long been felt that this description of Roman society and Roman history bears an uncomfortably close resemblance to what is assumed to have been Rostovtzeff's own opinion of the events that had sent him into exile from his homeland, and even Rostovtzeff himself soon came to question the aptness of his description. Nonetheless, the enormous scope of the work, the foregrounding of economic considerations, and especially the

Primary Source

Box 1.1: Hugh Last's assessment of Michael Rostovtzeff's *The Social and Economic History of the Roman Empire*, in his obituary for Rostovtzeff. *Journal of Roman Studies* 43 (1953): 133–4, quote from 133.

Rostovtzeff's interpretation of Roman imperial history is to some extent misconceived . . . Of the achievements of Rome none is greater than the creation of the Corpus Iuris [Roman law] . . . and though Rostovtzeff was almost thirty-three and had already been at Berlin when Mommsen died, he never showed himself so far a disciple as to seek access to the Roman mind through the Private Law, which is its fullest and most detailed expression.

marshalling of evidence of all kinds (archaeological, art historical, papyrological, epigraphical, numismatic, and literary) to make his argument were new and deeply impressive.

The second historian is Moses Finley. Though most of his publications date to the 1960s and beyond and focus on the Greek world, his approach to ancient history developed earlier, and his influence on history and historians of both Greece and Rome has been profound. An American, he earned a BA (with a major in psychology) from Syracuse University at age 15, an MA (in public law) from Columbia University at age 17, and shortly thereafter began to pursue a doctorate in ancient history at the same university.[26] Through contacts at Columbia, Finley became interested in economic and social theory. He would come to believe that ancient history was poorly served by the habits of his contemporaries, who in his opinion merely reiterated the words of the ancient literary sources and asked only those questions that were prompted by such sources. He instead advocated the productive potential of approaching ancient society through the consideration of a wide array of different kinds of sources, with the help of "models." Models in this sense are questions raised in, and theories drawn from, other disciplines (such as anthropology, economics, and sociology).

In Finley's opinion, historians, not ancient sources, could raise questions and their answers were not immutable truths but only an interpretation of the sources. He also felt that the sources could not provide answers without the help of theoretical hypotheses, and he protested against the isolated consideration of historical phenomena or institutions. Finley's own work was notably influenced by social theorist Max Weber, though it was an interest in Marxist theory that, in the 1950s, led to suspicions of him having communist sympathies and to his subsequent dismissal from his position at Rutgers University. Unemployment led him to seek a position at the University of Cambridge, where he eventually became Professor of Ancient History.

It goes without saying that the Professor of Ancient History at Cambridge could wield a great deal of influence over the way ancient history was studied. At the same time, social history in general was attracting the interest of an increasing number of ancient historians, thanks in no small part to the social upheavals of the 1960s and 1970s. Some historians (who, not surprisingly, often had backgrounds or interests in different disciplines) saw the potential of opening lines of inquiry that were simply not possible if single-minded dependence upon traditional approaches was maintained. For example, Keith Hopkins, a key figure in this movement and another who would later become Professor of Ancient History at Cambridge, was trained and employed as a sociologist as well as an ancient historian. In a series of controversial studies in the 1960s and 1970s, Hopkins used sociological methods to investigate the life cycles and consequences for social structures of the general Roman population (see Box 1.2 for Hopkins's justification for his methods). His studies sparked a lively interest in demography (population studies),[27] which continues to thrive.

See Chapter 15, pp. 332–3, for further discussion of Rostovtzeff, Finley, and Hopkins and their approaches to ancient and Roman economies.

Primary Source

Box 1.2: Hopkins, K. 1978. *Conquerors and Slaves: Sociological Studies in Roman History*, vol. 1. Cambridge: Cambridge University Press, x.

One objective is to experiment with methods borrowed from sociology in order to gain new insights into changes in Roman society—not new facts, but a different way of understanding the relationship between various changes . . . Throughout this book I try to explore some of the long-term consequences of repeated actions, for example, the consequences of importing slaves into Italy during the period of Rome's imperial expansion, or of allocating colonial plots to emigrant Italian peasants. I want to explore the consequences of these actions independently of the intentions of individual actors . . . The ancient source, if we are lucky, tells us only what an ancient author thought was happening and how he felt about it, or how he thought that others felt about it. That is obviously important, but partial. In the face of this difficulty, we have to look out for other methods by which we can validate analyses . . . That is where sociological methods can be helpful. And that is why these two books make use of sociological concepts and arguments, set out explicit hypotheses, and seek to support those arguments with models, figures and coordinates, as well as with quotations from the sources.

The willingness to consider non-literary sources opened the possibilities further. Focus could turn to elements of ancient society that were either under- or indirectly represented in literary sources, such as women, slaves, ex-slaves (**freedmen** and **freedwomen**), children, the poorer citizenry, and non-citizens.[28] Relationships between different social elements—marriage, familial relations, bonds of **patronage** between ex-slaves and their former masters, and relationships between slaves—could also be considered.[29] Historians with these interests did not meditate on the "achievements" of the ancient Greeks and Romans. Instead, they explored concepts in antiquity that had contemporary relevance. This pursuit came at the expense of losing undiluted admiration for the ancients, but such a price was no longer considered too high (see, for example, Box 1.3, where Keith Bradley describes the benefits of considering Roman slavery in light of current understandings of human rights).

New areas of investigation continue to be identified as current society's concerns change. For example, in the last 20 years, interest in the Roman provinces and their experiences of the "coming of Rome" has been growing. This focus surely reflects modern interest in cultural exchange stemming from the removal of trade barriers between different countries (a result of, for example, the North American Free Trade Agreement and the development of the Eurozone) and the consequent ease of movement of goods. At the

Primary Source

Box 1.3: Bradley, K. 1992. "'The Regular, Daily Traffic in Slaves': Roman History and Contemporary History." *The Classical Journal* **87 (2): 136.**

The kinds of impact on slaves made by the traffic in human merchandise . . . are symptomatic of what in contemporary affairs we should now call violations of fundamental human rights. If the current sensitivity to that concept sharpens perception and understanding of the past, then that to my mind marks a true historical advance. It does not follow that what is admirable from the past is any the less admirable; it simply means that the price of the admirable—an incalculable degree of human misery and suffering—is given its full historical due. It is in this sense, accordingly, that one might assert that the best history is very much contemporary history.

same time, advances in technology that have given unprecedented rise to social networking have also played a significant role in cultural communication. Of current concern in an expanding world is the fate of traditional cultural forms (such as language, food, manners, and social habits). Do they persist or are they simply discarded by individuals in favour of something "better"? Do they continue without government intervention to ensure their survival? Can such mandates be successful? It has become clear that the answers to these questions are far more complex than a simple "yes" or "no." Studies of the Roman provinces reflect this awareness, and gone are the days when historians spoke heedlessly of "Romanization," a term that suggested that Roman culture paved over previous traditions in newly conquered areas. This concept has been replaced with a sensitivity to the methods of, limits to, and motives for cultural "blending" in the provinces and a recognition that all provincial communities in the Roman empire did not have one common experience of Roman rule.

Social History and the Classics: Debates and Problems

The aims and approaches to ancient history embraced by social historians were not met with unmitigated enthusiasm or even approval in all academic circles.[30] Consider, for example, the opinion of Hugh Last (then Camden Chair of Ancient History at Oxford) on the usefulness of other disciplines—in this case, anthropology—in the study of classics: "An acquaintance with the habits of savages is not an education."[31] Nor were the pioneers of social history in ancient history endlessly open-minded about its potential. One can note Finley's pronouncement to then-student Richard Saller on his desire to study the Roman family: "Why? The lawyers have already written everything that needs to be said."[32] Over the years, a series of related and recurrent concerns over the conduct of social history has developed within the broader field of ancient history. It should be noted here that these criticisms were and are not levelled only by traditionalists but by social historians as well.

First and foremost among these problems is the proper relationship between the historian and the ancient sources, particularly the literary sources. Some have been resolute that the historian must follow the sources. In a critical review of Hopkins's *Conquerors and Slaves* (1978), Ernst Badian writes: "The lack of what one might call the historian's basic humility before his sources . . . leads to uncertainty in evaluation, to misinterpretation, indeed to sheer invention, of the evidence."[33] In the introduction to his tour de force *The Emperor in the Roman World*, Fergus Millar (1997), who would later become Camden Chair of Ancient History, similarly champions a reading of the sources uninfluenced by any sort of extraneous theory (see Box 1.4). Others (such as, unsurprisingly, Hopkins) have been equally adamant that the treatment of the sources as "sacred texts" is misguided, not least of all because writing about these works in languages other than Latin or ancient Greek means that historians cannot avoid interpreting the words. Hopkins writes: "The historian interprets a lost world to modern readers through the medium of a living language."[34] Put simply, our language is the product of our society, which is different from ancient society; therefore, our words and their words are loaded with, and carry, different meanings (see further Box 1.5, an excerpt from Hopkins's review of Millar's *The Emperor in the Roman World*).

Yet other historians, being less certain about the appropriate treatment of the sources, fall in between the extremes. Believing that ancient sources convey "the unvarnished

Primary Source

Box 1.4: Millar, F. (1977) 1992. *The Emperor in the Roman World*, 2nd edn. London: Duckworth, ix.

In preparing the work I have rigidly avoided reading sociological works on kingship or related topics, or studies of monarchic institutions in societies other than those of Greece and Rome. I am perfectly conscious that this will have involved considerable losses in percipience, and unawareness of whole ranges of questions which I could have asked. None the less, I am confident that the loss in the opposite case would have been far greater. For to have come to the subject with an array of concepts derived from the study of other societies would merely have made even more unattainable the proper objective of an historian, to subordinate himself to the evidence and to the conceptual world of a society in the past.

Primary Source

Box 1.5: Hopkins, K. 1978. "Review: Rules of Evidence." *Journal of Roman Studies* **68: 180, 182.**

I regret that Millar has written a socio-political analysis of Roman emperors without explicit consideration of power, legitimacy and authority . . . In sociological literature, power is often conceptualized as the capacity either to make people do what you want against their will, or to shape their desires so that they want to do what you want. Let me stress straight away that I am not advocating that all history should be sociological history, nor do I intend to enter here even a short essay on power. I want only to raise some of the questions to which a conceptual awareness could and in my view should have led Millar . . . One of my main dissatisfactions with Millar's history is the absence of explicit problems. He seeks only to describe, not to explain. Once again, I have not been completely fair. Millar sets himself one problem repeatedly; at the beginning of each section, he typically studies the origins of a practice of institution . . . [but] explanations of origin are only partial; they do not explain persistence . . . Millar completely overlooks what we call structural functional explanations, that is explanations of how Roman institutions and practices, values, expectations and beliefs related to each other in enabling the Roman political system to function and persist . . . One problem is that the ancient sources, the evidence, are elevated to the level of sacred texts . . . On the whole, Millar seems to assume that the sources by and large faithfully reported the world in which they lived. But it is conceivable that ancient sources, like modern newspapers, reported the abnormal more often than the normal . . . The evidence is not holy; it is itself a social construct and so should not be taken at face value any more than one should take *The Times* or a contemporary academic political scientist as necessarily right. The historian should interpret his sources actively, by trying, for example, to understand what the ancient sources took for granted and so systematically under-reported.

truth" (to quote Fowler) is now uncommon, but how should they be interpreted? Do they describe what was normal or what was exceptional? If they describe stereotypes, what is their relationship to reality? If different sources give contradictory impressions of society, which one is to be followed? And which should have priority: the sources or the theoretical framework used to interpret them? In other words, should the sources be subordinated to the theory to form a sort of "best fit"? Or should the theory be subordinated to the sources, such that the former is proven unsuitable if enough sources seem to contradict it? If so, how many contradictory sources should suffice? One? Two? A dozen?

Other concerns arise as a consequence of the attempt to deal with source interpretation. Some scholars occasionally chastise others for using ill-defined terms or concepts, which (they say) result in narrow or superficial studies (see, for example, Box 1.5 for Hopkins's criticisms of Millar for an insufficiently nuanced concept of power). However, other scholars' care to describe their interpretative frameworks precisely can lead them to use words whose meanings are not immediately obvious to their audience (or to use words in senses that are unusual). Readers may feel that these words conceal rather than illuminate meaning. Indeed, accusations of the use of jargon are a commonplace of academic criticism. Applause of the exceptions underlines what is sometimes felt to be the rule. Consider, for example, the compliment Peter Brunt (then Camden Chair of Ancient History) paid to Geoffrey de Ste. Croix in his review of the latter's *The Class Struggle in the Ancient Greek World from the Archaic Age to the Arab Conquests* (1982), a work heavily influenced by Marxist theory: "The approach is sociological. But [Ste. Croix] does not envelop us with cloudy metaphors and ill-defined abstractions or suppose that impenetrable verbosity will be taken for profundity of thought."[35] The unwritten end to this sentence is clearly "as others do."

Theory and incomprehensibility are not necessarily conjoined twins of scholarship, however. To no small extent, theory can be understood as a self-conscious method by which questions may be asked and a recognition that only certain, or limited, answers may be derived. On this understanding, theoretical approaches may be "named" (for example, Michel Foucault's theory of power), historians might use specific vocabulary that the theorist has laden with meaning, or a theoretical approach may be simply an explanation of the stance that the historian will take regarding his or her use of the ancient sources. Consider, for example, Saller's approach, or theory, regarding the use of anecdotes as historical evidence: Saller carefully defines what he understands the term *anecdote* to mean, considers the purpose of anecdotes in antiquity, and concludes that they cannot be taken as reflection of fact but as indicators of ancient ideologies and expectations of behaviour.[36]

Next is the use of cross-cultural comparisons.[37] This method is an attractive way to investigate the lives of poorly attested segments of the ancient population because, by considering their better documented counterparts in other societies, it is perhaps possible to recapture something of the ancient experience. The personal accounts of slaves in the antebellum American South have been used, for example, as ways to think about the lives of ancient Roman slaves and to suggest modes of resistance.[38]

As promising as the approach might be, however, cross-cultural comparisons are often problematic. The comparison of the practices or ideologies of two different societies demands that the societies compared be internally homogenous to some extent. But most societies experience either local variation or change over time, which raises the question of which places and times are being compared. Even if these details could be narrowed down, the choice of such-and-such society at such-and-such a time as a comparative situation often risks being criticized as arbitrary. What is the common element that suggests that the comparison is apt, and why should it be more important than the differences? For example, do all preindustrial societies present as possible points of comparison for the structures and values of ancient society? Are economics and technology the only factors that drive social and cultural characteristics? Or are there other, possibly even more important, factors? If so, what are they?

Finally, there is the charge of anachronism in the study of ancient societies. Those who import descriptive terms, theories, or models drawn from other disciplines or who employ the observance of other cultures or historical societies to investigate ancient history risk using concepts that are entirely inapplicable to the societies they seek to understand (see Box 1.4 for Millar's concerns about this topic). For others, anachronism can never be avoided, regardless of the acceptance or rejection of a theoretical framework (consider once again the opinion that anachronism is an unavoidable function of writing history in a modern language). We are back where we began, and in more ways than one, since a frequent criticism is that a new methodology results in a conclusion quite similar to one from previous scholarship.[39] Therefore, do we really need all the careful vocabulary and impenetrable theories? Or is history more like math class, where we are told that the answer is less important than how we reach it, particularly since we might gain insights along the way?

The difficulty with all these problems is not that someone must be wrong but that no one can be entirely right. Far from being a damper on history, this situation is instead a productive force: problems generate discussion, the lifeblood of academic disciplines. As this chapter demonstrates, scholarship in ancient history is an ongoing debate among interested parties rather than a race to have the final word.

Social History and This Volume

Given the foregoing discussion, two issues of particular relevance to the present volume must be addressed. First, the reader may be left with the impression that the historian G.M. Trevelyan's (now notorious) 1944 definition of social history as "history with the politics left out" is correct. This view is now widely rejected, as it has become increasingly clear that politics and society did not function in isolation from each other and that, consequently, political history and social history have much to offer each other. For one thing, sensitivity to one increases understanding of the other.[40] Later chapters will demonstrate the close connection between, for example, political concerns, legal actions, and social changes in the Augustan period. Here, we will use another example.

See Chapter 3, pp. 54 and 60; ←
Chapter 4, p. 90;
Chapter 5, pp. 104–6; and
Chapter 8, pp. 184–6, for
Augustan social legislation.

Roman success in war often meant an influx of new slaves into the Roman economy, thereby inextricably binding the history of Roman slavery to Rome's political expansion. In turn, it is possible to detect the poignancy of political imagery and rhetoric at the end of the Republic only if one is sensitive to the nature of Roman slavery. We can see this relationship in a coin minted by Marcus Brutus, one of Caesar's murderers, to commemorate Caesar's assassination on the Ides of March 44 BCE (see Figure 1.1). One side of the coin features daggers framing a *pilleus*, the cap ex-slaves wore on special occasions.[41] Clearly, the coin is a celebration of Roman freedom regained, but the image of the little egg-shaped *pilleus* speaks greater volumes if we are attuned to hear them. Roman ex-slaves were expected to display eternal gratitude and loyalty to the one who had bestowed upon them the great benefit of freedom. Usually, this was their former master, but in the metaphor of **manumission** that the coin invokes, the Romans should be grateful and loyal to Brutus and his co-conspirators.

Figure 1.1 This coin celebrates one of the most famous dates in history, 15 March 44 BCE, when Julius Caesar, dictator of Rome, was assassinated by his former friends Brutus and Cassius. They were dedicated republicans who resented Caesar's rise to almost monarchical power after his victory in a civil war against Pompey the Great. © The Trustees of the British Museum

Around the same time, Cicero launched oratorical attacks upon Marcus Antonius (Marc Antony). In one delivered in 43 BCE, he declared that the long enslavement of the Roman people, which had begun with Caesar's dictatorship, could finally near its end (Cic. *Phil.* 8.32). The invocation of slavery is intended to nurture indignation in his audience. Cicero's implication is that Romans—masters of others by virtue of political and military superiority—have been unable to speak or act freely and instead have laboured in a state of forced compliance under an unworthy master (Caesar) and his unworthy sidekick (Antony).

These attempts to control Romans' perception of events and influence the direction of their loyalty were only partially successful: both Brutus and Cicero would soon be dead, casualties on the losing side of civil war. But the event of civil war itself is made more explicable if we are able to comprehend the images and rhetoric which, by activating and manipulating Roman awareness of the realities of slavery, aimed to polarize opinion. For a further example of how social history can shed light on political history, see Box 1.6.

Second, a perusal of this book's contents may lead to the question of why there are no chapters devoted to "daily life" or the lives of women. Bewilderment is natural, since daily life is surely an integral part of social experience and investigations of the experience of women and the social construction of "woman" have been important elements of the movement towards social history and cultural studies in the classics.[42] As will become clear in subsequent chapters, however, Roman society was composed of individuals with different social identities and legal privileges. At the same time, the Roman empire encompassed different communities, each with its own history and local traditions. Each individual's

Political History

Box 1.6: Gracchan Reforms and Women's Labour

Tiberius Sempronius Gracchus's tribunate in 133 BCE, his proposed reforms to land ownership in Italy, and the bloody aftermath of the plan are generally regarded by historians as the beginning of the late Republic, a period characterized by chronic violence and political upheaval in Rome and Italy. The reforms are understood to have aimed at alleviating the plight of the Italian peasant farmer. However, they spawned such a negative response among segments of the Roman elite that a state of emergency was called, and Tiberius (along with many of his supporters) was bludgeoned to death by an angry mob of senators.

But what had caused the distress of the farmers in the first place? The long-accepted explanation is rooted in the expectation that Rome's foreign wars and expansion in the second century BCE demanded that Italian conscripts undertake long tours of duty far from their small farms, a situation that exposed families to starvation and wrought a decline in population of free landholders. This explanation, however, does not take into account the possibility that men were not the only people who could, and probably did, perform agricultural labour.

Ancient ideals of female behaviour did not include the performance of farm work, but Walter Scheidel argues for the probability of female participation in light of anthropological studies, cross-cultural comparisons, and the evidence of ancient literature and art. He notes that "the wide gap between ideological claims and actual practice deserves our special attention," particularly since, if agricultural work was regularly done by females, this would have had a significant impact on the economic role of women, in addition to marriage patterns, food and health care allocations, and "what might be called their personal freedom."[1]

Nathan Rosenstein demonstrates that female agricultural labour also has importance in our understanding of political history.[2] Using demographic techniques to estimate female work potential and model marriage patterns, he argues that the impression of Italian peasant destitution and population decline in the second century BCE is incorrect; the population actually increased during this time, making it difficult for larger families to sustain themselves. With this line of reasoning, the reasons for Gracchan reforms and the violence associated with them (itself a harbinger of the bloodshed that was to come for the next century) lie in quite different circumstances than those long held to have been the case.

Notes

1. Scheidel (1995, 1996a); quotes from Scheidel (1995: 209, 204).
2. Rosenstein (2004).

daily experience of the most mundane activities—eating, bathing, dressing, socializing—was influenced to some degree by his or her location, age, gender, and social, economic, and legal **status**. Whose life, where, and at what time should be the focus of a chapter on daily life? Such a chapter would be either impossible due to insufficient evidence for everyone but a select few individuals or misleading if focused on those few individuals only. Instead, topics for chapters have been chosen that, when considered together, give a sense of the variety of individual experience.

A chapter on the experience of women might also give a false impression. Roman women did not have one common experience. There is no reason to imagine that empathy of "sisterhood" was shared between women of disparate rank, though perhaps there is one trait common to all Roman women: their lives were heavily influenced by their connections to men. Otherwise, women's experience was informed by their location, age, and social and legal status. However, it must be admitted that the choice not to include such a chapter is rather arbitrary. After all, no social category enjoyed one single, common experience. Different slaves, for example, could have radically different lives, and yet a chapter on slavery has been included.

The omission of a separate chapter on women is, however, consistent with what we consider one of the primary purposes of history: to engage with its audience in ways that lead to deeper contemplation of issues of current importance. Women, unlike slaves, compose approximately half of the modern population and of the envisioned readership of this book. Isolating Roman women as a "topic" to be "covered" in a separate chapter in an introductory volume risks giving newcomers to Roman studies the idea that Roman women were also somehow compartmentalized in ancient society. Diffusing a discussion of women's experience throughout several chapters is preferable, not least of all because this broader approach is more useful for the contemplation of the present heterogeneity of women's experience and social influence. That said, women do not figure in the discussion of every chapter. Readers are encouraged to consider the absence of women to be as significant as their presence, since the former also points to fruitful areas of contemplation and comparison with the present. Furthermore, although there was no single female experience in Roman antiquity, "woman" as a concept, social construction, and category of imagination, did exist. For this reason, a chapter on gender and **sexuality** has been included in preference to one on women per se.

Summary

As the ancient Greek word *historia* ("inquiry") suggests, the pursuit of history is an inquiry into the past. But it is often also a reflection of contemporary concerns and interests, as these tend to influence the questions any given historian seeks to answer. This tendency is a major justification for history as an academic study: history provides a safe context in which to consider today's issues, and the similarities and differences between then and now are both useful in our understanding of our own society. The study of ancient history has always been undertaken as an education for the present, but earlier historians traced only what they considered the admirable qualities of the Romans for the purposes of emulation. More recent historical investigations focus on the experience of members of the population beyond the elite to investigate issues that are of contemporary relevance.

Social historical studies in ancient history employ a wider base of evidence than was traditionally used: literary evidence is no longer the exclusive window into the past nor are the words of ancient authors considered a mirror of past reality. The benefits of epigraphic, archaeological, iconographic, numismatic, and papyrological evidence are now widely recognized. In addition, methods drawn from different disciplines such as anthropology, sociology, literary theory, and political studies are used to illuminate investigations into antiquity. These methods are problematic, but the debate surrounding their appropriateness is a productive force in studies of ancient Roman history and society.

Questions for Review and Discussion

1. Are there benefits and purpose to studying a society that is not wholly admirable? Why or why not?

2. Create an argument that refutes and another that supports the following statement: It is possible to have a full understanding of social structures and dynamics without an awareness of political history and vice versa.

3. Which cultural, social, economic, or political characteristics must be shared between two societies in order for a cross-cultural comparison to be possible? Give reasons to support your answer.

4. Which elements of today's society will elude the socio-historical record of evidence? Why will these groups be overlooked? What approaches or methodologies could future social historians use to illuminate the lives of such under-represented people?

5. Are the reasons given for excluding a chapter on the lives of women in Roman society compelling or should a separate chapter on this topic have been included in this book? Why or why not?

Suggested Reading

Barchiesi, A., and W. Scheidel. 2011. *The Oxford Handbook of Roman Studies*. Oxford: Oxford University Press.

This recent collection of essays by leading scholars on a wide range of areas germane to the study of Roman history, society, and culture includes individual chapters devoted to the consideration of different types of evidence.

Bradley, K. 1992. "'The Regular, Daily Traffic in Slaves': Roman History and Contemporary History." *The Classical Journal* 87 (2): 125–38.

Bradley makes the case for exploring issues of modern importance in ancient society, even at the expense of exposing some abhorrent aspects of ancient culture.

Burke, P. 2005. *History and Social Theory*, 2nd edn. Ithaca, NY: Cornell University Press.

As the title suggests, this book considers the evolving relationship between history and social theory as both are practised by academics. Attention is given to the usefulness of different theoretical approaches and to the problems encountered by those who pursue them in studies of historical societies.

Golden, M. 1992. "The Uses of Cross-Cultural Comparison in Ancient Social History." *Échos du monde classique/Classical Views* 36: 309–31.

This article discusses the advantages and difficulties of using cross-cultural comparisons in ancient history by critiquing some well-known studies that have used them.

Hopkins, K. 1978. "Review: The Rules of Evidence." *Journal of Roman Studies* 68: 178–86.

In his review of Fergus Millar's *The Emperor in the Roman World*, Hopkins lays out clearly the mounting objections to the traditional methods of writing history.

Peachin, M. 2011. "Introduction: The Study of Ancient Roman Society." In *The Oxford Handbook of Social Relations in the Roman World*, edited by M. Peachin, 3–36. Oxford: Oxford University Press.

In his introduction to a large collection of essays on various aspects and manifestations of Roman social relations, Peachin provides a brief and clear account of the development of social history as a field.

Saller, R. 1980. "Anecdotes as Historical Evidence for the Principate." *Greece & Rome* 27: 69–83.

Saller discusses the problems associated with using anecdotes as reflections of "true" history and, in so doing, provides a useful example of the steps involved in creating an interpretive approach to literary sources.

Scheidel, W. 1995. "The Most Silent Women of Greece and Rome: Rural Labour and Women's Life in the Ancient World (I)." *Greece & Rome* 42 (2): 202–17.

————. 1996. "The Most Silent Women of Greece and Rome: Rural Labour and Women's Life in the Ancient World (II)." *Greece & Rome* 43 (1): 1–10.

In the absence of much direct ancient evidence, these essays consider ways of exploring the realities of female agricultural labour and the implications for studying both ancient women and ancient society.

Treggiari, S. 1975. "Roman Social History: Recent Interpretations." *Histoire Sociale/Social History* 8: 149–64.

Treggiari offers an excellent bibliographical essay on seminal works in the budding field of Roman social history as of 1975. Many of the works mentioned have been surpassed or their subjects significantly expanded in the intervening years, but full appreciation must be given to these pioneering efforts, which have opened up inquiries and methodologies for subsequent scholars.

Notes

1   Fowler (1909: 135–67), subsequent quotes from pp. 144–5, 148, 154, and 158.
2   On the "new woman," see Ledger (1997).
3   For the development and relationships between social history and cultural studies, see Peachin (2011: 12–13) and Roller (2011).
4   Peachin (2011: 5–6); Burke (2005: 13–16).
5   Eck (2011: 148–52) provides an overview of the development of prosopography in the field of Roman history. See also Treggiari (1975: 150–1).
6   Peachin (2011: 5).
7   Treggiari (1975: 149).
8   It should be noted that, since 1863, enthusiasts of Roman history also had the *Corpus Inscriptionum Latinarum* (the abbreviation, *CIL*, is more commonly used), an on-going collection of Latin inscriptions from the Roman world begun by Theodor Mommsen.
9   Kitto (1951: 8–9).
10   Barrow (1949: 209).
11   Kitto (1951: 222).
12   Ibid.: 219.
13   Ibid.: 222.
14   Ibid.: 224.
15   Mattingly (2011: 13–22).
16   Barrow (1949: 101).
17   Ibid.: 100–02; see also Carcopino (2003: 56–61) for the eagerness of the Roman to manumit his slaves, whom he loves and who love him. Bradley (1992) discusses more recent attempts to overlook Roman slavery in order to focus on "admirable" traits of the Romans.
18   For example, Kitto (1951: 223).
19   Carcopino (2003: 92–4). Compare Barrow (1949: 102–03) for similar approaches to ex-slaves based on the descriptions of Petronius, a first-century CE elite novelist, who "exposes" their behaviours.
20   Fowler (1909: 165).
21   Ibid.: 167.
22   Roller (2011: 239–47) provides discussion and case studies.
23   Treggiari (1975: 150).
24   See Shaw (1992) for a discussion of Rostovtzeff's contributions, along with suppositions (and their limits) about the influence of his personal experience on his views of Roman history.
25   Ibid.: 217.
26   Whittaker (1997) provides an overview of Finley's life and works.

27 Scheidel (2001a: 1) notes that "'hard core' demography" and population studies are not exactly synonymous: the first is "the scientific study of human populations, primarily with respect to their size, their structure and their development"; the second is a study of "the relations between demographic events and social, economic, or cultural phenomena." See Scheidel (2001a) for a survey of the pursuit of demography (primarily in the first sense) in Roman studies.

28 Treggiari (1975) provides a bibliographic essay on Roman social history up to the mid-seventies and discusses many seminal works in these areas.

29 The bibliography is too vast to be included here, as is a list of scholars dealing with these topics. This volume's suggested readings lists (in each chapter) and the list of works cited direct students to important works in the various areas. See also the recent essays and associated bibliographies in Peachin (2011).

30 See Shaw (1982) for an account of the hostility of ancient historians towards the social sciences and a thorough, sometimes sympathetic, critique of Hopkins (1978), a particularly controversial work.

31 Quoted in Brown (1988: 431).

32 Quoted in Golden (2011: 177).

33 Badian (1982: 164).

34 Hopkins (1978: 180).

35 Brunt (1982: 158).

36 Saller (1980).

37 See Golden (1992) for a more in-depth discussion of the benefits and difficulties of using cross-cultural comparisons.

38 Golden (1992: 312 n. 9) lists relevant bibliography.

39 See, for example, Shaw (1982: 49–50).

40 See further Treggiari (2002: 5).

41 Compare also App. *B Civ.* 1.119, which states that one of Caesar's assassins paraded a *pilleus* on the end of a spear immediately after the slaying.

42 See Milnor (2011) for a brief summary of the issues surrounding the study of women in Roman antiquity and for a useful bibliography.

2

A Summary of Roman History

Matt Gibbs, Milorad Nikolic, and Andrew Sherwood

"In the beginning, Rome was ruled by kings; then Lucius Junius Brutus brought free-dom and established the consulship."[1] The Roman historian Tacitus begins his *Annals* (1.1) with this succinct statement, which identifies a number of themes critical to the Romans' understanding of their own history and political character. Romans were meant to be free, not to labour under the power of arrogant kings. According to trad-ition, Tarquinius Superbus, the last king of Rome, was expelled from Rome at the end of the sixth century BCE, after his son had violated Lucretia, the virtuous wife of a leading Roman citizen.

Brutus led the movement to eradicate the Monarchy and to establish in its stead the Republic, which meant that Rome would be under the leadership of magistrates who were lawfully elected by the citizenry and advised by the senate. Addressing the assembled body of Roman citizens in the Roman Forum, the very heart of the city, Brutus displayed the bloody body of Lucretia (who had killed herself lest she provide an example and an excuse for other Roman women to be unfaithful to their husbands) and laid bare the events that had led to her heroic demise. The outraged citizens begged him to lead them into arms against their monarch, but he (already a good republican) demanded that first the citizens vote: they must confirm that any-one who attempted to restore the Monarchy would be put to death and, in place of the Monarchy, agree to elect annually two consuls to divide the powers of the king between them. The citizenry unanimously voted in favour of these proposals; Romans would ever after have an aversion to the very idea of Monarchy.

The historians Livy (1.58–9) and Dionysius of Halicarnassus (*Ant. Rom.* 4.64–85) both tell versions of the disgraceful tyranny that brought the end to the Monarchy and of the unanimous desire for dignity and freedom that ushered in the Republic. It is interesting to note that each wrote at the very time that the Republic was giving way to the Empire (that is, when Rome would fall under the leadership of a single ruler, who would be very careful not to call himself a king). Indeed, far from shedding the presence of Monarchy from the Roman political system, the expulsion of kings ensured that the spectre of autocracy would cast a long shadow over the rest of Roman history—first as something to be avoided and rejected and then, in turn, desired, adopted, and adapted.

Timeline

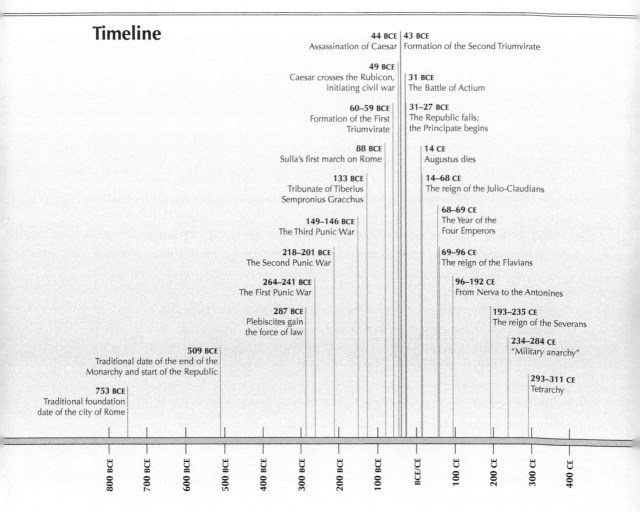

44 BCE
Assassination of Caesar

43 BCE
Formation of the Second Triumvirate

49 BCE
Caesar crosses the Rubicon, initiating civil war

31 BCE
The Battle of Actium

60–59 BCE
Formation of the First Triumvirate

31–27 BCE
The Republic falls; the Principate begins

88 BCE
Sulla's first march on Rome

14 CE
Augustus dies

133 BCE
Tribunate of Tiberius Sempronius Gracchus

14–68 CE
The reign of the Julio-Claudians

149–146 BCE
The Third Punic War

68–69 CE
The Year of the Four Emperors

218–201 BCE
The Second Punic War

69–96 CE
The reign of the Flavians

264–241 BCE
The First Punic War

96–192 CE
From Nerva to the Antonines

287 BCE
Plebiscites gain the force of law

193–235 CE
The reign of the Severans

509 BCE
Traditional date of the end of the Monarchy and start of the Republic

234–284 CE
"Military anarchy"

753 BCE
Traditional foundation date of the city of Rome

293–311 CE
Tetrarchy

800 BCE 700 BCE 600 BCE 500 BCE 400 BCE 300 BCE 200 BCE 100 BCE BCE/CE 100 CE 200 CE 300 CE 400 CE

Introduction

Although the aim of this volume as a whole is to address issues in Roman society thematically, full appreciation of these matters requires some knowledge of the chronological framework in which they occurred. This chapter sketches that frame. Concentration falls upon the period from approximately 200 BCE to 200 CE, the time span that is the major focus of the following chapters, but some attention is given to both previous and subsequent events. Discussion begins with the tradition of the city of Rome's foundation in 753 BCE under Romulus, its first king, and continues through the expulsion of the Monarchy and institution of the Republic in 509 BCE to consider major political events during the early, middle, and late Republic. The events of the last hundred years of the Republic, which set the stage for the shift to Empire during the Augustan period, are also explored. The problems and accomplishments of the imperial dynasties and rulers of the first, second, and third centuries (the period often referred to as the Principate[2]) are discussed next. The chapter ends with a brief summary of the events that led to the division of the Empire into eastern and western halves and its reunification under one emperor, Constantine.

It is important to note that, while different expanses of time in Roman republican history have been given different labels (for example, the early, middle, and late Republic), the dates associated with these eras are often disputed and the eras themselves are the backward projections of historians. The Romans did not know, for example, that they were living in the "late Republic." Historians choose benchmark dates—dates after which there was significant political, economic, or social change—to mark the beginnings or ends of eras in history, but historians have different opinions about the relative importance of such dates and events. In this chapter, for example, the beginning of the Augustan period is given as 31 BCE (the date when Octavian, who would become Augustus, defeated his last significant rival), but others might have chosen 27 BCE (the date when Octavian took the name Augustus and was invested with extraordinary powers and honours by the senate).

---·◆·---

Early Rome: Legends and Kings

As far as the Romans were concerned, the city of Rome sprang into existence in the middle of the eighth century BCE. Roman chronology would begin from this date: 753 BCE for us; 1 AUC (year one *ab urbe condita*, or "from the foundation of the city") for the Romans.[3] Rome was named after its legendary founder and first king, Romulus, a descendant of the Trojan hero Aeneas, who had escaped from the ruins of Troy to settle in Italy. It was Romulus who built Rome's walls and secured a population for his new city, first by accepting thieves and runaway slaves into its citizenry and then by snatching the womenfolk of the neighbouring Sabine population to provide the new citizens with wives and the promise of children.

A non-hereditary kingship remained the rule for the next two and a half centuries, during which six other kings are said to have held power in succession. Several of these kings had names that sound Etruscan, not Latin. The Etruscans were Rome's closest

⇥ See Chapter 17, pp. 380–1, on Etruscan influence on Roman architecture.

foreign (i.e. non-Latin) neighbour on the Italian peninsula, which might explain some of the influence that Etruscan culture had on Roman culture from an early period. For example, religious architecture and several Roman deities shared much with their Etruscan counterparts.

During the monarchical period, the early development of many Roman religious rituals, some political institutions (such as the **senate** and a popular assembly), and urban infrastructure began. The "great drain," or *cloaca maxima*, was built; the area of the Roman **Forum** was drained; and the Forum was given its new role as the geographic and figurative heart of the city. But the Monarchy was not to last. As mentioned at the outset of this chapter, the last king was expelled in 509 BCE by Romans jubilant to be out from under the thumb of a cruel autocrat and eager for a new political system—a Republic—in which the powers of the king would be shared among the citizenry.

The Early Republic (508–287 BCE)

The Republic's system of government did not distribute the powers of the king among all citizens. Instead, it was divided between two magistrates, the **consuls**, who were elected annually by the voting assemblies of adult male citizens and who had the senate as their advisory board. During this time, the other major Roman magistracies—**praetor**, **quaestor**, *aedile*, **tribune**, and **censor**—were also established. The republican system is often regarded as a combination of monarchic, aristocratic, and democratic elements

⇥ Compare Chapter 10, pp. 219–37, on republican political structures.

represented respectively by the consuls, senate (and elected magistrates), and popular voting assemblies.

In the early Republic, access to the magistracies and priesthoods lay solely in the hands of the **patricians**, members of privileged "clans" or "families" (*gentes*) that may have been given some form of special **status** during the Monarchy. The rest of the citizenry, the **plebeians**, began to chafe against their inability to hold high office and what they considered arrogant abuses of power by some patricians. The early Republic is therefore characterized by the so-called struggle of the orders, during which the plebeian population made incremental legal gains at the expense of the patricians' exclusive privileges. For example, in 494 BCE the plebeians established their own voting assembly,

⇥ See Chapter 10, pp. 223–4, 229–31, and 234, on plebeian political gains.

at which they elected their own officers (tribunes of the plebs) whose mandate was to protect them from arbitrary treatment by patricians. In 367 BCE the **Lex** *Licinia Sextia* allowed (wealthy) plebeians to be elected to the consulship. The final blow in the struggle was delivered by the *Lex Hortensia* of 287 BCE, which invested the plebeian assembly's decisions (*plebiscita*) with the force of law.

The Middle Republic (287–133 BCE)

Unlike the early Republic, the middle Republic is characterized not so much by internal political tensions as by foreign wars and territorial expansion beyond the Italian peninsula. During the early Republic, Rome had begun to expand its influence in the peninsula, coming into conflict with (and ultimately emerging victorious over) the neighbouring Latin and Etruscan communities, as well as the Samnite peoples in southeastern Italy. By the late 270s BCE Rome was the undisputed power in the region. Different relationships were extended to defeated Italian communities. Some were granted the right to intermarry with the Romans, for example, while others were merely made military allies, or *socii*.

Wars with Carthage, the great Punic city on the coast of North Africa, also loom large in this period. The first of these Punic wars, fought between 264 and 241 BCE, was over control of Sicily. Rome was ultimately successful, and Sicily became its first "overseas" province. Peace with Carthage, though, was not to last. The Second Punic War (218–201 BCE), the so-called Hannibalic War, broke out in Spain. Carthage had expanded its interests in the Iberian peninsula after its defeat in the First Punic War, and conflict with Rome arose when the Carthaginian general, Hannibal, captured Saguntum, a Spanish town purported to be under Roman protection. Rome declared war, and Hannibal (in a daring offensive endeavour) crossed the Alps and invaded Italy. Despite Hannibal's significant success in the battlefield, most of Rome's Italian allies remained unwavering in their support, and Hannibal's force gradually weakened. The Carthaginian senate recalled Hannibal in 204 BCE, and he was finally defeated two years later, by Scipio Africanus in the Battle of Zama in North Africa.

Compare Chapter 14, pp. 310–15, on the Punic wars.

Rome's victory over Carthage at the end of the third century BCE allowed it to concentrate on its interests in the eastern Mediterranean. A series of Illyrian and Macedonian wars had broken out prior to and during the Second Punic War, and, with the Carthaginian threat suppressed, Rome's power on the Greek mainland steadily increased. Annexation of the area, however, did not occur immediately. In 196 BCE, in a spectacular ceremony at the Isthmian Games (held near Corinth), Titus Quinctius Flamininus—the general responsible for the defeat of the Macedonian king Philip V— announced the withdrawal of the Roman forces and declared that the Greeks were "free, ungarrisoned, not subject to tribute," and able to use their own laws (Polyb. 18.46.5; cf. Livy 33.32.5). What the Romans meant (and what the Greeks understood) by "free" is disputed, but freedom in any of its definitions was fleeting. The crushing defeat of Macedonian forces at the Battle of Pydna in 168 BCE was another step towards the eventual transformation of Greece into the Roman provinces of Macedonia (in 146 BCE) and Achaea (in 27 BCE). In 146 BCE the Romans also razed the cities of Carthage, following victory in the Third Punic War (149–146 BCE), and

Corinth. King Attalus III of Pergamum bequeathed his kingdom to the Romans, which became the Roman province of Asia (133 BCE). Cilicia was soon added to the growing list of Roman provinces (101 BCE), as was Cyrene, which had been bequeathed to Rome by Ptolemy VIII of Egypt in 96 BCE and annexed as a province in 74 BCE.

While Rome was enjoying unparalleled success in expansion and military endeavours, things were less prosperous in Italy. Although Rome's overseas achievements had enriched the political elite and increased its power at home, small Italian landholders were experiencing growing economic difficulties. Traditional explanations of the plight of Italian peasant farmers have recently been called into question. Literary and archaeological sources are contradictory, yet tensions between the rich and poor were certainly rising. The late Republic is another period characterized by political problems at home.

→ See Chapter 1, p. 17, for recent objections to traditional explanations of the Italian peasant farmers' plight in the second century BCE.

The Late Republic (133–31 BCE)

Most begin the late Republic with the plebeian tribunate of Tiberius Sempronius Gracchus in 133 BCE because it foreshadows consistent themes of the century to come: civil unrest, bloodshed, and conflict between the senate and individuals suspected of courting the people's interests to achieve their own political ends. Indeed, the history of the late Republic can be depicted as a drawn-out struggle between members of the **senatorial** order who sought to ensure its leadership of the state (the *optimates*) and other ambitious men (the *populares*)—for the most part also members of the senatorial establishment—who sought to circumvent the traditions of the senate by drawing power from the support of the people and loyal soldiers. The terms *optimates* and *populares* should not be taken to suggest the existence of political parties in the sense of modern politics, however. They indicate political strategy more than political conviction.

After being elected tribune, Gracchus attempted to resolve a series of connected problems that threatened Roman social stability. The situation was very complex, and the evidence is contradictory, but Gracchus's law essentially proposed a radical redistribution of land in Italy so that the difficulties (the precise nature of which is disputed) facing Roman farmers could be assuaged. Under this law, individuals were permitted to hold no more than 500 *iugera* of state-owned land (an allocation that had been instituted much earlier but, by this period, was ignored); surplus land was found, seized, and redistributed in much smaller parcels to the poorer Roman citizens by a board of commissioners established for precisely this purpose. Unsurprisingly, there was vehement opposition from the senatorial elite, to which Gracchus refused to bow. Ultimately, Publius Scipio Nasica, an ex-consul of 138 BCE and the **pontifex maximus**, led a group of senators and their supporters in the murders of Gracchus and 300 of his followers.

From 123 to 121 BCE, Gaius Sempronius Gracchus, Tiberius's younger brother, attempted to introduce even more daring reforms. He too would end up dead (apparently by his own hand), and 3,000 of his supporters were executed without trial. In the course of these events, a new political tool was introduced that would see heavy use in the decades to come: the **senatus consultum ultimum** ("final decree of the senate"), a warning to the consuls that the state was at risk and that the senate supported whatever actions they might take to save the Republic.

The decade following Gaius's death was relatively calm under senatorial control, but the second century ended with a series of problems. War with King Jugurtha in Numidia (111–104 BCE), slave uprisings (103–101 BCE), and an invasion of northern Italy by German tribes all caused anxiety. Gaius Marius's success in the face of these dangers swelled his popularity with the Roman people, who elected him consul numerous times (107 BCE, 104–100 BCE). In an attempt to tackle the continuing shortage of soldiers, he allowed men who lacked property (previously a requirement for conscription) to enrol in the army. This radical step transformed the Roman military by providing subsequent commanders unprecedented influence with the army and thus the power to effect political change. Landless soldiers looked to their generals for booty, land, and retirement: a soldier's loyalty to the commander, not to the state, became the rule. This relationship would have significant consequences for the Republic's stability in the coming decades.

See Chapter 13, pp. 294–5, on Marian reforms and the professionalization of the army.

Soon after, Rome was troubled by the Social War (91–88 BCE), an armed rebellion in which its Italian allies demanded Roman citizenship and attempted to establish a state to rival Rome. This bitter conflict began at Asculum in startling fashion when an arrogant praetor who had been sent to evaluate the allies' discontentment was murdered and resident Roman citizens subsequently massacred. Numerous commanders won great prestige during the Social War, but two are most noteworthy: Lucius Cornelius Sulla and Gnaeus Pompeius Strabo, father of Pompey the Great. The war concluded in 88 BCE after only two years, largely the result of the *Lex Julia*, a political concession passed in 90 BCE. Through this law, Roman citizenship was granted to allied communities that either had not joined the revolt or had joined but were willing to lay down their arms. Other laws soon extended citizenship to all Italians south of the river Po.

No sooner had the Social War concluded than fresh conflict developed in the city of Rome. Indeed, the effects of Marian reforms were keenly felt in the 80s BCE, when Marius and his political rival Sulla competed for command of the Mithridatic War, a conflict that promised to be glorious and rich in spoils. In contrast to Marius, whose popularity with the Roman people made him an object of suspicion among the senatorial old guard, Sulla staunchly aligned himself with the establishment. Command of the Mithridatic War volleyed back and forth between the contenders amidst a startling array of brutal events in the city of Rome. Riots occurred, magistrates were murdered, and, most astonishingly,

Sulla took the unprecedented step of marching on Rome with his army of loyal soldiers. Once in control of the city, Sulla proceeded to "proscribe" wealthy citizens, publishing their names as enemies of the state and thereby rendering their lives and property forfeit (see Box 2.1).

Though Sulla was ultimately successful in gaining supreme power in Rome, he did not retain it. Ever the republican, he reasserted the necessity of obeying the traditional republican order of office-holding (rules of the *cursus honorum* had been neglected in recent enthusiasm to bestow office upon favoured individuals), curbed what he considered to be the erosive powers of the people and plebeian tribunes in an attempt to return power to the senate, and retired in 79 BCE to write his memoirs. He died a year later.

→ See Chapter 10, p. 228, on the *cursus honorum*.

Sulla's desires to re-establish the old ways were, ironically, soon undercut by one of his own supporters, Gnaeus Pompeius. Later known as Pompeius Magnus (Pompey the Great),

Primary Source

Box 2.1: Plutarch, *Life of Sulla*, 31.1–5.[1]

Sulla now busied himself with slaughter, and murders without number or limit filled the city. Many, too, were killed to gratify private hatreds, although they had no relations with Sulla, but he gave his consent in order to gratify his adherents . . . Sulla at once proscribed 80 people, without communicating with any magistrate; and in spite of the general indignation, after a single day's interval, he proscribed 220 others, and then on the third day, as many more. Referring to these measures in a public harangue, he said that he was proscribing as many as he could remember, and those who now escaped his memory, he would proscribe at a future time. He also proscribed anyone who harboured and saved a proscribed person, making death the punishment for such humanity, without exception of brother, son, or parents, but offering anyone who slew a proscribed person two talents as a reward for his murderous deed, even if a slave should slay his master, or a son his father. And in what seemed the greatest injustice of all, he took away all civil rights from the sons and grandsons of those who had been proscribed, and confiscated the property of them all. Moreover, proscriptions were made not only in Rome, but also in every city of Italy, and neither temple of god, nor hearth of hospitality, nor paternal home was free from the stain of bloodshed, but husbands were butchered in the embraces of their wedded wives, and sons in the arms of their mothers.

Note

1. This excerpt is slightly adapted from Perrin (1916).

he gained extraordinary popularity during the 70s BCE thanks to his involvement in subduing piracy, dealing with problems with Mithridates and the East, and crushing a series of
revolts, including that of the slave Spartacus and his servile supporters. In 67 BCE Pompey
was given extraordinary powers by the Roman people through a tribunician plebiscite to
resolve the ongoing problem of piracy in the Mediterranean and, a year later, to deal with
Mithridates and finally settle affairs in the East. The senate was vociferous in its attempts to
deny Pompey these powers, but its attempts were for naught. Pompey had the support of
the people and of young ambitious men (among them Gaius Julius Caesar) who perhaps
saw the potential to further their own aims by supporting Pompey's.

The opportunity for a stronger alliance soon came. By 60 BCE Pompey's hopes for land
for his veterans had been thwarted by the senate, while Caesar discovered that he was
unable to obtain senatorial permission to hold a **triumph** and run for consul at the same
time (he reluctantly forfeited the triumph). Marcus Licinius Crassus
was also denied his request for renegotiation of a tax contract for
Asia on behalf of the *publicani*. Frustrated and embittered with the
senate, the three men formed an unofficial, private coalition to work for each member's
political benefit. Modern scholars commonly refer to this group as the First Triumvirate.

See Chapter 15, pp. 340–2, ←
on taxation.

As consul in 59 BCE, Caesar began to implement measures conducive to his fellow
triumvirs and managed to secure for himself a special, extended command of three
legions to wage war in Gaul. However, triumviral relations deteriorated quickly in
the 50s BCE. The politically provocative activities of plebeian tribunes Publius Clodius
Pulcher and Titus Annius Milo served to antagonize the triumvirs against each other and
led to violent clashes in Rome. In 52 BCE, in an attempt to quell the trouble, the senate
appointed Pompey sole consul, and he quickly passed retroactive laws concerning corruption and gang violence, along with other laws to curb corruption and regularize the
procedure for holding offices and commands (although, notably, exemptions were made
for Caesar). By this point, however, the triumvirate had already dissolved, as Crassus
had been killed during an unsuccessful invasion of Parthia the year before. Pompey soon
decided to throw his lot in with the senate to work towards neutralizing Caesar, who
had gained extraordinary military influence thanks to his activities in Gaul and who was
seeking a second consulship. A series of political wranglings ended with the proposal that
both Pompey and Caesar give up their respective commands and disarm; the proposal
was barred by a small group of senators. One consul asked Pompey to save the Republic
(from Caesar), and Pompey accepted.

The senate passed a *senatus consultum ultimum* on 7 January 49 BCE. Within days,
Caesar had led his soldiers across the Rubicon River to invade Italy, initiating another
civil war. In the years immediately following, and by a series of remarkable military
campaigns, Caesar gained control of the Roman world. Pompey, defeated at Pharsalus in
northern Greece (48 BCE), fled to Egypt, where he was killed as he disembarked from his

ship. The remaining Pompeian forces, under the command of his sons, were defeated in 45 BCE at the Battle of Munda in Spain.

Throughout the civil war and until the end of his life, Caesar held an extraordinary array of offices (for example, **dictator**, consul, *pontifex maximus*) and exercised supreme power in Rome and Italy. Thanks to the support he enjoyed from the military, no one dared to resist as he implemented a variety of administrative reforms, increased the size of the senate (by making some of his supporters members), founded colonies (for both citizens and veterans), and instituted the Julian calendar. In his will, he adopted his great-nephew, Octavian (who would later become Augustus) as his son. Caesar was suspected of aspiring to be made king, to be deified, and to create a lasting Julian dynasty.

Caesar was stabbed to death on the Ides of March (15 March) 44 BCE by a throng of senatorial conspirators led by Marcus Junius Brutus and Gaius Cassius Longinus. Their hope that the removal of Caesar would lead to the restoration of the Republic under senatorial control was not realized. Anger rather than gratitude met the so-called tyrannicides, who were quickly ushered out of Rome. Conservative republicans' initial hope that Octavian might be manipulated to act in the interests of the senate and against Caesar's friend and commander, Marc Antony, were also disappointed. Although they were not natural friends, Octavian, Antony, and Marcus Aemilius Lepidus formed a coalition (referred to as the Second Triumvirate by modern historians) in 43 BCE. Unlike the First Triumvirate, this alliance was formalized by statute and was officially known as the Triumvirs for the Restoration of the State (*Triumviri Rei Publicae Constituendae*); its purpose ostensibly was to pursue Caesar's assassins. Brutus and Cassius would die in 42 BCE after defeat at Philippi in Greece; other wealthy and leading men, including Marcus Tullius Cicero (the famous mid-first-century BCE orator and republican states-man who had denounced Antony in a series of speeches) were proscribed in Italy.

→ Compare Chapter 1, p. 16, on Cicero's denouncement of Antony.

After the defeat of Brutus and Cassius, the triumvirate divided control of the empire, its resources, and its armies between its members. The chief beneficiary was Antony, who took the eastern area. Octavian was given the west (including Italy), and Lepidus received Africa. By the mid-30s BCE, however, Lepidus was marginalized, Octavian and Antony were estranged, and conflict between the latter two was inevitable. Both men, in fact, could claim legitimacy with Roman soldiers and citizens by demonstrating the favour shown to them by Caesar: Octavian was his heir and Antony his most trusted military officer. It was not clear that one had more right to supremacy than the other.

Octavian, however, cleverly exploited Roman moral sensibilities and the traditional abhorrence of Monarchy. Antony, who was married to Octavian's sister, rejected her in favour of the Egyptian Queen Cleopatra, who by this time was not only the mother of his children but also his military ally. This relationship provided Octavian with the opportunity to advertise a distinction between himself and Antony: he was the saviour and defender of Roman culture, while Antony was an eastern potentate under the spell of an Egyptian queen. Defamation devolved into actual conflict, and in 31 BCE Octavian's forces defeated those of Antony and Cleopatra in the Battle of Actium, off the west coast of Greece. Antony and Cleopatra escaped to Egypt, where they soon committed suicide; Egypt and its wealth were added to Rome's empire. In reality, the massive forces barely came into conflict at Actium, but the battle still represented a defining moment in Roman political history. One man, Octavian, was now in control. A century of revolution and the Republic were gone. The **Principate** had begun.

For centuries, the dominance of an individual (that is, the emperor) remained unchallenged in this new system. The senate continued to play a role in Roman politics, but its power was largely transferred to the emperor and his advisors. The voice of the Roman people—the plebs—could also still be heard and bring about change, but the ability to elect magistrates dwindled as selection increasingly became the prerogative of the emperor. Although emperors often veiled their powers and deeds behind republican rhetoric (and several claimed to be saviours or restorers of the Republic), the Republic would not return.[4]

Augustus

Octavian, who took the name Augustus in 27 BCE, led the political shift from the combination of aristocratic and democratic systems in place during the Republic (represented by the senate and the Roman people, respectively, or *SPQR*, *Senatus Populusque Romanus*) to the autocracy of the Empire. By building on the successes of his predecessors, avoiding their mistakes, and utilizing all their weapons (legal or illegal, traditional or novel, moral or immoral), he gained absolute power and forged something new and lasting. Augustus was astute enough to cloak his powers with inoffensive vocabulary (he was the ***princeps***, "leading man", and *primus inter pares*, "first among equals") and to create the impression that power and honours were shared almost equally between him and the senate.

In consultation with his trusted advisors, most notably Marcus Agrippa, Gaius Maecenas, and Statilius Taurus, Augustus transformed or revitalized almost all aspects of society. Augustan rhetoric made much of his "revival" of Roman religion, further promoting Roman religious ideology that connected well-cultivated Roman gods with political stability and economic prosperity. By 12 BCE Augustus had become *pontifex maximus*, a position that he and all successive emperors would hold and that would focus religious authority in the person of the emperor. He also restructured the Roman state's economic foundation, establishing a provincial **census** upon which a system of direct taxation could be built.

See Chapter 9, p. 200, on ⬅ re-evaluations of Augustus's religious "revival".

See Chapter 15, pp. 340–4, on ⬅ provincial taxation.

Augustus's array of powers evolved slowly over the time he was *princeps* (27 BCE–14 CE). Underlying everything, however, was his control of the armed forces, which he accomplished

by taking responsibility for soldiers' pay, rewards, and retirement and by choosing commanders personally. Augustus deployed the military forces in their traditional pursuit of
waging war against foreign enemies. In addition to keeping them
out of Italy, this move also allowed for conquest, expansion, and
colonization and for the provision of land for his veterans. By 6
CE Augustus had not only established a military treasury that was
funded in part by taxes and in part by funds from his personal fortune but also the practice
of pensioning off discharged soldiers.

→ Compare Chapter 13,
pp. 289 and 291–2, on military
retirement practices.

The new regime also led to significant administrative changes. In the city of Rome,
public offices were created and assigned to the previously apolitical but wealthy **equestrian** order. In the provinces, further positions were open to equestrians in the administrative sphere. **Procurators** watched over financial matters, and success in these positions
could lead to significant career opportunities, such as the equestrian governorship of
Egypt (the *praefectus Aegypti*).

Augustus certainly faced significant difficulties, however. His plans for succession
were severely hampered by the fact that he was predeceased by several men who could
have been his heirs: his nephew, Claudius Marcellus; his friend (and son-in-law) Marcus
Agrippa; and his grandsons (Agrippa's sons) Lucius and Gaius. In fact, he held out for
some time before acknowledging his stepson Tiberius as his successor, doing so only
when Tiberius had adopted Germanicus, Augustus's great-nephew on his sister's side and
the son of Tiberius's brother Nero Drusus (who had also died). Another problem occurred
in 9 CE, when the Roman army suffered one of its most notable defeats in the Battle of
the Teutoburg Forest in Germany. The force under the command of Publius Quinctilius
Varus—made up of the 17th, 18th, and 19th legions—was annihilated once it had been
betrayed by Arminius, the Roman-educated son of a Germanic tribal chief. According to
Suetonius (*Aug.* 23.2), Augustus was inconsolable.

When Augustus died in 14 CE, his successors walked into a socio-political world quite
different from the one he had entered in the first century BCE. Some of the changes Augustus
wrought had already been tried or previously imposed in some form. However, he instituted
them with great finesse, which, in addition to a universal reluctance to return to civil war,
convinced most Romans to accept them. Resistance to Augustus was minimal thanks to his
repeated claim that he had returned Rome to the traditional republican ideal, in which pre-
eminent men guided rather than dominated the state. After 27 BCE Augustus's power was
not his *potestas* (military might) but his *auctoritas* (influence won from esteem; see Box 2.2).

The Julio-Claudians (14–68 CE)

Despite his repeated protestations that he exceeded his peers in influence only and was
a "first man" rather than an emperor or king, Augustus clearly intended that a member

Primary Source

Box 2.2: Augustus, *The Deeds of the Divine Augustus*, 34.

In my sixth and seventh consulships, after I had quenched the civil wars, and having become master of all affairs through universal consent, I transferred the Republic from my power to the authority of the senate and the Roman people. For my service, I was named Augustus by *senatus consultum*, and the doors of my house were publicly adorned with laurel, and a civic crown was fixed above my door, and a golden shield was placed in the *Curia Julia*, which—as the inscription of the shield testifies—the senate and Roman people gave to me on account of my courage, mercy, justice, and piety. After that time, I surpassed all others in influence (*auctoritas*), although I had no greater power (*potestas*) than the others who were my colleagues in each magistracy.

of his family succeed him upon his death. Having but one daughter from an earlier marriage, he and his third wife, Livia (of the Claudian clan), arranged the marriages of their descendants, often to each other. The descendants of the imperial house of Augustus and Livia therefore became known as the Julio-Claudians. Four would occupy the throne in the decades to come: Tiberius (14–37 CE), Gaius (37–41 CE), Claudius (41–54 CE), and Nero (54–68 CE). The fundamental issues of this period were different from Augustus's reign. They focused on the relationship between the emperors and the political elite and on the continued succession of the Julio-Claudian house. External wars and expansion continued; however, our literary sources are occupied with fascinating tales of trusted but self-interested (or downright malevolent) advisors to the emperors and of conspiracies (real or alleged) within the vast network of those with some claim to Julio-Claudian blood and the descendants of prominent republican families.

As previously mentioned, Tiberius (Livia's son and Augustus's stepson) succeeded Augustus as emperor. Although the beginning of his reign was marked by general discontent and military revolts, Tiberius appears to have been a reasonably good leader at first. But he soon took as confidante and agent the notorious Lucius Aelius Sejanus, whom many of the ancient sources report to have had an insalubrious influence on the emperor. Ultimately, Tiberius's rule was marred by accusations of treason (*maiestas*) and conspiracy, as well as trials and executions of several high-ranking Romans.

When Tiberius died in 37 CE, his great-nephew Gaius (known to history as "Caligula") became emperor. The son of the popular Germanicus (who had been a favourite of Augustus), Gaius's ascension to the imperial throne met with broad approval, but he was not able to fulfill the high expectations. Having lost the restraining influence of his grandmother Antonia

See Chapter 13, p. 302, on the source of the nickname "Caligula."

when she died in 37 CE, his behaviour became increasingly cruel and bizarre. By 40 CE enemies among the Roman elite were conspiring against him. The plot was crushed, but the remaining year of his sovereignty was branded by increasing brutality, autocracy, and megalomania. In early 41 CE he was murdered, along with his wife and daughter.

After Gaius's murder, his uncle Claudius was selected as emperor, reputedly by soldiers. Perhaps as a result, Claudius ensured that his dealings with the senate were largely civil. Unlike Gaius, he seemed genuinely interested in politics and government and in the welfare of the Roman populace and provincial populations, among whom he was liberal with grants of Roman citizenship. The empire expanded under his rule, with several provinces (including Britain) added; however, notable failures in Judea and with the Parthians tempered the expansion to a degree. In late 54 CE Claudius died. He was remembered as being insecure and excessively influenced by scheming wives and self-promoting **freedmen**, all of whom nurtured their own aims by cultivating Claudius's paranoia about conspiracy.

See Chapter 3, pp. 64–5, for examples of the activities of Claudius's freedmen and the negative responses to them.

See Chapter 12, pp. 269–70, on Nero's interest in the performing arts.

Claudius's stepson and great-nephew, Nero, succeeded him. During his reign, Nero managed to alienate the Roman elite by transforming the role of the emperor from one of guidance to something very different. He neglected the military in order to indulge his private interests, and he bankrupted the treasury. In the spring of 68 CE Julius Vindex, the governor of Gaul, revolted. Although the initial rebellion was quashed, the support of Servius Sulpicius Galba (then governor of Spain) for the rebels seriously damaged Nero's senatorial support. Nero saw only one way out and committed suicide that same year. Leading senators vied for the position, and the state was plunged into civil war once again for a year and a half, a time often referred to as the Year of the Four Emperors. In 68 and 69 CE Galba, Otho, Vitellius, and Vespasian rapidly succeeded one another as emperor, often with the help of the provincial armies. As Tacitus (*Hist.* 1.4) famously put it, "The secret of Empire was out: emperors could be made in places other than (the city of) Rome."

The Flavians (69–96 CE)

With the ascendancy of Vespasian, the Flavian dynasty began. The consolidation of the empire, the strengthening of the emperor's position, and the entwined motifs of the restoration of discipline and loyalty in the Roman military and the senate were all central themes under Vespasian's reign. He promoted building programs in the city of Rome, including the beginning of the monumental Flavian Amphitheatre, today better known as the **Colosseum**. He also added numbers to the senate from both Italian and provincial

See Chapter 12, pp. 273–4, and Chapter 17, pp. 390–1, on the Colosseum.

communities and awarded privileged status to some communities in the provinces, most notably in Spain. Moreover, he attempted to recoup some of the imperial treasury's financial losses, caused by Nero's outrageous spending and the devastation of the civil wars, by increasing provincial taxation and revoking grants of immunity from taxation.

In 79 CE Vespasian died. He was succeeded by his capable elder son, Titus, who was intellectually and physically gifted, good-natured, generous, and a distinguished soldier by the time he became emperor. His dealings with the senate were cordial, and he continued the construction projects that his father had set in motion (including finishing the Colosseum) and provided expensive public spectacles. His brief reign, however, was also marred by great calamities (the eruption of Vesuvius in 79 CE and a serious outbreak of plague in Rome), the effects of which he attempted to alleviate. Titus died in 81 CE at the age of 42, apparently of natural causes, although allegations of murder were inevitably made against his brother and successor, Domitian.

Despite the hostility shown to him by ancient sources, Domitian performed his imperial duties well, at least as they concerned the people and the military. He sponsored a variety of lavish, magnificent spectacles, ranging from races and infantry battles to gladiatorial shows and animal fights. He also continued the Flavian building program by completing, restoring, and creating several projects, including the Capitol (which had burned during the civil war in 69 CE) and a palace on the Palatine Hill. He

Compare Chapter 9, p. 212, on ← Domitian's building projects on the Capitoline Hill.

increased the military's pay by a third, and his decisions in both provincial administration and the legal sphere were generally accepted. He was also the first emperor since Claudius to go on military campaign, and he enjoyed several triumphs linked to his campaigns on the Rhine and the Danube.

Nevertheless, Domitian was autocratic, obstinate, and undiplomatic. He failed spectacularly in his attempts to work with the senate for various reasons. His inflated belief in his own political position—he held 10 consulships as emperor and became *consul perpetuus* in 85 CE—alongside his insistence on being regarded as a god and on being addressed as such in both documents and orations, only resulted in senatorial resentment. The banishment or execution of several important and influential senators at his orders alienated the senate even further. Domitian's behaviour perhaps caused the open rebellion of Lucius Antonius Saturninus, the governor of Upper Germany, in 89 CE. The uprising itself was quickly quelled and Saturninus was killed in battle, but the revolt made Domitian even more tyrannical. In 95 CE Domitian's end was preceded by his executions of close family members. The following year, a plot was hatched in the emperor's household, perhaps with the complicity of his wife, Domitia; in mid-September 96 CE the Flavian dynasty that had begun so promisingly with Vespasian ended in a bloody coup when Domitian was stabbed to death by several assailants.

From Nerva to the Antonines (96–192 CE)

After Domitian's death, the senate recognized Marcus Cocceius Nerva as the new emperor. He faced the difficulty of making a clean break with Domitian's policy while preventing a revolt of the soldiers, with whom Domitian had been very popular. Nerva was willing to co-operate with the senators, who declared **damnatio memoriae** over Domitian. This process involved the removal of his image and name from all public monuments. During Nerva's reign, individuals whom Domitian had exiled were recalled to Rome, and the *alimenta*, a state-sponsored support system to feed orphans, was initiated. To prevent a repetition of the Year of the Four Emperors, it was desirable that Nerva name an heir. In 97 CE he adopted as his son, co-ruler, and successor Marcus Ulpius Traianus (Trajan), a man in his mid-forties who was governor of Upper Germany, had a distinguished military career, and was popular with the soldiers. Nerva died the following year.

Trajan, who had been born in Spain, was the first Roman emperor not born in Italy. His adoption by Nerva began an unprecedented period of stability for the Roman Empire. Since four successive emperors (beginning with Nerva) had no sons, they kept a quasi-dynastic succession intact by adopting the individual(s) who would become their successor(s). This pattern lasted for 84 years (96–180 CE). The time of the reigns from Nerva to Marcus Aurelius is sometimes referred to, after Machiavelli, as the period of the five good emperors.

Under Trajan, the Roman empire saw its biggest territorial expansion and a subsequent period of consolidation, infrastructure development, and general prosperity. Presenting himself in deliberate contrast to Domitian, Trajan treated the senate with respect, a quality explicit in Pliny the Younger's *Panegyric*, an official speech in praise of the emperor. Trajan also expanded Nerva's *alimenta* and the distribution of free grain to the plebs in Rome. A series of surviving letters between Pliny the Younger and Trajan, written when the former was governor of the eastern province of Bithynia, is a valuable source of information about the even-handedness of the Trajanic administration. The letters also give a glimpse into the nature of provincial administration in the early second century CE.

→ See Chapter 16, p. 374, for an excerpt from Pliny and Trajan's correspondence.

→ See Chapter 13, p. 299, and Chapter 17, p. 393, for an image and discussion of Trajan's Column.

→ See Chapter 16, pp. 361–3 and 366, on road and harbour construction.

Trajan waged two wars in Dacia (modern Romania), scenes of which are depicted on Trajan's Column. He also built a new harbour for Rome at Ostia and the Via Traiana, extending the Via Appia from Beneventum to Brundisium. In 106 CE the province of Arabia was added to the Roman empire, and Armenia, Mesopotamia, and Assyria followed by 116 CE as a result of a campaign against the Parthians. Trajan died in 117 CE, after he had transferred his command over the Syrian armies to his successor and distant relative, Publius Aelius Hadrianus (Hadrian), who like Trajan was also born in Spain.

The exact details of Hadrian's succession are not quite clear, although Trajan's wife, Plotina, may have staged Hadrian's adoption shortly after her husband's death. Hadrian had been a member of Trajan's staff for some time and, as emperor, soon recognized that it was difficult to hold his predecessor's conquests, as the new provinces were by no means secure. Emperors were traditionally supposed to expand the empire gloriously, not forfeit parts of it, but Hadrian took the unpopular step of abandoning Armenia, Mesopotamia, and Assyria and withdrawing to the Euphrates. He may have had a more easily defensible boundary in mind, but there were also internal problems—notably the Bar Kokhba revolt in Judea in 135 CE—that likely led to a rethinking of the expansionist policy.

Hadrian rebuilt the **Pantheon** (originally constructed by Marcus Agrippa between 27 and 25 BCE), inaugurated the Temple of Venus and Roma in 121 CE (a temple he designed), and built his own mausoleum in Rome (now the Castel Sant'Angelo). However, he spent relatively little time in the city of Rome. He is known as the "restless emperor," as the unstable situation on the **frontiers** required him to travel extensively. He inspected and fortified the *limes* (border area) in Germany and built Hadrian's Wall in Britain. Known as a philhellene, a lover of Greek culture, he also spent significant time in Greece.

In the mid-130s CE Hadrian fell ill and began to make provisions for his succession. After the death of his first adopted successor, Lucius Aelius Caesar, he adopted Aurelius Antoninus Pius, who, in turn, was required to adopt Marcus Aurelius and Lucius Verus. This arrangement ensured continuity of succession for two generations. Hadrian died in Baiae in 138 CE. During his reign, he secured the frontiers, brought about a rebirth of Hellenic culture in the Roman empire, and ensured a smooth transition to his successor.

Antoninus Pius continued Hadrian's external policy of consolidation, with the exception of one major engagement in the north of Britain, after which the Antonine Wall was built some 160 kilometres north of Hadrian's Wall. In contrast to Hadrian, though, Antoninus Pius never travelled outside of Italy while he was emperor. He tried systematically to prepare Marcus Aurelius for his role as future emperor so that, when he died in 161 CE, the Empire would have a capable new ruler. Indeed, at the beginning of Marcus Aurelius's reign, all seemed prosperous. The Mediterranean Sea was referred to as *mare nostrum*, "our sea," and shipping routes—the arteries of the Roman economy—crisscrossed it. The empire was protected by an army that, since the reign of Hadrian, had focused mainly on defence, not expansion. Concord marked the relationship between the emperor and the senate and that between Marcus Aurelius and Lucius Verus. In fact, Marcus Aurelius began his reign with a novelty: he elevated his adoptive brother to the rank of co-emperor—in theory his equal in every respect—as had been intended by Hadrian. The only formal difference was that Marcus Aurelius was also *pontifex maximus*.

Yet the reign of Marcus Aurelius foreshadowed the beginning of a multi-layered crisis in the empire. The relationship of the co-emperors with the senate was calm, but trouble was brewing externally. In northern Britain, Germany, and Armenia, the frontier garrisons came under attack. Hadrian's *limes* system nearly collapsed. The Parthians, after seizing Armenia, attacked Syria as well. Lucius Verus set out to deal with the situation and managed to retake Armenia. The Romans were equally successful in Syria and converted **Dura-Europos** into a frontier fortress. However, the troops in the east were being ravaged by plague, and the Parthians were attempting to regain lost territory. The eastern frontier turned into a chronic zone of conflict within the first decades of the third century CE.

→ See Chapter 14, p. 320, on Dura-Europos.

Problems were also beginning to arise on the Danube. Since troops were drawn off to deal with the eastern frontier, the Danube frontier was under increasing pressure from the Quadi and other Germanic tribes. The Roman army successfully warded off an attack in 167 CE by the Quadi and the Marcomanni; Marcus Aurelius and Lucius Verus decided to travel to the Danube themselves. Their headquarters were located at Aquileia, in northern Italy, where they spent the winter of 168 CE. Shortly after, however, Lucius Verus died. The Romans finally concluded the so-called Marcomannic Wars in 174 CE.

Just one year later, Avidius Cassius staged a revolt in Syria and was declared emperor. Marcus Aurelius and his teenage son, Commodus, set out to deal with the usurper but received en route the message that Cassius had been killed by one of his own soldiers. Meanwhile, the situation on the Danube was anything but safe after the emperor's departure. A revolt of several Germanic tribes prompted a Roman declaration of war, and Marcus Aurelius and Commodus together launched the "second Germanic campaign." After the Roman victory in 179 CE, Marcus Aurelius fell ill and died in Vindobona (modern Vienna) the following year. With his death, the almost century-old tradition of choosing a successor according to his merits rather than his blood relations came to an end. Having been introduced as co-regent in 176 CE, Commodus became sole ruler and arrived in Rome four years later.

Commodus seems to have had a highly unstable personality. He ascribed the "good fortune of the times" to his mere presence as ruler, became obsessed with performing as a **gladiator**, and menaced the senate (see Box 2.3). He began to style himself as a living god, Hercules Romanus, who had his own priest (*flamen Herculaneus Commodianus*). Threatened by his unpredictable character, individuals in his immediate environment—his lover, Marcia, his servant Eclectus, and the praetorian prefect Aemilius Laetus—conspired to poison him. When the plan failed, they had him strangled by a young wrestler one night in December 192 CE. The senate immediately voted for *damnatio memoriae* for Commodus. Because his murder had not been an act committed by a political opposition or with a successor in mind, a new *princeps* had to be presented to the empire and the legions.

The Severans (193–235 CE)

Commodus's immediate successor was Publius Helvius Pertinax, a senior senator who, as prefect of the city (**praefectus urbi**) of Rome, took power temporarily. After only three

Primary Source

Box 2.3: Cassius Dio 73.21.1–2.[1]

Here is another thing that Commodus did to us senators that gave us every reason to look for our death. Having killed an ostrich and cut off his head, he came up to where we were sitting holding the head in his left hand, and in his right hand he raised his bloody sword. Though he did not say a word, he wagged his head with a grin, suggesting that he would treat us in the same way. In fact, many of us would have been slain on the spot for laughing at him (for it was laughter rather than indignation that overcame us), if I had not chewed some laurel leaves. These I got from my garland, and I persuaded the others who were sitting near me to do the same, so that we might conceal the fact that we were laughing by the steady movement of our jaws.

Note

1. Adapted from Cary (1925).

months as emperor, he was killed for being unable to make promised payments to the **praetorian guard**, the very force that was
supposed to protect him as emperor. The wealthy senator Marcus
Didius Severus Julianus took his place. The imperial succession
See Chapter 13, p. 293, on ←
Severus's punishment of the
praetorian guard for their
actions in 193 CE.
reached a low point as the praetorians simply auctioned off the imperial throne to the highest bidder. Almost simultaneously, Pescennius Niger (in Syria), Clodius Albinus (in Britain),
and Lucius Septimius Severus (in Upper Pannonia) were declared emperor by their respective troops. Septimius Severus prevailed against his rivals and founded the Severan dynasty.

Septimius Severus, born in Lepcis Magna (modern Libya), was the first emperor of
African origin. He elevated his family by associating it with the Antonines, calling himself
"son of the deified Marcus Aurelius." To reduce the power of individual provincial governors, Severus divided Syria and Britain into two new provinces each. In 199 CE he defeated
the Parthians in the East and created the new province of Mesopotamia. Ten years later,
he had to go to Britain, where the Scots and the Picts had been entering Roman territory
beyond Hadrian's Wall. The wall was repaired over its full length, and the frontier area
south of it was brought back under Roman control. Severus also fortified and enhanced
Hadrian's *limes* system, increased the overall number of legions, and strengthened the role
of the equestrian order in the imperial administration at the expense of the senate.

Severus's Syrian wife, Julia Domna, gave birth to two sons, Bassianus (Caracalla) and
Geta. Anxious that they should succeed him, Severus declared the elder co-emperor (or
"Augustus") in 198 CE and bestowed the same honour upon the younger in 209 CE. When

Severus died in Eboracum (modern York) in 211 CE, his famous last words to his sons were to "get along with each other, pay the soldiers, and despise all the others" (Cass. Dio 77.15.2). Caracalla and Geta, however, did not get along. The sibling rivalry of their youth mutated into outright loathing. Finally, in 212 CE, Caracalla had his brother killed and presented himself to the praetorian guard as sole ruler. His rule is most notable for the *Constitutio Antoniniana*, an imperial decree probably dated to 212 CE, which granted Roman citizenship to every free inhabitant of the Roman empire (*Dig.* 1.5.17). The motivation for the *Constitutio* is not entirely clear, but it appears to have increased the number of people liable to pay certain kinds of taxes. Aside from this order, Caracalla was remembered for being a dangerous and delusional megalomaniac. He was murdered in 217 CE by a member of his own bodyguard. Macrinus, the prefect of the praetorian guard (who might have been the instigator of Caracalla's assassination), declared himself emperor and was acclaimed by his troops.

Macrinus reigned as emperor for only one year before being removed. In 218 CE Elagabalus, the 14-year-old son of Caracalla's cousin on his mother's side, was declared emperor by troops in the East. Elagabalus's reign was short-lived and marked by bizarre scandals. He was assassinated after only four years by the praetorian guard (reputedly with the complicity of his grandmother), and his cousin Severus Alexander succeeded him. Although his reputation as emperor was better, Alexander was also assassinated, in 235 CE, marking the end of the Severan dynasty.

"Military Anarchy," or "Crisis of the Third Century" (235–284 CE), and Tetrarchy (293–311 CE)

Fifty years of notorious "military anarchy" followed the demise of Severus Alexander, a half-century in which perhaps more than two dozen men were declared emperor in various parts of an empire ravaged by political unrest, economic difficulties, threat of invasion from hostile tribes on the borders, and plague. The chaos ended in 284 CE, with the accession of Diocletian. He reorganized the empire's administration, military, and economy. Most important, he introduced a system called the **tetrarchy** ("rule of four"), a system composed of two "senior" emperors, called *Augusti* ("Augustuses"), and two "juniors," called *Caesares* ("Caesars").

Soon after his accession, Diocletian chose Maximian as co-ruler and his equal in the rank of Augustus. The empire was divided into two halves, an eastern and a western one, each governed by an Augustus. In 293 CE two junior colleagues, Constantius and Galerius, were given the rank of Caesar to constitute the complete tetrarchy, with each of the four emperors governing one-quarter of the empire with his own court and capital city. Each Augustus had one Caesar as a designated successor, which was meant to eliminate the danger of usurpation. Each Augustus was also supposed to withdraw from office after a certain period of time, and his Caesar was supposed to take his place and choose his own Caesar in turn.

The system, however, collapsed soon after its inception. Constantius died in 306 CE, only one year after he became Augustus, and his son Constantine was declared the new Augustus by his own troops. Shortly afterwards, Maxentius, son of Maximian, elevated himself to the rank of Augustus. After a number of years of confusion, with more individuals claiming titles, Constantine prevailed as the sole emperor of Rome in 324 CE.

Constantine's reign is best remembered not for the reunification of the empire but for the toleration of Christianity. But this act was perhaps less revolutionary than might be imagined. Constantine's ability to dictate official religion depended upon the tradition, instituted by the first emperor Augustus, of concentrating religious authority in the person of the emperor. Moreover, the reasons for Constantine's deathbed conversion to Christianity were rooted in an ideology that extended back to the very beginning of Rome, which dictated that one should cultivate the gods who aided military victory. Constantine claimed that the Christian God had helped him win his victory over Maxentius in 312 CE. Constantine may therefore be seen as equally falling into line with his predecessors and breaking ranks with them.

Summary

The events discussed in this chapter cover more than a millennium, and their effects continued, in one form or another, for much longer. Interest in ancient Rome has continued from the medieval period until today, as has the civilization's influence on many social, economic, and political aspects. This brief historical prelude is not meant to be exhaustive but to present a sketch of the chronology of Roman history relevant to the following thematic chapters.

Questions for Review and Discussion

1. Find and read Livy's and Dionysius of Halicarnassus's accounts of the Lucretia incident and subsequent events, the tale that opened this chapter (see specifically Livy 1.58–9 and Dion. Hal. *Ant. Rom.* 4.64–85; the appendix of this volume provides information on locating translations). Compare the two accounts and suggest reasons for their differences.

2. Examine the connection between land ownership and military service during the Roman Republic. How did this connection shape the development of Roman politics and the transition from Republic to Empire?

3. What changes did Augustus make to Rome and the empire?

4. Consider the changes in military and foreign policy between the reigns of Vespasian and Hadrian. How was the empire affected?
5. What crisis did the reign of Marcus Aurelius foreshadow? What were the main reasons behind it?

Suggested Reading

Barrett, A.A., ed. 2008. *The Lives of the Caesars*. Oxford: Blackwell.

This collection of essays by leading scholars addresses the individual lives of Rome's emperors from Augustus to Constantine and also provides further bibliographic information.

Dmitriev, S. 2011. *The Greek Slogan of Freedom and Early Roman Politics in Greece*. Oxford: Oxford University Press.

This study examines the evidence for the use of "freedom" as propaganda before and during the Roman conquest of Greece in the late third and second centuries BCE. It also considers the Roman policy in Greece in 229 BCE— the first Illyrian intervention—and the use of freedom propaganda between the Second Macedonian War and the war with Antiochus III, between 197 and 189 BCE.

Pagán, V.E. 2004. *Conspiracy Narratives in Roman History*. Austin: University of Texas Press.

Pagán's study considers how our sources present conspiracies during the Republic and the Empire.

Potter, D.S., ed. 2006. *A Companion to the Roman Empire*. Oxford: Wiley-Blackwell.

This volume provides both a historical narrative and a thematic treatment of several elements of Roman society during the Roman Empire.

Rosenstein, N., and R. Morstein-Marx, eds. 2006. *A Companion to the Roman Republic*. Oxford: Wiley-Blackwell.

This volume provides both a historical narrative and a thematic treatment of several elements of Roman society during the Roman Republic.

The Cambridge Ancient History, 2nd edn. 1970–2005. Cambridge: Cambridge University Press, esp. vols 7–13.

This series provides a narrative history of Rome from its beginning through to the late Empire (ending in 425 CE) and several thematic chapters by leading scholars. Volumes 8 through 12 contain the material most relevant to the period 200 BCE–200 CE and offer an excellent array of bibliographic information.

The Cambridge Companions to the Ancient World. 2004–2013. Cambridge: Cambridge University Press.

This series examines topics in the civilization and history of ancient Greece and Rome. Of interest to those studying Rome and its history are *The Cambridge Companion to the Roman Republic* by Harriet Flower (2004), *The Cambridge*

Companion to the Age of Augustus by Karl Galinsky (2005), and *The Cambridge Companion to the Age of Constantine* by Noel Lenski (2nd edn, 2012).

The Fontana History of the Ancient World. 1976–1993. London: Fontana.

This series by several authors considers the history of ancient Greece, the Hellenistic world, and Rome. For Roman history in particular, Michael Crawford's *The Roman Republic* (2nd edn, 1992) and Colin Wells's *The Roman Empire* (2nd edn, 1992) will prove useful.

The Lancaster Pamphlets in Ancient History. 1992–2012. London and New York: Routledge.

This series by various authors considers both specific periods of Roman history and the lives of particular emperors. Notable among them are David Shotter's *The Fall of the Roman Republic* (2nd edn, 2005), *Augustus Caesar* (2nd edn, 2005), *Tiberius Caesar* (2nd edn, 2004), and *Nero* (2nd edn, 2005), as well as Sam Wilkinson's *Caligula* (2004).

The Routledge History of the Ancient World. 1995–2011. London and New York: Routledge.

This series by various authors considers the history of the ancient world. Notable titles regarding Roman history are *The Beginnings of Rome* by Tim Cornell (1995), *The Roman World 44 BC–AD 180* by Martin Goodman (1997), and *The Roman Empire at Bay, AD 180–395* by David S. Potter (2004).

Notes

1   Unless otherwise indicated, translations are those of the authors.
2   The term *Principate* is used to describe not only the regime established by Augustus as *princeps* ("first man") but also the Roman historical period between Augustus and the late third century CE, with the *dominate* (admittedly a term now rarely used) traditionally beginning in 284 CE with the accession of Diocletian. The term *Empire* is often used to refer to the time covered by both of these periods.
3   The major literary sources for the history of early Rome and the Republic are the Latin works of historians Livy and Sallust; the Greek works of the historians Appian, Dionysius of Halicarnassus, Cassius Dio, and Polybius; the biographies of the Greek author Plutarch; and the letters and speeches of the late republican statesman Cicero.
4   Among the major literary sources for the history of the Principate are the autobiographical *Deeds of the Divine Augustus* (*Res Gestae Divi Augusti*) by Augustus; the biographies of the emperors of the first century CE, written by Suetonius; those of the later emperors, by the so-called *Scriptores Historiae Augustae*; the works of the historians Velleius Paterculus, Tacitus, Cassius Dio, Josephus, and Herodian; and the letters of Pliny the Younger.

3

Class and Status

Pauline Ripat

An ancient gag book called *The Laughter-Lover* (*Philogelos*) includes the following jokes: "A provincial was trying to sell a pot without a handle or spout. 'Why did you cut off its appendages?' asked someone. 'So that it wouldn't hear that it was going to be sold, and so run away!'" and "An officer saw a carter driving his wagon through the marketplace, and ordered him to be blinded. But the latter protested that he was a Roman citizen, so it was against the law to blind him. Whereupon, the officer ordered his oxen to be flogged."[1] Although these jokes are found in a collection that dates to the fourth or fifth century CE, earlier generations of Romans would have undoubtedly found them funny too. But they strike the modern audience as distasteful and perhaps even incomprehensible. Humour is among the most culturally specific forms of expression, and "getting" the joke usually depends upon first-hand familiarity with not only social values but also the many ways those values are used, abused, or ignored.

These jokes, therefore, underline two issues of critical importance in the study of Roman society. First, our social values are often very different from the ancient Romans': the Romans are not just like us, and we are not just like them. We certainly recognize the presence of violence and social inequality today, but the social values we publicly embrace lead us to find jokes about life-altering physical violence as a deterrent or punishment distasteful rather than hilarious. Second, these jokes demonstrate the vital influence of status upon an ancient individual's experience. In the first, the intellect of slaves and kitchen utensils are "humorously" equated, but the joke depends upon the fact that slaves and kitchen utensils were both property to be bought and sold by others. Any imagined attempt at escape earns mutilation, not sympathy. In the second, the "crime" (a minor traffic infraction) remains the same—it is the punishment that changes. The perpetrator is revealed to be protected from physical violence by his legal status as a Roman citizen. The violence required to right the wrong must be unleashed upon the oxen, who have merely obeyed the orders of their master and whose suffering demonstrates (and this, presumably, is the funny part) that oxen are not Roman citizens.

Timeline

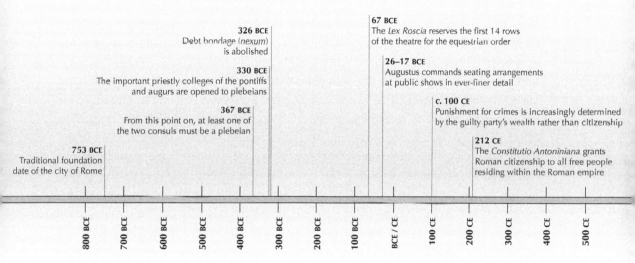

753 BCE
Traditional foundation date of the city of Rome

367 BCE
From this point on, at least one of the two consuls must be a plebeian

330 BCE
The important priestly colleges of the pontiffs and augurs are opened to plebeians

326 BCE
Debt bondage (*nexum*) is abolished

67 BCE
The *Lex Roscia* reserves the first 14 rows of the theatre for the equestrian order

26–17 BCE
Augustus commands seating arrangements at public shows in ever-finer detail

c. 100 CE
Punishment for crimes is increasingly determined by the guilty party's wealth rather than citizenship

212 CE
The *Constitutio Antoniniana* grants Roman citizenship to all free people residing within the Roman empire

800 BCE   700 BCE   600 BCE   500 BCE   400 BCE   300 BCE   200 BCE   100 BCE   BCE / CE   100 CE   200 CE   300 CE   400 CE   500 CE

Introduction

Considerations of wealth (class) and legal standing (status) reached all areas of Roman life. Some aspects are obvious: the poor were more likely to live in rented, cramped apartment space than the more affluent were, and the wealthy enjoyed a more varied and abundant diet than the poor did. Other aspects are possibly less expected, such as the fact that not all members of Roman society enjoyed the same access to the justice system or an equal right to vote. Perhaps more surprising is that status dictated names, clothing, and the kind of food and drink one was served at another's house. But most startling is the high value placed on social stratification. As Pliny the Younger (*Ep.* 9.5.3) wrote, "Nothing is more inequitable than equality."

Social disparity was not an evil to be lessened whenever possible but was encouraged by law and fostered by social practice. This is not to say that social mobility was impossible. On the contrary, Roman society was rather unusual in antiquity in that avenues of economic and social improvement existed (although how many could take advantage of them is another matter). But a society that extends opportunities for social mobility is not necessarily one that considers widespread equality a desirable goal. In

Roman society, those who achieved higher social and economic standing did not pave the way for others but slammed the door on them. Given the pervasive presence of concerns over class and status in Roman social life, this chapter introduces some of the themes and concepts that will re-emerge or underlie the topics of subsequent chapters.

————•◆•————

This chapter illuminates some of the historical and legal questions surrounding issues of **class** and **status** in Roman society and considers the ways that status in particular was experienced. Five subjects will be addressed, beginning with definitions. As with many important historical concepts, the Latin terms used by Romans to describe class and status are numerous, less precise than we would like, and somewhat different in meaning from the English words used to represent them. The second topic is history. For most of its existence, the Roman world was expanding. Newcomers—individuals and whole communities—had to be incorporated into the social and political entity that was the Roman empire. At the same time, expansion brought new military, political, and economic opportunities to people who were already established members of Roman society. These changing circumstances shaped the criteria that decided social standing (in the sense of social experience, opportunity, and the treatment one received from others). The third deals with social mobility, both upward and downward. The fourth considers the impact of status on the ordinary lives of individuals. How much, and in what ways, did status matter? The final subject is the persistence of social disparity throughout Roman antiquity.

Before proceeding, it is important to note some complications involved in the consideration of class and status in Roman society. As Roman society changed over time, the factors that invested individuals with privilege or social esteem also changed. But the old factors did not give way entirely to the new; instead, a whole series of factors of greater or lesser importance were in play at any given time. As a consequence, it is impossible to sketch a tidy social hierarchy. For example, a Roman citizen might be poor, and certainly might be poorer than a **freedman** or **freedwoman** of a wealthy master, but citizens generally enjoyed greater legal privileges and fewer social stigmas than ex-slaves. Who had the better social existence? How do we plot the social positions of the poor citizen and the wealthy freedperson relative to each other? Should we imagine two parallel social hierarchies, one that describes the social value granted by status and the other by wealth?

Even if we were to imagine two such social hierarchies, we still run into a problem: two hierarchies are not enough to account for all the factors that affected social experience. Historians must often generalize to make sense of larger social trends, but surely social experience was often very personal, even among those whose social status and wealth were the same. For instance, all slaves were the same in the eyes of the law, and no slave could own property. But a slave consigned to the silver mines of Spain must have had a very different quality of life than one who lived in the imperial household and dressed the hair of the emperor's wife.

This dilemma is exacerbated by the nature of our sources. Very little direct evidence regarding anyone beyond the wealthiest and most prestigious survives. We are left to patch together a sense of social existence for the vast majority of the population from sources such as tombstone inscriptions, Roman law, and (often negative) anecdotes featuring social inferiors as told by their social superiors. All of these impart an impression of what was possible, not a clear image of what was usual.

In fact, the evidence for all aspects of Roman society is just a minute fraction of what once existed. The result is that evidence for the importance and experience of class and status in Roman antiquity is somewhat contradictory. Some sources suggest that class and status were of the utmost importance; others indicate that there was a good deal of casualness towards maintaining these social distinctions. Although this chapter suggests possible ways of resolving contradictory information, the inconsistencies we perceive are themselves a function of limited sources. We see contradictions because information that might have provided the shades of grey between the black and white is lost to us.

Terms

To begin with the English terms that form the themes of this chapter, both *class* and *status* are suggestive of social hierarchy but are not synonymous. Instead, they raise related and complementary issues. As we shall see, gaining the fullest impression of the forces that shaped Roman social experience and relations requires a consideration of both terms.[2]

Class

The English term *class* has two general connotations. "Economic class" is explicitly concerned with wealth; "social sophistication" is less obviously so. However, it is common to hear behaviour described as (for example) middle class, which suggests that attitudes and actions can be popularly understood, or stereotyped, as the direct result of economic standing. Both English meanings of *class* are widely recognized as relevant to the consideration of Roman society, since wealth influenced the nature of the moral and intellectual qualities attributed to individuals and was also a significant factor in social organization. For example, the citizen army in Rome's earliest history was divided into categories that were determined by wealth and established one's role in military deployment. (In fact, each category was called a *classis*, a term from which *class* derives but which, given its relevance to the army, does not have precisely the same meaning as the English term.) Although the army would not maintain this system for most of the rest of Roman history, the divisions were transferred to the political realm and became the basis of the voting units of the **comitia centuriata**, the popular assembly responsible for electing higher magistrates during the Republic. The effect was to endow the wealthier (but less numerous) members of Roman society with greater electoral influence than their poorer (and vastly more numerous) counterparts. Already we can see that class mattered.

Nonetheless, there has been some resistance to the use of *class* as an investigative term. The objection is that Marxist theory has hijacked the economic meaning of the word, forever rendering it a description of the relationship to the means of production. The result (the argument goes) is that a class analysis of Roman society would artificially group together people who perform similar economic roles (say, the freeborn rural poor and rural slaves as workers) but whose actual social experience could have been quite different because of other factors, such as legal status or prestige. A sense of belonging to a common community, or class consciousness, among such disparate individuals was probably absent. However this may be, the importance of class in the sense of wealth as an important element in understanding Roman social divisions can hardly be discounted. It is clear, though, that we cannot understand Roman social stratification by considering class alone.

Status

Like *class*, *status* has two meanings for us. The first points to one's legal standing (for example, citizen or legal alien); the second refers more casually to social prestige. As we shall see later in this chapter, this second sense applies to Roman society. But the word *status* comes to us directly from the Latin word of the same spelling, a term most often used to describe the degree to which the law protected one's privileges and rights. The Roman jurist Gaius (*Inst.* 1.9–11) identifies the primary division between people as being one of freedom or slavery; a third category is then created by subdividing free individuals into those who were freeborn (**ingenui/ae**) and those released (manumitted) from slavery (**freedpersons, liberti/ae**).

Legal status, however, was not confined to these three broad groups. Free birth did not necessarily equal Roman citizenship; much of the political history of Rome describes the gradual extension of Roman citizenship, or degrees of citizenship, to communities and individuals who lived within its bounds.[3] Until the emperor Caracalla granted citizenship to all free people in 212 CE, there were significant numbers of free non-Roman citizens residing within the empire.[4] As a category, however, freeborn Roman citizens enjoyed the greatest number of legal privileges. These included the ability to pass citizenship on to one's children (provided the children were born of a recognized union between citizens), the right to make a will, and (for males) the right to vote in the popular assemblies in the city of Rome and to bear the symbolic markers of citizenship—the toga and three names (*tria nomina*; for instance, Gaius Julius Caesar). Since Roman citizens were legally protected from suffering physical abuses without trial, they could even protect themselves from physical violence with the cry "I am a Roman citizen!" (*civis Romanus sum!*).[5]

Slaves (*servi*) existed on the other end of the spectrum of legal privilege. Slavery and citizenship were entirely incompatible: a slave was never a citizen and, as such, had none of the citizen's legal benefits. Slaves owned nothing—even their own bodies belonged to their owners. Slaves had few legal protections against physical abuse (those that existed were generally created to protect the master from loss of property, not the slave from harm or humiliation) and could be branded, whipped, or held in chains. In some situations, they were even required by law to be tortured. What we would call sexual abuse was undoubtedly common, as slaves' bodies were thought to exist for the use, profit, and enjoyment of their masters. Slaves' children were also slaves and belonged to their mother's master, at whose whim they might be sold. Slaves had but a single name, imposed at their master's will.

Freedpersons existed in the divide between freeborn citizen and slave. Freed status was the only status that was not hereditary. Citizenship was granted with formal **manumission**.[6] Freedpersons, however, did not enjoy all the rights of freeborn citizens (although children born to them after manumission did). For example, freedmen could not run for elected office, even if they met all the other criteria for eligibility. Freedwomen had to wed their ex-masters if they had been manumitted for that purpose, and their ability to divorce their husbands was curtailed. The law allowed former masters to continue to inflict physical punishment upon their ex-slaves, who continued to owe their ex-masters both a deferential attitude (***obsequium***) and a certain amount of (free) labour (***operae***) per year. The continuation of this relationship, which we might think should have been severed with manumission, was reflected in the freedperson's very name. Citizenship came with the right of three names: the first two mirrored the former master's first two names and the third was the ex-slave's servile name.

Compare Chapter 4, p. 85, and Chapter 5, p. 108, on slave families.

See Chapter 4, p. 89, on *obsequium* and *operae*.

Just as there is difficulty using *class* as an investigative term, *legal status* also fails to describe the full range of ancient individuals' social experience. The citizenry, for example, was not an undifferentiated mass, and not all civic opportunities or legal privileges were extended to everyone.[7] Some citizens living in the city of Rome were at times eligible to receive free grain (the *plebs frumentaria*), while others were not. The wealthiest citizens had the greatest access to political office and the machinery of justice, but these things could be denied to those who did not display the moral behaviour suitable to a citizen, regardless of wealth. As we have already seen, we also cannot posit a common social experience for slaves. With their absolute dependence upon their masters ensured by law and social custom, slaves might be treated with relative kindness or brutality, depending on the demeanour of their master (see, for example, Plin. *Ep.* 8.16). Similarly, freedpersons might or might not prosper, depending not only on their own energies but also on the identity of their ex-masters. The ex-slaves of the rich, powerful, and well-connected might become the same, while those of non-descript masters were less likely to soar to great social or economic heights.

Given the inability of each class and status to provide a full description of social experience in Roman society, it is unsurprising that, when referring to social gradations, the Romans generally avoided using terms that had strict connotations of only wealth or legal standing. *Ordo*, for example, was often used and can be translated to mean "rank," "class," "station," or "condition."[8] Other terms are suggestive of wealth but presuppose the presence of citizen status and include connotations of moral qualities or behaviour. Take, for example, the use of **honestiores** to describe the wealthy and **humiliores** to describe the poorer ("the more honourable" and "the more humble," respectively). These examples are far from exhaustive,[9] and clear difficulties are posed to anyone who wishes to write about Roman society in English rather than in Latin. Modern historians therefore often speak of the Roman "elite" and "non-elite." These terms are useful because of, rather than in spite of, their relative imprecision. Generally, the elite includes the three wealthiest classes of freeborn Roman citizens: the **equestrians** (those who had a minimum of 400,000 **sesterces** of annual income), the **senatorials** (equestrians who had been elected to a public magistracy and had consequently gained life-long membership in the **senate**), and the **decurions** (the wealthiest members of urban communities outside of the city of Rome, who were eligible for local magistracies and entry into local town councils; the amount of wealth required varied from place to place).[10] The non-elite includes everyone else.

Class and Status: Changes over Time

Social disparity was such an integral feature of Roman society that it features in the foundation legends of the city of Rome. Romulus, the city's founder and first king, was said to have divided his population of citizens into two categories, **patricians** and **plebeians** (Livy 1.6–8; Dion. Hal. *Rom. Ant.* 2.8–9). The first he created by selecting 100 *patres*, or "fathers," to serve as the senate, his advisory board. These men were, we are told, quite literally fathers (and it was their descendants who would become known as patricians) but also men of particular authority due to their notable birth, remarkable wealth, or outstanding virtue. The remainder, which legendarily comprised such humble folk as shepherds, freedpersons, and runaway slaves, became known as the plebeians, a designation that also became hereditary.

Tradition aside, it appears that clans of patricians (the hereditary aristocracy whose wealth was dependent upon landownership) monopolized priesthoods and magistracies and provided the cavalry of the Roman army in the early Republic. This situation did not last. Roman expansion over the Italian peninsula (which was accomplished between roughly the fifth and early third centuries BCE) perhaps inspired among plebeians a greater awareness of their military importance and a sense of common identity.

At the same time, it created new opportunities for trade (and wealth) for some of them. Resentment over positions of political and religious power being reserved for patricians also increased. During the consequent "struggle of the orders" that characterized the early Republic, plebeians formed their own popular assembly (the **concilium plebis tributum**), elected **tribunes** (*tribuni plebis*) to protect and advocate for their interests, and made legal recommendations (**plebiscita**, which were granted the force of law in 287 BCE). But it was wealthy plebeians who really benefited from the changes of this period, as wealth rather than aristocratic birth came to be the prerequisite for traditional positions of political and religious power.[11] It is important to note that this expansion of eligibility did not result in greater social equality but greater opportunity for power and prestige among the wealthy, regardless of the hereditary designation of patrician or plebeian.

See Chapter 10, pp. 219–37, on popular assemblies and magistrates.

The avenue to membership in the most prestigious echelon of society was now open, at least in theory, to any wealthy male citizen who met the minimum property requirement of equestrian rank. In reality, no throng of "self-made men" began to populate public offices. Instead, "new men" (**novi homines**), men who were of wealthy but previously non-political families, aimed to distinguish themselves and their families by getting elected to public office and admitted to the senate. An exclusive society of just 300 men, the senate developed its own internal hierarchy during the middle Republic with the appearance of the **nobiles** ("nobles"; literally, "famous ones"), men who had been elected **consul** and particularly those who undertook famously successful military campaigns while holding that office.[12] Descendants of such men would ostentatiously display the waxen masks (*imagines*) of their famous ancestors in their homes as a permanent reminder of familial glory.[13] Since they were of wax, none of these masks survive, but the *Togatus Barberini*, a first-century BCE statue of a man carrying the busts of his ancestors, provides as close a visual impression of this proud display of the dead as we can get (see Figure 3.1).

See Chapter 7, pp. 150–1, and Chapter 10, pp. 231–3, on novi homines.

It was possible to be both a new man and a **nobilis**. However, a degree of snobbishness on the part of established senatorial families towards newcomers, even militarily successful consuls, is palpable in our sources. As the historian Sallust (*BJ* 63.7) remarked with reference to Marius, a famous general of the late Republic and a new man, "There was no new man so illustrious or marked by famous deeds that he was not considered (by those of senatorial families) unworthy (of the consulship) and considered a kind of stain upon it." But prestige was not a birthright, nor was senatorial rank hereditary—a senator's son who did not win office at the popular assemblies remained an equestrian. Consular ancestry, though it might help one's chances at the polls, did not guarantee electoral success. By the late Republic, if not before, popularity (in the very literal sense of being admired by the population at large) was an important element of political success and was perhaps even an end unto itself: the applause of the crowd was avidly sought by

Figure 3.1 The *Togatus Barberini*, part of the Capitoline Museum Collection in Rome. © Erin Babnik/Alamy

→ See Chapter 4, p. 90, for restrictions on manumission.

→ See Chapter 5, pp. 104–06, on Augustan marriage legislation.

ambitious men at the **theatre** and games.[14]

When rivals for power, prestige, and popularity brought civil war to the Roman world in the late Republic, many took advantage of the upheavals to increase their wealth and to enjoy privileges of status to which they were not legally entitled.[15] When Octavian finally emerged victorious and became the first emperor (under the name Augustus), he devoted a good deal of attention to what was advertised as the re-establishment of the old system of Roman values. This restoration included measures to define social distinctions more clearly and to regulate access to citizenship. For example, since manumission often came with citizenship, the number of slaves who could be freed in a master's will was restricted.[16] Citizens of the senatorial order, their children, and their grandchildren could not marry freedpersons. The minimum property requirement for senators was raised to one million sesterces.[17] Furthermore, markers of senatorial status, if not membership in the senate itself, became hereditary rights (for example, sons of senators had the right to wear the distinctive clothing of the senatorial rank).[18]

The prestige attached to the senatorial order continued under the Empire, although its composition and powers changed. Augustus's reforms might have been expected to restrict senatorial membership to a select group of Italian families, but this was not the long-term effect. Many senators were neither joined nor replaced by their sons and grandsons: some families could not maintain the minimum property requirement; others were bereft of living adult sons; and some senatorial descendants declined the position. By the second century CE, the percentage of provincials in the senate was increasing as members of wealthy, ambitious provincial families vied to fill the vacancies and gain the cachet of membership in the most prestigious rank of imperial society (on provincial elites, see p. 56–7). According to estimates, perhaps as many as two-thirds of senators came from the provinces in the third century CE. Gone, however, were the days when the senate as a body wielded real political authority. While individuals of particular military talent (often provincial senators with no senatorial pedigree) were granted strategically important positions by the emperor, those who had inherited their positions were often free of any real responsibility. Members of the equestrian rank, whose public service during the Republic was confined to jury duty, became a source of salaried imperial administrative and military agents;

those so selected were also more often provincials. By the fourth century, the difference in prestige between senators and politically active equestrians had narrowed to become virtually non-existent.[19]

From early in the Empire, slaves and freedmen of the imperial house were also given administrative responsibilities,[20] since the loyalty they owed to the emperor was enshrined in traditional expectations of the master–slave relationship and they (unlike senators) were of explicitly subservient status to the emperor. Imperial freedmen could become fabulously wealthy and politically powerful as advisors or agents, and imperial slaves were granted special privileges. They might, for example, marry freeborn women of high status. But imperial rule also brought opportunities for wealthy freedmen who were unconnected to the imperial house. Although forever barred from public office, they could become *Augustales* (priests of the imperial cult), positions of no small prestige.

Indeed, although different statuses—senator, equestrian, freedman, slave—persisted throughout the Empire, the history of status under the emperors conveys the impression that these differentiations were gradually subordinated to a single division of wealth (*honestiores* and *humiliores*) for the citizenry. The relevance of this division was felt in the area of justice. By the second century CE, if not earlier, punishment and access to justice came to be determined according to the category one belonged to. *honestiores* received lighter punishments for crimes than *humiliores* and were more likely to have their grievances heard. *Humiliores*, for their part, could be subjected to punishments that, during the Republic, were reserved for slaves only.[21] Recent studies, however, conclude that consideration continued to be given to the more traditional social divisions. For example, citizens had greater access to trial than non-citizens, freedpersons were never considered to be among the *honestiores*, and *humiliores* were subjected to servile punishments in only exceptional circumstances (slaves did not count as *humiliores*).[22]

Compare Chapter 11, ⟵
**pp. 249–50, on punishment
for the poor.**

In sum, although the rights and privileges associated with different economic brackets and legal statuses changed over the long course of Roman history, social disparity persisted throughout. However, the whole story has hardly been told. The foregoing discussion has primarily focused on the social and political hierarchies of the centre of the empire, Rome. This Romanocentric view might imply that the provincial populations were simply undifferentiated masses whose social and legal existence did not begin until the extension of Roman citizenship in 212 CE. Such an impression is false. Every provincial community recognized economic, political, and religious hierarchies that invested a few people with more political power, religious authority, or social value than others.[23] The infinite variation among provincial communities makes it very difficult to describe provincial social hierarchies as a general topic. It is also clear that the experience of incorporation into the larger Roman empire varied drastically from province to province and from community to community.[24] Furthermore, and as usual, we often have very little information regarding anyone but urban dwellers and provincial elites, and even these groups are sparsely and sporadically represented in the sources.

Despite the lack of knowledge about rural populations, we can hazard a few general suggestions. It can be said with some confidence, for example, that social equality reigned nowhere: slavery was ubiquitous, although the number of slaves probably varied from one place to another. Furthermore, provincial communities had their own assemblies in which citizens of the community could participate, their own councils, and their own magistrates. Indeed, Roman provincial administration, the kernel of which consisted of only a governor and a small staff sent from Rome, largely depended upon the ability of provincial communities to continue to take care of themselves as they had done before inclusion in the empire.

→ See Chapter 4, p. 76, on the uneven distribution of slaves.

It is not the case, however, that local political and social hierarchies remained absolutely unchanged by the coming of Rome. Roman rule generally brought with it grants of Roman citizenship to local individuals (sometimes to whole communities) that had been supportive of Rome. The less Roman citizenship was shared within a community, the greater the prestige. But of greater impact on local hierarchies was the fact that local land was also often redistributed to Roman supporters. Perhaps little changed if these supporters happened to be the pre-existing community elites, but the practice meant that new provincial elites could rival or displace the previous ones.[25] Members of this new (or remade) wealthy and powerful echelon were the communicators, or "mediators," between their native communities and the Roman administration.[26] They could nurture good relations with both their own communities and the Roman authorities by undertaking expensive local public works—the construction of public buildings or amenities, for example. These same works also served as permanent reminders of their benefactions and consequently nurtured the posterity of their family's fame and status.

→ Compare Chapter 16, pp. 358–9, on public building and prestige.

Some provincial elites had ambitions of influence beyond their own communities, and, as previously discussed, the imperial senate was increasingly populated by wealthy provincials. In the quest for positions of standing and power in Rome itself, elites of the eastern provinces had the advantage that the Greek language and culture already occupied a place of high regard at Rome. In contrast, the languages and culture of the western provinces did not enjoy such esteem. It has long been observed that the elites in the western provinces tended to "Romanize," that is, to adopt Roman cultural habits such as dress, to learn Latin, and to be educated in a Roman-style curriculum, thereby rendering themselves more familiar (or at least less foreign) to the Roman authorities. These efforts perhaps eased the path to positions of influence at the centre of the empire. Certainly, such positions were not granted to those who adopted no Roman traits. However, Romanized provincial elites did not turn their backs on their local identity entirely, a consideration that should make us question

→ See Chapter 6 on education.

whether this term is precisely apt. Instead, they seem to have engaged in a sort of cultural bilingualism by cultivating two identities, one Roman and the other intensely local, each to be adopted as the context demanded.[27]

What about the provincial non-elite? Did they also develop two identities? It seems that less wealth meant less opportunity to learn or practise Roman cultural habits. As a general rule, local traditions and cultural traits remained strong among non-elite provincial populations. While statements in Roman literature praising whole provincial communities for "becoming Roman" (see, for example, Strabo 3.2.15) exist, such descriptions are probably exaggerated. Nevertheless, there was certainly awareness of Roman culture or power among the provincial non-elite. The necessity of paying Roman taxes would have been one perpetual and ubiquitous reminder, and, for some provincial populations, the presence of soldiers would have been another. Urban dwellers in particular would have come into contact with infrastructures that were Roman in form and built as benefactions by the provincial elite (the Theatre of Herodes Atticus in Athens provides a famous example).[28]

Compare Chapter 13, pp. 289–92 and 300–2, on the army in provincial society and Chapter 15, pp. 340–4, on provincial taxation.

Compare Chapter 16, pp. 361–2 and 368–70, on Roman architecture and technology in the provinces.

The results of contact with Roman power and culture manifested in different ways and degrees in different areas. In rural communities of North Africa, for example, letters of the Latin alphabet were used in inscriptions to represent the native Punic language, which was in common use there. In some areas of the Danube provinces, images inscribed on tombstones celebrate local traditions and identities, but the very act of engraving a tombstone reflects Roman funerary habits.[29] In short, Roman cultural technologies might have provided a medium, but local traditions provided the content of provincial expressions of identity. Local integration of Roman cultural forms, to the varying degrees that it took place, must therefore be understood within the context of local social structures and concerns, such as the desire to get along with, impress, or surpass one's neighbours. The aim was not to curry the favour of Rome's ruling elite. That goal was left to the wealthy.

Mobility

Upward social and economic mobility was possible in Roman society. As mentioned earlier, slaves could be freed and become Roman citizens; freedmen and freedwomen, although they could never become members of the equestrian order or hold public office, could become extremely wealthy;[30] freedmen of the imperial house could exert considerable political power as advisors or agents;[31] sons of equestrian families could gain public office to become senators, as might (eventually) the descendants of freedmen;[32] and Romans of undistinguished ancestry might work very hard and become leading citizens in their own communities.[33] To communities incorporated into the expanding empire and to individuals who were felt to merit it, citizenship was granted relatively generously. For non-citizen men, the army also provided an avenue to citizenship, which was awarded upon honourable discharge. Furthermore, retirement pay could be translated into property ownership in frontier settlements and, in turn, eligibility for membership in local government.[34] The extension of the citizenship to conquered peoples has been understood in both ancient and modern times as a strategy that ensured Rome's historic superiority (note Tac. *Ann.* 11.24, for example). Under the Empire, some enfranchised provincials rose to power at its very heart,[35] gaining entry to the senate, or even gaining the imperial throne (as did, for example, the emperors Trajan, Hadrian, and Septimius Severus).

→ Compare Chapter 13,
pp. 289–92, on soldiers'
retirement.

These examples suggest a rosier picture of opportunity and social acceptance than is perhaps deserved. Mobility was certainly possible, but was it common?[36] It once was thought, for example, that Romans freed their slaves in such great numbers that the majority of slaves ended their lives as freedpersons.[37] This impression is encouraged by tombstone inscriptions, which commemorate freedpersons three times more often than freeborn. It is now thought, however, that social, emotional, and ideological reasons made the former more likely to commemorate themselves on tombstones than the latter.[38] Some slaves might gain their freedom, but as Keith Hopkins wrote, "Most Roman slaves were freed only by death."[39]

Although there are examples of individuals skyrocketing through the ranks thanks to their good services or exceptional talents,[40] most families probably experienced social advancement more slowly, over the course of several generations. And how long did lowly or servile ancestry follow one around? The poet Horace (*Sat.* 6.65–99) says that he is not ashamed, as others might be, to have a freedman for a father. But, tellingly, his father had ensured that, in his student days, Horace gave no visual impression of being from lowly stock. If anyone had seen him on his way to school, Horace says, they would have thought him a descendant of a wealthy, established family. Before Octavian became the emperor Augustus, even his ancestry was held up for public scrutiny. He claimed to come from an old equestrian family, but his political rival Marc Antony said that Octavian's great-grand-father was a freedman and a rope maker, his grandfather a money-changer (Suet. *Aug.* 2).[41]

Moreover, admittance into the citizen body was not necessarily accompanied by a warm welcome. Freeborn Romans might begrudge the successes of freedmen as won at the expense of their own misfortunes (for example, Plin. *HN* 35.58.200). Although provincials would be incorporated into the political power structures with increasing frequency over the course of the Empire, some prejudice against them would remain on the part of the old Italian establishment, and the tendency to ridicule provincial habits and accents extended back to the Republic. The poet Catullus (39), for example, famously versified: "Egnatius, because he has white teeth, smiles all the time . . . But Egnatius, you are from Spain, where it is the habit to brush your teeth with urine. So the shinier your teeth are, the more pee we know you have drunk."[42]

Demotion was also possible but, like promotion, was probably a rare occurrence. The best-known cases and causes involve the higher orders. Senators could be ejected from the senate by a **censor**—an ex-consul elected by popular assembly—for behaviour that was considered unsuitable to the status. This conduct often involved public or private activities that hinted at poor morals. Sallust is a famous example of senatorial demotion, but there were others.[43] Augustus undertook three purges of the senate to remove those he considered unsuitable, reducing the numbers from 1,000 to merely 600 (thereafter, emperors regularly assumed the role of censor).

But it was not just senators who were expected to display appropriate behaviour. The censor might also impose certain legal restrictions (such as the inability to hold public office or to enrol in the army) on other citizens, such as pimps and **gladiators**, who were felt to be engaging in professions inconsistent with Roman moral standards.[44] Debt bondage (**nexum**), in which a freeborn citizen might be reduced to slavery by using his or her body as collateral for a loan, had been abolished in the fourth century BCE, but in the first century CE free women who became involved with slaves could find their status reduced to that of slave or freedwoman. By the next century, if not earlier, *humiliores* found guilty of crimes could be stripped of the protection promised by citizenship.[45]

Compare Chapter 8, pp. 172–3, on *infamia* and Chapter 12, pp. 270 and 281–3, on Roman attitudes towards gladiators.

Less formal routes to demotion also existed for those who were kidnapped by pirates. This scenario, which sounds like a Hollywood fiction, was a recognized problem in the late Republic. Pirates made raids at sea and even inland, making off with human booty to ransom or to sell as slaves in distant markets. Victims included freeborn men and women, sometimes even those of high status, such as a young Julius Caesar (Suet. *Iul.* 4; see also Plut. *Pomp.* 24–6).

Compare Chapter 11, p. 244, Chapter 14, p. 316, and Chapter 16, p. 364, on piracy.

Did Class and Status Matter?

So far, we have looked at class as a measure of wealth and status as a legal designation. We have seen that the law differentiated between people based on their wealth and status, that both reflected and protected pre-existing social divisions, and that laws regulated social mobility and the benefits it conferred.[46] Efforts were also made to ensure that social differences were recognized on visual and behavioural levels as well. For example, equestrians were barred from loitering in the crowds of commoners that gathered around entertainers in the Forum.[47] The toga with a wide purple stripe was the dress for senators, one with a narrow stripe for equestrians, and one with no

Political History

Box 3.1: Seating at Public Entertainments

Historians have long been intrigued by how the seating arrangements at Roman public entertainments came to reflect social stratification.[1] In 194 BCE senators were formally given front-row seating at the theatre, probably right in the orchestra (Val. Max. 2.4.3, 4.5.1; Livy 34.44.5, 34.54.4). In 67 BCE, by the terms of the *Lex Roscia*, the first 14 rows (directly behind the senators) were reserved for equestrians. Both of these measures were unpopular with poorer members of the audience (Val. Max. 2.4.3; Plut. *Cic.* 13), and encroachment upon the privileged seating was rampant during the civil wars of the late Republic, when the bounds of status were regularly overstepped (see, for example, Suet. *Aug.* 14). Augustus was not only determined to put a stop to such ill behaviour but also to make seating arrangements yet more specific as part of his agenda to define different social strata and groupings more clearly (Suet. *Aug.* 40, 44; Cass. Dio 53.25.1). In addition to privileged seating for senators and equestrians, everyone else was assigned an area based on status, adherence to Augustan family values (married male citizens were allocated special space), age (young male citizens had their own area), and gender (women were sent to the back).

Seating arrangements at spectacles might seem frivolous to us, but it must be kept in mind that public entertainments in the Roman world were intrinsically political, as they provided the people at large with the opportunity to communicate their wishes to, and their approval or disapproval of, those who governed them (Cic. *Sest.* 106; *Att.* 1.16.11, 2.19.3; *Fam.* 8.2.1). It was, therefore, felt to be of tantamount importance that all be quite literally reminded of their relative place in society.

Note

1. Rawson (1991: 508–45) provides more detailed discussion.

→ See Figure 1.1, p. 16, for an image of a *pilleus*.

→ Compare Chapter 12, p. 282, on social organization at the games.

→ See Chapter 11, pp. 248–9, for circumstances that could deny justice.

stripe for the regular citizenry,[48] while freedmen wore a special hat (the *pilleus*) on certain occasions, such as their ex-master's funeral.[49] Seating at public entertainments also came to be dictated by status (see Box 3.1).

But how much difference did status really make in people's ordinary lives? For example, although the degree of access to the justice system (and the experience of punishment) depended upon wealth and status, how often did most people want to take someone to court or discover themselves dragged into one?[50] Even prior to the second century CE, the protection that citizenship was supposed to offer from physical violence sometimes vanished when magistrates' arrogance or greed outweighed their sense of responsibility to the law.[51] Furthermore, one's reputation could dictate the degree of punishment suffered, quite apart from wealth or status.[52] Documentary proof of legal status (such as birth or manumission certificates) could be attained, but there reigned a surprisingly casual attitude towards attaining it, with many choosing to rely on neighbours' testimony if proof was required.[53]

Did the privileges and markers of status really do much to ensure that the various statuses had different social experiences or lifestyles? There was no profession or education specific to citizens that distinguished their lifestyles from non-citizens: the real difference was probably between city dwellers and country dwellers.[54] Senators were barred from taking part in trade, but many were involved through agents; at the same time, equestrians could engage in trade but generally preferred to be landowners (as were senatorials).[55] Freedmen could not hold political office, but neither could most freeborn citizens, since they did not meet the minimum property requirement.[56] Although only adult male citizens could vote, some scholars have argued that disenfranchised elements of society, such as women, might have influenced the outcome of elections.[57] The toga was the distinctive dress of citizen males, but Augustus had to insist that they wear it, at least in the Forum and at the theatre (Suet. *Aug.* 40.5), and Juvenal (3.171–2), writing about a century later, says that no man wore it except at his own funeral.[58] At the same time, wall paintings suggest that striped tunics, the kind supposedly reserved for magistrates, were worn by every Tom, Dick, and Harry (or Gaius, Marcus, and Publius).[59] Graffiti from **Pompeii** conveying electoral support (for example, "All the worshippers of Isis call for Gnaeus Helvius Sabinus as **aedile**" [*CIL* 4.787] or "The spectators in the **amphitheatre** ask for Holconius Priscus as duumvir with judicial power" [*CIL* 4.7585])[60] suggest that individuals might draw identity not from their legal status but from membership in groups focused on common interests and composed of all elements of society.

Compare Chapter 15, pp. 334–0, on the ideological importance of land ownership.

Furthermore, perhaps privileged status was not the sacred social commodity we think it was. There are, for example, notorious incidents when citizenship was not bestowed upon those deemed worthy to join the club but sold to high bidders by members of the imperial household and military commanders.[61] It is possible, however, that many did not even desire to increase their status, despite the (sometimes unfulfilled) promise of superior legal privileges and prestige. Men of high rank bemoaned the crushing responsibilities and dangers of their positions and praised what was, in their opinion, the carefree existence of the destitute and enslaved.[62] While it is unlikely that any of these complainers would have willingly traded places with the poor and powerless, examples exist of individuals refusing the chance to "move up" when the offer was extended because they saw greater opportunity and security in their inferior positions. Melissus, a slave of Augustus's friend Maecenas, is one famous example: he chose to remain the slave of the great man even when it was discovered that he was freeborn.[63] Although slaves and freedpersons might embrace some of the values perpetuated by members of free society in general (such as the ideals of familial relationships), funerary commemorations indicate that they did not necessarily emulate the pretensions of the freeborn elite. Economically successful freedmen took pride in their occupations and advertised them on their tombstones, in contrast to the illustrious, who saw no honour in paid labour of any kind.[64]

→ Compare Chapter 16, pp. 373, on professional pride.

In short, sometimes great efforts were made to maintain social distinctions, while no effort was made at other times. To resolve the contradictions in the evidence, it is best to ask *when* class and status mattered in the lives of individuals. In doing so, it is important to recognize that status was more than just a legal designation but was also manifested as the treatment that one regularly received from others. It was the respect or deference one expected to—indeed, felt entitled to—command from others. Respect and deference (or lack of either) could be displayed by etiquette and demeanour, that is, in a variety of ways that were not legally enforceable. For example, an evaluation of other people's social value could be made by the tone and volume of voice used when addressing them, by making or avoiding eye contact, by offering an opinion or waiting for it to be solicited, by waiting seconds or minutes before acknowledging their presence, by elbowing or giving way in a crowded street, or by serving them first or last at a shop or better or worse food at a dinner party (see, for example, Sen. *Brev. Vit.* 14.4; Juv. 3.164–267; and Box 3.2, where Pliny's attempts to foster an air of equality at the dinner table clearly went against the tide). Every individual would experience hundreds of these tiny exchanges every day, and each would be a pronouncement on his or her relative social worth. This is probably the level at which status primarily functioned for most people.

→ Compare Chapter 8, pp. 179–82, on stereotypes of appearance and behaviour.

Discrimination based on skin colour was rare in Roman society, but judging people by their appearance was not. Stereotypes prevailed about appearance, behaviour, and moral qualities thought to characterize different classes and statuses, although daily experience must have undermined them at every turn: the wealthy and illustrious were good-looking, smart, and honest, while the poor and servile were ugly, stupid, and dishonest.[65] The strength of these stereotypes inspired many to adopt the trappings of a status higher than their own, along with the behaviours and mannerisms associated with it. The visual signs of higher status presumably improved the treatment that the usurpers received from strangers, and the cultivated behaviour possibly increased the respect they commanded from acquaintances. We are told of slaves and freedmen wearing iron rings with gold-plating—that is, the costume version of the ring that signified membership in the equestrian order—and of freedmen massaging their last names into something more "freeborn Roman."[66] Houses also might be adorned in such a way as to suggest that their owners were well educated and, as a result, culturally

Primary Source

Box 3.2: Pliny the Younger, *Letters*, 2.6.

I ended up dining at the house of a man whom I don't know very well . . . He served himself and a few others some rich dishes, and put cheap food, and in small portions, in front of the rest. Even the wine he had divided into three types, in little bottles—not so that there would be the ability to choose, but rather so that there was no possibility of refusing. There was one for himself and for us, another for his lesser friends (for he ranked his friends), and another for his and our freedmen. The man next to me noticed this and asked me if I approved. I said no. "What habits do you follow, then?" he asked. "I place the same things in front of everyone, since I invite people to dinner, not to grade them, and I treat in all ways the same those whom I have made equal with table and seating." "It must cost you a lot," he said. "Not at all." "How not?" "Because my freedmen don't drink what I drink, I drink what they drink."

sophisticated, even if the sometimes rather poor technical quality of the decorations betrayed the household's economics as modest.[67]

The record for the majority of innumerable little details, exchanges, and experiences that promoted and reflected individuals' social value is lost to history. But literary and other sources include two situations in which specific status concerns were stressed. The first is the acquisition of a new and better status. The upwardly mobile tended to advertise their newly achieved status in a variety of ways, such as by adhering to the behaviour and trappings that were deemed proper to that status. Ridicule met those who failed to do so seamlessly: members of the Gallic elite, newly minted as senators by Julius Caesar, were mocked as trouser-wearers-turned-toga-wearers (Suet. *Iul.* 80). Even emperors were not immune from the need to conform with the cultural characteristics thought to be appropriate for (in their case) the ruling class. For example, Hadrian is said to have worked hard to lose his provincial accent (SHA *Hadr.* 3). Septimius Severus apparently achieved the proper accent but is said to have squirmed in embarrassment when his sister visited from their hometown in North Africa and mangled her Latin (SHA *Sev.* 15).[68]

The upwardly mobile might have also ostentatiously observed the rights and privileges that came along with their new status and defended its traditions. Freedpersons, for example, regularly advertised their familial connections—that is, their newly found right to have spouses and legitimate children, something denied to slaves—on their tombstones.[69] While holding a minor magistracy, Septimius Severus had a man from his hometown who had dared to embrace him beaten for showing insufficient

See Chapter 5, pp. 107–08, for examples of freedpersons advertising familial connections on tombstones.

respect to a Roman official (SHA *Sev.* 2). Vedius Pollio, himself descended from slaves, notoriously threw his own slaves to deadly eels as punishment for their clumsiness (Cass. Dio 54.23.1–6). As these actions suggest, desire to exercise the powers invested in the new status might outweigh empathy.

The second situation that called attention to status was lack of recognition (either real or perceived) by peers or social inferiors. Most probably accepted the treatment that society deemed appropriate to their legal status without particular outrage, or so Roman assumptions about slaves lead us to suspect. It was felt that home-born slaves (**vernae**) were better slaves because they had known nothing else, but newly enslaved freeborn foreigners were more likely to object to their new existence and attempt to run away or otherwise resist.[70] These feelings presumably were rooted in the recognition that *vernae* accepted their treatment unquestioningly, while the newly enslaved thought that they still deserved to be treated as free people and therefore felt degraded by being treated as slaves.

Compare Chapter 4, pp. 86–7, on modes of resistance.

Members of other statuses might also take what they considered inappropriate treatment very hard. Consider the error of etiquette made by Julius Caesar. The story goes that Caesar failed to stand when a group of senators approached to present him with special honours. His defenders claimed that he was unable to get up because he was suffering from a terrible bout of diarrhea—evidently no less an excuse sufficed for such shoddy treatment of men who were supposed to be Caesar's peers—but the suspicion persisted that he had been disdainful on purpose. Some thought that the affront was enough to inspire his murder (Cass. Dio 44.8; compare Suet. *Iul.* 78).

A suspected attempt to force a deferential attitude from one's peers was certainly terrible. But equally awful were situations when insufficient deference was shown by social inferiors, either individually or collectively. The law sometimes stepped in to attempt to squelch inappropriate behaviour, dictating in 4 CE that freedpersons who showed insufficient gratitude to their ex-masters should be exiled beyond the hundredth milestone from the city of Rome (Tac. *Ann.* 13.26–7) and, later, that equestrians could not insult senators (Suet. *Vesp.* 9.2). However, the law was powerless to check all situations of social affront, since these were limitless. Pliny the Younger (*Ep.* 8.6; compare 7.29), for example, whipped himself into a rage when he learned that Pallas—the emperor Claudius's freedman but a freedman nonetheless—had been so cheeky as to refuse some of the honours that the senate had voted to him. Who was this freedman to contradict the decision of his betters?

Nor did "uppity" freedmen offend only those of senatorial rank. Narcissus, another of Claudius's freedmen, earned the resentment of rank-and-file soldiers (who were reluctant to listen to their freeborn commander and leave Gaul) when he was sent by the emperor to convince them to undertake the campaign to Britain (Cass. Dio 60.19). Given the option of following their commander or an ex-slave, the soldiers became only too happy to choose the former. When Narcissus attempted to address them, the soldiers even jeered him with the cry "Hey, it's the Saturnalia!" (*io Saturnalia!*). The Saturnalia was a December religious festival that was celebrated by, among other ways, having masters and slaves switch positions.

The very existence of a festival that inverted social roles might suggest that a rather casual attitude towards social difference generally prevailed. On the contrary, the setting aside of specific days when slaves did not have to defer to their masters underlines the fact that they had to submit the rest of the time. We might also wonder how much licence slaves really enjoyed, even on the days of the Saturnalia. Prudent slaves would probably have done well to keep their mouths shut then too. "Come on!" Horace (*Sat.* 2.7.1–5) imagines saying to his slave, "Take advantage of the freedom of December . . . tell me". Even in this fictional exchange, the earful his slave delivers about Horace's (*Sat.* 2.7.116–18) habits is received with threats of punishment. Slaves must have been ever mindful that, although the Saturnalia promised a break from having to show deference, it did not promise forgetfulness or forgiveness when January arrived.

The Persistence of Hierarchy

Another question now presents itself. Why did social hierarchy, a system that benefited the few at the expense of the many, persist throughout Roman history? The question is particularly worth posing given that all examples of Romans offended by treatment inappropriate to their status are also examples of individuals resisting the system by not concerning themselves about giving offence. Yet social stratification was a constant of Roman society. Surely there was a combination of factors that ensured the maintenance of social hierarchy. Let us look at three possible elements.

First, significant social change would require a strong sense of community between social equals. Individuals would have to share goals first and foremost with their social equals and owe their loyalty primarily to their peers in order to work together for their common good. Social ties in Roman society, however, appear to have formed vertically (between members of different classes and statuses) as often, if not more so, than horizontally (between social equals). For example, slaves might feel more loyal to their masters, with whom they lived, than other slaves with whom no common experience might have existed.

Also worth considering is the Roman institution of **patronage**. Once thought to be a life-long social connection between an elite male (the patron, ***patronus***) and a collection of his non-elite social inferiors (his clients, *clientes*), patron-age has more recently been assessed as a more dynamic system of possibly even short-term and mutually beneficial relations between social unequals who did not necessarily

Compare Chapter 4, p. 89, ←
Chapter 7, pp. 154–5,
Chapter 10, p. 237, and Chapter 17,
p. 384, on patronage.

know each other well (the exception was freedmen, whose ex-masters would be their life-long *patroni*).[71]Members of different classes and statuses formed a variety of short- and long-term relationships with each other, and such relationships might have often been of greater emotional, economic, or social importance than the bonds with their peers.

Second, in a society that adheres to social and economic hierarchies yet allows for mobility, social success equals the attainment of the next rank up. Gaining social superiority mattered only if there were social inferiors. The upwardly mobile probably had no wish for their experience to be universally shared, and, as already stated, individuals quickly adopted the demeanours and habits appropriate to their new status. Ex-slaves, for example, often became slave owners; at no point do we hear of any becoming champions for the universal eradication of slavery.

Indeed, social equality for all would never have occurred to anyone in Roman society as possible or even desirable. This is not simply because Roman law sought to defend social inequalities. As subsequent chapters will demonstrate (and this is the third factor), all Roman social systems and cultural forms suggested the rightness and naturalness of social stratification, as did popular wisdom.[72] In addition to the kind of jokes with which this chapter began, urban myths and other popular tales undoubtedly circulated as instructive stories promoting correct social attitudes and behaviours towards both superiors and inferiors. We get whiffs of them in ancient literature[73] and in the moral tales attributed to Aesop (who was, according to legend, once a slave himself). Aesop's fables, beloved by Greeks and Romans alike, expounded lessons that supported the social status quo (see Box 3.3). For example, they encouraged their audience not to attempt

Primary Source

Box 3.3: Two Fables by Aesop

An ass put on a lion's skin, and both men and animals took him for a lion and fled from him. But when a puff of wind stripped off the skin and left him bare, everyone ran up and began to beat him with sticks and cudgels.[1]

A fowler spread his nets and tied his tame pigeons to them . . . In due course some wild pigeons came up and got entangled in the mesh . . . They reproached the tame birds for not giving warning when they saw their kindred walking into a trap. "In our position," the others replied, "it is more important to avoid giving offence to our masters than to earn the gratitude of our kindred."[2]

Notes

1. Handford (1954: 113 [no. 109]).
2. Ibid.: 89 (no. 85).

to rise above their station and expounded the appropriateness of helping their superiors rather than their peers.

Roman social inequity, therefore, was in no danger of being removed. No one was unmindful of its omnipresence and the social etiquettes that fed it. Those who over-stepped the bounds of proper behaviour towards their peers or superiors did so in full knowledge of the offence they would cause, in approved contexts—the licence of the Saturnalia, for example—or, like Claudius's freedmen, with the support of a yet higher social power than those they were insulting.

Summary

Social divisions according to wealth and legal status existed throughout the entire history of Rome, and both class and status must be considered in order to gain the fullest under-standing of individual experience at any given time. Change over time did occur, however. In earliest Rome, birth dictated how much ability an individual would have in the political process, but wealth soon became the more important factor. As the Roman world expanded, the favoured status of citizen was unevenly distributed to newly incorporated peoples. For the enslaved, freedom often brought citizenship, though freedpersons suffered life-long legal restrictions. With the death of the Republic, emperors came to transfer many of the respon-sibilities traditionally invested in the senate to equestrians and to their slaves and freedmen. Yet wealth continued to be an important factor in the determination of legal privilege for the Empire's citizenry, with the division of the citizen body (which, by the early third century CE, included all free members of the empire) into *honestiores* and *humiliores*. Upward and downward social mobility were possible, although both were unlikely to have been common experiences. The effects of status in the ordinary lives of people were probably most keenly felt when a new (higher) status was achieved or when one was treated with less respect by peers or inferiors than was felt to be consistent with one's status. Social disparity persisted throughout Roman antiquity mainly because all social systems supported it, such that no one appears to have ever questioned its continued presence.

Questions for Review and Discussion

1. Do the multiple English meanings of *class* and *status* make them more or less use-ful in describing the factors that shaped Roman social experience? Why?
2. What non-extant evidence would be useful in recapturing more clearly the social experience of the non-elite in Roman society? What kind of information would

such sources provide, and what aspects of life or experiences would this information illuminate?

3. Explain how and why the following statement is true: Freedpersons were never entirely free of their servile background.

4. In this chapter, the attitudes of home-born slaves and newly captured slaves regarding their treatment were contrasted (p. 63). Discuss whether this difference is compelling evidence that most ancient Romans were content with the treatment deemed appropriate to their accustomed status.

5. What forces in our own society discourage social change? How might some, if any, of them be relevant to Roman antiquity as additional factors that fostered the maintenance of social disparity?

Suggested Reading

Alföldy, G. 1988. *The Social History of Rome*. Translated by D. Braund and F. Pollock. Baltimore: Johns Hopkins University Press.
 A chronological study of social changes in Roman history, this work clearly describes the mutually supporting cycle between social divisions and the political context.

Edmondson, J., and A. Keith, eds. 2008. *Roman Dress and the Fabrics of Roman Culture*. Toronto: University of Toronto Press.
 This collection of articles by various authors (including four from the present volume) investigates the multiple meanings of dress as social and status statements in Roman antiquity.

Gardner, J.F. 1993. *Being a Roman Citizen*. London and New York: Routledge.
 Gardner investigates the experience of Roman citizenship from the perspectives of women, freedmen, and people with disabilities.

Garnsey, P. 1970. *Social Status and Legal Privilege in the Roman Empire*. Oxford: Clarendon Press.
 Garnsey studies the nature of Roman justice for the inhabitants of different wealth and status in the Roman empire in the first century CE and beyond.

Morley, N. 2006. "Social Structures and Demography." In *A Companion to the Roman Republic*, edited by N. Rosenstein and R. Morstein-Marx, 299–323. Malden, MA, and Oxford: Wiley-Blackwell.
 This chapter discusses the benefits and drawbacks of the concepts of status and class (with reference to modern theories of the terms) for our understanding of ancient society.

Peachin, M., ed. 2011. *The Oxford Handbook of Social Relations in the Roman World*. Oxford and New York: Oxford University Press.
 This collection of essays by leading scholars addresses the nature of specific

interactions between individuals or collectives (or interactions between specific collectives) within the traditions and structures of Roman society.

Reinhold, M. 1971. "Usurpation of Status and Status Symbols in the Roman Empire." *Historia* 20 (2–3): 275–302.

Reinhold's study gathers the evidence for the appropriation of higher status by individuals and the responses (legal and otherwise) to these practices.

Sherwin-White, A.N. 1980. *The Roman Citizenship*. Oxford: Clarendon Press.

This work is an exhaustive study of the extension of citizenship in Roman history to individuals (freeborn and servile) and communities.

Toner, J. 2009. *Popular Culture in Ancient Rome*. Cambridge: Polity.

Toner provides (especially at pp. 123–61) an engaging discussion of how sensory details—for example, body odours, colours of clothing, and accents—worked as stereotyped characteristics of class and status.

Notes

1 Slightly adapted from Baldwin (1983: 23, 26, nos. 122 and 138), who has translated the collection. All other translations are mine unless otherwise noted.

2 For discussion of the applicability of these terms to Roman society, their benefits, and their inadequacies, see Alföldy (1988: 149–50); Garnsey and Saller (1987: 109); and Harris (1988).

3 Sherwin-White (1980) is the classic study of the extension of Roman citizenship and its permutations.

4 These could be recognized as citizens of their own communities. It was also possible to be a Roman citizen and a citizen of another community within the empire.

5 Cicero (*Verr.* 2.5.147, 165) presents a case in which this ideal was not met; however, Acts 22:25 of the Bible describes a situation in which the claim of citizenship allows St Paul to avoid a flogging.

6 Freed slaves, their place in Roman society and ideology, and their expressions of

identity have enjoyed a good deal of recent attention. For recent treatments and further bibliography, see Mouritsen (2011) and Bell and Ramsby (2012).

7 See Nicolet (1980) and Gardner (1993).

8 Harris (1988: 600); Morley (2006: 303–04). Rawson (1991: 508) notes that "the basic *ordines* . . . were those of the senators, *equites*, and *plebs*."

9 See, for example, MacMullen (1974: 192–3 n. 51); Harris (1988: 601); and Morley (2006: 303–04).

10 Alföldy (1988: 128).

11 Membership in a patrician family always carried with it a certain social cachet, but the actual power invested in that membership dwindled, as did the number of patrician families itself. Only 14 of the original patrician clans were in evidence by the end of the Republic.

12 Alföldy (1988: 32–3).

13 For the display, meaning, and use of *imagines*, see Flower (1996).

14   Hopkins and Burton (1983a: 44).

15   Cassius Dio (48.34), for example, records a remarkable tale in which a slave managed to gain public office but was recognized and hauled away by his master before actually taking up the position.

16   See Suet. *Aug.* 40.3–4 for further restrictions.

17   Although Cassius Dio (55.13.6) says that Augustus personally fronted the money for those he deemed worthy but who lacked the necessary extra funds.

18   Hopkins and Burton (1983b: 125).

19   Ibid.: 120–200, especially 171–84; Garnsey and Saller (1987: 123); Alföldy (1988: 121, 163–8, 193–4); Mennen (2011).

20   See Weaver (1972) in particular.

21   Garnsey (1970) is the classic study.

22   See Aubert (2002).

23   See Ripat (2006b) for an example of the ways that provincial (in this case, Egyptian) socio-religious hierarchies accommodated Roman rule.

24   See Hope (2000: 130–8) for an orienting discussion. Different studies have focused on different provinces: see, for example, Alcock (1993) on Greece; Woolf (1998) on Gaul; and Mattingly (2011) on North Africa and Britain.

25   Mattingly (2011: 151) notes yet other possibilities: "Army recruitment, supervision of native peoples by Roman prefects, and the recognition of specified settlements as administrative centers could all be used to undermine traditional power structures within a community."

26   Woolf (1998: 33).

27   See Mattingly (2011: 240–1).

28   Garnsey and Saller (1987: 189–90) provide other examples.

29   For these and other examples, see Garnsey and Saller (1987: 186–95) and Mattingly (2011: 203–45).

30   Consider the fictionalized Trimalchio of Petronius's novel *Satyricon*, a parody of the wealthy freedman.

31   Tac. *Ann.* 11.38, 12.2; Suet. *Claud.* 28–9.

32   Hopkins and Burton (1983a: 31–119); Tac. *Ann.* 13.27.

33   For example, *CIL* 8.11824, an example called "highly exceptional" by Garnsey and Saller (1987: 124).

34   Garnsey and Saller (1987: 124); Alföldy (1988: 124); McGinn (1998: 44).

35   Hopkins and Burton (1983b: 120–200).

36   Alföldy (1988: 151) notes that urban dwellers would have had more opportunity for social advancement than country dwellers but that the incidence of mobility either way should not be overestimated.

37   For example, Barrow (1949: 101). See also Hopkins (1978: 115–16, nn. 31 and 32).

38   See, for example, Mouritsen (2005).

39   Hopkins (1978: 118).

40   See, for example, Alföldy (1988: 114), citing Tac. *Dial.* 8.2, Plin. *HN* 18.37, and Cass. Dio 53.30.2.

41   Note that Mouritsen (2004) finds from tombstone commemorations that descendants of freedpersons would generally focus on this identity to only the second generation.

42   See also the discussion in Mattingly (2011: 211–12) for Roman "protoracist" attitudes that rested upon ideas about ethnic identities.

43   See, for example, Val. Max. 4.5.1.

44   McGinn (1998: 26–44, 68).

45   Aubert (2002: 101–02).

46   See MacMullen (1974: 105) and Reinhold (1971: 284–7).

47   Porphyrio on Hor. *Sat.* 1.6114 and Tac. *Ann.* 1.77.

48   Regarding the regular white toga, Toner (2009: 154) remarks that a "hierarchy of whiteness will have operated, a threadbare greyness acting to show the lower status of the wearer."

59   Petersen (2009: 204). Note that there was no specific costume for slaves; see Bradley (1994: 97–9) and, for example, App. *B Civ.* 2.120. See Olson (2008) on the significance of dress for Roman women.

50   Garnsey (1970: 275–6).

51   For example, Cic. *Verr.* 2.5.65–7; Plin. *Ep.* 2.11.

52   Garnsey (1970: 260).

53   Gardner (1986).

54   Morley (2006: 307); MacMullen (1974: 28–56); Alföldy (1988: 133).

55   Plut. *Cat. Mai.* 21.5–6; Morley (2006: 306).

56   Alföldy (1988: 136); Morley (2006: 300).

57   Mouritsen (1999) recounts the arguments and disagrees.

58   On the significance of the toga in particular contexts, see further Edmondson (2008) and George (2008).

59   Petersen (2009: 200–01).

60   Cooley and Cooley (2004: 87 [E7] and 118 [F28]).

61   Reinhold (1971: 290).

62   Cic. *Dom.* 1, *Rep.* 2.39–40; Hor. *Sat.* 1.1; Tac. *Ann.* 14.60.3; Artem. 4.17; Mart. 9.92; Arr. Epictetus *Disc.* 4.1.33; cf. Val. Max. 9.1.3 and Artem. 1.50.

63   Suet. *Gram.* 21; see also Hopkins and Burton (1983b: 168–9).

64   On family values, see Bradley (1987: 48–9). On freedperson funerary monuments, see Mouritsen (2005) and Stewart (2008: 63–7). On elite disdain of work, see Cic. *Off.* 1.42.150.

65   Bradley (1994: 142–3); George (2002).

66   See Reinhold (1971) for these and other examples; on names, see also MacMullen (1974: 104–05) and Mouritsen (2004: 284).

67   Stewart (2008: 39–62, esp. 50–1).

68   MacMullen (1974: 30–1) discusses disdain of provincial accents.

69   Mouritsen (2005: 61).

70   Bradley (1994: 34).

71   Tacitus (*Hist.* 1.4) indicates that not all non-elites were clients of great men.

72   See Ripat (2006a) for discussion of the role of omens and portents in this capacity.

73   For example, Cic. *Div.* 1.55; Livy 2.36.2–8; Dion. Hal. *Rom. Ant.* 7.68; Val. Max. 1.7.4.

4

Roman Slavery

Leslie Shumka

Any viewer of the television series *Rome*, which aired in the mid-2000s, will notice the number of scenes featuring slaves, either in the foreground or background. One such scene is remarkably instructive regarding the role of slaves. It involves a tryst between Atia, virago of the Julian clan, and her lover, Marc Antony. As the scene opens, we find the pair on a sumptuous bed, their naked bodies entwined and glistening from their sexual exertions. They gaze at one another for a moment before Atia languidly raises one arm, snaps her fingers, and hoarsely calls for water. Antony rolls away from her at the same instant and the camera follows suit, cleverly directing our attention to Atia's body slave, Merula, who has been sitting mutely in a corner of the room—or so we are meant to understand. As a passive observer of the couple's intimacy, Merula personifies an essential paradox of Roman slavery: slaves were ubiquitous yet invisible. When we reflect on their presence and contributions in virtually every realm of Roman life, questions naturally arise. For example, how did Rome become a slaveholding society, and how did it manage to sustain a vast supply of slaves?

Introduction

This chapter offers an introduction to the history of Roman slavery and to some of the methodological approaches specialists use in its reconstruction. Slavery was an established feature of life in the Mediterranean basin long before Rome's ascendancy and played a crucial role in the economic and social life of many cultures, as it did in Roman society.[1] Comprehending Roman slavery involves defining its form (for example, chattel slavery or debt bondage), obtaining an idea of slave numbers, and recovering something of the slave experience. To write its history is to appreciate that

Timeline

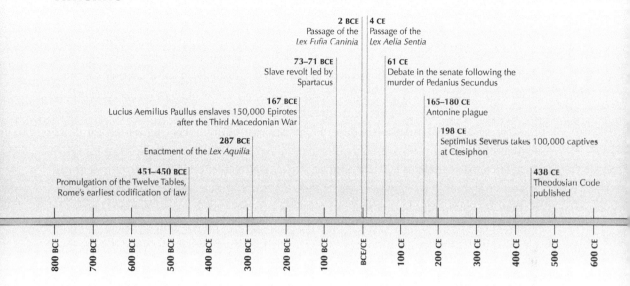

2 BCE
Passage of the
Lex Fufia Caninia

4 CE
Passage of the
Lex Aelia Sentia

73–71 BCE
Slave revolt led by
Spartacus

61 CE
Debate in the senate following the
murder of Pedanius Secundus

167 BCE
Lucius Aemilius Paullus enslaves 150,000 Epirotes
after the Third Macedonian War

165–180 CE
Antonine plague

287 BCE
Enactment of the Lex Aquilia

198 CE
Septimius Severus takes 100,000 captives
at Ctesiphon

451–450 BCE
Promulgation of the Twelve Tables,
Rome's earliest codification of law

438 CE
Theodosian Code
published

800 BCE   700 BCE   600 BCE   500 BCE   400 BCE   300 BCE   200 BCE   100 BCE   BCE/CE   100 CE   200 CE   300 CE   400 CE   500 CE   600 CE

written and material evidence from the early and middle Republic is limited and that this inadequacy makes us more dependent on information from the central period of Rome's history (200 BCE–200 CE). Yet even material from this era cannot tell us everything we wish to know, and so we are obliged to seek practical ways of mitigating its shortcomings (such as engaging in cross-cultural analysis). The challenges of investigating this subject are significant but surmountable.

The following discussion is thematic; however, specific texts have been highlighted to illustrate slavery's chronological breadth and intensification. These excerpts have been selected for their perspectives on legal developments and influential events, but it must be acknowledged that they cannot offer a highly nuanced picture of Roman slavery's evolution. For example, they may create the impression that Rome's transformation was carefully engineered and that, once deeply rooted, the institution of slavery remained unchanged. If, however, we consider slavery against the vast sweep of Roman history, we see that it developed more organically. Effort was certainly expended on maintaining distinctions between free person and slave, securing slave owners' rights, and regulating manumission, but it is essential to remember that this effort was often a response to unforeseen societal stresses (for example, the growth of Christianity or the economic troubles of the third century CE).

As a field of study, Roman slavery has engrossed ancient historians for over half a century, and this engagement shows no sign of abating. It is often hard to fathom the appeal of a history that is fundamentally one of dehumanization, desocialization, and oppression, but a part of this narrative is also the extraordinary story of the extent to which slaves, despite their marginalization, made their mark upon Roman society. A brief but graphic demonstration of their impact is found in the *Digest of Justinian*, a sixth-century CE codification of Roman law. As we might expect, a cursory survey of its contents reveals that jurists provided legal opinions on matters of concern to slave owners: the care of slaves, the freeing of slaves (**manumission**), the punishment of runaways (*fugitivi/ae*), and the regulations governing slave interrogation and torture. But in a broad spectrum of topics—legacies, noxal actions (illegal or injurious acts), commerce, finance, prerogatives of the head of the household, dowries, and other commonly litigated matters—slaves are both at the centre and on the periphery of juridical discussions. Roman law alone makes it abundantly clear that slaves were indispensable to society. But when the legal evidence is coupled with other primary sources (for example, commemorative monuments), we find that the public and private lives of Romans and their slaves were very closely entwined. The fundamental importance of slavery to Roman society will become fully apparent in the following discussion of the definitions of slavery, determination of slave numbers, slave trade, and slave experience and resistance.

Definitions

Before turning to a discussion of slavery in the Roman context, it is helpful to examine how historians understand and use key terms such as *slaveholding society* and *slave*.[2] Quantitative and qualitative techniques are employed in defining these terms, and while scholarly opinion is often divided on the application and outcome of each method, both have their merits. Where statistical or documentary evidence exists, a quantitative approach can help us define a slaveholding society. Specialists calculate slave numbers and use these figures to distinguish between actual slave societies, where involuntary or slave labour is the dominant form, and societies with slaves, where it is not. These designations are not moral assessments but distinctions that reveal a great deal about the internal dynamics of slavery.

In a genuine slave-owning society the proportion of slaves in the total population reaches a critical mass of 20 per cent or higher and familial, gender, and economic relationships are deeply affected by slaves' presence. For example, between 1750 and 1860, black slaves comprised approximately one-third of the American South's total population.[3] In addition to working field and farm, these slaves served in a range of domestic roles, from child-care provider to body slave (the individual who bathed and dressed the master).

In a society with slaves, the number of enslaved people is comparatively low (perhaps

5 per cent of the entire population) and social relationships are relatively unaffected by their existence. Slaves certainly serve in a variety of capacities, from farmhands to domestics, but their low numbers diminish their impact on free society. By this definition, the part of Canada once known as New France was a society with slaves. Between 1681 and 1818, slaves in French Canada (predominantly *panis* or Aboriginal slaves but also black people) numbered approximately 4,100, which was less than 1 per cent of the population.[4] This figure hardly approaches the staggering statistics from the American South; nonetheless, it indicates that slaves were a real and visible presence in New France.

Compared to the broad categories yielded by a quantitative approach, a qualitative approach to slavery (that is, consideration of the qualities of slaves) provides insight into different types of slaves. The term *chattel slave* is applied to the individual who is "socially dead." This person is denied any kind of physical autonomy, as well as the legal and social privileges accorded to regular citizens, such as the freedom to marry, have a family, and form kinship ties.[5] Such controls ensure that owners gain slave labour for little cost and have extraordinary flexibility in managing their slaves. There are, in practice, no familial relationships to consider when selling or trading one's slaves because they are legally kinless. Chattel slaves are usually captives transferred into another society, an act that literally and legally transforms them into property. They may also be born in slavery, the result of sexual relations between fellow slaves or a master and his bondswoman. Moreover, the relationship between chattel slave and master is essentially "a relation of domination": the owner's power is unconditional and the slave's non-existent.[6] This situation differs from that of debt slaves, free individuals whose poverty compels them to serve their creditors until their financial obligations are discharged. In spite of this situation, however, these individuals retain their civic privileges.

Neither the quantitative nor qualitative approach reflects the conceptions or paths of enslavement in all cultures across time and place. Yet they can help us to understand the characteristics and dynamics of Roman slavery. Calculating the population of Rome's empire or its urban centres at any point in its history is a challenge: our statistical and documentary evidence is woefully incomplete, leading ancient historians to employ tools (for example, model life tables) used by demographers when studying modern populations. Attempts to quantify ancient slave numbers have produced some interesting results but have also created strong disagreement about how these figures should be formulated and interpreted (some conclude slave numbers are high; others argue that they are low) and whether ancient sources can be relied upon to bolster demographic approximations.[7] We need not engage further with the specifics of these divergent opinions. What must be recognized is that estimates are complicated by a dearth of dependable information and even more so by the vastness of the geographical empire and its chronology.

For example, one estimate puts as many as 1.5 million slaves in Italy by the end of the first century BCE, out of a total population of nearly 6 million (i.e. 20 to 30 per cent). In contrast, prior to the Antonine plague (165–180 CE) there were 6 million slaves outside of Italy, where the free population may have totalled 45 to 60 or 70 million (i.e. approximately 10 per cent). According to **census** returns for Roman Egypt—an admittedly small sample size but the only province for which real data is available—slaves comprised only 11 per cent of the entire population and were found mainly in the hinterland (*chora*) of large urban centres.[8] Another evaluation claims that, when all the statistical information is thoroughly weighed and we try to formulate the slave population empire-wide, we arrive at a figure of 16 to 20 per cent.[9] And still another presents a more conservative estimate of 5 to 10 per cent in a population of 50 to 100 million in the central era of Rome's history (approximately 200 BCE–200 CE). While some of these calculations suggest that ancient Roman society does not meet the demographic standard for a genuine slave-owning society, others indicate that it meets the criteria at only specific times and places. What all these figures and comments make clear is that the pattern of slaveholding was far from uniform across the Roman world.

If, on the other hand, we consider the qualities of Roman slaves, we find a good deal of similarity with those from other cultures. None of the surviving legal evidence includes a precise definition for the term *slave*, but it is plain that Roman slaves were chattel slaves in the period 200 BCE–200 CE. There are numerous regulations that refer to them as both *persona* (a person) and *res* (a thing).[10] To the modern mind, this designation seems ambiguous and even offensive since, on principle, we find it difficult to accept the objectification of human beings. The Roman legal view was not so morally fraught. The law of persons stated categorically that one was either free or slave (Gai. *Inst.* 1.9) and thus tacitly acknowledged the slave's *persona*. But because slaves laboured for their owners and the law regarded their labour as a commodity, they were also classified as corporeal things (Gai. *Inst.* 2.1, 12–14). Consequently, they were enumerated among their owners' material possessions, just like land, livestock, farm equipment, and domestic paraphernalia.

The ***Lex Aquilia*** makes this situation clear. Enacted in 287 BCE, this law was concerned with damage to private property and, more specifically, damage that was inflicted illegally: "If anyone kills unlawfully a slave or female slave belonging to someone else or a four-footed beast of the class of cattle, let him be condemned to pay the owner the highest value that the property had attained in the preceding year" (*Dig.* 9.2.2).[11] Roman law also recognized that this person–object had to be clothed, fed, and (in some instances) protected from excessive abuse by his or her owner (Gai. *Inst.* 1.53). On the face of it, such stipulations seem to recognize the slave's humanity and safeguard his or her well-being. But these laws, which were difficult to enforce, were designed to prevent masters from diminishing their own property through negligence or inattention. Lastly, like their counterparts in other societies, Roman slaves were socially dead:[12] they had no parents, no family connections from which they derived a social identity, and no **conubium** (the ability granted to Roman citizens to contract a legal marriage), which would have enabled them to create their own kin networks.

The other predominant form of slavery at Rome, at least in its early history, was **nexum**, or debt bondage. Legal evidence, more specifically the **Twelve Tables** (451–450 BCE) and the *Lex Poetelia Papiria* (326 BCE), seems to indicate that this form of slavery was limited to the first 150 years (approximately) of the Republic's existence and was not a phenomenon of the central period of Roman history. A reading of the Tables quickly reveals that early Rome was an agrarian society and that the unpredictability of nature frequently caused economic hardship for smallhold and tenant farmers.[13] *Nexum* made it possible and legal for indigent Romans to pledge themselves (or, more precisely, their labour) as collateral if they were in danger of defaulting on a loan; it required individuals to perform labour for their creditors or to hand over any fruits of their labour.

Compare Chapter 15, pp. 335–7, on the risks involved in agricultural investment.

Debtors' relationships with their creditors were undoubtedly burdensome, but debtors did not relinquish their citizenship or the privileges it conferred, except in extreme circumstances (such as an inability to pay within a reasonable period of time). This fact, however, did not prevent creditors from physically maltreating their bondslaves. Indeed, the historian Livy (8.28) suggests that, by the end of the fourth century BCE, the practice of *nexum* was so widespread and caused such incredible hardship that it had to be abolished. The *Lex Poetelia Papiria* forbade creditors from privately imprisoning debtors, which effectively meant that affluent Romans could no longer economically exploit those individuals who lived hand to mouth. Although property, not person, had to be used as a form of collateral, Roman law still permitted creditors to seek redress by taking the insolvent to court. Whether slave or bondsman, the individual was generally subject to another who monopolized political and economic power.

Sources of Slaves

It is generally agreed that slavery in the Italian peninsula did not fully take shape until the beginning of the third century BCE, even though we know from textual sources that the inhabitants of Rome probably practised some form of slavery as far back as the Etruscan monarchy (753–510 BCE). This is suggested by Dionysius of Halicarnassus (*Ant. Rom.* 4.1.1–3) and Livy (1.39), two historians who wrote long after this period. Both state that the mother of Servius Tullius (who, according to tradition, was king from 578 to 535 BCE) was a Latin princess whom the Romans had enslaved. The difficulty with such anecdotes is that they describe a kind of semi-mythical era in Rome's history for which we have very little evidence.

We find more solid proof for the earliest beginnings of slavery if we again turn to the Twelve Tables. These are chiefly a collection of regulations—reasonable at times and just plain curious at others—that governed marriage, inheritance, crimes, and other matters of import to the small agrarian community that was Rome. To judge from the information in the Tables,[14] Rome's slave population in the mid-fifth century BCE was small (although actual numbers cannot be measured), and general attitudes towards slaves were consistent with what we know from later periods. That society did not value slaves as highly as citizens is evident from a number of regulations, especially one on noxal actions stipulating that a person who causes harm or injury to a citizen must pay a penalty of 300 *asses*; if he injures a slave, however, the fine is only 150 (12.2). A minor but nevertheless important reference in a section on inheritance points to the existence of manumission, where we read of a slave being freed through a will on the condition that he remunerate the heir with an agreed-upon sum (7.13). A great disparity between free person and slave in terms of penalties for contravening the law is also apparent. Free individuals caught in the act of theft could be whipped and then handed over to the plaintiff for additional punishment. Slaves, however, forfeited their lives: after flogging they were thrown to their death from the Tarpeian Rock, a precipice in the middle of the city of Rome (8.8).

The utter lack of security for the slave's person, his or her need to reimburse his or her master (or master's heir) in return for emancipation, and inequitable treatment under the law all point to a rather fully conceived form of slavery by the mid-fifth century BCE. But how and when did slavery really begin to intensify? If we analyze thoroughly the great era of expansion (the fourth through second centuries BCE), we find that a confluence of events and conditions fostered the intensification of slavery. First, Rome went to war on such a regular basis during this time that its citizens became habituated to annual military operations. Second, while Rome's elite profited both socially and politically from imperialism, their economic gains were equally profound and gave them the capacity to purchase large numbers of slaves. Third, military success resulted in the transport of captives back to Italy as slaves on a previously unprecedented scale. Literary accounts convey something of the magnitude of enslavement: Lucius Aemilius Paullus, for instance, allegedly took 150,000 Epirotes prisoner at the close of the Third Macedonian War (Livy 45.33.8–34.6). If we tally up all reported instances of mass enslavement linked to military campaigns conducted between 297 and 167 BCE, the total number falls somewhere between 672,000 and 731,000.

It is helpful to remember two things about such figures: we cannot substantiate them, and it is highly probable that they are approximations and may even under-represent the actual number taken captive.[15] During the late Republic and the first two centuries of Empire, enslavement on a grand scale occurred only periodically. The imperial biographer Suetonius (*Iul.* 15.3), writing in the early second century CE, claims that nearly one million Gauls had lost their freedom by the time Julius Caesar concluded his wars in the west, and the emperor Septimius Severus is said to have taken 100,000 inhabitants of Ctesiphon captive in 198 CE (Cass. Dio 75.9.4). We should also remember that not all captives were transported to Italy. Some were ransomed, some were given to soldiers as booty, and others were sold to itinerant dealers who conducted informal sales after campaigns. Less fortunate captives were summarily executed.[16] Whether those sent to Italy during the early and middle Republic ever became the dominant labour force is a matter of some debate. That they played a fundamental role in agricultural production, particularly on the **latifundia** (plantations of the wealthy), is not in doubt.

As Republic gradually turned to Empire and geographic expansion slowed, the Romans were compelled to obtain slaves through means other than warfare. For our purposes, it might be more instructive to think qualitatively rather than quantitatively to gain some perspective on the slave supply.[17] In discussing the emergence of the republican *latifundia*, the ancient historian Appian (*B Civ.* 1.1) remarked on the advantages of slaveholding: slaves were ineligible for military service and they produced children, so one's holdings could be maintained and even expand considerably. In one of his books on agriculture, the Roman polymath Varro (*Rust.* 2.10.6) expressed concern for keeping slaves content and working to capacity; he recommended that slave-herdsmen, who had to be absent from farmsteads for extended periods of time while they pastured animals, be given female companions with whom there would be offspring. The first-century CE agronomist Columella (*Rust.* 1.8.19) may have had breeding in mind when he proposed incentives (for example, a reduction in work responsibilities, manumission) for slave women who bore a certain number of children. None of these texts explicitly advocates breeding, but the authors clearly recognize that children are a natural outcome of slaves' sexual and emotional relationships.

Offspring from relations between female slaves and their owners also increased holdings because Roman law stipulated that these children take the **status** of their mothers. Legal evidence, in fact, offers support for the thesis that natural reproduction was a key source of slaves, for it contains frequent references to the juridical problems created by the children of slave women (when it came to legacies, for instance).[18] Nevertheless, home-born slaves, or **vernae**, held considerable appeal for owners because, in large measure, they presented fewer challenges than other slaves (Sen. *De Ira* 3.29).

Compare Chapter 3, p. 64, and Chapter 5, pp. 103 and 107, on *vernae*.

Born in slavery and unfamiliar with the life of freedom, they were more easily habituated to a life of servitude than freeborn captives. But like other slaves, *vernae* were still regarded with suspicion, for they were deemed capable of manipulating their privileged position within the household for personal gain.[19] Whatever their perceptions, owners were not blind to the financial benefits that accrued from home-born slaves, and this knowledge must have led some to actively encourage sexual relationships among their slaves.

A second source of slaves resulted from the abandonment and exposure of children. Historians contend that these practices were common, and evidence of imperial date supports this assertion.[20] Parents' decision to discard their children was probably fuelled by their inability to provide the necessities of life rather than by concern for a child's legitimacy or deformity.[21] Plutarch (*Mor.* 497E),

Compare Chapter 5, p. 104, on the exposure of children.

writing in the late first or early second century CE, hints at this conclusion when he says that the poor did not rear their children for fear of consigning them to a life of destitution, but this comment also universalizes among the poor a practice whose frequency cannot be measured. By the reign of Constantine, in the fourth century CE, the discarding of children was certainly taken as entirely normative. The fifth-century CE Theodosian Code contains a law, enacted by Constantine, which reinforced the judgments of previous emperors on the subject of abandoned and exposed children.[22] It instructs that anyone who purchases a new-born in good faith is entitled to enslave the infant and further specifies compensation for the buyer if, in the future, someone claims that the child is actually freeborn and so entitled to be set free (*Cod. Theod.* 5.10.1). The law's protection of the buyer—rather than the slave or the individual attempting to recover the enslaved—indicates that, however socially repugnant the discarding of children may have been, it was tolerated.

We possess few details about the methods by which children were exposed or abandoned. How many slaves were acquired in this manner is difficult to say. Even if we could gain some sense of the number, it would have to be considered in the context of the horrific infant and child mortality regime of Roman society. Some historians estimate that nearly 33 per cent of children died within the first year of life, while nearly 50 per cent did not live to see their tenth birthday. Given the precariousness of infancy and childhood under the best of conditions, the survival of exposed children must have been significantly reduced and their contribution to the slave supply lessened by this fact, although arguments are made to the contrary.[23]

Romans also obtained slaves through importation. Literary evidence on this subject is reasonably abundant and has been fundamental in identifying specific communities and ports that facilitated trade between various points within Rome's empire and along its **frontiers**. At Tanais, nomadic peoples of central Europe and western Asia and traders who crossed the Sea of Azov from the Bosphorus met to exchange slaves and other commodities (Strabo 11.2.3). Slaves abducted in central Anatolia (now the interior of Turkey) were transported to Side on the south coast (Strabo 14.3.2), and shipped to many destinations, including Alexandria in Egypt. On the island of Delos, in the southern Aegean, tens of thousands of slaves were delivered, sold, and sent to other markets every day, and the high frequency of this activity purportedly led to the saying: "Trader, dock here, unload, your cargo's already been sold" (Strabo 14.5.2).[24] Inscriptions from commemorative monuments (for example, statue bases and altars) of Hellenistic and imperial date confirm the presence of slave markets (***stataria, venalicia***) in well-known communities along the coast of Asia Minor and in the city of Rome.[25] Inscriptions from the latter are unique in that they mention the *genius venalicium*, or guardian spirit, who presided over the slave market.[26] In spite of the fact that our best literary and epigraphic evidence is connected chiefly to the traffic in slaves in the empire's eastern half, it is essential to keep in mind that the slave population included individuals from a variety of geographic locales, including Western Europe, sub-Saharan Africa, and even India.[27]

Rather surprisingly, self-enslavement provided another source of slaves. The very idea of enslaving one's self was abhorrent to Romans because it defied the cherished ideal that no citizen be divested of his or her freedom or rights without his or her consent (Cic. *Dom.* 29). Yet evidence for the practice is abundant and spans nearly four centuries of the imperial period, which suggests that the need for self-enslavement was chronic. One can easily imagine that acute poverty and the consequent fear of starvation induced significant numbers of Romans, at different times, to enter slavery voluntarily or to sell their children into slavery in the vain hope of a better life: at least the bare necessities would be provided. The individuals who made these difficult decisions had few options. Public grain doles were sporadic, as were special food programs for children, and there was never in the whole of Roman history a concerted state-sponsored relief plan that might have discouraged self-enslavement to some degree.

The Romans obviously drew on different sources to maintain their slaveholdings, but could the yearly demand for slaves be met? It has been argued that, in the final stages of the Republic, roughly 100,000 slaves were required per annum, while this need reached far greater proportions in the early Empire. The historian William Harris conservatively estimates that, in order to maintain a servile population of 5 to 8 million, 250,000 to 400,000 slaves were required every year. Walter Scheidel pushes this number as high as 500,000.[28] Like computations of the slave population, those for the supply are complicated and controversial and should be considered together with the logistical challenges of the slave trade.

One might expect that the annual demand and volume of sales in major cities or trade depots necessitated the construction of buildings that integrated all aspects of the business: short-term housing and latrines for slaves, a place for auctioning and selling, and space for legal and financial transactions. Archaeologists have attempted to locate the remains of *venalicia*, and eight structures—two in Asia Minor, five in Italy, and one in North Africa—have been identified as such. Recently, however, a persuasive reassessment of their form and function has rejected the theory that these structures are *venalicia* and asks whether the slave trade ever required dedicated or purpose-built facilities. Auction or sale could have taken place on the ships that brought human cargo to market or in multi-purpose commercial spaces. Practically speaking, in small towns where the need for slaves was far lower and the trade in slaves seasonal, the community would hardly commit to the construction and maintenance of a building that might be used only periodically.[29] A more efficient approach was for municipal officials to make arrangements when needed; slave sales could have been conducted in any open or conveniently located area where display platforms (*castatae*) could be hastily constructed and dismantled (or omitted altogether). The notion of ad hoc arrangements is attractive. In fact, it is consistent with the reputed practices of itinerant slave dealers who expedited the sale of war captives in similar fashion.[30]

Slave Experience and Resistance

A fundamental challenge in writing the history of Roman slavery is overcoming the fact that we rely almost entirely on information provided by an affluent, well-educated, slave-owning elite. Slave memoirs, letters, and documents (which might provide a unique perspective on the slave experience) do not exist, and this absence complicates our efforts to reconstruct a precise picture of slavery. How are we able to think of slaves as people or breathe life into their daily experience when our knowledge of them is limited and filtered through the writing of the very people who owned them? Consider the case of a Phrygian slave girl who is known to us through a bill of sale. The fragmentary contract, dated 8 July 151 CE, runs as follows:

> In the consulship of Sextus Quintilius Maximus and Sextus Quintilius Condianus, 8th day before the Ides of July, at Side, when the priest of . . . Demonikos son of Myros was *demiourgos*, 16th of the month Panemos. Artemidoros son of Kaisios, an Alexandrian, has bought from Lucius Julius Protoketus, in the market, a girl, Sambatis renamed Athenais or whatever other name she may be called by, a Phyrgian by race, 12 years old, for a price of 350 silver denarii. Hermias son of Hephaistas confirms (the transaction) and bids it take place on his own guarantee.[31]

The contractual language is formulaic. The date and place of sale, names of witnesses to the transaction, those of vendor and purchaser, and particulars about the slave (age, origin, price) are stated in a detached manner, underscoring the fact that the sale of the girl was nothing more than a routine business deal: a "prosaic aspect of Roman life."[32]

We have little more than a hint of what enslavement may have meant to Sambatis. Side, the town in which she was sold, was a familiar port of call for slavers (**venalicii**) but was situated some distance south and east of her native Phrygia. She may eventually have been transported across the Mediterranean for resale since the purchaser, Artemidoros, hailed from Alexandria, a city known for its slave market. After a journey of this length, could the 12-year-old have known where she was? Did she understand the local language well enough to ask? We have no idea at what age Sambatis first became a slave and suffered what is termed **deracination**, physical separation from her natal family and removal from her homeland. But it is evident that she experienced deracination a second time, when she was renamed Athenais, an act that expunged her previous identity and severed any remaining ties she may have had with her natal family or the household of a previous owner.

If we speculate on the practical circumstances of her sale, we might ask whether she, like others before her, was made to stand on a *castata* in the market. Did she wear the customary placard (*titulus*) around her neck, bearing information for potential buyers, including mention of her physical and moral defects (for example, epilepsy or a propensity to run away)? Did Artemidoros and other customers physically examine the 12-year-old, as they were perfectly entitled to do? What did Sambatis feel at the time of her sale? Numbness? Humiliation? Resignation? Defiance? The girl's experience cannot have differed radically from the hundreds of thousands of nameless slaves who were marched from their homelands in coffles or chained gangs (see Figure 4.1) or transported to bustling slave markets where they were sold like livestock. But how do we know for certain?

Documentary, epigraphic, legal, and literary evidence—much of it indirect—provides significant insight into the daily reality for slaves. Individuals at all levels of society owned slaves, with poorer Romans holding perhaps one or two and others holding more according to their economic status. The most affluent might own several hundred, as was the case of the **praefectus urbi** and former **consul** Pedanius Secundus, who was murdered by one of the 400 slaves he kept in his townhouse in Rome (Tac. *Ann.* 14.42; see Box 4.1). Different factors naturally shaped the experiences of ordinary slaves: age, sex, place of residence (urban or rural), possession of technical or much-needed skills (such as literacy, midwifery, or carpentry), the social and economic status of the owner, and even an owner's character.[33] Work began in early childhood with age-appropriate tasks such as herding geese and continued well into old age, with elderly slaves serving in less-taxing posts such as doorkeeper. The number and range of tasks to be performed was generally commensurate with the size of the household or estate.

Where estates were large and agricultural production diverse, vast numbers of slaves were essential for keeping them productive. This much is suggested by Columella (*Rust.* 1.9.1–8). To ensure maximum efficiency, he advised owners to have slaves perform one job rather than several concurrently. As needed, slaves could help with tasks outside their areas of expertise. We hear of harvesters, vintagers, herdspeople, beekeepers, animal doctors, provisioners, smiths, and managerial staff, the most prominent of which were the estate manager (**vilicus**) and his wife (**vilica**). Additional slaves saw to domestic tasks such as child care (of slave children), food preparation, laundry, and clothing manufacture for outside workers. Still others were needed to serve in and maintain the owner's villa, which was at the heart of the estate.[34]

In large urban households a cadre of slaves met the basic demands of owners. Epitaphs for those who worked for some of Rome's leading families, such as the Statilii and the Volusii, attest to extreme job specialization. Affluent Romans might have one slave to dress them, one to style their hair, another to hold their grooming implements, another to fold clothes and put them away, and still another to mend them. At their dinner tables, there might be waiters, carvers, cupbearers, and

Figure 4.1 Chained slaves. Ashmolean Museum

Political History

Box 4.1: The Murder of Pedanius Secundus and Its Aftermath

In 61 CE, the city prefect Pedanius Secundus was murdered by one of his 400 slaves. Roman tradition dictated that all the slaves in the household where such an event had occurred must be put to death, but the vast number of those who would be killed in this case incited the pity of large numbers of the Roman population. Crowds thronged the **senate** house where the matter was being debated. Some senators argued for mercy, but most were opposed. Tacitus (*Ann.* 14.43–4) reports the speech reputedly made by Gaius Cassius, one of those who stood by the blanket death penalty:

> Do you believe that a slave took the resolution of killing his master without an ominous phrase escaping him, without one word uttered in rashness? Assume, however, that he kept his counsel, that he procured his weapon in an unsuspecting household. Could he pass the watch, carry in his light, and perpetrate his murder without the knowledge of a soul? A crime has many antecedent symptoms. So long as our slaves disclose them, we may live solitary amid their numbers, secure amid their anxieties, and finally—if die we must—certain of our vengeance amid the guilty crowd. To our ancestors the temper of their slaves was always suspect, even when they were born on the same estate or under the same roof, and drew in affection for their owners with their earliest breath. But now that our households comprise nations—with customs the reverse of our own, with foreign cults or with none, you will never coerce such a medley of humanity except by terror. "But some innocent lives will be lost!" . . . All great examples carry with them something of injustice—injustice compensated, as against individual suffering, by the advantage of the community.[1]

Gaius Cassius and his supporters won the day, and the 400 slaves of Pedanius Secundus's household were crucified.

Note

1. Translated by Jackson (1937).

food tasters, in addition to entertainers such as musicians and dancers. Job specialization in such elite households did not necessarily aim at efficiency. Slaves often functioned as visible wealth, with their significant numbers enhancing the social status of their owners. There also existed an upper stratum of highly skilled slaves who were connected to a particular household but who worked outside it. They contributed to an owner's financial income by working as craftspeople, providing financial services, or overseeing commerce.

Many owners mistreated their slaves, but there were some who recognized that a family life might keep slaves content and thus encouraged slave unions (Mart. 4.13; Juv. 11.146). The evidence from inscriptions is particularly strong on this subject and reveals that a desire for family life was most definitely present among slaves. Of course, Roman law forbade a bona fide marriage between two individuals of servile status, but slaves could and did form de facto unions (**contubernia**) that produced children. Consider the family life of ex-slave Psyche Herennia, who died at age 70 (*CIL* 11.6998). Despite beginning life as a slave, she enjoyed some semblance of family life, for she was commemorated by Cresimus, who refers to her as his wife; her daughter, Aiecta; and her son-in-law, Alexander. Pointed references to personal relationships in epitaphs like this one are intentional; they created a veneer of respectability and solid membership in a community that was otherwise closed to the deceased and her family.

Compare Chapter 5, ←
pp. 102–3, on *contubernium.*

Even with the reasonably abundant information we have on how slaves were employed in Roman society and what sort of family life they had, we are still left with the feeling that we do not fully comprehend their experiences, especially when these could vary so dramatically with time and place. For instance, Ovid (*Ars am.* 3.239–40) describes the misfortunes of his lover's hairdresser (*ornatrix*), whose perceived ineptitude impelled her owner to stab her in the arm with a hairpin. There is also the instability endured by young slaves, as revealed through bills of sale: one girl was sold twice by the age of 11 and another three times by the age of 14 (*P.Vind.Bosw.* 7; *P.Mich.* 9.547). Two of the Younger Pliny's letters, which are meant to show him as a benevolent owner, reveal that he allowed his slaves to celebrate at festival time, partake of recreation when chores were done and make wills, with the proviso that the heirs be members of his household (see *Ep.* 2.27, 8.16). If all these slaves could speak, what would they tell us about their lives?

Historians' methodological response to the lack of slave narratives and other gaps in evidence is to engage in cross-cultural analysis. More specifically, they compare New World slaveholding systems (those of Brazil, the Caribbean, and the American South) with practices in Roman antiquity, and this approach has proven fruitful. For the most part, historians concentrate on the memoirs and narratives of ex-slaves from the American South that were recorded primarily during the mid-1930s as part of a Depression-era make-work scheme. Despite originating in a culture vastly removed in time, place, and character, these accounts reveal striking similarities between the attitudes of American and Roman slaveholders. They also contain sentiments that might easily be attributed to Roman slaves: resentment at inhumane treatment; anger at being stereotyped as lazy, immoral, ignorant, and dishonest; genuine fear at knowing that their bodies were subject, both physically and sexually, to the authority of another; and anxiety at the knowledge that owners might arbitrarily dissolve their affective relationships by the sale of their partners and children. In the New World, as in Rome, slave life was marked by hardship and insecurity.

Attitudes that characterize Roman slavery recurred in other slave systems, appearing, for example, in much later historical periods in the West. An evocative comparative example is found in the story of Marie-Joseph Angélique, a Portuguese-born black slave who was tried and convicted in June 1734 of setting a fire that destroyed her owner's home and, indeed, most of Old Montreal.[35] Glimpses into Angélique's life emerge from the trial transcripts and record of her final interrogation and torture. We do not know whether she was born in slavery or at what age she was first sold, but we learn that a Flemish man purchased her and that she may have passed through his native Flanders before the transatlantic journey to New England, possibly via New York.

In 1725, at about age 20, she was sold to François Poulin de Francheville, a Montreal businessman, and taken to New France. It was common practice among the French to have slaves baptized and renamed, and this is how the young woman came to be called Marie-Joseph Angélique. She worked chiefly as a domestic for the family, as was typical of slaves in New France, but also helped as needed on their small farm. Between 1731 and 1732, she bore three children, all of whom died in infancy, to a slave from Madagascar. A friend of de Francheville's owned the Malagasian father of Angélique's children, and it is possible that the friends intended the couple to breed. On the death of Sieur de Francheville, Angélique passed into the control of his widow. Theirs was a troubled relationship, and details of the friction between them surfaced as Angélique gave her responses during her trial. She was clearly a spirited individual who could not be intimidated. Mild and unruly by turns, she sassed her owner often and was far too outspoken for a slave, which provoked the Widow de Francheville and the court. As further evidence of her rebellious nature, the inquisitors heard that Angélique had run away once and, at the time of the fire, had been planning a second attempt with an indentured servant of the widow's.

In comparison with the bulk of existing Canadian and American slave narratives, Angélique's story is undeniably sensational. Yet on a basic level, many of her experiences exemplify those of other North American slaves: deracination, verbal and physical maltreatment, attempted escapes, and capture. It is useful to think about these as we contemplate the Roman slave experience. This is not to say that Angélique's life and that of a Roman slave such as Sambatis were identical or that we can speak of a monolithic slave experience—far from it. But there are clear parallels that cannot be dismissed and that allow us to speculate in an informed manner about slave life in Roman antiquity.[36] At a young age, both Angélique and Sambatis were taken great distances from their homelands, sold more than once, and renamed. Angélique formed an attachment with a fellow slave, whether strictly sexual or emotional we cannot say, and had children. If they had survived, the children would have taken the status of their mother, as did home-born slaves in Roman society. From our perspective, perhaps the most interesting question prompted by the trial transcripts concerns Angélique's response to being a slave. She was disobedient, insolent, and troublesome. Is this a coincidence of personality or the behaviour of someone who chafes at being a slave? The fact that she was undaunted by recapture after she first ran away is telling. A natural question to ask at this point, then, is whether we can detect the same resistance to servitude in the ancient record.

There were, undoubtedly, benevolent slave owners in Roman antiquity, but many slaves still endured harsh treatment and laboured under horrific conditions. As a result, there were revolts. Between 135 and 71 BCE, the Romans had to quell three mass slave rebellions in Sicily and South Italy, the best-known being the one led by the slave–gladiator Spartacus. As insurrections go, they caused a great deal of damage and consternation in the late Republic. There was little repetition of these events during the imperial era, although individuals tried periodically to exploit the discontent of slaves, and runaways sometimes gravitated to the robber gangs that roamed virtually unchecked in the countryside (Tac. *Ann.* 4.27; Cass. Dio 77.10). Intractable slaves also set fire to their owners' property and even took their own lives to resist their position. According to Columella (*Rust.* 1.7.6–7),

See Chapter 11, pp. 241–2, 244, 253 and 256, on brigandage.

there were other acts of "sabotage" carried out by agricultural slaves, which endlessly annoyed slave owners:[37] renting out or selling off the master's livestock, neglecting crops, and idleness. Perhaps the best example of non-violent resistance occurs in an amusing anecdote from Plutarch, recounted in Box 4.2. This exchange shows that Roman slaves, like Angélique, clearly devised ways of coping with their enslavement.

Primary Source

Box 4.2: Plutarch, *Moralia*, 511D–E.[1]

If anyone will but review and recollect constantly these and similar instances, he may conceivably stop taking pleasure in foolish chatter. But as for me, that famous case of the slave puts me utterly to shame when I reflect what immense importance it is to pay attention to what is said and to be master of our purpose. Pupius Piso, the orator, not wishing to be troubled, ordered his slaves to speak only in answer to questions and not a word more. Subsequently, wishing to pay honour to Clodius when he was a magistrate, Piso gave orders that he be invited to dinner and prepared what was, we may suppose, a sumptuous banquet. When the hour came, the other guests were present, but Clodius was still expected, and Piso repeatedly sent the slave who regularly carried invitations to see if Clodius was approaching. And when evening came and he was finally despaired of, Piso said to the slave, "See here, did you give him the invitation?" "I did," said the slave. "Why hasn't he come then?" "Because he declined." "Then why didn't you tell me at once?" "Because you didn't ask me that."

Note

1. Translated by Helmbold (1939).

The Success of Slavery at Rome

Finally, we come to the question of how Roman society maintained the institution of slavery for nearly a millennium. One would have thought that developments such as the growth of Christianity, with its emphasis on equal treatment for all (slave and free person, rich and poor) and its claim that God made no distinction between free person and slave, might have led to the abolition of slavery, or at least undermined it.[38] Yet even Christ himself encouraged his followers to be slaves to one another (Mark 10:43–4).[39] The best answer is that Roman slaveholders employed an effective combination of punishments and incentives that served as control mechanisms. Unmanageable slaves were punished severely by beatings and were kept in check by intimidation. A common threat, so the ancient sources say, was to tell one's slave that he would be packed off to a mill. Here—as in other workplaces—human beings rather than draft animals such as donkeys or oxen regularly powered the heavy machinery. For slaves consigned to a mill, the working environment was horrific and life a constant toil. The North African writer Apuleius, working in the second century CE, provides a detailed description of dreadful mill conditions in his novel *The Metamorphoses*. A quick reading of this text explains why some slaves may have thought twice before acting out: the workers were dressed in rags, brutally scarred by regular beatings, and barely recognizable as human beings (see Box 4.3).

Owners often employed professional slave-catchers to track runaway slaves. Once apprehended, the fugitives were identified as problematic individuals by being branded upon the face (Petron. *Sat.* 103) or being forced to wear a slave collar. To judge from

Primary Source

Box 4.3: Apuleius, *The Metamorphoses*, 9.12.[1]

Good gods, what stunted little men they were! The whole surface of their skin was painted with livid welts. Their striped backs were merely shaded, not covered, by the tattered patchwork they wore: some had thrown on a tiny cloth that just covered their loins, but all were clad in such a way that you could discern them clearly through their rags. Their foreheads were branded, their heads half-shaved, and their feet chained. They were hideously sallow too, and their eyelids were eaten away by the smoky darkness of scorching murk until they were quite weak-sighted; like boxers who fight sprinkled with dust, they were dirtily white-washed with a floury ash.[1]

Note

1. Translated by Hanson (1989).

the surviving few, the collar was a simple device comprising an iron circle and pendant affixed permanently around the slave's neck. Pendants were sometimes inscribed with the acronym *TMQF*, meaning *tene me quia fugio* or "Hold me, because I flee" (*ILS* 9454); others bore the owner's name and mention of a reward for the fugitive's return.[40]

Inducements for good behaviour varied. Slaves could receive favours or kindnesses (*beneficia*), such as permission to have sexual relationships or create family units, but by far the greatest "carrot" was the hope of emancipation, or so frequent references in our sources suggest. Manumission was a formal procedure by which a master freed a slave, consequently transforming him or her into a **libertus** (freedman) or **liberta** (freedwoman). Freedom was granted to select slaves, often those who interacted closely with an owner, such as the young slave girl Peina, mentioned in a petition to a local official in Roman Egypt (*P.Oxy.* 50.3555). Although her owner, Thermouthion, sought compensation from the careless donkey driver who maimed the girl while she was on her way to a singing lesson, the petition's tone makes it apparent that their relationship was closer to that of a mother and daughter than one of an owner and slave. Peina's situation differed dramatically, however, from that of public slaves who swept the streets or collected garbage and wretched mine slaves who might be worked to death. Their chances for achieving freedom were greatly diminished.

Manumission conferred most of the Roman citizen's privileges on freed slaves: the legal capacity to marry and to have any children born after emancipation recognized as freeborn citizens (**ingenui** and **ingenuae**) and the ability to enter into contracts, engage in litigation, and write wills that were legally binding. **Freedmen**, like freeborn men, gained the right to vote, although they could not run for public office. It is essential to note that manumission was always granted at the discretion of the owner: it was never a promise or a right, and it did not bring complete legal or personal autonomy. Nor did it guarantee security. For this reason, we might characterize manumission as an ambiguous benefit.

Emancipation certainly reduced the degree of control that owners legally held over their slaves. But because this deed was regarded as a kindness, a reciprocal act on the part of the freed individual was essential. Roman laws ensured that ex-slaves remained socially and economically indebted to those who had set them free. Owners became patrons (**patroni**) of their newly freed slaves and were therefore owed proper deference and respect (**obsequium**). For instance, the law stipulated that freedmen and **freedwomen** could not retaliate when patrons verbally or physically abused them or criticized them openly because doing so was disrespectful (*Dig.* 47.10.7.2). Former slaves were expected to labour annually for those who freed them, performing **operae**, work obligations that had been agreed upon by both parties prior to manumission. Alternatively, the obligations might be waived in exchange for a specified sum of money. That patrons could and did make unreasonable demands upon former slaves where *operae* were concerned is suggested by the opinions of Roman jurists. Gaius (*Dig.* 38.1.19), working probably in the late second century CE, held that labour demands could not be so onerous that they inhibited the freed individual's ability to earn an adequate personal income, while Paulus (early third century CE; *Dig.* 38.1.17) believed that patrons could not make impossible demands upon aged or infirm freedmen and freedwomen that were detrimental to their way of life.

Although these laws aimed to protect freed individuals, there were other inequities within the system. A freedman or freedwoman may have gained the right to make a will, but in principle the heir was his or her patron. Similarly, **freedpersons** had no legal claim to partners or children who remained slaves, and familial dislocation might result when slaves were freed but their partners and children were not. Owners looking to reduce their costs might also manumit aged or infirm slaves and leave them to fend for themselves. With little knowledge of freedom or practice in making their own way in the world, how did these slaves cope?

→ See Chapter 5, p. 108, on manumission and its impact on slave families.

Despite its ambiguous benefits, manumission was an important technique of social control in that it offered slaves hope of freedom if they demonstrated the proper deference, obedience, and loyalty.[41] At the same time, emancipation helped to perpetuate slavery by theoretically ensuring that only "quality" slaves—those with a demonstrated commitment to Rome and its social ideals—were admitted to the citizenship. How often enfranchisement occurred is much debated, since we have no real quantitative evidence to help us determine its frequency. We do know that attempts were made to restrict manumission. The *Lex Fufia Caninia*, passed in 2 BCE, sought to limit the numbers of slaves who could be emancipated through a will (Gai. *Inst.* 1.1.42–3), while the *Lex Aelia Sentia*, enacted in 4 CE, fixed the minimum age of the manumitter at 20 and the minimum age of the slave at 30 (Gai. *Inst.* 1.1.38, 1.1.20). Scholars generally agree, however, that the practice was common and effective.[42]

Summary

Roman slavery can be usefully approached through quantitative and qualitative methods, though each provides a different perspective. While it is difficult to be certain about statistics regarding the ancient world, it appears that Roman society would not have qualified as a slave society at all times and places throughout its history. However, qualitative approaches underline that slavery was a central and chronic element of Roman society throughout its history. Warfare provided slaves, as did the reproduction of those already enslaved, importation, and self-enslavement. Servile experience is difficult to recapture, but comparisons with more recent slave-owning societies can provide some valuable insights. In general, the experience of slavery in Rome appears to have been one of exploitation, degradation, and humiliation, conditions to which Roman slaves devised modes of resistance that resonate with those of slaves from more recent periods. Though not every slave experienced freedom, the very prospect of manumission was a strong force in ensuring the success and perpetuation of the system as a whole.

Questions for Review and Discussion

1. What were your ideas of Roman slavery prior to reading this chapter? How did the discussion in this chapter confirm or subvert them?
2. Would Rome have become a slaveholding society if the wars of expansion had not brought thousands of slaves into Roman society? Why or why not?
3. What are some of the ways that we calculate the slave population at Rome?
4. How markedly did the Roman slave experience vary? Give examples to support your answer.
5. Why was slavery so successful in Roman society?

Suggested Reading

Bradley, K.R. 1984. *Slaves and Masters in the Roman Empire: A Study in Social Control.* New York: Oxford University Press.

This pioneering work on the mechanics of Roman slavery demonstrates how owners used various methods to maintain the institution of slavery.

———, and P. Cartledge, eds. 2011. *The Cambridge World History of Slavery*, vol. 1. Cambridge: Cambridge University Press.

This weighty volume comprises a comprehensive series of articles on Greek and Roman slavery that address topics of current interest and employ a variety of methodological approaches.

Garnsey, P.D.A. 1996. *Ideas of Slavery from Aristotle to Augustine.* Cambridge: Cambridge University Press.

Anyone wishing to understand the philosophical underpinnings of Greek and Roman slavery should begin with this book.

George, M. 2010. "Archaeology and Roman Slavery: Problems and Potential." In *Antike Sklaverei: Rückblick und Ausblick. Neue Beiträge zur Forschungsgeschichte und zur Erschließung der archäologischen Zeugnisse. Redaktion: Andrea Binsfeld.* (Forschungen zur antiken Sklaverei Bd. 38), edited by H. Heinen, 141–60. Stuttgart, Germany: Franz Steiner Verlag.

In recent years, specialists have begun to consider more seriously the significant contributions of archaeology to the study of Roman slavery. This article offers a much-needed assessment of these contributions, their limitations, and the direction of future research.

Joshel, S. 2010. *Slavery in the Roman World.* Cambridge: Cambridge University Press.
  The scholarship on Roman slavery is vast, but this compact monograph offers a sound introduction to the subject and includes discussion of and references to seminal and innovative work.

McKeown, N. 2007. *The Invention of Ancient Slavery?* London: Duckworth.
  Deliberately polemical, this book offers an overview of problems, methods, and concepts in current studies of ancient slavery.

Patterson, O. 1982. *Slavery and Social Death: A Comparative Study.* Cambridge, MA: Harvard University Press.
  This book is fundamental for anyone wishing to understand the usefulness of cross-cultural analysis in the study of ancient slavery.

Thompson, F.H. 2002. *The Archaeology of Greek and Roman Slavery.* London: Duckworth.
  This book offers the only detailed survey of the archaeological evidence of ancient slavery.

Notes

1   Snell (2011: 4–21) is a short but useful introduction to Egyptian, Israelite, Hittite, Aegean, and African slavery.
2   See Dal Lago and Katsari (2008: 3–11) on definitions. They also offer a valuable and concise overview of scholarship on slavery by ancient and modern historians and historical sociologists.
3   Wahl (2010).
4   Donovan (1995: 5).
5   Patterson (1982: 38–45). Compare Finley (1980: 74–6).
6   Patterson (1982: 334).
7   McKeown (2007: 124–40) has a useful summary of the main arguments and a brief description of the demographic tools.
8   Bagnall and Frier (1994: 48); Scheidel (2005: 64; 1997: 158, n. 16).
9   Harris (1999: 65); McKeown (2007: 11).
10 Garnsey (1996: 26).
11 The translation is from Mommsen, Krueger, and Watson (1985).
12 For criticism of this formulation when applied to Greek and Roman slaves, see McKeown (2007: 33–4).
13 Cornell (1995: 272–92) is a solid introduction to the Twelve Tables, their reconstruction, and textual idiosyncrasies. For the text of the Tables, see Crawford (1996: 584–721).
14 Crawford (1996: 584–721).
15 Scheidel (2011: 294–5).
16 Bradley (1994: 33).
17 Compare Bradley (1994: 31).
18 Bradley (1994: 34).
19 Scheidel (2011: 306).
20 Laes (2011: 201, nn. 170 and 171).
21 Harris (1994: 1), and especially Vuolanto (2003).
22 Compare Harris (1994: 6).
23 Harris (1994); Scheidel (2011).
24 The translation is from Wiedemann (1981: 110).
25 Trümper (2009: 20–4). The others are Sardis, Magnesia on Maeander, Thyatira, and Acmonia.
26 Ibid.: 27.
27 Scheidel (2011: 304, with references). On the sub-Saharan slave trade in particular, see Bradley (2012: 164–80).

28 Harris (1980: 118; 1994: 18); Scheidel (2011: 293).
29 See Trümper (2009: 83–4).
30 Harris (1980: 125–8). Compare Bradley (1987: 33).
31 Tcherikover, Fuks, and Stern (1964: no. 490). In the analysis of this contract I follow the approach of Bradley (1994: 4) on the sale of a 10-year-old girl named Abaskantis at Side in 142 CE (*P.Turner* 22) and Joshel (2010: 79–80) on the epitaph of Gaius Julius Mygdonius, an ex-slave from Parthia (*CIL* 11.137).
32 Bradley (1994: 2).
33 Joshel (2010: 129–30).
34 For a comprehensive list of estate workers, see Joshel (2010: 168), following Bradley (1994: 60, Table 2).
35 Beaugrand-Champagne (2004) and Cooper (2006) offer compelling yet different accounts of Angélique's life, trial, and conviction.
36 Bradley (1994: 44).
37 Ibid.: 115–17.

38 See for instance St Theodoret's discussion of St Paul's first letter to the Corinthians (7.22; translation from Wiedemann [1981: 245]):
> It is our custom to call someone who is an ex-slave a freedman; Paul applies this term to the slave who has been blessed by Faith. He calls the free man Christ's slave, and the slave his freedman, both in order to teach those who are free that they have a master, Christ, and similarly to teach slaves that they have attained true freedom.
39 For a thoughtful response to the question of why Christian slaveholders did not oppose slavery, see Glancy (2010).
40 Joshel (2010: 120, Figure 35).
41 Bradley (1984: passim); Joshel (2010: 129).
42 Compare here the attitudes of Canadian slave owners (Trudel 1960: 295–7, 309–10; Winks 1971: 96–113) who resisted government attempts to regulate manumission or abolish slavery. Many American slaveholders were similarly opposed to the manumission of their slaves (Harrill 1995: 53).

5

The Roman Household

Alison Jeppesen-Wigelsworth

Literary evidence of Roman family life exists for only a limited segment of the population: the upper classes. Death, however, was common to all, and there was great social pressure to bury and commemorate the deceased in Roman society. Epigraphical sources in the form of funerary commemorations—that is, tombstone inscriptions or epitaphs—are, therefore, reflective of a wider population. All could afford at least a modest burial, with the exception of the very poorest of Romans (who might be given anonymous burials in open pits that also contained dead animals and garbage). Since tombs tended to house the remains of many members of individual households, epitaphs are among the best sets of evidence for the family life of the non-elite. It must be admitted that epigraphical evidence presents its own interpretive problems, often raising as many questions as it answers. For example, epitaphs tend to be expressed according to accepted formulas, making it difficult to gauge the sincerity behind the sentiments. Nonetheless, funerary commemorations present unique evidence for non-elite families and can help to illuminate the realities of household relationships.[1]

The following inscription demonstrates the potential of tombstone epitaphs to tell us about the realities of the familial relations and dynamics of the non-elite:

> May malicious evil be absent from this monument. To the Spirits of the Dead: Scribonia Attice made this for herself and for Marcus Ulpius Amerimnus, her husband, and for Scribonia Callityche, her mother, and for Diocles, and for all her freedmen and freedwomen and their descendants, with the exception of Panaratus and Prosdocia. This monument must not follow an external heir.[2]

This inscription is found on a household tomb at Isola Sacra, a necropolis (literally, "city of the dead") about 30 kilometres from Rome. As we shall see, the Roman

Figure 5.1 Photo of Tomb 100, Isola Sacra. Tomb of Scribonia Attice, a midwife, *c.* 140 CE. Left panel: Relief of Scribonia's husband bathing a patient's foot. Centre panel (not shown, text given above): Inscription. Right panel: Relief of Scribonia Attice delivering a child. © Alison Jeppesen-Wigelsworth

household was expected, in Roman law and ideals, to circle around a male authority figure—the *paterfamilias*—while women existed to fulfill supporting roles of dutiful wife, mother, or daughter. Yet here we have Scribonia Attice, a midwife, as the dedicator of the tomb. The tomb depicts equally her work (delivering a baby) and her husband's (he was a physician) in two relief panels (see Figure 5.1). She commemorates her husband, but he had nothing to do with the building of the tomb (he may have died before she had it built). It is *her* mother who is also included in the inscription. No children of her own are mentioned; perhaps Scribonia Attice was not a mother or was a mother no longer. Instead, the tomb would welcome the remains of others: a male (whose single name suggests that he was a slave), Scribonia Attice's former slaves, and *their* children. Scribonia Attice, childless professional woman, wife, daughter, slave owner, and patron of her freedmen and freedwomen, is at the centre of this familial unit. This family would be deemed atypical in light of literary and legal evidence, but it was probably, in reality, very ordinary.

Introduction

To investigate the Roman household is, in many ways, to investigate Roman society itself. The ancient household cannot be explored in isolation from either the private or public aspects of Roman society, given that the family and familial concerns have relevance to all facets of Roman life. It is therefore unsurprising that, in the last 40 years, studies of the Roman household and family have formed a cornerstone of Roman social history. Topics of interest have ranged from Roman marriage and divorce to children and childhood, intergenerational relationships, bonds between

Timeline

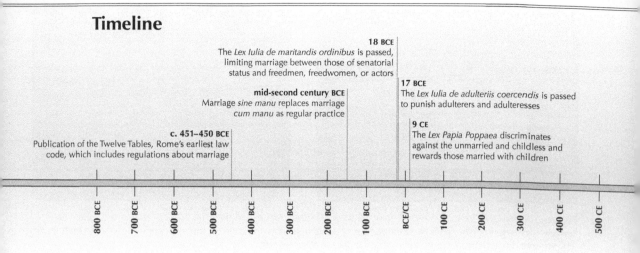

18 BCE
The *Lex Iulia de maritandis ordinibus* is passed, limiting marriage between those of senatorial status and freedmen, freedwomen, or actors

mid-second century BCE
Marriage *sine manu* replaces marriage *cum manu* as regular practice

17 BCE
The *Lex Iulia de adulteriis coercendis* is passed to punish adulterers and adulteresses

c. 451–450 BCE
Publication of the Twelve Tables, Rome's earliest law code, which includes regulations about marriage

9 CE
The *Lex Papia Poppaea* discriminates against the unmarried and childless and rewards those married with children

800 BCE | 700 BCE | 600 BCE | 500 BCE | 400 BCE | 300 BCE | 200 BCE | 100 BCE | BCE/CE | 100 CE | 200 CE | 300 CE | 400 CE | 500 CE

free and servile household members, demographic considerations (such as the age at first marriage), and the "shape" of the Roman family (was it nuclear, as ours tend to be, consisting of parents and children, or extended, embracing step-parents, half-siblings, slaves, and freedpersons?). These studies have exploited sources of information that stretch beyond the legal texts and male-authored literature that have generally informed more traditional historical investigations. They have made use of, for example, inscriptions, papyri, and archaeological findings, revealing a more nuanced impression of the family and household in the ancient Roman world than is evident in the literary sources alone. These same sources and studies have also allowed for some perspective on the families and households of the Roman non-elite. This chapter explores different aspects of the Roman household—its members, their relationships, and its physical structures. It examines the stereotypes of the Roman family and presents the more recent arguments that have overturned them.

———•◆•———

Terms, Concepts, and the Shape of the Roman Family

Suetonius (*Ner.* 50.1; *Dom.* 17.3) includes a fascinating detail in his biographies of two of the most hated Roman emperors, Nero and Domitian: their childhood nurses ensured their proper burial, since they were the only people who still cared for them. This information points to a critical difference between modern and Roman society. For us, the concept of "family" is probably more relevant than "household," but when we discuss the Roman family we almost always end up discussing the Roman household. The reason for this is simple. Members of a Roman household do not always correspond to members of a modern family, as illustrated by the example of Nero's and Domitian's wet nurses, non-blood relations with whom bonds could nonetheless be important and lasting.

There are two Latin terms used to indicate the household: *familia* and **domus**. These words have overlapping but not identical meanings. *Familia* is often translated as "family" but more often means the members of a household who were under the legal power (**patria potestas**) of the "father of the household," or **paterfamilias**. As the eldest free male in the household, the *paterfamilias* had legal authority over free and non-free members of his household (*Dig.* 50.16.195–6; see more on this power below), but the absolute nature of *patria potestas* should not be exaggerated. Few adult Romans were likely to have a living *paterfamilias*, and few women entered into their husbands' *potestas*, much less that of their husbands' fathers. Domineering *patresfamilias* were unlikely to have been common during the period under consideration here. Furthermore, the entirety of a Roman family was not made up only of those biologically tied to the *paterfamilias*. Although the word *familia* included the biological descendants of the *paterfamilias* and, by the second century BCE, usually excluded his wife (although she might be referred to as the **materfamilias**[3]), it was often used to refer specifically to the household's slaves.

Domus, on the other hand, is closer to our understanding of family as it implies the members of the household widely defined (children, spouses, slaves, and other relatives on both the father's and mother's sides). But it also includes the physical house where the members lived.[4] As the concepts of both *familia* and *domus* suggest, the Romans in many ways had a wider understanding of family than we do. Furthermore, it is clear that the family did not consist simply of parents and children; that is, the Roman family was not strictly nuclear but extensive. It was most probably marked by divorces, deaths, remarriages, step- and half-children, siblings, and parents and was a conglomeration of free, freed, and servile persons, bound both legally and (often) emotionally.[5]

The potential complexity of household membership is evident on tombstone inscriptions, which are sometimes perplexing to the modern reader. Consider the following epitaph from Rome:

> Titus Pompeius Reginus, son of Titus, made this for himself and for Titus Pompeius Reginus, son of Titus, his brother, and for his mother, Valeria, daughter of Gaius, and for his father, Gnaeus Pompeius, and for Gnaeus Pompeius, son of Sextus, his stepfather, and for his wife, Posilla. (*CIL* 6.24501)

This inscription leaves us with more questions than answers. Why does Titus Pompeius Reginus have the same name as his brother? Was the name reused because the brother was older and died young? Why is their father referred to as Titus, then Gnaeus? Did Valeria remarry after her husband's death, or were all still alive at the time of commemoration?

Even with these questions, the epitaph is an excellent demonstration that the Roman family could be convoluted.

Household Members and Relationships

Cicero tells us that the degrees of respect and duty that a free male Roman citizen owes to the members of his household vary and exist in descending order: he is responsible first to his parents, then to his dependants (children and slaves), and, lastly, to his other relatives (see Box 5.1). It is interesting to observe that, although she is ranked first for companionship elsewhere (Cic. *Off.* 1.54), a wife (*coniunx/uxor*) is not explicitly included on the list of those deserving dutiful attention. Certainly a man must have a wife: in order to have legitimate children, he had to be legally married to their mother. A man could, of course, have illegitimate children, but legitimate offspring were required for the perpetuation of the familial name(s) and the transmission of property and familial ritual. Indeed, the goal of any Roman household was the continuation of that household. This meant legitimate children and legal marriage, although, as previously stated, a wife was rarely a legal member of her husband's *familia* after the second century BCE.

Wives and Marriage

For marriage to be considered legitimate, three criteria usually had to be met by the partners. First, they had to be Roman citizens (or belong to a community that had been granted the right of intermarriage with Roman citizens). Second, they had to be of minimum age, probably 14 for boys and 12 for girls. (The average age at which people actually got married is unknown, although estimates range between early and late twenties for boys and mid-teens to early twenties for girls.[6]) Third, they could not be too closely related. If the couple met these requirements, they were considered to have the legal capacity to marry (**conubium**).[7]

Primary Source

Box 5.1: Cicero, *On Duties*, 1.58.

But if there were a contest or a comparison about who should get most of our dutifulness, then first would be our country and our parents to whom we are obligated for the greatest benefits. Next would be our children and our whole household (*domus*), who look to us alone and who have no other shelter. And finally, our relatives who are well disposed to us and with whom our fortune is held in common.

There were two possible forms of Roman marriage. Historians call the first and older form **marriage *cum manu*** and the second **marriage *sine manu*** (the Romans did not use titles to describe the two categories). Although the latter was the norm for most of Roman history (certainly by the first century BCE), its unique nature can be understood only in the light of the former. The word *manus* means "hand" and, by extension, "authority" or "control." In the context of marriage, it is used to indicate the legal authority, *potestas*, of a husband over his wife. If a woman entered into a marriage *cum manu*, she was henceforth under the legal authority of her husband (or his *paterfamilias*, were he still living). She would be a legal part of her husband's *familia* and would worship the same household gods as her husband. If her husband died without a will, she would stand to inherit as if she were his daughter, but she would not inherit from her own father's family. This form of marriage, however, became increasingly rare over the span of the Republic.[8] By the end of the second century BCE, it was used only for the marriages of certain priests, such as the *flamen dialis*.[9]

Compare Chapter 9, pp. 209–10, on household religion.

Marriage *cum manu* was largely replaced by marriage *sine manu*. The differences between this form and its predecessor concern the amount of independence that a woman had from her husband and inheritance patterns. A woman who entered into marriage *sine manu* did not pass into the power of her husband and was not a legal member of his *familia*. She retained the worship of her birth family's household gods and, perhaps most important, inherited from her father. Legally and financially, she was independent of her husband and would be independent (*sui iuris*) upon her father's death, although she would still technically have a legal guardian (*tutor*). This form of marriage also invested her with a greater ability to divorce her husband. Although she required her father's permission to do so, the law considered his consent to be given if he did not explicitly object.[10]

Since a woman was under her own *paterfamilias' potestas*, her father could also legally force her to divorce her husband and marry another man. It is unlikely that this practice happened often, although there is evidence of a situation of political jockeying in which a would-be bridegroom attempted to persuade a father to do just that (Plut. *Cat. Min.* 25, 52). Quintus Hortensius, seeking an alliance with Cato the Younger, asked to marry his daughter Porcia, even though she was already married with two children. Once Porcia gave him a son, Hortensius was willing to divorce her and allow her to return to her previous husband. Cato refused to force Porcia's divorce, perhaps recognizing, given what we know of Porcia's personality from other sources (see, for example, Cic. *Att.* 15.11), that the potential fight with his daughter was not worth it. Instead, Cato divorced his own wife, Marcia, so that she could marry Hortensius. He did so with the consent of Marcia's father, who would not give her in marriage to Hortensius without her ex-husband's agreement and presence at the wedding; the two men, father and ex-husband, jointly gave her in marriage. Six years later, Hortensius died. Marcia, who had never produced a child for Hortensius, inherited the bulk of his estate and returned to Cato.

Though Plutarch could find nothing wrong in this situation, it is clear that Cato's political enemies did.[11] Indeed, Plutarch quotes Julius Caesar's accusations of wife-trafficking: If Cato loved Marcia, why would he divorce her? If he did not want to be married to her, why would he take her back? According to Plutarch (*Cat. Min.* 52), Caesar believed that this was a political alliance cemented by the exchange of a woman. It is hard not to agree that this tale, one of the most bizarre stories of Roman marriage, was a most blatant case of marriage-seeking for political advantage and heir production. It also demonstrates both the continued legal authority of a father over his adult daughter if she married *sine manu* and the fact that some, like Cato (if not Marcia's father), might be hesitant to use it.

When contemplating women's experience of marriage *sine manu*, it is likely that the continued legal authority of a father over his daughter was less important than the financial considerations. Couples married *sine manu* were financially separate; therefore, the property of the wife's natal *familia* was never at risk of alienation. A woman married *sine manu* did provide a dowry to her husband to cover her living expenses, and he could use it for the duration of their marriage. However, it was legally hers or her family's; in the case of divorce, it had to be paid back to her or her father. Husband and wife were not even normally permitted to give gifts to one another, as doing so clouded ownership. This is not to say that generosity between spouses was completely absent or that a wife did not contribute to the family. Indeed, wives performed critical economic duties. A wife was the guardian (*custos*) of the household. In a small household, a wife's ability to estimate the family's usage of its products could mean the difference between survival and starvation. In a larger household, this economic role would be even more complex, involving the management of multiple houses and large numbers of slaves as well as significant amounts of personal property.[12]

Terentia and Cicero provide a good example of how separate finances might work within a marriage and how much a wife might contribute. Terentia was married *sine manu*, and she appears to have been *sui iuris* for much (if not all) of her marriage. She owned a great deal of property (including various farms and blocks of buildings), some of which she sold in order to aid her husband while he was in exile (Cic. *Fam.* 14.1; *Att.* 2.4). Cicero was horrified at this decision. He could not stop Terentia from selling her property, but he was guilt-ridden over the fact that his actions had made it necessary for her to try to support him and thereby possibly put her financial security (and their children's future inheritances) at risk. In supporting her husband, Terentia proved herself to be Cicero's "very faithful" (*fidelissima*) wife, but her faithfulness is illustrated through actions she took autonomously for the good of the family in a perilous situation.

As the laws of Roman marriage differ from modern unions, so do the ideals of marriage. Roman unions were not supposed to be based on notions of romance or passion, although these elements might be present or develop later. Marital relationships were supposed to be formulated for the good of the broader family, to produce legitimate offspring. An ideal marriage was one characterized by harmony between the spouses (**concordia**). It is possible that the concept of *concordia* is best described in the negative— it might imply uncomplaining attitudes or a lack of arguing rather than the presence of emotional warmth—but it also suggests a mutually respectful attitude between partners, one based on the recognition that each put familial concerns above the personal. Partners should confide in each other and seek each other's advice.[13]

The ideal of marital *concordia* should not be taken to indicate, however, that Roman marriages could not be affectionate. There are many examples marked by the sort of happiness that resonates with modern readers. Cicero's devotion to, and reliance upon, Terentia is one; their seemingly abrupt divorce after 35 years of marriage continues to surprise readers of his letters to her. Augustus and Livia were married for 53 years (Suet. *Aug.* 62). Livia's son from her first marriage, Tiberius, so deeply loved his wife, Vipsania Agrippina, that care had to be taken to keep them apart when he was forced by Augustus to divorce her and marry his stepsister, Julia (Suet. *Tib.* 7). Pliny the Younger's third wife, Calpurnia, was so devoted that she slept with his letters under her pillow (Plin. *Ep.* 6.7). Examples such as these can easily be found, and they indicate that affection between spouses was fostered and found social approval.

Cicero's family exemplifies both the presence of marital *concordia* and its absence. Terentia, for example, acted as Cicero's friend and partner in all aspects of the *familia's* interests, advising Cicero on personal and even political matters until their divorce in 46 BCE.[14] In contrast, Cicero's brother Quintus did not enjoy the same marital harmony in his marriage to Pomponia, the sister of Cicero's friend Atticus (see Box 5.2). Quintus and Pomponia married, probably at the suggestion of Atticus and Cicero and in keeping with normal marital practice, to forge a family bond between two friends.[15] The marriage, as Cicero's letter indicates, was fraught with squabbles and bad feelings. It reached the point that Cicero and Atticus felt that they should intervene in their siblings' relationship in order to establish (or restore) a measure of *concordia*, showing that concerns over marital harmony clearly extended beyond the married couple to include siblings and in-laws. This situation also indicates how complex family relationships could be. When Cicero's brother was unhappy, Cicero was unhappy. When his daughter, Tullia, was distressed in her marriage to Dolabella (her third husband), Cicero was beside himself. Concern over family members' marital contentment is palpable.

It is safe to say that divorce existed in Roman society, but it is impossible to tell how often it occurred or by whose standards it was "common." For example, should it be measured by contemporary North American standards? Absolute percentages of marriages ending in divorce in Roman society cannot be guessed at, nor can we tell if divorce rates were higher among the elite or non-elite. But certainly divorce was not unknown, and remarriage was usual, either after divorce or the death of a spouse. Despite the Roman ideal, death and divorce made it difficult to achieve a long marriage, and women

Primary Source

Box 5.2: Cicero, *Letters to Atticus*, 5.1.3.[1]

To Atticus at Rome, from Minturnae, May 51 BC

I have never seen anything more gentle and pacific than my brother's attitude towards her (his wife and Atticus's sister, Pomponia) . . . Quintus said, in the kindest way, "Pomponia, will you ask the women in and I'll get the boys?" Both what he said and his intention and manner were perfectly pleasant, at least it seemed so to me. Pomponia, however, answered in our hearing "I am a guest myself here." . . . Quintus said to me "There! That is the sort of thing I have to put up with every day." You'll say "What was there in that, pray?" A good deal. I myself was quite shocked. Her words and manner were so gratuitously rude . . . In a word, I felt my brother could not have been more forbearing nor your sister ruder. And I have left out a number of things that annoyed me at the time more than they did Quintus . . . Well, you may tell her to her face that in my judgement her manners that day left something to be desired. I have told you about this, perhaps at greater length than was necessary, to show you that lessons and advice are called for from your side as well as from mine.

Note

1. Translated by Shackleton Bailey (1999, 2.24–7).

were unlikely to remain unmarried, especially given that marriage was often necessary for their economic stability.[16] It was once thought that remarriage by Roman women was a contravention of a closely held ideal of female behaviour, the *univira*, or the woman who was married just once. However, Hanne Sigismund Nielsen's recent work on inscriptional evidence suggests that this ideal, although an element of the moralizing ideology of the Augustan period, was not really in full force until the later Christian period. There are 71 epitaphs that use this term (or a variation of it) to commemorate women, only 29 of which date between 200 BCE and 200 CE, with only three pre-dating the Augustan period. The remaining 42 date to the Christian period.[17]

To this point, discussion has focused on legal marriage, which was just one of the affective relationships present in Roman society. As mentioned above, marital relationships needed to meet three requirements to be considered legitimate. Intent, however, was also needed, particularly on the part of the male: he needed to consider himself married in order to be married. If intent was lacking—a situation that appears to have been normal in relationships between men and women of different **status** (often, but not exclusively, freeborn men and their **freedwomen**)—the relationship was not called marriage but **concubinage**.[18] A union in which one (or both) of the partners lacked not the intent but the legal capacity to marry, often because one or both were slaves, was called **contubernium**. Slaves might, therefore, not call themselves spouses (*coniunges*) but companions (*contubernales*, literally, "tentmates"), a term that recalls the basis of their relationship as fellow slaves.[19]

Compare Chapter 13, p. 287, on the use of similar terminology in a military context and Chapter 4, p. 85, on slave families.

The realities of both concubinage and *contubernium* can be quite difficult to discover. Did they mimic legal marriage or were they something quite different? For example, legal sources occasionally indicate that a concubine who was the freedwoman of her partner was to be held to the same standard of behaviour where sexual fidelity was concerned, while a *contubernalis* was explicitly not held to this account by the law. But, as Susan Treggiari observes, the fact that the law "could raise the question of adultery at all shows how *contubernium* was compared with marriage." On the other hand, funerary inscriptions praise wives and concubines with different terms, suggesting that ideals of behaviour were not identical.[20] Sources perhaps do not contradict each other so much as they present the breadth of possibility.

While the continuation of concubinage depended upon the intent of the male partner, the continuation of slaves' quasi-marital relationships depended entirely upon the goodwill of their master (*dominus*). He might choose to allow the couple to live as though they were married or he might decide to sell one or both partners or their children in different directions (children born to servile parents belonged to their parents' master and were known as **vernae**, "home-born slaves"). Slave partners might attempt to reunite or to impart legitimacy to their relationships if one member gained his or her freedom and could buy (and then free) the other. This transaction, however, also depended upon the goodwill of the master to sell the slave and to set an achievable price.[21]

Parents and Children

Since the purpose of Roman marriage was the production of legitimate offspring, children were an essential element of the Roman household, the means of providing a continuous line of inheritance and ensuring the maintenance of familial ritual. We can see the centrality of the parent–child relationship in Cicero's hierarchy of duty (see Box 5.1): children must be dutiful to their parents (*parentes*, their *pater* and *mater*) first and foremost, a responsibility that is reciprocated in a measure greater than to all others, save only that shown to their own parents (should they be alive). This ideal is witnessed on tombstone inscriptions, as commemorations of children often state that they were most dutiful (*pientissimus*). As the funerary medium of this evidence suggests, however, the spectre of death (of either child or parent) was ever-present and, as we shall see, influenced both Roman child-rearing practices and our understanding of intergenerational relationships.

In the study of Roman familial relations, the relationship of the *paterfamilias* to his descendants has received special attention, as he had the greatest responsibility for the preservation of his *familia* and was therefore also endowed with the greatest legal powers over its members. The legal meaning of the term *paterfamilias* had less to do with emotional relationships and more to do with property ownership; the *paterfamilias* was, as far as the law was concerned, an estate owner.[22] The concept of ownership, however, extended to the living members of his household who were under his *patria potestas*, as the law appears to have invested him with the power of life and death (*vitae necisque potestas*) over his slaves and his children throughout his life.[23] Despite evidence pointing to fond fathers (Cicero, for example, doted on his daughter Tullia; he affectionately referred to her as "Tulliola," or "little Tullia," in his correspondence and was devastated by her death),[24] scholars long embraced the vision of the Roman household led by a cruel and heartless *paterfamilias*. In reality, however, his power was circumscribed by his own mortality and by law. Many Romans would not have had a father living by the time they were 15 years old[25] and instead might be raised by a widowed or remarried mother, a stepfather, or a group of extended family members. Upon the death of the *paterfamilias*, his freeborn children would henceforth be under their own legal authority (*sui iuris*), although daughters of any age and pre-pubescent sons would have a guardian to oversee any legal transactions.

Even fathers who survived to see their children grow up did not exert the power to kill their children on a whim, as has been previously imagined. A Roman father had to call a council of extended relatives (*consilium*) and present evidence in order to kill his grown child. Even so, there are very few examples of fathers actually killing their adult children and, in most of these, the father was justified by the fact that his child was committing a crime against the state.[26] Augustus's adultery laws of 18 BCE (see Box 5.3) also asserted that a father could kill his daughter, but only if she was caught in the actual act of adultery in her father's house or that of her husband and if her father killed her lover at the same time, a confluence of events that is unlikely to have occurred very often.[27]

→ Compare Chapter 8, pp. 172–3 and 184–6, on Augustan legislation concerning sexual conduct.

Where a father retained the right of life and death, it was in his power to expose (abandon to die) or kill an infant newly born into the *familia*. There were many reasons for exposing a child—physical deformity, its sex, and doubts about its paternity, for example—but it is unknown how prevalent infanticide was in Rome. The evidence is not conclusive, but it is possible that girls were abandoned more often than boys (see for example, Ov. *Met.* 9.669–81; *P.Oxy.* 4.744). If so, this might have been because females were simply valued less than males and because girls would need to be given dowries and therefore might be seen as a financial drain on a household's resources.[28] Exposed children might die or be picked up by others and raised as servile or free foster children (*alumni*).[29]

Political History

Box 5.3: Roman Marriage and Morality: The Legislation of Augustus

Between 18 BCE and 9 CE, Augustus passed a series of laws to curb adultery and to encourage marriage and the production of legitimate (and upper-class) children.[1] These laws were ostensibly designed to revitalize Roman morals and promote the stability of the Roman *familia*, but the underlying purpose (or at least one of them) was perhaps to increase the population of the upper *classes* in order to fill administrative positions and the military.[2] The legislation limited marriage between social groups, specifically between the **senatorial order** and **freedmen**, freedwomen, or actors. Freeborn men of any class were forbidden to marry prostitutes, brothel owners, the freedwomen of pimps (since it was thought that they had most likely been prostitutes while in servitude), actresses, condemned women, and adulteresses.

Although the law limited marriages between certain statuses, it penalized the unwed and childless and rewarded marriage and the production of legitimate children. A childless person could lose half the sum of an inheritance to which he or she was otherwise entitled, while bequests were null and void if contingent on the inheritor not marrying. In contrast, benefits of the law passed to those who were engaged or married. As a result, some men became engaged to very young girls so that they could reap legal benefits without actually marrying. In 9 CE the Papio-Poppaean law closed this loophole: a man now had to marry his betrothed within two years. This meant that he could not become engaged to a girl under the age of 10 (12 was the minimum legal age at which a girl could marry).[3]

The legal benefits of child-bearing (*ius liberorum*) were various. For example, political prestige while holding the consulship was now earned not by age but by children: the senior **consul** would no longer be the elder but the one with more children. Three children earned freeborn women freedom from perpetual guardianship (*tutela*) and freeborn men from having to be guardians. Freedmen who had two or more children born to them after they were freed, or one child who had survived to age five, no longer had to provide services to their patrons (*Dig.* 38.1.37 pref. 1), while freedwomen were released from the guardianship of their ex-masters, now patrons, if they gave birth to four children following their manumission (Gai. *Inst.* 1.145).

It is unknown how well these laws actually worked, in part because it is uncertain how much incentive the benefits offered. For example, as the **Lex** *Aelia Sentia* of 4 CE set the minimum age of manumission at 30, it is doubtful that many freedwomen were able to produce four children following emancipation. It is also not clear that freedom from guardianship would have made much of a difference to many freeborn women, whose guardians do not appear to have intervened much in their lives. The benefits, however, to a young man entering political office were greater if he married, and there is some evidence that the age of first marriage for men dropped after these laws were enacted (Tac. *Agr.* 6.1, 3; Plin. *Ep.* 7.24.3, 8.23.7). The emperor also had the ability to grant dispensations from the laws, and there is evidence that these were courted. Pliny (*Ep.* 2.13) reports that he had obtained the *ius liberorum* for a friend who did not have three children. Pliny himself, although he married three times, also failed to have the required three children.

Notes

1. For more on the adultery laws, see Chapter 8 of this volume.
2. Treggiari (1991: 60–80).
3. Cass. Dio 56.1.2, 6.6, 10.1; Gai. *Inst.* 2.286a.

Parents who exposed newborn children, however, ran the risk of eventual childlessness, even if they had a number of older, living children. Death rates for young children were high, with one-third dying by the age of one year and only half of all children born likely to live to age five.[30] The *familia* bereft of a younger generation might adopt an heir or heirs in order to preserve itself, but Romans tended to adopt full-grown adults, those who had survived the perilous years of childhood. The adult son, now adopted, took the name of his new father (although, were his natal family politically illustrious, an element of his original name might be retained as an aid to his own political career) and cut legal ties to his natal family.

An example of this phenomenon is the complex story of the Cornelii and Aemilii Paulli families. When Publius Cornelius Scipio (son of the great Publius Cornelius Scipio Africanus, who had defeated Hannibal in 202 BCE) had no son, he adopted one of Lucius Aemilius Paullus Macedonicus's four sons. The child took the name Publius Cornelius Scipio Aemilianus (to which were eventually added Africanus Numantinus, after subsequent military successes). Although the newly adopted child had no legal entitlement to his natal family's property, he did not necessarily cut emotional ties or snuff out all sense of duty to his birth parents (nor did they to him). For example, when Scipio Aemilianus inherited from his adoptive family, he immediately gave his inheritance to his birth mother, Papiria, who had been left destitute after his natal father had divorced her (Polyb. 31.26–8). Papiria returned the property to him upon her death, an inheritance that he then gave to his birth sisters. As for Lucius Aemilius Paullus Macedonicus, he died without a male heir: he had given his two elder sons up for adoption, and his remaining two sons died in childhood. He left his property to the former, thereby passing it out of the family. With his death, the *familia* of the Aemilii Paulli ceased to exist.

As Cicero tells us, children—whether freeborn blood relations to the *paterfamilias*, *alumni*, or adopted adults—had responsibilities to their parents and broader *familia*. As discussed above, children were supposed to be amenable to marriages contracted with political, economic, and/or social advantage of the larger *familia* in mind. Children were also expected to care for their elderly relatives and ensure their proper burial and commemoration.[31] Those born to illustrious families should maintain or increase the family's wealth and political glory; those born to more humble families should contribute to its financial well-being, starting from youth. All children, whether freeborn, foster, or servile, might be trained from a young age to do useful work.[32] The expectation that children would work does not negate the care felt for children or the grief at their loss. Parents who lost a child described themselves on tombstones as miserable or most unlucky (*infelicissimi*): "To the Spirits of the Departed Calpurnius Trygetus. Calpurnius Trygetus and Calpurnia Hermione, his most unlucky parents, made this for their very dutiful son who lived 10 years, 6 months, 10 days, and 11 hours."[33]

Slaves and Freedpersons

Slaves and **freedpersons** were recognized as integral elements of the *familia* and the household by both law and custom. Large households might have hundreds of slaves living on various properties, while the running of even a relatively small Roman household could not survive without slaves. However, the economic value of slave labour was not always visible to the Romans. The historian Richard Saller, for example, compares the work of slaves, particularly female slaves, to that of the modern housewife: with no wage associated with the work, Romans did not fully recognize the significant contribution to their economy.[34] Individual Romans were perhaps more inclined to value the emotional relationships that often developed between free members of the household and some of its slaves. *Vernae*, for example, might be treated better and could be raised as companions for the household's freeborn children, a situation that could blur the line between children and slaves in the Roman household. Indeed, their favoured positions might earn *vernae* their freedom more often than other slaves.[35] It is probable that some *vernae* were even fathered by free members of the household, an (unintentional, perhaps) economic spin-off of the regular sexual use of slaves by their masters.

See Chapter 3, p. 64, and Chapter 4, pp. 79, on *vernae*.

Upon **manumission**, freedmen and freedwomen were expected to continue to contribute economically to the household: they had a responsibility to perform certain duties (*operae*) for their former masters (who were now their **patroni**). They might even perform the same occupations as they had before manumission, either in a lesser or equal capacity. This was certainly the case for Cicero's personal secretary, Tiro, who was his trusted aide and companion in both servitude and freedom.[36] Ex-masters, for their part, also had responsibilities to their freedmen and freedwomen, who became to some extent their legal, social, and economic protégés. In some situations the relationship was even closer; freed slaves might be adopted by or even marry their former masters, who might have freed them specifically for these purposes. Naming practices further demonstrate that freed slaves were expected to continue to be members of the households that had owned them. A freed slave, who had previously had a single name, took his or her former owner's first name (*praenomen*) and family name (*nomen*) and retained his or her servile name as a sort of surname (*cognomen*).

Within the larger *familia*, as we have already seen, slaves might attempt to form their own family units by taking another slave as a companion and having children. These slave families often appear to have adopted ideals of duty similar to those of free society and could experience and sustain strong emotional bonds, despite the difficulty of staying together. As unity depended upon the whim of the master, slave families were always at risk of separation. Unity of the slave family was not assured even when mother and child stayed in the same household: sources suggest that newborn slaves were often separated from their mothers to be suckled by wet nurses in order to allow their mothers to resume work.[37] The possibility that servile parents or children might be sold away from each other, however, was ever present. In addition, the *Digest* (40.7.3), a legal source, suggests that some masters might allow a slave woman to gain her freedom after producing three children for him (female slaves had their highest value during child-bearing years). In such a situation, the mother would be freed, leaving her children in slavery and with no guarantee that she would be able to maintain contact with them or purchase their freedom in the future.[38]

There is also evidence, however, that some servile parents and children might, against the odds, maintain contact even when sold to different households. In a funerary inscription, three sons who were born as slaves into different households jointly commemorated their deceased mother, a freedwoman (*CIL* 6.2318). Apparently, at some point after giving birth to her first two sons, the woman was sold to another house, where she had another son before being freed. Yet the three sons were aware of each other and had sufficient contact with each other to commemorate their mother together. How they managed to maintain a family unit from seemingly separate households is a mystery that again illustrates how complex and flexible the Roman understanding of family could be.

Another tombstone inscription from Rome reveals the complicated legal history of another slave family: "To the Spirits of the Departed Decimus Publicius Antiochus and Publicia Musa, his wife. Publicia Albana, their illegitimate daughter, made this for her most worthy father and mother, together with Marcus Caesonius Primus a freedman" (*CIL* 6.25122). Publicia Albana's self-identification as illegitimate tells us that she was born before her parents were legally married. Given that all three have the same *nomen* (Publicius/ Publicia), her parents were likely both freed from the same household. The mother was freed before their daughter was born, but the father was not (or else Publicia Albana would be listed as his daughter rather than as his illegitimate offspring). To make matters more interesting, Publicia Albana commemorates her parents together with a freedman, Marcus Caesonius Primus, whose name indicates that he did not belong to any of the others mentioned on the tombstone and whose relationship to them is, therefore, entirely unclear.

Primary Source

Box 5.4: Vitruvius, *On Architecture*, 6.5.1–2.[1]

Those rooms which no one is allowed to enter without an invitation are considered "private": bedrooms, dining rooms, bathrooms and so on. But the public rooms are those which people have a right to go into without being invited: entrance halls, courtyards, porticoes and so on. It follows that men of average wealth do not need wonderful entrance halls, vestibules and courtyards, since their social obligations consist in going to pay their respects to others rather than receiving their own clients. Those whose wealth comes from agriculture must have room to keep their livestock and produce on display in their entrance hall . . . Those who lend money or are engaged in government contracts need houses that are both pleasant and impressive, and safe from thieves . . . Those of the highest status, who are involved in politics and the struggle for office and have to appear in public, must have high and impressive entrance halls, wide courtyards and wide porticoes lined with trees to show off visibly how important they are.

Note

1. Translation slightly adapted from Gardner and Wiedemann (1991: 9–10).

The Physical House

The physical structures in which the households of Roman society lived varied widely according to social status and wealth (see Box 5.4). A dwelling, called an *aedes* or *domus*, could range in size and opulence from a small unit in an apartment building (*insula*) to an urban mansion or country villa, depending on the family's social standing and wealth. Many urban dwellers lived in modest apartments.[39] Wealthy families often had both urban and rural properties, between which the free members of the *familia* moved at will. Slaves tended to belong to either the urban or the rural household (members of the *familia urbana* or *familia rustica*, respectively) as their jobs dictated.

In his treatise on architecture, Vitruvius, an architect and engineer, presents idealized visions of Roman houses. In reality—or at least as the remains of the Italian towns of **Pompeii** and **Herculaneum** suggest—these ideal forms were rarely realized: the physical remains of Roman houses are much more varied, and it is clear that even preference for basic designs changed over time. For example, the atrium/peristyle house (discussed in greater detail below) was a popular design during the Republic but fell out of favour in the imperial period and was replaced by a design featuring a single courtyard surrounded by elaborate chambers for entertaining.[40]

Most striking to the student of ancient domestic architecture is the fact that public and private spaces were never as clearly defined by function for the Romans as they are for us. Even *cubicula*, rooms that are usually translated as "bedrooms" and which Vitruvius tells us could not be entered without an invitation from the house's inhabitants, could be multi-functional rooms used for dining, entertaining, and storage, in addition to (possibly) being used for sleeping. Different rooms might be used in different seasons, and furniture could be moved to repurpose a chamber.[41] As discussed further below, it is also often very difficult to tell which rooms were used by which members of the household.[42] There is, moreover, evidence that owners of large-scale houses may have rented out rooms on the second or third floors as apartments and that their houses were closely associated with nearby commercial buildings. Andrew Wallace-Hadrill has argued for "moving away from the standard image of the Roman *domus* as a 'single-family unit' and towards thinking of it as a 'big house' inhabited by a 'houseful' rather than a household," which included everyone from extended family to slaves to commercial tenants.[43] The lines between public and private, free person and slave, and rich and poor blur when it comes to Roman domestic space.

Despite the variations possible for the atrium/peristyle house—Wallace-Hadrill notes that the design implied by this label was the "ideal rather than typical"[44]—it is possible to reconstruct a generic floor plan of this type of dwelling (see Figure 5.2). The Romans traced this style, which tended to house the elite, to their Etruscan predecessors (Varro *Ling.* 5.161). Houses from Pompeii, such as the House of Sallust and the House of the Prince of Naples, provide evidence of this style (with variations) and are the same type that Vitruvius describes in Box 5.4.[45]

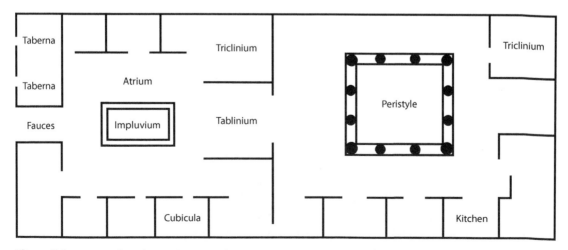

Figure 5.2 Generic Plan of an Atrium/Peristyle House

In this type of house, access was gained through the entrance hall, or *fauces*. This hall could be flanked by *tabernae* (restaurants or taverns) or small shops. The House of Sallust, for example, featured six rooms that flanked the entrance hall and had doorways into the street, spaces that were likely used as shops. Houses could also include exterior stairs leading to additional lodgings, which perhaps provided housing for a family's slaves or freedpersons or were rented out to lower-status families. The less wealthy might also have dwelt behind or above their shops and businesses with their slaves and apprentices.

The atrium was the central room of the house and was visible from the street through the *fauces*. It often had a roof that sloped inward from a rectangular opening (*compluvium*) to allow light and water to enter. The water then fell into a central basin called the *impluvium*. It was in the atrium that the master of the house would meet his clients and welcome visitors. Literary evidence can supplement archaeological remains to provide information about the typical contents of the atrium. For example, we learn of an assault made on the home of a Roman politician during the late Republic. When the attackers entered his atrium, they smashed the wax images of his ancestors (*imagines*) on display there, turned over his wife's couch, and tore out the weaving from her loom (which was likely there for decoration or the use of her slaves rather than for her own use).[46] Archaeological remains suggest that the family's shrine to its ancestral deities (*lararium*) might also be placed in the atrium, although *lararia* frequently turn up in other rooms, too.

See Chapter 3, p. 53, and ← Chapter 17, p. 384, on *imagines*.

See Chapter 9, p, 209–10, ← on domestic shrines and cult.

Cubicula surrounded the atrium and could serve as bedrooms or dining chambers (*triclinia*). In the House of the Prince of Naples, however, the rooms on one side of the atrium, because they had less light, have been identified as servants' quarters. In this example, there is also a kitchen and toilet off the atrium, along with a small chamber (likely belonging to the doorman) that contains stairs to the second floor, which perhaps featured more slave quarters. Often *triclinia* opened on to the atrium in its far corners, and the back of the atrium gave way to the *tablinum* (the office of the *paterfamilias*). The *tablinum* was open to the peristyle at the back of the house. The peristyle was a colonnaded porch surrounding a garden that allowed light into the house; the kitchen and latrine (which were regularly located next to each other) often opened on to the peristyle.

We would like to know where different members of the *familia* slept (and with whom) because information about sleeping habits could potentially reveal a great deal about the nature of different relationships between members of the household. Unfortunately, the archaeological evidence is inconclusive: bed frames and bed niches remain, but there is no easy way to distinguish between what we would call single and double beds. Thus, it is hard to pinpoint the room occupied by the *paterfamilias* and his wife as opposed to the rooms occupied by children, slaves, and other members of their *domus*.[47] Whether spaces designated as slave quarters functioned as bedrooms is also uncertain. Indeed, it is possible that slaves often did not have dedicated areas in which to sleep but slept wherever there was space and whenever there was opportunity.

That said, it is clear that some slaves might be expected to sleep with free members of the household, suggesting that the latter, including the married couple, neither had nor desired much privacy, even in their bedchamber. Sources such as Tacitus (*Dial.* 59) describe children sleeping with their nurses.[48] We also have evidence of slaves sleeping in the same room as their (adult) masters; for example, the *Digest* (29.5.14) describes a slave girl (*ancilla*) sleeping in her mistress's chamber when other slaves entered to assassinate her mistress. They threatened to hurt her if she cried out, so she stayed silent while they murdered her mistress—a choice for which she was later punished by death so that slaves would know "not to look to themselves" when their owner was in physical danger.[49]

In short, there was little physical separation between household members of different status; there was also a good deal of physical proximity between landlords and renters and between domestic and commercial activity. The physical space of the Roman household, characterized by its lack of space demarcated for specific functions or for people of specific status, reflects the heterogeneous nature of the *familia*.

Summary

The Roman household was complex. It included people of various statuses, the property belonging to the freeborn members of the household, and the physical structure of the dwellings in which the members of the household lived. The Roman household does not precisely equate to our understanding of a family, although we often merge the Roman household and the Roman family in discussions. There was also no single, typical "Roman household" in the way that we might consider the nuclear family to be typical of modern contemporary society. The human element of the Roman household consisted of complex arrangements of married couples, their children, other relatives, slaves, and freedmen and freedwomen. The composition of any given household, furthermore, fluctuated over time. Although every *familia* had to be headed by a *paterfamilias*, family members could be separated by death or divorce, and new families and stepfamilies formed. Slave families were at even greater risk of separation. There was little to stop a slave master from selling off various members of a slave family to other households. And yet, as inscriptional evidence demonstrates, slave families might be able to keep in contact with one another and find each other later in life, although this was not guaranteed.

Economically, the various members of the household worked together for the good of the household, but not all work was valued equally. Property divisions between husband and wife were also clear. Although the husband and wife would form a partnership for the *familia* and *domus* that contained their mutual children, their individual property and wealth remained individual.[50]

Just as familial composition was variable, so was the structure and room usage of the physical house. It is difficult to tell from the archaeological remains of houses where the various household members slept, worked, dined, or relaxed with each other or with friends and associates. Our very inability to pinpoint these behaviours (and our desire to do so) points to real differences between Roman family life and contemporary expectations of our own.

Questions for Review and Discussion

1. What are the key Latin terms related to the Roman family, household, and their members? How do they compare to modern conceptions?
2. How did slaves and former slaves contribute to the household? What was the family experience for slaves?
3. What were the expectations of children in the household? How does the treatment of children compare with that in modern society?
4. Did the Roman concept of family change? If so, in what ways?
5. What did a Roman house look like and how did it function?

Suggested Reading

Bradley, K. 1991. *Discovering the Roman Family*. Oxford: Oxford University Press.
     Each chapter in this book is a self-contained examination of different aspects of family life. Topics include the role of men, remarriage, child labour, and the social role of nurses.

Dixon, S. 1992. *The Roman Family*. Baltimore: Johns Hopkins University Press.
     Dixon provides a clear introduction to the topic of the Roman family by focusing on the definition of the family, Roman law and the family, marriage, children, and life cycles within the family.

Frier, B., and T. McGinn. 2003. *Casebook on Roman Family Law*. Oxford: Oxford University Press.
     This sourcebook of case law related to the Roman family includes detailed explanations.

Gardner, J., and T. Wiedemann, eds. 1991. *The Roman Household: A Sourcebook*. London and New York: Routledge.
     Arranged thematically, this sourcebook brings together a host of well-translated sources on the family.

George, M., ed. 2005. *The Roman Family in the Empire: Rome, Italy, and Beyond*. Oxford: Oxford University Press.

This collection of essays examines the family in the light of literary, iconographic, epigraphic, and papyrological evidence, both within Italy and in provincial regions such as Africa, Lusitania, Pannonia, Egypt, and Judea.

Rawson, B., ed. 2011. *A Companion to Families in the Greek and Roman Worlds*. Oxford: Wiley-Blackwell.

This monumental work brings together 32 chapters on all aspects of families and family life in the ancient Mediterranean basin, covering Classical Greece through early Christianity. The bibliography is also extensive.

Saller, R.P. 1984. "*Familia, Domus* and the Roman Conception of the Family." *Phoenix* 38: 336–55.

Saller's article on the differences between the terms *familia* and *domus* is very important to understanding the Roman household.

———, and B. Shaw. 1984. "Tombstones and Roman Family Relations in the Principate: Civilians, Soldiers and Slaves." *Journal of Roman Studies* 74: 124–56.

This article uses evidence from commemorative tombstones to examine the Roman family.

Sigismund Nielsen, H. 2001. "The Value of Epithets in Pagan and Christian Epitaphs from Rome." In *Childhood, Class and Kin in the Roman World*, edited by S. Dixon, 165–77. London and New York: Routledge.

By comparing pagan and Christian epitaphs from Rome, this article demonstrates a change in Roman attitudes to family as the use of morally charged terminology increased. This shift included a new focus on women's chastity.

Treggiari, S. 1991. *Roman Marriage: Iusti Coniuges from the Time of Cicero to the Time of Ulpian*. Oxford: Clarendon Press.

The definitive book on Roman marriage, this text covers every aspect of the subject, from betrothal to divorce or death.

Notes

1   See Sigismund Nielsen (1996: 35–60) for the limitations of epigraphical evidence.
2   *IPOstie*-A, 00222 = *ISIS* 00133. All translations are mine, unless otherwise stated.
3   According to Ulpian, any woman could be termed a *materfamilias* whether she was married, widowed, or divorced, provided she lived a respectable lifestyle (*Dig.* 50.16.46.1).
4   Saller (1984: 336–55).
5   Free and freed members of the household often shared a tomb. See, for example, *CIL* 6.24658, from Rome: "To the Spirits of the Dead. For Pomponia Fortunata, her mother, and for Aulus Aulienus Iustus, her brother, and for Aulus Aulienus Saturninus, her father, Auliena Iusta, daughter of Aulus, made this, they were well-deserving, and for herself and for all their freedmen and freedwomen and descendants."

6   See Scheidel (2007b) for a summary of estimates and the problems involved in accepting any of them.
7   Treggiari (1991: 37–49).
8   Even in the Twelve Tables, the earliest Roman law code, a wife had options for staying out of her husband's power: she must spend three nights each year away from her husband (Gai. Inst. 1.111).
9   Treggiari (1991. 22–5).
10 Ibid.: 445.
11 For more on the Stoic view of Cato's actions, see Luc. 2.326–89.
12 See Saller (2003: 190) and Columella Rust. 12. pref. 7; compare Xen. Oec. 7–10.
13 On various interpretations of the expectations of marriage, see Bradley (1991: 126–8); Dixon (1992: 83–90); and Treggiari (1991: 229–61).
14 See further Jeppesen-Wigelsworth (forthcoming).
15 Nep. Att. 5.3; Treggiari (1991: 109).
16 On "serial marriage," see Bradley (1991: 130–9).
17 See Sigismund Nielsen (2001: 170, 173–5, Table 10.2; forthcoming ["Killing the Univira"]); I am grateful to Dr Sigismund Nielsen for permitting me access to this material.
18 Treggiari (1991: 51–2); Dixon (1992: 93–4).
19 Treggiari (1991. 52–4); Dixon (1992: 90–2). Note that the term contubernalis in the context of slave unions had mostly dropped out of use by the second century CE.
20 Treggiari (1991: 52–3, 180–01 [quote from p. 53]). Bradley (1987: 48–9) comments on the use of similar phrasing in inscriptions to describe slave and free unions, and Jeppesen-Wigelsworth (2010: 258–330) contrasts the portrayal of concubinae and contubernales with that of legal wives (coniuges and uxores).
21 On the slave family, see Bradley (1987: 47–80).
22 Saller (1999: 182).

23 The fourth of the Twelve Tables includes this formula, but it is unclear how absolute it was originally. Some saw it as all-encompassing (Gell. NA 5.19.9; Dion. Hal. Ant. Rom. 2.26.4), but Cicero (Leg. 3.8.19) tells us that it applied only to deformed children. Gaius (Inst. 1.52, 1.55) states that a master has the power of life and death over his slaves, who are in his potestas, and points out that children are also in a father's potestas; therefore, the two laws are often read together. Even if this understanding is correct, few fathers likely ever exercised this power, and it may truly have been symbolic. See Saller (1994: 114–21).
24 See Bradley (1991: 139–40) for examples.
25 Saller (1994: 52) estimates that 37 per cent would have lost their fathers by age 15.
26 Dixon (1992: 47). Spurius Cassius tried to become a king (Val. Max. 5.8.2; Livy 2.41.10), and Aulus Fulvius tried to join Catiline's conspiracy (Val. Max. 5.8.5; Sall. Cat. 39.5; Cass. Dio 37.36.4).
27 For more on the realities of the paterfamilias versus the Roman myth of the paterfamilias, see Dixon (1992: 31); Saller (1984: 336–55; 1999: 182–97); Shaw (2001); and Frier and McGinn (2003).
28 See Harris (1994). For the view that female infanticide was not prevalent in antiquity, see Engels (1980).
29 Dixon (1992: 128–9).
30 Gardner and Wiedemann (1991: 88). For more discussion, see Scheidel (2001b). Children's tombstones often express parental sorrow and affection; see Bradley (1991: 139).
31 Parents might also remark on their own dutifulness. See, for example, AE (1902, 00081), from Rome: "To the Spirits of the Departed Titus Flavius Heliodorus, a son who was very sweet and who lived 3 years, 10 months, and 9 days. His father, Titus Flavius Maximus, an evocatus (recalled veteran) of the emperor, and his mother, Aurelia Antonia, made this (together) as very dutiful parents."

32 Dixon (1992: 108–12); Sigismund Nielsen (2007: 39–54). As far as the law was concerned, slave children under the age of five had no value but gained it thereafter, as they were expected to work (*Dig.* 7.7.6.1–2).

33 *CIL* 6.14202. Numerous other examples can be found on Roman tombstones.

34 Saller (2003: 185–204).

35 This manumission did not necessarily occur any earlier, however. For example, a tombstone inscription records a *verna* who died at age 27 (*CIL* 6.5195).

36 Cicero frequently mentioned Tiro in letters to Atticus. Twenty-seven letters written to Tiro survive (all of Book 16 of Cicero's *Epistulae ad familiares*) and highlight Cicero's concern for Tiro's bad health and the work that he continued to perform for Cicero as a freedman. See Cic. *Fam.* 16.13, 16.14 for health concerns and *Fam.* 16.22 for some duties performed by Tiro.

37 Dixon (1992: 128).

38 Gardner and Wiedemann (1991: 148); Saller (2003: 201–04).

39 The *c(o)enaculum* largely equates to the modern understanding of a multi-room apartment (see Storey [2004: 51–2]), but *insula* could also indicate "an independent unit within the structural fabric of some other edifice" or an entire city block (Storey 2004: 54–5). For more on Roman *insulae*, see Packer (1971); Storey (2004: 47–84); and Bergmann (2012: 237–40).

40 Wallace-Hadrill (1994: 82–5, 51–7).

41 For example, Suet. *Aug.* 72 and Plin. *Ep.* 2.17.

42 Wallace-Hadrill (1994: 8–14, 50–61).

43 Wallace-Hadrill (2003: 4). On experimenting with population density, Wallace-Hadrill has argued for seven to eight people per house. For more on the "public" versus "private" aspect, see Riggsby (1997: 36–56).

44 Wallace-Hadrill (1994: 82–5, 51–7 [quote on p. 83]). For further examples and an analysis of the remains found in Roman households, see Allison (2004) and Allison's *Pompeian Households: An On-line Companion*, available at www.stoa.org/projects/ph/index.html.

45 For more on the House of the Prince of Naples (VI.15.8), see Wallace-Hadrill (1994: 26, 47–51). For more house plans from Pompeii, see www.stoa.org/projects/ph/houselist.html. For a detailed example of a "typical" *domus*, see www.vroma.org/~bmcmanus/house.html.

46 Asc. *Mil.* 38.

47 Wallace-Hadrill (1994: 91–117). On the survival of beds, Wallace-Hadrill notes that there is one exceptional child's cot/crib that survives. From Suetonius's description of the rift between Tiberius and Julia, it is clear that married couples often shared a bedchamber. See Suet. *Tib.* 7.3 and Fantham (2006: 83).

48 See also Sor. *Gyn.* 2.12.19 and Bradley (1991: 13–36).

49 Compare also *Dig.* 29.5.1.28 for a slave boy (pre-adolescent) who slept at the foot of his master's bed and was also put to death as punishment for not crying out (out of fear) when other slaves entered the room to kill their master.

50 For more on the multiple aspects of ancient families, see Rawson (2011).

6

Education in the Roman World

Fanny Dolansky

In the mid-second century CE, Lucian of Samosata wrote *The Dream* (*Somnium*), a speech about how he came to pursue a career in literary studies.[1] When he had finished school, his father and his father's friends discussed his future. Further studies would be costly, as he came from a family of modest means, so it was determined that he acquire a trade instead—one that would be easy to learn, provide him with a decent living, and be suitable for a man of free birth. They decided that he should apprentice with an uncle to become a sculptor and stonemason. Initially, Lucian was happy about this plan, but that changed on his first day of training. Striking a stone tablet too hard with his chisel, he broke it; his uncle flew into a rage and beat him with a stick. Lucian ran home crying. That night, he dreamt that the figures of *Technē* (Craft) and *Paideia* (Education) were vying for his allegiance. *Technē*, appearing as a dusty worker with calloused hands and dirty hair, made her pitch. Then *Paideia* countered. A sculptor's life, she claimed, would be a life of poverty, obscurity, and constant service. But a life of learning would yield great moral and material benefits:

> I shall adorn your soul, the most essential part of you, with many noble ornaments—moderation, justice, piety, gentleness, fairness, understanding, endurance, love of beauty, and a yearning to achieve the sublime. For these are the purest adornments of the soul . . . You are now poor and the son of a nobody, and you thought of taking up such a sordid craft. Soon everyone will admire and envy you; you will be praised and honoured, enjoying high esteem for the finest qualities, respected by the rich and the noble, wearing clothes like this (pointing to her own brilliant attire) and considered worthy of office and precedence. If you go abroad, not even on foreign ground will you be unknown or unnoticed. I shall put such identification marks on you that everyone seeing you will nudge his neighbour and point to you, saying, "That's the man." (Lucian *Somn.* 10–11)[2]

Lucian was persuaded and decided to devote himself to *Paideia*, which he hoped others, inspired by his story, would also do.

Timeline

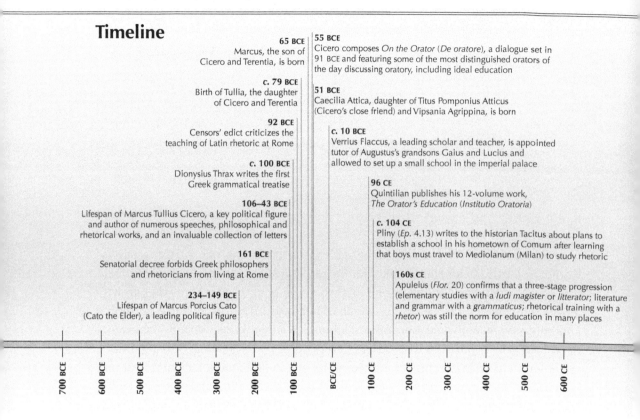

65 BCE
Marcus, the son of Cicero and Terentia, is born

55 BCE
Cicero composes *On the Orator* (*De oratore*), a dialogue set in 91 BCE and featuring some of the most distinguished orators of the day discussing oratory, including ideal education

c. 79 BCE
Birth of Tullia, the daughter of Cicero and Terentia

51 BCE
Caecilia Attica, daughter of Titus Pomponius Atticus (Cicero's close friend) and Vipsania Agrippina, is born

92 BCE
Censors' edict criticizes the teaching of Latin rhetoric at Rome

c. 10 BCE
Verrius Flaccus, a leading scholar and teacher, is appointed tutor of Augustus's grandsons Gaius and Lucius and allowed to set up a small school in the imperial palace

c. 100 BCE
Dionysius Thrax writes the first Greek grammatical treatise

96 CE
Quintilian publishes his 12-volume work, *The Orator's Education* (*Institutio Oratoria*)

106–43 BCE
Lifespan of Marcus Tullius Cicero, a key political figure and author of numerous speeches, philosophical and rhetorical works, and an invaluable collection of letters

c. 104 CE
Pliny (*Ep.* 4.13) writes to the historian Tacitus about plans to establish a school in his hometown of Comum after learning that boys must travel to Mediolanum (Milan) to study rhetoric

161 BCE
Senatorial decree forbids Greek philosophers and rhetoricians from living at Rome

160s CE
Apuleius (*Flor.* 20) confirms that a three-stage progression (elementary studies with a *ludi magister* or *litterator*; literature and grammar with a *grammaticus*; rhetorical training with a *rhetor*) was still the norm for education in many places

234–149 BCE
Lifespan of Marcus Porcius Cato (Cato the Elder), a leading political figure

700 BCE 600 BCE 500 BCE 400 BCE 300 BCE 200 BCE 100 BCE BCE/CE 100 CE 200 CE 300 CE 400 CE 500 CE 600 CE

Introduction

Whether as formal study or vocational training, education was an important component of childhood and adolescence throughout the central period (200 BCE to 200 CE) in both Italy and the provinces. Because it intersects with several areas of social life, education has considerable relevance to the study of Roman social history. Perhaps most obviously, the examination of education overlaps significantly with historical interests in childhood and the family. Parents' attitudes and responsibilities towards their children's education and slave owners' approaches to educating domestic slaves add to our understanding of both Roman educational practices and the dynamics of family life. The roles that servile childminders (such as nurses and pedagogues) and private teachers (who were generally of servile background) played in the intellectual development of their young charges contribute to the pictures that emerge about Roman childhood and domestic slavery, as well as educational practices. As the excerpt from Lucian's autobiographical sketch illustrates, ancient authors' discussions of education in its various forms often included commentary on the values and expectations that society held concerning juridical status (whether a person was of free birth, a slave, or a former slave), gender, and socio-economic standing. For example, a fitting course of study for a poor freeborn boy such as Lucian differed from those approved for the son or the daughter of a senator.

Studying Roman education is often more about ideology than practice. That is, it is more about what people (particularly elite males) thought was appropriate for individuals of different backgrounds and less about what those individuals actually knew or did. These insights into elite attitudes can inform our appreciation of Roman society beyond the sphere of education to help answer questions about literary culture, the economy, slavery, and much more.

———— • ◆ • ————

This chapter focuses on two interrelated subjects regarding education: its contents (what students learned, as well as when, where, and how) and its objectives (what people sought to achieve through education, depending on a student's age, gender, and **status**). The chapter begins with formal education, exploring what elementary studies, advanced studies in literature and grammar, and rhetoric entailed. It also examines evidence for training slaves and poor freeborn children in skilled occupations and presents an overview of Roman education as it pertains to children and youth of both sexes from different **classes** and of different statuses. The second part concentrates on the goals that ancient authors articulate about educating children, particularly the ethical aims and desired outcomes. In doing so, it also considers the roles and attitudes attributed to parents, slave attendants, and teachers, who were each involved in the educational process in unique ways. For upper-class boys, training in literature, grammar, and rhetoric was believed to help shape them into good citizens who could participate in politics and the law courts. For upper-class girls, freeborn children of the lower classes, and slaves, such avenues were unavailable. Education, therefore, assumed different forms with distinct aims.

This chapter draws primarily on textual evidence, namely papyrological and literary sources. In many ways, these sources are complementary and reflect the chapter's two main interests. School exercises on papyri produced by students and teachers' models offer testimony of content and shed some light on pedagogy. The writings of educationalists and other literary sources tend to be theoretical and express ideals, especially regarding the impact that education could have on character formation and development. Such authors also concentrate on elite boys who were being groomed to be future orators and leaders and tell us much less about elite girls, children of the lower classes, and slaves.

Although there is a substantial amount of surviving evidence that concerns education, it can be fragmentary. Sources from a range of genres and geographical locations sometimes have to be drawn together carefully to form a coherent, though generalized, picture. This chapter adopts such an approach in seeking to present a view of Roman education that is not specific to a time or place but is broadly representative of practices and beliefs during the central period. Certainly Roman society was not homogenous chronologically or geographically but featured significant cultural and structural differences from region to region. Yet there is a considerable degree of consistency in the evidence for education from different genres, eras, and locales. The evidence of school texts, which come mainly from Roman Egypt, confirms theoretical notions found in literary sources from Italy, Greece, and Asia Minor. Similarly, much of what Quintilian, a rhetorician, prescribes in Latin for schoolboys in first-century CE Rome is compatible with ideas expressed by Plutarch, writing decades later in Greek and in his hometown of Chaeronea.

"Letters are a good start to life."[3]

The First Elements: Early Education at Home and School

Before formal studies began, a great deal of valuable learning took place at home. Recognizing this, some authors stressed the importance of the home environment in children's intellectual development, especially in the upper classes. Quintilian, who wrote a 12-volume work titled *The Orator's Education* (*Institutio Oratoria*), offers advice concerning various influences in the life of an elite boy and future orator. Nurses (**nutrices**), who oversaw much of the very young boy's care, must speak properly because he will hear and try to emulate their words first. The slave boys in the household, with whom he is reared, should also speak correctly.[4]

Pedagogues (**paedagogi**), male slaves responsible for the boy's early training and behaviour, should be highly educated. Failing that, they should know the limits of their knowledge. Finally, both parents should be as educated as possible since children model parental speech (Quint. *Inst.* 1.1.4–9). Before Quintilian, Cicero (*Brut.* 210) had written comparable sentiments in one of his treatises on oratory, insisting that whom children heard and spoke to (and how they spoke) at home every day was of great importance. He singled out fathers, *paedagogi*, and mothers, in that order. Though some worried about the influence of slave caregivers, nurses and pedagogues were nevertheless fixtures in the lives of upper-class boys and girls throughout childhood and into adolescence. They were sometimes present in the lives of children of other classes as well.[5]

➔ Compare Chapter 5, p. 107, on relations between servile and free members of the household.

➔ See Chapter 5, 96–7, for an example of the continuing relationship between nurses and their charges.

Beyond these interactions, some elite children enjoyed other domestic opportunities that fostered an early appreciation for learning. Many wealthy Roman men had private libraries and invited scholars to make use of their collections. Cicero's correspondence with his friend Atticus in the mid-first century BCE contains many discussions of their respective libraries and efforts to expand them and mentions resident scholars and visiting intellectuals who were guests at dinners and readings. Cicero's children, Tullia and Marcus, as well as his nephew Quintus (who spent much time with them) and Atticus's daughter, Attica, most likely had access to all these cultural resources, which no doubt enriched their childhood experiences.[6]

Compare Chapter 7, pp. 154–8, on the relationship between poets and their elite patrons.

Regardless of juridical or socio-economic status, most children presumably learned a considerable amount through play, which helped them learn about the world around them while developing important motor, communication, and social skills. Both archaeological and literary sources provide evidence of a wide variety of toys, ranging from rattles for babies and animal pull toys for toddlers to dolls and hoops for older children.[7] Many boys' games involved assuming social and political leadership roles, such as playing at judges or generals. Some reflected current events, as when boys in Rome staged a two-day contest of "Octavians and Antonians" prior to the Battle of Actium in 31 BCE.[8] There is also evidence to suggest that it was common for children to keep pets, a practice that, as Keith Bradley proposes, likely yielded significant psychological and emotional benefits.[9]

One of the first steps in the more formal educational process, which ideally began at home, was learning the alphabet. Quintilian (*Inst.* 1.1.25) believed that children should learn the letters' shapes and names together, followed by their order so that they could recognize letters out of sequence. School exercises show how beginning students were encouraged to master the alphabet by learning to follow different alphabetical sequences, such as starting from the last letter and working towards the first or skipping a fixed number of letters. In one second-century CE exercise from Roman Egypt, a student was supposed to create two alphabets, one in regular order and the other reversed, thereby pairing the first letter (*alpha*) with the last (*omega*) and so forth. But as Raffaella Cribiore's analysis reveals, the student struggled to complete the exercise as required and instead produced one alphabet in its entirety before proceeding to the other.[10]

To reinforce knowledge of the alphabet and cultivate an early love of learning, wealthy children were given letter shapes crafted from ivory or boxwood, a practice Quintilian (*Inst.* 1.1.26) reports from his day. Jerome (*Ep.* 107.4) mentions this same practice more than three centuries later when discussing the studies of one little girl; he suggests she learn a song to master the letters' proper order. Cookies and cakes were recommended as rewards and incentives to help children learn their ABCs, which were called *prima elementa* or "first elements" (Hor. *Sat.* 1.1.25–6; Jer. *Ep.* 128.1).[11]

Children began more serious studies at about age seven, some at public schools and others at home with tutors.[12] Parents who kept their sons out of school are said to have worried mainly about corruption by a teacher of bad character or insufficient individual attention (Quint. *Inst.* 1.2.2). Quintilian felt that such worries were valid but did not out-weigh the benefits of group learning. Nevertheless, a number of elite boys—and girls—are known to have had private tutors. Cicero's letters mention several teachers who worked in his home, beginning with Aristodemus of Nysa, an esteemed grammarian and rhetorician who tutored his son, Marcus (who was then nearly six), in the spring of 59 BCE. Cicero does not indicate whether his daughter, Tullia, also engaged in studies, but it seems prob-able considering that other upper-class girls of this era did. For instance, we know that Attica had a *paedagogus* who was responsible for her elementary education when she was about five or six. Pompey the Great's daughter, Pompeia, appears to have made impressive progress with her tutor, for, when she was only eight or nine, she apparently welcomed her father home from the East by reading aloud from Homer's *Iliad*.[13] Papyrus letters record that privileged girls in Egypt likewise enjoyed private education. Heraidous, the daughter of a civil administrator, is associated with a teacher (*kathēgētēs*) in several letters, one of which reports to her mother that she is "persevering with her studies."[14]

While upper-class girls may have generally acquired basic reading and writing skills at home, limited evidence suggests that other freeborn girls sometimes attended schools. The funerary monument for Furius Philocalus, an elementary school teacher (**ludi magister**) from Capua near the Bay of Naples, depicts him seated between the standing figures of a boy and a girl.[15] More substantial is the poet Martial's (9.68.1–2) reference, late in the first century CE, to the *ludi magister* who is hated by boys and girls alike. This work also lends the impression that lessons were conducted outdoors—Martial complains that, even before dawn, the sounds of the teacher's shouting and thrashing of his students can be heard by the neighbours. Dio Chrysostom (*Or.* 20.9) notes that teachers sit in the streets with their pupils and "nothing hinders them in this great throng from teaching and learning."[16] A wall paint-ing from **Pompeii** shows what may not have been an unusual scene: before a colonnade in the **forum**, a boy is being beaten by the teacher while other students sit demurely, their books or writing tablets on their knees.[17] Though open-air teaching seems to have been common at the elementary level, schools were also held in private and public buildings.[18]

Like those tutored at home, the freeborn children who attended school initially focused on mastering the alphabet. Some school exercises from Egypt feature models written by a teacher and copied by a student. To help develop proper handwriting, Quintilian (*Inst.* 1.1.27–8) recommended inscribing the letters on a tablet so that they could be traced with a pen (*stylus*) and within well-defined grooves. Jerome (*Ep.* 107.4) later offered similar advice regarding a six-year-old named Paula: "When she begins with uncertain hand to use the pen, either let another hand be put over hers to guide her baby fingers, or else have the letters marked on the tablet so that her writing may follow the outlines and keep to their limits without straying away."[19]

Students then learned to combine letters into syllables, a preparatory step to both writ-ing and reading. They recited various syllabic sets inscribed on teachers' models and wrote down letter combinations following a system, such as starting with two-letter combinations that paired a consonant with each vowel (for example, *ba*, *be*), then forming three-letter (*bra*, *bre*) or four-letter sets (*bras*, *bres*), and eventually working through the entire alphabet.[20] Ancient authorities highly approved of this practice, insisting that syllables had to be learned by heart and drilled repeatedly (Dion. Hal. *Comp.* 25; Quint. *Inst.* 1.1.30). Students also copied lists that included the names of rivers, animals, or mythological characters.[21] One first-century CE exercise contains 24 groups of four disyllabic words, the first group starting with *alpha*, the second with *beta*, and so forth to those beginning with *omega*, some of which appear to have been made up for the occasion, presumably by a teacher.[22]

For a student's initial reading and copying exercises, maxims and sayings (***sententiae***, or ***gnōmai***), such as the phrase used as this section's title, were considered the best material. Verses from Homer and the Greek playwrights Euripides and Menander were especially popular. Students copied short excerpts—often just a few verses—to practise penmanship, then learned to read these texts with the syllables marked and words separated.[23] Cribiore calls these "user-friendly" texts, prepared for the student still grasping the complexities of reading. In antiquity, reading could be very challenging since manuscripts other than school texts lacked features that modern readers take for granted, such as separation between words and punctuation. Instead, one encountered "only an ensemble of letters in need of interpretation."[24] Dionysius of Halicarnassus (*Comp.* 25), a Greek historian and teacher of rhetoric in the Augustan period, offers some insight into the lengthy process of learning to read:

> When we are taught to read, first we learn by heart the names of the letters, then their shapes and their values, then, in the same way, their syllables and their effects, and finally words and their properties . . . When we have acquired knowledge of these things, we begin to write and read, syllable by syllable and slowly at first. It is only when a considerable lapse of time has implanted firmly in our minds the forms of the words that we execute them with the utmost ease.[25]

By completing this phase of studies, a student would have achieved some important goals. These might seem modest by modern standards, but given the low levels of literacy that persisted in the Roman world and the fact that schooling was neither mandated nor regulated by the state, gaining even the basics was no small accomplishment.[26]

To this point, the focus has been on freeborn boys and girls, particularly of the upper classes. As previously mentioned, one of Quintilian's concerns for the future orator's development was how those around him spoke, including slave children. In *On the Education of Children*, an essay attributed to Plutarch (*Mor.* 3F), a similar point is made: young slaves chosen to be a child's servants and companions should be "distinct of speech." This theory raises the question of whether slave children also received formal elementary education. Surely there were economic incentives for doing so, as educated and well-trained slaves were assets for the skilled jobs they performed and the high value they could garner at sale.[27] Perhaps that is why some owners assumed responsibility for their slaves' education themselves. Cato the Elder preferred to buy slaves still young enough for him to raise and train (Plut. *Cat. Mai.* 21.1). Crassus, one of the wealthiest Romans in the late Republic, is said to have directed the education of his sizeable slave staff (Plut. *Crass.* 2.6), and Atticus similarly oversaw the training of his slaves, among whom were very learned boys, accomplished readers, and secretaries (Nep. *Att.* 13.3–4). Presumably, these young slaves acquired critical foundations before progressing to specialized training.

→ Compare Chapter 4, pp. 80–3, on the sale of slaves.

Of course, not all masters were interested in or had time to educate slaves themselves. Martial (10.62) attests to young slave boys attending lessons with the *ludi magister* and others studying under teachers of accounting and stenography.[28] Male slaves may have also attended in-house schools since the imperial household and very large private households are known to have had special training establishments called *paedagogia*. Although these seem to have focused on preparing boys for dining-room service (important given the prominence of dinner parties in elite social life), scholars maintain that their training was likely more comprehensive, as attendance at dinners sometimes involved tasks such as reading, taking notes, and reporting on financial accounts. Indeed, the more important functions in an urban household would have required a high degree of literacy and practical knowledge of arithmetic.[29]

Beyond the Basics: *Grammaticē*, Rhetoric, and Vocational Training

It is not clear how long a child typically spent on the first stage of education, perhaps two to three years. Ability rather than age determined advancement for those who continued to the next stage, which is generally called *grammaticē*. This phase aimed at developing skills in reading, writing, and speaking and was taught under the direction of a **grammaticus** (sometimes translated as "grammarian," though his teaching focused on more than simply Greek and Latin grammar). Some upper-class boys studied privately with a *grammaticus*. Marcus and Quintus Cicero began working with Tyrannio, a teacher from Amisus on the Black Sea, in 56 BCE. Two years later, Quintus (then 13) was ready to begin rhetorical studies, but Marcus (who was younger) needed further instruction in literature, so Cicero hired respected scholar Marcus Pomponius Dionysius to tutor both boys in the areas required.[30] The emperor Augustus likewise employed a successful *grammaticus* for his grandsons Gaius and Lucius, in the figure of the eminent scholar Verrius Flaccus. Emily Hemelrijk plausibly suggests that Flaccus might have instructed Augustus's granddaughters, Julia and Agrippina, as well.[31] Certainly other upper-class girls are known to have continued their studies, such as Attica, whose secondary education was overseen by Quintus Caecilius Epirota, a famous *grammaticus*.[32]

Suetonius's *On Teachers of Grammar and Rhetoric* (*De grammaticis et rhetoribus*), a collection of short biographies dating to the early second century CE, indicates that arrangements for *grammatici* varied, with some primarily offering individual instruction in children's homes

Figure 6.1 A second-century CE relief showing three boys in a school setting. © Bridgeman Art Library Ltd./Alamy

and those who were in great demand teaching in schools and tutoring privately (see Figure 6.1). How large classes were is not clear. Quintilian (*Inst.* 1.2.15) held that "a good teacher will not burden himself with a bigger crowd of pupils than he can manage"[33] and devoted considerable attention to addressing imagined remarks about the potential impact of class size, which suggests that genuine parental concerns probably existed.

Studies under a *grammaticus* were based predominantly on literature, specifically poetry, as Quintilian's reading list and school exercises reflect (see Box 6.1).[34] It was felt that students should concentrate on Greek first, even if their dominant language

Primary Source

Box 6.1: Quintilian, *The Orator's Education*, 1.8.4–6, 8.[1]

Above all, these tender minds, which will be deeply affected by whatever is impressed upon them in their untrained ignorance, should learn not only eloquent passages but, even more, passages which are morally improving. The practice of making reading start with Homer and Vergil is therefore excellent. Of course it needs a more developed judgement to appreciate their virtues; but there is time enough for this, for they will be read more than once. Meanwhile, let the mind be uplifted by the sublimity of the heroic poems, and inspired and filled with the highest principles by the greatness of their theme. Tragedy is useful; and even lyric poets are educative, so long as you select not only the authors but the parts of their works to be read, because the Greeks have a good deal that is licentious, and there are some things in Horace that I should not care to explain in class . . . But with boys, the texts to be read should be those which will best nourish the mind and develop the character.

Note

1. Translated by Russell (2002).

was Latin, and Homer was deemed best for all ages (Quint. *Inst.* 1.4.1; cf. 1.1.12–14). Quintilian (*Inst.* 1.8.5) thoroughly approved of starting with Homer for improving oral reading abilities, and Plutarch's (*Mor.* 14D–37B) essay *How the Young Man Should Study Poetry* is replete with examples from the *Iliad* and *Odyssey* for more advanced students. Some truly revered Homer—one school exercise declares, "Homer was a god, not a man" (*P.Mich.* 8.1100)—though Augustine's recollections of his own education in the late fourth century CE are less enthusiastic (see Box 6.2). Despite the many differences in education, one constant appears to have been the primacy of Homer. Recall that Pompeia greeted her father with a recitation from the *Iliad* (Book 3), while a second- or third-century CE letter from Oxyrhynchus (*P.Oxy.* 6.930) reports that a boy named Ptolemaios had been reading Book 6. The *Iliad*, especially the first two books, was consistently preferred to the *Odyssey* in educational contexts, and the most advanced students would read to the poem's end.[35]

Grammaticē encompassed a number of areas of study. As Quintilian (*Inst.* 1.4.2) put it, "Although this subject comprises two parts—the study of correct speech and the interpretation of the poets—there is more of it behind the scenes than meets the eye." *Grammatici* used poetic texts to teach students several subjects considered distinct from literature today (including grammar, pronunciation, linguistics, and history), all with an eye to helping them become eloquent speakers, proficient readers and writers, and, ultimately, better people.

The next logical step for aristocratic boys was to study rhetoric, which usually occurred in their early to mid-teens, though no fixed age was set (Quint. *Inst.* 2.1.7; see Box 6.3). Specialized teachers (**rhetores**) existed, but initial instruction sometimes began under a *grammaticus* (Quint. *Inst.* 2.1.1–6). The crowning achievement of this phase was

Primary Source

Box 6.2: Augustine, *Confessions*, 1.13–14.[1]

Not even now am I sure why it was that I hated Greek literature, in which I received instruction as a young boy; for I loved Latin literature—not that taught by the elementary teachers, but that taught by the so-called *grammatici*. In fact, I found my elementary Latin instruction—learning to read, write and count—as tiresome and painful as the Greek . . . So why is it that I hated *Greek* literature? For Homer, too, is a skilful weaver of tales like that [i.e. Vergil] and is pleasantly inconsequential; yet as a boy I found him unappetising. I expect Greek boys find the same thing with Vergil, when they are forced to learn him by heart, as I did with Homer.

Note

1. Translated by Joyal, McDougall, and Yardley (2009: 244–5, no. 108).

Political History

Box 6.3: Rhetoric at Rome

The study of rhetoric in Latin was common in Rome by the time Quintilian published his treatise on educating an orator in the late first century CE. Yet early in the first century BCE, when Cicero was a youth, there was considerable resistance because it was seen as a threat to Roman traditions. Paradoxically, the teaching of Greek rhetoric was not deemed problematic then, although attitudes towards it in the previous century had varied. Suetonius (*Gram.* 25.2) preserves an edict of the **censors**, Gnaeus Domitius Ahenobarbus and Lucius Licinius Crassus, dated to 92 BCE:

> We have been informed that there are persons who have established a novel sort of instruction and that the youth gather at their school; these persons have styled themselves "Latin rhetoricians," and that young persons idle away whole days there. Our ancestors established what manner of things they wished their children to learn and what manner of schools they wished them to attend. These new practices, which do not accord with ordinary custom and the way of our ancestors, are vexatious and wayward-seeming. Therefore we have determined to make our judgement plain both to those who preside over these schools and to those who have become accustomed to attending them: we do not approve.[1]

Though it expressed strong sentiments, the edict did not have the force of law and could not prevent rhetoricians from teaching.

Note

1. Translated by Kaster (1995).

declamation, the delivery of a piece of oratory. But before he could reach that stage, a boy had to complete preliminary training exercises (*progymnasmata*). As primarily written compositions on set themes, *progymnasmata* were designed to develop argumentation and style and were often later given orally so that the boy could work on delivery.

The earliest and easiest exercises made use of materials learned previously and were based on an instructive saying, maxim, fable, or mythological narrative that the student had to reproduce in his own words, explain, and expand upon in a composition. More advanced exercises had themes related to praise and denunciation or involved impersonating a literary or historical character and expanding on his or her speech or action in a particular situation.[36] Practising declamation began in earnest through composition and delivery of mock speeches, of which there were two main types at Rome.[37] The first, called *suasoriae*, were exercises in deliberative oratory in which a literary or historical figure debates two or more courses of action and the declaimer urges one. The second, called **controversiae**, were exercises in forensic oratory, essentially fictive legal cases in which one or more laws are cited, a situation involving a problematic application of the law is proposed, and the declaimer argues one side of the case. Thorough training in rhetoric could take several years, and it was not unusual for boys who were serious about becoming orators to spend most of their teenage years learning from a "teacher of eloquence" (Quint. *Inst.* 2.8.4).

Boys from **senatorial** and **equestrian** families who wished to pursue careers in politics or law normally followed their rhetorical studies with one to two years of apprenticeship called *tirocinium fori* ("recruitment to the forum"). The *tirocinium* often began soon after a boy had celebrated his coming-of-age ceremony, where he received the *toga virilis* ("toga of manhood") to mark his attainment of adult status.[38] The apprenticeship was designed to prepare an upper-class boy for entry into public life. It paired the boy, a *tiro* ("novice"; literally "recruit"), with an established orator who served as a mentor. Cicero (*Amic.* 1.1) recalled how his father had brought him to study under Quintus Mucius Scaevola, an esteemed lawyer and **augur**, early in the first century BCE. Once Cicero (*Cael.* 4.9) became an influential advocate, he mentored Marcus Caelius Rufus.

In his speech in defence of Caelius some years later, Cicero (*Cael.* 5.11) indicates that upper-class boys usually spent some time during their *tirocinium fori* engaged in military training. This involved performing physical exercises on the **Campus Martius** to acquire basic skills with weaponry and other aspects of soldiering. Boys were subsequently assigned to prominent generals during an additional apprenticeship called *tirocinium militiae* ("recruitment to the army") and designed to give boys experience in battle. Even if they were intent on careers in the forum or law courts rather than the battlefield, all boys had to complete some military service. Moreover, serving in the army was an important duty for Roman men. Pompey the Great apprenticed with his own father, "a very accomplished general" according to the historian Velleius Paterculus (2.29.5), then mentored Cicero's son, who served under him as a cavalry officer in 49 BCE (Cic. *Off.* 2.13.45).

Since upper-class girls could not participate in the law courts or politics as speakers, it seems unlikely that many received training in rhetoric. However, women such as Cornelia, the mother of the Gracchi, were celebrated by later sources for their elegant manner of writing and speaking (see, for example, Cic. *Brut.* 211, *De or.* 3.45; Quint. *Inst.* 1.1.6; and Figure 6.2). This praise suggests formal study in rhetoric in addition to careful modelling by their fathers, who were accomplished speakers.[39] At the age when their brothers and male cousins were beginning rhetorical studies, many elite girls were betrothed or already married, yet this did not necessarily signal the end of their studies. Attica, who married Marcus Agrippa in her early teens, was then taking lessons from a *grammaticus*. Minicia Marcella, whose death Pliny (*Ep.* 5.16.3) laments, was soon to marry at nearly 13 and had been devoted to her teachers and studies. There is no indication who would have overseen her education had she lived, but perhaps it would have been her husband. Plutarch (*Mor.* 145–6), for instance, believed it was a husband's responsibility to educate his wife, particularly in philosophy, though his remarks to a pair of newlyweds about the wife's knowledge of mathematics point to a broader course of study.[40]

For children of the upper classes, especially boys, childhood and early adolescence were normally spent becoming well versed in literature and eloquent in expression. For the lower classes and slaves, such formal education was a luxury very few could enjoy. Lucian, with whom this chapter began, indicated that formal education was limited for boys from modest backgrounds. He seems to have completed studies with a *grammaticus* before it was deemed time to acquire more practical skills. His apprenticeship being short-lived, he was fortunate to find an alternative career path. For others, learning a trade was perhaps the only option available, unless they wanted to enlist in the army, which offered steady wages and other benefits but required a 25-year service commitment.[41]

Figure 6.2 A first-century CE wall painting of a woman with a stylus. © VPC Travel Photo/Alamy

Apprenticeship contracts from Egypt document arrangements for training freeborn boys and slave children of both sexes mainly in weaving, though there is evidence for a range of occupations related to construction, coppersmithing, and nail making, as well as jobs in music and shorthand. Training generally began at age 12 or 13, and periods of apprenticeship spanned six months to six years.[42] For some apprentices, working condi-

Compare Chapter 13, pp. 287–89, on the career of legionary soldiers.

tions appear to have been harsh. A contract dated to 183 CE for a freeborn boy apprenticed to a weaver stipulates that he work "from sunrise to sunset" over 5 years and have only 20 holidays a year (*P.Oxy.* 4.725). One from the middle of the second century CE outlines terms for training a slave boy in shorthand; his master had high expectations and intended to pay the bulk of the teacher's salary only after the boy had achieved certain milestones (*P.Oxy.* 4.724). Though similar contracts do not survive outside Egypt, Christopher Forbes plausibly suggests that apprenticeships likewise existed in Rome and cities in the western Mediterranean.[43]

A variety of sources attest to the many jobs that slave children had, and funerary epitaphs are especially helpful in this regard. Rather young slaves were often already skilled artisans, such as 9-year-old Viccentia, a gold worker, and 11-year-old Gaius Valerius Diophanes, a silver engraver. A slave accountant (*calculator*) named Melior, who died at 13, was already celebrated for his great expertise. Jurists disagreed over the age by which a slave should be productive, some arguing 5 and others 10 (*Dig.* 7.7.6; *Cod.* 6.43.1). In some spheres, such as entertainment, they might have been well below those limits. Inscriptions record the deaths of three acrobats who were brothers, two aged 5 and the third just 17 months.[44]

It might seem surprising that many occupations that are deemed highly respectable today (including medicine, architecture, and teaching) were once considered beneath the dignity of the upper classes (see, for example, Cic. *Off.* 1.42.151). Consequently, "a large proportion of the brain-workers in ancient society were of servile status."[45] Medicine, like other professions, was scorned because one received payment for services and the work was associated with manual labour. No authority regulated qualifications or "schools," and experience rather than education indicated who was a capable physician. Students apprenticed with established doctors, observing them during visits to patients, and eastern cities such as Ephesus and Alexandria became known as centres of medical expertise. Sources record periods of study from six months to six years, though the average may have been two to three years. This figure accords with inscriptional evidence of young men (and a few women) who died in their late teens and early twenties as already practising physicians. Galen, perhaps the best-known doctor from the Roman world, appears to have been an exception. His extensive training took a total of 12 years between studies in Pergamum, Smyrna, Corinth, and Alexandria.[46]

➔ See Chapter 5, pp. 94–5, for the funerary inscriptions of a doctor and a midwife.

"A proper education is the source and root of all goodness."[47]

In the Roman world, education had clear ethical aims that varied depending on the juridical status, socio-economic circumstances, and gender of the learner. Educationalists such as Quintilian, Plutarch, and the unknown author of an essay on child-rearing (which lends this section its title), repeatedly emphasize the moral objectives underlying lessons in reading and writing. At each stage, shaping character was paramount. Content, instruction, and supervision all contributed to a desirable finished product: a young adult who was not simply knowledgeable about literature and grammar but also displayed moral excellence. In Lucian's dream, *Paideia* promises to bestow precisely the "many noble ornaments" that would distinguish and empower their recipient.

Even in the beginning of a child's formal education, the materials selected were designed to achieve moral as well as practical goals. According to Quintilian (*Inst.* 1.1.35–6), the maxims a teacher selects for copying should not be meaningless but convey a moral lesson, for "the memory of such things stays with us till we are old, and the impression thus made on the unformed mind will be good for the character." These short texts would play a role in each successive stage of education (see, for example, Quint. *Inst.* 1.9.3–5), and their lessons would ideally be deployed later when delivering political or forensic speeches.

The *gnōmai* preserved in school texts from Egypt cover topics such as wealth, virtue, intellect, women, and self-control.[48] "Love justice and do not be greedy for anything," one advises (*P.Oxy.* 42.3004). "Bad habits distort one's nature," claims another (*P.Mon. Epiph.*

2.615). The usefulness of literacy is a theme that recurs with the sense that education is important, though it is not necessarily linked to wealth. Instead, it potentially betters one's situation, for "the man who knows his letters has a superior mind" (*P.Mon. Epiph.* 2.615).[49] A large category of *gnōmai* concern women and marriage; most are negative, as examples such as "trust a woman and open your tomb" and "marry in haste and repent" reflect. Teresa Morgan, who discusses these and other maxims in detail, rightly questions the impact that such sentiments might have had on children of both sexes who presumably had regular contact with adult women among their kin.[50]

The ethical focus continued, and perhaps became more obvious to students both in terms of content and methods, when they proceeded to *grammaticē*. It is less in the elements related to their acquisition of proper and eloquent speech (such as correct grammar and pronunciation) and more in the study of literature that we find a clear emphasis on ethical instruction. The Greek and Latin authors Quintilian recommends for study at this stage are all chosen because they are edifying, and any of their works that might be problematic for a "tender mind" were simply to be excluded (see Box 6.1). As discussed in the previous section, Homer enjoyed unparalleled status in antiquity and was considered not only the best poet but also a moral and religious authority. Plutarch's essay on studying poetry offers numerous examples of how, with a *grammaticus* as a guide, the Homeric **epics** could instruct boys in virtue, teaching them how to manage their emotions, discern truth from lies, and speak and conduct themselves well, all through reference to specific passages and phrases. He also shows how the words of Achilles can teach boys to control their anger and how descriptions of men and gods, both their strengths and flaws, can help them understand appropriate uses of commendation and criticism (*Mor.* 31A-D, 35A-C).

Anthony Corbeill has recently proposed that education in Roman society served "to replicate or re-produce the already existing social system."[51] This idea certainly holds true for rhetorical education and applies to earlier educational stages as well: some of the maxims were decidedly misogynistic, and the texts chosen for interpretation—mainly epic poems and Greek **tragedy**—were dominated by aristocratic warriors and noble queens, not ordinary citizens and slaves. For the boy who studied rhetoric, training in declamation not only taught him how to compose and deliver a speech but also how to exercise the prerogatives associated with being an elite male. Through the mock speeches he performed, he rehearsed the future roles he would play as a **paterfamilias** and patron who had to manage social subordinates. The plots of these speeches, which generally concern domestic and civil problems, feature the well-scripted voices of characters such as slaves, **freedpersons**, and women. The student imagined their words and tried to assign them appropriate responses and motivations. W. Martin Bloomer maintains that "the role playing of declamation trained the rather insulated upper-class adolescent in a sort of situational ethics. To a degree the student learns how others, specifically those denied the right to speak, might speak and feel in some period of crisis."[52] Yet while declamation encouraged sympathy with others, it ultimately reinforced the boy's current and future position of privilege.

The progression from acquiring the elements to *grammaticē* to studying rhetoric was called *enkyklios paideia* in Greek, which modern scholars variously translate as "common/ general education" or "circuit of education." The adjective *enkyklios* means "circular," which Cribiore suggests points to "the completeness of a program that had to envelop a student."[53] In Latin the phrase *liberalia studia* ("liberal studies") is used, reflecting a degree of exclusivity not apparent in the Greek but nevertheless shared in concept. Seneca (*Ep.* 88.2) encapsulated elite opinion when he remarked that *liberalia studia* are studies worthy of a free man. In actual fact, educationalists were not interested in freeborn children overall but only wealthy freeborn boys who would one day be the state's leaders. Poor parents were urged to do their best to provide some education to their children (Plut. *Mor.* 8E), but *enkyklios paideia* was unaffordable and unnecessary. Perhaps surprisingly, the situation is less straightforward for slaves. Though there were no legal restrictions on providing slaves a liberal education, they were generally trained only in basic literacy and vocational skills instead. There were exceptions, as we have seen, but hostility to the idea of educating slaves in the manner of the freeborn persisted (see, for example, Philo *Leg.* 166).[54]

This is similarly the case for women, as Juvenal's (6.434–56) attacks on those he deems *too* educated exemplify. Authorities seem to have agreed, though, that upper-class girls should be educated to a reasonable degree for moral purposes. For instance, philosophers were especially insistent that studying philosophy would help girls become good wives, mothers, and housekeepers who could manage their emotions.[55] Musonius Rufus, a prominent Stoic teacher of the first century CE, expounds such views in his third and fourth lectures, "Women Too Should Study Philosophy" and "Daughters Should Have the Same Education as Sons," respectively.[56] Plutarch (*Mor.* 145A–146A) likewise reminds Eurydice, a new bride, of the lessons she learned with him as a girl and encourages her to continue studying philosophy, as well as mathematics, under the tutelage of her husband because such studies will keep her from immoral behaviour.

For both sexes, provision of good role models and careful supervision were important to ensuring proper development. Seneca (*Helv.* 18.8) echoes familiar sentiments when he tells his mother, Helvia, who was raising her granddaughter Novatilla, that "now is the time to order her character" and insists that "you will give her much even if you give her nothing but your example."[57] Several authors record considerable parental involvement in children's education, though some portraits are undoubtedly idealized. For instance, the young Augustus's mother and stepfather are said to have asked his teachers and slave attendants about his studies, activities, and companions on a daily basis (Nic. Dam. 3.6). Fathers traditionally took an active role in their sons' education, as Cicero did in arranging successive teachers for Marcus and Quintus. Cato the Elder, however, was probably atypical in undertaking all of his son's education from early childhood, apparently because he did not want him to be criticized by a slave or indebted to one for his knowledge (Plut. *Cat. Mai.* 20.3–4).

Many upper-class parents, however, relied heavily on slave childminders, whose influence on children was thought to be significant and therefore a source of great concern (see, for example, Quint. *Inst.* 1.1.4, 1.1.8; Plut. *Mor.* 4A). Seneca (*De ira* 2.21.9) aptly summed up prevailing worries: "Every young thing attaches itself to what is nearest and grows to be like it; the character of their nurses and pedagogues is presently reproduced in that of the young men."[58] Pedagogues especially had to be reliable and exhibit moral integrity because they accompanied children to school through streets filled with dangers, particularly for boys who might be the target of unwanted sexual advances.[59]

Concern for the welfare of children while under their teachers' care seems to have only increased. Sources routinely complain about teachers' questionable behaviour and suggest that it was difficult to find ones above reproach. Instructors' use of corporal punishment and anger, such as Martial's (9.68) *ludi magister* displays, are actually among the lesser offences that troubled people.[60] Quintilian (*Inst.* 1.2.2–5) contends that, at school or at home, a child's morals could be corrupted by the wrong sort of teacher. This statement seems to refer to some form of sexual impropriety, as was apparently the reason for the dismissal of Caecilius Epirota (Suet. *Gram.* 16.1).

Compare Chapter 8, p. 182–3, on concerns about predatory teachers.

Some teachers were notorious for misconduct. For example, Suetonius (*Gram.* 23.2) claims that the emperors Tiberius and Claudius publicly declared that Quintus Remmius Palaemon was the last person who should be entrusted to educate boys or young men. No doubt because of the prevalence of these concerns, those who were free from scandal celebrated that fact. The epitaph of Furius Philocalus boasts that he behaved towards his students with the highest morality (*CIL* 10.3969).

Teachers could also be the target of criticism, and sometimes contempt, on account of their low socio-economic standing. Many of the *grammatici* and *rhetores* in Suetonius's *On Teachers of Grammar and Rhetoric* were slaves or former slaves. While some are known to have received large salaries, teachers generally seem to have been poorly paid and might

Compare Chapter 7, pp. 147–8, on servile and foreign tutors.

have supplemented their teaching income. Cribiore suggests that Furius Philocalus did so by "faithfully [writing] out wills."[61] A character in Juvenal's seventh *Satire* (7.150–78) complains bitterly about the stinginess of parents who do not want to pay fair wages for their children's teachers. He also rails against other indignities teachers suffer. Some had to teach in places that even blacksmiths or wool carders would not use for training apprentices, areas lit by smelly lamps that covered the students' copies of Vergil and Horace with soot (Juv. 7.219–27). Others must deal with unreasonable expectations of parents who insist *grammatici* have vast knowledge at their fingertips and who test them by asking questions concerning minor literary characters or obscure events (7.229–36).

Juvenal surely exaggerates, but presumably readers found some degree of truth in his portrayal.

Summary

The combination of literary, papyrological, and epigraphic sources from across the Roman world help to create a vivid picture of teaching and learning during the central period. Given the bias of authors in the period with which this chapter is concerned, we are well informed about the educational experiences of freeborn children of the upper classes, particularly boys (who, as budding orators and future leaders, were the authors' main focus). Children began the learning process at home, through exposure to the alphabet and, ideally, the proper ways of speaking by listening to their parents, slave companions, and the nurses and pedagogues who spent a great deal of time overseeing their activities. Formal studies, either at home with a private tutor or in school, began around the age of seven and focused on the foundations of reading and writing.

Several years of studying *grammaticē* under the direction of a *grammaticus* followed, often until boys were in their early teens. This stage concentrated on developing oral communication and studying literature, chiefly poetic texts that were used to teach many subjects, including grammar, linguistics, and history. Upper-class girls generally appear to have studied privately with *grammatici* rather than to have attended public schools, and some continued their studies at this stage even after marriage in their early teens. For elite boys, the pinnacle of their education was the study of rhetoric and declamation, in which they learned how to compose and deliver speeches of the sort they hoped to give in a courtroom or political forum once they reached adulthood.

Less affluent freeborn children and slaves of both sexes pursued a rather different course. Basic education in reading and writing was probably attainable for many, and some boys of modest means were able to complete studies in *grammaticē*. Certainly some slaves, such as those whose jobs involved intellectual tasks, received education beyond the basics, whether they attended schools, special training establishments in *paedagogia*, or were instructed by their masters. Yet most slaves and poor freeborn children did not have the opportunity to proceed with formal education. Instead, they engaged in vocational training, sometimes through long and arduous apprenticeships, to become weavers, stonemasons, or artisans.

While these children needed to learn useful skills to contribute economically to their households or, in the case of slaves, to become valuable assets at sale, the goal of education for those of means (especially the upper classes) was predominantly ethical. At all levels, teachers chose material that would simultaneously allow students to improve reading and writing skills and improve themselves. Early exercises entailed copying and reading maxims that were intended to remain with students for life. Many firmly believed that children needed character formation and that early childhood, when their minds were still pliable, was the time to begin. Of course, this malleability was also cause for concern, given that children spent considerable time in the company of nurses and peda-gogues, not to mention teachers, many of whom had suspect reputations. The potential influence of childminders, teachers, and companions was always a consideration, even as students continued to receive ethical instruction through the study of grammar and lit-erature (especially of Homer, a moral authority in his own right). When aristocratic boys reached the final phase of their studies, they put some of the lessons they had learned into practice by fashioning speeches in the personae of elite men who had enjoyed the benefits and privileges that status and education afforded.

Questions for Review and Discussion

1.   What roles were slave nurses and pedagogues thought to play in children's early intellectual development? What concerns, if any, did parents have about this in-volvement in their children's education?
2.   Contrast the education of upper-class girls with that of boys. Are these differences significant? Why or why not?
3.   Did slaves have opportunities to acquire skills in literacy? What types of jobs did they perform and how were they trained?
4.   How did the content of the first two stages of education pertain to the goals set out by educationalists such as Quintilian and Plutarch?
5.   What place did poetry, and the Homeric epics in particular, have in Roman education?

Suggested Reading

Bloomer, W.M. 1997. "Schooling in Persona: Imagination and Subordination in Roman Education." *Classical Antiquity* 16: 57–78.

This article explores the contribution of school declamation exercises to the socialization of elite boys.

Cribiore, R. 2001. *Gymnastics of the Mind: Greek Education in Hellenistic and Roman Egypt.* Princeton, NJ: Princeton University Press.

Cribiore presents a very accessible and engaging study that combines lit-erary and papyrological sources for the content and goals of each stage of education, as well as evidence for students, parents, and teachers.

Forbes, C.A. 1955. "The Education and Training of Slaves in Antiquity." *Transactions of the American Philological Association* 86: 321–60.

This article builds on an earlier examination of the subject and covers topics such as *paedagogia*, apprenticeships, and medical training.

Hemelrijk, E.A. 1999. Matrona Docta: *Educated Women in the Roman Elite from Cornelia to Julia Domna*. London and New York: Routledge.

Hemelrijk's book is a good discussion of evidence for the education of elite girls, especially attested aims and probable motives, as well as male attitudes towards well-educated women.

Joyal, M., I. McDougall, and J.C. Yardley, eds. 2009. *Greek and Roman Education: A Sourcebook*. London and New York: Routledge.

This sourcebook offers a very useful collection of literary, papyrological, and art historical sources, each prefaced by a helpful introduction that discusses pertinent details and includes select bibliography.

Morgan, T. 1998. *Literate Education in the Hellenistic and Roman Worlds*. Cambridge: Cambridge University Press.

This study is particularly helpful regarding the ethical aims of *enkyklios paideia* and the relationship of content to objectives and outcomes in educating the freeborn, especially wealthy males.

Rawson, B. 2003. *Children and Childhood in Roman Italy*. Oxford: Oxford University Press.

The lengthy chapter on education covers all the areas treated here substantially, though its focus on Italy precludes the evidence of papyri school texts.

Too, Y.L., ed. 2001. *Education in Greek and Roman Antiquity*. Leiden, The Netherlands: Brill.

This collection offers more detailed analysis of some topics considered here (for example, declamation) and explores others, including philosophical studies and the relationship between Christianity and traditional Roman education.

Notes

1   I am grateful to the Humanities Research Institute at Brock University for an award in 2010–11 that facilitated research for this project.
2   Translated by Costa (2005: 9–10).
3   *P.Bour.* 1.
4   These children might be "milk-mates" (*collactanei*), children nursed by the same woman. See Bradley (1991: 149–54).
5   On childminding figures, see Bradley (1991: 13–75).
6   On private libraries and girls' education, see Hemelrijk (1999: 54–5) and Rawson (2003: 200).
7   Shumka (1993).
8   Wiedemann (1989: 150–1).
9   Bradley (1998: 523–57).
10 Cribiore (1996: 184, no. 44; 2001: 166).

11 Students seem to have learned numbers only after cementing knowledge of the alphabet, according to Cribiore (2001: 183).

12 There were no fixed ages for schooling, and attendance was not required by the state.

13 Bonner (1977: 24–33) examines evidence for tutors, particularly in the late Republic; Hemelrijk (1999: 21–2) treats Attica and Pompeia's early education.

14 See Cribiore (2001: 94–7) for discussion of these letters.

15 Pictured in Rawson (2003: 161).

16 Translated by Cohoon (1939).

17 Bonner (1977: 117–18, with Figure 11).

18 Cribiore (2001: 21–8).

19 Translated by Wright (1933).

20 Johnson (2011: 446); Cribiore (2001: 172–3).

21 Morgan (1998: 101).

22 Cribiore (1996: 197, nos. 100 and 101).

23 Cribiore (2001: 179).

24 Ibid.: 190.

25 Translated by Usher (1985).

26 Cribiore (2001: 183). While one estimate for Italy proposes a low 15 per cent, Rawson (2003: 146) notes that others are more optimistic.

27 Rawson (2003: 187).

28 For this convincing interpretation, see Booth (1979: 11–19).

29 Mohler (1940: 279); Rawson (2003: 189–90).

30 For the boys' teachers, see Bonner (1977: 28–30).

31 Hemelrijk (1999: 22).

32 Suet. Gram. 16.1.

33 Translations of Quintilian are from Russell (2002).

34 Among Greek authors, Homer, Euripides, and Menander were the most common: Morgan (1998: 313, Table 15 [for numbers of texts]) and Cribiore (2001: 194–201).

35 Morgan (1998: 105); Cribiore (2001: 194–7).

36 See Bonner (1977: 250–76) and Cribiore (2001: 220–30) for progynmasmata and literary texts previously studied.

37 Cribiore (2001: 232–4) examines differences between Latin and Greek declamatory exercises.

38 On the *toga virilis* ceremony, including its connections with advanced studies, see Dolansky (2008).

39 Hemelrijk (1999: 24, 76–7).

40 For husbands teaching their (often much younger) wives, see Hemelrijk (1999: 31–6).

41 Watson (1969: 54–74) discusses what training entailed for new recruits. Only Roman citizens could serve in the army, so boys did not serve until they had come of age and received the *toga virilis*, which distinguished them as citizen men; this often took place around the age of 15 or 16, though there was no fixed age.

42 Bradley (1991: 107–12) assesses the apprenticeship contracts, such as the examples that follow. These can be found in the Loeb Classical Library (*Select Papyri*, vol. 1).

43 Forbes (1955: 333).

44 Bradley (1991: 112–16).

45 Mohler (1940: 263).

46 Kleijwegt (1991: 156–63) details medical training and Galen's career.

47 Plut. *Mor.* 4C. Translated by Babbitt (1927).

48 Morgan (1998: 125).

49 Ibid.: 131.

50 Ibid.: 135–7.

51 Corbeill (2001: 262).

52 Bloomer (1997: 63).

53 Cribiore (2001: 129). *Enkyklios paideia* was not, however, comprehensive. Morgan (1998: 33) proposes that mathematics, music, philosophy, and astronomy were commonly grouped under this term, yet ancient opinions varied regarding the extent to which such subjects should receive attention. See Corbeill (2001: 261–87) for concerns over some subjects' Greek origins.

54 On slaves and *liberalia studia*, see Booth (1979: 15); Mohler (1940: 264); and Forbes (1955: 322–3).

55 For other motives, see Hemelrijk (1999: 64–75).

56 Both lectures are in Lutz (1947), with the Greek text and corresponding English translation. Excerpts from Musonius's fourth lecture can also conveniently be found in Joyal, McDougall, and Yardley (2009: 185–6, no. 8.18).

57 Translated by Basore (1932).

58 Translated by Basore (1928).

59 Rawson (2003: 166–7) discusses female pedagogues.

60 Rawson (2003: 175–7) and Cribiore (2001: 65–73) discuss corporal punishment in education, which some Romans staunchly opposed for freeborn children.

61 See Cribiore (2001: 61, 59–65) on the socio-economic status of teachers in Graeco-Roman Egypt. Rawson (2003: 177–9) provides details for teachers in Italy.

7

Latin Literature

Luke Roman

> Although I am separated from home . . . and fatherland, and though every-
> thing that can be taken from me has been taken, yet my literary talent still
> accompanies me, I still have recourse to my talent: Caesar was not able to
> wield power over this. (Ov. *Tr.* 3.7.45–8)[1]

In 8 CE the Roman poet Ovid was relegated by imperial decree to the shores of the
Black Sea. According to Ovid, the emperor Augustus sent him there for two reasons:
a poem—the notorious *Art of Love* (*Ars Amatoria*), which went against the grain of
the emperor's moral legislation—and a "mistake." The exact nature of the mistake
remains unknown, but it is possible that Ovid had knowledge of some treasonous
behaviour that he did not report to the emperor. Even in this remote outpost, relegated
to a land he considered deeply "uncivilized," Ovid continued writing poetry, seeking
pardon from the emperor and, at the same time, maintaining contact with his literary
public in Rome and throughout the empire. It is impressive testimony to the power of
literature in ancient Rome that Ovid, deprived of his home and everything he once
considered important, continued to promote his image as poetic author through a
medium of expression that eluded even the emperor's control: the creation and circulation of literary works.

This chapter examines the literature of ancient Rome. Literature, as shall be made
clear in the course of the discussion, was not a pursuit consigned to the margins of
Roman history and society. Roman literature formed part of, contributed to, and
reflected on the social, political, and historical phenomena that furnish the topics of
this book. Literary activity was connected to Roman politics, the history of Roman
imperialism and cultural interchange with the Greek world, issues of social class and
social mobility, the circulation of Roman culture and language throughout the provinces, and the self-definition and self-promotion of the Roman elite.

Timeline

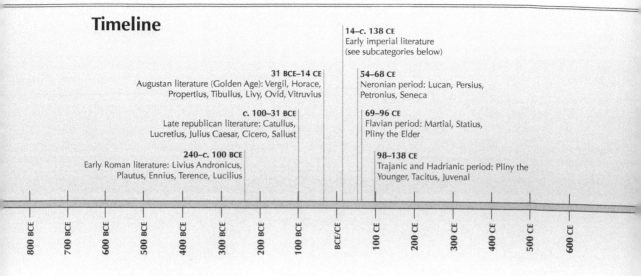

14–c. 138 CE
Early imperial literature
(see subcategories below)

31 BCE–14 CE
Augustan literature (Golden Age): Vergil, Horace,
Propertius, Tibullus, Livy, Ovid, Vitruvius

54–68 CE
Neronian period: Lucan, Persius,
Petronius, Seneca

c. 100–31 BCE
Late republican literature: Catullus,
Lucretius, Julius Caesar, Cicero, Sallust

69–96 CE
Flavian period: Martial, Statius,
Pliny the Elder

240–c. 100 BCE
Early Roman literature: Livius Andronicus,
Plautus, Ennius, Terence, Lucilius

98–138 CE
Trajanic and Hadrianic period: Pliny the
Younger, Tacitus, Juvenal

| 800 BCE | 700 BCE | 600 BCE | 500 BCE | 400 BCE | 300 BCE | 200 BCE | 100 BCE | BCE/CE | 100 CE | 200 CE | 300 CE | 400 CE | 500 CE | 600 CE |

Introduction

This chapter offers a critical examination of the basic terms, concepts, and narratives relevant to the understanding and interpretation of Roman literature. A consideration of the term *literature* and its applicability to ancient Rome is followed by a brief critical overview of the chronology and periods of Roman literature as well as some of the historical narratives that have been used to characterize the different phases of Roman literary production. A section on Greece and Rome explores the trajectory of Roman literary history in greater detail, with a focus on the relation between Roman writers and their Greek models. The chapter then considers the social dynamics of Roman literature and the roles and functions of literary practices among the Roman elite. The final section examines narratives of literary decline in the early imperial period.

———•◆•———

Defining *Literature*

Pliny the Younger was a member of the elite **class** and an active participant in public life under the emperors Domitian and Trajan. He was also an author, most notably of the *Epistulae*, a highly polished collection of letters addressed to his friends and colleagues but intended for a broader audience. In a letter addressed to his friend Caninius Rufus, Pliny evokes the splendid elegance of his friend's villa—the setting *par excellence* for literary pursuits among upper-class Romans (see Box 7.1). In the traditional Roman

Primary Source

Box 7.1: Pliny, *Letters*, 1.3.[1]

I wonder how our darling Comum is looking, and your lovely house outside the town, with its colonnade where it is always springtime, and the shady plane trees, the stream with its sparkling greenish water flowing into the lake below, and the drive over the smooth firm turf. Your baths which are full of sunshine all day, the dining-rooms large and small, the bedrooms for night or the day's siesta—are you there and enjoying them all in turn, or are you as usual for ever being called away to look after your affairs? If you are there, you are a lucky man to be so happy; if not, you do no better than the rest of us. But isn't it really time you handed over those tiresome petty duties to someone else and devoted yourself to literary studies in the peace and comfort of your retreat? Let this be your business, this your leisure, this your toil, this your rest; to these pursuits let your wakefulness be devoted, to these pursuits devote even your sleep. Shape and hammer out something to be yours for all time; for everything else you possess will fall to one or another master after you are dead, but this will never cease to be yours once it has come into being. I know the spirit and ability I am addressing, but you must try now to have the high opinion of yourself which the world will come to share if you do.

Note

1. Adapted from Radice (1963).

view, literature was an occasional diversion of *otium* ("leisure"), subordinate to *negotium* ("business") and *officia* ("duties"). Yet Pliny's letter presents literature as an elite Roman's deeper, truer occupation, the site of his most important ambitions. Although Pliny recognizes that a man of Caninius Rufus's standing must have many important occupations, he hopes that his friend will find time and inspiration to devote himself, more deeply and thoroughly, to an existence of literary withdrawal (*secessus*). Pliny's paradoxical wording suggests the extent to which literary pursuits, by the early second century CE, might be seen as forming part of a Roman man's public reputation: "Let this be your business, this your leisure, this your toil, this your rest; to these pursuits let your wakefulness be devoted, to these pursuits devote even your sleep."

Pliny's letter in some sense represents the culmination of an ongoing debate—some three centuries in duration—over the question of the place and value of literature in Roman society. Literature was for a long time seen as the province of Greek professionals and not as an activity appropriate for Romans of

Compare Chapter 6, p. 130, ⬅
Chapter 15, pp. 329–30 and 336–7,
Chapter 16, p. 373, and
Chapter 17, p. 378, on pursuits
considered suitable or unsuitable
for men of the Roman elite.

any standing. Over time, however, aristocratic Romans began to take an interest in producing works of literature, albeit within the circumscribed frame of leisure. Pliny's deliberate blurring of the boundaries between *otium* and *negotium* is all the more striking when read against the background of the long negotiation of literature's shifting place within Rome's social and cultural hierarchies. Whereas literary pursuits generally belong to the time of leisure and the space of the villa, some Roman writers came to harbour literary ambitions that exceeded an amateur's amusement.

→ Compare Chapter 6, pp. 125–6, on literature as part of education and Chapter 12, pp. 266–8, on the performance of plays.

The broader impact of literature extended beyond the sphere of elite leisure practices. Literature was also at the core of the Roman educational system both in Italy and throughout the empire, and other practices that might be defined as literary—the performance of plays, for example—enjoyed a large audience. Even if literature was initially defined as belonging to the space of leisure, literary competence and literary works played important roles in spheres of activity categorized as *negotium*. Politicians and orators employed rhetorical techniques deriving from their literary education and circulated texts of their speeches, letters, and other works that contributed to their public image; works of literature embodied exemplary moral values that influenced political and moral behaviour; and Roman literary texts copied and circulated throughout the empire played a crucial role in the diffusion of Roman culture and the Latin language.

It is not only the time and space of literature that were subject to change and varying definitions but also the very content of the term *literature*. Roman literature might equally encompass works of technical instruction, such as Frontinus's *On Aqueducts* and Vitruvius's *On Architecture*; the love poetry of Ovid; the philosophical works of Cicero; or the *Annals* of the

→ Compare Chapter 16, pp. 359–60, on Frontinus and Vitruvius.

historian Tacitus. All these works might have been designated by Pliny's catch-all term *studia* ("studies," or "literary/intellectual pursuits"). Other terms that might approximate our word *literature* are likewise broad in meaning: *litterae*, which is simply the plural of the Latin word for "letter," signifies literature in a very general sense but also means "written records," "history," "learning," "scholarship," and "liberal culture." Comparably, a *monumentum* is anything that provides a memorial. Thus *monumenta* might refer to buildings, tombs, historical chronicles, or works of literature.

While internal divisions between different genres are carefully marked in Roman literature, there is no blanket criterion distinguishing between essentially literary traits and more utilitarian scholarly and scientific works. Tacitus is often hailed as a highly scrupulous historian who discusses his sources and makes a show of rejecting lurid rumours and anecdotes, yet he is also clearly a master stylist who offered his spin on historical material already well known in the elite circles that constituted his prime audience. Did people read him to learn the lessons of history or to enjoy his dense, elliptical prose style and devastating **sententiae** ("one-liners")? In the modern world, fictionality is an important criterion that separates works of literature such as novels from reportage and other forms of non-fiction. For the Romans, however, there was not always a clear divide between mythology and history. History was often mythologized and mythology rationalized and treated as history. Ovid's *Metamorphoses*, for example, is an **epic** poem that extends from the creation of the universe to the author's own times and includes tales drawn from the vast repertoire of Classical and Near Eastern mythology (Daphne, Echo and Narcissus, Midas), Roman historical legend (Romulus, Remus, Aeneas), and recent historical events (the death and subsequent deification of Julius Caesar).

About half a century later, under the emperor Nero, Lucan's epic poem *Civil War* narrated the conflict between Julius Caesar and Pompey the Great in the dying decades of the Roman Republic. Lucan's magnificently grim epic takes relatively recent history as its subject matter and avoids the usual poetic device of Olympian gods manipulating the destinies of mortals. So conspicuous was Lucan's break with poetic conventions that some people wondered aloud whether he was truly a poet. To them the **epigrammatist** Martial (14.194) wittily responded that Lucan's bookseller does not doubt his status as a poet. Fictionality, it seems, does not provide a hard-and-fast criterion of ancient Roman literariness.

The fact that Roman literary production is so diverse and lacks a clear set of criteria has led some modern scholars to deny that the Romans had a concept of literature. Such wholesale denial may be going too far, however. It is worth recalling that, even in the modern world, "literature" can have a broad and slippery significance and can include works as varied as the plays of Shakespeare, the Harry Potter novels, the works of Jane Austen, the satires of Jonathan Swift, *Beowulf*, short stories published in *The New Yorker*, the latest winner of the Man Booker Prize, Gibbon's *Decline and Fall of the Roman Empire*, the personal correspondence of a famous author, and a slim volume of obscure postmodern verse published by a university press. The latest critical approaches display a fondness for "decentring" canonical texts and eroding the boundary between the literary and the subliterary. Some contemporary avant-garde works are explicitly devoted to undermining such boundaries. The impulse to set quotation marks around the term *literature* applies no less to the modern world than to ancient Rome.

What *does* define Roman literature, then? Perhaps there is a clue in the passage cited in Box 7.1: Pliny exhorted his friend to "hammer out something" of eternal value. The specification of content and mode is vague, but the emphasis on perennial endurance is marked. At the core of Roman literary practices, and Roman culture more generally, is an emphasis on commemoration, tradition, preservation over time, and memory. The literary "monuments" of Rome are the works of authors deemed important enough to preserve and remember. These works exemplify key aspects of Roman society, preserve the memory of exceptional individuals, and constitute a contribution to Rome's cultural fabric. The Roman consciousness of the passage of time, and the capacity of the literary work to withstand time's destructive force, is striking and unusual. In the first poem of his collection, the late republican poet Catullus introduces his "spruce new book" with the wish that it might endure "more than one generation." In another poem (95), he condemns the atrociously bad works of a contemporary poet to a humiliating, short-term use: Volusius's *Annales* will be recycled as wrapping for fish. The Augustan poet Horace (*Carm.* 3.30) states that he has built "a monument more lasting than bronze," that his poetry will be read as long as Rome's social fabric endures, and that "the greater part of him" will survive death. Finally, in the closing lines of the *Metamorphoses*, Ovid (15.879) claims, simply and magnificently, "I shall live" (*vivam*).

This fierce determination to conquer time through the power of literary eloquence may be the single most important idea contributed by Rome to the traditions of Western literature. Furthermore, it constitutes a key point of contact between our own concept of literature and the Roman conceptions of literary activity that continue to inform literary practices today.

Chronology

It is important to be aware of the traditional periodization of Roman literature and to understand its limitations. The following pages offer a brief consideration and critique of such chronological divisions. Most of the literary texts discussed in this chapter were written between the second century BCE and the second century CE. The earliest major Roman authors (Livius Andronicus, Ennius, Plautus, Terence) were active from the late third century BCE to the earlier half of the second century BCE. During this time, Rome was at the height of its glory in military terms—the Carthaginian Wars and the subsequent conquest of the great Hellenistic kingdoms in the Greek East—but Roman literature was in its infancy. It is not until the late Republic, which corresponds roughly to the first century BCE, that we begin to see the authors more commonly taught in high school and university courses and more commonly admired in scholarly articles: Catullus, Lucretius, Cicero, and Julius Caesar. While political culture in these years was violent, disordered, and increasingly dysfunctional, literary culture was rising to new heights of sophistication. Works written in this period are by turns learned and obscene, technical and colloquial, provocative and urbane, self-promoting and self-effacing. Late republican literature has all the uneven brilliance of a period of discovery and experimentation.

An especially important development of this period is the increasing influence of Hellenistic poetry, that is, poetry written in Greek during the post-classical period, mostly in Alexandria in the third century BCE. The Alexandrian Greek poet Callimachus had announced certain orienting principles of poetics in the prologue to his *Aetia*. Specifically, he declared his preference for erudite, intricate, and densely worked poetry, often on exotic topics, and his disdain for less refined, more conventional, and more popular works. Hellenistic literature had exerted influence on Roman writers from the earliest period of Latin literature, but in the mid-first century BCE Roman writers articulated (or invented) their own version of Callimacheanism with more explicit enthusiasm. At the same time, they distanced themselves from the public poetic genres that were traditionally accepted in Rome. The poets of this generation, such as Catullus, have been dubbed *neoteroi* (Greek for "the more recent ones") or "new poets" by modern scholars on the basis of some stray remarks in Cicero's writing (see *Att.* 7.2.1, *Orat.* 161, and *Tusc.* 3.45). The fierce devotion to aspects of Hellenistic aesthetics—at the time a relatively new and provocative enthusiasm—was subsequently incorporated as a regular feature of Roman poetry.

The following period saw a new form of government emerge out of the wreckage of republican civil conflict. The young Octavian, later called Augustus, managed to defeat his sole remaining rival, Marcus Antonius (Marc Antony), in 31 BCE at the Battle of Actium and became Rome's first emperor (or, as he put it, *princeps*). It is often justly observed that Augustus concealed the immense transformations that he was bringing about in Roman society behind the facade of conservative republicanism, respect for the *mos maiorum* ("the way of the ancestors"), and the restoration of Rome's pristine, archaic *virtus* ("manly excellence"; "valour"). Literature produced during the Augustan period manifests a similar tendency: some of the boldest, most innovative, and even baroque works in the Roman tradition were nonetheless devoted to promoting the image of a "new age" imbued with the serene elegance of classical Greece. Poets wrote on grand contemporary themes, such as Augustus's military victories and his pacification of the known world.

At the same time, citing the literary ideals of Callimachus, these poets declared their refusal (*recusatio*) to write dull **panegyric**. Now Rome could boast an array of canonical works rivalling the Greek masterpieces in the major genres. Examples of poetic works include Vergil's *Aeneid* (epic), Horace's *Odes* (**lyric**), Ovid's *Medea* and Varius's *Thyestes* (**tragedy**), Vergil's *Georgics* (**didactic**) and *Eclogues* (**pastoral**), and Ovid's *Fasti* and *Propertius* Book 4 (**aetiological elegy**). Among the prose works produced in this period were Livy's monumental history of the city of Rome and Vitruvius's influential *On Architecture*. Many of these works are brilliantly eccentric, and every Augustan author seems to have approached the question of how to write a classic work from his own unique angle.

Employing a metaphor that derives from the Augustan writers, modern scholars have come to refer to the Augustan cohort of poets, along with some select predecessors, as constituting the Golden Age of Latin literature. According to this simplifying scheme, the following age of literature is inevitably inferior and hence is called the Silver Age. As we shall see, the literature of the early imperial period (the first and second centuries CE) can hardly be classified as inferior in blanket terms, although authors working under the Julio-Claudian and Flavian emperors do engage intensely, persistently, and at times anxiously with the now canonical works of the Augustan period. The extent to which the assessment of modern scholars has been influenced by the self-description of the ancient authors themselves is striking. The Augustans heralded themselves as the denizens of a new Golden Age, but their successors often denigrated their own abilities and lamented the decline of literary culture. The Augustans also succeeded in demoting middle republican authors from the pedestal of revered antiquity by referring to their rough, "unkempt" style and lack of metrical sophistication. More recent scholarship has scrutinized these inherited categories and narratives. It is important to both appreciate the ways in which Roman authors describe their own literary history and recognize the limits of those narratives, especially in cases where acceptance would involve underestimating works of significant interest and value.

Finally, we should at least briefly ponder one simple question whose answer is unexpectedly elusive: When does Latin literature end? Traditionally, the classical period extends no further than the second century CE, concluding with the brilliant, intricate, and strange *Metamorphoses*, or *Golden Ass*, a novel written by the North African writer and rhetorician Apuleius. The social and political instability of the third century CE, followed by the distinct governing style of the **tetrarchy** and the subsequent Christianization of the Roman Empire in the fourth century CE, have been traditionally identified as developments that initiated a radical break with the social structures, political culture, and geographical disposition of the classical Roman Empire. On the other hand, the works of the so-called Church Fathers Augustine and Jerome in the third and fourth centuries CE betray a deep immersion in classical literary culture. In a particularly harrowing dream, a heavenly voice famously intoned to Jerome (*Ep.* 22.30): "You are a Ciceronian, not a Christian."

We could go yet further. Medieval authors such as the Archpoet continued to write in Latin and to mark their participation in the classical Roman tradition, while Latin plays written in the twelfth century by clerics in the Loire valley recall the comedies of Plautus and Terence. Finally, humanist writers of the Renaissance, such as Petrarch, Poliziano, and Giovanni Pontano, considered themselves the peers and successors of Cicero, Catullus, and Vergil. In one striking instance, Petrarch addressed letters, in Latin, to classical Latin authors, employing the characteristic themes and tropes of their own writings in order to engage them in a dialogue across centuries.[2]

Greece and Rome

The traditional date given for the beginning of Latin literature is 240 BCE, when Livius Andronicus is said to have presented a tragedy at the *Ludi Romani*, the "Roman Games" (Cic. *Brut.* 18.72–4, *Sen.* 50). To many scholars, such a beginning seems suspiciously abrupt. Drawing on scattered hints (such as those in Cic. *Tusc.* 4.2.3 and *Brut.* 75), they have reconstructed, or at least tried to imagine, earlier literary practices. It is worth considering, however, that literature in Rome may have emerged quite suddenly through a series of calculated actions rather than through a gradual, "natural" development.[3]

⇥ Compare Chapter 12, pp. 268–70, and Chapter 17, pp. 380–3, on the adoption of foreign literary themes and architectural styles.

Repeated acts of deliberate but controlled adoption of foreign cultural practices are a discernible pattern in the development of Roman culture. One example is especially instructive. According to Livy (29.10–110), in 210 BCE—a time of serious military threat and the height of the Second Punic War—the Romans solicited divine advice through oracles. On the strength of the gods' responses, they moved the aniconic black stone representing the Anatolian goddess Cybele, or Mater Magna ("the Great Mother"), from Pessinus in Asia Minor to the Temple of Victory on Rome's Palatine Hill. The Romans subsequently instituted her cult and established her festival, the *Ludi Megalenses* ("Megalesian Games"). Because of her orgi-

Compare Chapter 9, pp. 204–7, on the Mater Magna and the integration of foreign cults into the city of Rome and Chapter 12, p. 266, on the *Megalenses*.

astic rites, however, Cybele was viewed with suspicion at Rome. Romans were forbidden to serve as her castrated ritual attendants (*Galli*); for this task, Easterners had to be imported.

Although Cybele was viewed as foreign, dangerous, and therefore something to be contained within certain boundaries, she was enthusiastically appropriated by the Romans and incorporated into the urban and religious fabric. Plays were often performed on the occasion of Cybele's festival and, according to one scholar's reconstruction, before the steps of her temple on the Palatine Hill.[4] The links are suggestive and the comparison instructive: literature was also an import that the Romans first began to appropriate during the period of the Punic Wars, when Rome went from being the major power in Italy to the dominant power in the Mediterranean.

Moreover, the authors who created Roman literature were, in almost every instance, not born in Rome but often hailed from other regions of Italy and were fluent in two or more languages. Italy in the middle republican period was militarily dominated by Rome but remained highly diverse both culturally and linguistically, with non-Latin languages (including Greek) flourishing throughout the various regions of the peninsula. Rome's earliest writers were men such as Livius Andronicus, who, according to some versions of his biography, came from the city of Tarentum (originally a Greek colony in southern Italy) as a captive of war and was a slave tutor to the conquering general's children before eventually being freed. It is hard to know if any of these details are true—in general the biographies of ancient poets are notoriously unreliable—but Livius's life story fits the pattern of other early Roman writers. According to ancient biographical tradition, they came from outside Rome (in some cases from major centres of Greek culture, such as Tarentum), had a low and even servile social **status** in Rome and were involved in the education of aristocratic youth.

Compare Chapter 6, pp. 120, 125 and 133, on the role of slaves as educators.

It is not enough to suggest that Rome was influenced by the precedent of Greek literature. The appropriation of literature and literary practices by the Romans was at once more deliberate, more decisive, and, in some instances, more

Compare Chapter 14, pp. 309–17, on Roman expansion in the Republic.

violent. The Roman importation and institution of literature and literary practices need to be understood within the context of war and imperialism during the middle Republic. As they conquered Italy, then Carthage (their major Mediterranean rival), and the Hellenistic Monarchies, the Romans not only annexed lands and brought home plunder of the usual sort but also imported books, entire libraries, art objects, architectural forms, and even Greek intellectuals who had been captured in war. In many cases, the aristocratic captors developed an admiration for the learning and cultivation of their educated Greek slaves, rewarded them with freedom, and, as time went on, began to develop literary interests themselves.

→ Compare Chapter 4, pp. 77–9, on warfare as a source of slaves.

Later, in the first century BCE (when literature was a more familiar pursuit among the educated classes), Horace (*Epist.* 2.1.156) observed with irony that "captive Greece took its brutal conqueror captive." Another example of this pattern is the great historian of the Roman Republic, the Greek writer Polybius. A supporter of the Achaean League, Polybius originally opposed Rome, was imprisoned, and ended up in Rome as a captive of war. Eventually, however, he developed a friendship with one of the leading aristocratic Roman statesman of the age, Cornelius Scipio Aemilianus. Remaining in Rome, Polybius wrote a penetrating history of Rome's rise to power in the Mediterranean.

→ Compare Chapter 5, p. 106, on Cornelius Scipio Aemilianus.

For the first Roman writers and audiences, literature simply was a Greek thing because Greece was the one civilization that Rome had close and sustained cultural contact with and the only one that had a literature. Therefore, when the Roman elite began to appropriate and import certain literary practices, they hewed very closely to Greek categories, in part because the professional literary artisans they hired came from a Greek background. The forms of Roman literature produced in the third and second centuries BCE corresponded to major Greek poetic genres: tragedy, **comedy**, and epic. These genres, however, were also carefully selected from a much broader range of possibilities. The Romans displayed a particular interest in genres with a strong public appeal, such as plays for performance at public festivals (**ludi**) organized by Roman magistrates and epic poetry that commemorated the deeds of Roman heroes, celebrated the greatness of the Roman state, and promoted the convergence of elite and communal values.

The pattern of appropriation at this stage is hardly one of wholesale importation of Greek literary practices and modes. As in the carefully controlled adoption of the cult of Cybele, the uses and contexts of literature in the early Roman milieu are closely circumscribed. The situation of Roman **drama** is a good example. Greek comedy adapted to the Latin stage (*comoedia palliata*, "comedy in Greek dress") was immensely popular among Roman audiences, yet, despite a few failed initiatives, the Romans did not complete a permanent stone **theatre** structure until the Theatre of Pompey in 55 BCE. The **senate** was presumably reluctant to concede that dramatic spectacle was part of civic life to the point of altering the public face of the city.[5] The progress of Greek culture among Romans of the Republic follows a familiar pattern: continual acts of importation, incorporation, translation, and acquisition accompanied by a no less continual expression of disdain for such Greek refinement

→ Compare Chapter 9, p. 200, and Chapter 12, pp. 266–7, on the Theatre of Pompey.

as unbefitting Romans or being more appropriate for their occasional diversion than for serious devotion.

Ultimately, the drive to appropriate was more powerful and consequential than the impulse to express contempt for or limit the adopted practices. One indication of the Romans' genuine enthusiasm for Greek literary culture is the ferocious originality with which they approached the task of imitation. The early Roman playwrights Plautus and Terence wrote comedies usually based on specific Greek exemplars, yet all the evidence we possess suggests that they altered, cut, expanded, and transformed their models with extraordinary freedom and even a certain playful impudence. From the beginning, Roman versions of Greek genres displayed a distinctive spirit of play (*lusus, ludere*; Eng. *ludic*), which sometimes included rambunctious wordplay and a fascination with misrule, mischief, and the subversion of everyday normality. It is significant that Latin has many finely graded terms for *wit, humour,* and *playfulness,* such as *ioci, facetiae, urbanitas, ineptiae, nugae,* and *lusus.* Supposedly serious and pragmatic Roman audiences evidently appreciated boisterous imagination and constantly inventive and surprising verbal expression. A further example is provided by a Roman genre without Greek precedent: the verse satire, which seems to have been invented by the wealthy and well-born Italian writer Lucilius in the late second century BCE. In the surviving fragments of his works, he mocks the foibles and pretensions of the Roman elite with great verbal panache.

Roman literature of the first century BCE manifests no less an inclination to urbane wit and verbal invention than early Roman comedy and satire, but it also features a new intellectual intensity and an ambition to emulate Greek achievement in the arena of philosophy. For example, Julius Caesar, a man normally associated with political ambition and military conquest, was one of the brilliant writers and thinkers of the time. Most famous as the author of "commentaries" (campaign accounts written by Roman generals), he is known to have also written a treatise on the linguistic principle of analogy. Cicero wrote a series of philosophical works imitating those of the Greek philosopher Plato. Like Plato, Cicero frames philosophical debate in dialogue form, in some cases locating his own dialogues in topographical settings that specifically recall similar passages in Plato. Yet, even as he echoes the form and settings of Plato's works, he carefully positions his philosophical activities to answer the concerns of a Roman audience.

Cicero must work hard to respond to the objections of those who associate intellectual activity of this type with Greek experts, who are their social inferiors. At the other end of the spectrum, he must also contend with philosophy snobs who believe that Latin philosophy has nothing to offer. To this latter type of critic, Cicero (*Leg.* 1.5, *Fin.* 10) insists that he does not wish to yield to the Greeks nor does he want his fellow citizens to feel a lack of something that the Greeks enjoy in plenty. He declares that the Romans do not lack ability; they have surpassed the Greeks in all areas, at least those deemed *worthy* of their labour (Cic. *Tusc.* 1.1). Cicero implies that the challenge is to raise the standing, the *dignitas*, of philosophy in the eyes of his countrymen. To this end, he claims that the Latin language is not, as is commonly believed, inferior to Greek in its richness of vocabulary (Cic. *Nat. D.* 1.8). He even argues that it is not Rome that lacks force in such areas. Greece is in decline and Rome in a position to appropriate Greek prestige:

> I encourage all, who have the ability, to wrest the glory of this field of endeavour from Greece, now in decline, and to transfer it to this city, just as our ancestors transferred, by their zeal and hard work, all other forms of endeavour that were worth pursuing. (Cic. *Tusc.* 2.5)

Cicero's claims and exhortations are indeed striking, particularly when he goes so far as to suggest that Greek cultural prestige be replaced with Roman and to insist, however gently and urbanely, that the search for wisdom (*sapientia*) has no limits.

   Cicero's ambition is nothing less than the incorporation of Greek philosophy into Roman life. A similar drive informs the main poetic work of his contemporary Lucretius, the *De Rerum Natura* (*On the Nature of Things*). Lucretius's grand didactic poem in six books is a lively and rhetorically powerful exposition of the ideas of the Hellenistic philosopher Epicurus. Philosophy in the ancient world comprised ethics but also what we might call **natural philosophy** or science. As a result, Lucretius expounds both Epicurus's ethics, at the heart of which is the pursuit of "an untroubled state of mind" (*ataraxia*), and his scientific atomism. He chooses the poetic medium, and a sublime style reminiscent of epic poetry, to articulate these philosophical theories. This choice is all the more interesting when we recall that Epicurus did not highly recommend poetry or other literary pursuits. The poem's chief addressee is the aristocratic statesman Gaius Memmius, who also stands in for readers of the poem, presumably members of the Roman elite, who have an interest in philosophy yet also want it presented to them in an attractive and comprehensible fashion. Poetry itself is likened, in Lucretius's memorable figure, to the honey smeared around a cup's rim to facilitate the ingestion of the bitter but curative medicine inside (Lucr. 1.931–50). Like Cicero, Lucretius adapts Greek philosophical ideas to the Latin language and Roman social contexts.

   Literary activity in the late Republic could be intensely erudite and technical at times and at other times (or even simultaneously) intensely engaged with contemporary politics and society. Cicero, for example, was best known as an orator. His multi-faceted eloquence was employed in court cases, both for the prosecution and the defence, and in political contexts. As a **novus homo** ("new man"), a political aspirant without a significant family history of public office-holders, Cicero was able to pursue a ferociously ambitious career largely on the merits of his capacity for public speaking. His prosecution of Gaius Verres, a governor of Sicily, for corruption propelled him to public visibility early on.

See Chapter 3, p. 53, and Chapter 10, pp. 231–3, on "new men."

Throughout his career, which culminated in the highly coveted office of the consulship, Cicero used the medium of oratory to publish his positions, advertise his accomplishments, and pillory his enemies. His orations exerted their effect both in their initial oral performance and, later, in their circulation as carefully revised published texts. As orator, Cicero drew upon the art of public speaking (rhetoric) as developed in ancient Greece and modelled himself, at times quite explicitly, on famous Greek orators

Compare Chapter 6, ⬅
pp. 126–8 and 131–2, on
rhetoric as a part of education.

such as Demosthenes. (In fact, it was a work modelled on Demosthenes—the *Philippics*, in which Cicero attacks the politician and general Marc Antony—that led to his death, as described in Box 7.2.) Even as Cicero closely imitated Greek models and techniques, he adapted them to the political dynamics of the Roman Republic, the social and moral categories of his Roman audiences, and his own shifting self-representational projects.

Cicero's contemporary Sallust was similarly a participant in public life, and his literary activity was also closely related to his public career. Sallust wrote works of history that were often devoted to relatively circumscribed historical episodes of exemplary significance, such as the failed *coup d'état* of Lucius Sergius Catilina in 63 BCE and Rome's war with Jugurtha of Numidia in 110–104 BCE. Sallust appears to have been disillusioned with contemporary politics at least in part because of his own failed career and subsequent retirement, and he inevitably views the episodes of Roman history that form his

Political History

⬥⟩═◉═⟨⬥

Box 7.2: The Death of Cicero

Cicero's death offers a good example of the power of literature in ancient Rome, specifically how an influential work could damage public reputations and even endanger its author's life. In the wake of the assassination of Julius Caesar in 44 BCE, three men in particular sought to inherit Caesar's power and prestige: Gaius Octavian (later the emperor Augustus), Marcus Lepidus, and Marc Antony. While they each had their own interests at heart and were effectively rivals, in 43 BCE they agreed to form a triumvirate (an alliance of three) as a strategic ploy to defeat Caesar's assassins. They began their reign with a proscription, that is, by composing a list of their enemies to be killed.

Meanwhile, Cicero had been writing the *Philippics*, a series of orations in which he fiercely attacked Antony. The title of the orations was modelled on those delivered by the Greek orator Demosthenes, who similarly attacked Philip II of Macedon, a man whom Demosthenes saw as a dangerous tyrant. On Antony's orders, Cicero was killed and his head and hands were brought to the Roman **Forum** to be displayed on the speaking platforms (*rostra*). It was with his hand, after all, that he had written the *Philippics* (Plut. *Cic.* 48).

subject matter with the expertise, intensely engaged perspective, and at times tendentious bias of an insider. Sallust was influenced by the Greek historian Thucydides, who affords one model for Sallust's deliberately irregular and dense prose style, yet his historical writings focus on the moral concerns of first-century BCE Rome and, in particular, the connection between the moral degeneracy of Roman aristocrats and the dysfunctional political climate of the late Republic. History, for Sallust, was at once an inherited Greek form of writing and inquiry and an outgrowth of his own political experience and career.

Perhaps the most ambitious and extensive literary imitation of Greek works occurred during the Augustan period. As previously discussed, writers of this time heralded a new Golden Age, an integral element of which was to be the creation of canonical works of Latin literature to rival the Greek classics. This aspiration had an important architectural embodiment: next to his own residence on the Palatine Hill, Augustus built a splendid new Temple of Apollo, which included library buildings adjoining the porticoes that surrounded the precinct. According to one scholarly reconstruction, there were shelves containing the Greek classics and, elsewhere, corresponding (but still largely empty) sections for Latin works in the same genres.[6] It is perhaps for this reason that Horace (*Epist.* 2.2.214–18) spoke of the empty shelves in the Palatine library acting as a "spur" to poets to fill the shelves with their own literary creations.

The Augustan poet Propertius (2.34b) had this basic set of ideas in mind when he wrote that "something greater than the *Iliad* is coming into being." This "something" was, of course, Vergil's *Aeneid*. Vergil's epic tells the story of the legendary Aeneas, a Trojan prince who fought in the Trojan War and, in the wake of Troy's destruction, escaped with his son and aged father, eventually making his way to Italy, where he founded Roman civilization. The *Aeneid* is a truly Roman epic insofar as it concerns the very origins of the Roman race. At the same time, Vergil models his poem on the works of his Greek predecessors Homer and Apollonius of Rhodes. The structure of the epic announces his ambitions: books 1 to 6, which detail Aeneas's wanderings at sea and adventures in diverse lands, correspond to Homer's *Odyssey*, while books 7 to 12, which tell of Aeneas's war against a federation of native Italic peoples following his arrival in Italy, represent the *Iliad*. Vergil's *Aeneid* thus aims to provide a Roman answer to both Homeric epics. The forward drive of the plot, moreover, functions as a dynamic correlative of his Homeric emulation. Just as Aeneas travels, laboriously yet inexorably, from the Homeric world of Troy towards the future site of Rome, so do Vergil's poetic labours bring Homeric epic poetry to Italian shores and the Latin tongue. Finally, Aeneas is a distinctly Roman hero: his central quality is not the magnificent intensity of spirit and sublime violence of the Homeric epic hero Achilles or the tactical shrewdness of Homer's Odysseus but *pietas*, "dutifulness" towards the gods, his (prospective) fatherland, and his family.

As Vergil explored Rome's origins in epic verse, his contemporary Livy was producing a monumental prose history of Rome, significantly entitled *From the Foundation of the City* (*Ab urbe condita*). Livy's vast work, now surviving in substantial fragments, extended from the mythic age of Aeneas to contemporary times. Livy, like his predecessor Sallust, wrote in a genre deriving from the pioneering work of Greek historians such as Herodotus and Thucydides, yet he too adapted this form of writing to a Roman context and Roman concerns. Livy's focus on "the City"—prominently featured in the work's title—is informed by the distinctly Roman concept of the city of Rome and its topographical landmarks as immoveable, sacred, and central to Roman identity. The city constitutes the enduring, concrete link between past and present, between the legendary period of foundation and the emperor Augustus's "re-foundation" of Rome's pristine moral integrity. Livy's city-based history is a highly original project when viewed in relation to his Greek predecessors.

Compare Chapter 17, pp. 385–90, on Augustus's architectural program of renewal.

While Herodotus, Thucydides, and other Greek historians certainly awarded attention to the history and traditions of city-states throughout the Greek world, Livy contributes a new element in his exploration of the "cultural history" of Rome's urban fabric, namely the dense interconnections between rites, Latin words, topographical sites, historical events, and social structures.

Roman writers were both the inheritors of Greek genres and the inventors of new literary modes responsive to contemporary needs and social circumstances. For example, Horace effectively invented the lyric genre in his *Odes*. There were Greek poets whose work might be loosely defined as lyric; that is, recitation was accompanied by the lyre in performance, but there was little in the way of an explicit recognition of the lyric genre as such. Horace defined the genre in terms of a canon of lyric predecessors, certain recurrent ethical tendencies, and themes. In his *Eclogues*, Vergil accomplished a similar feat in regard to pastoral poetry. In the third century BCE, the Alexandrian poet Theocritus included in his collection of *Idylls* both poems defined by their pastoral setting and other compositions with urban settings. Vergil imposed a coherent character on the pastoral genre, heightening its identification with the countryside, formulating a recurrent set of pastoral markers and themes, and systematizing the Theocritean metafictional scenario of herdsmen singers.

In many cases, it is the Roman exemplars of a given genre that set the norms adopted by later European authors. Lyric, pastoral, epigram, and satire are all genres transmitted in a basically Roman form. Renaissance tragedy betrays the influence of Seneca more than that of Aeschylus, Sophocles, or Euripides. The Roman tradition of epic informs Milton's *Paradise Lost*. This phenomenon is explained not only by the broader diffusion of the Latin language in post-classical Europe but also by the tendency of the Romans to distill, systematize, and develop a sophisticated awareness of generic traits.

Literature and the Roman Elite

In the text quoted in Box 7.3, the Neronian satirist Persius evokes a dreadful dinner party, complete with poetic after-dinner entertainment. The attendees are rich and aristocratic, but they appear to be accompanied by their socially inferior hangers-on. The

Primary Source

Box 7.3: Persius, *Satires*, 1.30–9.

Behold, the descendants of Romulus, after they've dined, inquire amid their cups what divine poesy has to say. And here's one with hyacinthine cloak around his shoulders who mutters something rancid from his snivelling nose, burbles forth "Phyllises," "Hypsipyles"—any tear-jerking poetic theme you like—and trips out words on ladylike palate. The worthies have bestowed applause! Now the poet's ash is happy, is it not? Does not the stone now press more gently on his bones? The (humbler) guests applaud in turn: now, from his shade, now from his tomb and fortunate ash, shall not violets spring?

entertainment is a poetry recitation on obscure Greek mythological topics in the most superficial and ornamental modern style. These pretentious grandees, however, do not know the difference between fake poetry and the real thing: they applaud enthusiastically for the verbal equivalent of a poster of a Monet painting.

Later in the same satire, Persius complains that some of these aristocratic Romans seek to add to their cultural capital by composing and reciting poetry themselves. But how can they expect an objective response when the audience consists of their clients, who hope to gain something by their flattery? "I love the truth, tell the truth about me," these rich poetasters insist, while their dependents mock them with humorous gestures behind their backs (Pers. 1.55–62).

As always in such characterizations, there arises the problem of literary representation and social reality. Persius, as a satirist, tends to bring out the dark, unflattering aspects of the relationship between writers and their upper-class supporters. At the other end of the literary spectrum are idealized representations of the same relationship, which emphasize equality and mutual respect. Complicating the issue is a question of terminology. Modern scholars and critics habitually employ the terms *client* and *patron* in describing the affiliation between Roman writers (especially poets) and their socially superior connections. They appear to be all the more justified in doing so given that these words come from Latin (*cliens* and **patronus**, respectively) and were key Roman social concepts. Other scholars have argued, however, that this usage is misleading[7]: ancient Roman poets rarely, if ever, referred to their upper-class acquaintances as patrons or themselves as their clients but almost always employed the terms *amicus* ("friend") and **amicitia** ("friendship"). They tended to shun the notion of a *quid pro quo* exchange of benefits—poetic encomium in return for material rewards, for example—and instead would emphasize shared interests in literary culture, a shared set of attitudes towards elite leisure, and commonality of ethical values.

Of course, simply accepting the picture projected by Roman writers carries its own problems. In reality, the relation between poets and powerful members of the political class was inevitably asymmetric, despite protestations of equality. In texts other than those of the poets, we do occasionally hear of substantial material rewards bestowed for poetic compositions. These facts still do not justify, however, an unreflective or unqualified use of the word **patronage**. This term almost always applied to very special instances of Roman social relations: the relationship between a **freedman** and his former master, for example, or between a defendant and his legal representative in court. The term may have been more broadly and figuratively applied in some cases to include the notion of an asymmetric relationship between social inferiors and their upper-class supporters, but examples of this usage are rare and ambiguous in our sources.

Compare Chapter 3, p. 65, Chapter 4, p. 89, Chapter 10, p. 237, and Chapter 17, p. 384, on patronage.

Moreover, whereas *patronage* in modern English implies a pattern of consistent material support for a writer or artist of modest or negligible means, it is far from clear that such an institution ever existed in ancient Rome. Almost all writers we know anything about were independently wealthy—not necessarily at the top of the Roman wealth pyramid but rich enough to have pursued a life of leisure and literary studies. Patronal support, if we believe Martial, was more likely to take the form of individual occasions of benefaction—the gift of a new cloak or some special act of generosity—rather than a regular stipend or income (see, for example, Mart. 2.43, 4.61, 7.86, 8.28, 12.36; compare Pliny *Ep.* 3.21).

Within the broader picture of relations between writers and the Roman elite, the Augustan period once again merits special attention. In this period, Maecenas, a close associate of the emperor, developed a rapport with leading poets of the age. Some scholars have interpreted the poets' conspicuous association with a figure closely involved in the new imperial regime as propagandistic in its purpose and have accordingly identified Maecenas as Augustus's minister of propaganda. There is at least some basis for this view: all these poets wrote, at least occasionally, on patriotic, contemporary themes; some are known to have received substantial gifts from Maecenas and Augustus; and several appear to have lived in the same neighbourhood near Maecenas's elegant estate on the Esquiline. More recent scholarship, however, has viewed this relationship in more nuanced and complicated ways and questioned whether the poets offered unambiguous support to the regime. Maecenas, after all, was not the emperor, and the poets, by their own description, were merely friends of Maecenas—they certainly did not hold any kind of permanent official positions as paid writers for the regime. They were independently wealthy and hence not dependent on patronage for their immediate needs.[8]

A key issue in modern scholarship has been the extent to which the content of a given work written in the Augustan period can be identified as pro- or anti-Augustan.[9] While some individual passages in their work resound more patriotically and propagandistically than others, these poets did not normally write imperial panegyric, and the ideolog-ical tenor of their poetry is hard to reduce to a simple message. To take two major instances, both Vergil and Livy focus on Rome's past and legendary origins while remain-ing engaged with the contemporary figure of Augustus and his transformation of Roman society. Whether this engagement was largely one of approval or contained a critical or even subversive element has been a central topic of debate among modern scholars. Vergil praises Augustus in his epic and represents his rule as the culmination of Rome's historical destiny yet, at the same time, devotes conspicuous attention to the victims of Rome's destiny and the darker aspects of Roman power. Livy also appears to contribute to the contemporary project of rewriting Roman origins as a propagandistic backdrop to Augustus's reign, but it is also reported by Tacitus (*Ann.* 4.34.3) that his treatment of late republican history inspired Augustus to call him a Pompeian, a supporter of Pompey the Great, rival and enemy of Julius Caesar (Augustus's adoptive father).

Whatever the precise import of this comment, it seems unlikely that Livy's version of contemporary history (which, unfortunately, has not survived) was pro-Augustan in any simple or unproblematic way. Even in the sections on early Roman history that are extant, Livy does not flinch from exploring harsher aspects of the development of Roman power, such as the violent career of Rome's founder, Romulus, a figure with whom Augustus was associated. Similar questions of interpretation apply to the writers of the early imperial period. Literary works that praise contemporary emperors—for example, the epic poetry of Lucan or Tacitus's historical writings—have also been inter-preted as offering critical reflections on the imperial system and, implicitly, the emperors under which the authors themselves lived.

Even critical and independent poets, of course, might be interpreted as serving the emperor's interests in some larger sense. In the case of Augustan Rome, the very auton-omy of contemporary writers arguably placed the emperor in a good light: the goodwill and participation of literary men of integrity reflected well on him. Maecenas's status as intermediary between Augustus and these writers created the conditions for a mutually beneficial balance: both the emperor's need for literary recognition and the writers' need for independence were accommodated.

An important shift occurred, however, in the latter part of Augustus's reign. For rea-sons that are debated, Maecenas appears to have receded from prominence as a patron of poets, and Augustus took a more active role as direct addressee and patron of writers. A key example is Horace's *Epistle* 2.1, usually called the *Epistle to Augustus*. Apparently chided by Augustus in a personal letter for not addressing any of his poetic compositions directly to him, Horace offers the emperor an unusual and fascinating discussion of poetry's role in contemporary Roman society, insisting, with subtlety and firmness, on the necessity of high aesthetic standards. Citing the negative example of Alexander the Great, who failed to insist on rigorous standards of quality in the poems written about him, Horace (*Epist.* 2.1.232–70) argues that inept praise is worse than no praise at all. It is evident from Horace's epistle that addressing Augustus required a careful combination of deference towards the emperor and tactful insistence on one's own priorities as a writer.

A more negative view of the same basic situation is furnished by Ovid's exile poetry, the *Poems of Sorrow* (*Tristia*) and *Letters from the Black Sea* (*Epistulae ex Ponto*). As mentioned at the opening of this chapter, Ovid was sent into exile by the emperor Augustus in 8 CE. One ostensible reason for the sentence was the immorality of some of his poetry. (Ovid's brilliant and notorious *Art of Love* [*Ars Amatoria*], published in 2 BCE, was condemned by Augustus for "teaching adultery.") Ovid's exile and its supposed reason could have only a chilling effect on the relationship between writers and imperial power. The fact that Ovid went on writing throughout the long years of his exile, pleading for his return and examining and re-examining the basis for his relegation, resulted in an indelible literary portrait both of the poet in exile and of the angry, authoritarian emperor who had sent him there. As in Horace's *Epistle to Augustus*, the emperor looms as a major presence for poets, and the mild-mannered, cultivated Maecenas no longer exists as a buffering figure.

See Chapter 8, pp. 175–6, for an excerpt from Ovid's *Ars Amatoria* and pp. 172–3 on Augustan adultery laws.

From this point on, the emperor is at the centre of literary activity, and his tastes and inclinations have a major impact on contemporary literary production. Augustus's successor, the reclusive Tiberius, had little interest in playing the role of literary patron in Rome, and the Tiberian period is indeed fairly meagre in terms of literary output. The next major literary renaissance significantly occurred under the emperor Nero, who was known for being a consummate showman and highly public literary enthusiast. Nero's involvement in the literary scene, however, was an ambiguous benefit. While many writers undoubtedly drew inspiration from the hyper-charged cultural atmosphere of Neronian Rome, the emperor appears to have resented the writers he viewed as his competitors for literary prestige. In the wake of the **Pisonian conspiracy** in 65 CE, several major figures—the

---

Primary Source

Box 7.4: Martial, *Epigrams*, 1.107.

Often you say to me, dearest Lucius Julius: "Write something big. You are a lazy man." Give me leisure of the sort that Maecenas once made for his Flaccus (i.e. Horace) and his Vergil. I would try to fashion works that would live through the ages and snatch my name from the flames. Oxen are not willing to bear the yoke into barren fields. A rich soil is tiring, but the very labour is enjoyable.

philosopher and tragedian Seneca, the epic poet Lucan, and the novelist Petronius, for example—ended up being forced by Nero to commit suicide.

A comparable set of tensions characterizes the next major period of literary activity under the Flavian emperors. The dominating figure of this dynasty, the emperor Domitian, had substantial literary interests, instituted and presided over literary festivals, and attempted large-scale patronage of the arts and urban building on the Augustan model, but he also required outrageous flattery from both courtiers and contemporary writers. Writers of this period were caught between Domitian, an unusually powerful patron who could make or break their careers, and numerous lesser patrons who could not provide the degree of protection and public prominence afforded by Maecenas under Augustus. Literary production was subject to the whim of a single formidable arbiter.

Tradition, Intertextuality, and Decline

In a poem from Martial's *Epigrams* (see Box 7.4), as in Pliny's letter to Caninius Rufus, one elite Roman male encourages another to produce the "something" (*aliquid*) that we call literature. In this case, however, Martial's friend Lucius Julius wants him to write something quite atypical: a grand (*magnum*) work, such as an epic poem. But Martial writes epigrams, which are known for their brevity and wit—they are the very opposite of "something big." Martial, who writes under Domitian and must seek the support of many individuals to secure his social prominence as a poet, nostalgically recalls the financial security and uninterrupted leisure enjoyed by poets of the Augustan period. He lacks both the autonomy and the continuous state of tranquility required to devote oneself to a work of true depth, a work of exhausting but ultimately rewarding labour.

Martial's complaint, of course, is at least partially a consciously insincere ploy: he knows—and his reader knows—that he is making a play for precisely such large-scale, long-term patronage, perhaps bestowed by the emperor himself. He also knows that his genre, although notionally humble, hardly lacks ambition or literary value. Martial put epigram on the literary map, both in terms of the Roman tradition and posterity. (Indeed, Martial provides the model of epigrammatic poetry in the Renaissance.) There is an element of sociological truth, however, in his self-denigrating conceit. The conditions of literary leisure were not necessarily the same under Domitian as they had been under Augustus, and poets certainly did not enjoy the protective shelter of Maecenas's unique form of patronage. Martial nevertheless makes consistently brilliant poetry about the brave new literary world he inhabits. Playful and corrosive, flattering and at the same time sarcastic, deferent and occasionally vicious, Martial depicts a Rome in which poets beg for their bread on the streets, the emperor inhabits a dazzlingly remote realm far from ordinary mortals, and the endlessly fascinating, deplorably nasty City extends as far as the eye can see.

Martial's poetry offers just one example of a broader pattern of narratives of cultural

decline in the post-Augustan literature of the early Empire. In
Tacitus's *Dialogus de oratoribus* ("Dialogue on Oratory"), several
elite Romans in the time of the emperor Vespasian discuss the

Compare Chapter 10,
pp. 227, 231–3 and 237–8, on
political careers under the empire.

nature and possibilities of the contemporary literary field. Under the imperial system of
government, which concentrates power in the hands of the emperor, civic debate is no
longer imbued with the same urgency and importance as it was under the Republic. Given
such conditions, is oratory still a fruitful arena of ambition, or should one turn to the more
secluded, tranquil pursuits of poetry?

Casting a shadow over this entire discussion of literary activity is the consciousness of
the superiority of the past. The very form and language of Tacitus's dialogue are based on
Ciceronian models, and the names of Augustan writers such as Vergil evoke a level of literary achievement that is beyond the reach of Tacitus and his contemporaries. If writers of
the Republic and the Augustan period oriented themselves towards the daunting challenge
posed by Greek literary accomplishments, the writers of the early
Empire oriented themselves towards the Augustan classics. These
works imprinted themselves as master texts on the cultural fabric of the Roman Empire at a crucial moment in Roman history

Compare Chapter 3, pp. 56–7,
on Roman education and the
provincial elite.

and were absorbed throughout the provinces by schoolboys learning Latin and becoming
Romans. These formidable works, it was felt, could be neither equalled nor ignored.

Yet even a quick perusal of Roman literature produced in the so-called Silver Age
reveals an astonishingly fertile literary field. Much of this brilliant work derives its
force from subverting, tarnishing, and dismantling Augustan literary ideals and ideologies.
The satirist Juvenal, like his older contemporary Martial, assumes the persona of "client
poet." Instead of shoring up his autonomy and authority as a poet, he subsumes his literary image to degrading routines of clientage, tarnishing the very concept of literary activity and liberal studies in the process. In the Neronian period, Lucan wrote the *Civil War*,
an epic poem that some scholars have characterized as an "anti-*Aeneid*." Rather than reach
back into the legendary past to recall Rome's pristine origins, Lucan looks to the civil conflicts of the late republican period to explore evil, futility, and the origins of the imperial
system of government. In the same period, Persius alludes to Horace's verse satires, even
as he adopts a more cynical tone and assumes a more isolated position vis-à-vis Roman
society. Finally, another Neronian work, Petronius's *Satyricon*, recounts the adventures of
three characters in what looks like Italy in the first century CE. The protagonists are evidently poor vagabonds but moderately well educated, and thus the novel's satirical effect
pivots around a constant ironic contrast between their low-life surroundings and their
frequently paraded smattering of high-literary conceits and reminiscences.

Philosophy and history in the early imperial period likewise provide examples of fertile
engagement with earlier Roman models. The letters and treatises of Seneca stand alongside
Cicero's dialogues as contributions to Roman philosophy, while Pliny the Younger, in his

Epistulea, fashions himself as a post-Ciceronian man of letters and a public figure for the early Empire. Tacitus, the author of the *Dialogus*, is even better known for his works on Roman history, such as the *Histories* and *Annals*. He draws on Sallust's epigrammatic sharpness and moral critique while offering a consciously cynical interpretation of key aspects of imperial politics: the tense, intricate relations between emperor and senate, the sometimes treacherous dynamics of the imperial house, the impact of the emperor's personality on political culture, and the deformation of language and rhetoric in an age when a large part of the workings of political power were withdrawn from public view. So compelling is Tacitus's vision of the claustrophobic world of the imperial Roman elite and so authoritative is his literary manner that he has profoundly influenced modern historians of the ancient world and, consequently, our own view of imperial Rome. He inherits, in some sense, Livy's mantle as imperial historian but explores the altered political landscape of the first century BCE through the lens of a highly original perspective and an inimitable literary style.

Roman literature of the early imperial period is informed by a tense, sharp-edged confrontation between tradition and innovation, authority and subversion. Perhaps for the very reason that tradition and exemplarity enjoyed a central status in Roman culture, innovating within a system defined by strongly established authorities could be precarious. The task of creating an original work, as Pliny observed to his friend Caninius Rufus, demands hard work and long stretches of time. It also requires daring, talent, and a willingness to reshape and even dismantle the ideals of the past.

Summary

This brief discussion has suggested the great variety and depth of the Roman literary tradition. In ancient Rome, the term *literature* encompassed a broad range of texts, and "literary" status was not necessarily determined by the criteria of practicality versus non-practicality or fictionality versus non-fictionality. This chapter also considered questions of chronology and literary history, with specific emphasis on how, in many cases, the self-promoting narratives of the Roman writers influenced the terms employed by modern scholars.

The interaction between Greece and Rome is another important factor in the history of Roman literature. For Roman writers, it was never simply a case of "translating" or "reproducing" Greek models. The history of literature was entangled in the history of aristocratic culture, military conquest and imperialism, and the Romans' patriotic interest in establishing their own literary achievement as valuable and original. Part of the effort to define literature in specifically Roman terms involved adapting literary practices to Roman modes of social interaction. Accordingly, this chapter examined the ways in which Roman writers were involved in relations of friendship (*amicitia*) among the Roman elite. Finally, the issue of "decline" was discussed. Writers of the early imperial period found themselves in the challenging position of defining their originality in relation to the seemingly insuperable masterworks of the Augustan period—a challenge they nonetheless managed to face with considerable creative brilliance.

A civilization known for its pragmatism and devotion to the arts of war paradoxically produced many of the central works of Western civilization. Roman authors are commonly viewed as the creators of serious, high-toned, dusty "classics" remote from the interests of modern readers. (The image that most readily comes to mind is a row of marble busts in a museum.) By contrast, this chapter has attempted to emphasize their surprising wit, playfulness, originality, and subversive irony. The Romans not only redefined the central Greek genres with immense zest and brilliance, but they also went on to rewrite and dismantle the guiding assumptions of their own canon of revered classics.

Questions for Review and Discussion

1. How does the Roman conception of literature differ from our own? How are the two perspectives similar?
2. Give three examples of Greek genres imitated by Roman authors in the early period of Roman literature. Why do you think they chose those genres?
3. Were there literary patrons in ancient Rome? What is the difference between a patron and a friend?
4. What consequences did the emergence of the imperial system have for Roman literary activity? Describe the importance of the figure of the emperor in literature.
5. Did Roman literature decline from its height under the emperor Augustus? What challenges were faced by post-Augustan writers? Give evidence to support your answers.

Suggested Reading

Braund, S.M. 2001. *Latin Literature*. London and New York: Routledge.

This book provides a compact introduction to basic issues in the interpretation of Latin literature. Thematically organized chapters consider themes such as gender, multiculturalism, performance, patronage, literary allusion, and the relation of Roman writers to their Greek models.

Conte, G.B. 1991. *Latin Literature: A History*. Baltimore: Johns Hopkins University Press.

This book, which features an excellent treatment of individual authors and periods, is probably the best chronological history of Latin literature currently available. The English-language edition includes a bibliography and brief treatment of the later reception of Roman authors.

Fantham, E. 1999. *Roman Literary Culture: From Cicero to Apuleius*. Baltimore: Johns Hopkins University Press.

The focus of this book is Roman literature in the context of Roman society. The book is chronologically organized and includes discussion of literary recitation and performance, literary careers, patronage, and the social class and position of writers.

Feeney, D. 1991. *The Gods in Epic: Poets and Critics of the Classical Tradition*. Oxford and New York: Oxford University Press.

This book traces the representation of the Olympian gods in epic poetry from ancient Greece through Flavian Rome. It affords an outstanding example of literary criticism on Roman literature that combines sensitive reading of a broad range of texts with an awareness of social, political, and religious background.

———. 1998. *Literature and Religion at Rome: Cultures, Contexts, and Beliefs*. Cambridge and New York: Cambridge University Press.

This book provides a compact introduction to the interaction of literature and religion in ancient Rome. Feeney challenges received ideas about Roman culture and the relation between text and ritual.

Hardie, P. 1993. *The Epic Successors of Virgil: A Study in the Dynamics of a Tradition*. Cambridge and New York: Cambridge University Press.

This book investigates a set of related themes that inform the tradition of Roman epic poetry as definitively established by Vergil's *Aeneid*. It provides excellent insight into the workings of a Roman literary tradition, its development over time, and its relation to imperial ideology.

Harrison, S., ed. 2005. *A Companion to Latin Literature*. Malden, MA: Blackwell.

This handbook is composed of a number of essays written by leading experts in the field of Roman literature. It examines periods, genres, and themes in Roman literature and offers up-to-date discussion and bibliography.

Hinds, S. 1998. *Allusion and Intertext: Dynamics of Appropriation in Roman Poetry*. Cambridge and New York: Cambridge University Press.

This book examines, through a series of case studies, the workings of literary allusion in Roman poetry. It provides an ideal starting point for students interested in how literary texts define themselves through comparison with earlier and/or contemporary works.

Taplin, O., ed. 2001. *Literature in the Roman World*. Oxford and New York: Oxford University Press.

This book is composed of a series of essays by leading scholars in the field of Roman literature. The authors examine poetry and prose of the Republic and Empire and consider themes such as the beginnings of Latin literature, literary space and time, and the relation between poetry and politics.

Notes

1 All translations are my own, unless otherwise noted.
2 See Hinds (2004).
3 Feeney (2005).
4 Goldberg (1998).
5 See the discussion of Gruen (1990: 205–10).

6 Horsfall (1993: 62–5).
7 See, for example, White (1993).
8 See White (1993).
9 The most important treatment of the question is Kennedy (1992).

8

Roman Sexuality and Gender

Kelly Olson

As you step through the doorway of the House of the Vettii in Pompeii, you see a colourful fresco of the Roman god Priapus weighing his enormous phallus against a bag of gold (see Figure 8.1). A graffito below catches your eye: "Eutychis (a female), Greek, nice-mannered, for two *asses*" (*CIL* 4.4592; an *as* was the smallest denomination of Roman currency).[1] Farther back in the house, in the garden, you glimpse a fountain in the shape of a well-endowed young man, the water flowing through his penis into the basin. And as you walk through the house, various graffiti draw your attention: "Isidorus (a male), slave of the household, from Puteoli, cuntlicker" (*CIL* 4.4699); "Ampliate (a male) is a cocksucker" (*CIL* 4.4580). Elsewhere, you read that "Eros (a male) is a *cinaedus*" (*CIL* 4.4602) and that Constans and Priscus (males) charge two and a half *asses* for their sexual services (*CIL* 4.4690). Based on these sights, you might think that the building is a brothel. It is, in fact, a lavish private residence whose contents provide a valuable glimpse into the sexual world of the ancient Romans.

Introduction

Figure 8.1 Wall painting of Priapus (Roman god of fertility), House of Vettii, Pompeii. © Cobie Martin/Alamy

It is important to begin with the assumption that ancient Roman sexual culture is different from ours. As Craig Williams points out, the Romans lived in a society where men were free to pursue sexual contacts outside of marriage (as long as they kept away from citizen women), where it was always possible to go out and purchase a sexual partner in the form of a male or female slave from the slave market, where adultery generally raised more concerns than pederasty, where a man whose masculinity had been

Timeline

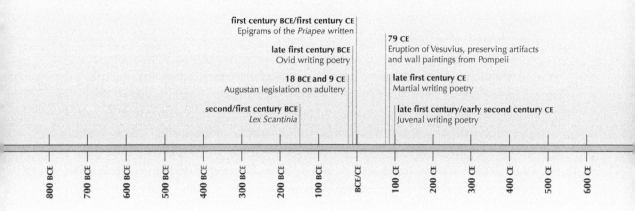

impugned could cite as proof of his manhood the fact that he had engaged in sexual relations with his accuser's sons,[2] where images of penises were placed on walls and carved into paving stones, and where males and females of all ages could look on explicit images of sexual intercourse. In this chapter, we will encounter radically unfamiliar values, forms of behaviour, and social practices. Roman sexuality is a foreign domain. To illustrate this point, some of the language and photos in this chapter may be considered strong; however, they are used to give precise translations of original works and/or representations of the attitudes and vernacular common in the period under study.

One way in which the ancients were different from us is that they seem not to have recognized "sexuality" or "sexual identity," concepts to which modern analysis of sex and sexual acts have given rise. In addition, our ideas of what is pornographic, sinful, or shameful do not hold for the ancient world. Sexual pleasure had a positive social value in Roman antiquity. The ancients had a goddess of sexual pleasure (Venus or Aphrodite), and erotica was displayed openly as an indication of high status and luxury. Sex was a blessing from the gods, in whatever form it took.

———— • ◆ • ————

Literary Sources

The study of Roman **sexuality** and sexual attitudes is made difficult by the limitations of the ancient evidence. There is no connected narrative remaining from the ancient world on sexuality—ancient erotic handbooks, often illustrated, unfortunately have not survived. Consequently, we find pertinent information about Roman sexual matters in all sorts of ancient literature: legal texts, history, poetry, and political discourse. Because the majority of our authors are elite males and information about sexuality is rarely central to their primary concerns of politics, war, and the battlefield, they present only a certain (very limited) viewpoint.

While some literary sources (such as personal poetry and satire) may give us more information, each literary genre has its own specific caveats. Satire, for example, may exaggerate social ills or situations for its own purposes. Love poets look more favourably on sexual practices than do the moralists. We must also remember that the ancient literary evidence that talks about **sex** is often discursive or idealizing. That is, it encapsulates a set of sexual standards (for example, that citizen men should not be anally penetrated) that the authors, and probably society in general, wished to see upheld in Roman antiquity. The reality was much more complex, and there was a multiplicity of ancient practices and notions regarding what was "right" and "wrong" in terms of sex, as we shall see.

We also have many artistic representations of sex, including wall paintings, vases, lamps, and mosaics that depict sexual scenes (see Figure 8.2). But there are also stipulations concerning ancient art and archaeology as evidence for sexual practices. Art is neither a slice of life nor a photographic portrait of the event depicted: it embellishes, omits, or highlights aspects of the visual for its own purposes. For example, the missionary position is not a sexual posture represented in art because it affords no titillating

views of body parts, and yet we know that the ancients had sex in this position (see, for example, Archil. *Cologne Epode, P.Colon.* 7511). Caution is therefore essential. We also need to beware of placing twenty-first-century values or conceptions on ancient erotica. There is a value judgment inherent in labelling a piece of art "pornographic" (in which sex is equated with power and violence) or even "erotic" (tending to arouse sexual desire). These modern terms can obscure ancient meaning.

Moreover, due to archaeological methods current in the eighteenth and nineteenth centuries (and beyond), we do not know the find spot of many erotic ancient statues and paintings, as many were removed and shipped off to museums without the provenance being recorded. This makes it difficult to answer questions of audience, context, and function—Who looked at this object? Where did they look at it and under what circumstances?—and to reconstruct the decorative program of houses.[3] In addition, and more

Figure 8.2 Roman oil lamp with erotic scene, Carthage. © François Guenet/ Art Resource, NY

seriously, our extant collection of Roman artistic erotica probably represents only a very small percentage of what was actually produced in ancient times, due to the deliberate destruction of such objects by later archaeologists, often in the very place where the material was found.

Prudery and Expurgation[4]

Why would archaeologists in past centuries have destroyed ancient erotic art? The answer lies in their own contemporary culture, which was one of prudery and expurgation. Until as late as 1970, scholars of antiquity had a habit of whitewashing Greece and Rome, choosing to ignore or suppress those aspects of the ancient civilizations that they found disturbing, immoral, or unpleasant. The classification of antiquity on moral, as opposed to strictly scholarly, grounds can be traced back to early archaeological discoveries at **Pompeii** and **Herculaneum** at the end of the eighteenth century. Almost as soon as excavations began, the field notebooks record with ill-concealed embarrassment the discovery of more and more "obscene items": amulets, lamps, murals, and reliefs depicting sex, explicit and often in the style of caricature. At first the objects were shown openly to Grand Tour visitors in the Museum Herculanense in Portici. The existence of the first *secretum* ("secret museum") in the Herculaneum Museum was recorded in 1795. This room (number XVIII) was reserved for "obscene" antiquities and could be visited only by those in possession of a special permit.

In February 1819 the heir to the Neapolitan throne, the future Francesco I, visited the museum (by then transferred to the Palazzo degli Studi) with his wife and daughter. He suggested that "it would be a good idea to withdraw all the obscene objects, of whatever material they may be made, to a private room." To this room, at first prosaically named the Cabinet of Obscene Objects and in 1823 more coyly called the Reserved Cabinet, only those people of mature years and sound morals (which in practice meant educated males) would be admitted. According to a contemporary guidebook, the collection contained 202 "abominable monuments to human licentiousness" when it was first installed.

Restricting access inevitably helped to promote the collection. In 1822 only 20 requests for visits were made; two years later the number had increased to 300. By 1861, after decades of uncertainty, the Museo Borbonico was transformed into the National Museum of Naples. Five years later, libertarian zeal drove the publication of a catalogue of the "Pornographic Collection," compiled by Giuseppe Fiorelli, who was then the director of the excavations at Pompeii. Despite Fiorelli's obvious discomfort with the vocabulary used to describe the artifacts, the catalogue's arrangement forms the first nineteenth-century attempt at scientific classification of sexual material, the first experiment in the formalization of the secret museum as a curatorial concept. The *Gabinetto Segreto* continued on even into the twenty-first century. As late as 2003, one still needed a special appointment to visit the room. Only since 2009 has the room been completely open to the public.

At the British Museum, such a room was also established in 1865, in the wake of the Obscene Publications Act (1857). Concern with "pornography" became especially pronounced in nineteenth-century Britain with the onset of the Industrial Revolution and the rise of the middle classes, who (it was felt) had to be protected from depraved material that might inflame the sexual passions. In addition, the male establishment felt that exposing women to the sexual culture of the ancient world might provoke an imbalance in the relationships between men and women and hence a breakdown in the social order.[5] These concerns meant that, as in the National Museum of Naples, "indecent" objects were separated from the objects on public display and hidden away in a cabinet or small room.[6] The register of the British Museum's *secretum* indicates that some antiquities from the ancient Egyptian, Near Eastern, and Classical civilizations were segregated from the collections on the basis of their obscene nature as early as the late 1830s, with many more joining them during the next two decades. Many derive from collections donated by some of the foremost antiquaries of the day, including Sir William Hamilton. Admittedly, the *secretum* started to break down even before World War I, and today the indecent objects are on display with the rest of the collection.

Sexually explicit material was not confined to the visual arts but was in the literary sources as well. There were several ways of dealing with this material in English translations of classical texts. In some (especially in school study editions), erotic or disturbing parts were left out altogether, with no indication that text had been removed; in others, an ellipsis (. . .) showed where the editor had omitted part of the text. Sometimes, such parts were kept in the original Latin or even translated into Italian (considered a bawdy language) in an attempt to conceal their content.

These strategies successfully hid the meaning of the less common obscenities from even professional scholars while allowing the curious reader to locate confidently the passages in which they occurred. Such prudish measures continued as late as 1930, when A.E. Housman, a poet and leading classical scholar, proposed to clarify the meaning of various sexual acts in Roman literature and explicate Roman attitudes to sexual acts between males. His essay was in Latin, but it was still too explicit for *Classical Quarterly*, which rejected his submission. The essay was finally published (in Latin) in 1930 in the German classical periodical *Hermes*.

Since 1970, however, the field of classical studies has witnessed a scholarly explosion of interest in erotic art and artistic objects, sexual literature and language previously thought too "indelicate" to be discussed or published, as well as the development of sophisticated studies of related topics (such as gender in antiquity). With the publication of Michel Foucault's *Histoire de la sexualité* (1976–1986), scholarly excitement over erotic ideologies in antiquity really began. Influenced by Kenneth Dover (author of the ground-breaking *Greek Homosexuality* [1978]), Foucault was the first scholar to state that male sexuality was a true cultural construction, divorced from nature, and not a biological constant. After his study appeared, scholars began to formulate new questions: How was sexual experience constituted in a given culture? Were sexual pleasures and desires configured differently for different members of society? In what terms was sexual experience constructed? Feminism and feminist or woman-centred studies, as well as queer studies (that is, the study of homosexuality) also contributed greatly to the knowledge of sexuality in antiquity.

Terminology

Before we look at sexuality in antiquity specifically, we need to define our terms. *Sex* may be characterized as an individual's biological status as male or female, or as a sexual act. *Sexuality* is the sexual knowledge, beliefs, attitudes, values, and behaviours of individuals. Its dimensions include the anatomy, physiology, and biochemistry of the sexual response system; identity, orientation, roles, and personality; and thoughts, feelings, and relationships. The expression of sexuality is influenced by ethical, spiritual, cultural, and moral concerns. For modern thinkers (especially Freudians), sexuality is thought to provide a key to unlocking the mysteries of the self: sexual activity is considered in a psychological and self-reflexive way. The ancients did not consider it in that respect, as we shall see.

Although the Romans, as far as we know, never posed the following kinds of questions, it may be useful to look briefly at the sorts of social and scholarly controversies currently raging about sexuality (and more specifically, **sexual orientation**, a characteristic determined by the preferred sex of one's sexual partners). This will provide an introduction to sexuality studies and the concept of sexual identity, as well as lay the groundwork for comprehending a very different sexual value system from our own.

One ongoing scholarly debate concerning sexuality is whether or not it is a product of continuity or change, views embraced by essentialists and constructivists, respectively. **Essentialism** is the belief that people (or phenomena) have properties that are essential to what they are. Such properties are viewed as definitive of identity because they are "natural," "inherent," or "inborn," existing before or beyond acculturation. Essentialists believe that the concept of people being homosexual or heterosexual accurately reflects an unchangeable reality that holds true for all cultures in all of history and that a person's homosexuality or heterosexuality constitutes an unchangeable "essence" rather than a socially constructed characteristic. Therefore, sexual categories and sexuality have remained relatively unchanged over time and are the products of biology. For example, gay men and women as we understand them today (who take their personal identity from their sexual preference) have existed throughout history.

Constructivism, in contrast, is the theory that different times and places produce different results. So sexuality as we understand it today has little to do with the sexualities of people in other historical periods. Therefore, constructivists can say that sexuality and sex (in terms of what is thought to constitute a sexual act) are "cultural constructions." Sexuality is not a universal or a given but differs from community to community and from historical epoch to historical epoch. Sexuality and gender roles are learned depending on one's time and culture and are not internal constants. For example, social constructivists believe that, although same-sex love has occurred in all cultures and chronological periods, the concept of certain people being predisposed to love only one sex (and consequently being identified, either by themselves or by society, as homosexuals or heterosexuals) is a concept invented by modern Western society and does not accurately describe how human sexuality developed in other cultures. Constructivists would argue, then, that homosexual *behaviour* is universal, while a homosexual *identity* is historically specific. They believe that those who describe themselves as homosexual or heterosexual and orient their sexual behaviour towards one gender do so only because their culture has fed them certain ideas about sexual identity.

These two viewpoints may be better understood as possible critical standpoints that different people take at different times. For some purposes, essentialism's arguments are best; for others, constructivism's. In fact, the views are not all that different: they concern the content and character of sexual identity, and the debate is over the most appropriate description of that identity. This debate asks: What does it mean to be "straight" or "gay"?[7]

The essentialism versus constructivism debate should not be confused with two other current debates over the *causes* of homosexuality: the **nature versus nurture debate** and the **determinism versus voluntarism debate**. Both debates concern the extent to which people choose their sexual orientation. Regarding the former, do genetics and/or hormones produce sexual orientation in the fetus, thus determining a person's desires before he or she even emerges from the womb (nature)? Or do later psychoanalytic causes, such as family dynamics, determine sexual orientation (nurture)? Concerning the latter, determinism holds that a person has no power to control his or her sexuality and that sexual orientation cannot be changed. Voluntarism holds that one can choose one's sexual orientation or choose to change it without great difficulty. Clearly these two debates are closely connected, as nature and nurture are the primary forms of determinism. (In other words, both hold that people cannot choose their desires but are given them, either by biology or upbringing.) But note that these two debates ask *how one becomes heterosexual or homosexual*, while essentialism versus constructivism asks *how sexual categories are formed and given meaning*. These are not the same things. It is a case of cause versus identity, debating how a person becomes gay versus debating whether or not gay identity always existed and how it has been given meaning.

In addition, an essentialist or determinist view of sexuality is not the same as a biological constant. A biological constant is a quantity that, under stated conditions, does not vary with changes in the environment or society. An example of a sexual biological constant is that males ejaculate on climaxing. This statement is not the same as the contention that there have been gay men and women (as we understand them today) in all historical periods. Biological constants concern physiological facts; other assertions deal with questions of sexual identity and cause.

Gender Identity versus Sexual Orientation

The sexual categories of modern Western society (heterosexual, homosexual, bisexual) do not map onto those of the ancient Roman world. Roman culture did not assign an identity to individuals based on their sexual orientation, something underlined by linguistic differences. In fact, Latin has no words for the terms *heterosexual*, *homosexual*, or *bisexual*. A man's desire for a woman, girl, or beautiful boy was considered quite normal, and both sexes exerted a powerful erotic appeal. No stigma was attached to sex with one or the other. Instead, the important sexual categories at that time were "penetrated" and "penetrator." The penetrator, or "active" partner, was perceived as manly and dominant; the penetrated, or "passive" partner, was emasculated and placed on a par with women and slaves. This theory came about because social and sexual roles were closely linked in ancient understanding. Sexual roles and sexual activity were ideally supposed to correspond to a person's gender and social **status**. For example, pleasure in sexual submission should disqualify a male citizen from assuming a role of social and political mastery. An assault on the body or an invasive punishment

Compare Chapter 3, pp. 51 and 55, ⇐ Chapter 4, p. 78, and Chapter 11, pp. 249–50, on status and corporal punishment.

(whipping, torture, penetration) was a humiliating mark of low status. Interestingly, it was sometimes possible to lose that inviolability, as in the case of the adulterer (see Box 8.1).

One can say, then, that the Romans operated on a system of **gender identity** (deriving one's primary identity from a sense of self as male or female and adhering to the behaviours inherent in a socially constructed gender category) rather than sexual orientation. Clearly the two can be related, but Roman ideas of masculinity and manhood included the penetration of other men. Note also that the "penetrative" or "phallocentric" model was the "normal" one in antiquity; hence, there is the tendency to recognize as "sexual" only those acts in which a penis was involved. This practice may explain why there is so little information on lesbianism in visual and literary sources: it did not count as sex under the penetrative model.

The Romans were such a phallocentric society that many of their sexual terms presuppose penetration. In fact, the Romans used different verbs according to whether or not the subject was inserting or receiving the penis and which orifice was penetrated. For example, to insert a penis into a vagina was *futuere* but to receive a penis in one's vagina was *crisare*. To insert one's penis into someone's anus was *pedicare*; to receive it, *cevere*. To insert one's penis into someone's mouth was *irrumare*; to receive it, *fellare*. The use of such terms has the interesting result of making the person with the penis the dominant, active agent. A heterosexual woman in ancient Rome, for example, could not say "I fucked him" (*futuere*) but only "I received him" (orally, anally, or vaginally).

Political History

Box 8.1: Augustus's Adultery Laws

During the Republic, which seems to have had no law on general sexual misconduct, the family handled cases of adultery. An adulterous woman was dealt with by her husband, **paterfamilias**, or a family council. As for her lover, public opinion from all time periods often held that certain punishments were perfectly legitimate. The enraged husband could beat him up, castrate or anally rape him, pass him on to kitchen slaves to be beaten or urinated upon, or shove a foreign object into his anus.

This system changed when Augustus instituted a *quaestio de adulteriis*, the forum for sexual offences in general.[1] For the first time in Roman history, adultery was a criminal offence. The *Lex Julia de adulteriis coercendis* ("the Julian Law on restraining adulterers") was passed in 18 BCE as part of Augustus's program of moral reform. However, this law did not apply equally to both sexes. *Adulteria* meant "sex with a married woman"; the status of the man was irrelevant. Thus slave women by definition could not commit adultery with their married masters, but male slaves could with their married mistresses. A husband could prosecute his wife for adultery, but she could not do the same because—in the eyes of the law—he had not committed any offence against their marriage. She could, however, still obtain a divorce.

With the **ius occidendi** Augustus made it legal for a father to kill his daughter and her adulterous partner if he caught them *in flagrante delicto* at his own or his son-in-law's house, but he had to kill both or neither. If he killed only the lover, he was liable for homicide. Perhaps this directive was meant to discourage the killing of male lovers. A husband had the right to kill *only* the lover if the latter was caught in the matrimonial home and if he was of a lower status or a slave. If the wronged husband killed his wife, he could be liable to a murder charge. To prosecute a wife for adultery, her husband had to divorce her without delay or he could be subject to a charge of pimping (*lenocinium*).

Not every woman caught in adultery went to court: the law stated that a husband had to divorce a guilty wife but not necessarily prosecute her. If they simply suspected infidelity but had no proof, many husbands may have preferred a quiet divorce to the expense and notoriety of a public trial and the possibility of making enemies of the accused man's friends and relations. The severity of the consequences for the wife may also have been a deterrent.

The penalties for convicted adultery were severe. The woman lost half her dowry and one-third of her property, the man lost half of his property, and, at a later stage, they were relegated to different islands. Part of the money went to the **delator** (the person who had brought the accusation, whether the husband or a third party) and part to the Roman state. The wronged husband could keep a further one-sixth of the dowry as compensation for his wife's misconduct. Women convicted of adultery in the strict sense (that is, caught in the act) could not remarry free-born citizens and thus could not receive outside legacies. They also incurred a degree of **infamia** ("evil reputation"; a diminution of status that carried with it certain legal penalties) and were not

Continued . . .

allowed to testify in court. Men, if convicted of adultery, could not witness formal acts of law or receive or bequeath legacies.

We may assume that the primary purpose of the Augustan legislation was to protect those in the upper classes, given that the penalties would be felt mainly by them. All the adultery trials we know of concern **senatorial** or **equestrian** families, and a good number also have a political basis.

Note

1. For the Augustan legislation on adultery, see McGinn (1998: 140–215), from which much of this text is drawn.

The Phallus

The terminology used to describe sexual intercourse underlines the fact that ancient Rome was a male-dominated society; that is, men had most of the direct or formal power and influence, and Rome supported institutions of male rule and privilege. Women could not vote, hold public office, or have highly visible careers, such as being lawyers. The male organ was spoken of more freely than the female in Roman antiquity, and there existed more jokes and metaphors concerning it. There are also more words in Latin for the penis than for female genitalia.[8] The phallus excited fear, admiration, and pride (but not disgust) and was a symbol of power. Size was a preoccupation: huge *phalloi* in Rome were a source of amusement or awe, and size was also presumed to be a concern to women and *cinaedi* (on this term, see pp. 179–81). The patriarchal nature of Roman society may also be detected on statues. While penises are carved in loving detail, female genitalia are often given no definition at all, remaining a smooth, blank, wedge-shaped plane.

The phallus was also an **apotropaic** object. In other words, it had a protective function.[9] As John R. Clarke has noted, the Romans believed that their world was full of demons (much as we believe our world is full of germs, although our belief is based on scientific evidence).[10] These demons could direct the Evil Eye—a gaze that emanated particles that surrounded and entered the victim—at a human out of ill will or envy (*invidia*). This stare would cause harm or mischance, make the recipient ill, or place a curse on or even kill him or her. Humans also had the power to direct the Evil Eye, with similar results. The phallus, along with other apotropaic objects (such as hands and eyes, still considered to ward off evil in modern Greek and Turkish cultures), was thought to attract this harmful gaze and deflect it from its intended victim. Moreover, many apotropaic images were also humorous, as laughter was also thought to dispel the Evil Eye. Apotropaic images were, therefore, placed in particularly dangerous spots where accidents could occur (crossroads, doorways, bridges, corners). Phalluses carved into walls, floors, and buildings from Roman antiquity are not "erotic graffiti" in our sense of the phrase but protective images (see figures 8.1, 8.3, and 8.4). Images of the phallus, in the form of amulets and jewellry called *fascina*, were also

Figure 8.3 Phallic plaque, Pompeii (original in a baker's shop). © Erich Lessing/Art Resource, NY

Figure 8.4 Phallic tintinnabulum, Pompeii. © Vanni/Art Resource, NY

worn by both women and men for extra protection. Babies of both sexes, being especially vulnerable, were given small rings and pendants carved with *phalloi*.

Why was the penis rather than the female genitals selected as this powerful and protective image? It is true that male genitals are easy to represent and easily recognizable even when stylized. However, in this male-dominated society, notions of male primacy were not only everywhere but were also taken for granted. The phallus as the usual apotropaic device is just another confirmation of this reality.

Female Sexuality

Despite the phallocentric nature of ancient Rome, women were not denied sensuality. Ancient authors provide several different impressions of female sexuality, many of them unflattering. Sexually active women are portrayed as nymphomaniacs (*Priapea* 26 and most of the other poems), unfaithful (Ov. *Am.* 3.14), frigid (Mart. 11.60), or sexually transgressive in some way (see Apul. *Met.* 10.19–22, in which a woman eagerly has sex with a donkey). Citizen men, even if they were married, could have sex with whomever they liked, whenever they liked, but were supposed to keep away from married or marriageable citizen women and citizen boys. Sex with foreigners, slaves, and prostitutes of

Primary Source

Box 8.2: Ovid, *The Art of Love*, 3.769–812.[1]

What's left I blush to tell you; but kindly Venus
      Claims as uniquely hers
All that raises a blush. Each woman should know herself,
      pick methods
To suit her body: one fashion won't do for all.
Let the girl with the pretty face lie supine, let the lady
      Who boasts a good back be viewed
From behind. Milanion bore Atalanta's legs on
      His shoulders: nice legs should always be used this way.
The petite should ride horse (Andromache, Hector's Theban
      Bride, was too tall for these games: no jockey she);
If you're built like a fashion model, with willowy figure,
      Then kneel on the bed, your neck
A little arched; the girl who has perfect legs and bosom
      Should lie sideways on, and make her lover stand.
Don't blush to unbind your hair like some ecstatic maenad
      And tumble long tresses about
Your upcurved throat. If childbirth's seamed your belly
      With wrinkles, then offer a rear
Engagement, Parthian style. Sex has countless positions—
      An easy and undemanding one is to lie
On your right side, half-reclining. Neither Delphi nor Ammon
      Will tell you more truth than my Muse:
Long experience, if anything, should establish credit: trust my
      Art, and let these verses speak for themselves!
A woman should melt with passion to her very marrow,
      The act should give equal pleasure to them both:
Keep up a flow of seductive whispered endearments,
      Use sexy taboo words while you're making love,
And if nature's denied you the gift of achieving a climax,
      Moan as though you were coming, put on an act!
(The girl who can't feel down there is really unlucky;
      Missing out on what both sexes should enjoy.)

Only take care that you make your performance convincing,
       Thrash about in a frenzy, roll your eyes,
Let your cries and gasping breath suggest what pleasure
       You're getting (that part has its own private signs).
After the pleasures of sex, though, *don't* try to dun your lover
       For a present: such habits defeat
Their own ends. And don't open all the bedroom windows:
       Much of your body is better left unseen.
Our sport is ended: high time to quit this creative venture,
       Turn loose the swans that drew my poet's car.
As once the young men, so now let my girl-disciples
       Inscribe their trophies: *Ovid was my guide.*

Note

1. Translated by Green (1982: 237–8).

either sex, however, was normal and uncensured, unless indulged in excessively. Citizen women and girls, on the other hand, were not supposed to have sex outside the confines of marriage and, when married, were restricted to sex with their husbands only. This is not to say that illicit female sexual activity never occurred (it gets plenty of mention by ancient authors, since women were thought to be unable to control their sexual appetites); it just was not condoned by social convention.

Female orgasm was recognized and encouraged, and many medical writers thought that it was necessary for a woman to conceive. But our existing authors offer no instructions on how to bring a woman to orgasm; it was simply supposed to happen during intercourse (the poet Ovid encourages a woman to fake her orgasm if she cannot achieve a real one, as doing so will heighten the man's sexual pleasure; see Box 8.2). It was also thought that conception meant that the woman had had an orgasm, which in turn meant that she had enjoyed the sexual act. Unfortunately, this line of thinking was applied even in instances of rape.

The ideal female body was soft, plump (one woman is described as a beautiful round little berry; Petron. *Satyr.* 61), smooth, and completely hairless—women were encouraged to depilate even their pubic hair. Breasts were not supposed to be large but small and well shaped. Thus the poet Martial (14.49) imagines a breastband (the ancient equivalent of a brassiere) saying, "I fear big-breasted women."[11] Large breasts were possibly considered ungainly and barbaric. On the other hand, erotic poets considered large hips very desirable, an ideal borne out by depictions of women in wall paintings (see Figure 8.5). The modern erotic ideal of full breasts, small waist, and rounded hips has, therefore, not been a cultural constant.[12] In the passage from Ovid in Box 8.2, we notice that women are encouraged to show off their best bodily feature and conceal their less-than-perfect body parts to heighten the sexual pleasure of their partner. There is no corresponding section on how men should go about concealing or showing off their bodies for the visual delectation of women. However, it seems that Roman men were held up to a physical ideal that began in Classical Greece and is still with Western culture today: slender and long-legged, with well-defined chest and pectoral muscles and a handsome face.

Sexual Scenes

Private Houses

Ovid's *Ars Amatoria* (see Box 8.2) recommends various sexual positions for a heteroerotic couple: woman on her back, on top, on all fours, or kneeling at the edge of the bed, with her legs over her lover's shoulders. Many of these positions are shown in Roman art. Sexual scenes of varying explicitness are often found painted on the walls of private houses in a technique called **fresco**. As we might expect, numerous erotic paintings are found in bedrooms (*cubicula*)—perhaps reflecting the real-life activity within the room. However, many are found in dining rooms and hallways. The painting in Figure 8.5 was originally located on the outside wall of a room opening off the *triclinium*, or dining room, of

Figure 8.5 Sexual scene, House of Caecilius Iucundus, Pompeii. © Erich Lessing/Art Resource, NY

the House of Caecilius Iucundus at Pompeii. Such paintings were never meant to be private or secreted away from visitors or other occupants of the house. Some *cubicula* even open right onto the atrium, the main reception room in a Roman house. All statuses would have seen these pictures, as well as both sexes and children. Such paintings may have functioned as didactic paradigms, aphrodisiacs, or sexual aids. The emperor Tiberius, for example, supposedly used paintings and statues for sexual stimulation (Suet. *Tib.* 43–44).

But as Clarke has recently pointed out,[13] such paintings were likely meant to be "high art," signifying elite status and refined taste. They are, in fact, depictions of lovely and well-fed young people enjoying the blessings of Venus. These elevated images of lovemaking are meant to be seen by visitors because they illustrate the owner's elite pretensions and a life of luxury and high status. Because of this intention, such scenes are even found in the lower-status areas

See Chapter 5, p. 110, on ⬅
the atrium/peristyle
house design.

Figure 8.6 Sexual scene, "cook's bedroom," Pompeii. © Scala/Art Resource, NY

of a house. The House of the Vettii at Pompeii has a set of erotic scenes (see, for example, Figure 8.6) in the room next to the kitchen (possibly the cook's bedroom but, in any case, clearly the service area of the house). The painting is crude and hastily done over a plain whitewashed wall but nonetheless indicates a desire for some of the status and luxury found in upper-class areas of the house.

Public Places

Due to the connection with status and luxury, scenes of sexuality are also found in public spaces. The best-known example is the brothel, in which the sexual scenes painted above each prostitute's cell were not designed to be depictions of the inhabitant or her sexual specialty but, as Clarke has deduced, romanticized and luxurious pictures of sexual couplings, meant to give the squalid surroundings some high-class ambience.[14]

Another reason for the placing of such scenes in public spaces is indicated by Figure 8.7. This erotic picture is part of a series displayed in the *apodyterium* (change room) of the large and luxurious Suburban Baths, located outside the city walls of Pompeii and built in the early first century CE. Both sexes used the same change room at the baths, as there were no separate quarters for men and women. The erotic paintings were atop the wooden cupboards designed to hold clothes while

Figure 8.7 Sexual threesome (man/man/woman), change room of the Suburban Baths, Pompeii. © Scala/Art Resource, NY

the patrons bathed (and sometime later were painted over, which explains their poor state of preservation). They mostly represent sexual acrobatics and include many activities condemned or ridiculed by Roman authors. The scene in Figure 8.7, a threesome, was likely meant to be apotropaic given that the baths were especially dangerous places. One could slip on the wet floor, be burned on hot pipes or tiles, have one's clothes stolen, or fall victim to the Evil Eye emanating from envious demons or humans. Such pictures invoked laughter and protected the viewer from misfortune.

Oral Sex

Several of the pictures in the Suburban Baths depict oral sex, either cunnilingus or fellatio. Oral sex was not generally looked upon favourably in Roman antiquity, at least by elite authors. The mouth was the organ of speech, public oratory, and social interaction—Romans kissed upon meeting—and the Romans were very concerned with its purity and care.[15] A Roman citizen male *receiving* oral sex from a male or female was of course perfectly normal, as such behaviour was in keeping with the gender identity of being the dominant, active partner. Although some men or women very likely took pleasure in giving fellatio or cunnilingus to their partners, giving oral sex was viewed by many authors as an enjoyable activity only for those who were impotent or sexually perverse (for examples of this view, see Box 8.3). In literature, to fellate or give someone cunnilingus sometimes leads to the *os impurum*, the "filthy mouth" that can never be "clean" again.

Figure 8.8 is another painting from Pompeii's Suburban Baths. It is unique as it shows a scene of cunnilingus. Note that the woman is depilated and wears jewellery and that the man is small, subservient, and unmanly, which corresponds to literary descriptions of the *cunnilinctor*. From graffiti at Pompeii we have an advertisement that male prostitutes would give women oral sex for two *asses* (*CIL* 4.3999). This might be actual sexual practice, or it might be libel.

Same-Sex Couplings[16]

In Rome, male–male contact was normal (it was common to desire a woman or a boy, and the services of both kinds of prostitutes were available), but certain rules prevailed. Again, Roman culture did not assign an identity to individuals based on their sexual orientation, and a man's predilection for homosexual activity was thought to be almost perfectly compatible with heterosexual marriage (although it is implied by a few authors that a man would give up his male sexual partners on marriage so that he could focus his sexual energies on impregnating his wife).[17] One of Martial's epigrams upbraids a wife for caring that her husband has affairs with slave boys (*pueri*), as though they were her rivals. "Such affairs are short and fleeting," says the poet (Mart. 12.96; see also the example of Lygdus on p. 182).

Clearly, what bothered the Romans most in male homoerotic behaviour was assimilation to the female role

Figure 8.8 Scene of cunnilingus, Suburban Baths, Pompeii. © Scala/Art Resource, NY

Primary Source

Box 8.3: Martial, *Epigrams*.[1]

In the springtime of your cheeks when the down was still dubious, your shameless tongue licked male middles. Now that your sorry head has earned the scorn of undertakers and the disgust of a wretched executioner, you use your mouth otherwise; delighted by excess of spite, you bark at whatever name is put to you. Better that your noxious tongue stick in genitals. It was cleaner when it sucked. (2.61)

That over-active cock, well known to girls not a few, has ceased to stand for Linus. Tongue, look out! (11.25)

Husband with his tongue, adulterer with his mouth, Nanneius is dirtier than Summemmian lips. When foul Leda sees him naked from a window in the Subura, she closes the brothel, and she prefers to kiss his middle rather than his top. Well, he that lately used to go through all the inner tubes and declare confidently as of personal knowledge whether boy or girl was in a mother's belly (rejoice, cunts, this is to your advantage) cannot raise his fornicating tongue. For while he was stuck deep in a swelling womb and heard the infants wailing inside, an uncomely disease relaxed the greedy member. Now he can't be either clean or unclean. (11.61)

CIL.[2]

On a column in a private house:
Yes, Sabina, you are sucking it, but you aren't doing it right. (4.4185)

On a wall inside the *lupanar*:
Myrtis, you suck it so well. (4.2273)

Outside a shop entrance:
Vote Isidorus for aedile. He licks cunts fantastically. (4.1383)

Note

1. Translated by Shackleton Bailey (1993).
2. Translated by Varone (2002: 77, 81).

(see Box 8.4). To be penetrated was thought to be incompatible with a fully masculine image. Ideally, the citizen male was the active partner and the penetrated a smooth, hairless younger male who was not a free citizen. Thus the philosopher Seneca (*QNat.* 1.16) writes with disgust of a rich citizen man named Hostius Quadra, who, "with his whole body spread in position for submitting to them," enjoyed being penetrated by grown men and even had a room fitted up with mirrors so that he could watch these "monstrous couplings."[18] The most important questions for the ancient viewer would not be if the sexual act was heterosexual or homosexual but of what status the participants were and, most importantly, who was doing the penetrating. The voices of men who chose to be penetrated or to fellate—the passive, as the Romans would have called them—are absent from our source material, though surely we can assume that some of those who took on the receptive or passive role received pleasure from doing so. Evidence of established and respected sexual relationships between grown men is also not to be found in the works of Roman authors. Homosexual acts are represented in Roman literature less as loving contact between two partners and more as something that one does to another person.[19]

Passive-Sexual Labels as Abuse

As Williams has noted,[20] one of the most common accusations in graffiti, political slogging matches, lampoons, and courtroom attacks is one of "pathic" homosexuality, attempting to discredit another man by claiming he is sexually passive. This allegation takes the form of one of three types of behaviour: as a citizen, having previously been the sexual partner of an older man; continuing as an adult to enjoy being penetrated anally; or enjoying performing fellatio. Attacks of this nature occur everywhere in Roman society and seem to have been something of a communal preoccupation. Consequently, Cicero (*Phil.* 2.44) could scathingly say that Marc Antony had been "married" to Gaius Curio in his youth. A graffito from Pompeii (*CIL* 4.10232A) declares: "Lucius Habonius mutilates Caesonius Felix and makes him suck it."

A more negative aspect of the Roman stereotype of male sexuality involves the proclivities attributed to the effeminate man.[21] The Greek word *kinaidos* referred to an

Primary Source

Box 8.4: Martial, *Epigrams*, 2.51.[1]

Often you have one silver coin in your entire strongbox, Hyllus, and that worn smoother than your arse. And yet you won't lose it to the baker or the innkeeper, but to someone who boasts an outsize cock. Your unfortunate belly watches your arse's banquet. The one hungers miserably all the time, the other guzzles.

Note

1. Translated by Shackleton Bailey (1993).

effeminate eastern male dancer who entertained the audience by clashing a tambourine and lasciviously shaking his hips in such a way as to suggest anal intercourse. Some of those characteristics are transferred to the Roman *cinaedus*. It was thought that *cinaedi* could be identified by such unmasculine characteristics as their curled hair, use of perfume, mincing gait, coloured clothing, long or short unbelted tunic, and tendency to dance at parties. Consequently, to call a mature man a *cinaedus* was to call him soft, eastern, a dancer, and apt to be anally penetrated and to enjoy it, although what made a man a *cinaedus* was not specifically a predilection for anal penetration. In Petronius's novel, the *Satyricon*, the protagonist, Encolpius, is attacked by an old *cinaedus*:

> (After spouting poetry, the man) befouled me with a slobbery kiss. Then he got up on my bed and in spite of my resistance forced the covers off of me. He laboured long and hard over my groin—in vain! The makeup caked on his face melted and streamed off in rivulets; there was so much rouge in his wrinkles you'd have thought of an old wall battered by a rainstorm.[22]

The *cinaedus*, then, was a man who had abandoned his masculinity through action and appearance. Not every man who submitted to anal penetration (for instance, through rape) could be labelled in this way.

Cinaedi were not outcasts. Although they were targets for ridicule and censure, they were also handy and pleasurable sexual outlets for other men. While the figure might look to us like a proto-homosexual identity, the effeminacy of the *cinaedus* was sometimes said to be a veneer for excessive heterosexual activity. Many *cinaedi* are also described as lovers of women. Martial depicts Lygdus, the *cinaedus* and sexual plaything of a Roman citizen male who is also having an affair with the man's wife and has fathered a child by her. Interestingly, Martial describes this situation "without suggesting that such a combination of behaviours in one man is at all striking or in need of explanation."[23]

What is paramount in the definition of a *cinaedus*, then, is not his love of any one type of sexual act or gender but his lack of sexual self-control and loss of interest in masculinity. To be indiscriminate in one's sexual partners, to be more open to sexual experiences of any kind (with either sex) than other men, to be overactive with both sexes (even orally), or to dress effeminately was to fail to live up to the central imperatives of masculinity: control and dominion, "both of others and of oneself."[24] That is what made a man a *cinaedus*.

Pederasty

Even though homoerotic relations were considered natural in Roman society, such activities were condemned when the passive partner was freeborn. Unlike ancient Greece, in which couplings of older and younger citizen males were enshrined in social convention, Roman social ideology does not seem to have tolerated sexual contact between male citizens of any age. There is even some indication that an early law, the *Lex Scantinia*—dating to the second or first century BCE—attempted to restrict pederasty (sex with citizen boys).[25] Quintilian (*Inst.* 2.2.14), a first-century CE orator, matter-of-factly warns parents against sending their (free or freed) sons to schools, hotbeds of sexual activity with known pederasts as teachers. The satirist Juvenal (7.238–41, 10.224) presents us with two vignettes: one of students masturbating in the classroom and another of a teacher "bending a boy over." Adults clearly feared that these things might happen, and there was apparently enough evidence to warrant notice.

But there seems to have been little to censure in a man pursuing a slave or a non-Roman male. A pronounced fondness for boys or too many boys could make a citizen the subject of malicious gossip. Nevertheless, the keeping of slave boys, like the keeping of mistresses, was a common practice and perhaps one that was emulated and envied. The praise of beautiful boys in erotic epigram is commonplace (see Box 8.5). Dozens of funerary epitaphs to cherished male sexual partners remain. It seems that, while sexual intercourse with citizen boys was deplorable and illegal, sexual intercourse with young slave boys, non-citizens, or prostitutes was acceptable.

Female Homosexuality[26]

Unfortunately, there is little in the way of literary and visual evidence for female homo-sexuality in ancient Rome. Lesbians who enjoyed penetrating other women by means of a dildo or "rubbing" each other were called *tribades*. Such women were exposed to censure because they failed to align themselves with the fundamental insertive or receptive split

---

Primary Source

Box 8.5: Catullus, *Poems*, 48.[1]

If someone would let me keep kissing
your honeysweet eyes, Juventius,
I'd keep kissing up to three thousand,
and never feel close to satiety,
not even if the crop of kissing
were denser than the ripe fields of wheat.

Note

1. Translated by F.W. Cornish; see Goold et al. (1913).

(like citizen males who prefer the passive role in homoerotic intercourse). In other words, they took pleasure in performing activities inappropriate to their gender and so transgressed the boundaries of acceptable gender identity. Interestingly, their female partners performed normally and were not censured. Martial has several epigrams on this topic, both attacking lesbians and drawing attention to the mechanics of their lovemaking. The "monstrous organ" he mentions in Box 8.6 probably refers to a strap-on dildo and not, as some scholars have puzzlingly maintained, an outsized clitoris.

Again, it is difficult to pinpoint the Roman attitude to homosexuality because the voices we have to work with present the opinions set out by the dominant discourse. It is problematic to try to decide how closely the values that Latin literature assigned to different homosexual practices reflected reality.

Sexuality and the Law: *Stuprum* and Rape

Stuprum was the generic Latin term for "sexual misconduct." In the Republic, cases of *stuprum* were handled within the family, with most centring on the containment of female sexuality. Consequently, there are a few extreme examples of fathers killing their daughters for their sexual misconduct (because the girls' behaviour was thought to imperil their chances of marriage). One Aufidianus killed his daughter rather than marry her to her freed lover, the implication being that no one else would have married her because of this relationship (Val. Max. 6.1.3). Sometimes women were punished for activities that were thought to lead to *stuprum*. In one instance, a woman was fined the amount of her dowry for drinking wine.

After Augustus reformulated adultery as a separate criminal offence (in the *quaestio de adulteriis*; see Box 8.1), *stuprum* took on a more restricted meaning: sex with a freeborn boy,

Primary Source

Box 8.6: Martial, *Epigrams*, 1.90.[1]

I never saw you close to men, Bassa, and no rumour gave you a lover. You were always surrounded by a crowd of your own sex, performing every office, with no man coming near you. So I confess I thought you were a Lucretia, but Bassa, for shame, you were a fornicator. You dare to join two cunts and your monstrous organ feigns masculinity. You have invented a portent worthy of the Theban riddle: where no man is, there is adultery.

Note

1. Translated by Shackleton Bailey (1993).

virgin, or widow, unmarried woman, or divorcee (that is, any marriageable woman). It was an offence on the part of both partners, and both men and women could be prosecuted. (That said, ancient Rome had nothing like a modern police force or crown prosecutor. Any lawsuit had to be brought by an interested third party; otherwise, the charge did not go to court.) But like adultery, it is the woman's status that matters in a charge of *stuprum*—there was no crime if the woman was a slave or a prostitute. Sexual relations between betrothed couples would also technically be *stuprum*, but the concerned parties (that is, the parents) would be unlikely to prosecute. A prosecution might be brought against a jilting lover to force him into marriage or punish him, but then the woman was open to prosecution as well. The Roman jurists thought it safest for men to avoid taking women who might fall under the laws for *stuprum* as their concubines. They recommended a slave, prostitute, or woman convicted of adultery instead.

Compare Chapter 5, pp. 104–6, on other Augustan legislation.

See Chapter 5, pp. 102–3, on concubinage.

Although someone with a grudge against both parties, such as a widow's or divorcee's former in-laws or family or a failed or disappointed suitor, might benefit from a *stuprum* prosecution, it is unlikely that this part of the Augustan legislation did much to restrain the Romans' sexual activities. But accusations of *stuprum* and adultery often masked political enmity: they were good and quick ways of getting rid of opponents, or at least of discrediting them. *Relegatio* (temporary exile) was the usual penalty for *stuprum*, accompanied by a monetary fine but no loss of status or confiscation of property. Serious cases were resolved by *deportatio* (permanent exile). The sources, legal and otherwise, are far more concerned with the penalties for adultery, which was a much graver crime in Roman eyes because it could potentially introduce an illegitimate child into the hereditary line.

Another sexual act addressed in Roman law is rape, technically known as *per vim stuprum*, or "seduction through force." Julius Caesar made the rape of free women and boys a crime (before this, rape was prosecuted under *iniuria*, a law that punished bodily injury and offences to good reputation). The victim could bring a charge if he or she was *sui iuris* (that is, if his or her father were dead). A woman's husband or father could prosecute, as could outsiders. There was no statute of limitations on rape.

We have no way of detecting the level of incidence of rape in Roman antiquity. The subject rarely appears in the historical sources, but this is unsurprising given their nature. Even today rape is an underreported crime due to personal trauma or a fear of stigma, and this must have held in the Roman world as well. The Roman woman or man who was raped was subject to no penalty and was allowed to marry. But if the rapist claimed that the victim had consented, they could both be accused of adultery or *stuprum*. If a female victim was married and found guilty, her husband would have to divorce her, a requirement that may have prevented some rape charges from going to trial. Under Augustus the maximum penalty for rape

See Chapter 2, pp. 23–4, for the legend of the Rape of Lucretia, the paragon of Roman female virtue.

was death. Hadrian advocated leniency for anyone who had committed murder trying to stop a rape.

On a more interesting note, rape was generally a criminal charge against only the freeborn or freed. If a slave was raped by anyone other than his or her owner or someone who had the owner's permission, his or her master or mistress could prosecute the rapist but only under the Roman laws for damage to property. If the rapist was a slave, the action was brought against his master or mistress.

Summary

This chapter has given some idea of sexual culture in Roman society and has detailed the problems of using ancient literary and artistic evidence to explore this topic, the expurgation of literary and artistic erotica, and the relatively recent explosion of interest in sexual material. Our own sexual categories cannot be imposed on the Roman sexual blueprint, as it operated on a system of gender identity rather than sexual orientation. In addition, the Romans saw the phallus in part as an apotropaic object rather than as merely a sexual organ, and some sexual pictures in public buildings (such as those in the Suburban Baths at Pompeii) functioned as images designed to ward off ill will, or *invidia*. Sexual scenes in private houses and brothels functioned as signs of luxury and status.

But the Romans also censured certain sexual acts. The *os impurum* was thought to come about as a result of giving oral sex; homoerotic relations between adult citizen males were frowned upon, as were men who took citizen boys as sexual partners; and the figure of the *cinaedus* was ridiculed for having abandoned his masculinity. Some sexual offences, including adultery, *stuprum*, and rape, were enshrined in Roman law as criminal acts. Nevertheless, we have to remember that the voices of the passive are missing from our sources. The elite authors are extremely concerned with sexual transgression because sexual "perversion" meant moral, political, and social perversion as well. Their statements represent a very simple view of Roman sexuality; the reality was likely much more complex.

Questions for Review and Discussion

1. What is the difference between an essentialist and a constructivist? How does this relate to the determinism/voluntarism and the nature/nurture debates regarding sexual orientation?

2. What were the important sexual categories in Roman society? How do they differ from our own and why?
3. Define the term *apotropaic* and give an example of an apotropaic image. How did the Romans think such images worked?
4. What is the *os impurum*, and from what does it result?
5. In Roman society, what did "pathic" homosexuality include?

Suggested Reading

Clarke, J. 1998. *Looking at Lovemaking: Constructions of Sexuality in Roman Art 100 BC–AD 250*. Berkeley: University of California Press.

This outstanding and beautifully illustrated book examines sexuality in Roman art.

———. 2003. *Roman Sex 100 BC–AD 250*. New York: Harry N. Abrams.

This book is a shorter, perhaps more accessible, version of *Looking at Lovemaking*.

Flaherty, J. 2000. "O Profligate Youth of Rome, Ye #*!, Ye @#! (See Footnote)." *New York Times*, 28 Sept. www.nytimes.com/2000/09/28/arts/28ARTS.html.

Flaherty offers an interesting history of the expurgation in the Loeb Classical Library volumes.

Gaimster, D. 2000. "Sex and Sensibility at the British Museum." *History Today* 50 (9): 10–15. www.historytoday.com/david-gaimster/sex-and-sensibility-british-museum.

Gaimster's essay examines the expurgation of ancient erotica.

Hallett, J., and M. Skinner, eds. 1997. *Roman Sexualities*. Princeton, NJ: Princeton University Press.

This volume contains an excellent series of essays on various aspects of Roman sexuality.

Hubbard, T. 2003. *Homosexuality in Greece and Rome: A Sourcebook of Basic Documents*. Berkeley: University of California Press.

Featuring outstanding accompanying notes, Hubbard's book presents the ancient sources on homosexuality.

Johns, C. 1982. *Sex or Symbol: Erotic Images of Greece and Rome*. London: British Museum Publications.

This text is a general work on ancient Greek and Roman erotic culture, with illustrations.

Johnson, M., and T. Ryan, eds. 2005. *Sexuality in Greek and Roman Society and Literature*. London and New York: Routledge.

Johnson and Ryan provide a translated book of primary sources on Greek and Roman sexuality.

Ortiz, D. 1993. "Creating Controversy: Essentialism and Constructivism and the Politics of Gay Identity." *Virginia Law Review* 79 (7): 1833–57.

This excellent article lucidly sets out the details of the debates surrounding gay identity, as well as the causes of sexual orientation and their relation to one another.

Skinner, M. 2005. *Sexuality in Greek and Roman Culture*. Oxford: Blackwell.
This textbook is a general examination of Greek and Roman sexuality.

Varone, A. 2002. *Erotica Pompeiana: Love Inscriptions on the Walls of Pompeii*. Translated by R.P. Berg, with revisions by

D. Harwood and R. Ling. Rome: L'Erma di Bretschneider.
Varone's book is a fascinating collection of the erotic Latin inscriptions from the ancient city of Pompeii.

Williams, C. 2010. *Roman Homosexuality: Ideologies of Masculinity in Classical Antiquity*, 2nd edn. Oxford: Oxford University Press.
This book is an exhaustive, fascinating, and detailed discussion of sexuality in Roman antiquity, particularly homoerotica.

Notes

1 Translations of the *CIL* are from Varone (2002).
2 Williams (2010: 3).
3 After Clarke (1998: 11).
4 Johns (1982: 15–35) is excellent on this topic and is the source of much of what follows, along with Gaimster (2000) and Kendrick (1987: 3–14).
5 Clarke (2003: 12); Gaimster (2000); Kendrick (1987: 69–70).
6 Gaimster (2000); Kendrick (1987: 69–70).
7 The following draws heavily on Ortiz (1993).
8 Adams (1982).
9 See Johns (1982: 61–75).
10 Clarke (2007: 67).
11 Translated by Shackleton Bailey (1993).
12 Olson (2008: 69).
13 Clarke (2003: 28–33).
14 Clarke (1998: 196–206).
15 Ibid.: 220–5.
16 See Williams (2010), which is the source of much of the following.
17 Williams (2010: 54–6).
18 Translated by Corcoran (1971).
19 Williams (2010: 179).
20 Ibid.: 179–97.
21 See Ibid.: 137–76.
22 Translated by Hubbard (2003: 403, 9.13).
23 Williams (2010: 229).
24 Gibson (2003: 275); self-control was seen as a masculine province. See Williams (2010: 139, 156–70); Edwards (1993: 78); and Cic. *Fin.* 2.47.
25 This is a fragmentary and confusing law. See Williams (2010: 130–6).
26 On this topic, see Rabinowitz and Auanger (2002).

9

Religion at Rome

Andreas Bendlin

A lead curse tablet, or *defixio*, from Raraunum in Roman Gaul (near modern Poitiers) was found near a spring. It was rolled up and, as was a common feature of ritual manipulation of curse tablets, pierced by a nail. It asks otherwise unknown deities or persons to "bind" a group of mimes with whom the tablet's commissioner or commissioners appear to have been in competition. Particularly remarkable is the request that one rival be unable to sacrifice, that is, be rejected by the gods, should he ever try to approach them in this way again:

> Apecius, he shall bind Trinemetos and Caticnos. He shall strip bare Seneciolus, Asedis, Tritios, Neocarinos, Dido. Sosio shall become delirious. Sosio shall burn with fever. Sosio shall suffer pain every day. Sosio shall be unable to speak. Sosio shall not triumph (?) over Maturus and Eridunna. Sosio shall be unable to sacrifice. Aqanno shall torment you. Nana shall torture you. Sosio shall be unable to outshine the mime Eumolpus. He shall be unable to play . . . He shall be unable to sacrifice. Sosio shall be unable to snatch the victory from the mime Fotios.[1]

Other curses from the Roman world were clearly formulated with the purpose of retaliation, even though the texts adopt quasi-juridical language. The following is from the temple of the goddess Mater Magna ("Great Mother") in Mogontiacum (modern Mainz) in the Roman province of Upper Germany:

> I request from you, mistress Mater Magna, that you vindicate me (or: take revenge on my behalf) regarding the goods belonging to Florus, my husband. He who has defrauded me, Ulattius Severus, just as I write this unfavourably, so may everything for him, whatever he does, whatever he attempts to do,

may everything for him turn out unfavourably. As salt (disperses in) water, so may it turn out for him. Whatever he has taken away from me from the goods belonging to Florus, my husband, I request from you, mistress Mater Magna, that you vindicate me regarding this matter. (*AE* 2005, 1122)

Vengeful curses such as this one, sometimes called prayers for justice and directed towards the gods (who served as the final arbiters of justice and righteous behaviour), seem particularly appropriate in a society whose legal system was inadequately equipped to deal comprehensively with the enforcement of justice or may have been disinterested in doing so. In the Roman period, it is sometimes difficult to draw a clear distinction between purely competitive *defixiones* to bend the future (one's own or that of others) and prayers for justice to mend past wrongs. However, each demonstrates the critical role that the gods played for ancient individuals, even in aspects of life that we now tend to think of as secular, such as competition and justice. As this chapter will demonstrate, the gods and the rituals through which humans communicated with them were ubiquitous presences in Roman society, in both public and domestic settings.

→ Compare Chapter 11, pp. 249, 251 and 255–8, on the accessibility of the justice system.

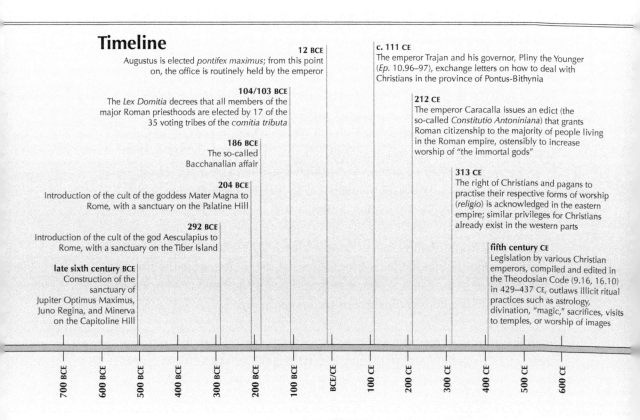

Timeline

12 BCE
Augustus is elected *pontifex maximus*; from this point on, the office is routinely held by the emperor

104/103 BCE
The *Lex Domitia* decrees that all members of the major Roman priesthoods are elected by 17 of the 35 voting tribes of the *comitia tributa*

186 BCE
The so-called Bacchanalian affair

204 BCE
Introduction of the cult of the goddess Mater Magna to Rome, with a sanctuary on the Palatine Hill

292 BCE
Introduction of the cult of the god Aesculapius to Rome, with a sanctuary on the Tiber Island

late sixth century BCE
Construction of the sanctuary of Jupiter Optimus Maximus, Juno Regina, and Minerva on the Capitoline Hill

c. 111 CE
The emperor Trajan and his governor, Pliny the Younger (*Ep.* 10.96–97), exchange letters on how to deal with Christians in the province of Pontus-Bithynia

212 CE
The emperor Caracalla issues an edict (the so-called *Constitutio Antoniniana*) that grants Roman citizenship to the majority of people living in the Roman empire, ostensibly to increase worship of "the immortal gods"

313 CE
The right of Christians and pagans to practise their respective forms of worship (*religio*) is acknowledged in the eastern empire; similar privileges for Christians already exist in the western parts

fifth century CE
Legislation by various Christian emperors, compiled and edited in the Theodosian Code (9.16, 16.10) in 429–437 CE, outlaws illicit ritual practices such as astrology, divination, "magic," sacrifices, visits to temples, or worship of images

700 BCE 600 BCE 500 BCE 400 BCE 300 BCE 200 BCE 100 BCE BCE/CE 100 CE 200 CE 300 CE 400 CE 500 CE 600 CE

Introduction

Religion is a vast and varied subject whose tendrils reached into every part of Roman life. This chapter introduces the shape and contexts of religion at Rome and gives some sense of its significance and function for a polytheistic society. To these ends, focus falls upon deities, religious ritual (sacrifice, prayer, vows, and dedications), location (temples, shrines), and specialists (priesthoods, religious functionaries, and "ritual experts"). State-approved religious activity (called civic religion in this chapter) supported traditional concepts of authority and public order; it is for this reason that public disorder and suspected political subversion could sometimes be described in religious terms. However, polytheistic Rome was also a place of religious options, and our discussion includes the individual religious choices made by worshippers. Although this chapter concentrates on religion in the city of Rome, it also addresses the religious traditions of Rome's trans-Mediterranean empire in so far as these traditions, deities, and cults migrated to (and thus shaped the religious life in) Rome as an inadvertent result of Roman imperialism and expansion.

———— • ◆ • ————

Practice, Belief, and Divinity:
Some Salient Features of Religion at Rome

At the beginning of the political year (1 January in the late Republic), the newly elected **consuls**, accompanied by members of the major priestly **colleges**, the senators, and the people, ascended to the sanctuary of Jupiter Optimus Maximus ("Best and Greatest"), Juno Regina ("Queen"), and Minerva on the Capitoline Hill (for the location of sacred sites of deities discussed in this chapter, see Figure 9.1). The purpose of their procession was to fulfill the vows (***vota***) that the consuls of the previous year had undertaken on behalf of the well-being of the state (the *res publica* of the Roman people) and to pronounce new ones for the following year. Under the Empire, the ritual's date was moved to 3 January and, more importantly, the imperial vows focused on the well-being of the ruling emperor and his family as representatives of the people. This is a telling reminder that neither rituals (*sacra*) nor their meanings were fixed in time or resistant to change. On the contrary, both action and meaning were highly adaptable to social or (as in this case) political transformations.

The celebration of these vows is attested among civilian and military populations in Rome, Italy, and the provinces.[2] Vows dating to 3 January 87 CE are preserved in the annual protocols of the **Arval Brothers**, a priestly college in the vicinity of Rome known for its cult of the goddess Dea Dia. The college's painstaking documentation of all its ritual activities proffers a highly detailed glimpse of religious practices and beliefs at Rome in the imperial

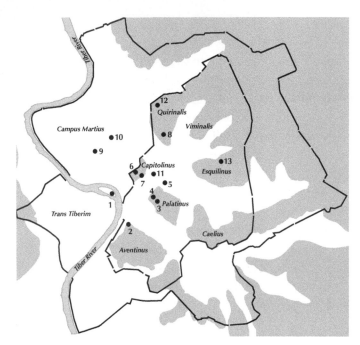

Figure 9.1

Map of Sacred Topography

1 Aesculapius, on the Tiber Island
2 Ceres (with Liber and Libera),
   on the Aventine Hill
3 Apollo, on the Palatine Hill
4 Mater Magna, on the Palatine Hill
5 Vesta, on the margins of the Forum
6 The Capitoline Triad (Jupiter, Juno,
   and Minerva)
7 Jupiter Tonans, on the Capitoline Hill
8 Diana Planciana, on the Quirinal
9 Theatre of Pompey, in the Field of Mars
10 Isis (with Serapis), in the Field of Mars
11 Divus Vespasian (and Divus Titus),
   in the Forum Romanum
12 Salus Publica, on the Quirinal Hill
13 Tellus, on the Esquiline Hill

period. In this example (see Box 9.1), the Arval Brothers acknowledge that the emperor Domitian, his spouse, his niece, and the imperial house are alive and safe. Through sacrifice, they fulfill the vows made on 3 January of the previous year on behalf of the imperial family's well-being. They also pronounce the vows for the next year: if the gods continue to preserve

Primary Source

Box 9.1: *CFA* no. 55, col. I.

When the Emperor Caesar Domitian Augustus Germanicus was consul for the thirteenth time and Lucius Volusius Saturninus was his fellow consul (87 CE), three days before the Nones of January (3 January), the Arval Brother Caius Salvius Liberalis, officiating in lieu of the *magister* Caius Julius Silanus, reported to the college of Arval Brothers on the Capitoline Hill in the porch of (the Temple of) Jupiter Optimus Maximus: since the immortal gods, their power made propitious, have lent their ears to the vows of the entire world which were eagerly undertaken for the well-being of the Emperor Caesar Domitian Augustus Germanicus, son of god Vespasian, *pontifex maximus*, for Domitia Augusta his spouse, for Julia Augusta, and for their entire house, that it was fitting for the college to fulfill the previous vows and pronounce new ones. The college decreed: that this should be favourable, propitious, happy and salutary! Concerning the vows, that the previous ones should be fulfilled and new ones pronounced for the well-being and safety of the Emperor Caesar Domitian Augustus Germanicus, son of god Vespasian, for Domitia Augusta his spouse, for Julia Augusta, and for their entire house: to Jupiter Optimus Maximus a bull, to Juno Regina a cow, to Minerva a cow, to Salus Publica of the Roman People the Citizens a cow.

On the same day, there on the hill, Caius Salvius Liberalis, officiating in lieu of the *magister* Caius Julius Silanus, sprinkled incense and poured wine into the fire on the portable altar and sacrificed with wine, ground spelt, and the knife: to Jupiter Optimus Maximus a bull, to Juno Regina a cow, to Minerva a cow, to Salus Publica of the Roman People the Citizens a cow. The entrails were cooked in a pot, after which he returned them (to the deities).

On the same day, there in the porch of (the temple of) Jupiter Optimus Maximus the Arval Brother Caius Salvius Liberalis, officiating in lieu of the *magister* Caius Julius Silanus, in the presence of the college of the Arval Brothers undertook the vows for the well-being and safety of the Emperor Caesar Domitian Augustus Germanicus, son of god Vespasian, *pontifex maximus*, holder of the tribunician power, censor for life, father of the fatherland, for Domitia Augusta his spouse, for Julia Augusta, and for their entire house in the name of the college of Arval Brothers, using the following words: Jupiter Optimus Maximus, if the Emperor Caesar Domitian Augustus Germanicus, son of god Vespasian, *pontifex maximus*, holder of the tribunician power, censor for life, father of the fatherland, and Domitia Augusta his spouse, and Julia Augusta, whom I intend to name, are alive and their house is safe on the third day before the Nones of January that will be next for the Roman People the citizens, and the *res publica* of the Roman People the citizens, and if you have preserved that day and them safe from any dangers occurring now or in the future before that day, and if you have given as favourable an outcome as I intend to name, and if you have preserved them in the same or better condition in which they are now, if you have done this in this way then I vow that in the name of the college of Arval Brothers there will be an offering to you consisting of an ox with gilded horns. Juno Regina, with the words I have employed to vow that there will be an offering to Jupiter Optimus Maximus consisting of an ox with gilded horns, which vow I have made today, if you have done this in this way then using the same words I vow in the name of the college of the Arval Brothers that there will be an offering to you consisting of an ox with gilded horns. . . .[1]

In the college were present Caius Salvius Liberalis, Nonius Bassus, Aulus Julius Quadratus, Lucius Maecius Postumus, Lucius Veratius Quadratus, Publius Sallustius Blaesus, and Lucius Venuleius Apronianus.

Note

1. The words used for the vow to Juno are also used for the vows to Minerva and Salus Publica.

the lives of the emperor and his family, sacrifices will be offered on 3 January 88 CE.

The Arval Brothers' account details the documentary practices and administrative routines of a Roman priestly college and thus provides an excellent example of the issues under discussion in this section. It is often stated that Roman religion, like most other religious traditions in the ancient world, operated without sacred books or theological truths revealed through authoritative writings, which contrasts markedly with some of today's world religions. To a certain extent, this statement is undoubtedly correct. But there existed extensive priestly archives at Rome, most of them lost. Some, like the protocols of the Arval Brothers, contained detailed prayer formulas and elaborate depictions of ritual procedure; others, like the books kept by the college of pontiffs (**pontifices**), laid down rules and regulations to serve as a blueprint for ritual action and as a reference in cases of ignorance or disputes over correct procedure.[3] But in 213 BCE, at the height of the Second Punic War, the urban **praetor** confiscated unsanctioned books containing prophecies, prayers, or sacrificial instructions and banned illegitimately conducted sacrifices (Livy 25.1.6–12). The emperor Augustus also ordered the collection and destruction of more than 2,000 compilations of prophetic writings in Greek and Latin that were privately owned and hence deemed to be without sufficient authority (Suet. *Aug.* 31; Tac. *Ann.* 6.12). Arguably, religion at Rome was not characterized by a lack of texts that claimed to possess some religious authority but by an abundance of them. It was also marked by competition over who possessed sufficient authority and power to interpret the will of the gods.

The peculiarly repetitive structure of the Arval Brothers' protocol underlines another critical feature of Roman ritual practice: the practitioners of religion at Rome, like those in most other religious traditions in the ancient world and in many current traditions, regarded the scrupulous and correct performance of ritual utterances, gestures, movements, and actions as vital. Some scholars have therefore argued that the Romans were more concerned with observing an orthopraxy ("correct action") than with following an orthodoxy ("correct opinion") of faith; that is, practices mattered more to the Romans than beliefs did. It is furthermore sometimes held that the primary aim of all Roman ritual practice, at least in the public domain, was to maintain a correct if somewhat legalistic relationship between the Roman people (or, under the Empire, the emperor and the Roman people) and their gods, thus assuring an equilibrium sometimes called the *pax deorum* ("peace of the gods," or "peace with the gods").[4] As long as the Romans scrupulously kept their side of the "contract," the gods would stick to theirs and support Rome.

The following objections to these two claims may be raised. First, so that we do not see religion at Rome merely as a punctilious, "ritualistic" system mired in its own religious tradition, we must understand that ritual is exceedingly flexible and adaptable to the most variable circumstances. The practitioners of ritual decide how fastidiously or how casually they follow the rules to achieve their desired goal, namely to communicate their aims and wishes to the gods successfully. Both strict and casual attitudes to religious performance are amply documented in the ancient Roman world.

Second, it is true that, for example, the vow of the Arval Brothers given in Box 9.1 is framed in quasi-legal terms, spelling out conditions and obligations in precise detail like the fine print of a contract. Yet their vow is less suggestive of a contractually binding arrangement than of a more dynamic and complex relationship: the gods need to be obliged, reassured, and even cajoled before they "(make) their power propitious" and deign to listen to human requests. Similarly, in the curse text from Roman Mogontiacum (introduced in the chapter's opener) the defenceless woman can only request an act of vindication from the goddess. The Arval Brothers' statement that "the immortal gods . . . have lent their ears to the vows of the entire world" implicitly acknowledges that the gods may take the liberty of doing the exact opposite of their past propitious behaviour. In other words, the gods, all powerful as is their nature, can be expected to assist those deserving of such benefaction, but they may equally frustrate human expectations or fail to reward faithful observance of religious ritual. They may make individuals suffer for no apparent reason and punish those who do not deserve such chastisement. In this context, *communication* (a dialogue between two or more parties in which the responses are not predetermined) is an appropriate term to describe the ritual interaction between humans and gods of the kind named in the Arval Brothers' protocol. But as some scholars in the field of cognitive studies have suggested more recently, it is often the counterintuitive nature of what the gods do or fail to do—a communication where they set the rules—that establishes the powerful beliefs that people hold in them.

It would therefore be wrong to think that these beliefs lie merely in the efficacy of ritual practice, as scholars reluctant to apply a more comprehensive notion of "belief" to religion at Rome would hold. Ancient Roman beliefs in the value and efficacy of ritual communication with the divine were formed on the basis of, and therefore cannot be separated from, people's beliefs about the existence, power, and justice of the gods independent of their communication with worshippers.[5]

There was another crucial form of communication with the gods, one which (unlike the vow) was not primarily verbal: sacrifice. Again, the Arval Brothers' protocol provides an excellent example. Before committing himself and the college to new vows for the following year, Caius Salvius Liberalis fulfills the previous year's ritual obligation by offering an animal sacrifice. He would have performed this sacrifice with part of his toga drawn over his head, a ritual gesture known as *capite velato* ("with his head veiled") and commonly seen on sacrificial representations from Rome and Italy. He begins by sprinkling incense and pouring wine over a small, portable altar. The name of this phase of the ritual was *praefari* ("to speak beforehand"), suggesting that it combined verbal and non-verbal actions to make the deity inclined to listen to the purpose and intention of the sacrifice.

Caius Salvius Liberalis then sprinkles the animal's head, the sacrificial knife, and the altar with salted ground spelt (*mola salsa*; hence the Latin for "to sacrifice," *immolare*), pours wine over the animal's forehead, and uses the knife to draw an imaginary line from the animal's head to its back. The protocol outlines this complex ritual sequence with only a few words because everybody would be able to fill in the missing activities. Similarly, everybody would understand that the protocol omits several other crucial stages of the sacrifice: the actual killing of the animal, which was the responsibility of sacrificial assistants, and the inspection of the animal's entrails (the heart, liver, lungs, and peritoneum) by the *haruspex*. This divinatory expert inspected these innards to ensure that their shapes and appearances were regular, as regularity indicated that the sacrifice was accepted by the deity. In this way, the gods communicated their response to the sacrificer non-verbally.[6]

Finally, we come to the gods themselves. The protocol of the Arval Brothers demonstrates the diverse character of the Roman pantheon (that is, all the divinities worshipped in the city of Rome). The Arval Brothers made sacrifices and vows to the traditional anthropomorphic deities of the **Capitoline Triad**, namely Jupiter, Juno, and Minerva. But sacrifices and vows were also made to the goddess Salus Publica, or "Civic Well-Being of the Roman People, the Citizens," whose very name is a potent reminder of the rituals' original purpose: the plea for the well-being of Rome's political community of citizens. The creation of a deity to represent a quality that is being sought from the gods through ritual means (a prominent device of constructing divinity at Rome)[7] is witness to the creativity of the Roman religious system. Such innovation might bother us more than it did the Romans, who worshipped the goddess with statues, prayer, and sacrifice. As early as 302 BCE, a sanctuary was dedicated to Salus on the Quirinal Hill as the protectress of the well-being of the Roman people (Livy 10.1.9). In the first century CE her cult became even more diversified, as the worship of the Well-Being of the Roman Body Politic (Salus Publica) and the Well-Being of the Emperor (Salus Augusti or Augusta) and his family mirrored the ideological foundation of the imperial age. It is significant that the ritual of the Arval Brothers recognizes no difference between the traditional gods and the deified quality—Salus Publica is accorded the same female sacrificial victim that Juno and Minerva receive.

But there is yet another kind of deity mentioned in the Arval Brothers' protocol: *divus* ("god") Vespasian, a once-human emperor consecrated as a god by decision of the Roman **senate** after his death in 79 CE.[8] Vespasian's alleged last words—"Woe, I believe I become a god" (Suet. *Vesp.* 23.4)—have sometimes been interpreted as a criticism of the practice of divinization and of the notion that any human (especially the emperor, whom many regarded as the most powerful person on earth) might become divine and receive cult like all the other gods. Yet such a notion was widely established among the ancients. Vespasian's words may have been little more than a witty reflection on his unlikely rise to supreme power. By common understanding, such power and immortality distinguished the gods from mere mortals. But the divide was neither as insurmountable nor as categorical as it is held to be in some of today's world religions. In the eyes of many of his contemporaries, the Roman emperor's superior achievements, spectacular military successes, and benefactions would have rendered him divine during his lifetime (see, for example, Suet. *Aug.* 98; *AE* 2007, 1505). Even the purported working of some "miracle" could lead to spontaneous acclamations of divine status in the Graeco-Roman world (see, for instance, Acts 14:8–18).

The worship of Roman emperors, either alive or deceased, occurred in many different guises in cities and provinces across the empire. For all intents and purposes, it was a local religious phenomenon like all the other cults existing in the Roman Mediterranean. Yet the Arval Brother's protocol shows that the imperial cult, as it is sometimes called, neither emerged as a "religion" of its own nor replaced the traditional cults in Rome and elsewhere. Instead, it was integrated into the fabric of, and coexisted with, traditional religious practices and beliefs.[9] The cases of Salus Publica and *divus* Vespasian bring into sharp focus *our* preconceptions and prejudices about the nature of divinity, which were not shared by the Romans.

Civic Religion

Along with the practices and beliefs discussed in the previous section, the Romans also believed that their *res publica* was constantly being "augmented by the resources and councils of the immortal gods," as a Roman statute of 58 BCE bluntly states.[10] Indeed, Romans thought that their well-being was at least partly determined by the gods as a divine response to their piety, which the people showed through their meticulous attention to worship. The Romans, incidentally, were not alone in making this claim. Yet the political and military successes that they enjoyed throughout their history could legitimately be taken as proof of divine favouritism, just as domestic crises and military disasters were sometimes explained as the consequences of divine anger. The vows of 87 CE point to this attitude when they link the emperor's and the political community's well-being to the power of the gods made favourable.

The belief that the affairs of the city state were dependent on the divine world may explain the enormous effort, financial and otherwise, that the civic community at Rome (like other ancient city-states) undertook to maintain a sophisticated religious infrastructure. This endeavour comprised the financing and maintenance of the city's civic temples, festivals, games, and rituals.[11] The last category included the sacrifices, dedications, and vows made by magistrates and *sacerdotes publici* ("civic priests") on behalf of the city-state and its citizenry and, as was the case with the vows of 87 CE, on behalf of the emperor and his family. Taken together, these religious activities were referred to as **sacra publica populi Romani**, the "civic rituals of the Roman people" (Festus *Gloss. Lat.* 4.350).

Late republican and imperial authors record the tradition that all matters of civic religion were established when the *res publica* was young. They state that Romulus (*augur* and first king of Rome) inaugurated the site of Rome (Lutatius frg. 11 *HRRel*; Cic. *Div.* 1.30–1) and that Numa, the second king, organized the *sacra publica*, thereby putting Roman ritual practices on a permanent footing (Livy 1.20.5). In historical actuality, however, religion at Rome was a dynamic organism that underwent constant transformation over the centuries.[12] The administrative and ritual structure of civic religion persisted until the later fourth and early fifth centuries CE, when those responsible for overseeing the rituals of organized religion—the emperors and the political elites—came to prefer Christianity over traditional religious practices and beliefs, which were outlawed as "superstitious" and illicit. This change brought about the gradual disappearance of the rituals and underlying beliefs of what we now call paganism, at least as it was publicly practised in the civic domain.[13]

The details regarding civic religion in all sources of information—literature, epigraphy, numismatics, and archaeology alike—are so vast that some scholars have argued that civic religion *was* religion at Rome, that all religious practices and beliefs were undertaken in the context of public "state religion." While this theory is debatable (see pp. 203–13), civic religion unquestionably provided a powerful and pervasive frame of reference for all religious activity in the city and beyond. It is therefore necessary to sketch its most important elements.

A striking feature of Roman civic religion is its massive cost, as well as the implications that cost had on the relationship between religion and political success (and, as we shall see, political authority) for the Roman elite. The civic maintenance of temples, the personnel required to take care of cult images and the paraphernalia of daily ritual routine, and the huge number of animals needed for public sacrifice added up to colossal expense. The four animals that the Arval Brothers sacrificed in 87 CE are but the tip of the iceberg: 300 oxen, for instance, were offered to Jupiter in 217 BCE (Livy 22.10.7). Civic religious observances might also extend over many days and could be repeated many times. An extreme example is offered by the 55 rituals of thanksgiving (*supplicationes*) decreed by the senate during Augustus's lifetime on account of his successes. These rituals amounted to 890 days altogether, averaging 16 days of celebration for each (*RG* 4.1).

Annual public games in honour of the gods were also extremely costly. Evidence cited on an early imperial calendar from the Italian town of Antium (*Inscr. Ital.* 13.2, pp. 208–10) suggests that the Roman celebration of the games in honour of Apollo in July might cost the state close to 400,000 **sesterces**, an **equestrian** fortune; 600,000 sesterces were expended on the Plebeian Games in November and a staggering 760,000 sesterces on the Roman Games in September. Yet public funds were regularly supplemented by the magistrate organizing the event during the Republic. Such sponsorship served to augment the magistrate's renown among the populace and to increase his chances when running for higher magistracies. In the imperial period, the emperor's role as sole patron of the city of Rome meant that he subsidized the public games.[14] The joint contribution of civic funds and individual elite benefaction not only served to diffuse financial responsibilities (although some magistrates of the first century BCE managed to bankrupt themselves in the event) but also to underline the symbiotic relationship between the religious affairs of the *res publica* and the interests of its political elites.

➜ Compare Chapter 10, pp. 228–9, and Chapter 12 in general on games and political figures.

Costs for temples, shrines, and altars were similarly shared between state coffers and individual benefactors, a further illustration of the political elite's personal interest in civic religion. Public funds were generally used for the construction of religious build-ings. Civic responsibility applied even if, as happened on several occasions throughout the second and first centuries BCE, it was a Roman magistrate on military campaign who vowed a shrine to a deity.[15] During the Republic, the state often determined what was a necessary repair and paid for it. Consider, for example, the restoration of a decrepit altar rebuilt in Rome to a deity whose name and identity the Romans no longer remembered:

> Sacred to the god or goddess. Caius Sextius Calvinus, the son of Caius, praetor, restored (this altar) on a vote of the senate. (*CIL* 1².801)

This practice does not imply, however, that individuals did not construct or at least repair civic temples in Rome. For instance, Marcus Tullius Cicero (*Har. Resp.* 31), one of the two consuls of 63 BCE, was commissioned to rebuild the Temple of Tellus in 55/54 BCE. The Temple of Diana Planciana on the Quirinal Hill (see the inscriptions in Box 9.2) was either restored or, more likely, built by a member of the elite family of the Planci (or Plancii).

With the rise of imperial rule in Rome, the construction and restoration of sacred buildings, like public building in the city in general, became the prerogative of the emper-ors. But such activities undertaken by the state and individuals during the late Republic

---

Primary Source

Box 9.2: *AE* 1971, 31.

A dedication of a temple warden's wife to the god Silvanus:

> Sacred to Silvanus. Julia Sporis, spouse of Hymetus, warden of the temple of Diana Planciana, (set up this dedication).

Both Julia Sporis and her husband reappear in the dedicatory inscription of a funerary monument by another woman.

CIL 6.2210.

To the propitious gods. Claudia Quinta, daughter of Tiberius, built this tomb for Caius Julius Hymetus, warden of (the temple of) Diana Planciana, her pedagogue and instructor, also her legal guardian since the time she became an orphan, because he rendered to her his services as her guardian most faithfully, and for Caius Julius Epitynchanus, his brother, and for Julia Sporis her mommy (or foster mother?), and for their freedmen and freedwomen, and for their descendants.

should cast doubt on the long-accepted view that this period was a time of religious decline and that only the Augustan settlement restored the religious institutions, rituals, and temples in the city of Rome.[16] Scholars have only recently come to terms with the fact that the writers of the Augustan period deliberately minimized the religious commitment of the late Republic so as to present the sacred building projects of Augustus as a favourable contrast. His aggrandizing projects—such as the new Temple of Apollo on the Palatine and the new Temple of Jupiter Tonans on the Capitoline Hill (*RG* 19; Suet. *Aug.* 29)—served the purpose of legitimizing the new imperial power. But here, too, the actions of Augustus (and similar actions of later emperors) were continuations of precedents, as his republican predecessors also used religious building projects as attempts to further their own political position at the expense of their peers. The Theatre of Pompey, which included a temple to Venus Victrix ("Victress"),[17] is one striking example of that tendency: the monumental complex, which occupied a vast amount of space in the Field of Mars, commemorated Pompey's military achievements and served as an investment in his struggle for recognition as the foremost Roman of his day.

Given the correlation between religious responsibility and political power, it is unsurprising that Rome's religious officials were primarily drawn from the political elite and were male. There were, however, a few female religious functionaries from elite families, such as the Vestal Virgins, whose duties included maintenance of the cult of the goddess Vesta; the wife of the Flamen Dialis, or "priest of Jupiter," with whom she shared certain ritual obligations and responsibilities; the Roman priestesses of Ceres; and the priestesses in the imperial cult. In a speech delivered in 57 BCE, Cicero emphasizes the desirability of having the same people, the members of Rome's economic and political elite, administer the city's affairs in their dual roles as magistrates and priests (*sacerdotes*). It is interesting to note, however, that his rhetorical attempt to erase the division between the responsibilities of these positions implicitly confirms their conceptual differentiation:

→ Compare Chapter 10 p. 236, on the social identity of Roman priests.

> While our ancestors . . . have invented and established many things under divine guidance, there is certainly nothing more distinguished among these than their decision to put the same men in charge both of the *religiones* (i.e. rituals) owed to the immortal gods and of the most pertinent affairs of their polity—so that the most excellent and most illustrious citizens through proper administration of their polity might safeguard the rituals and through wise interpretation of these rituals might safeguard the polity. (Cic. *Dom.* 1)

During the late Republic, the members of Rome's political elite were eager to occupy any vacant spaces in the major priestly offices, filled by election since the **Lex** Domitia of 104/103 BCE. Cicero was proud of securing his own membership in the college of augurs by election in the late 50s BCE. Under the Empire, membership in a priestly college was also sought fervently, particularly when the candidate could secure nomination through the emperor or become his colleague in the college. The Arval Brothers' vows of 87 CE remind us of the colleges' ideological proximity to the emperor.

Yet the case of the major Roman priesthoods provides another area where a republican tradition was rewritten under the exigencies of imperial realpolitik. The accumulation of different priesthoods by a single individual was shunned by the political establishment in the second and first centuries BCE, but the increasing tendency of individuals to monopolize political power was inevitably mirrored by a tendency to monopolize priesthoods. Julius Caesar was elected **pontifex maximus** ("chief pontiff") in 63 BCE and both *augur* and *quindecimvir* during his second dictatorship in 47 BCE (on these priesthoods, see the following paragraphs). Augustus added to his portfolio membership in a fourth priestly college, the college of *epulones* (seven men who were in charge of the *epulum Iovis*, a feast for Jupiter held at the Roman Games and the Plebeian Games), thereby single-handedly establishing the tradition of the emperor's membership in all of the "four most renowned colleges" (*quattuor amplissima collegia*; see, for example, *RG* 9.1 and compare 7.3). As a matter of fact, he established the very tradition of counting four such colleges. Until then, the most prestigious priesthoods had been only three in number.

As will have already become clear, there were many different Roman priesthoods. It is beyond the scope of this chapter to discuss all of them in any detail; therefore, we will focus on only the major types. Roman authors identify three (Cic. *Nat. D.* 3.5) and sometimes four (Val. Max. 1.1) domains of priestly duty, overseen respectively by the colleges of the pontiffs, augurs, **(quin)decimviri sacris faciundis** ("Ten [later Fifteen] Men for the Performance of Rituals"), and *haruspices*.[18] The supervision and guidance concerning all matters of ritual was the responsibility of the pontiffs (Dion. Hal. *Ant. Rom.* 2.73.1–2). This area included such matters as sacred places, the Roman calendar, the correct performance of rituals, and the care of tombs. The pontiffs' central role concerning the *sacra publica* also explains the importance that the Romans attached to the office of *pontifex maximus*.

The augurs' controlled the **auspicia** (the means by which divine will was determined) and the "inauguration" (for the procedure, compare Cic. *Leg.* 2.21) of places, priests, and rituals. The Roman antiquarian writer Festus (*Gloss. Lat.* 4.367) distinguished five categories of *auspicia*: the observation of signs "from the sky" (*ex caelo*; celestial signs such as thunder and lightning), from the sound and flight of birds (*ex avibus*), from the feeding behaviour of the sacred chickens (*ex tripudiis*), from four-hoofed animals (*ex quadrupedibus*), and unfavourable signs of other natures (*ex diris*). The taking of the auspices was not the sole prerogative of the augurs, however. Curule magistrates (magistrates who had **imperium**, such as praetors and consuls) also held the *auspicia*: they sacrificed before certain public events and took the *auspices* before assemblies and at specific political ceremonials. During the *auspicium ex tripudiis*, which on military

See Chapter 10, pp. 227–8, for ⬅
magistracies with *imperium*.

campaigns was a more expedient form of auspication than the observation of birds in the sky, the assistant reported the chickens' feeding habits to the magistrate, who interpreted the results and informed the army. Famous examples exist of republican magistrates neglecting the chickens' refusal to eat (an unfavourable sign) immediately before a military conflict. In these examples, the Romans invariably lost the battle (see, for example, Cic. *Nat. D.* 2.7–8).

A distinction was made between *auspicia* that the observer had actively looked out for (*auspicia impetrativa*) and those that had been received but not sought (*auspicia oblativa*). The former category established a direct link between the auspiciant and the gods; the latter, by contrast, needed to be examined to determine what and whom they might concern. But there existed yet another category of unsolicited divine signs in need of interpretation. This function was the task of the other two major priesthoods. The (*quin*)*decimviri sacris faciundis* were in charge of the **Sibylline Books**, state-approved Greek oracular texts. Unusual natural occurrences might be deemed to be *prodigia* ("prodigies"; signs of divine displeasure), and the prophetic texts encapsulated in the Sibylline Books were thought to hold instructions to remedy such situations. The Etruscan *haruspices* were also sometimes consulted in the case of such occurrences and suggested viable ritual solutions to mitigate the divine displeasure that the political community had incurred. These could include sacrifices, festivals, or the introduction of new deities into the city's civic pantheon (see pp. 204–7). It must be noted, however, that discretionary power concerning religious affairs, including extraordinary events, new cults, and the restoration of altars, rested with the senate.

Two further observations about priests are important. First, civic priests were not religious experts nor was ritual expertise a prerequisite for nomination to one of the major priesthoods. The cases of Appius Claudius Pulcher and Marcus Valerius Messalla, Cicero's fellow augurs and writers of treatises on augury and the interpretation of the auspices, are the proverbial exceptions that prove the rule (Cic. *Fam.* 3.4.1, 3.9.3; Gell. *NA* 13.15.3–4). Ritual authority did not rest with individual priests but with the college as a body drawing upon a wealth of accumulated knowledge. Second, Roman civic priests were not full-time priests. Although Cicero appears to have made a regular effort to attend the augurs' meetings to participate in the duties required of the college, the case of Crassus, who died in battle away from Rome (leaving vacant his position as augur, which Cicero then filled),

→ See Chapter 2, p. 31, and Chapter 14, pp. 316–17, on Crassus's eastern campaign.

illuminates the sometimes insurmountable conflict between the different roles of magistrate and priest. Under the Republic, there were several telling instances of conflicts between magisterial and priestly roles, normally centring on the issue of which role should take precedence. For instance, in 189 BCE a praetor's departure to his assigned province of Sardinia was vetoed by the *pontifex maximus* on behalf of the pontifical college because the praetor also held the flaminate ("priesthood") of the god Quirinus. In this case, the senate decided in favour of the pontifical argument that the priest had to stay in Rome to honour his sacrificial responsibilities towards the deity (Livy 37.51.1–6). No such conflict of interest is ever reported for the *pontifex maximus*, either during the Republic or under the Empire (when the emperor held this office).

This example addresses the more fundamental question of who held supreme religious authority at Rome. The view that the civic priests in general or the *pontifex maximus* in particular was invested with such authority or with some religious charisma presupposes a model of priesthood developed in the Judeo-Christian tradition, which scholars have unwittingly imposed on the ancient evidence. Contradicting such a model, the emperor Vespasian received authorization from the senate to handle the Roman state's religious affairs the very moment that body conferred upon him a whole range of other constitutional powers and privileges in 69 CE, before he was elected *pontifex maximus* and thus became entitled to exert "priestly" influence (*CIL* 6.31207). Similarly, Augustus's election to the office of *pontifex maximus* took place in 12 BCE, rather late in his political career.

Moreover, as we have just seen, ancient pagan "priests" would not claim superior theological knowledge—they were neither the privileged mediators of religious truths nor the arbiters on questions of faith. In historical actuality, technical or theological expertise was rather widely dispersed. There existed a wide range of divinatory and ritual service providers, "magical" specialists, common diviners or seers (*vates*), fortune tellers, necromancers, dream interpreters, augurs, *haruspices*, and astrologers, all of whom operated outside the bounds of the state-controlled *sacra publica* (see, for instance, Cic. *Div.* 1.132). In the non-civic cults of the goddess Isis (see, for example, Apul. *Met.* 11.21) and the god Mithras, as well as other "mystery" cults in which initiation was practised and independent religious hierarchies and offices existed, a significant amount of ritual and theological expertise was also required. Ritual and theological competency characterized the officials of the Judean communities in Rome and the nascent Christian collectives.

In fact, the generic words *priest* and *priesthood* are used in this chapter for the sake of expediency, not to suggest that this modern terminology aptly characterizes religious authority in the ancient Roman world. There was no single term for our word *priest*; the title *sacerdos*, which is often translated as such, is only one of several names used to designate religious officials. Furthermore, applying our notion of *priest* or *priesthood* may invite the belief that priestly authority in the Roman world is roughly comparable to the authority that today's priests hold. However, ritual agency was more diversified in the ancient world and religious authority more widely dispersed.[19] Our notion of what "religion" entails may not be entirely relevant to the variety of practices and beliefs or the diffusion of religious authority that characterized religion at Rome.

From Roman Religion to Religion at Rome

To this point, this chapter has focused more or less on religion in the public realm. Arguably, this focus is too narrow to capture the full spectrum of religious activity in the city of Rome and beyond. What about, for instance, the religious practices and beliefs of those inhabitants of Rome that civic life largely left on the sidelines—**freedpersons**, slaves, and women? Or the many foreigners living at Rome and practising religion? And what about Roman citizens such as St. Paul of Tarsus, who did not (as far as we can tell) worship any "Roman" gods?

These questions are not to suggest that civic religion at Rome was fundamentally different from what "ordinary" people did or believed. Most people held the same beliefs in the power of the gods over their lives, regardless of their respective political or social **status**. In the same way that the Arval Brother's vows addressed the well-being of the emperor and the political community, concerns for well-being (be it personal physical health or economic success or that of family and friends) underpinned the countless prayers, sacrifices, vows, and dedications that the freeborn, freedpersons, slaves, and foreigners—both men and women—would perform every day. Historians' focus on the civic aspects of religion in the city of Rome has sometimes obscured the real, and often independent, religious responsibilities and contributions of, for example, women sacrificing or making dedications to the gods (such as those in Box 9.2).[20] Furthermore, we should not assume that the religious institutions of the civic community were of no interest to its individual members. Epigraphic evidence suggests, for example, that people in Rome enquired with the pontifical college in cases regarding the transfer of corpses to a new tomb (*CIL* 6.2120).[21] The authority of the *quindecimviri* extended to those cults that had been introduced to Rome on the recommendation of the Sibylline Books, and the col-

➔ Compare Chapter 7, pp. 146–7, on the adoption of the cult of Mater Magna.

lege was consulted, for instance, in matters pertaining to the cult of Mater Magna ("Great Mother"), which had been adopted by Rome in 204 BCE (*CIL* 10.3698, 3699; compare *CIL* 13.1751). We do not know whether such evidence indicates a common practice or whether only a few people in Rome, Italy, or Roman provincial communities took the effort to consult the authorities.

In fact, the latter is much more likely, since religion in the Roman Mediterranean was a predominantly local and regional phenomenon: deities had different names, cities patronized different cults, and different ritual norms and expectations existed from one place to another. When Pliny the Younger (*Ep.* 10.49–50; compare Gai. *Inst.* 2.1–11), as governor of Pontus-Bithynia, found that the local procedure of temple dedication in the town of Nicomedia was different from that in Rome, the emperor and *pontifex maximus* Trajan assured him that, in this particular instance, Roman custom was inapplicable to "foreign soil." Elsewhere, Trajan confirms that it would be hard on provincials if they were obliged to consult the pontiffs in Rome about tomb transfers (*Ep.* 10. 68–9). Compatible underlying beliefs and ritual patterns are discernible and similar religious practices can be identified across the Roman empire: witness the curses from two of the empire's western provinces with which this chapter began or the vows and sacrifices that people undertook across the Roman Mediterranean.

Yet it is advisable to conceive, as this chapter does, of religion at Rome as the local religious practices and beliefs of Rome's inhabitants and their diffusion across the empire rather than as the totality of the religious cults and beliefs of the empire as a whole.

It is important to understand that ancient polytheism did not recognize conceptual and spatial separation of secular and sacred realms, as we tend to do. The divine world densely populated the world of the living: the gods inhabited temples and shrines, cross-road altars and cult niches along the streets, and domestic spaces, shops, basilicas, and crowded piazzas. Divinities were carried along in processions, gazed out at passersby from wall paintings, appeared on reliefs and altars, and literally accompanied people wherever they went since everyone carried coins or wore rings, brooches, fibulae, and amulets with images of the deities of their choice.

An examination of Figure 9.2 can perhaps give us a glimpse into this world. This piece, painted on one side of the entrance to a shop on **Pompeii**'s Via dell'Abbondanza, shows a procession of 18 wreathed figures. In front of the procession, four male litter-bearers clad in white tunics with purple mantles carry an enthroned statue of Mater Magna with turreted crown and lion cubs at her feet. The group appears to have momentarily paused to pay homage to the god Bacchus, whose bust is on display in a small shrine on the far left. (It was common for processions to follow the major features of a town's or city's sacred topography, such as the temples of other deities.) Note how both Mater Magna, whose lifelike appearance denies the lifelessness we tend to ascribe to statues, and the three worshippers behind her litter reverently turn towards Bacchus. They are clad in white and carry ritual objects, which may give away their identity as officials in the Mater Magna's cult. Are these three figures male? Behind them follows a group of what seem to be female adult worshippers and children in coloured attire: the painting carefully reproduces the gender differentiation and hierarchy that must have been conspicuous elements of cult life in the ancient world.

What emotions and concerns do these worshippers have as they follow the throne of Mater Magna? Were the shopowner commissioning these paintings and his family particularly attached to the goddess? Were they hoping for divine protection of their commercial and domestic fortunes? Are they perhaps portrayed in this painting? And why is Bacchus included? The god had a sanctuary outside Pompeii, which the procession in this painting is seen passing by. On the other side of the shop's doorway is a painting of Venus Pompeiana ("Pompeian Venus"), Cupid, and a group of Amorini; above the doorway the painter has also depicted Jupiter, Apollo, Diana, and Mercury. We happen to know that a statue of Mater Magna was set up in the porch of the Pompeian Temple of Venus Pompeiana. In nearby **Herculaneum** in 76 CE, Vespasian restored the local Temple of Mater Magna, which had been damaged by the earthquake of 62 CE (*CIL* 10.1406). The painting thus invites a multitude of associations as the painter encourages viewers to link the scenes to their own experiences both in the local sacred landscape of Pompeii and with a view to the wider imperial world.

Figure 9.2 Procession scene painted on one side of the entrance to shop IX.7.1, Via dell'Abbondanza, Pompeii, before 79 CE. Photo courtesy of Drew Baker, www.pompeiiinpictures.com.

But the parallels and points of contact between civic and non-civic religious activities in the city of Rome may hide a deeper-seated difference. People's concerns often pertained to their own affairs, not necessarily to those of the state. There existed a rather unregulated religious field in which shared practices and common beliefs concerning the gods did not necessarily translate into a homogenous field of civic religion. It is only quite recently that scholars have begun to consider the history of Roman religion, at least in part, as a result of imperial expansion and the consequent creation of a culturally heterogeneous empire, the latter being reflected in the diversity of religious cults and activities at Rome. As the Mediterranean metropolis par excellence and home to perhaps close to a million inhabitants, the urban space of imperial Rome provided a backdrop to the most variable forms of cultural and religious exchange and communication.

Only continuous migration sustained Rome's grandeur, but this constant also accelerated the problems of accommodation and cohabitation of different human populations, deities, and cults in the city. By the early imperial period, there was already a perception of the capital as the preferred destination of all the deities contained by Rome's empire (Ov. *Fast.* 4.270). Supplementary evidence supports this sentiment: dedications and sanctuaries in the city of Rome to deities from as far away as Gaul, Germany, and Britain; Northern Africa and Egypt; Syria and Palestine; and Thrace and the Danube region populated a diversified urban landscape. Consideration of civic religion is too narrow to account for the rich and varied religious life of the city. It is for this reason that the phrase "religion at

Rome" is preferred to "Roman religion" in this chapter; the latter suggests a unified system of Roman religious practices and beliefs that misrepresents the reality.

To be sure, the arrival of new deities and cults was always a prominent feature of Rome's urban landscape.[22] For instance, in 292 BCE the cult of the Greek healing god Aesculapius was imported from his healing sanctuary at Epidaurus after the Sibylline Books recommended him as a suitable remedy to the plague affecting the city (Livy 10.47.6–7; *Per.* 11). In 204 BCE, on the brink of victory in the Second Punic War, the cult of the Mater Magna (which we have already encountered at Pompeii and Herculaneum) was fetched from the East when a prodigy in the form of frequent showers of stone resulted in another consultation of the Sibylline Books (Livy 29.14.10–14). The ancient gods, together with their worshippers, travelled widely and freely across the Mediterranean.

These imports were quickly accommodated to the populace's diverse ritual needs. Dedications since the third century BCE document the gratitude that worshippers felt for Aesculapius after the restoration of their health, and individual cases of temple incuba-tion in his sanctuary on the Tiber Island are attested. The pull of his sanctuary was such that construction work could occasionally be financed entirely from donations and fees received from ordinary worshippers (*CIL* 1².800). The case of the Mater Magna poses a similar scenario: second-century BCE statuettes of her divine consort, Attis, in her sanctu-ary on the Palatine Hill anticipate his official invitation into civic cult in the first century CE. Clearly, the institution of an official cult invited people to pursue their own variations on the established theme, resulting in the further diversification of religion. Civic religion would therefore create the infrastructure in which a differentiated religious life evolved.

Roman epitaphs, which generally include the name (and sometimes the age) of the deceased and the names of those who set up the funerary monument, also illustrate the variability of religious beliefs in the metropolis. Epitaphs are usually dedicated to the **Di Manes**, who were understood to be the spirits of the dead but were also seen as the gods of the underworld—as the word *di* ("gods") suggests (see, for example, *CIL* 6.13388). In Roman antiquity there circulated several learned and often incompatible opinions on what the word *manes* actually signified. One view was that the dead were euphemistically

Primary Source

Box 9.3: *CISem.* 2.159.

To the *Di Manes*. Abgarus, son of Eutyches, from Petra (has set up this monument) for Abdaretas, son of Esteches, his blood relative. He lived for 30 years. For him, who deserved this. This is the *nefesh* of Abdaretas.

called "the good gods," probably because the dead were known to have the ability, and sometimes the intention, to harm the living (Festus *Gloss. Lat.* 4.266). Additional sentiments expressed in epitaphs provide fascinating information about the urban population's adoption of the new and retention of the old religious attitudes. Consider the epitaph in Box 9.3, from the late first or early second century CE. Neither the deceased nor his relative bears a Roman name; they hail from Nabataean Petra and can be identified as eastern migrants to Rome without Roman citizen status. Yet the epitaph adopts the local Roman convention of funerary commemoration, including the adaptation of the local belief in the *Di Manes*. Even so, the bilingual inscription ends in Aramaic, with the identification of the tomb as the *nefesh* (literally, "life," or "soul") of the deceased, thereby importing beliefs concerning death and the afterlife that were prevalent in their homeland.

Or consider the sarcophagus of Marcus Aurelius Prosenes, a **freedman** of the imperial household. This tomb features traditional urban Roman iconography and an inscription documenting the deceased's impressive career, which culminated in the position of chamberlain under the Antonine emperors. On the top rim of the sarcophagus's right small side, Prosenes's ex-slave Ampelius carved a second inscription that gives the date of death as 217 CE and states that his former master was "received unto God"—a clear if rather surreptitiously placed indication of the Christian belief in the afterlife that Prosenes and his ex-slave, both apparently members of Rome's growing Christian community, expected to experience.[23]

Epitaphs also constitute a dialogue concerning contemporary views on death and the status of the dead, ranging from assertions of the existence of the *Di Manes* to denials.[24] For example, in an epitaph from late first-century CE Rome, a couple professes their belief in the *Di Manes* after their two daughters, deceased at the respective ages of 9 and 15, had appeared to them in a dream and reassured their parents of their post-mortal existence among the *Di Manes*. As a result, the parents erected a tombstone with busts of their children and the inscription "You who read this and doubt that the Manes exist . . . call upon us and you will understand" (*CIL* 6.27365). One may compare a similar sentiment expressed

Primary Source

Box 9.4: *CIL* 6.14672.

There exists in Hades no dinghy, no ferryman Charon, no Aikaos holding the keys, no dog Cerberus. No, all of us who are dead below have become bones and ashes but nothing else whatsoever . . . Do not grace this stele with myrrh and garlands; it is a stone. Do not feed the fire; the expenditure is in vain. If you have something, let me partake in it while I am still alive. Making ashes drunk you turn them to mud, and the dead does not drink.

by the Roman poet Propertius (4.7.1) towards the end of the first century BCE: "The Manes are something; death does not put an end to everything." In contrast, on another funerary monument (see Box 9.4) a freedman named Marcus Antonius Encolpus commemorates his deceased spouse of 40 years and stipulates who else may have her or his ashes placed in the tomb. The inscription then switches from Latin to Greek to divulge philosophical sentiments that deny the existence of the underworld or a life in the beyond and question the necessity of funerary ritual such as libation and sacrifice to the deceased at the tomb.

Given the bewildering range of deities at Rome, how did people actually choose deities to worship? Scholars have often assumed that there was an expectation to worship a fairly well-established pantheon of particularly "Roman" gods. It is true that the Roman **senatorial** elite generally displayed rather conservative religious tastes in public dedications. Moreover, there are no overtly foreign deities in sight in the Arval Brothers' protocols. But are the religious tastes of the Roman political elites truly indicative of wider trends? To answer this question, we might consider the evidence available from the Roman communities of Pompeii and Herculaneum. Thanks to their entombment and consequent preservation by the eruption of Mount Vesuvius in 79 CE, these towns provide a glimpse at the domestic religious practices of their inhabitants.[25]

In several houses, domestic shrines and small cult niches have been preserved, the former usually in the living areas of the house and the latter in the kitchen and work

Figure 9.3   Domestic sacrificial scene, wall painting beside a cult niche for domestic worship, so-called House of Sutoria Primigenia (I.13.4), Pompeii, before 79 CE.

areas. In some cases, entire ensembles of statuettes of the deities worshipped in these domestic contexts have survived; more rarely, scenes of actual domestic worship are portrayed, as in Figure 9.3. In this painting, two oversized *lares familiares*, the protective deities of the household's *familia* (of whom only one is shown here), flank the other participants and are in all likelihood the prime addressees of the ritual depicted. At the centre of the sacrificial scene, the master of the household, the toga partly drawn over his head (*capite velato*), sprinkles incense from a flat bowl over a burning altar; one may compare the Arval Brothers' sacrifice. On the left stands his wife, wearing the *stola* typical of Roman matrons. A double-flute player accompanies the sacrifice, and 12 males clad in white tunics, probably representing the household's *familia* of slaves and freedmen, make identical gestures of reverence. Individuals of different ages are shown: there is a thirteenth male figure, a boy standing immediately to the right of and intently observing the sacrifice. This detail points to the reality that the religious socialization of the young was achieved through participation in the ritual, either through active involvement—for instance, as double-flute player or sacrificial assistant—or through observation and close adherence to the ritual behaviour of others in the group.[26]

→ Compare Chapter 5, p. 97, on the *familia*.

This painting has sometimes been interpreted as the depiction of a religious festival, when the entire household would sacrifice together. Yet there may be more to this painting than meets the eye. A freeborn Roman had his or her own divine guardian—males had their Genius and females their Juno. These guardian deities were often depicted worshipping at the altar in domestic contexts. Therefore, are the two central figures (the sacrificers) perhaps also the implied recipients of worship, representing the Genius and Juno of the master and his wife? The household's slaves and freedpersons frequently made dedications to these two deities (for instance, *CIL* 10.860, 861). This suggests that the religious scene, painted on the wall of a kitchen where the house's slaves worked and worshipped, must also be read as further reflection and reinforcement of the social hierarchies of the household rather than as a mere "realistic" depiction of household cult.

This is not to say that domestic worship was thoroughly regulated. Rather, it mirrored the decentralized religious landscape outside. Dedications by slaves and ex-slaves in the houses' working quarters exist to suggest some autonomy of religious choice (for instance, *CIL* 10.882, 930; *AE* 1980, 247). In addition, two issues deserve closer consideration. First, the deities chosen by the inhabitants of these houses, while encompassing a wide range of divine choices, resemble those worshipped in the local pantheons of Pompeii and Herculaneum. But the ensembles of deities in these domestic shrines and niches are almost never identical, and the inhabitants mix and match more traditional deities with relative newcomers. For instance, the Egyptian goddess Isis, who had an old temple in Pompeii, is represented fairly prominently, but Venus, Cupid, Jupiter, Apollo, Diana, Mercury (all of whom the painter of Figure 9.2 depicts), and many more are equally present. No conspicuous guiding principle can be identified: whoever assembled his or her domestic pantheon (and there is often more than one shrine in a house, with different ensembles of deities) appears to have picked and chosen the deities rather freely from a range of locally acceptable divine commodities. Second, the number of statuettes found in houses is relatively limited, averaging three to six deities per place of worship. This does not necessarily imply that worshippers would turn to only a few divinities. After all, public temples, shrines, and altars provided countless additional avenues for worship. However, these figures do suggest that people selected their religious portfolio carefully and according to very particular needs, predilections, family or other traditions, personal tastes, and political or cultural trends.

Religious activity was therefore often a matter of personal preference, although the nature of individual observance might be guided by the infrastructure of civic religion. This system encouraged a remarkable diversity of cult at Rome and in Roman communities. However, the civic authorities sometimes attempted to impose their political will on the increasingly differentiated landscape of religion at Rome: witness only the senatorial suppression of certain rituals in the cult of Bacchus (the so-called Bacchanalian affair) in Rome and Italy in 186 BCE; the expulsion of the worshippers of the "foreign" god Sabazius, Jews, and Chaldeans ("astrologers") from Rome in 139 BCE by official edict; the repeated destruction of altars and small shrines dedicated to the Egyptian deity Isis on the Capitoline Hill in the 50s BCE; or the empire-wide persecution of Christians in the third century CE. Ampelius's inscription on Prosenes's sarcophagus is placed almost as if to hide this confession of Christian allegiance from unobservant passersby, who would rather notice Prosenes's career. In a political climate where people were persecuted for belonging to Christ-groups, which were notorious for their alleged disloyalty to the authorities and for the various crimes they were reputed to commit—charges the Christians would deny—people like Prosenes and Ampelius had to be on their guard.[27]

Roman polytheism was not tolerant, but bouts of suppressing cults and practices were normally short-lived. The urban sacred space could not be policed adequately, and Prosenes at least managed not only to survive but also to enjoy a respectable career at the imperial court. While the persecution of the members of Christ-groups was as much owed to their beliefs as to their disobedience to political authority, the general disapproval of foreign cults and practices is easily located in the Roman elite sources, which distinguish between *religio*, an acceptable, traditional form of religious behaviour, and *superstitio*, the deviant religious behaviour of the ethnographic "other." The foreign religious practices and deities migrating to Rome were thus denounced as "superstition."[28] Of course, deciding what belonged to each category was always at the discretion of the beholder (compare Box 9.5).

Although the term *superstitio* was generally indicative of a dismissive attitude towards a set of actions, there were practices that were seen as harmful and threatening to the existing socio-political order. The cursing of others provides an example of religious behaviour that was considered antisocial. As we saw at the outset of this chapter,

Political History

Box 9.5: Domitian, Divine Protection in the Year of the Four Emperors, and Religious Pluralism in Imperial Rome

On 19 December 69 CE on the Capitoline Hill, the future emperor Domitian narrowly escaped a siege by soldiers of then emperor Vitellius. Disguised in the linen tunic characteristic of religious officials and initiates in the cult of the Egyptian goddess Isis, Domitian joined a procession of the deity's followers, who were collecting alms in the streets (Suet. *Dom.* 1.2). His rebuilding of the sanctuary of Isis in the **Campus Martius** following a fire in 80 CE has been seen as an indirect testament to the emperor's indebtedness to the goddess.

Yet Isis was not the only deity to protect Domitian from the soldiers. The warden of the temple of the Capitoline Triad proffered shelter to Domitian after the Vitellians had taken control of the hill. Domitian's later allegiance to the Roman god Jupiter materialized not only in the reconstruction of the Capitoline Temple but also in the addition of a shrine to Jupiter Conservator ("Preserver") on the spot where Domitian had received shelter (it was later replaced by a shrine to Jupiter Custos ["Guardian"]). The Arval Brothers' vows to Jupiter Optimus Maximus highlight the Capitoline god's role in lending divine legitimacy to an emperor's rule. But the Capitoline cults of Jupiter Conservator and Jupiter Custos, distinct from that of Jupiter Optimus Maximus, also emphasize the almost symbiotic relationship between the emperor and *his* guardian god (Tac. *Hist.* 2.74).

Domitian and the many divinities dwelling on the Capitoline Hill serve to recapitulate some of this chapter's salient topics. First, different religious traditions coexisted in the city of Rome, an occurrence epitomized by the Roman god Jupiter on the one hand and the migrant cult of Isis on the other. In the early second century CE, the biographer Suetonius (*Dom.* 1.2) still reflects elite sentiments when he characterizes the followers of Isis, the *Isiaci*, as worshippers of a superstition. Second, a bewildering array of differentiated cults existed. Worshippers such as Domitian did not choose one deity over another but incorporated the worship of both, and many more, into their religious portfolios. Third, Jupiter Optimus Maximus exemplifies the civic face of religion at Rome. But Domitian's example also proves that a more personal, even privileged, relationship between an individual and his or her deity could be envisaged, collapsing the division between civic and individual or between public and private. Therefore, we would be wise not to look for one Roman religion but to appreciate the plurality of religion at Rome.

employing the help of the divine world was a common device to attack one's enemies, further one's own aims, or retaliate against injustice. Curses aimed to "bind" the victim or parts of the victim's body—the Latin word *defigo* ("to transfix, affix") gives us the technical term *defixio(nes)*, "binding spells" or "curses." A leaden tablet with the person's name would be attached to tombs, buried in graves, or deposited in springs, wells, or caverns to deliver the object to the gods of the underworld, the dead, or demons. Curse tablets could also be hidden in the house of the target (see the famous example of the mysterious death of Germanicus, the adopted son of the emperor Tiberius; Tac. *Ann.* 2.69) or left in sanctuaries to make the local deity carry out the practitioner's wishes.

The targets of such curses could be various. Litigants might aim to bind their opponents so that they might fall silent in court and be incapable of rendering their case; athletes, **gladiators**, and charioteers might target their competitors (and their horses); tradesmen might bind the trades and skills of others to make their businesses fail; and women could be rendered unable to love or have sexual intercourse with anyone but the one who commissioned the curse.[29] Modern scholars sometimes classify such curses as examples of "magic." The definition of *magic* in contrast to *religion* proves elusive, however, and the identification of an action as one or the other, as in the case of *religio* and *superstitio*, usually depends on the perspective of the speaker. In spite of these difficulties, *magia* nonetheless became legally actionable in the course of the Empire.[30] For all that the religious history of Rome appeared to be one of adoption, adaptation, innovation, and diversification, it was also at times marked by suspicion and disdain of the relationships others claimed to have with the gods.

Summary

Religion at Rome is sometimes understood as "civic religion," the state-approved ritual activities (vows, sacrifices, games, temple building and repair) undertaken for the welfare of the broader Roman community and overseen by members of official priesthoods, magistrates, and the senate. Concern for precision of ritual action (a concern which is not always attested) should not obscure the adaptability and significance of civic religion; the Romans were not mired down in a cycle of ritual for ritual's sake. Instead, the relationship with the divine was vital and uncertain, and the welfare and success of the Roman community depended upon it. Civic responsibility for nurturing this relationship was therefore often placed in the hands of the same people who occupied positions of political power. Indeed, the effort and expense poured into civic religion not only demonstrated its importance to the political community of Rome, but it also created a situation that further strengthened the relationship between political and religious authority. For example, religious activities and buildings depended upon both state funds and the private benefactions of the Roman elite.

However, to consider only civic religion at Rome is to miss much of the diversity of the city's religious activity. The rituals of "ordinary" people, many of whom were immigrants or descendants of immigrants with their own religious traditions, were varied and creative. Even the worship of civic deities by ordinary people diversified the nature of those deities' cults. Religion at Rome was therefore innovative and composed of innumerable cults and rituals, decentralized and largely unregulated, and the matter of personal choice. This is not to say that non-civic religious activity rivalled civic religion or that religion at Rome was an either–or situation. However, non-civic religious activity sometimes came under the negative scrutiny of civic religious and political authorities when it appeared that non-state cults might undermine the political and social hierarchies that civic religious activity mirrored, supported, and justified.

Questions for Review and Discussion

1. The Latin term *religio* is not exactly synonymous with the English term *religion*. What does each term suggest, and how do the terms differ from each other?
2. To what extent would the ancient notion of *sacerdos* comply with modern ideas of priesthood, and what are the differences between the two concepts?
3. Religion at Rome is sometimes defined as the system of civic religion. What are the advantages of such an approach, and what are its pitfalls?
4. Discuss the connection between religious and political authority at Rome. Why did members of the political elite, eventually including the emperor, tend to occupy the most important priesthoods of civic religion?
5. What active role could women, children, or foreigners take during religious rituals?

Suggested Reading

Beard, M., J. North, and S. Price, eds. 1998. *Religions of Rome. Vol. 1: A History. Vol. 2: A Sourcebook*. Cambridge: Cambridge University Press.

    The first volume is a comprehensive history of Roman religion from its archaic origins to late antiquity. The second volume offers a generous selection of pertinent literary texts and inscriptions, as well as illustrations of coins, reliefs, frescoes, and architectural remains.

Bendlin, A. 2000. "Looking beyond the Civic Compromise: Religious Pluralism in Late Republican Rome." In *Religion in Archaic and Republican Rome: Evidence and Experience*, edited by E. Bispham and C.J. Smith, 115–35, 167–71. Edinburgh: Edinburgh University Press.

    This article proffers a critique of the scholarly focus on civic religion.

Feeney, D. 1998. *Literature and Religion at Rome: Cultures, Contexts, and Beliefs*. Cambridge: Cambridge University Press.

    Feeney considers religious practice and belief in the context of the literature of the late Republic and the Augustan period.

North, J.A. 2000. *Roman Religion* (Greece and Rome New Surveys in the Classics 30). Oxford: Oxford University Press for the Classical Association.

    North provides a comprehensive introduction to Roman civic religion (the *sacra publica*), its functionaries, and its cults.

Rives, J.B. 2007. *Religion in the Roman Empire*. Malden, MA: Blackwell.
Rives provides an excellent introduction to religion in the Roman Empire, focusing on the most salient elements of religious practice and belief.

Rüpke, J. 2007. *Religion of the Romans*. Cambridge: Polity Press.
This book is a comprehensive consideration of religion at Rome and modern ideas about Roman religion.

————, ed. 2007. *A Companion to Roman Religion*. Oxford: Blackwell.
This volume comprises specialized treatments of aspects of Roman religion and modern interpretations.

Scheid, J. 2003. *An Introduction to Roman Religion*. Edinburgh: Edinburgh University Press.
Scheid introduces the major elements of Roman civic religion.

Scott Ryberg, I. 1955. *Rites of the State Religion in Roman Art* (Memoirs of the American Academy in Rome 22). Rome: American Academy in Rome.
This study embodies invaluable insights derived from the consideration of religious practice as depicted on Roman monuments.

Turcan, R. 1988. *Religion Romaine. 1: Les Dieux. 2: Le Culte* (Iconography of Religions 17: Greece and Rome 1). Leiden, The Netherlands: Brill.
Like Scott Ryberg's work, Turcan demonstrates the value of studying iconographic material for understanding Roman ritual.

Warrior, V.M. 2006. *Roman Religion*. Cambridge: Cambridge University Press.
Warrior provides a basic introduction to Roman civic religion.

Notes

1   All translations in this chapter are mine. This *defixio* is found in Gager (1992: 74–5).
2   See, for example, Plin. *Ep.* 10.35, 10.100.
3   See North (1998) and, more generally, Beard (1998).
4   In fact, the phrase *pax deorum* occurs infrequently in the sources. For a critical reassessment of the phrase's significance in the study of Roman religion, see Santangelo (2011).
5   There is a lively scholarly debate as to whether a more comprehensive notion of "belief" is applicable to religion at Rome. For a recent assessment, see Versnel (2011:

539–59), which, although addressing Greek religion, is closer to the view held here than Feeney (1998: 12–46) or King (2003) is. For Roman popular beliefs about the gods as arbiters of justice and moral behaviour, see Morgan (2007).
6   On Roman sacrifice, see Beard, North, and Price (1998: vol. 2, 148–65); Scheid (2003: 79–110); and Bendlin (2012). For sacrificial imagery, see also Scott Ryberg (1955) and Turcan (1988: vol. 2).
7   For other instances of such "divine qualities" from the republican period, see Clark (2007).

8   The translation of *divus* with the adjective *deified*, though widespread, is incorrect.

9   The deification of the emperor and the status of the so-called imperial cult in the Roman empire are still controversial. For an introduction, see Beard, North, and Price (1998: vol. 1, 140–9, 348–62); Bosworth (1999); Rives (2007: 148–56); and Galinsky (2011). On the local character of the imperial cult, see Mellor (1992).

10 Crawford (1996: no. 22, lines 5–6).

11 On the Roman festivals and games in particular, see Scullard (1981).

12 Compare North (1976) and Bendlin (2013).

13 On the Christianization of the urban Roman elites since the mid-fourth century CE and its consequences, see Cameron (2011). Sandwell (2005) contextualizes the imperial legislative measures of the fourth century that outlawed various "illicit" religious practices—from astrology, divination, and "magic" to sacrifices, visiting temples, or worshipping images.

14 Crawford (1996: no. 25, chs. 70–1) provides an example of the expectation that magistrates would personally finance games or theatrical shows in the Roman colony of Urso in Spain: the minimum contribution expected of them was 2,000 sesterces, more than what the colonial administration was obliged to contribute. Magistrates in Roman Pompeii were expected to pay for games or building projects during their year of office (*CIL* 10.829, 854-7, 1064).

15 On such temple dedications, see Orlin (1997).

16 Against that long-held view, see Beard, North, and Price (1998: vol. 1, 117–34).

17 See Packer (2010).

18 For a detailed overview of the different civic priesthoods and their duties, see Beard and North (1990: esp. 20–1); Beard, North, and Price (1998: vol. 1, 18–30, 99–108); North

(2000: esp. 23–4); and Scheid (2003: 111–46, esp. 134–5). Rüpke (2008) lists and discusses all known religious officials in the city of Rome.

19 There is controversy among scholars as to whether one should use the modern term *priest* in discussions of Graeco-Roman religion. Compare the views of Beard and North (1990: 1–14) with those of Henrichs (2008: esp. 1–9).

20 But see Schultz (2006) and Flemming (2008). For the religious role of the Roman matron during the festival of the Matronalia, see Dolansky (2011).

21 See Beard, North, and Price (1998: vol. 2, no. 8.3) for a translation of this inscription.

22 Compare Orlin (2010).

23 *CIL* (6.8498). See Beard, North, and Price (1998: vol. 2, no. 12.7c[i]) for a translation and Markschies (1999: Plate 1) for an illustration of the sarcophagus. For discussion, see Lampe (2003: 330–4).

24 For the wide range of funerary practices and beliefs, see the collections and discussion in Lattimore (1962); Toynbee (1971); and Hope (2007).

25 On domestic worship, see also Bodel (2008). On senators' religion, see Várhelyi (2010).

26 On this aspect, compare Mantle (2002) and Prescendi (2010).

27 For the charge of belonging to the *nomen Christianum* and court proceedings against *Christiani*, see Plin. *Ep.* 10.96–7. For a discussion of the legal foundation of these persecutions and the charges raised against Christians, see Ste. Croix (2006: 105–45).

28 Compare Gordon (2008).

29 For a wide range of texts and discussion, see, for example, Tomlin (1988); Gager (1992); and Versnel (2010). The curse tablets from Roman Britain are available at http://curses.csad.ox.ac.uk/index.shtml.

30 Compare Rives (2011, esp. 102–03).

10

Roman Government in the Republic and Early Empire

John Vanderspoel

> Do not evaluate what happens at Sparta by comparison with your own laws and institutions. There is no need for point-by-point analysis. You select cavalry and infantry on the basis of an assessment by censors, and you want a few men to have outstanding wealth, with a subjected population. The goal of our founder was that the state should not be in the hands of a few, whom you call the senate, and that no one order or another should be ascendant in the city. He believed that an equalization of wealth and position would ensure that large numbers would be able to serve their country under arms. (Livy 34.31.17–18)[1]

When the Roman historian Livy wrote these words for Nabis, king of Sparta in the second century BCE, the Rome that Nabis knew had long since disappeared. Rome had become a Mediterranean empire, and the political and social troubles of the first century BCE had led to the creation of an imperial system of government. A more favourable assessment of Roman politics in the second century BCE is found in the work of Polybius (6.43–58), who first experienced Rome as a hostage and eventually became an associate of the famous family of the Scipios. His appraisal of the Roman constitution intimates that the Roman political system was a perfect combination of monarchy, aristocracy, and democracy. Moreover, Polybius notes that Rome had not only incorporated all three into its political structure but had also selected the best aspects of each.

Historians have often cited Polybius's assessment as an accurate depiction of both the Roman political structure and the favourable attitude to it outside of Rome. This reference is not surprising: Polybius is the only non-Roman contemporary whose thoughts are still extant. On the other hand, Nabis's remarks and those of Calgacus in Tacitus's *Agricola* ("Where they create a desert, they call it peace" [30.6]) are the words of Romans who wrote what they supposed a foreigner might say. Presumably, these assessments of Rome in the mouths of foreigners reflect criticisms found at Rome itself. Rome's political structures developed out of constant internal controversy and conflict throughout its history. At any given point, there were people who complained that all power was in the hands of the wealthy few. Livy's cleverness thus lies not so much in the ascription of complaints about plutocracy to Nabis but in having him offer a contrast to the Spartan form of government—not contemporary Spartan government, which had devolved to Hellenistic monarchy, but the ancient system that the legendary Lycurgus supposedly established at Sparta. Interestingly enough, Nabis (that is, Livy) compares the Lycurgan system to Rome's so-called Servian Constitution, contrasting founder with founder. It is perhaps worth pointing out, though, that the large citizen armies created by Sparta's system were thoroughly defeated several times by legions of Roman citizens under arms.

Timeline

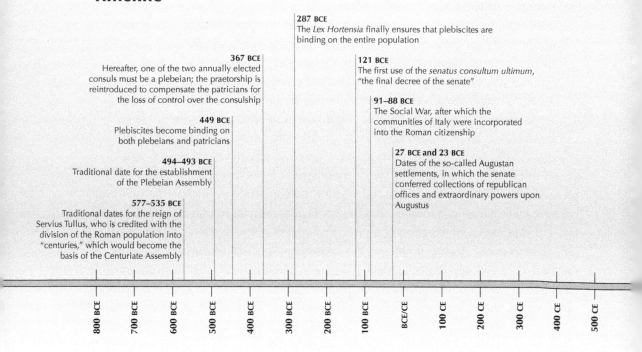

287 BCE
The *Lex Hortensia* finally ensures that plebiscites are binding on the entire population

367 BCE
Hereafter, one of the two annually elected consuls must be a plebeian; the praetorship is reintroduced to compensate the patricians for the loss of control over the consulship

121 BCE
The first use of the *senatus consultum ultimum*, "the final decree of the senate"

449 BCE
Plebiscites become binding on both plebeians and patricians

91–88 BCE
The Social War, after which the communities of Italy were incorporated into the Roman citizenship

494–493 BCE
Traditional date for the establishment of the Plebeian Assembly

27 BCE and 23 BCE
Dates of the so-called Augustan settlements, in which the senate conferred collections of republican offices and extraordinary powers upon Augustus

577–535 BCE
Traditional dates for the reign of Servius Tullus, who is credited with the division of the Roman population into "centuries," which would become the basis of the Centuriate Assembly

800 BCE 700 BCE 600 BCE 500 BCE 400 BCE 300 BCE 200 BCE 100 BCE BCE/CE 100 CE 200 CE 300 CE 400 CE 500 CE

Introduction

The following pages outline the Roman political system by providing brief accounts of political structures and political life. Naturally, Romans saw this system as a single entity and understood intrinsically how it operated. It is therefore important to remember that the system was always more than the sum of its constituent parts, that it was an organic unit that developed as conditions demanded. To provide a basic understanding of Roman politics, this chapter describes the major components of the system—the popular assemblies, the senate, and the various magistracies—and the changes that they underwent over time. The role of the people of Rome (the plebs) in the governing of the state is also considered. As will become clear, an awareness of these issues is important for a fuller appreciation of Roman society, particularly with regards to its composition, the terms used to describe different social categories (for example, the *equites* or the *plebs*), and the privileges of public life associated with different classes and statuses.

————— • ◆ • —————

The Voting Assemblies

The "Servian Constitution"

The process of building Rome's political structure began with Servius Tullus, whose reign as Rome's sixth and penultimate king is traditionally dated from 577 to 535 BCE. He is credited with the development of a political and social system that allowed Rome to create its armies. This accomplishment is often called his constitution, but Rome never had a written constitution in the modern sense. Its political mechanisms were a nebulous combination of tradition and precedent that was sometimes given a bit of structure by individual laws on specific points. Though it is unlikely that Servius Tullus developed the entire system credited to him in Rome's schematized early history, it is convenient to consider the system as a whole.

The Spartan King Nabis, with whose purported words this chapter began, was correct to note a link at Rome between wealth and military service. At some early period, the leadership of Rome divided the population into "centuries." These were not units of 100 men but groups of citizens that could annually provide that number for military service. Since citizens furnished their own equipment and wealthier citizens could afford better arms and armour, a smaller number of wealthy citizens could more easily supply 100 well-armed men than a larger number of poorer citizens. Put another way, wealthier men could more easily afford equipment and time for military service, and they could serve more often. Poorer men could not take as much time away from acquiring the necessities of life or spend money on equipment. In recognition of this fact, the citizens of Rome were allocated into groups that could reasonably be expected to provide this requirement.

As Rome's population grew, men continued to be allocated to the same number of centuries. With each century containing more citizens, it might be expected to provide more than 100 men if military needs increased. We do not know how many men were enrolled in each century at the various levels of wealth, but we do know that there were 193 centuries at Rome. Therefore, the theoretical army, or perhaps the maximum capacity that the Romans of the time could imagine, was 19,300 men. By the time Rome had completed its conquests, however, much larger armies had traversed Italy and the Mediterranean in search of enemies to fight.

Male citizens were allocated to the centuries of the Centuriate Assembly (*comitia centuriata*), a political structure that heavily favoured the older, wealthier inhabitants of Rome. This assembly was primarily a voting procedure, although speeches and discussions might occur before the process began. Each century voted internally and, by simple majority, cast a single vote on the issue at hand. Since the centuries voted consecutively, this could be a long process. For that reason, voting stopped when a majority was assured (that is, when one side had won 97 centuries). The first to vote, in a sequence determined by lot, were the 18 centuries of **equites**. Next were the 40 centuries of the *seniores* ("elders") of the population's wealthiest segment, followed by the 40 centuries of the *iuniores* ("juniors") of the same **class**. If all these centuries voted the same way, a majority would be achieved with the next-to-last century. If the vote was split, the process would continue. By and large, the wealthy generally discovered that their interests coincided more with those of their own group than with those of other elements of Roman society. Consequently, the middle, lower, and lowest classes rarely voted in the Centuriate Assembly.

Table 10.1 outlines the centuries and wealth requirements for each class in a system based on the principle that the greatest contributors to security should have more influence in the political process. Minimum property requirements for different classes of infantry reflect the same principle, given the different military usefulness of individuals with different equipment. The *equites* in the Centuriate Assembly are not the exact equivalent of the more familiar *equites* of the social class system, though the continued use of the term suggests some continuity. These early *equites* were among the wealthiest citizens and were given horses that were maintained at public expense. The specific connection later disappeared, and eventually the *equites* simply represented those wealthy individuals who were either not rich enough to pursue a **senatorial** career or chose not to do so. The difference between *iuniores* and *seniores* was age. The former were the potential fighting men, and the latter were men past the normal maximum age for military service (that is, over 45) but who might serve regardless, perhaps primarily as defenders of the homeland when other armies fought enemies farther away. Engineers and musicians (for bugles, flutes, and drums) were presumably allocated on the basis of skill, without regard for property requirements. The *capite censi*, on the other hand, were not even identified individually in the **census** rolls, the basis of service in the military. As the name suggests, they were "counted by head" like so many cattle. Those at the top of that group, with property near 11,000 *asses* (the *as* was a relatively low-valued unit of currency) were,

Table 10.1: The Classes of the Centuriate Assembly

Type		Seniores	Iuniores	Total	Minimum property requirement (in asses)
Equites				18	N/A
Infantry	Class 1	40	40	80	100,000
	Class 2	10	10	20	75,000
	Class 3	10	10	20	50,000
	Class 4	10	10	20	25,000
	Class 5	15	15	30	11,000
Engineers				2	N/A
Musicians				2	N/A
Capite censi				1	<11,000
				193	

Based on Livy (1.43) and Dionysius of Halicarnassus (4.16–18).

nevertheless, wealthy men in comparison to the poorest among Rome's population. It was the task of the **censors** to count citizens and allocate them to their places in the Centuriate Assembly.

In his *Republic*, Cicero (2.22.39–40) offers numbers different from those given in Table 10.1. He puts 6 centuries of *equites* together with 1 century of carpenters and the entire first class in a group that adds up to 89 centuries. Barring an error or problems in textual transmission, the first class presumably accounted for 82 centuries in the late Republic. As Cicero remarks, eight centuries of the second class would therefore be needed to achieve a majority if all the votes went the same way. He also notes that each of the remaining 96 centuries contained more citizens than the entire first class. The difference in numbers may be an indication that the details of the Centuriate Assembly were modified from time to time, but evidence for specific changes is rare and difficult to interpret.

The Tribal Assembly

Another voting assembly was the Tribal Assembly (***comitia tributa***). The tribes in this body were geographically based. As Rome added more territory, it accommodated this newly acquired land and its inhabitants by adding more tribes to the assembly. In the later period, the number of tribes was fixed at 35, of which 4 were urban and 31 were rural. Henceforth, new territory was allocated to existing tribes.

Because tribes were based on geography, each included citizens of every level of wealth. In principle, this arrangement should have meant that the greater number of poorer citizens could outvote the wealthier citizens, but the ubiquitous presence of **patronage** and the late introduction of the secret ballot circumscribed the citizens' ability to vote as they pleased. The voting procedure was similar to that in the Centuriate Assembly—each tribe voted internally and cast a single ballot, in a sequence determined by lot. The process was, if anything, even more time-consuming than the voting in the Centuriate Assembly, where the centuries were small in terms of the number of voters. By contrast, each tribe would represent (theoretically) nearly 3 per cent of the population. As in the Centuriate Assembly, voting stopped once a majority had been achieved. The lot setting the voting sequence partly ensured that different tribes would appear among the first 18 that could generate a majority; otherwise, some tribes might rarely, if ever, vote.

Like the Centuriate Assembly, allocation to tribes was done by censors. Most often, citizens belonged to the same tribe for life, even if they moved from one place to another, and tribal affiliation was passed down from generation to generation. For that reason, the original geographic basis of the tribes became somewhat muddied over time. Nevertheless, enough inscriptions and other evidence survive to plot the initial locations of the tribes. Each tribe also had a name that became part of a citizen's identity; however, once newly acquired territory and citizens were allocated to existing tribes, this identity could no longer be used on its own to determine a citizen's origin or place of residence. The system of tribes continued well into the imperial period and beyond Rome and Italy. Inscriptions from all over the empire identify Roman citizens as members of specific tribes, but tribal identification was no longer used for voting purposes.

That Romans valued their votes in the Tribal Assembly is evident from two points. Disputes between the elite and the other citizens often revolved around the issue of which voting assembly was employed for which types of decisions. For instance, the voting process used to declare war was an important matter. In the Centuriate Assembly, the decision belonged exclusively to the elite; in the Tribal Assembly, Roman society as a whole contributed to the decision, though the elite nevertheless had influence beyond their individual right to vote. Over the course of republican history, there was a slow migration of decision-making from the Centuriate to the Tribal Assembly.

When Rome was forced to grant citizenship to its Italian allies after the Social War (91–88 BCE), the problem of what to do with all the new citizens arose. One suggestion was to create a few new tribes. Given the voting procedure, the new citizens would not have a significant influence on the decisions made at Rome. A second proposal would have distributed the new citizens among 10 existing tribes. Again, the influence would be minimal because only a few new citizens might be at Rome to vote in fewer than a third of the tribes. In the end, Rome was forced to allocate the new citizens among all 35 tribes,

→ Compare Chapter 2, p. 29, and Chapter 14, p. 316, on the social war.

which spread their impact somewhat more broadly but perhaps also less effectively, since only a few might be at Rome for any specific vote. Besides, the censors of 86/85 BCE, who were in office after the decision to add the new citizens had been taken, left office before completing their work, and it appears that no censors were elected for about 15 years (70/69 BCE). This situation is usually regarded as a consequence of Rome's political disturbances of the period, but it may have been a deliberate decision: the enrolment of new citizens could be avoided if there were no censors to allocate them to centuries and tribes.

The Plebeian Assembly

In a move traditionally dated to 494/493 BCE, the **plebeians** established an assembly that excluded the **patricians**, with whom they were at odds. This political body initially voted by clans or kinship groups known as *curiae*. Beginning in 472 BCE, it voted by tribes (apart from the patrician members) and hence became known as the Tribal Assembly of the

Compare Chapter 3, pp. 52–3, on plebeians and patricians.

Plebeians (*concilium plebis tributum*). At first its decisions, called *plebiscita* ("plebiscites") were binding on plebeians only. After 449 BCE, however, by the terms of the *Lex Valeria Horatia* (see Box 10.1), the decisions were binding on the entire population of Rome, including patricians.

Some restrictions imposed by this law may have been removed partly by the *Lex Publilia* of 339 BCE and completely by the *Lex Hortensia* of 287 BCE, but these later laws may have been reaffirmations of laws that were sometimes ignored. When Rome was experiencing internal harmony, important decisions were usually made by the political and economic elite after discussion in the **senate** and ratified by the population as a whole in any of the assemblies, depending on the issue involved and the period of Roman history. Nevertheless, the Plebeian Assembly remained an important element in Roman politics and retained the right, even when it declined to practice it, to make decisions that were binding on Rome as a whole. Among other things, the Plebeian Assembly annually elected 10 **tribunes** (see pp. 235–6), whose task it was to represent the interests of the plebeians to the patricians.

By securing a majority in the Plebeian Assembly, tribunes could impose legislation upon all Roman society. When Tiberius Sempronius Gracchus and his brother Gaius Sempronius Gracchus introduced legislation in this assembly in 133 BCE and 123–121 BCE, respectively, they created internal strife at Rome. They did not do anything illegal, though the people had for generations left politics to the politicans and had merely ratified legislation put before the various assemblies. Many senators took the threat to precedent as dangerous enough to require the deaths of the brothers while they were still in office as tribunes. Subsequently, unscrupulous men used the assembly for all manner of purposes, particularly for political gain. Indeed, it became necessary for aristocrats to seek out tribunes to operate in the Plebeian Assembly on their behalf, and politics in the late Republic became a contest

---

Primary Source

Box 10.1: Livy, 3.55.1–7.

Through an *interrex*, Lucius Valerius and Marcus Horatius were then elected consuls and took up the consulship immediately. The consulship was popular, without injury to the patricians, although these nevertheless guarded against any freedom for plebeians, which they regarded as a loss of their own privileges. First, because there was some controversy about whether patricians were bound by plebiscites, they passed a law in the Centuriate Assembly that measures passed by the plebeians in their tribes were law for the entire population. With this law, a very sharp weapon was given to the proposals of tribunes. Then they not only restored but confirmed for the future another consular law on appeals, a defence of liberty that the *decemviri* had overturned, specifying that no one should create a magistracy without a right of appeal; if anyone did, by law he was to be put to death, with the killer not guilty of murder. After they strengthened plebeians with the right of appeal and the assistance of tribunes, then they renewed sacrosanctity for the tribunes themselves, which had nearly disappeared from memory, with specific ceremonies summoned from a distant past, and made them inviolate by religion as by law, by sanctioning that the head of anyone who harmed tribunes, aediles, and decemviral judges would be handed over to Jupiter and that proceeds of his property would go to the temple of Ceres, Liber, and Libera.

between various groups for supremacy, with the Plebeian Assembly as the theatre of operations (see pp. 235–6).

The Curial Assembly

It may be useful to mention the Curial Assembly (*comitia curia*), the earliest assembly based on the clans or kinship groups that initially comprised the Roman citizen body. This assembly never possessed binding power but was used to determine the majority opinion among the populace. In modern terms, it acted more like a poll than an election or referendum. Each *curia* voted internally and offered a single vote, as in the other assemblies. Once *curiae* were no longer employed as units for voting in the Plebeian Assembly, they lost most of their political influence. However, the *curiae* remained important as social units, and occasionally some remnant of their former significance surfaces, mostly in matters of religion.

The Centuriate, Tribal, and Plebeian assemblies, then, were the main voting assemblies at Rome. Even if ascendancy fluctuated among them, all three were important at all times. Therefore, it is impossible to state categorically which was the most vital. Most often, the assemblies were bodies that (relatively harmoniously) ratified decisions taken in the senate. In fact, though it was not a voting assembly in the sense of the three discussed in this section, the senate may well have been the most important decision-making body.

The Senate and Senators

The origins of the Roman senate can no longer be recovered. Almost certainly, it began as an advisory body during the regal period (753–509 BCE), but its composition is unclear. Presumably, it was at first a small group, perhaps including heads of the families that initially established Rome, heads of the *curiae* that comprised the Roman citizens, or heads of the patrician families (groups that may have essentially contained the same people). For much of the Republic, the senate was a body of about 300 men, but it became larger in the first century BCE and beyond.

Senate membership was not usually automatic and depended on several factors. A senator needed to possess a sufficient amount of property. Though the specific amount was surely lower in earlier times, the standard by the Augustan period was property worth at least a million **sesterces**. This requirement naturally limited the pool, and Roman society offered many wealthy men unable to become senators. Those whose wealth exceeded 400,000 sesterces were called *equites*. (As previously discussed, these men were not the cavalry at the top of the so-called Servian Centuriate system.) All those with less than 400,000 sesterces of wealth were the **plebs**, a group that was neither limited to the poor (as the usual misunderstanding has it) nor the equivalent of the plebeian families. Roman society was divided in different ways for different purposes, and some of the same terminology was applied to different divisions. The same terms possibly described the same thing at some point in Rome's past, but that is little consolation for the modern student.

Compare Chapter 3, p. 52, on the non-elite.

Rome's senators were therefore among its wealthiest citizens, but not all wealthy individuals became senators. Some preferred to stay out of politics and perhaps engage openly in livelihoods other than land ownership. The *equites*, often considered Rome's business class, thus included men who possessed sufficient property to be senators in terms of wealth but were not senatorial in **status**, often by choice.

Compare Chapter 15, pp. 334–38, on ideas about land ownership.

Senators were also required to be men of upstanding moral character. The censors, who were responsible for selecting senators, decided whether a man possessed the appropriate character and whether to exercise their right to remove unsuitable men from the senate, as they did on a few occasions. Typically, new senators were chosen from men who had been **quaestor**. In fact, election to the quaestorship carried with it some expectation of future selection as senator, and one reason for the expansion of the senate may simply be that more quaestors were elected annually in the late Republic than earlier.

Despite its prominence, the senate had no legally defined authority for most of its history. It was an advisory body to the **consuls**, who, as senators themselves, would regularly convene it to discuss the issues that lay before them. Such consultation ensured that consuls governed the state in a manner that was consistent with the wishes and perspectives of the Roman aristocracy to which they belonged. More significantly, discussions in the senate and the decisions taken there offered consuls the advice of a large group of men who all had experience of government. The senate was also important for continuity. Given that consuls were elected annually, the senate was well placed to ensure adherence to sensible policies over a period of time and could endeavour to achieve the harmonious operation of the state when consuls were at odds with each other.

Over time, the senate usurped power. It came to regard itself (perhaps correctly) as the only body competent to decide issues of finance and foreign policy but also (incorrectly) as the only body entitled to decide these matters. All decisions properly belonged to the people, but this group tended to limit itself to the ratification (or rejection) of matters put before it. This allowed the senate, consuls, and sometimes others to propose specific legislation and policies. It also established precedent and gave the senate a sense of power that it was unwilling to give up when, for example, Tiberius Sempronius Gracchus bypassed traditional procedure to achieve his political aims in 133 BCE. Working with a group of senators, he introduced legislation that had not met with the approval of the senate as a whole. Presumably, he and his supporters chose to employ unorthodox, though fully legal, means only as a last resort. But this break with precedent was too much. The consul Publius Cornelius Scipio Nasica, along with some other members of the senate, eventually killed the offending tribune. In doing so, Scipio Nasica operated within his authority as consul to preserve the state from danger. While it is possible to quibble with the decision that Tiberius Gracchus posed that kind of threat, Scipio Nasica's right to act on that conclusion cannot be legitimately questioned.

➔ Compare Chapter 2, pp. 28–9, on Tiberius and Gaius Gracchus.

A few years later, the senate issued a ***senatus consultum ultimum*** (the so-called final decree of the senate) that resulted in the killing of Tiberius Gracchus's brother, Gaius. The legality of this edict has been endlessly debated. The senate had the right to advise the consuls to eliminate Gaius Gracchus and to give the advice in strong terms, but it is not entirely clear whether they had the authority to order the consuls to do so. A few generations later, Cicero acted against Catiline only when he was certain of senatorial support but, when his political circumstances changed, he discovered that he could still be prosecuted for executing Roman citizens without trial.

Even a strong show of senatorial support was merely advice. The final decision, and responsibility for it, rested with consuls and other magistrates. By communicating its decisions as advice, the senate could achieve its wishes without the authority to act on its own. Most often, fear of consequences would ensure that the magistrates' final decisions agreed with those of the senate. Furthermore, reminders of the senate's power, as contrasted to its authority, occasionally appeared to ensure the co-operation of magistrates. On his way to exile, Cicero must have wondered why he needed to be one of those reminders.

In the early Empire, the senate shrank from dispensing advice. As emperor, Tiberius (Augustus's stepson and successor) wanted it to undertake a governing role, but it was unwilling to offend an emperor disinclined to state his views at the outset of any discussion. Too many senators had died in the civil wars and too many others of questionable eligibility had been retired by Augustus for the senators of this period to do anything that threatened their comfortable positions. As a result, the senate quickly became little more than a group of men pleased with their standing and with very little to do to maintain their status. Individual senators did regularly undertake important tasks and assume administrative positions, and in that way the senate continued to contribute to the government

Compare Chapter 3, pp. 54–6, ←
on the senate in the empire.

of Rome's empire. Occasionally, the senate might attempt to make a decision on its own but usually only when the emperor had become ineffective.

One reason for the change was simply that the imperial senate was not the direct descendant of the republican senate, since civil wars and proscriptions had wreaked havoc on senatorial families. A high proportion of the senate no longer belonged, in the male line, to families that had once regularly provided key senators. Daughters of republican senatorial families had had to marry into lesser families. Their children might become part of the new political aristocracy, but many men of insignificant family backgrounds also became senators. As such, the heritage of political involvement was lacking. This deficiency, along with an unwillingness to oppose emperors, created a mostly passive senate.

The Elected Officials of the State

Naturally, Rome needed officials to govern and manage its population, finances, military, foreign relations, and many other areas. In republican Rome, most officials were elected annually and served for a year, to ensure that a man could not accumulate enough power and influence to remain in power indefinitely. In most magistracies, including consuls in the earliest period, men could not be re-elected to the same office until two years had passed. Eventually, consuls had to wait 10 years after their first term to serve again. Continuity could be difficult to achieve, but the influence of the senate and the shared values among the elite were usually sufficient to prevent complete discontinuity.

Most elected officials at Rome are called magistrates, a term that derives from *magister* ("master") and is not as specifically judicial as the modern word (even though Roman magistrates regularly performed judicial functions). Magistrates who possessed **imperium**, essentially the authority to command, were entitled to sit on a *sella curulis* ("curule seat") and are called curule magistrates. They include curule **aediles**, **praetors**, and consuls, as well as **dictators** and masters of the horse—censors sat on curule seats but did not possess

Figure 10.1 Coin (denarius) representing Brutus the Elder with attending lictors. © Photos 12/Alamy

imperium. Curule magistrates with *imperium* were also entitled to be attended by **lictors**, the bodyguards who cleared a path for magistrates and who were regularly accused of excessive violence. Lictors also carried the symbols of office, the *fasces*, a bundle of rods with a protruding axe head that symbolized the magistrates' authority to inflict physical punishment (see Figure 10.1).

Once a *cursus honorum* ("sequence of offices") was established, men held office in a specific sequence. The *Lex Villia* of 180 BCE set out minimum ages for the holders of each office; this *lex annalis* ("law on years") was reaffirmed by Sulla in the first century BCE. Though details were different in an earlier period, the following sections describe the later requirements. From time to time, the populace ignored the rules and elected a person who had not held the required previous position or was younger than the minimum age. Pompey is an example: he was elected to the consulship for 70 BCE although he was well below the minimum age and had not held the praetorship. Such situations happened quite rarely and in unusual circumstances.

Annually Elected Magistrates

Quaestor

The first magistracy was the quaestorship, which required a minimum age of 30. The main task of quaestors was the management of finances. Some quaestors would be assigned to the treasury; others would be allocated to praetors and consuls as assistants. As the state grew and as more and more officials were needed, the number of quaestors increased, eventually reaching 20 in total. As noted earlier, the quaestorship generally led to a seat in the Roman senate.

Aedile

The aedileship lay outside the *cursus honorum*: it was held by men at least 36 years old, but a year as aedile was not a requirement for the praetorship. Aediles mainly undertook responsibility for the city's facilities (streets, sewers, public buildings), commerce (weights and measures), and public festivals, including games. The office was expensive because aediles paid for many repairs and some games from their personal resources and were not reimbursed; therefore, many men preferred not to hold the office.

→ Compare Chapter 12, pp. 279–80, on the aedileship and spectacles.

On the other hand, expensive games and extensive repairs could help aediles from less prominent families generate enough popularity to get elected to higher office more easily, as happened in the case of Julius Caesar.

To provide assistants to tribunes, the Plebeian Assembly annually elected two plebeians as aediles. These men were not curule magistrates since they were elected by the plebeians alone. When the plebeian aediles refused to fund an extra day of games in 367/366 BCE, patricians offered to fund the games if two curule aediles were elected. Initially, both new aediles were patrician. Patricians and plebeians were later elected in alternate years, and, in the final variation, any combination of patricians and plebeians was elected each year. Since the Plebeian Assembly also continued to select its two aediles, Rome had four aediles each year.

Praetor

The praetorship was recreated in 367/366 BCE to compensate patricians for the *Lex Licinia Sextia*'s provision that one consul had to be plebeian (for the original office of praetor, see the next section). To hold this magistracy, men had to have been quaestors and be at least 39 years of age. The first praetor was a patrician named Spurius Furius, and only patricians held this office until 337 BCE. Praetors relieved some of the burden on consuls, primarily by undertaking judicial work, but from the beginning they shared with consuls the right to lead armies (although a praetorian army was smaller than a consular one). Praetors were high officials who had almost as much authority as the consuls and could satisfy the requirement that one high official be at Rome at all times. As early as the First Punic War (264–241 BCE), the need for more praetors led to the creation of additional praetorships, and eventually eight men were elected annually. Julius Caesar raised the number even further, first to 10, then to 14 and 16.

Nearly from the beginning of this magistracy, two praetors, the *praetor urbanus* ("urban praetor") and the *praetor peregrinus* ("foreign praetor"), were designated for specific duties that included oversight of the legal system for citizens and foreigners. At first, the *praetor peregrinus* may regularly have served on embassies to foreign states, but he eventually remained at Rome, like the *praetor urbanus*. As the Roman world expanded, praetors were often appointed to govern provinces that required a military force. Sometimes—in fact quite regularly in the late Republic—a praetor's term was extended for a year, when he would serve as *pro praetor* ("with the authority of a praetor") and thereby offer some continuity of government in a given province.

Consul

Former praetors could seek the consulship at a minimum age of 42. Two consuls were elected every year, and this number did not change. These men, called ordinary consuls (*consules ordinarii*), gave their names to their year of service. For example, the date of an event in 55 BCE could be specified by using the Latin phrase for "in the consulships of Gnaeus Pompeius Magnus and Marcus Licinius Crassus" because these two men were the consuls in that year. The consulship was the quintessential Roman magistracy, created to replace the king when monarchy gave way to Republic; therefore, each consul possessed the authority and powers of a king. Consuls were thus equally heads of state for their year in office. They were empowered to conduct military operations, were responsible for the operation of the judicial system and could make legal decisions on their own authority, and ensured that sacrifices were performed and that religious activity took place properly. In short, they had full oversight of the state.

Among their duties, the consuls were required to ensure that elections for their replacements and for other officials took place correctly. Even when a praetor remained at Rome as the required high official in the city, at least one consul had to stay in Italy and be at Rome for the elections. Because of their importance, a new consul (*consul suffectus*, "suffect consul") was usually appointed if a consul died in office, unless the death occurred late in the year. When both consuls died in office, an ***interrex*** ("between kings") was appointed to hold elections for new consuls; his term of office was five days.

By annually electing two consuls who could veto each other, Romans hoped to have sufficient checks and balances in their new form of government and to prevent any attempt to establish a power base for tyranny. These precautions were not always effective, for the Republic did not always operate smoothly. Leaving aside disagreements on policy, its first two centuries were punctuated by irregular outbursts, serious social and political disturbances, and periods when no consuls could be elected.

Though both ancient and modern historians generally speak of the consulship as originating in 509 BCE, the chief magistrates were first called praetors, a term that fell into disuse until it was restored for the magistracy previously discussed. From approximately 445 BCE to 367 BCE, consular tribunes regularly appear in the consular list. These tribunes with consular power, often more than two in a given year, were plebeians. In some years no names appear, but at one point the same group of consuls and suffect consuls reappears for several consecutive years. At least one dictator shows up, and an *interrex* or two was appointed to conduct consular elections because of civic strife or the death of the consuls. Other irregularities are also evident.

These difficulties began with the creation of the **Twelve Tables** (the early Roman law code), itself a response to a crisis: in 451 BCE a group of 10 men, *decemviri*, took over the magistracies by universal agreement and generated Ten Tables of laws. A second group of *decemviri* handed down Two Tables the next year but refused to leave office until 449 BCE, when an uprising caused by Appius Claudius (1 of the 10) induced a pair of senators, Lucius Valerius Potitus and Marcus Horatius Barbatus, to force the group's resignation and take up the chief magistracy for the rest of the year. Though many consular tribunes followed them, this pair was the first to be known officially as consuls rather than praetors.

Compare Chapter 11, pp. 246 and 256, on the Twelve Tables.

The Twelve Tables failed to achieve social and political order. However, when Gaius Licinius Stolo and Lucius Sextius were consular tribunes from 371 to 367 BCE, a sense of a need for compromise emerged. One result was passage of the *Lex Licinia Sextia*, in 376/366 BCE. In this law, patricians gained a restoration of the praetorship with a slightly different role and the creation of the curule aedileship. The consulship remained the chief magistracy; henceforth, at least one of the two was supposed to be plebeian (although pairs of patricians still appear on occasion). The first plebeian consul was Lucius Sextius, in 366 BCE. From 342 BCE until the early second century BCE, pairs of consuls included a patrician and a plebeian, with the first pair of plebeians elected in 172 BCE.

For a long period after the compromises, only Manius Curius Dentatus was consul for two years running (275 and 274 BCE). A few held second consulships as early as three years after their first, since the two-year interval applied to consuls until the *Lex Villia* of 180 BCE changed it to a decade. Thereafter, fewer were consul twice. Given the high minimum age, death might prevent a second term, and new ex-praetors constantly refreshed the pool of candidates. When men were consul at close intervals, it was usually for military reasons. Before 104 BCE, when Gaius Marius began a series of consecutive consulships only three years after his first term in office in 107 BCE (see the following section), this happened only three times: Marcus Claudius Marcellus (166, 155, and 152 BCE); Publius Cornelius Scipio Nasica, father of the man who killed Tiberius Gracchus (162 and 155 BCE); and Gaius Marcius Figulus (162 and 156 BCE). The case of Scipio Nasica and Figulus is odd. Elected as colleagues in 162 BCE, they were forced to abdicate and were replaced by suffects. Tiberius Sempronius Gracchus (Tiberius and Gaius's father), consul in 163 BCE, recalled a failure to conduct the religious ceremonies properly before the elections, which were therefore declared null and void. Presumably, the need to prevent someone else from taking his **triumph** triggered Tiberius's recollection of faulty procedure (see Box 10.2).

The consulship was the pinnacle of most political careers, though men continued to sit in the senate and often served as the governor of a province. A consul sometimes remained in a governorship as a "proconsul" (*pro consule*). This happened more frequently as Rome needed more commanders for its expanding empire. In the last years of the Republic, men were sometimes given extended proconsulships of five years. The proconsulship was also regularly held by emperors. The power and authority, though not the honour and glory, of the consulship dissipated rapidly in the imperial period. As early as the reign of Augustus, the office was employed mainly to honour the elite, as deemed necessary or desirable. Many years offered multiple consuls, as ordinary consuls abdicated to make room for suffects, who did the same for more suffects. Election to office now consisted mainly of the senate's ratification of the emperor's choices, and even that devolved to straightforward appointment. By the later Roman Empire, the appointment of multiple pairs in a given year had ceased. The last western consul was Decimus Theodorus Paulinus, in 536 CE. In 541 CE the last consul, Flavius Basilius, was appointed in the Byzantine East.

"New Men"

Until Julius Caesar became dictator, Gaius Marius was the last consul to serve in consecutive years. He was a **novus homo**

Compare Chapter 3, p. 53, and ← Chapter 7, pp. 150–1, on *novi homines*

Political History

Box 10.2: Tiberius Sempronius Gracchus and the Consulship for 162 BCE

In *De Natura Deorum* (*On the Nature of the Gods*), Cicero uses the election of consuls for 162 BCE to argue that elite Romans respected the pronouncements of the priests, *augures*, and *haruspices*. However, the series of events was not quite so straightforward. Manius Iuventius Thalna, a consul for 163 BCE was assigned to Sardinia and Corsica but died while in his province. Meanwhile, Tiberius Sempronius Gracchus, the other consul, conducted the elections for 162 BCE, overriding the senate and *augures* in the process. In the words of Cicero (*Nat. D.* 2.10):

> In fact, events themselves proved the validity of both our augury and the divination of Etruscan *haruspices* in the consulship of P(ublius) Scipio and G(aius) Figulus. When Ti(berius) Gracchus, consul for the second time, was conducting the election of these successors, the first returning officer suddenly died in the very act of reporting them as elected. After Gracchus nonetheless proceeded with the election and then sensed that the incident had become a religious matter among the people, he brought the issue to the senate, which decided that it should be referred "to the customary officials." The *haruspices* who were brought in stated that the returning officer for the elections had not been in compliance.

Gracchus responded that, as consul and an *augur* himself, he had conducted the election and taken auspices properly. He dismissed the *haruspices* and went to Sardinia to replace Iuventius. Later, with the new consuls already heading to their provinces, Gracchus discovered an error. Cicero offers the details (*Nat. D.* 2.11):

> Later, however, he sent a letter from his province to the *augures* stating that while reading the sacred books it occurred to him that there had been a fault in setting up his tent in Scipio's gardens because after he had crossed the **pomerium** to convene the senate and then crossed into the *pomerium* a second time, he had forgotten to take the auspices and that the elections for consuls were therefore not conducted properly. The *augures* brought the matter to the senate, which decided that the consuls should abdicate; they abdicated. What better examples could you wish for? A very wise man, perhaps the most outstanding of all, preferred to admit a mistake that he might have concealed rather than allow an error of religion to hang over the state, and the consuls preferred to give up the highest office immediately rather than hold it for the slightest moment against religious sanction.

Whatever the validity of his point about respect for religion, Cicero surely knew about the attending circumstances. Gracchus stayed in Sardinia and was awarded a triumph for his successes. Clearly, he used the sacred books to ensure that, with victory and a potential triumph in sight, he would not be replaced, even by his brother-in-law Scipio (assigned to Sardinia and Corsica). An *interrex*, by the way, conducted new elections for suffect consuls for 162 BCE.

("new man"), one of the first in some time, since the Roman elite treated any attempt to join their ranks unfavourably. A small number of families held most of the consulships, with other elite families controlling almost all the remaining positions. Outsiders could be quaestors and praetors (and thus senators), but the consulship was safeguarded against intrusions. This attitude is clear in the excerpt in Box 10.3 (see also Plut. *Mar.* 8). Even though Marius was in his late forties and had been quaestor (120 BCE?), tribune (119 BCE), and praetor (115 BCE) beyond the minimum ages, he was advised to wait before seeking a consulship. Choosing to ignore this advice, Marius was successful in his bid and replaced his former commander in Africa. Military success, measures to ensure popularity and eliminate rivals, and fear at Rome of the Cimbri and Teutones secured him repeated annual election to consulships from 104 through 100 BCE.

In 106 BCE, while Marius was still in Africa, a woman in his hometown gave birth to a baby who would also become a *novus homo*. This child was Marcus Tullius Cicero, who proudly proclaimed that he had held his magistracies *in anno suo* ("in his year," or at the minimum ages). He was later exiled for executing Roman citizens without a trial. His status as a new man and his egocentric boasting were among the reasons that the senatorial establishment was willing to abandon him.

Civil wars and proscriptions meant that many new men appeared in the Augustan period. As time progressed, men from all over the empire became consuls and senators, but the number of new men in the republican period was quite small.

Primary Source

Box 10.3: Sallust, *The War with Jugurtha*, 64.1–4.

When Marius saw that the *haruspex*'s words pointed in the direction that his own burning desire was urging him, he asked Metellus for leave to become a candidate. Though Metellus had plenty of valour, renown, and other qualities to be desired by good men, yet he had a disdainful and proud spirit, a common evil in the nobility. Initially, then, annoyed by the unusual request and surprised at Marius's plan, he, pretending friendship, advised him not to pursue an irregular course or behave above his station and said that not all men should seek all things, that he should be satisfied with his place, and finally, that he should be careful of asking from the Roman people something that they would justifiably deny. After Metellus made this and similar points without changing Marius's mind, he finally replied that when the state's business permitted he would do what he asked. Later, after Marius had regularly made the same request, Metellus reportedly told him not to be in a hurry to leave, that it would be soon enough to seek the consulship when his son did. He was at that point about 20 years old and in Numidia on his father's staff.

Other Elected Officials

Censor

Censors have already been mentioned as officials responsible for several matters, including the counting of citizens, allocation of citizens to tribes and centuries, and appointment of new senators. From time to time, censors expressed their views (sometimes by edicts) on the lifestyle of Roman citizens. In particular, censors were responsible for ensuring that Romans did not live in too luxurious a manner. They might, for example, limit the amount of money spent on funerals or the amount of silver plate permitted in Roman households.

➔ Compare Chapter 3, p. 59, on the activities of the censor.

Two censors, almost inevitably men of great influence and high political standing, were elected every five years for an 18-month term (the office remained vacant for the remaining time). The elder Tiberius Gracchus was consul in 177 and 163 BCE and censor in 169 BCE. Not all the censors of the Republic are known, and it is possible that internal strife may at times have resulted in a failure to elect censors when they should have been. The last full pair of non-imperial censors was Lucius Minutius Plancus and Lucius Aemilius Lepidus Paullus in 22 BCE, but they accomplished little.

Though few details are known, citizens were counted from time to time in the imperial period, possibly still in accordance with the five-year cycle (but perhaps not every five years; censors may have taken office in a year that was a multiple of five since the last cycle). Other than Augustus (28 BCE, with Agrippa; 8 BCE, alone; 14 CE, with Tiberius), few imperial censors are known specifically. The task perhaps became part of an emperor's general responsibilities and was allocated, naturally, to the bureaucracy. Claudius (with the non-imperial Lucius Vitellius) in 47/48 CE and Vespasian (with Titus) in 73/74 CE seem to have used the censorship mainly to remove and add men from and to the senate. Since no figures survive, it is not known whether either of them organized a census. Domitian (alone) assumed the role of perpetual censor (*censor perpetuus*) in 85 CE, and again the sources note mainly his attention to membership of the senate. Around 251 CE, Decius attempted to revive the non-imperial office, with the choice of candidate left to the senate. It selected Valerian for the position, but he declined.

Tribune

Closely associated with the people of Rome is the office of tribune, which was not a magistracy because tribunes were elected by only the plebeians. As previously mentioned, the tribunate began with the creation of the Plebeian Assembly, which chose 10 tribunes each year. (Given the size of the plebeian population compared with patricians, this number is unremarkable.) The plebeians also promoted their own triad of deities—Ceres, Liber, and Libera—whose temples stood on the Aventine Hill, as opposed to the **Capitoline Triad** on the Capitoline Hill. In some sense, the story of Rome's political development is the amalgamation of the state with this "state within a state." In the process, patricians tended to give and plebeians to take because the latter was able to employ larger numbers and withhold services as soldiers and voters. Without these groups, patricians could accomplish little unless they perpetrated violence, as they sometimes did.

Like magistrates, tribunes could veto the actions and policies of their fellow officeholders; in time, they also gained the right to veto actions and policies of all other magistrates. As noted earlier, consular tribunes were sometimes elected instead of consuls, until the *Lex Licinia Sextia* resolved at least some disagreements between patricians and plebeians. In periods of stability, the people and their tribunes generally co-operated with the elite and their senate, many of whom were plebeians. Indeed, most tribunes were wealthy men of leading families, and many pursued full careers through the *cursus honorum*. In some cases, men whose families or who themselves were not well known might seek election to the tribunate as an avenue to generate recognition and enough popularity to stand for further office.

Among the duties of tribunes was the smooth operation of the Plebeian Assembly. The senate or consuls might encourage tribunes to introduce legislation on their behalf, or others might prepare the legislation that was brought to the Plebeian Assembly by the tribunes. Unsurprisingly, tribunes, who were often of the senatorial class, usually sought the prior approval of consuls and senate before introducing any legislation of their own. As previously discussed, Tiberius Gracchus's actions in 133 BCE changed this practice. Subsequently, other tribunes (such as Gaius Gracchus) also began to use the assembly for legislation not approved by the senate as a body.

To harness this new sense of political power among the people, the elite began to court tribunes. Different aristocrats were more or less willing to adopt this tactic; the more willing were called *populares* ("populists") and the others *optimates* ("best men"). Not political parties in a modern sense, relations between them (which were usually terrible) and their interactions are nevertheless sometimes called party politics by historians. Particularly late in the second century and the 80s BCE, politics at Rome devolved into utter chaos, with murder a frequent event as each group sought to control the political process and to use the opportunity to eliminate rivals by semi-legal murder and assassination. Throughout, tribunes remained the political operatives who, by fair means or foul, passed most of the legislation that governed the state.

The power of the tribunate continued in imperial times as one of the positions that emperors would adopt. The fiction of Empire was that the Republic continued to exist because the magistracies and offices endured (at least at first). In fact, magistracies and offices were altered enough that the men appointed to them had few of the duties and little of the authority of their republican counterparts. In 23 BCE Augustus allowed himself to be given *tribunicia potestas* ("tribunician power"), which gave him authority to lead and guide the people and to make legislation on their behalf. Combined with his proconsular powers, this title essentially allowed him to rule as emperor in the guise of a republican magistrate and office-holder. It was a pleasant illusion designed to counteract sentiment for the restoration of the Republic. No one was fooled, but most accepted the fiction.

Dictator

From time to time, the senate would appoint a *dictator rei gerundae causa* ("dictator to do what needs to be done") or, perhaps specifically to put down rebellion, a *dictator seditionis sedandae causa* ("dictator to settle sedition"), with a *magister equitum* ("master of the horse") as assistant. Holding virtually unlimited power, dictators were appointed for a normal term of six months to restore order and arrange for the election of consuls (if necessary). In the later Republic, the dictatorship might be a method of staying in power. Sulla held the position in 82–81 BCE, as *dictator legibus faciendis et rei publicae constituendae* ("dictator to make laws and to reconstitute the state"). Julius Caesar became *dictator rei gerundae causa* in 49 BCE and, through extensions, held the office until his assassination. After his death, the triumvirate of Marc Antony, Augustus (then called Octavian), and Marcus Lepidus was basically a triple-headed dictatorship (*triumviri rei publicae constituendae consulari potestate*; "board of three with consular powers to restore the state") sanctified by the *Lex Titia* of 43 BCE for a term of five years and eventually renewed for an additional five.

Priesthoods

Many priesthoods existed at Rome, and a few remarks about their role in politics are in order. Everything at Rome was to be preceded or accompanied by religious sanction or ceremony. Elected officials wanted the gods' favour for their activities. Furthermore, legal proceedings, elections, meetings of the senate, declarations of war, and many other deeds

→ Compare Chapter 9, pp. 200–03, on priesthoods.

needed prior divine approval. When that was not assured, activities were postponed or cancelled. As is clear from the forced abdication of the consuls for 162 BCE (discussed in Box 10.2), the religious rites needed to be conducted in the prescribed manner in order to be valid; otherwise, serious consequences might occur.

Clearly, with most priesthoods populated by the same elite as the magistracies and senate, priests could use religion as political tools. Such was the case with Tiberius Gracchus, as related in Box 10.2. To supervise Roman religion, the Roman elite selected from amongst themselves a ***pontifex maximus***, a position held for life.

The People in the Late Republic and Early Empire

By the late second century BCE, the population of the city of Rome had become large, as individuals from all over the empire flocked to it. Many came because they could not provide for themselves and their families. Since the situation at Rome was not much better, a crowd of unemployed people populated the Empire's capital. This crowd could be, and was, mobilized by politicians seeking voters in the Tribal and Plebeian assemblies or rioters to threaten their political opponents. Above all, the people needed food and distraction, and it is commonplace to link the distribution of grain and the provision of games to this purpose. While this connection is not entirely accurate, these programs were amplified as the unrooted population at Rome increased.

One form of control was the system of patronage. Every aristocrat constantly attempted to increase his number of clients, and many became patrons (*patroni*) of poorer citizens who required assistance. Typically, a patron provided bread or a small allowance; in turn, clients supported their patrons in political and other endeavours. Groups of patrons

Compare Chapter 3, p. 65, ⇐
on patronage.

might pool clients on behalf of a politician with a specific agenda. That assistance would include votes, of course, but might also include violence or the threat of it. Curiously, the elite despised the lower-class population, in part because of its propensity for violence; however, they instigated and encouraged this tendency when it suited their interests.

The question of whether the behaviour and participation of the people represents democracy has regularly arisen, especially in recent years. The answer depends heavily on how democracy is defined. In the imperial period, when politics no longer included the active participation of voters, the people nevertheless continued to express their views on issues, either with an occasional riot in the streets or more often by applause

Compare Chapter 12, pp. 281–3, ⇐
on games as occasions for
political manifestations.

and chanting at the games. As such, the people remained a problem that needed attention. Partly because the population was no longer mobilized by politicians, an adequate supply of food and regular distraction at the games was usually enough to keep it quiet.

The Imperial Period and Beyond

Under the Empire, the roles of many officials changed. They were appointed (with appointments perhaps ratified) rather than elected, and any right to engage in independent decision-making was circumscribed by the wishes of the emperors. Men continued to have an interest in holding office, and emperors continued to appoint men of senatorial status. Among other things, these opportunities helped to retain the support of the elite, who desired honour and glory. Naturally, many performed

See Chapter 16, p. 374, ⇐
for an example of Pliny's
correspondence with Trajan.

their tasks conscientiously. Pliny the Younger, for example, worked hard while serving as governor of Bithynia, as his letters to Trajan and the emperor's responses clearly attest.

Nevertheless, senators were no longer the government. Instead, they were a decorative element that disguised the fact that Rome was a military dictatorship. On occasion, the senate or one or more senators might raise an issue, object to something, or even plot against an emperor, but such behaviour became increasingly dangerous and rare. Curiously perhaps, emperors continued to add to the senate, which numbered 2,000 members in the fourth century CE. It had no real power by then, but it remained beneficial for emperors to maintain harmony with the elite as represented in the senate. The Roman senate's importance declined with the rise of a second senate at Constantinople in the fourth century CE. As the western part of the empire collapsed and even Italy fell in the sixth century, the senate as the Romans of the Republic and Empire had known it disappeared.

In imperial times, the most important person was the emperor. To rule, Augustus accumulated a package of positions, including tribunician status, proconsulships (for 5- or 10-year terms), and the post of *pontifex maximus*. He was also sometimes consul and/or censor. Individually, the offices and their lengthy terms and renewals had precedent; nonetheless, the aggregate was unrepublican. Essentially, Augustus could legislate as tribune, rule with his *imperium* as proconsul, and ensure the religious and moral health of state and people as *pontifex maximus* and censor. His right to make the first motion in the senate (*ius relationis primae*) inevitably generated control of that body's discussions. By the time he died, Augustus had ensured that Tiberius already possessed sufficient powers to become the emperor fully and completely. The Romans were not favourably disposed towards inherited rule in the manner of kings, and this first transition needed to be handled carefully. Attitudes changed as time went on, and the senate more or less automatically granted imperial powers, in a package similar to what Augustus had accumulated, to a designated successor (often a son) or to a candidate who presented himself in such a manner that he could not be denied. This process, in its simplest formulation, is how one emperor succeeded another.

Emperors were responsible for every aspect of the management of the Empire. While some preferred to tackle many details personally, others delegated more readily. They all made decisions on policy and appointed men to carry out their wishes, selected men to govern provinces and perform other administrative tasks, and promoted men to high military command and sometimes led the armies themselves, against external and internal threats. Rulers responded to petitions from their citizens and passed judgment on legal matters. As much as possible, emperors sought and took the advice of the senate and of the leading citizens of the cities around the empire. The Empire, in short, was able to keep emperors as busy as they wanted to be.

Historians have often ended the line of emperors with Romulus Augustulus in 476 CE. By that time, the Eastern Empire had become an entity of its own. We know it as the Byzantine Empire, but its rulers saw themselves as the successors of Augustus. On that reading, the last Roman emperor was Constantine XI Palaeologus, who died on 29 May 1453 CE, in the battle for Constantinople. Long before then, however, the duties and roles of a Byzantine emperor had changed dramatically from the responsibilities and functions of the position that Augustus had established.

Summary

This chapter has addressed the Roman system of politics and government by considering its various parts. Attention has been given to the following subjects: the three main voting assemblies and their procedures; the annually elected officials; the less regular offices of censor and dictator; and the senate, its influence, and the difficult question of the legal extent of its powers. Because the Roman system was never a static entity, the discussion has also attempted to give some sense of the government's development during the Republic, with additional remarks outlining the changes generated by the creation of a new system, imperial rule.

Questions for Review and Discussion

1. Who were the most important elected officials at Rome, and why?
2. Was disagreement between politicians at Rome healthy or unhealthy? Why or why not?
3. Discuss whether the collapse of the republican system of government was inevitable.
4. What role did violence play in the development of the Roman political system?
5. Were the lower classes pawns or manipulators of the elite? Give reasons to support your answer.

Suggested Reading

Beck, H., A. Duplá, M. Jehne, and F. Pina Polo, eds. 2011. *Consuls and Res Publica: Holding High Office in the Roman Republic.* Cambridge: Cambridge University Press.

> In this volume, the editors present a series of very recent studies on various aspects of the consulship.

Brennan, C.T. 2001. *The Praetorship in the Roma Republic,* 2 vols. Oxford: Oxford University Press.

> Brennan offers a very thorough study of the praetorship in these two volumes.

Cornell, T.J. 1995. *The Beginnings of Rome: Italy and Rome from the Bronze Age to the Punic Wars (c. 1000–264 BC).* London and New York: Routledge.

> A thorough but clear account of Rome's earliest history, Cornell's book outlines the development of Rome's political system and its magistracies.

Millar, F. 1992. *The Emperor in the Roman World (31 BC–AD 337),* 2nd edn. London: Duckworth.

> Millar offers a detailed study of the duties

undertaken by emperors and examines the changing nature of the role of emperors during the imperial period.

———. 1998. *The Crowd in Rome in the Late Republic*. Ann Arbor: University of Michigan Press.

This volume is one of the earliest studies of the behaviour of the plebs in the late Republic.

Mouritsen, H. 2001. *Plebs and Politics in Late Republican Rome*. Cambridge: Cambridge University Press.

In this book, Mouritsen reacts to the ideas found in Millar's book on the plebs and offers some new ideas of his own.

Pina Polo, F. 2011. *The Consul at Rome: The Civil Functions of the Consuls in the Roman Republic*. Cambridge: Cambridge University Press.

This book is a very recent and thorough study of the consulship.

Suolahti, J. 1963. *The Roman Censors: A Study on Social Structure* (Annales Academiae Scientiarum Fennicae, ser. B, torn. 117). Helsinki: Suomalainen Tiedeakatemia.

This work is a very detailed study of censors and their activities.

Taylor, L.R. 1966. *Roman Voting Assemblies: From the Hannibalic War to the Dictatorship of Caesar*. Ann Arbor: University of Michigan Press.

Taylor's book remains a thorough and useful treatment of Rome's voting assemblies.

Yavetz, Z. 1969 (rev. 1988). *Plebs and Princeps*. Oxford: Oxford University Press.

This study is an early analysis of the behaviour of the crowd in Rome, mainly of the early imperial period but with some treatment of the republican background.

Note

1   All translations in this chapter are my own.

11

Crime, Law, and Order

Benjamin Kelly

In the early third century CE, there was allegedly a serious outbreak of brigandage in Italy led by a certain Bulla.[1] An account of this has survived in the writings of the historian Cassius Dio, who was a contemporary of the events he claims to describe. The story illustrates one kind of public order problem faced by the Roman authorities and some of the ways in which they would respond to it:

> At this time, a certain Bulla, an Italian, put together a band of brigands numbering around 600. He plundered Italy for two years, right under the noses of the emperors and numerous soldiers. He was pursued by many men, with (the emperor Septimius) Severus zealously hunting him, but he was neither seen when seen, nor found when found, nor caught when caught—so much bribery and cleverness did he use . . . And once he approached the centurion tasked with eliminating his band, and accused himself, just as if he were someone else. He undertook to hand the brigand over to the centurion, if the latter would follow him. Pretending he was leading the centurion to Felix—Bulla was called this too—he led him into a bushy ravine, and easily seized him. After this Bulla put on the regalia of a magistrate and ascended a tribunal, and summoning the centurion, he caused his head to be shaved and said: "Tell your masters this: 'Feed your slaves, so they don't become brigands.'" For Bulla had a great many imperial freedmen with him, some who had been underpaid and some who had been completely unpaid. When Severus learnt of these events, he was angry that, although in Britain he was winning wars through others, in Italy he was losing to a brigand. In the end, he sent a tribune from his bodyguard with many horsemen, threatening him with a terrible fate if he did not bring Bulla back alive. Thus the tribune, learning that Bulla was sleeping with somebody else's wife, convinced the woman through

her husband to co-operate with the authorities in return for immunity. Bulla was therefore arrested while sleeping in some cave. Papinian the (Praetorian) Prefect asked: "Why did you become a brigand?" He answered: "Why are you a prefect?" After this he was thrown to the wild beasts accompanied by a herald's proclamation, and his band was dissolved—thus it seems that the whole strength of the 600 was in this one man. (Cass. Dio 77.10.1–2, 4–7.)

Timeline

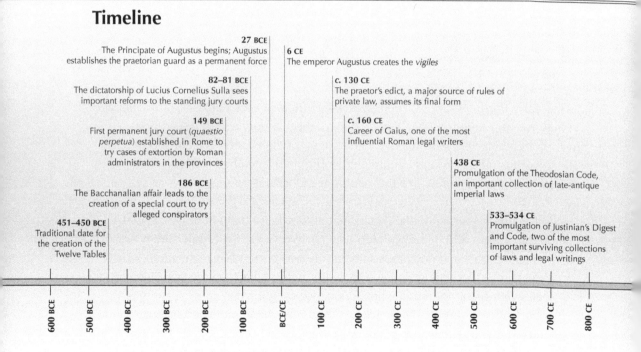

27 BCE
The Principate of Augustus begins; Augustus establishes the praetorian guard as a permanent force

6 CE
The emperor Augustus creates the *vigiles*

82–81 BCE
The dictatorship of Lucius Cornelius Sulla sees important reforms to the standing jury courts

c. **130 CE**
The praetor's edict, a major source of rules of private law, assumes its final form

149 BCE
First permanent jury court (*quaestio perpetua*) established in Rome to try cases of extortion by Roman administrators in the provinces

c. **160 CE**
Career of Gaius, one of the most influential Roman legal writers

438 CE
Promulgation of the Theodosian Code, an important collection of late-antique imperial laws

186 BCE
The Bacchanalian affair leads to the creation of a special court to try alleged conspirators

451–450 BCE
Traditional date for the creation of the Twelve Tables

533–534 CE
Promulgation of Justinian's Digest and Code, two of the most important surviving collections of laws and legal writings

600 BCE 500 BCE 400 BCE 300 BCE 200 BCE 100 BCE BCE/CE 100 CE 200 CE 300 CE 400 CE 500 CE 600 CE 700 CE 800 CE

Introduction

The Romans were proud of their legal system. They claimed to have brought law and order to the peoples of their empire and used this claim to try to justify the violence and repression that imperialism inevitably entailed.[2] Their jurisprudence has had a lasting impact on the modern world, since Roman law shaped the "civil law" legal systems of many countries in continental Europe and beyond.[3] One of the most enduring visual reminders of Roman civilization in the modern world refers to an especially gruesome criminal punishment ordered by the Roman governor of Judea in the 30s CE: the sign of the Cross. In short, law, crime, and punishment are central to our conception of the Romans, just as they were to the Romans' conception of themselves.

The history of Roman law is an expansive field. To exhaust it, one would have to outline the development not only of procedural and substantive rules but also of legal codes, handbooks, and other kinds of legal writing—a process that unfolded over more than a thousand years. Roman legal history is often harrowingly technical; many aspects of it are of interest only to specialists and are not enormously important to how we imagine life in the societies that made up the Roman empire. Consequently, as its title suggests, this chapter focuses on two questions that are centrally relevant to social history: How did the Roman justice system seek to prevent the sort of serious wrongs against people and property that we would call crimes? How successful was it in doing so? Raising and addressing these questions provokes two others: How much do we really know about "crime" as a social phenomenon in the Roman world? What did the inhabitants of the Roman empire do when the courts and the imperial administration failed to protect them?

In approaching these questions, the story of Bulla is a good place to start. It involves a category of crime often mentioned in the ancient sources (brigandage) and shows some of the ways in which the state sought to limit major crime (through the deployment of soldiers and through trials and terrifying public executions). The difficulties involved in catching Bulla illustrate the problems that the authorities sometimes faced in keeping order. The story also demonstrates some of the problems that historians face in studying crime and its repression in the Roman world. For one thing, like most cases of crime and punishment reported in Roman literary sources, it was a glamorous and spectacular episode with implications for political history and is therefore probably atypical. Furthermore, Dio's account of Bulla's career is charged with social and political critique, a feature shared with many other accounts of crimes from the Roman world.[4] In this society, as in most others, crime was rarely presented in a straightforward, dispassionate way. For these reasons and others, social historians face considerable hurdles when attempting to understand crime and punishment as it actually was.

———— ♦ ————

"Crime" in the Roman World

There are two main ways in which we can begin to study "crime" in the Roman period. First, we can examine it as a real social phenomenon: What kind of crimes took place in the Roman world, and what was their actual frequency and impact? Secondly, we can approach it as an intellectual category: How did the Romans think about and define "crime"?

It is clear that people in the Roman world faced many of the threats to their persons and property that we do today. The literary and documentary sources contain general mentions and specific allegations of murders, rapes, assaults, and thefts of the sort that would not be out of place in modern police reports or in the pages of a tabloid newspaper. One instance is that of Plautius Silvanus, a prominent Roman who supposedly killed his wife by ejecting her from a window in 24 CE, only to have his guilt demonstrated by the personal investigations of the emperor Tiberius. For today's reader, Tacitus's (*Ann.* 4.22) report of the incident conveys an instantly recognizable thrill, with its combination of celebrity misbehaviour and inspired detective work. Moreover, various larger-scale threats to person and property faced by the Romans still exist in our world. For example, dozens of riots are reported from the cities of the Roman empire. The technologies of organization and repression may have changed, but the angry chants, flying stones, and burning property of a Roman riot would not be out of place in a more modern setting.[5]

On the other hand, some Romans clearly faced security threats that do not loom large in our own society. **Brigandage** is a good example here because, while criminal gangs are a feature of modern urban life, the chance of being robbed by bands of desperadoes when travelling in the countryside or at sea is not something that often enters our conscious-ness. For the Romans, things were rather different: brigandage was a ubiquitous feature of their culture. All manner of ancient sources—poems, historical works, legal manuals, medical textbooks, tombstones, and documentary papyri—are peppered with references to bandits and pirates and the possibility of being attacked by them.[6]

So it is clear enough that what we would call "crime" did actually happen in the Roman world, some of it recognizable, some of it alien to our experience. The historian must acknowledge, however, that we do not know nearly as much about the general phe-nomenon of crime in the Roman world as we might assume. We cannot be sure about the crime rates in this society or about the social and economic impact of crime. The prob-lem is that the famous cases recorded by historians such as Cassius Dio or in law-court speeches by advocates such as Cicero are probably not representative of the day-to-day reality of crime. Furthermore, crime reports are often shaped by political, moral, and literary agendas. Again, brigandage provides a good example. In the Roman world, the term *brigand* was sometimes used for people not because they were in a straightforward sense outlaws living off violent property crime but as a term of abuse against political opponents.[7] Tales of brigandage could also be used to make sophisticated points about political power. Take the reported exchange between Bulla and the prefect Papinian— "'Why did you become a brigand?' . . . 'Why are you a prefect?'". This reproduces a well-worn ancient cliché: that political authority was really just a form of brigandage. Indeed, there was a story that when Alexander the Great asked a pirate what wickedness caused him to infest the seas, the latter replied: "The same that caused you to infest the land."[8] Thus, Dio's report is a highly stylized version of reality, not an artless account of how things actually happened. The same can be said of many other crime reports.[9]

Moreover, even if our literary authors were trying to give straightforward descriptions of "crime" in their society, they lived in a world where there was no scientific criminology.

In the absence of rigorous criminal statistics and the methods needed to interpret them, our sources can convey only unreliable popular beliefs and rumours. To be sure, our own world is awash with unreliable popular beliefs and rumours about crime, but serious researchers can use statistical and criminological methodologies to obtain a somewhat more accurate picture of modern crime. Ancient authors had no such tools at their disposal.

Scholars of Roman social history can sometimes partly correct the distorted picture provided by literary texts by employing documentary sources such as inscriptions and papyri. There are certainly documentary sources referring to wrongs against persons and property: especially numerous are petitions preserved on papyri.[10] In these documents, victims or their families complain of a variety of wrongs, including murder, assault, theft, and malicious damage to property. For example, a petition from the Egyptian village of Karanis, which probably dates to the reign of Claudius,[11] complains of assault, false imprisonment, and theft (see Box 11.1). The difficulty is, however, that such petitions preserved on papyrus come from just a few regions of the empire (mainly regions of Egypt, which was not under Roman control until 30 BCE). It cannot be assumed that they accurately reflect the phenomenon of "crime" in other periods or places. Furthermore, they are quite stereotyped, since they were mostly written by scribes who described wrongs using certain stock phrases. They were also written at the request of the victim or his or her family, so we only get one side of the story.[12] Something similar can be said of

Primary Source

Box 11.1: *P.Mich.* 6.421.

On the night of the [. . .] of Pharmouthi (March/April) in the present [. . . year of . . .] the emperor Claudius Caesar Augustus Germanicus, certain persons in the manner of brigands dug through into the courtyard where we keep our asses and once inside led off two of my white, adult asses, worth 280 drachmas. I submitted a petition concerning these matters to Pankrates, the *archephodos* of <Karanis>, and with him I loaded up one ass with water and another with food. We set off, tracking the offenders from the place where we discovered their route, which went into the region of Bakchias and back again into the desert. But just as we were about to capture the offenders in their lair, the *archephodos* of Bakchias, Pasion, and the collectors of customs duties prevented us. They detained me and the *archephodos* of Karanis, smashed our water jars, seized our staves, and then imprisoned us for three days, until such time as we could not capture the offenders. Then, once they had taken away our two packsaddles, our bread, a sheepskin, and two fodder bags (?), they mistreated me with blows. The village secretary and elders talked to them and forced them to let us go. I ask that you help me.

→ Compare Chapter 9, pp. 189–90
and 211–13, on curse tablets.   certain other types of documentary sources, such as the tombstones that claim that the deceased was murdered by bandits or the curse tablets complaining of thefts.[13] Documentary sources do not, therefore, bring us much closer to understanding the social history of "crime" in the Roman world.

It is somewhat more promising to study "crime" as an intellectual or cultural category. It is clear enough that the Romans sometimes treated some deviant actions in a way that was not dissimilar to our treatment of crimes. This immediately raises the question of what we mean by "crime" in our own society. A formal, legal definition would see a "crime" as an act or omission by which a person violates the criminal law, thereby being subject to punishment by the state. Criminologists have raised theoretical problems with this description,[14] but most people would probably agree that such a definition, crude though it is, captures at least part of what we mean when we talk about "crime." If we accept this, it is meaningful to talk about "crime" in the Roman context, since some acts potentially made wrongdoers liable to be sentenced to fines payable to the state or to other kinds of punishments administered by it. Furthermore, at least during some periods of Roman history, the courts that pronounced sentences did not use the same procedures as courts dealing with private law litigation, just as modern criminal and civil courts are often distinguished by procedure.[15] This is not to say that the Romans always had an overarching theory of crime[16] or that there was a Latin term that correlates precisely with the English word *crime*. But some actions were treated by the Romans in such a way that one can meaningfully call them "crimes."

Upon closer inspection, however, matters become more complicated. For one thing, the Romans obviously never criminalized exactly the same combination of actions that our society does. Furthermore, the range of actions that Roman law criminalized broadened with time. The archaic law code of the fifth century BCE, the **Twelve Tables**, prescribed penalties for a number of wrongs. These included assaults, thefts, malicious magic, some forms of criminal damage, and certain treasonous actions.[17] From the mid-second century through to the end of the first century BCE, there was a flurry of new criminal statutes. These created additional crimes or gave more precise definition to existing ones. The consulships and dictatorships of Sulla and Caesar and the **Principate** of Augustus were especially important for this process (for Sulla, see Box 11.2).

Of particular concern during this era were crimes of a political nature and crimes involving members of the **senatorial** elite. So, for example, extortion by Roman administrators in the provinces, electoral bribery, political violence, and new forms of treason all came to be criminalized in this period.[18] The criminal statutes of the late Republic and the reign of Augustus by no means marked the end of the expansion of the criminal law, since decisions and enactments of subsequent emperors, senatorial decrees, and interpretations offered by legal experts widened its scope still further. As a result, historians have to be careful to differentiate the many stages of the development of the criminal law:

Political History

Box 11.2: Lucius Cornelius Sulla and the Criminal Law

Having been victorious in a civil war against Marius and his supporters, Sulla was **dictator** in 82–81 BCE and **consul** in 80 BCE. Amongst his reforms were measures concerned with criminal courts, which were of crucial importance to the development of the permanent jury courts in Rome (the *quaestiones perpetuae*). Although there had been several such courts previously, Sulla reorganized them and added to their number, thus increasing the scope of the criminal law. These "Cornelian Laws" (*leges Corneliae*) included statutes on treason (*de maiestate*), murder (*de sicariis et veneficis*), and counterfeiting and forgery (*de falsis*). They also possibly included statutes on electoral bribery (*de ambitu*), embezzlement of public money (*de peculatu*), and extortion by Roman officials in provinces (*de repetundis*). Furthermore, there was a Cornelian law concerning outrages (*de iniuriis*), although it is unclear whether it transformed the delict of *iniuria* into a crime in the modern sense of the word. Several of Sulla's statutes came to form the basis of their particular branches of the criminal law for centuries to come.

The composition of juries had been a cause of political controversy for decades. As part of his reforms, Sulla gave the job of sitting on juries in the permanent jury courts back to senators. Not long after his death, however, senators once again lost their monopoly on the juries.

just because something was a crime at one stage of Roman history does not mean that it was at an earlier point.

Further confusion is caused by the fact that Roman law had a second category of wrongs against persons and property known as delicts (*delicta*). In many respects, these wrongs were not "crimes" in our sense of the term. Only the victim or his or her family could bring a suit in the wake of a delict. If the suit was successful, the defendant had to pay damages to the plaintiff, not to the state. These damages, however, were not purely compensatory but, depending on the delict, would be a sum representing twice, three times, or four times the cost of the damage. They therefore had a clear penal element, much like a fine imposed by a criminal court. Furthermore, many of the things that we would regard as everyday crimes were mainly dealt with as delicts, especially during the earlier parts of Roman history. So, *iniuria*, which encompassed assault and battery as well as other forms of insulting treatment, was purely a delict until at least the 80s BCE and perhaps later.[19] This meant that the law of delict was the main method of dealing with petty assaults for much of the Republic.[20] Theft was also primarily a delict during the Republic and early Principate, unless the thief was caught red-handed. It was only later that it was treated by lawyers as fully criminal.[21] The tension between the civil and criminal character of delict was evident to the Romans, just as it is for us. When they discussed such wrongs, laymen (and occasionally lawyers) employed words typically used for full-fledged crimes.[22]

Courts, Justice, and Terror

As Roman history progressed, changes in the courts available for prosecuting crimes were made.[23] In the early days of the Republic, criminal offences were tried before popular assemblies, although magistrates possibly also heard some cases alone or with a panel of advisors.[24] In the second century BCE, special judicial inquiries (*quaestiones*) were set up by the **senate** or the people on occasion to try particular outbreaks of criminality. For instance, the senate established a special *quaestio* in 186 BCE to punish various offences allegedly committed by adherents of the cult of Bacchus, offences that included forgery, perjury, rape, and murder (Livy 39.8–19). In the mid-second century BCE permanent jury courts began to be instituted. These were called *quaestiones perpetuae* ("permanent jury courts") and sometimes also *publica iudicia* ("public courts"). There were multiple permanent jury courts, each with competence over a particular type of offence or group of offences.[25] The statutes that established these courts were in fact the same that gave increased definition and breadth to the range of criminal offences (see the previous section).

→ Compare Chapter 9, pp. 194 and 210–11, on actions taken against religious cults.

The Principate of Augustus was a time of further change when it came to the criminal courts. The permanent jury courts continued to exist for a period during the Principate, although the precise date of their disappearance is debated. But the senate came to hear criminal cases as well. As far as we can tell, these were mostly cases involving high-status people accused of political offences. At the same time, the emperor and various magistrates began judging criminal matters according to a procedure known as *cognitio* (literally, "inquiry").[26] In doing so, they were often guided by the definitions of crimes contained in the statutes that set up the permanent jury courts, but they also had some discretion in deciding what counted as crime and what the penalty should be. It was sometimes the practice for the emperor or magistrate exercising *cognitio* to have a panel of advisors to help with the task. Ultimately, however, one man made the decision. Under the Republic, governors of Roman provinces had judged criminal cases themselves using a similar procedure. During the Principate, provincial governors exercised *cognitio*, hearing cases in the capitals of their provinces or in regional towns during their annual tours of inspection (*conventus*). It is also important to realize that not every criminal case that arose in a province was heard before the governor: some local communities had the right to try cases before their own courts.[27]

If we view them as arenas for crime victims to obtain justice and defendants to be judged with fairness, Roman criminal courts clearly had many shortcomings. During the Republic, the courts were sometimes used as venues for political battles and personal vendettas between aristocratic politicians. Bribery, on occasion, swayed juries. Since it was possible in many situations for any male citizen to prosecute a crime, and because success could bring financial and political rewards, some prosecutors acted out of a desire for personal gain. The sources relating to the Principate in particular stress the abuses perpetrated by these so-called *delatores*.[28]

Even when criminal courts were not being abused by people with ulterior motives, the quality of justice delivered was variable. In the Roman world, as in our own, access to legal advocacy no doubt improved one's chances in court. But the right social connections or adequate financial resources were needed to obtain the services of an advocate.[29] There are also signs that, during their tours of inspection, some provincial governors were swamped with cases and lacked the manpower to resolve them swiftly. Justice would have, therefore, been slow in coming—if it came at all.[30] Then there was the fact that the jurymen of the standing courts in Rome and the officials who exercised *cognitio* were not necessarily legal experts and did not always have the benefit of expert legal advice. Thanks to ignorance, favouritism, or malice, proper procedure was sometimes ignored, and verdicts did not always adhere to the strict letter of the law.[31] We are told, for example, that the future emperor Galba, when serving as governor in Spain, sentenced a Roman citizen to crucifixion and responded to the man's attempts to invoke his legal rights by crucifying him regardless, but snidely gave him the distinction of an elevated cross decorated with white paint (Suet. *Galb.* 9). Additionally, as a general proposition, it might well have been the case that people of higher social **status** were treated more favourably by the courts.[32] More specifically, during the Principate an officially sanctioned practice developed whereby upper-class people (*honestiores*) received more lenient punishments than their social inferiors.[33]

Although the quality of justice delivered by criminal courts was probably quite variable, they did fulfill other functions. Historians of several pre-industrial societies have remarked on the importance that spectacular, erratically applied punishments—especially executions—had in asserting the power of the state and keeping order in the absence of a professional police force. The same can be said of the Roman world, where criminal justice could certainly be a bloody and spectacular experience. Even during an actual trial, there could be blood. Slaves who were called as witnesses were routinely tortured in an attempt to verify their testimony; torture was also occasionally applied to free people. Torture also had other roles in Roman courts: in accounts of Christian martyrdoms, one finds depictions of judges torturing Christians in an apparent attempt to terrorize them and their brethren into recanting their faith.[34]

The punishments that awaited those who were found guilty would often have reinforced the terror and majesty of the law. During the republican period, many convicted criminals escaped lightly, with exile being the usual result of a guilty verdict. Even then, however, there were some examples of extreme punishments. The punishment for parricide used at some points during the Republic was for the criminal to be sewn up in

➜ Compare Chapter 12, pp. 274–5,
on the punishment of criminals
as a spectacle.

a sack and drowned in a body of water.[35] Under the Principate, there was an escalation in the number and frequency of brutal executions. The most infamous of these is crucifixion; also notorious is the punishment of being thrown to wild beasts.

During the republican period, it was mostly slaves and foreigners who suffered these gruesome punishments, but under the Principate they came to be inflicted on citizens as well.[36] It is important to note that executions tended to be public and that the Roman authorities were quite conscious of their potential to deter crime. In a speech delivered in 80 BCE, Cicero claims that drowning people convicted of parricide in a sack was meant to have a deterrent effect (see Box 11.3). Several centuries later, the legal author Callistratus (*Dig.* 48.19.28.15) wrote that "most authorities have preferred to affix notorious brigands to gallows where they used to prowl about for victims, so that others might be deterred from the same crimes by the spectacle." Consequently, when studying the social impact of criminal courts, it may well be more important to think about their capacity to provoke terror than their tendency to deliver justice.

Roman "Policing Officials"

In most modern countries, the criminal courts would not be able to operate without the assistance of a police force. The police track down criminals, arrest them, and assist in

Primary Source

Box 11.3: Cicero, *In Defence of Sextus Roscius of Ameria*, 70–1.

Our ancestors . . . invented a remarkable punishment for people who committed parricide, so that those whom Nature herself could not keep true to their duty might be deterred from crime by the gravity of the punishment. They determined that they should be sewn up alive in a sack and thrown into a river. O remarkable wisdom, judges! Can they not be seen to have removed and torn this person out of nature? From this person they suddenly took away the sky, the sun, water, and earth, so that someone who had slain the person to whom he owed his birth might lack all those things from which everything is said to have been born. They did not want to toss the body to wild animals in case we should find even the beasts who had touched such wickedness more savage. Our ancestors did not want to throw such people naked into a river without further ado, in case, when they had been carried down into the sea, they should pollute the sea itself—the sea, by which other things that have been defiled are thought to be purified. In short, there is nothing so contemptible or common that our ancestors left them any portion of it.

their prosecution and punishment. Police also deter crime and coerce criminals in more direct ways, without the involvement of the courts. But not all historical societies had "police" in the modern sense of the word. In fact, professional, specialized police forces were very rare prior to the nineteenth century, although in some past societies there were state officials who had at least some of the functions that we now associate with "police." What can be said of ancient Rome?

To coin a phrase, Rome can be said to have had some "policing officials," even if it did not really have "police" in the modern sense.[37] In the city of Rome during the Republic and early Principate, the responsibilities of **aediles** included the supervision of markets and baths, the repression of dicing, the exercise of coercive powers (including the exaction of fines), and the prosecution of crimes before popular assemblies.[38] At the same time, aediles had other functions not carried out by modern police, such as putting on public games and ensuring the good repair of roads and public buildings.[39]

Compare Chapter 10, pp. 228–9, ←
and Chapter 12, pp. 266 and
279–80, on duties of the aedile.

Furthermore, in the city of Rome during the same period, there was a board of three minor magistrates known as the *tresviri capitales*. Their functions included the supervision of the city's prison and the executions carried out there, and overseeing the rounding up of thieves and escaped slaves during nightly patrols.[40] They apparently also sometimes held hearings in criminal cases, and it has been suggested that the *tresviri capitales* exercised summary criminal jurisdiction over citizens of low status and slaves. It may sound plausible that, during the Republic, the popular assemblies and the *quaestiones* did not have the time or inclination to try low-status people accused of crimes and that such people must have been dealt with in some other way. There is, however, little clear evidence of the *tresviri capitales* (or anyone else) routinely exercising criminal jurisdiction over low-status citizens and slaves; indeed, the hearings they held may have been only preliminary.[41] Whatever the true extent of their role in maintaining law and order, these magistrates clearly had duties not directly related to this rule, such as organizing fire prevention.[42] Nor were aediles or *tresviri capitales* professional, career policemen: each office lasted for only one year and was unpaid.

The transition from Republic to Empire brought with it a significant increase in the manpower available for policing Rome.[43] In 6 CE, the emperor Augustus created a paramilitary body of approximately 3,500 men called the **vigiles**, partly to help protect the city against fires. The prefect in charge of these men developed the jurisdiction to punish some kinds of crimes, and the ranks of the *vigiles* included officials in charge of the incarceration of suspects.[44] These facts suggest that the *vigiles* fought crime as well as fires, no doubt apprehending thieves, escaped slaves, and arsonists during their nightly patrols. Under Augustus, two military forces came to be stationed in and around Rome: the urban cohorts and the **praetorian guard**. The urban cohorts had an initial complement of approximately 1,500 men, which rose perhaps as high as about 4,000 by the late second century CE; the praetorians in Rome initially numbered approximately 1,500 as well and might have been as many as 10,000 by the late second century CE.[45] The prefects in charge of the urban cohorts and the praetorian guard also developed jurisdiction over various crimes,[46] which again suggests that these forces had a role in policing petty criminality.

Compare Chapter 13 , pp. 292–4, on the praetorian guard.

There is explicit evidence that these military forces were stationed at public spectacles to prevent disturbances. They also are found repressing riots and assisting with the persecution of Christians.[47]

Unlike their republican counterparts, the new policing officials of the Principate were professional in the sense that they were career soldiers or *vigiles*. They were not necessarily specialist policemen, though, since they had other tasks. Firefighting would have made considerable demands on the resources of the *vigiles*, especially on occasions when large fires were raging.[48] For its part, the praetorian guard had the challenging task of ensuring the security of the imperial family and had some tax collection functions. At times, detachments from the praetorian guard and urban cohorts were deployed outside the city of Rome.[49]

Compare Chapter 15, pp. 341–5, on tax collection.

The effectiveness of the *vigiles*, urban cohorts, and praetorian guard as policing bodies would have been partly dependent on the trust and co-operation of the civilian population. There are some signs of a distant and difficult relationship between the people of Rome and the military and paramilitary forces in the city.[50] When it came to riots, the ancient sources assume that the urban and praetorian cohorts were no silver bullet, since attempts to stop riots are often depicted as resulting in bloody battles between soldiers and civilians, as well as extensive damage to Rome's physical fabric.[51] Augustus's new military and paramilitary forces were, therefore, by no means a cure-all for public order problems in the city of Rome.

Outside of the city of Rome, "policing officials" fell into two categories. First, soldiers were sometimes deployed to carry out policing duties, at least in certain parts of the empire during some periods.[52] Second, local communities would often appoint "policing officials," with little or no involvement by the imperial authorities.

Several of the empire's larger cities had military forces permanently stationed in or around them. Such forces were sometimes used to put down riots.[53] The emperors Augustus and Tiberius also initiated the practice of posting soldiers along the roads of Italy to repress brigandage, and soldiers were used later in a similar way in other parts of the empire.[54] The soldiers performing this task were sometimes referred to as *stationarii* ("post-holders"), but soldiers with a variety of other titles performed essentially the same duties. The epigraphic record suggests that many of these soldiers assigned to posts were guarding roads that had a strategic importance for the Roman government or

Compare Chapter 13, pp. 300–01, on soldiers performing policing duties in the provinces.

were securing publicly owned, revenue-generating enterprises, such as mines, quarries, and estates.[55] We also learn from inscribed potsherds (ostraca) that in southern Egypt civilians served stints in watchtowers located on key routes, overseen by soldiers.[56] One of the main dangers to such strategic routes and imperial assets was, of course, brigandage. A pronouncement of 176–180 CE by the emperors Marcus Aurelius and Commodus also required *stationarii* to help owners of runaway slaves in hunting them down.[57] This task was probably linked to brigandage as well, since this would have been one of the few career options open to an escaped slave. If *stationarii* and other soldiers posted in small contingents could not handle an especially grave outbreak of brigandage, larger military units were sometimes dispatched to deal with the problem, as Septimius Severus eventually did to capture Bulla.[58]

Some modern historians have suggested that the Roman authorities assigned policing duties to soldiers only to protect the interests of the central government.[59] They see the policing role of soldiers as deeply intertwined with the army's more general goal of ensuring Rome's continued political control of the provinces. This view is made plausible by the fact that soldiers were deployed in places that were strategically important or productive of revenue for the imperial authorities. It is also supported by the sources' emphasis on the role of soldiers in repressing brigandage, which was often thought to be linked to slave revolts and uprisings against Roman rule (some of the leaders of such movements were said to have been brigands, and their guerilla tactics were considered to be similar to the activities of brigands).[60] Also relevant is the fact that *stationarii* and other soldiers were used in the third and fourth centuries CE to track Christians down and bring them to trial:[61] at this stage, the imperial authorities deemed the repression of Christianity a priority.

With all of this said, there are also signs that, whatever the intentions of their superiors, soldiers posted on policing duties found themselves dealing with petty wrongs against persons and property that did not threaten the interests of the central government. Among the Egyptian papyri are dozens of petitions addressed to soldiers complaining of petty assaults, thefts, damage to property, and the like.[62] Furthermore, a second-century CE wooden tablet from **Vindolanda** in Britain contains a petition mentioning previous complaints made to soldiers regarding an assault (see Box 11.4). It is not entirely clear just what soldiers would, in fact, do upon receiving these petitions, but the very persistence of the practice makes it evident that they must have sometimes taken steps to help victims of petty crime.[63]

As for policing officials appointed by local communities, the most detailed evidence is from Asia Minor and Egypt. The inscriptional evidence from Asia Minor makes it clear that there was a wide range of local "policing officials" in this region and that these officials bore a rich variety of different titles.[64] Some of these were full-fledged magistrates, holding office in a city or a league of cities. Others were apparently recruited to deal with particular public order issues as the need arose.

The evidence regarding the precise responsibilities and activities of these officials is thin, and we must sometimes deduce functions from the name of an official. Occasionally,

Primary Source

Box 11.4: *T. Vindol.* 2.344, lines 4–19.

I beseech Your Majesty not to permit me, a blameless man, to have been thrashed with rods and, my lord, [in so far as] I could not make a complaint to the prefect because he was detained by illness I made a complaint to the *beneficiarius* [and . . .] to the centurions [. . .] of his unit, [accordingly] I beseech Your Mercifulness not to permit me, a blameless man from overseas, about whose good faith you may make inquiries, to have been bloodied with rods as if I had perpetrated some crime.

however, we do get specific information about the activities of policing officials in particular places. In one inscribed decree, local policing officials (in this case called *paraphylakes*) are given the task of punishing with whippings or fines people who pasture animals illegally in vineyards (*MAMA* 4.297). (For a depiction of a *paraphylax* and his assistants at work, see Figure 11.1.) From another inscription, we learn that *mastigophores* ("whip-bearers") were recruited in one city to keep order in the **theatre** during a particular festival (*SEG* 38.1462.63–5). There is also evidence of eirenarchs ("chiefs of peace") and their assistants hunting down brigands and Christians, interrogating them, and producing them before the governor for judgment.[65] We also happen to know of cases from Asia Minor and elsewhere in which private citizens of towns were involved in hunting down bandits.[66] Presumably local magistrates such as eirenarchs had called upon the assistance of the public to cope with an especially bad outbreak of banditry.

In Egypt, documents preserved on papyrus show the existence of a variety of policing officials, again with quite diverse titles. Different communities had different combinations of officers.[67] In the *poleis* (Greek-style cities), policing officials were sometimes local magistrates; in villages and regional capitals, they tended to be local men of substance drafted into the job as a compulsory public service. The papyri contain several concrete examples of these Egyptian officials at work. So, for example, we find them being deployed in a preventative capacity, watching public places, roads, and buildings.[68] We find them physically intervening to prevent crimes that are still in progress. In the immediate aftermath of crimes, we find them assisting victims to discover the identity of perpetrators (see Box 11.1,

Figure 11.1 A relief depicting a *paraphylax* and his assistants discovered in the Cayster Valley, near Ephesus (first or second century CE).

an example from the first century CE), bearing witness to the details of the crime, or arresting perpetrators caught red-handed.[69] In other cases, once victims had launched prosecutions, the presiding magistrate would order a policing official to ensure that the defendant appeared before the court.[70]

Various Egyptian papyri also show people making allegations of brutality and corruption against civilian policing officials.[71] Furthermore, complaints were made about corrupt behaviour by eirenarchs and *paraphylakes* in Asia Minor.[72] A number of allegations of brutality by soldiers with policing duties have also been pre-

served.[73] The difficulty is, however, that we do not even know if the particular complaints were true, let alone whether their contents are a good indication of the behaviour of policing offi-

Compare Chapter 13, p. 301, on provincials' complaints about soldiers.

cials in general. But one thing that we can say for certain is that the "policing officials" appointed by local communities in Asia Minor and Egypt were not professional policemen.[74] They were either holding a magistracy or performing compulsory public service for a short period (usually a year), or they were individuals recruited to deal with a particular public order problem. This lack of professionalization would have prevented "policing officials" from benefitting from the years of crime-fighting experience that modern police have at their disposal. Moreover, the ability of local "policing officials" to deal with crime would have varied according to place. These people were usually part of the administration of a city or village, so people living in remote rural areas would have been less protected. The posting of soldiers on policing duties would have compensated for the absence of civilian policing in some locales. But such soldiers were not spread evenly throughout the empire, and even if communities felt that they needed such a military presence, the imperial authorities could be reluctant to grant their wishes (see, for example, Plin. *Ep.* 10.77–8).

Self-Help

The Roman judicial and policing systems had many imperfections, just like the vast majority of similar systems in more recent times. This raises the problem of how people during the Republic and Principate reacted to the fact that the state was less than successful in preventing crime and deviance. Part of the answer is that people took whatever steps they could to enhance their own security and ensure that they did not become crime victims in the first place.

The architecture of houses was one obvious way to avoid being the victim of a crime. The remains of houses in Italian towns such as Ostia, **Pompeii**, and **Herculaneum** suggest that the houses of the wealthy would often have had high walls and few (if any) windows at street level. It has plausibly been suggested that these design features were intended to enhance security.[75] Doors of high-status houses were solidly constructed and sometimes flanked with porters' lodges; when open, they would have been guarded

→ Compare Chapter 5, pp. 109–12, on Roman house design.
by slaves.[76] Lower-class people living in the more ramshackle apartment blocks of large cities would perhaps have been less able to control who entered their buildings. We do hear, however, that during a spate of violent burglaries in the first century CE—or at least a panic about violent burglaries— apartment dwellers took to boarding up their windows to keep themselves safe (Plin. HN 19.59). Outside of the house, people who could afford it sometimes went about the streets of the city of Rome with entourages of slaves.[77] Among other things, this practice would have enhanced personal security. We also read about upper-class people being transported around Rome in sedan chairs carried by burly slaves who would have surely improved the safety of the occupant.[78]

In rural areas, people also had to take steps to ensure the security of themselves and their property. There is evidence from several parts of the empire of private security guards being employed to guard large estates.[79] On rural roads, travellers faced the danger of brigands and so took whatever precautions they could. Just as in the city, wealthy people often travelled with entourages of slaves and dependants along the highways of Italy and the empire, sometimes carried in sedan chairs,[80] although this was not always enough to guarantee security. From Pliny the Younger (*Ep.* 6.25) we learn about an **equestrian** and an army officer, both of whom (along with their escorts of slaves) disappeared separately while travelling on the roads of Italy; Pliny assumes that both men fell victim to brigands or perhaps to their own slaves. For those without slaves to escort them, steps could still be taken to reduce the risks. One source makes reference to the fact that the cautious traveller will delay his journey until he can attach himself to a Roman official travelling with a retinue, although even this practice was not a surefire guarantee of safety (Arr. *Epict. diss.* 4.1.91–4).

Of course, as much as people tried to avoid becoming victims of crime, crime nevertheless still happened. Some people were in the fortunate position of being able to fight back against their attacker, and Roman law gave certain rights in relation to self-defence. The Twelve Tables gave householders the right to kill thieves apprehended in their houses. Nocturnal thieves could be killed with impunity, and daytime thieves could be killed if they were armed and if the householder called on his neighbours as witnesses, presumably to prevent this right from being misused.[81] These rights to self-defence extended outside the home: the legal writer Gaius ruled that a person shall be immune from legal repercussions if he kills a slave who has become a brigand and is lying in ambush for him, "for natural reason permits someone to defend himself from peril."[82]

In cases when victims were not able to fight off an attack themselves, other members of the community would sometimes step in to protect them. At least in the early history of the city of Rome, when people were in the very process of being victimized, they would call upon the assistance of passersby; there were even apparently set Latin phrases that Romans would use in such situations.[83] For example, the comic playwright Plautus (who was writing around 205–184 BCE) imagines a scene in which two freeborn women, who have been captured by pirates and sold as prostitutes in North Africa, seek refuge in a temple. Their pimp tries to drag them out, but a friendly slave calls on the aid of people of Cyrene, prompting some passersby to come to the rescue. The scene is not evidence for what happened in Cyrene, which was not under Roman control in the second century BCE, but it probably does reflect a practice with which Plautus was familiar in Rome.[84]

If the community was not able to step in to prevent a crime, it might still band together to punish the criminal, or the victim could invoke communal censure to obtain redress. This could be done without any involvement of state magistrates or other officials. For example, there is evidence that, in the earliest days of the city of Rome, victims of wrongs would engage in *flagitatio* (shouting to demand the return of misappropriated property, often in front of the house of the wrongdoer or some other public place). The poet Catullus, in the mid-first-century BCE, wittily refers to this practice when he anthropomorphizes poems in hendecasyllabic metre and asks them to demand the return of some stolen writing tablets (see Box 11.5). The idea behind *flagitatio* was that the wrongdoer would be shamed into providing redress. There was a similar motivation behind the practice of *squalor*, whereby the victim would appear in public in a dishevelled state and follow the wrongdoer around to stir up communal disapproval.[85]

From the first century BCE onwards, the sources provide concrete cases of crowds in Rome displaying their outrage at individuals' behaviour with chants and violence. Some of these incidents look rather like lynchings attested for more recent societies. The philosopher Seneca, for instance, discusses the case of a member of the equestrian order

Primary Source

Box 11.5: Catullus, *Poem* 42.

Calling all Hendecasyllables, as many as you are, from everywhere, however many you are! A filthy adulteress thinks I'm a joke and says she won't give me back our writing tablets, if you can stand for that! Follow her and demand them back. Who is she, you ask? She's the one whom you see strutting foully, laughing in a stagy and annoying way with a Gallic puppy's mouth. Surround her and demand them back; "Rotten adulteress, give back the tablets; return, o rotten adulteress, the tablets!" She doesn't give a stuff? O filth, o bordello, or whatever is more depraved than that! But we can't think this is enough, for if we can do nothing else, we can extract a blush from the bitch's hard face. Shout again with louder voice: "Rotten adulteress, give back the tablets; return, o rotten adulteress, the tablets!" But we're going nowhere, she's unmoved. You need to change your strategy and method, if you are to get any further: "O chaste and virtuous one, return the notebooks!"

who flogged his own son to death, perhaps invoking the Roman father's controversial right to execute his own children. A crowd of people waylaid the man in the **Forum** and attempted to stab him to death with styluses, but he was res-

Compare Chapter 5, pp. 99–100 and 104, on the legal powers invested in the *paterfamilias*.

cued thanks to a timely intervention by the emperor Augustus (Sen. *Clem.* 1.15.1). These kinds of crowd response have been interpreted as evidence of how the community "policed" itself, although most of these crowds were reacting to actions that were politically or socially controversial and not to straightforward, day-to-day thefts, assaults, or murders.[86] Elsewhere in the Roman empire, one also finds crowds taking the law into their own hands and attacking deviants. The stonings described in Christian texts are perhaps evidence of a kind of lynch justice in the Roman province of Judea. We also read that, in 177 CE, a persecution of the Christian community of Lugdunum (modern Lyons) began when pagan mobs took the initiative and began assaulting Christians.[87]

Summary

Although the state of the evidence makes it very difficult to study crime as a social phenomenon, our sources do reveal how lawyers and others thought about serious harm to person and property. As time progressed, an increasing number of acts considered to be harmful to the community were punished by criminal courts. At the same time, some acts were treated as delicts, which gave rise to punitive damages but were not always subject to the same process as full crimes and could only be prosecuted by the victim or his or her family. Over time, there were changes in the particular courts before which crimes were prosecuted; very often political developments were linked to this. Roman criminal courts had many shortcomings as far as delivering justice was concerned: they were sometimes abused by unscrupulous litigants; judges and juries could be inexpert, malicious, or corrupt; and people of higher status probably fared better. The courts did, however, have another function: their ability to invoke terror, no doubt, helped to keep order.

Aside from providing courts, the Roman authorities and the authorities of local communities around the empire also appointed officials to carry out policing duties of various kinds. The repression of banditry and riots were important functions for such officials, but some of them found themselves dealing with minor crimes as well. It would be wrong, however, to think of these officials as the same as the professionalized, specialized police we encounter in modern societies. There is also some evidence that suggests a distant, hostile, or even abusive relationship sometimes existed between such officials and the people whom they policed. Because of the shortcomings of the state in ensuring order, individuals often took private measures to try to protect themselves and their families against crime. On occasion, communities would also spontaneously punish individuals felt to be guilty of certain kinds of deviance.

Questions for Review and Discussion

1. In Roman culture, was there a concept of crime similar to our concept of crime?
2. What difficulties does the historian experience in studying crime as a social phenomenon in the Roman world?
3. To what extent did the criminal courts of ancient Rome provide justice and contribute to public order?
4. Were there police in the Roman world?
5. What kinds of self-help measures did individuals and communities take in response to crime?

Suggested Reading

Grünewald, T. 2004. *Bandits in the Roman Empire: Myth and Reality*. Translated by J. Drinkwater. London and New York: Routledge.

Grünewald discusses banditry in the Roman empire, with particular attention to the political, literary, and rhetorical agendas that shaped the representation of bandits in the sources.

Harries, J. 2007. *Law and Crime in the Roman World*. Cambridge: Cambridge University Press.

In this book, Harries analyzes Roman discourses concerning "crime" and discusses the social and political context of several different categories of crime.

Lintott, A.W. 1999. *Violence in Republican Rome*, 2nd edn. Oxford: Oxford University Press.

Lintott discusses political violence in the late Republic and the various attempts on the part of the state and its agents to control violence. He also examines traditions of popular justice.

Nippel, W. 1995. *Public Order in Ancient Rome*. Cambridge: Cambridge University Press.

This text examines the various ways in which order was kept during both the Republic and the Principate. The focus is mainly on the city of Rome, but there is some discussion of the situation in the provinces.

Robinson, O.F. 1995. *The Criminal Law of Ancient Rome*. Baltimore: Johns Hopkins University Press.

Robinson summarizes the evidence of the Roman legal sources regarding criminal law.

Notes

1   Many thanks to Andrew Lintott, Angela Hug, and the editors of the present volume for reading and commenting on drafts of this chapter. All translations are my own.

2   See, for example, Cic. *Q Fr.* 1.1.24–5 and Just. *Epit.* 44.5.8.

3   It should be noted, however, that Roman law had comparatively little influence on the development of the second great "Western" legal tradition, the English common law, which forms the basis of the legal systems of most anglophone nations.

4   Shaw (1984: 46–52); Grünewald (2004: 111–20).

5   See Kelly (2007) for ancient evidence and modern literature.

6   See Shaw (1984: 8–12) for the "ubiquity" of brigandage.

7   Shaw (1984: 23–4); Grünewald (2004).

8   For references, see Shaw (1984: 51 n. 131) and Grünewald (2004: 118–19).

9   See, for example, Juv. 3.268–314 and Tib. 1.2.25–30.

10   Egyptian petitions: see the references in Kelly (2011: 335–64). Non-Egyptian petitions on papyri: *P.Euphrates* 1–5. Occasionally a petition is preserved on an inscription (see Hauken [1998]) or a wooden tablet (see *T.Vindol.* 2.344).

11   For the date, see *BL* 7.111, 8.214.

12   Kelly (2011: 7–9, 38–74).

13   Curse tablets: Ménard (2000) for references. Tombstones: Shaw (1984: 10–12 n. 25) for references.

14   For instance, one could object that advocates of such a legalistic approach face the difficulty that it is not always self-evident which parts of the law can be called criminal. Moreover, some criminologists have argued that this approach is not helpful in understanding crime as a social phenomenon. For discussion and further literature, see Law Commission of Canada (2004).

15   Lintott (1999a: 147–9; forthcoming).

16   Note that Riggsby (1999: 151), mainly on the basis of a reading of Cicero's speeches, claims that, during the republican period, the "sources show little interest in any overarching phenomenon we could call crime."

17   Treasonous actions: *Dig.* 48.4.3. Assault: Twelve Tables 1.13–15. Theft: Twelve Tables 1.19. Magic: Twelve Tables 8.1, 8.4. Criminal damage: Twelve Tables 1.16, 8.5–6. All references to the Twelve Tables are to Crawford's (1996: 2.578–83) text.

18   Robinson (1995: 2–3); Lintott (1999a: 157–62); Harries (2007: 16–18).

19   Robinson (1995: 49–51); Harries (2007: 49–50).

20   Note, however, Twelve Tables 1.13–15, to be read with Gell. *NA* 20.1.13–14.

21   Robinson (1995: 23–5); Harries (2007: 50–8). For the situation in relation to thieves caught red-handed, see Twelve Tables 1.17–20 and cross-reference Gell. *NA* 11.18.7–9.

22   Harries (2007: 4–5, 50–8).

23   Here I exclude developments in the courts in which suits concerning delicts were heard; these followed a different historical trajectory.

24   Lintott (1999a: 149–57).

25   Ibid.: 157–62.

26   Senate: Robinson (1995: 7–9). *Cognitio*: Robinson (1995: 9–11); Harries (2007: 28–33).

27   Republican governors: Lintott (1993: 54–69). *Conventus*: Burton (1975). Local jurisdiction: Lintott (1993: 55–6, 62–3).

28   Rutledge (2001); compare *OGI* 2.669.40–1.

29   Bablitz (2007: 77, 141–50).

30   Burton (1975: 99–102); Kelly (2011: 75–122).

31   Bablitz (2007: 108–10); Harries (2007: 38–41).

32   Garnsey (1970: 206–18); Burton (1975: 101–02); Bablitz (2007: 77–9).

33   Garnsey (1970: 103–78).

34   Ibid.: 213–16; Potter (1996: 148–51); Harries (2007: 33–5); Kelly (2011: 178, 183–4).

35 *Auct. ad Her.* 1.23; Cic. *Rosc. Am.* 70–1; Liv. *Per.* 68.

36 Garnsey (1970: 126–31).

37 For the terminological issue, see Fuhrmann (2012: 5–12).

38 Markets: Plaut. *Rud.* 372–3. Baths: Sen. *De vita beata* 7.3; *Ep.* 86.10. Dicing: Mart. 5.84.3–5, 14.1.3. Coercive powers: Tac. *Ann.* 13.28; Varro ap. Gell. *NA* 13.13.4 (Varro quoted by Aulus Gellius); Lintott (1999b: 92–101). Prosecutions: Lintott (1999a: 131–3; 1999b: 96–9).

39 Lintott (1999a: 129–31).

40 Prison and executions: *Dig.* 1.2.2.30. Rounding up of slaves: Lintott (1999b: 102).

41 The argument that the *tresviri capitales* exercised such jurisdiction has been pressed most strongly by the German scholar Wolfgang Kunkel. For discussion and evaluation of his views, see Nippel (1995: 22–6) and Lintott (1999a: 142–3, 154–6; 1999b: 102–6).

42 *Dig.* 1.15.1; Val. Max. 8.1. *damn.* 5.

43 For military policing in Rome, see Fuhrmann (2012: 113–18, 124–30).

44 *Dig.* 1.15.3.1, 1.15.4; Sablayrolles (1996: 225–6, 232).

45 Coulston (2000: 76–81).

46 Praetorian prefect: Durry (1938: 172–4). Urban prefect: Lintott (forthcoming).

47 See Kelly (2013: 413) for references.

48 Nippel (1995: 96–7).

49 Security of imperial family: Coulston (2000: 86–8). Tax collection: Suet. *Calig.* 40. External deployment: Durry (1938: 274–80); Coulston (2000: 88).

50 For references and discussion, see Kelly (2013: 415-16); compare Coulston (2000: 89–91).

51 Kelly (2007: 167–71).

52 For a full discussion of the phenomenon, see Fuhrmann (2012: 124–6, 151–7, 201–38).

53 See, for example, Dio Chrys. 32.72; Joseph. *BJ* 2.490–8; compare *SHA Tyr. Trig.* 22.2.

54 Suet. *Aug.* 32; *Tib.* 37; Tert. *Apol.* 2.8. For analysis, see Fuhrmann (2012: 99–103).

55 Brélaz (2005: 258–67), with further literature.

56 Bagnall (1977).

57 *Dig.* 11.4.1.2; compare *CIL* 9.2438, with *AE* (1983), 331.

58 Nippel (1995: 102); Brélaz (2005: 291–6).

59 See, for example, Nippel (1995: 100).

60 See Grünewald (2004: 33–71) for references and analysis.

61 Brélaz (2005: 261–2) for references.

62 See examples on theft: *BGU* 1.157, *BL* 1.23; *BGU* 2.454. Violence: *P.Amh.* 2.78; *SB* 6.9238. Property damage: *Chrest.Mitt.* 111; *Stud.Pal.* 22.87.

63 See Kelly (2011: 83–5) for literature and discussion.

64 The following discussion of policing in Asia Minor is indebted to the comprehensive treatment by Brélaz (2005: 69–230). See also Fuhrmann (2012: 66–75).

65 Christians: *Martyrdom of Polycarp* 6–8; *Martyrdom of Conon* 2. Brigands. *Dig.* 48.3.6.1; Xenophon of Ephesus 2.13, 3.9.

66 *AE* (1979), 624, with Brélaz (2005: 300–03) (Bubon, Lycia; 190 CE) and App. *B Civ.* 4.28 (Minturnae, Italy; 43 BCE).

67 Much of the following rests on Homoth-Kuhs (2005), which provides the fundamental collection of evidence regarding the various kinds of *phylakes*. See also Fuhrmann (2012: 75–82).

68 *P.Brem.* 23; *P.Petaus* 48; *SB* 20.14975; compare Bagnall (1977: 75–6).

69 Crimes in progress: *P.Fay.* 108; *SB* 14.12199 (partly reconstructed). Investigations: *P.Athen.* 38; *P.Mich.* 6.421; *P.Ryl.* 2.139; *SB* 3.6952, 4.7469, 16.12951, 20.15032; with *BL* 11.234. Witnessing: *P.Mich.* 9.525; *SB* 20.14975. Arrests. *BGU* 13.2240; *P.Gen.* 2.107

70 See, for example, *P.Ryl.* 2.136, 2.145, 2.150, 2.151 and *SB* 12.11107, 24.16005.

71 *P.Mich.* 6.421; *SB* 5.7523.

72 *Dig.* 48.3.6 pr.–1; *OGI* 2.527.

73 Hauken (1998: docs. 1.1.3, 1.1.4, 1.2.8); compare *SB* 6.9207; with *BL* 6.152.

74 With the possible exception of *phylakitai* in

Egypt, who were disbanded very early in the Roman period. See Bagnall (1977: 68) and Homoth-Kuhs (2005: 9–12).

75 Ellis (2000: 75); Hales (2003: 105–06).

76 Porters' lodges: Ellis (2000: 75). Doors: Tib. 1.2.5–14. Doormen: Mart. 5.22; Sen. *Constant.* 14.1–2.

77 Cic. *Mil.* 10; Gell. *NA* 2.13.4; Juv. 3.282–5; Prop. 2.29a.

78 *CIL* 6.6308; Cass. Dio 57.15, 60.2; Juv. 4.21; Plin. *Ep.* 3.5.15; Suet. *Aug.* 82; *Tit.* 10; for the later Empire, compare Amm. Marc. 14.6.16–17 (fourth century CE).

79 Brélaz (2005: 165–70, 227–8); Homoth-Kuhs (2005: 195–200).

80 Cic. *Phil.* 2.106; Suet. *Claud.* 25; Tac. *Ann.* 14.4.

81 Twelve Tables 1.17–18.

82 *Dig.* 9.2.4 pr.; compare Cic. *Mil.* 10–11.

83 Lintott (1999b: 11–16).

84 Plaut. *Rud.* 615–26, with Lintott (1999b: 13–14).

85 *Flagitatio*: Lintott (1999b: 6–10). Squalor: Lintott (1999b: 16–20).

86 Kelly (2013: 418–21).

87 Stonings: John 8.1–11; Acts 7.57–60. Lyons: Euseb. *Hist. eccl.* 5.1.7, compare 5 pr.1.

12

Entertainment in the Roman World

Michael Carter

The ancient Roman predilection for "bread and circuses" is well known. The phrase comes to us from Juvenal (10.78–81), a second-century CE satirist who famously complained that the Roman people had conferred consulships and military commands in their political assemblies during the Republic but, under the emperors, desired only *panem et circenses*. This statement conjures an unflattering picture and would seem to confirm our worst impressions of the ancient Romans by suggesting that they declined from the idealized purity of the Republic to the lazy decadence of the imperial period. Common current opinion holds that the Romans always preferred bloodshed and death and had little time for the nobler (Greek) pursuits of the theatre or athletics; we think of dying gladiators, crashing chariots, and Christians being devoured by lions, all performed before a mob roaring its approval. For a modern audience, even the concept of spectacle is pejorative, never mind attending a bloodbath. Where theatre requires an engaged and thoughtful audience and athletics promote wider participation and the pursuit of excellence, spectacle suggests the simple amusement of passive onlookers and implies a shallowness meant to thrill or titillate—to entertain—rather than a substantive undertaking meant to motivate a person to higher ideals.[1] If the Romans sank to such lows, the fall of the Empire could not be far off.

Yet we should weigh Juvenal's judgment against the great investment in resources—time, money, energy—made for such popular entertainment. Even today, the towering remains of Roman entertainment buildings stand as concrete testimony to the importance of what went on inside them: amusement, perhaps, but not simple pleasure. Far from being empty shows pandering to the lowest tastes of the mob, Roman entertainment spectacles offer scholars access to some of the fundamental priorities of the Roman people. To disregard these shows is to lose something of our understanding of Roman society as a whole.

Timeline

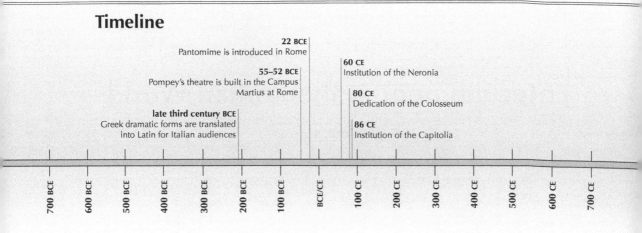

22 BCE
Pantomime is introduced in Rome

55–52 BCE
Pompey's theatre is built in the Campus
Martius at Rome

late third century BCE
Greek dramatic forms are translated
into Latin for Italian audiences

60 CE
Institution of the Neronia

80 CE
Dedication of the Colosseum

86 CE
Institution of the Capitolia

700 BCE — 600 BCE — 500 BCE — 400 BCE — 300 BCE — 200 BCE — 100 BCE — BCE/CE — 100 CE — 200 CE — 300 CE — 400 CE — 500 CE — 600 CE — 700 CE

Introduction

The ubiquity of information regarding Roman entertainment in the ancient sources is indicative of entertainment's importance in Roman society. In addition to literary sources, such as those already mentioned, we have epigraphy, which includes tombstones or honorific inscriptions and decrees, and material culture, ranging from buildings to mosaics and other graphic depictions. Juvenal's scorn for Roman *circenses* may seem strange: Why disparage popular entertainment if it was so important to his society? Other ancient authors do much the same thing. For example, the historian Cassius Dio (73.18.3) even apologized to his readers when he described at length the emperor Commodus's participation in the arena as a beast fighter and gladiator:

> Do not think that I am sullying the dignity of history when I write such things. Otherwise I would not have mentioned them. But since the spectacle was given by the emperor and I myself was present and saw, heard, and spoke all these things, I thought it proper to suppress nothing but rather to hand them over to the memory of those who shall come hereafter, as if they were something great and important.[2]

Clearly, Dio did not think such shows were worthy of historical discussion. Another historian, the Roman writer Tacitus (*Ann.* 13.31.1), explains this for us: history is about "brilliant accomplishments" (*res inlustres*) and specifically not about amphitheatres and gladiators. The sentiments of writers such as Juvenal, Dio, and Tacitus reflect their desire not to appear too interested in what was popular with the masses. Yet, if we were to take them at face value, we would find ourselves ignoring the vast majority of people who attended the shows by the thousands and cheered or jeered at what they saw. Whatever we may think of these shows, appreciating how and what a society celebrated and found entertaining is critical to understanding that society and its people. Mass public entertainments in Rome all had a religious character and a political aspect; they were the principal occasions during which the Roman community came together. What was common and popular with the masses, then, matters a great deal.

Moreover, Roman entertainment spectacles are linked to bigger themes in Roman society. For example, however bloody and often deadly gladiatorial combats might have been, they were governed by rules and standards of behaviour: martial victory was celebrated more than ostentatious homicide; spectacular executions were about the triumph of Roman justice over the enemies of Roman society; and chariot races and theatrical shows were directly tied to religious games (*ludi*) of the greatest antiquity and were thus sacred to the gods. The diffusion of traditionally Roman entertainment spectacles throughout the empire is also linked with the spread of Roman culture more generally as a sign of the cultural integration of provincial peoples into imperial society.

The Roman theatre also betrays bigger issues. Some of the earliest evidence for the impact of Greek culture in Rome ("Hellenization") is seen in the adoption of Greek theatrical genres and the production of Latin versions of original Greek plays. The same theme appears with the later adoption of Greek-style musical and athletic competitions (*certamines* in Latin and *agones* in Greek) and competitors in Rome. Entertainment spectacles, therefore, are found at the heart of some of the key issues in Rome's history.

————— • ◆ • —————

Public Entertainment

A diversity of mass public entertainment was available to the people of Rome, ranging from **chariot** races to musical and dramatic performances of various kinds, exhibitions of exotic wild beasts, staged combats, and executions. By the first century CE, a number of different purpose-built structures had been erected to accommodate these various forms of entertainment. These comprised some of the grandest buildings in the city: the **Circus Maximus** in the

Compare Chapter 17, pp. 391–2, ⬅ on Roman entertainment venues.

valley between the Palatine and Aventine hills could hold as many as 150,000 spectators and was considered the most beautiful building in the world (Plin. *HN* 36.102), and the iconic **Colosseum** (the Amphitheatrum Flavium) remains an architectural marvel to this day. Rome was also served by three large **theatres** and a stadium for athletic events. No other ancient city had such extensive amenities for the entertainment of its people.

Roman public entertainment falls into two broad categories: the **ludi** and the **munera**. Traditionally, *ludi* comprised public games in the circus or theatrical shows, ostensibly offered by the state as civic celebrations, while *munera* (*munus*, singular) were originally private productions, featuring gladiatorial contests especially. The Romans were undoubtedly able to watch smaller, localized forms of entertainment as well, such as jugglers, magicians, musicians, and poets, although evidence for this sort of street performance is limited. For that reason, this chapter shall focus, like Juvenal, on the larger forms of mass entertainment, which were meant to appeal to all Romans. It will also address the following question: What did Romans find entertaining and why?

Ludi

Games were a central feature of Roman religious festivities and were sponsored by the state. They were held annually in honour of different gods and could last for several days. Seven principal *ludi* marked the Roman calendar:

> *Ludi Megalenses* (in honour of Mater Magna): 4–9 April
> *Ludi Cereales* (in honour of Ceres): 12–18 April
> *Ludi Florales* (in honour of Flora): 27 April–3 May
> *Ludi Apollinares* (in honour of Apollo): 6–12 July
> *Ludi Romani* (in honour of Jupiter): 4–12 September
> *Ludi Victoriae* (in honour of Victory): 26–31 October
> *Ludi Plebeii* (in honour of Jupiter): 4–12 November

Other games could be held in thanksgiving for a military victory or in commemoration of a deceased emperor. Responsibility for the production of the *ludi* fell to various magistrates (the **aediles** in particular) and included both dramatic performances (**ludi scaenici**, from *scaena*, the Latin term for a stage-building) and chariot races (**ludi circenses**) in the Circus Maximus.

Throughout most of the Republic, there was no permanent theatre built to accommodate the *ludi scaenici* of the various festivals until Pompey the Great erected his massive theatre in 55–52 BCE. Pompey's theatre was followed by the Theatre of Marcellus and the Theatre of Balbus, both built during the reign of Augustus. All three stone theatres were located in the southern part of the **Campus Martius**, just outside the city proper but immediately accessible from it. Tacitus tells us that the **senate** had stopped earlier attempts to build a permanent building because it had feared the idle masses lingering in the theatres all day (see Box 12.1).

→ Compare Chapter 7, p. 148, and Chapter 9, p. 200, on the Theatre of Pompey.

Prior to the construction of these permanent theatres, all stage performances were held in wooden structures built specifically for the *ludi* and taken down after the celebrations. Especially in the later Republic, before Pompey's theatre was built, these temporary

Primary Source

Box 12.1: Tacitus, *Annals*, 14.20–21.

During the fourth consulship of Nero and that of Cornelius Cossus (60 CE), games to be held on a five-year cycle were established in Rome in the fashion of a Greek competition, with mixed reviews, as with nearly all innovations. There were those who said that Gnaeus Pompey had also been criticized by his elders because he had established a permanent theatre building. For before that time games were accustomed to be put on with provisional seating and a temporary stage and in even earlier times people stood to watch, lest (it was feared) if seated they would spend whole days in idleness. Old-style performances should be preserved when the praetor presided and with no expectation that citizens compete. Moreover (they added) ancestral morality which was being steadily eroded was now uttered overturned by imported degeneracy, with the result that whatever was corrupt or being corrupted was seen in the city, and the young people were becoming corrupt though foreign fashions: going to the gymnasium, wasting time, disgusting love affairs. The emperor and the senate were responsible, since they not only permitted these vices but even compelled Roman nobles to be defiled on stage on the pretext of delivering speeches or poetry. What else was there (they continued) but to put on boxing gloves and train in that sort of fighting in place of military training and weaponry? Perhaps justice would be advanced and the decuries of equestrians would better fulfill their important duties if they should hear falsetto notes and lovely voices. . . . Most were pleased with the licentiousness, yet they gave it a respectable name. Their ancestors had not turned away from pleasing spectacles, according to the resources that they then had. So actors had been brought from Etruria and horse racing from Thurii. And with the conquest of Greece and Asia more elaborate games had been put on, but no one of a respectable background had ever stooped to performing in the theatre, and this in the 200 years since the triumph of Lucius Memmius, the first man to have presented this sort of show in the city. There was also concern for financial prudence, since a permanent location for the theatre had been established, something much better than constructing and dismantling one at enormous cost every year. Nor indeed would magistrates deplete family fortunes or would there be cause for a Greek contest to be demanded by the people from their magistrates, since the state was paying the expenses.

theatres could be marvels of Roman engineering, constructed by ambitious politicians eager to win popular favour by their fantastic buildings (see Plin. *HN* 36.24). Since the *ludi scaenici* were intimately connected with the celebration of religious festivals, it is probable that the temporary staging and seating was constructed in some sacred space directly associated with the deity that was being celebrated. Even after the construction of permanent theatres, temporary

Compare Chapter 9, pp. 197–98, on *sacra publica*.

structures continued to be used for certain *ludi*, such as the **Ludi Saeculares** celebrated by Augustus in 17 BCE.

Although its origins are murky, the Roman **drama** staged in these theatres probably had its roots in the unscripted farces found in other Italian cities. We know these performances as **Atellanae fabulae**, named after the Campanian town of Atella. These farces used stock characters in comic situations improvised from everyday life. Attested character types include, for example, the Pappus (the old man), the Bucco (the fool), and the Dossennus (the glutton). It is likely that early *ludi scaenici* included such popular forms of entertainment. While Atellan farce survived into the late Republic and early imperial period, little is known about it and it is difficult to ascertain how it influenced later Roman drama.

The influence of Greek drama, however, is clear. Roman expansion throughout the Italian peninsula and the Mediterranean led to direct contact with the Greek city-states in southern Italy and Greece proper. In imitation of Greek drama, well developed by this time, scripted plays based on its genres (in particular **comedy** and **tragedy**) were introduced by the late third century BCE and a number of playwrights who wrote plays in Latin subsequently emerged.

Compare Chapter 7, pp. 144–53, on the influence of Greek literary genres on their Roman equivalents.

Related to these sorts of productions are two other Greek-inspired genres that became the most important form of theatrical performance in Rome: **mime** and **pantomime**. Mime artists are known to have performed during the Republic, perhaps initially as improvised street theatre. Like the Atellan farces, the topic of mime tended to be comic stock situations drawn from ordinary life (perhaps akin to modern-day soap operas, with themes such as adultery or the trickster), although these tended to be better prepared and rehearsed than the *Atellanae*. Mime artists included both men and women who were organized into troupes under the leadership of an *archimimus* ("mime leader"). Due to its popularity during the Republic, mime became one of the important forms of entertainment at the *Floralia*. Unfortunately, little evidence remains to allow a more complete reconstruction.

More is known about pantomime, a form of dance that primarily treated topics drawn from myth. This genre was introduced to Rome during the reign of Augustus, when two performers, Pylades from Cilicia and Bathyllus of Alexandria, were brought to the city to perform. Pantomime featured a solo dancer who, through postures and gestures, performed mythological scenes without voice (he wore a mask with the mouth closed) to the accompaniment of musical instruments and a chorus. Sometimes, these dances could be erotically charged. (We might think of modern ballet as an approximate parallel.) In public shows the performers danced in competition with one another, although they were also popular as solo entertainers in the houses of the aristocracy. In Latin, they were referred to as *histriones*, the same general word used for an actor, but the pantomimes styled themselves in Greek as "actors of tragic, rhythmic movements," a phrase that conveys both the dignity of tragedy and the gracefulness of the Greek

gymnasium. A measure of their "star power" is perhaps indicated by the fact that, in an inscription boasting about a series of games and spectacular entertainments given at **Pompeii** over the course of his career, the magistrate Aulus Clodius Flaccus lists only one performer by name: the pantomime Pylades (see Box 12.2).

As with much else, the Romans adopted foreign cultural institutions on their own terms. There was traditionally little interest in full-length, Greek-style dramatic competitions (*agones*); individual plays were performed instead. It was not until Nero introduced the *Neronia* in 60 CE that Rome had a festival with competitive dramatic performances (see Box 12.1). The festival, intended to be held every fifth year—much like the great games of the Greek world (Olympian, Nemean, Pythian, and Isthmian)—included musical and dramatic competitions and marked an innovation in the entertainment offered to the Roman people.

By this time, many of the competitive events comprised excerpts of the great tragedies, sung to the accompaniment of the lyre. This phenomenon seems to reflect a declining interest in complete dramatic performances in favour of a greater variety of shorter, more famous set pieces, what we might think of as the "greatest hits" of classical drama. These, moreover, were put to music and sung. For example, Nero was famous for singing "Canace Giving Birth," "Orestes the Matricide," "Oedipus Blinding Himself," and "The

Primary Source

Box 12.2: *CIL* 10.1074d = *ILS* 5053,4 (Pompeii).

Aulus Clodius Flaccus, son of Aulus, of the Menenian tribe, duumvir with judicial power three times, quinquennial, military tribune by popular demand.

In his first duumvirate, at the Games of Apollo (*Ludi Apollinares*) in the Forum, (he presented) a procession, bulls, bullfighters, and their fleet-footed helpers, three pairs of stage fighters, boxers fighting in groups, and Greek-style pugilists; also (he presented) games with every musical entertainment, pantomime, and Pylades; and he gave 10,000 sesterces to the public coffers.

In return for his second duumvirate, which was also his quinquennial duumvirate, at the Games of Apollo (he presented) in the Forum a procession, bulls, bullfighters and their fleet-footed helpers, and boxers fighting in bands; and the next day in the amphitheatre (he presented) 30 pairs of athletes and 5 pairs of gladiators, and with his colleague (he presented) 35 pairs of gladiators and a hunt with bulls, bullfighters, boars, bears, and other hunt variations.

In his third duumvirate (he presented) with his colleague games by a foremost troupe, with extra musical entertainment.

Insane Hercules"—and infamous for singing "The Fall of Troy" in a private moment as he witnessed the great fire of Rome in 64 CE (Suet. *Ner.* 21; Tac. *Ann.* 15.39). We may be reminded of today's great operatic arias, which are often better known than the operas from which they come. Like other performers, Nero sang these pieces before judges in competition in hopes of winning the crown. Unsurprisingly, the emperor was very successful, but his desire to perform in public was a cause of embarrassment and consternation for some of Rome's **senatorial** aristocracy.

Although the *Neronia* did not survive Nero's reign, in 86 CE the emperor Domitian established the *Capitolia*, a Greek-style agonistic competition in honour of Jupiter Capitolius (in the same way that the Olympian Games were in honour of Zeus Olympius). These games proved to be more enduring and included musical, athletic, and equestrian competitions. For his games, Domitian constructed a large Greek-style stadium in the Campus Martius, the oblong shape of which can still be seen in the outline of the **Piazza Navona** today. Besides Rome, other cities in the western empire, such as Carthage, established Greek-style sacred *agones* with athletic programs. It should also be noted that athletic competitions in the Greek, eastern half of the empire flourished during the imperial period as many emperors, especially Hadrian, encouraged them and offered imperial **patronage**.

But there is also evidence for what we would characterize as athletic events from the earliest days of Rome. According to the historian Livy (1.35), when the Etruscan king Tarquinius Priscus (who reigned from 616 to 579 BCE) first celebrated the *Ludi Romani*, he included equestrian events and **boxers** imported from Etruria. The nature of these boxing matches, however, is uncertain. Although boxing is clearly a competitive sport, the Romans considered these boxers to be professional performers paid to entertain the people. The Romans also maintained a distinction between Greek and native Italian boxers (see Suet. *Aug.* 45 and Box 12.2). Livy (39.22) later tells us that it was not until 186 BCE that the first proper **athletic contest** (*athletarum certamen*) took place at games organized by Marcus Fulvius Nobilior in honour of Jupiter Optimus Maximus. What Nobilior provided was a contest on the Greek model, probably with Greek athletes imported or invited for the purpose; however, the Romans preferred the more bruising *caestus* (studded boxing gloves) of the Italians. According to Cicero (*Leg.* 2.38), athletic events had become a regular feature of the Roman *ludi* by the late Republic.

The Roman attitude to athletics is complex and remained so throughout the Republic and into the imperial period. Although there was clearly an "athletic" tradition in Italy, the early Romans did not hold athletes and athletic competition in the same esteem as did the Greeks, for whom participation in the gymnasium and the world of athletics was a sign of elevated social **status**. In part, the Roman attitude has to do with their disdain for public performance, a similar contempt with which they branded charioteers and actors (and **gladiators**, as we shall see). For the Romans, athletes were simply yet more performers (see Box 12.1). Furthermore, although Roman culture celebrated martial excellence and recognized the importance of physical fitness in military training, the Romans found very little in athletic training that was valuable in this respect.

Nevertheless, events such as chariot racing were extremely popular in ancient Rome. The great religious festivals typically culminated with such races in the Circus Maximus, the largest and oldest entertainment structure in the city. According to Livy (1.9; see also Plut. *Rom.* 14), it was here that Romulus supposedly orchestrated the rape of the Sabine women at the *Consualia*, suggesting that there had been chariot races from the very foundation of the city. Another tradition, also recorded by Livy (1.35.8–9), suggests a somewhat later date. He explains that Tarquinius Priscus, the fifth king of Rome (616–579 BCE), laid out the circus in the valley, allowed the aristocrats to erect seating on the slopes, and celebrated games here to mark a victory over the nearby Latins. These games soon became a regular event: the *Ludi Romani*.

A chariot team usually included 4 horses (a *quadriga*), although as many as 10 horses are attested. The presiding magistrate (typically a **praetor**) indicated the start of the race by dropping a cloth, the *mappa*. The teams then raced from the starting gates down the track to complete seven laps around the central barrier, which was about two-thirds the length of the track. The hairpin turns at the posts (*metae*) were the most dangerous parts of the course and could be the cause of spectacular crashes, which the Romans came to refer to as shipwrecks (*naufragia*). The race concluded at about the halfway point along the northern straightaway. It was here, on the slopes of the Palatine Hill, that Augustus located the imperial box (**pulvinar**). From this ostentatious location, which was essentially a small shrine affixed with divine images, the emperors watched the races. As will be discussed later in the chapter, the spectacles were about both seeing and being seen.

While other Mediterranean cultures (like the ancient Greeks) also enjoyed chariot races, the overall organization of the Roman races was unique (see Figure 12.1). Chariot teams were arranged into one of four factions identified by colour: red, white, blue, and green. Among the "ordinary" people, allegiance to a faction was a source of pride and personal identity—one cheered for the greens or the blues, for example (see Box 12.3). As a key focus for people's affection, these factions became increasingly

Figure 12.1 Ancient Roman chariot race in the Circus Maximus. © Ivy Close Images/Alamy

Primary Source

Box 12.3: Pliny, *Letters*, 9.6.

I have spent the past few days quietly, but happily, involved with my notes and books. "In Rome?" you say. "How could you?" There were, of course, chariot races, but I am not in the least bit interested in that kind of entertainment. There is never anything new or different about them, nothing which you need to see more than once. And so I am amazed that so many thousands of men time after time have such a childish desire to see horses racing and men driving chariots. Now, if they were attracted to the speed of the horses or the skill of the drivers, this would not be unreasonable. But as it is, they are interested only in the team uniforms. It's the team colours they love. In fact, if, during the race itself, right in the middle, the team colours were suddenly switched, the spectators would immediately transfer their interest and support, and abandon those drivers and those horses which they recognized from afar and whose names they had been shouting just a moment before.

One cheap little tunic has so much power, so much influence, and not just with the rabble, which is cheaper even than the tunic, but with certain men of rank and dignity. When I consider these men, and their insatiable desire to see something so silly, so boring, and so common, I take some pleasure in the fact that I am not taken in by an interest such as that. And so, during the past few days, which other men have wasted on the most vacant pursuits, I have used my leisure time very cheerfully for literary work.

politicized, especially in the later Roman Empire, with different groups supporting different political interests. In their enthusiasm for the factions, ancient spectators have much in common with modern sports fans, whose die-hard loyalties lie with professional sports teams. Even when Greek-style agonistic competition was introduced in Rome by Domitian, the chariot races remained fundamentally Roman in character. Where the ancient Greeks credited the owner of the horses with the victory, the Romans awarded the prize to the charioteer (*auriga*) and his faction. Although often of lower status, individual charioteers such as Marcus Aurelius Polynices (*CIL* VI 10049 = *ILS* 5286,1) could become famous and, by the imperial period, extremely wealthy if they were successful. In this way, they were like most other performers in ancient Rome for whom success brought wealth and social standing (see Box 12.4).

Munera

While the great *ludi* were sponsored by the state and provided by its magistrates as part of religious observances, leading individuals could also provide privately funded shows

Primary Source

Box 12.4: *CIL* 6.10049 = *ILS* 5286,1.

Marcus Aurelius Polynices, born a slave,

who lived 29 years, 9 months,

5 days, won 739 palms

in this way: 655 in the red faction,

55 in the green faction, 12 in

the blue faction, 17 in the white faction.

He won prizes of 40,000 sesterces three times,

prizes of 30,000 sesterces twenty-six times, lesser prizes eleven times;

he won 8-horse chariots eight times, in 10-horse

chariots nine times, in 6-horse chariots three times.

(*munera*) as a gift to the people. For the most part, these private shows involved gladiatorial combats and were associated with funerary spectacles. Indeed, from the first recorded gladiatorial combat at the funeral of Decimus Iunius Brutus Pera in 264 BCE until the very end of the Republic, gladiatorial contests were almost exclusively given at the funerals of great men (Livy *Epit.* 16).[3] It was not until the imperial period that these events were detached from the funerary context and offered as regularly occurring spectacles.

It was also in the early imperial period that a permanent **amphitheatre** was constructed in Rome. Just as the Romans of the Republic were unwilling to construct a permanent theatre, they also refused to build a permanent amphitheatre. Instead, temporary wooden seating was constructed for the shows, which usually took place in the **Forum**. This construction would have resulted in an oblong or elliptical arena, which is thought to be the precursor to the shape typical of all amphitheatres. The form of the permanent stone amphitheatres therefore reflects their long evolution as provisional structures.[4]

Although the oldest stone amphitheatre is found at Pompeii (dedicated about 70 BCE), a permanent structure was not built in Rome until the reign of Augustus. This amphitheatre, of which nothing remains, was constructed by Statilius Taurus, one of Augustus's generals, and should be considered part of the larger program to supply Rome with entertainment complexes (the theatres of Marcellus and Balbus were constructed at about the same time). It was not until the reign of Vespasian that the Colosseum, the largest amphitheatre in the empire, was erected (see Figure 12.2).

Compare Chapter 17, pp. 390–1, ← on the Colosseum.

Figure 12.2 The Colosseum. ©iStockphoto.com/sndr

Compare Chapter 16, p. 367, and Chapter 17, pp. 390–1, on the Domus Aurea.

Built with proceeds from Vespasian's successful Jewish campaign, the Colosseum sits on the site of Nero's **Domus Aurea** ("Golden House"). It was thus a potent political symbol for the new regime: where Nero had constructed an enormous palace for his own use, the new emperor erected a structure for the benefit of the people of Rome. The Colosseum measures 188 metres by 156 metres, with a seating capacity of at least 50,000 people. The performance area, known as the *arena* (meaning "sand") is approximately 84 metres by 54 metres. The structure beneath the arena floor, with rooms for animals and gladiators, is still visible today. These participants could be lifted into the arena through trap doors. A subterranean passageway also connects the Colosseum with the large training school for gladiators—the **Ludus Magnus**—just to the north. This building had rooms for the gladiators as well as a smaller, elliptical arena for practice.

By the early imperial period, at about the same time that the first permanent amphitheatres were being constructed and gladiatorial contests were being removed from their strict funerary context, the typical program of the *munus* emerged. Displays and hunts (**venationes**) of wild beasts were usually in the morning, with the executions of convicted criminals (**damnati**) and gladiatorial combats held at the end of the day.

Venationes had long been a feature of spectacular entertainment in Rome, often as part of the interludes between races in the circus or as a feature in triumphal *ludi*. Acquiring and displaying wild animals was one way that an ambitious magistrate, charged with organizing the *ludi*, could embellish the spectacles he put on for the people and so win popularity for himself—a critical element in the production of entertainment (see the next section). Frequently, these animals were not simply put on display but were matched against each other or hunted and killed by professional hunters, sometimes by the thousands. In one victory celebration lasting 123 days, the emperor Trajan boasted that 10,000 gladiators fought and 11,000 animals were killed (Cass. Dio 68.15). Those numbers work out to an average of almost 90 animals killed per day, an astounding fig-ure—especially considering that the *venationes* took place for only part of the day.

While we may shudder at such exhibition and wanton destruction of animals, the Romans (and other peoples in the Mediterranean) saw it differently. As the Roman writer Seneca (*Clem.* 26) observes, the dangerous wild animals in the natural world were an enemy of civilization and it was right to kill them: "What would life be if lions and bears ruled, if power over us were given to snakes and all the other dangerous animals? Those creatures lack reason and have been condemned to death by us on the charge of their brutality." The public slaughter of exotic wild animals signalled that the sponsor was willing to spend considerable sums of money on the entertainment of the people watching. But, in the larger picture, it indicated the triumph of (Roman) civilization over the dangerous natural world.

Associated with the *venationes* in the arena were executions. At times, the convicts were made to dress as mythological figures and re-enact their death (a phenomenon that modern scholars have termed "fatal charades"); at other times they were brought out to be devoured by wild beasts (**damnatio ad bestias**).[5] Again, the desire to display executions publicly may seem to indicate a level of cruelty, but we should remember that doing so was typical in most cultures around the world, including—until only quite recently—modern Western culture. We should also remember that those being executed had been convicted and sentenced to death in the arena. Even the early Christians who met their end there had been properly tried and convicted. In the eyes of the Roman authorities and Roman people, those being executed were the enemies of Roman society. Just as the arena was the place where dangerous natural enemies were killed, so too was it the place where the human enemies of Roman society were visibly eliminated. Thomas Wiedemann concludes:

> The arena was the place where civilisation confronted nature, in the shape of beasts which represented a danger to humanity; and where social justice confronted wrong-doing, in the shape of the criminals who were to be executed there; and where the Roman empire confronted its enemies, in the persons of the captured prisoners of war who were killed or were forced to kill one another in the arena.[6]

It was only after several of these events that the crowd would have seen gladiators in action (see Figure 12.3). Although technically slaves who had been sold—or had sold themselves—into service under the **lanista** (an owner/manager of a *familia gladiatoria*, a troupe of gladiators), gladiators were nevertheless well-trained professionals. They were subdivided into a number of distinct types that could be found across the empire. Most classifications were of heavily armed gladiators who wore a helmet, one or two greaves on their shin(s), and carried a sword (typically a short *gladius*) and a shield. The most common types of heavily armed gladiators include the *murmillo*, the *secutor*, the *hoplomachus*, and the Thracian, although a number of other types are also attested. Lightly equipped gladiatorial types are less common, with the exception of the *retiarius* ("net-man"), who fought with a trident and a net. The speedy and agile *retiarius* was usually matched against the plodding but better-protected *secutor*. Their training in a gladiatorial school (*ludus gladiatorius*) was conducted under the supervision of a professional weapons instructor (a *doctor* or a *magister*) and was specific to type, at least in the larger schools. Thus we have epigraphical evidence of a *doctor secutorum* (a trainer of *secutores*) and a *doctor retiariorum* (a trainer of *retiarii*), suggesting that the different types of gladiators employed different tactics.

Within each type, the gladiators also seem to have been ranked, with the recruit (*tiro*) at the bottom. A *tiro* was not a raw novice but an extensively trained professional gladiator of particular type who had not yet fought in public. Ranking gladiators would have helped in establishing the relative costs of gladiators when an official and *lanista* arranged for the lease of gladiators for a show: the better the gladiator, the more he would have cost.[7]

Although current popular imagination often supposes that the gladiatorial combats were little more than spectacles of death and that the participants were either especially desperate men or homicidal maniacs, a closer look at our evidence indicates otherwise. Although gladiators could be compelled to fight to the death and gladiatorial combat was clearly a dangerous event, three things are clear. First, in the vast majority of cases, a gladiator could submit if he were wounded in a fight. Second, contests were governed by a series of rules and expected behaviour that gladiators generally followed. Third, fights to the death were exceptional.

If wounded or exhausted in the fight and nearing defeat, a gladiator could submit to his opponent. He did so by lowering his shield and weapon, perhaps even dropping to his knee, and raising a finger. Gladiators fought literally **ad digitum** ("to the finger"), an action frequently depicted in mosaics

Figure 12.3 Gladiators in the arena: *Secutor* vs *retiarius* with a *summa rudis* officiating. © The Print Collector/Alamy

and relief scenes of the arena. At this point, an official, who was present in the arena with the fighting gladiators, stepped in to separate the two. This official, known as the **summa rudis** (literally, "chief stick"), is often included in artistic representations of arena scenes. He always wears a white tunic with two red or purple stripes running down the front and carries a long stick or switch with which to signal to the gladiators. The decision to accept or reject the gladiator's request, however, was referred to the sponsor of the show—the person who was paying for it. The sponsor could end the fight or compel the gladiators to continue, but the matter was often passed on to the people, who would typically decide with "a turn of their thumb" (Juv. 3.36). If the submission was accepted, the gladiator was freed from the fight and said to have earned **missio** (release).

One striking aspect of this rule is the behaviour of the opposing gladiator. When the submitting gladiator dropped his shield and weapon, his opponent could easily have pressed the attack and seriously wounded or killed him. But this move was extremely rare. Gladiators fought for victory but not necessarily to wound or kill their opponents. Indeed, several gladiatorial epitaphs record the deceased's boast that he had "hurt no one" while fighting, an odd claim that makes sense only if we understand that victory in combat was the real goal, not homicide:

> I was called Meilesis and had the civilian name Mestrianos. I fought five times and hurt no one. Now I have been hurt. And from her own funds [. . .] Alexandra erected this in memory of her husband. Farewell, all you who pass by.[8]

 Beyond a general unwillingness to harm an opponent unnecessarily, an additional series of rules seems to have been in place to govern the combats. The nature of all these rules is difficult to ascertain, especially given the nature of our sources (gladiatorial rules are just not something that aristocratic writers were likely to discuss much.) But we can glimpse the rules' existence from the fact that the *summa rudis* seems to have been able to intervene in the fight to enforce them, which our sources refer to as the **lex pugnandi** ([Quint.] *Major Declamation* 9.9).[9]

Evidence from the provinces indicates that fights in which gladiators were compelled to fight to the death were exceptional. For example, an inscription from Beroia in the Roman province of Macedonia (240 CE) announces an upcoming three-day *munus* in which one pair would contend "for their lives in addition to the normal two pairs." To do this, the sponsors boast the authorization (*indulgentia*) of the reigning emperor Gordianus himself. These statements indicate that such fights were unusual, but we might also observe that the contests of the other two pairs, presumably not to the death, are called "normal" (see Box 12.5).

According to Suetonius (*Aug.* 45), Augustus had banned fights **sine missione** ("without release") at the beginning of the imperial period. Such attempts to limit the possibility of a gladiator dying in the arena may have been due to humanitarian concerns, but they

Primary Source

Box 12.5: *AE* (1971, no. 431).

With Good fortune! For the health and safety and victory and eternal endurance of the great and most holy and unconquerable lord the emperor Caesar Marcus Antonius Gordianus *Pius*, *Felix* Augustus, *pontifex maximus*, in the third year of his tribunician power, consul for the first time, *pater patriae*, and for the god of his house and the hallowed senate and hallowed armies and the Roman people and the eminent provinces of the hallowed *praetorium*, the macedoniarch and chief priest of the Augusti (?) and *agonothete* of the *koinon* of Macedonians for the Alexandrian games, sacred, *eiselastikoi*.[1] Lucius Septimius Insteianus Alexander and his wife Aelia Alexandra the chief priestess will present in the city of Beroia the most illustrious metropolis of Macedonia three days of hunts and gladiators, introducing as well each day of the spectacles a pair who will contend for their lives in addition to the normal two (pairs) by the indulgence of our lord, Marcus Antonius Gordianus *Pius*, *Felix* Augustus. They will begin their *munera* seven days before the Kalends of July, in the consulships of (Gaius Octavius Appius) Suetrius Sabinus, consul for the second time, and Ragonius Venustus, the year 271 of Augustus (Actian era) and 387 (Macedonian era), the seventeenth day of Panemos. Farewell.

Note

1. The reading here is uncertain. *Eiselastikoi* were games in which victors were awarded the honour of riding home in a chariot.

were more probably related to finances. As previously indicated, by the imperial period gladiators were generally well-trained professionals. They were also expensive. A legal passage from the jurist Gaius (*Inst.* 3.146), written in the late second century CE, indicates that gladiators were leased from a *lanista* for a relatively small sum, but if a gladiator was killed or seriously wounded in the combats, the lease converted to a sale. That is, the official who was putting on the show effectively had to purchase the gladiator. The new "selling price" was estimated to be 50 times what it cost to lease a gladiator. Despite this expense, many ambitious politicians were too willing to expend fortunes and even go into debt while putting on memorable spectacles because such sponsorship was a sure way to win popularity with the people.

Compare Chapter 10 , pp. 228–9, on the aedileship, spectacles, and popularity.

Plutarch (*Mor.* 823E) complains, "And so seeing this, we must not be humbled or impressed at the immediate reputation with the masses, since it lasts only a short time and ends immediately with the gladiatorial combats and dramas, since they have nothing honorable or dignified."

Compelling gladiators to fight without chance of *missio* was not so much seen as cruelty but as an enormous expenditure and an opportunity to advertise connections with the imperial house, since it was only through imperial indulgence that such a fight could be offered. The sponsors in Box 12.5, Insteianus and Aelia, show their wealth and their willingness to spend it on the people. But they also publicize their connections to the imperial powers. Moreover, the emperors were eager to limit unnecessary expenditure by having local and overly ambitious aristocrats pay for spectacles. Approval for such expensive shows was thus given only if the personal fortunes of the sponsors could bear the cost.

The possibility of submission, the various rules of combat, and the general prohibition against deliberately compelling gladiators to fight to the death may also suggest that the combats were not about the death of the gladiators but the fights themselves. While we should not deny the extreme violence of these contests, what seems to have been especially important was that gladiators demonstrated extreme bravery, martial skills, and strict discipline. It was the demonstration of these traits that the people came to see and considered when deciding for or against *missio*.

The Political Importance of Entertainment Spectacles

All forms of large-scale public entertainment had religious significance. Even gladiatorial *munera* became primarily connected to the celebration of the imperial cult during the imperial period.[10] A town charter from Urso, a town in southern Spain that was established as a Roman colony by Julius Caesar, indicated that the leading magistrates (the duumvirs and aediles) were to provide *ludi scaenici* or *munera* as part of their duties in honour of the **Capitoline Triad** of Jupiter, Juno, and Minerva (see Box 12.6; compare Box 12.2).

For these games, the duumvirs and aediles at Urso were provided with funds from the town treasury, a situation mirroring that of Rome. (State games were paid for with state funds.) The amounts provided, however, were often not enough. At Urso the duumvirs received only 2,000 **sesterces**, while the aediles received 1,000. The magistrates were then expected to cover extra costs themselves, which allowed them to take "ownership" of the games and, in a way, claim them for themselves. It is unclear whether priests of the imperial cult received funds for their *munera*, but it is probable that such funds would have also been insufficient. As at Rome, we find especially ambitious men going into great debt to outdo rival magistrates in order to gain popularity.

A remarkable mosaic from Smirat in North Africa commemorates a *venatio* put on by Magerius, a local magistrate, no doubt as part of the expectations of his office (see Figure 12.4). The mosaic shows a series of (named!) leopards being killed by professional beast hunters, a troupe identified as the Telegenii. In the centre of the mosaic stands a man holding a tray with four bags of money, each marked with the symbol ∞, presumably meaning 1,000 *denarii*. On either side of this figure we have two "inscriptions" that

Primary Source

Box 12.6: *CIL* 2.5439 = *ILS* 6087 (*Lex Ursonensis*), sections 70 and 71.

The duumvirs, except for those who were first appointed after this law, shall present during their magistracy at the discretion of the decurions either a gladiatorial show or dramatic spectacles in honour of the Jupiter, Juno, and Minerva [and] the gods and goddesses, over four days for the greater part of each day, or such part of the shows as shall be possible, and on the *ludi* or *munus* each of the said persons shall spend from their own money no less than 2,000 sesterces and for each duumvir it shall be lawful to spend a sum not to exceed 2,000 sesterces from the public funds, and it shall be lawful for this person to do so with prejudice to themselves, so long as no one shall expend or otherwise attribute that money, which according to this law shall be given or allocated for those sacrifices which are performed in public or in any other place.

The aediles shall present during their magistracy a gladiatorial show or dramatic spectacles in honour of the Jupiter, Juno, and Minerva [and] the gods and goddesses, over three days for the greater part of each day, or such part of the shows as shall be possible, and during one day games in the circus or in the forum to Venus, and on the *ludi* or *munus* each of the said persons shall spend from their own money no less than 2,000 sesterces, and for each aedile it shall be lawful to expend 1,000 sesterces, and a duumvir or a prefect shall provide that the money shall be given and allocated, and it shall be lawful for the aediles to receive this without prejudice to themselves.

describe the scene and record words heard in the amphitheatre that day. In a way, we can both see and hear this event (see Box 12.7).

In the first inscription, the herald asks the people to authorize the payment of 500 *denarii* for each leopard (presumably each leopard killed) to the Telegenii. The people are properly addressed with the greatest deference by being called my lords (*domini mei*). From the picture we may speculate that the four beast fighters have been paid a bag of money each. If so, then Magerius seems to have given twice as much as asked. The people's forceful and enthusiastic response to his generosity is recorded in a second inscription. Although their reply is long, their phrases are metrical and repetitive—"This is what it is to have money! This is what it is to have power! (*Hoc est habere! Hoc est posse!*)"—and so it may be easier to believe that a crowd could have shouted, even chanted, this sort of thing in unison. Moreover, since the vocative form of his name ("Mageri") also appears twice on the mosaic, it is probable that the people were also shouting his name. What a day for Magerius! His generous expenditure and deference to the people have earned him enormous personal popularity.

The Magerius mosaic also hints at the political power wielded by the people at these shows. They had the power to approve of what Magerius provided or to reject it and

Figure 12.4 A mosaic from Smirat in North Africa commemorating a *venatio*. © Gilles Mermet / Art Resource, NY

embarrass him. Loud chanting done in unison emphasized this power. The historian Cassius Dio (76.4), for example, recorded the sorts of chants that he heard at the Circus during the chaotic early days of the reign of Septimius Severus:

> When those races had finished and the charioteers were preparing to race again, the people first became silent and then suddenly all clapped their hands at the same time and also joined together in a shout, appealing for good fortune for the state. They cried for this first; then, applying the epithets "Queen" and "Immortal" to Rome, they shouted: "How long must we suffer such things?" and "How long must we wage war?"

The people could make their will known through such chants. Already in the late Republic, when the voting institutions were still in place, Cicero (*Sest.* 116) could describe political Rome as *Theatrum Populusque Romanus*, punning on the familiar *Senatus Populusque Romanus*. The people were consulted over the fate of gladiators and that of convicts who were paraded in front of the crowd before their execution. Approval of the execution implied support of the imperial authorities who handed down the sentence. In this way, such entertainment served to reinforce the established order and

Political History

Box 12.7: Mosaic from Smirat

Dunbabin, K. 1978. *The Mosaics of Roman North Africa*. New York: Oxford University Press. 67–8.

The mosaic not only provides a graphic depiction of a *venatio* put on by a local magistrate named Magerius, but also includes a lengthy written description of what was said in the amphitheatre on the day of the games. We hear first the herald announcing Magerius' decisions and then the acclamation shouted by the people. It is a powerful example of the importance of entertainment for members of the upper **classes** to win popularity.

'Proclaimed by the *curio* (herald): My Lords, in order that the Telegenii should have what they deserve from your favour, for each leopard give them five hundred *denarii*.'

The shout in reply: 'May future generations know of your *munus* because you are an example for them; may past generations hear about it. Where has such a thing been heard before? When has such a thing been heard before? You have provided a *munus* as an example to the other magistrates. You have provided a *munus* from your own resources." Magerius pays (the money). "This is what it is to have money! This is what it is to have power! Now that it is evening, they have been dismissed from your *munus* with bags of money.'

Roman values. The public's approval was important: jeers and discontent reflected negatively upon the sponsor.

The organization of seating at shows is also relevant. By a series of laws, the spectators were seated in a way that reflected their social status: front rows were reserved for the senatorial elite, and (in Rome) the next 14 rows were reserved for the **equestrians**. There were even attempts to classify and organize others in the upper seats.[11] The enforcement of such social hierarchies appealed to Roman sensibilities. Moreover, despite the obvious ranking system, the very fact that one had a seat to watch the shows clearly marked one's inclusion in society. For a community to exist as a community, it has to assemble in some way.

→ Compare Chapter 3, p. 60, on seating at spectacles.

Especially in the imperial period, after the voting assemblies had been shut down, mass public entertainment was one of the most important—and visible—ways that the Roman people gathered. The inclusion of the spectators is doubly emphasized when compared to the degraded legal status held by various performers, who were deemed to suffer from *infamia* ("ill repute") because they were thought to sell themselves for money. It is for that reason that the senators were so shocked at

Compare Chapter 8, pp. 172–3, ← on *infamia*.

Nero's desires to perform on stage and that many performers did not mention their monetary winnings but stressed their victory crowns or palms. Of course, concerns about *infamia* belonged especially to the aristocracy; it is difficult to say how the vast majority or "ordinary" Romans viewed such things. Certainly the charioteer Marcus Aurelius Polynices did not shy away from enumerating his monetary rewards in addition to his palms. Such successful charioteers, gladiators, athletes, and other performers were the heroes of the ordinary people.

Summary

Juvenal's famous line belittling contemporary (second-century CE) Romans for their desires to be entertained rings hollow. Not only does he willfully downplay the religious significance of such shows and the aristocracy's need to provide the people with this entertainment, but he also ignores the real political power that the masses could exert at the spectacles. The line may be good satirical poetry, but it does not reflect the importance or reality of entertainment in Roman culture.

Juvenal casts all the varied forms of entertainment together. There were multiple options for the Romans, from theatrical plays and other dramatic performances to chariot races in the circus and animal hunts and gladiatorial fights in the amphitheatre. Each had a large venue built specifically for these different types of entertainment. Indeed, few cities—even in modern times—could match the number of entertainment facilities available to the Romans. More important, however, is the social significance of a community coming together. People were seated according to social orders and watched spectacles provided by their magistrates for them and for their gods, shows that might include electrifying musical or theatrical performances, thrilling chariot races, hunts of wild animals, executions, or exciting gladiatorial combats where the gladiators demonstrated some of the martial values that had made Rome great. All of these events reaffirmed the dominance of Rome. Therefore, spectacle entertainment was an important element of Roman society.

Questions for Review and Discussion

1. In what ways did Roman theatrical productions differ from Greek performances?
2. What was the social status of performers in the Roman world? How might the ordinary people have viewed them?

3. In what ways were Roman chariot races unique?
4. What was the nature of gladiatorial spectacles? With what other sorts of events were these fights given?
5. What was the political importance of mass public spectacles? In what other ways were they important to Roman society?

Suggested Reading

Csapo, E., and W. Slater. 1995. *The Context of Ancient Drama*. Ann Arbor: University of Michigan Press.

Csapo and Slater present an excellent introduction to the study of ancient drama.

Dunkle, R. 2008. *Gladiators: Violence and Spectacle in Ancient Rome*. Harlow, UK, and New York: Pearson/Longman.

This book offers a good discussion of the world of the gladiator.

Fagan, G. 2011. *The Lure of the Arena: Social Psychology and the Crowd at Roman Games*. Cambridge: Cambridge University Press.

Fagan explores the spectacle of violent entertainment from a socio-psychological position and argues that, in their passion for violent spectacle, the Romans were not much different than people of all times, including today.

Futrell, A. 2006. *The Roman Games: A Sourcebook*. Malden, MA: Blackwell.

Futrell has collected many of the key sources in her sourcebook. Her focus is on the arena and, to a lesser extent, the circus.

Humphreys, J. 1986. *Roman Circuses: Arenas for Chariot Racing*. Berkeley and Los Angeles: University of California Press.

This book is still invaluable for information on the circus and chariot races.

Potter, D. 2009. "Entertainment." In *A Companion to Ancient History*, edited by A. Erskine, 381–91. Oxford and Malden, MA: Blackwell.

Potter provides the best introduction to Roman entertainment, in which he surveys much of the same material covered in this chapter.

Notes

1 Bergmann (1999: 11).
2 All translations are my own.
3 Ville (1981: 57–99).
4 Welch (2007: 30–101).
5 Coleman (1990).
6 Wiedemann (1992: 46).
7 For more on ranking, see Carter (2003).
8 Robert (1940: 84–5, no. 20).
9 For more on the rules governing gladiatorial combat, see Carter (2006/07).
10 The imperial cult refers to the worship of the divinity of the Roman emperors, a practice that became widespread during the imperial period.
11 Edmondson (1996).

13

The Roman Army

Conor Whately

In an early scene of the 2000 film *Gladiator*, we see a battlefield in Germania on a grey and dreary day. Scores of Roman soldiers are loosely arrayed around some wooden fortifications, ready for battle and eagerly greeting their general, the fictional Maximus (played by Russell Crowe). From across the plain, an angry and bedraggled barbarian with scraggly hair and dirty clothes shouts something incomprehensible at the Romans and tosses the severed head of a Roman scout in an act of defiance. Orders are given, the Romans array themselves for battle, and Maximus gives the ominous order, "At my signal, unleash hell." The infantry march in tight formations into position, while the artillery soldiers prepare to fire and archers ready their bows in unison. In the meantime, the aged emperor Marcus Aurelius (played by Richard Harris) watches from the safety of a hill behind the battlefield. Maximus gives a short and emboldening speech to the soldiers around him, complete with moments of humour and intimacy of the sort we might well find amongst contemporary "bands of brothers" and barks a few more orders at the troops. The opening volleys of arrows and fireballs commence; Maximus, on horseback, races into position with his unit; Marcus Aurelius anxiously watches from afar; and the Roman soldiers maintain their formations while commanders in the distance bellow commands. The battle proper begins soon after, and the angry barbarians charge in a disorderly manner at the tightly organized Roman troops. There are close-ups of Romans hacking and slashing their way through the barbarian ranks, without any sense that they are ever in danger of breaking their formation or losing this battle. Even after Maximus is knocked off his horse, his training and courage (far superior to his foes') are abundantly evident: the Roman victory is complete.

This scene is merely one of many in numerous films and television programs that depict Roman legions in battle. Such portrayals conform to modern stereotypes of the Roman army in action: the soldiers are well trained, courageous, disciplined, and robotically efficient—a marked contrast to their barbarian enemies. Is this an accurate depiction? Furthermore, was the field of battle the only place where the army made a contribution to Roman history and society?

Timeline

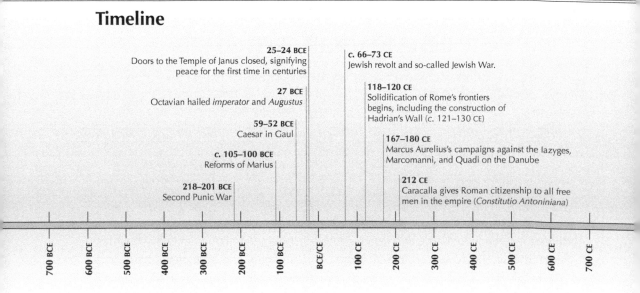

25–24 BCE
Doors to the Temple of Janus closed, signifying peace for the first time in centuries

27 BCE
Octavian hailed *imperator* and *Augustus*

59–52 BCE
Caesar in Gaul

c. **105–100 BCE**
Reforms of Marius

218–201 BCE
Second Punic War

c. **66–73 CE**
Jewish revolt and so-called Jewish War.

118–120 CE
Solidification of Rome's frontiers begins, including the construction of Hadrian's Wall (*c.* 121–130 CE)

167–180 CE
Marcus Aurelius's campaigns against the Iazyges, Marcomanni, and Quadi on the Danube

212 CE
Caracalla gives Roman citizenship to all free men in the empire (*Constitutio Antoniniana*)

700 BCE   600 BCE   500 BCE   400 BCE   300 BCE   200 BCE   100 BCE   BCE/CE   100 CE   200 CE   300 CE   400 CE   500 CE   600 CE   700 CE

Introduction

The Roman army is one of the best-documented elements of Roman society.[1] The varied, and in some cases voluminous, evidence paints a rich picture of the Roman military in its many capacities, from keeper of the peace to police force and from wager of war to instrument of imperial power. The Roman army was the largest institution in terms of manpower and expenditure in the Roman world. During the imperial period, it may have consumed 50 per cent of the Roman state's finances. In a world where war was a regular feature of daily life for many people—and the Romans were no more militaristic than their neighbours, only more successful—it is hard to overestimate the impact of the Roman army on wider society and its role within it.

This chapter provides some background to the organization and history of the Roman army, discusses its performance in war, and considers its role in society (within both local communities and the larger empire). Although some discussion will be devoted to the middle and late Republic (roughly 264–27 BCE), the majority will focus on the imperial period (27 BCE–235 CE). What will emerge is that the army was composed of individuals rather than identical automatons: it was an army full of both Romans and non-Romans, much like the Empire it served. In this and many other ways, the army reflected the society of which it was such a significant part.

———•◆•———

The Composition of the Roman Army

Fundamental to any discussion of the Roman army's activities in both warfare and society more generally is a basic familiarity with its major components: the **legions**, the **auxiliaries**, and the **praetorian guard**. The recruitment, careers, weaponry, and appearance of soldiers are described in the following sections. This discussion shows that the Roman army was not a single, homogeneous unit of interchangeable soldiers but an institution whose human components came from all over the empire and could continue to express their individual differences within the parameters allowed by the army's organization. The various elements of the army were also treated differently, with the praetorians (originally populated by Roman citizens from Italy) receiving better terms of service and salary than the legions (which were made up of Roman citizens from Italy and the provinces), and the legions generally faring better than the auxiliaries (which were made up of non-citizens). Furthermore, and as we shall see in later sections, patterns of deployment and retirement of soldiers in turn promoted both the spread of Roman culture and cultural diversity within the Empire.

The Legions

Of the components of the Roman army (*exercitus*), the legions—the heavy infantry—attract the most attention in both modern and ancient eras (see, for example, Tac. *Hist.* 2.22). The number of legions varied drastically over time. Under Augustus, for example, there were 25; under Diocletian, there were at least 67. It is difficult to say, however, how many legionary soldiers these numbers translated into, since we do not know if (or when) legions functioned at full strength. Ideally, and on paper, imperial legions each counted 5,000 soldiers (or 5,280 soldiers, as calculated by one scholar),[2] but the number increases to over 6,000 if we include the servants and other individuals who accompanied each legion. The soldiers of any given legion were organized in a series of ever-smaller subunits: a legion had 10 cohorts (*cohortes*); a cohort consisted of 5 or 6 centuries (*centuriae*); and centuries were composed of between 80 and 100 men each, who were further organized into *contubernia* ("tents"), groups of 10 men who shared a tent on campaign or barracks at the base.

Calculations based on ancient sources suggest that approximately 4,500 to 5,000 legionary recruits enrolled per year. Not everyone was permitted to join the legions, however. Only male Roman citizens could be legionary soldiers; freeborn non-citizen men might enlist in the auxiliaries (see pp. 289–92), but women and slaves were excluded from serving in the army altogether. Those convicted and condemned to the beasts, convicted of adultery, or convicted in a public court by a jury were also excluded from service (moreover, if found by military tribunal to be guilty of legal infractions while serving in the ranks, soldiers could face serious penalties, including execution).[3] Generally, those with any kind of physical deformity were also barred from service (Plin. *Ep.* 10.29–30). The *Digest* (49.16.4.pr.) stipulates, however, that a man born with one testicle was permitted to serve, thanks to permission given by the emperor Trajan (in recognition that the famous republican generals Sulla and Cotta both apparently shared this condition).

Legionary recruits were evaluated not only for their physical fitness but also for their literacy, although the latter determined their potential rank rather than their ability to enlist. Vegetius (*Mil.* 1.6), the author of a military handbook dating to the fourth or fifth century CE, writes that the recruiting officer examined the face, eyes, and physical condition of the recruits. He also stresses the advantages of certain physical traits, such as a broad chest, muscular shoulders, and a small waist.

Recruits did not become full-fledged soldiers until they had completed four months of probation (*probatio*) and, at the end of this period, had sworn a formal oath, the **sacramentum**, to the emperor. Vegetius (*Mil.* 2.5), writing at a time when the official religion was Christianity, has this to say about the *sacramentum* as it existed in his day: "They swear by God and Christ and the Holy Spirit and the majesty of the emperor . . . to carry out all the emperor's commands energetically, never desert their military service or shirk death on behalf of the Roman state." He also indicates that key elements of the *sacramentum* included the recruit's name, a statement of loyalty and one of obedience, and some reference to the emperor's—and possibly the state's—safety.[4]

Over the course of the army's long history, the legionary soldier's equipment and weaponry went through significant changes. By the late Republic, some of the distinct features most often associated with the appearance of those soldiers—and found in films and on television—had appeared. In the second and first centuries BCE, legionary armour included the helmet (*cassis*), the cuirass (*lorica*), and greaves. Legionaries carried a shield (*scutum*) that was rectangular and either flat or concave, a javelin (*pilum*), a short Spanish sword (*gladius*), and a dagger. A soldier's pride in his equipment was likely increased by the fact that he had paid for it personally out of his own salary (an arrangement that reduced cost to the state).[5] It also probably meant that the appearance of Roman soldiers of the same unit was not as uniform as we might have thought (particularly if one considers their presentation in popular culture, such as in *Gladiator*).[6] While from a distance legionary soldiers arranged for battle may have looked quite similar, some differences in the detail of their clothes would have become apparent with closer inspection. A slightly wealthier soldier, for example, could have afforded a more elaborate scabbard for his *gladius*. What is more, the various units would have had some features to distinguish them from other units and to promote *esprit de corps* within. Variety in the appearance of the Roman legionary, albeit on a small scale, was therefore common.[7]

Legionaries usually served about 20 years before retirement. Prior to the reign of Augustus, veterans might have received cash or, more often, land upon discharge. Available land in Italy became ever scarcer, but veterans were generally unwilling to settle far from Italy. When Augustus became emperor he introduced cash payments to legionary veterans, a practice that continued throughout much of the imperial period.[8] Land allotment endured as well, though outside of Italy, and some emperors used veteran settlements as a means of pacifying troubled or recently conquered territory. Money, however, seems to have been the primary reward. The amount, roughly 40 per cent of a legionary's career earnings during the reign of Augustus, had dropped to 22 per cent by 235 CE.[9]

During the Republic the ranks of the Roman army were filled with Roman citizens and their Italian allies. As peace settled into the heart of the empire at the end of the first century BCE, however, the number of Roman citizens from Italy serving in the legions (and the auxiliaries) started to drop, and continued to do so over the next two and a half centuries. The number of provincials with Roman citizenship enrolled in the legions increased in inverse proportion.[10] However, the high regard for Italy (and consequent preferential treatment of Italians) that marked the attitudes of many Romans was still reflected in legionary recruitment. While Italians generally no longer served in the ranks, they continued to be commissioned (higher-ranking) officers well into the third century, on the assumption that Romans from Italy were somehow better qualified.

The Auxiliaries

The legions deserve only part of the credit for Rome's military success, especially in the imperial period. Mention must also be made of the *auxilia*, or auxiliary forces, which were composed of non-citizens who resided in the empire. Their importance is not to be underestimated; since at least the third century BCE, allied contingents had fought alongside Roman citizen soldiers. The use of auxiliary units did not become formalized until the **Principate** (roughly 27 BCE through 235 CE), with the first set of major changes being instituted by Augustus. The number of auxiliary soldiers fighting for Rome was nearly equal to, and possibly more than, the number of citizen legionaries (somewhere between 150,000 and 200,000 auxiliary soldiers in service each year). There were two broad types of auxiliary unit, each of which had between about 500 and 1,000 soldiers: the cavalry wings (*alae*) and the infantry cohorts.

It is probable that the auxiliary forces adopted recruitment standards similar to those of the legions, though we have less evidence for them. In the first century or so of imperial rule (27 BCE–81 CE), auxiliary units primarily included men from the provinces and the **frontiers** of the Roman empire. At first each unit was generally composed of men from the same tribe or ethnic background and often bore the name of the specific tribe from which it was constituted (for example, the First Veteran Infantry Cohort of

Sugambrians, *Cohors I Sugambrorum Veterana*[11] and the Cavalry Wing of Dardanians, *Ala Dardanorum*).[12] However, in 26 CE, Thracian auxiliaries, who were about to be stationed abroad and possibly not in units composed of their fellow Thracians, rebelled (Tac. *Ann.* 4.4.46–51). In 70 CE some Batavians based in their native Germany rebelled as well, probably because they too were going to be stationed abroad.

Rebellions such as these brought an end to the practice of enrolling soldiers in units of their countrymen. An exception was made for ethnic groups with reputations for specific military skills, and these continued to be recruited as discrete units, although they were not necessarily based in their native territory (an example is the First Cohort of Cilician Archers, *Cohors I Cilicum Sagittaria*, which was based in Lower Moesia, roughly modern-day Bulgaria and Serbia, in 138 CE).[13] Unique traits and skills made auxiliaries prized soldiers during the Empire, as they were able to perform functions in combat that the legionaries could not. In fact, although ancient authors such as Tacitus often belittled the auxiliaries' contribution, their importance was recognized by those in positions of military authority and responsibility, including the emperors themselves.

Although enrolment in the legions was reserved for citizens, one did not have to be a non-citizen to enrol in the auxiliaries. Indeed, in the Empire, service in auxiliary units started to appeal to Roman citizens, who were probably attracted in large part by the financial benefits that accrued with service. Additionally, the sons of auxiliary soldiers often followed their fathers into the auxiliaries, even when the former had citizenship. In the first century CE, citizens made up perhaps only 20 per cent of the auxiliaries and tended to be in cavalry units. But the percentage of citizens in the auxiliaries increased over the next two centuries, making up roughly half the total number by the mid-second century CE. By the third century CE, when Caracalla had extended citizenship empire-wide, the majority of auxiliaries were already Roman citizens, although rarely from Italy.

Did the appearance of auxiliaries differ from that of the legionaries? In general, it seems that there were several distinct features of auxiliary equipment and weaponry. Many auxiliary infantry of the imperial period are identifiable in artistic evidence by the sword and spear (the *spatha* and *hasta*, respectively).[14] In comparison to the legionary soldiers, auxiliaries often appear to have been poorly protected; however, some are occasionally represented wearing metal plates or chain mail.[15] But the artistic evidence should perhaps not always be taken as reflective of reality, since ideological agendas were often at work. Trajan's Column, which depicts the emperor's wars in Dacia in relief sculptures, provides a good example. In some plates, such as those that depict the building of a camp, we find soldiers adorned in armour (*lorica segmentata* in particular). Presumably, these men are the legionaries. In other plates illustrating scenes of combat, we can see soldiers without such armour wearing tunics and carrying the circular shields that we tend to associate with auxiliaries (the legionaries' shields are more rectangular). But it seems that, in reality, some auxiliaries might have worn the *lorica segmentata*[16] and that the differences between legionary and auxiliary soldiers were exaggerated on the column. This was most likely done to empha-size the distinctions between the legionaries, valued for their technical skill, and the aux-iliaries, who did the bulk of the fighting, and consequently to glorify Trajan as a commander who spared Roman legionary blood at the expense of the auxiliaries.[17]

Compare Chapter 17, pp. 393, on Trajan's Column.

However, the appearance of some auxiliary units was quite different from the legion-aries and, indeed, from other auxiliaries. This was particularly true of those units of men of the same ethnic background, with the same distinctive skills, and under the command of a tribal chieftain.[18] An example is the First Cavalry Wing of Gallic and Pannonian Cataphracts (*ala Gallorum et Pannoniorum Catafracta*) that served throughout the Balkans (Moesia Inferior, Dacia Porolissensis, Pannonia). **Cataphracts** were heavily armed, mail-armoured cavalry soldiers who became more common in late antiquity and were similar to medieval knights with regard to their armour.[19] Most auxiliary cavalry were not armed so heavily.

Auxiliary soldiers served a longer term than legionaries, on average about 25 years. Box 13.1 is the text of a Roman **military diploma** of an auxiliary soldier, made of bronze and comparable to a modern passport in its function (see also Figure 13.1). These diplo-mas, which were usually given only to auxiliary soldiers,[20] are valuable for determining where individual auxiliary units were stationed at a given time. More important, they provide information about retirement practices. The auxiliaries generally received neither land nor money on discharge. As our sample diploma illustrates, an auxiliary veteran's great reward was Roman citizenship.[21] Each diploma was, in fact, a portable copy of an original document that was archived in Rome. Although citizenship was presumably

Primary Source

Box 13.1: *RMD* 5.335, Upper Moesia, 16 September 94 CE.

The Emperor Caesar Domitian, son of the divine Vespasian, Augustus, Germanicus, *pontifex maxi-mus*, tribunician power for the thirteenth time, imperator 22 times, consul for the sixteenth time, permanent censor, father of the fatherland, to the cavalry and infantry who served in the 3 *alae* and the 9 *cohortes* which are called the *II Pannoniorum*, the *Claudia nova*, and the *praetoria*, and the *I Cilicum*, *I Cisipadensium*, *I Cretum*, *I Flavia Hispanorum milliaria*, *I Antiochensium*, *II Gallorum Macedonica*, *IIII Raetorum*, *V Gallorum*, and *V Hispanorum* in Moesia Superior under Gnaeus Aemilius Cicatricula Pompeius Longinus . . . before the sixteenth day of the kalends of Domitian by the consuls Tiberius Pomponius Bassus and Lucius Silius Decianus . . .

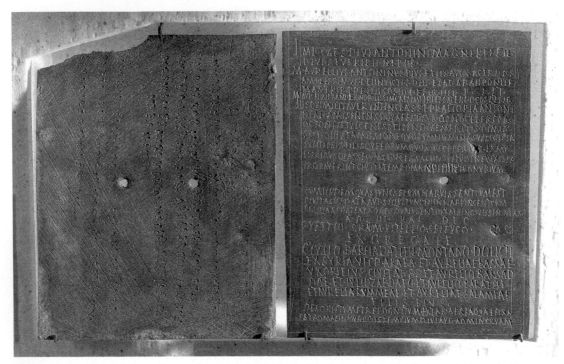

Figure 13.1 Military diploma, bronze, 29 November 225 CE, given by emperors Elagabalus and Alexander Severus to a sailor in the Misene Fleet. © De Agostini Picture Library / G. Dagli Orti / The Bridgeman Art Library

given to all non-Roman soldiers upon discharge,[22] it seems that such diplomas were issued only on request. Another reward for a veteran auxiliary (at least up until about 140 CE), was citizenship for his wife, if he had one (see pp. 303–05), and any children born while he was enlisted. Roman citizenship opened up new economic possibilities for these families and helped spread Roman culture throughout the empire.

The Praetorian Guard

Since the Republic, Roman commanders had been attended and protected by small units of soldiers, but it was Augustus who formalized their organization by establishing the praetorian guard. During the Empire, these soldiers were specifically responsible for the safety and security of the emperor, a function they often shared with German soldiers. The guard consisted of between 9 and 12 cohorts with 500 to 800 men per cohort, depending on the emperor, and were stationed in the city of Rome. At three times the salary given to a legionary, their pay was usually the highest within the Roman military. They tended to receive cash gifts (donatives) from the emperor much more often than the legionaries or auxiliaries, their term

→ Compare Chapter 11, pp. 251–3, on the functions of the praetorian guard.

of service was the shortest (16 years), and they received more money upon retirement than the other soldiers. They were recruited exclusively from Italy until the end of the second century CE, when their abuses of the privileged position and power they and their commanders (a pair of praetorian prefects) enjoyed caused the emperor Septimius Severus to disband them and replace the guard's ranks with provincials (see Box 13.2).[23]

As the preceding discussion illustrates, the Roman army was heterogeneous in nature. From the Republic through the imperial period, one of the significant trends is an ever-decreasing number of Italians serving in the army balanced by an ever-increasing number of men from the provinces. Roman soldiers hailed from all over the Roman world and beyond. Given this empire-wide recruitment, scholars now highlight the diversity of Roman soldiers rather than their uniformity and question the appropriateness of calling

Political History

Box 13.2: The Disbanding of the Praetorian Guard

Following the murder of the emperor Commodus (192 CE), civil war erupted. At one point the praetorian guard auctioned off the imperial throne to the highest bidder: the winner was Didius Julianus. He was eventually put to death on the orders of the **senate** after Septimius Severus had been declared emperor in 193 CE. Severus promptly disbanded the guard for its actions and probably filled its ranks with his own Danubian legionaries, who might be called regular soldiers. The historian Cassius Dio, a contemporary of the events, gives his opinion of the consequences for those who would have formerly filled the ranks of the praetorian guard and for Rome:

> Some found fault with him (Severus) particularly because he abolished the practice of selecting the bodyguard (i.e. the praetorian guard) exclusively from Italy, Spain, Macedonia, and Noricum—a plan that furnished men of more respectable appearance and of simpler habits—and ordered that any vacancies should be filled from all the legions alike. Now, he did this with the idea that he should thus have a guard with a better knowledge of the soldier's duties, and should also be offering a kind of prize for those who proved brave in war; but, as a matter of fact, it became only too apparent that he had incidentally ruined the youth of Italy, who turned to **brigandage** and gladiatorial fighting in place of their former service in the army, and had filled the city with a throng of motley soldiers most savage in appearance, most terrifying in speech, and most boorish in conversation.[1]

Note

1. Lewis and Reinhold (1990: 375, no. 104).

the Roman army of the Principate just that—an "army," as opposed to a collection of "armies."[24] It is clear that the military was composed of a host of provincial armies that often acted, and were referred to, as independent bodies. In addition, each provincial army was composed of a wide range of legions and auxiliary units. Consequently, we sometimes find references in modern scholarly literature to entities such as the *Exercitus Moesicus* (the Moesian army) or the *Exercitus Syriacus* (the Syrian army). The Roman army, like the Roman empire, was a diverse entity.[25]

Professionalization and the Roman Army

Until the late Republic, the army was composed of non-professional soldiers. The legions had been organized into the slightly more cumbersome maniples rather than cohorts, and Rome's Italian allies manned the *auxilia*. The citizen-soldiers serving in the legions would be recruited for individual wars and discharged at their close. However, as Rome's territory expanded and its wars came to be longer, more complex, and waged ever farther from Italy, the demographic demands imposed on the growing empire became significant. Although the men who served remained amateurs, the longer tours of duty paved the way for the advent of a professional military career, whereby many of these amateurs served in several consecutive wars.

At the end of the second century BCE, Gaius Marius undertook further important steps towards the military's professionalization and finalized a number of developments. These included enhanced training for individual soldiers, using techniques employed in gladiatorial schools (Frontin. *Str.* 4.2.2); the requirement that soldiers carry two weeks' worth of supplies in their packs while on campaigns (Frontin. *Str.* 4.1.7); and the recruitment of men without property. Hitherto there had been a property minimum for recruits in part because they were responsible for paying for their own equipment. This regular training, emphasis on discipline and fitness, and especially the hiring of men who owned no property meant that a body of soldiers depended on the commanders they served for their livelihood, not just during service but also during retirement. In other words, the army was well on its way to transforming from an amateur militia into a professional military.

Augustus advanced the process of professionalization considerably. After emerging victorious from the civil war with Marc Antony in 31 BCE, Augustus found himself in charge of almost 60 legions, each with varying loyalties. He discharged nearly half the soldiers and made the remainder permanent members of the new professional army. Terms of service were regulated, a military treasury (**aerarium militare**) was established, and remuneration for veterans was regularized. The majority of the soldiers were deployed to the empire's frontiers, where their units were to remain for the next four centuries (albeit with some modifications). This arrangement kept them well away from the centre of power, the city of Rome, and so less available to any ambitious individual who might wish to stage a coup. At the same time, they were also stationed in close proximity to Rome's most significant external threats, such as the Parthians in the east and the various Germanic peoples near the Rhine in the west. These changes also placed a group of individuals with disposable income in a position to impress the benefits of Roman rule upon non-Romans in the provinces and on the frontiers.

If the events of the late Republic and the civil wars that ended it had demonstrated that anyone who wished to rule Rome required the loyalty of the soldiers, the history of the Empire repeated the lesson time and time again. In many instances the Roman army attempted to raise generals and senators to the throne—sometimes successfully—and at other times soldiers played a significant role in the removal of emperors. When the emperor Caligula was assassinated in 41 CE, for instance, it was the praetorian guard who proclaimed Claudius, his uncle, successor. During the year of civil war that erupted following Nero's suicide in 68 CE, armies in the provinces and the praetorian guard in Rome were in turn the makers and assassins of short-lived emperors. It was, therefore, vital for an emperor to command the admiration and loyalty of the troops and to style himself as a fellow soldier, whether or not he was actually a military man.

Some emperors were more successful at this task than others. Active campaigning was a good way to win over the support of the soldiery, and those who undertook many campaigns tended to win good reputations. For example, Trajan, who waged successful wars in Dacia and Parthia, is remembered as one of Rome's greatest emperors. If he felt that there were no wars worth waging, a canny emperor might gain the goodwill of the troops with personal visits. Hadrian, on a tour of the provinces, made a point of witnessing the local soldiery performing manoeuvres and complimenting their skill. This event was even recorded for posterity in an inscription that details the drills carried out by the soldiers (both legionaries and auxiliaries) and Hadrian's approving pronouncement upon their abilities (see Box 13.3).

Primary Source

Box 13.3: *ILS*, 2487.

To the Cavalry of the Legion

Military exercises have their own laws somehow, and if something is added or taken away from them, the exercise would be easier or more difficult. But, as such difficult tasks are added, by so much is its esteem decreased. You have done the most difficult of the difficult manoeuvres, throwing the javelins while wearing corselets . . . furthermore I commend your spirit.

Warfare

It goes without saying that the Roman army is best known for waging war. It might come as a surprise, then, that some historians concentrate on the army's part in the creation and perpetuation of Roman society instead. Despite the charge that these scholars are in danger of straying too far from the focus on war, both roles are clearly important and deserve discussion.[26] This section will therefore focus on the Roman army at war and the next on the army and society.

Preparing for War

Roman soldiers practised rigorous drills in order to be well prepared for battle, and this is surely one of the reasons for the army's successes. Vegetius (*Mil.* 1.9, 1.10, 1.19, 1.23) describes the training in detail, including activities such as marching in step, marching with a heavy load, jumping, swimming, and using various kinds of weapons.[27] Roman soldiers may have trained regularly with wicker shields and wooden weapons, which were heavier than their regular equipment. Continuous repetition ensured that the soldiers were in the best possible shape in a serious engagement, something observed by Josephus in the aftermath of the Jewish War (see Box 13.4).

But the Roman army was also well prepared for conflict in other ways. Indeed, a large part of the army's success can be credited to its reliance on logistics and infrastructure. An elaborate system of roads criss-crossed the empire from Britain to Jordan. Rivers and the Mediterranean Sea served as a means for men to travel, supplies to be moved, and information to be communicated from one region to another relatively quickly, at least by ancient standards.

→ Compare Chapter 15, p. 346–7, and Chapter 16, pp. 361–3 and 365–6, on roads and transportation networks.

Primary Source

Box 13.4: Josephus, *The Jewish War*, 3.72–73, 74.

If someone looks into the entire organization of the (Roman) army it will be clear that they won this vast empire as a reward for their valour, not as a gift of fortune. For their nation is armed not only in war, and does not lie idle in times of peace and put on their armour only in times of need, but, as if they were born and grew with their armour on, they never receive a truce from their training, and they never wait until the critical moments . . . for they do not scatter in disorder from their customary formation, they are not paralyzed by fear, nor are they exhausted from hard work, and as a result of this they undoubtedly always win.

However, Roman response to an incursion would still have been rather slow. It might take several months to travel from one part of the empire to another, particularly if a considerable amount of that travel took place overland, through the interior of the empire. To shorten the response time, troops were often transferred from neighbouring regions. In the first and second centuries CE, individual legions or auxiliary units were moved in their entirety when reinforcements were required for war. From the latter half of the second century CE onwards, however, the Romans opted to move detachments of soldiers (called **vexillations**) rather than whole units. When offensives were undertaken, men and material were generally moved into position well in advance. The Romans also made full use of the resources in the immediate vicinity of their bases. Much of their food, for example, was produced locally,[28] and even their equipment was often produced on the spot. Only in the later Empire were the production and storage of such goods centralized.

One other significant aspect of Rome's success in combat was its devotion to security and its skill in field engineering. The Roman military was famous for erecting marching camps daily while on campaign. These temporary camps (they would be dismantled each day) included fortifications, ditches, and tents for the troops (Polyb. 6.26.10–6.34.6). Streets were marked out, and the tents were positioned according to centuries and legionary and auxiliary units.[29] These camps provided a means of defending the troops and their supplies while on campaign and a base from which they could launch operations and rest and recover afterwards (see Figure 13.2).

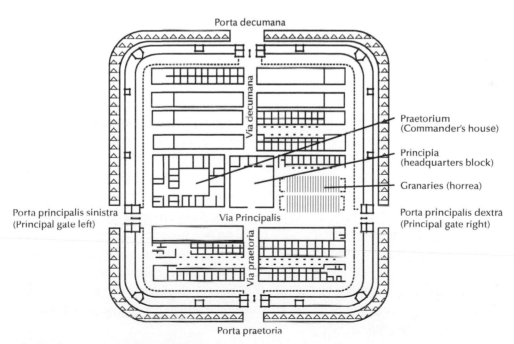

Figure 13.2 Plan of a Roman Military Base.

Permanent bases shared many of the features of the marching camps, including barracks for the rank-and-file soldiers, storage areas and granaries (*horrea*),[30] the general's quarters (*praetorium*), a headquarters building (*principia*), and two principal roads running at right angles to each other. Camps aside, the Romans sometimes went to extraordinary lengths in other ways while on campaign, providing other examples of their engineering mastery. Caesar (*BGall.* 4.17), for example, built a temporary bridge across the Rhine that was supported by piles driven into the riverbed.

Battle, Bravado, and Discipline

Battles were complicated and chaotic events. An initial flurry of missiles (arrows, javelins, and the like, such as lead balls from slings) accompanied taunts shouted from the opposing sides. After exchanging challenges and insults, units moved into position and began to advance. When the two sides collided the battle was fierce, loud, smelly, and potentially confusing. Frequently, the Romans emerged victorious from the heat of battle. Why? For some scholars the answer lies in the soldiers' discipline, a characteristic often highlighted in modern popular representations of the Roman army. Indeed, the army was known for its discipline in antiquity too.[31] For example, the practice of **decimation**, in which 1 out of 10 soldiers was chosen by lot and beaten (often to death) by his fellow comrades, made a deep impression on outsiders.[32] Polybius, a Greek author of the second century BCE who was captured by the Romans, came to admire soldiers and wrote an analysis of Rome's rise to Mediterranean domination. He stated that those on whose lot the punishment falls were beaten to death with cudgels, while the remainder of the guilty party (the other nine soldiers) received a milder punishment (Polyb. 6.38). In short, Polybius (6.39) argues that the army's system of rewards and punishments led it to such heights. In doing so, he reinforces the notion that the Romans combined individualism and group discipline in combat.

Other scholars, such as Ted Lendon, question strict adherence to rigid discipline as the ultimate answer and argue that the evidence suggests a combination of discipline, individualism, and bravado.[33] We do have examples in which Roman soldiers display considerable daring while acting as individuals rather than as part of a collective. Two of the main characters in the television series *Rome* are Titus Pullo, a bold and headstrong Roman legionary, and Lucius Vorenus, a conservative and dutiful Roman centurion. These fictional characters are based on two historical figures with the same names. They appear in a vivid episode from Caesar's *Gallic Wars*, in which the two men, both centurions, compete for honour while demonstrating a glaring lack of respect for traditional Roman discipline (see Box 13.5). The actions of men such as the historical Pullo and Vorenus cast doubt on the supposed rigid adherence to discipline for which the legions are famous.

Primary Source

Box 13.5: Caesar, *Gallic Wars*, 5.44.

There were in that legion the bravest of men, centurions, who were among the best in the ranks, Titus Pullo and Lucius Vorenus. These men were always arguing with each other over who would bear the attack first . . . one of them, Pullo, when the fighting was fiercest at the fortifications, said, "Why are you holding back, Vorenus?" "Or what opportunity are you expecting to prove your virtue? This day will decide our argument." When he had said this he went beyond the fortifications and attacked whichever part of the enemy forces seemed closest. Not even then was Vorenus himself contained by the wall, but he followed in fear of the opinion of all the others.

War: The Aftermath

After a victorious battle, the Romans buried their dead (usually in the area where they fell) and collected their equipment and any goods left behind by fallen enemy soldiers. There is no surviving record of post-traumatic stress disorder among ancient soldiers, but it is probable that individual soldiers were touched by the loss of their comrades, the experience of battle, and war more generally.[34] That said, it is noteworthy that the Romans were careful to preserve with monuments the memory of victories and only rarely honoured the dead in a similar manner. There is one lone surviving inscription from Adamklissi in Romania—in the provinces, that is—adjacent to Trajan's Trophy (*Tropaeum Traiani*) that may have listed 3,800 men who died fighting for Rome,[35] but this memorial appears to be exceptional, and there were no monuments to the fallen in the city of Rome.[36] In contrast, the city was filled with monuments to Roman conquests, including the triumphal Arch of Titus, erected in honour of Rome's victory in the Jewish Revolt (66–73 CE); Trajan's Column, erected in honour of Rome's victories in the emperor's Dacian Wars (101–102 CE, 105–106 CE; see Figure 13.3); the Flavian Amphitheatre (better known as the **Colosseum**); and the Altar of Augustan Peace.

This difference gives the impression that the Romans invariably celebrated victory while defeat was considered no more than an obstacle to overcome. To some degree this stubborn determination to win, even in the face of spectacular defeat, such as after the Battle of Cannae (216 BCE), is a good explanation of the ultimate success of the Romans. In a militaristic ancient world in which the Romans were the most successful state, generals, emperors, and citizens alike celebrated victory.

Figure 13.3 Battle scene from Trajan's Column. © Rod McLean/Alamy

The Army and Society

As important as combat was, the Roman soldier fought only part of the time. The relationship between the army and society was equally important and complicated. With the recent interest in the relationship between the army and the social formation during the Empire, as well as the growth in the body of evidence, it has become increasingly apparent just how complex this relationship was. In some cases the army acted as an instrument of power, carrying out—to the detriment of the inhabitants of the empire—the orders of the senate, the emperor, or provincial governors. In other cases soldiers were closely integrated into their neighbouring communities. Frontier military communities grew and flourished over time, and soldiers created families with local residents. Wives, partners, and children of the soldiery played an integral role in military life, both at the base itself and in the surrounding settlements (*vici* and *canabae*). For the people who inhabited the frontier regions, these Roman soldiers and their families were, for the most part, representative of Roman society itself.

The Army and Civilians: Policing and the Abuse of Authority

Roman soldiers were involved in a range of policing activities, from apprehending, escorting, and detaining brigands to quashing instances of civil unrest. Abundant evidence from the Levant[37] illustrates the rough treatment of civilians at the hands of the military.[38] Literary accounts reflect a similar impression of arrogant misuse of the authority wielded over the public by the soldiery. A notable example comes from an episode in Apuleius's novel, *Metamorphoses*, or *The Golden Ass*.[39] The hero of the story has been transformed into an ass. His owner, a gardener, rides him along a country road, where they are accosted by a Roman soldier who happens to pass them. The soldier barks some commands to the gardener who, ignorant of Latin, pays no attention to the demands. Enraged, the soldier knocks the gardener off the ass and shouts at him in Greek, proclaiming that he needs the ass to transport the governor's belongings. The gardener, however, flees with the ass to a neighbouring town, where they hide. Unfortunately for them, the soldier enlists the help of some comrades to track the pair down. They find the gardener in a chest and drag him out, thrust him in front of some Roman magistrates, and then haul him away to certain death while the ass is commandeered. Yet another fictional episode is perhaps also suggestive of reality: in Petronius's *Satyricon* (82) the character Encolpius rushes out from an inn into the street with sword in hand, only to be upbraided by a soldier who proceeds to steal that very sword.

Compare Chapter 11, pp. 252–5, on policing in the provinces.

Other, non-fictional examples of the mistreatment of civilians at the hands of soldiers also exist. The famous city of **Pompeii** was settled by perhaps as many as 2,000 of Sulla's veterans (plus their families) following the Social War between the Romans and Italians (91–88 BCE).[40] Besides losing much of their property, many of the city's original inhabitants also lost whatever influence they may have previously had in local affairs because the veterans managed the city.[41] We also have letters from Egypt in which civilians highlight the wrongs committed against them by soldiers, sometimes in conjunction with other members of the public. In the *Oxyrhynchus Papyrus* (19.2234) we find a complaint written to a certain Quintus Gaius Passer, a centurion, about being attacked by a group that included a few fishermen and at least one soldier.

See Introduction, p. xxix, on Roman colonization of Pompeii and consequent questions about the dedication of its amphitheatre.

Though ostensibly engaged in actions on behalf of the state, soldiers sometimes committed theft through the unlawful requisition of boats, animals, and persons. One of several attempts to combat this exists in a papyrus from Egypt dating to 133–137 CE (*PSI* 5.446). Extortion by soldiers was another problem (for example, Luke 3:14), and one papyrus (*SB* 6.9207) lists the blackmail "required" by a soldier. While the soldiers were meant to protect civilians and enforce law and order (and we have evidence in which they were called upon to do just that, such as *P.Ryl.* 2.141), it appears that they were at times, perhaps even often, the cause of the trouble.

The Army and Civilians: Women and Families

The Roman army has traditionally been thought of as a male institution, operating in a male-dominated community. Until relatively recently, the consensus was that Roman bases were filled almost exclusively with men, except for the occasional prostitute from the neighbouring *canabae* or *vici*. The rhetoric of Roman authors (for example, Juv. 6.398–402 and Hdn. 3.8.4), which stresses the negative influence of women on the effectiveness of soldiers, supports this view of an all-male camp. Further proof was to be found in Roman law, which barred soldiers (though not officers) from marrying. Scholars were inclined to believe that soldiers adhered to this stipulation.[42]

Prostitutes are generally thought to have been a staple of the *canabae* and *vici* near the bases, but there is also evidence that some may have actually worked on the bases. At the legionary fortress of Vindonissa in Switzerland, for example, a woman named Belica worked at a tavern (or brothel) within the base's walls.[43] Furthermore, for all that soldiers were prohibited from marrying, perhaps as many as 20 per cent of those serving in non-commissioned ranks formed unions that were, for all intents and purposes, marriages.[44]

Numerous papyri that have survived in the Egyptian desert and wooden tablets found in abundance at **Vindolanda** in the north of England document the lives of Roman military personnel, especially regarding their families. We have letters exchanged between soldiers, between soldiers and their parents, between soldiers and other members of the imperial government, between soldiers and civilians, and between the family members of the Roman military, including letters from the wives of officers in some units to their counterparts in others. Archaeological evidence also provides a wealth of information. For example, the small items occasionally found at such sites, including men's, women's, and even children's shoes, brooches, and spindle whorls, confirm that soldiers, slaves, women, and children were all present in these communities (see Figure 13.4). The fact that the emperor Gaius was given the nickname "Caligula" ("Little Boots") by the soldiery as he accompanied his father on military campaigns as a child (Suet. *Calig.* 9) also points to the presence of the wives and children of leading officers in military camps.

Although the evidence is far from conclusive, it does suggest that not all interactions between soldiers and civilians were negative. The letter quoted in Box 13.6 (a birthday invitation of Claudia Severa to Sulpicia Lepidinia) is one of many pieces of documentary evidence from Vindolanda, dating to the late first century CE and early second century CE, that shows the prominent role that women played in Roman auxiliary military life, at least amongst the officer class.

Figure 13.4 Examples of more elaborate footwear from Vindolanda, with the leather of the uppers cut away to produce a type of "fishnet" effect. Despite their flimsy appearance, such boots were hard-wearing. Credit: Vindolanda and Roman Army Museum, Northumberland, UK / Photo © Neil Holmes / The Bridgeman Art Library

Primary Source

Box 13.6: *T. Vindol.* 2.291.

Claudia Severa to her Lepidina, hello! I happily invite you, sister, to my birthday on the third day before the Ides of September, as you would make it a much better day if you come see us, me especially . . . say hello to your husband Cerialis. My husband, Aelius, and our little son pass along their greetings . . . I'll be expecting you, sister. So long sister, my dear soul.

The Army as Distinct Society[45]

Quite apart from the relationship between the army and wider society is the problem of whether the former should be considered a distinct society. Many of the elite writers of the imperial period who comment on political and social issues of their recent past or their present (for example, Tacitus and Juvenal) betray a marked distrust and dislike of the soldiery. It is fair to say that much of this negativity hinges on the army's changing character. As previously discussed, the army was originally made up of Roman and Italian citizen-soldiers with whom Roman writers could identify, but it came to comprise Roman citizens and foreigners from the provinces who had little connection with the **senatorial** elite, who wrote many of the surviving texts.

What is more, where Italy had witnessed a considerable degree of militarization during the republican period, especially during the civil wars of the first century BCE, this was not the case during the imperial period, when Italy experienced a time of relative peace. The bulk of Rome's soldiers were based on the distant frontiers, far removed from the political and social affairs in the heart of the empire and far away from the authors whose works survive. Legionaries and auxiliaries in uniform were therefore a rare sight in Italy. Those that were seen often looked quite different from the soldiers that made up the praetorian guard, and their appearances in the capital tended to coincide with civil war. The exception comes from the reign of Septimius Severus (193–211 CE), who filled the praetorian guard with soldiers from his own legions (see Box 13.2).[46] The historian Cassius Dio (75.2.6) complains bitterly about their presence in Rome, saying that they were crude in appearance and vulgar in speech. In general, many soldiers did not speak Latin or knew only a smattering of Latin commands. This was true not only for the auxiliaries but also for the legionary and auxiliary soldiers stationed in the eastern half of the empire, where the principal language of administration was Greek. These soldiers looked different, had accents, and, as far as many Roman writers were concerned, might as well have been from a different world.

Summary

During the imperial period, most of the Roman army's troops were based on Rome's frontiers. Soldiers spent the majority of their lives there, perhaps 20 or 25 years, if not more. The frontier regions were often complex and colourful areas where the local people tended to straddle the line between Roman and non-Roman. Despite the fact that the army operated in and was part of a land of the "other," the presence of women and children in and around military bases demonstrates that the Roman military community contained many of the elements of wider Roman society.

The Roman army was composed of individuals rather than human droids and was populated by Romans and non-Romans, much like the empire it served. Roman soldiers could make or break emperors and were prone to committing acts of cruelty against members of the public, the very public that celebrated the Roman army's victory in war. The Romans were usually victorious thanks to their meticulous preparations, strict discipline, bravado, and relatively arduous recruitment process that weeded out the less able. Ultimately, the historical Roman soldiers were not the soldiers that we usually find in movies but were, like their compatriots, individuals within complex communities.

Questions for Review and Discussion

1. What criteria were included in the Roman army's recruitment process?
2. What are the three divisions within the Roman army and how do they differ?
3. Why were the Romans so successful in combat?
4. Is it fair to characterize the Roman soldiers as faceless grunts? Why or why not?
5. Should the evidence that we have for the Roman army be characterized as limited? Why or why not?

Suggested Reading

Campbell, B. 1984. *The Emperor and the Roman Army 31 BC–AD 235*. Oxford: Clarendon Press.

Campbell's book is the definitive study of the relationship between the soldier and the emperor.

Erdkamp, P., ed. 2007. *A Companion to the Roman Army*. Oxford: Blackwell.

This collection of essays includes varied subject matter, such as military documentation, frontiers, and veteran settlement.

Goldsworthy, A. 1996. *The Roman Army at War 100 BC–AD 200*. Oxford: Clarendon Press.
    Modelled on Keegan's *The Face of Battle* (London, 1976), this book is a study of the Roman army in battle, particularly the experience of the common soldiery.

Isaac, B. 1992. *The Limits of Empire: The Roman Army in the East*. Oxford: Oxford University Press.
    This wide-ranging book looks at the impact of the army on civilians in the East, as well as the much-debated issue of grand strategy.

James, S. 2004. *The Excavations at Dura-Europos Conducted by Yale University and the French Academy of Inscriptions and Letters, 1928 to 1937. Final Report VII. The Arms and Armour and Other Military Equipment*. London: British Museum Press.
    More than simply a catalogue of the spectacular finds from Dura-Europos, this book explores soldierly identity, combat, and the transformation of the army.

Le Bohec, Y. 2000. *The Imperial Roman Army*. London and New York: Routledge.
    Le Bohec presents a detailed study of the organization, strategy, and fighting abilities of the imperial army.

Lendon, J.E. 2005. *Soldiers and Ghosts: A History of Battle in Classical Antiquity*. New Haven, CT: Yale University Press.
    A cultural history of Greek and Roman warfare, this text looks at the impact of cultural change on the nature of combat in antiquity.

Phang, S. 2001. *The Marriage of Roman Soldiers (13 BC–AD 235)*. Leiden, The Netherlands: Brill.
    Phang takes a wide-ranging look at the marriage of soldiers and also has much to say about the nature of broader military communities.

Roth, J. 1999. *The Logistics of the Roman Army at War (264 BC–AD 235)*. Leiden, The Netherlands: Brill.
    This text is a study of Roman military supply that focuses on food, goods, supply routes, and organization.

Sabin, P., H. Van Wees, and M. Whitby, eds. 2007. *The Cambridge History of Greek and Roman Warfare Volume II: Rome from the Late Republic to the Late Empire*. Cambridge: Cambridge University Press.
    Now the definitive overview of the Roman imperial army through late antiquity, this collection covers everything from international relations to battle, with two specific chapters entitled "War and Society."

Notes

1   All other translations are mine unless otherwise noted.
2   Roth (1994: 362).
3   *Dig.* 49.16.4–9, 11, 16.
4   Campbell (1984: 19–32).
5   See further Bishop and Coulston (2005: 260–7).
6   We might expect even more variety with regard to their camp attire, but it is hard to be certain given that organic materials tend not to survive in the archaeological record.

7   Gilliver (2007).

8   Rathbone (2007b: 162).

9   Ibid.: 163.

10   A notable exception comes from the reign of Marcus Aurelius (161–180 CE) when Italians, and possibly some Noricans, were enrolled in newly created legions of the *Legio II Italica* and the *Legio III Italica*. In this instance the unusual measure was taken because Marcus Aurelius was concerned that the Germanic Marcommani and Quadi might invade Italy.

11   *RMD* 2. The Sugambrians were a Germanic people from what is now the Netherlands.

12   *CIL* 3.7504. The Dardanians were from the Balkans.

13   *CIL* 16.22. Cilicia corresponds to Anatolia in modern-day Turkey.

14   The different terminology reflects the differences in these swords and spears from those used by legionaries.

15   Le Bohec (2000: 123).

16   Bishop and Coulston (2005: 254–9); Rankov (2007: 58, 62). The evidence, as it turns out, is not unequivocal one way or the other.

17   Bishop and Coulston (2005: 259). Tacitus (*Agr.* 35) presents a similar situation in his biography of his father-in-law, Agricola.

18   Rankov (2007: 52). Compare Tac. *Hist.* 4.12–3.

19   The first Roman encounter with Cataphracts dates back to the middle republican period in the wars with the Seleucids (Livy 35.48.3). Rome's foes in what is now Iran, whether Parthian or Sasanian, continued to use them, as did the Sarmatians.

20   Some were given to members of the fleet and some to the praetorian guard.

21   The number of surviving diplomas drops as the number of citizens enrolling in those auxiliary units rises. For those who were already citizens, money was likely the reward.

22   There is no direct evidence of this practice.

23   Compare Hdn. 2.14.5 and Rankov (207: 72–3).

24   For more on this issue, see James (2002).

25   Rankov (2007: 58) notes that soldiers, at least on parade, would have looked generally homogeneous while varying in detail. On the unique representations of soldiers of the Twentieth Cohort of Palmyrenes (*cohors XX Palmyrenorum*) on the "Terentius Painting," a mid-third-century CE fresco from Dura-Europos, see James (2004).

26   Goldsworthy (1996).

27   Veg. *Mil.* 1.1, 1.9, 1.10, 1.19, 2.23.

28   Stallibrass and Thomas (2008).

29   Rankov (2007: 67).

30   The granaries were restricted to permanent bases.

31   Watson (1969: 117–26).

32   Rankov (2007: 65). During the imperial period, decimation became increasingly unpopular (Phang 2008: 123–9).

33   Lendon (2005: 163–315).

34   Melchior (2011).

35   *CIL* 3.14214.

36   The majority of tombstones for Roman soldiers commemorate men who died in camp rather than in battle. See Hope (2003).

37   Roughly, Israel, Palestine, Jordan, Syria, Lebanon, and parts of Iraq.

38   Isaac (1992: 104–40, 269–82, 291–304).

39   Apul. 9.39–10.1.

40   Zanker (1998: 62).

41   Ibid.: 61–2.

42   See Tac. *Ann.* 14.27 and Cass. Dio 60.24.3. More definitive evidence for the existence of the ban is found in the *Cattaoui Papyrus*. A detailed overview of the evidence for a marriage ban among the soldiery is found in Phang (2001: 13–114).

43   Allison (2006: 3).

44   James (2006: 32). James arrived at the figure of 20 per cent on Scheidel's (1996b: 117–29) assumption that about 30 per cent of soldiers would have been over the age of 35 and Phang's (2001: 164–90) suggestion that ordinary soldiers tended to marry relatively late. On the other hand, nearly 70 per cent of auxiliary diplomas include a wife or partner, which suggests that the number who formed unions was perhaps much higher than 20 per cent. Compare Greene (2011).

45   Note MacMullen's (1984b) article of similar title.

46   Compare Hdn. 2.14.5 and Rankov (2007: 72–3).

14

Foreign Relations: War and Conquest

Greg Fisher

According to the Roman historian Cassius Dio, the emperor Trajan, at the end of his victorious campaign in what is now Iraq, stood at the entrance to the Persian Gulf and lamented his fate as an old man. Watching a ship leave for eastern ports, he declared: "I should certainly have crossed over to the Indi, too, if I were still young."[1] Like many Roman leaders, including Julius Caesar before and Caracalla after him, Trajan felt the heavy legacy of the ghost of Alexander the Great, who had conquered large swathes of Asia as far as Afghanistan and Pakistan nearly four centuries earlier. It was in fact the Romans who bestowed the epithet "the Great" on Alexander, and Dio imagines Trajan thinking that, if he were lucky, he would cross to India to see what Alexander had seen and to conquer further. Unable to do so because of his age, Trajan consoled himself with his exuberant claim to the Roman senate that he had gone further than Alexander. This statement was false, but under Trajan's reign the Roman Empire encompassed more territory than at any other time in its history. Few emperors better exemplify the central role that the conquest of neighbours and foreign enemies played in Roman political life and in society more generally.

Introduction

From the very beginning of Roman history, military virtue and the glory gained by the defeat of others were deeply ingrained into Roman social values and self-conception. The *cursus honorum* of the Republic encouraged ambitious aristocrats to compete with each other for the senior position of consul, through which they would lead armies into battle and gain the rewards of victory on the battlefield. Such ideas drove an ethos of conquest and ensured that Rome would not remain an isolationist power.

Timeline

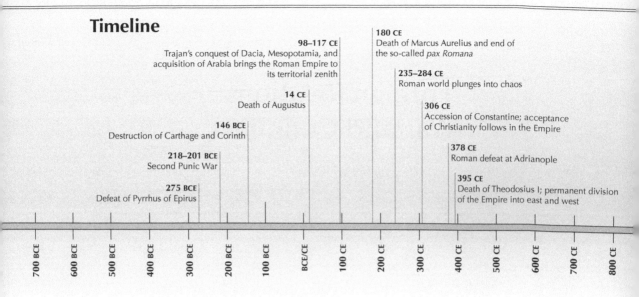

98–117 CE
Trajan's conquest of Dacia, Mesopotamia, and
acquisition of Arabia brings the Roman Empire to
its territorial zenith

14 CE
Death of Augustus

146 BCE
Destruction of Carthage and Corinth

218–201 BCE
Second Punic War

275 BCE
Defeat of Pyrrhus of Epirus

180 CE
Death of Marcus Aurelius and end of
the so-called *pax Romana*

235–284 CE
Roman world plunges into chaos

306 CE
Accession of Constantine; acceptance
of Christianity follows in the Empire

378 CE
Roman defeat at Adrianople

395 CE
Death of Theodosius I; permanent division
of the Empire into east and west

700 BCE 600 BCE 500 BCE 400 BCE 300 BCE 200 BCE 100 BCE BCE/CE 100 CE 200 CE 300 CE 400 CE 500 CE 600 CE 700 CE 800 CE

Yet as Roman armies defeated their neighbours and added territory, Roman society was changed by the wars and interactions with foreign peoples. The influx of wealth prompted ambitious attempts at social reform; alienated allies rebelled in a long and bloody civil war; and the acquisition of overseas territories provided the backdrop for new forms of political competition as republican government proved inadequate to the running of a foreign empire. As Rome conquered the ancient lands of the Near East, there began a slow shift in the political and cultural centre of gravity that, by the death of the emperor Constantine in 336 CE, relegated the city of Rome to a supporting role and introduced Greek, not Latin, as the dominant bureaucratic language of the Empire. A new capital was established at Constantinople (modern Istanbul), and, by the third and fourth centuries CE, new military capitals placed to oppose Rome's Germanic and Iranian enemies made the city of Rome—as well as the old heartlands of Spain, Gaul, and the Italian peninsula—increasingly irrelevant.

At the same time, the Empire's relations with its neighbours had significant consequences. In the west, Roman frontier policies towards Germanic "barbarians" (people who were neither Roman nor Greek) helped to create powerful groups of people who grew strong enough to challenge Roman dominion. In the east, Rome's wars with the Sassanids so weakened both parties that the Arab takeover of the Near East was greatly facilitated. Clearly, any understanding of Roman society and culture must also include an understanding of Roman expansion, conquest, and foreign relations.

This chapter will examine how the Roman Republic, and then the Empire, subjugated its neighbours and sought to intimidate and control them. Framed between the third century BCE (the period following the conquest of Italy) and the late fourth century CE (the end of attempts to hold the Empire united in the face of numerous enemies) and based around key events such as the defeat of Carthage and the rise of the Sassanid Empire, the chapter will show how the Romans conducted their foreign campaigns and conquered the lands around them. It will also consider some of the consequences of those actions.

———— • ◆ • ————

Foreign Relations and Expansion to the End of the Second Punic War: Concepts and Themes

Rome's relations with its neighbours during the early and middle Republic are marked by a number of concepts and practices that together informed its military actions and, ultimately, Rome's history in this period and beyond. However, the practical habit of creating alliances that assured the manpower necessary to undertake wars (and sometimes sparked war itself), the ideal of **bellum iustum** ("just war") that underlay conflict, and the fame attendant upon militarily successful leaders all complicate the issue of whether Rome's wars were defensive or offensive strikes.

In the words of Plutarch (*Pyrrh.* 25), the bloody defeat of King Pyrrhus of Epirus in a campaign between 282 and 275 BCE had given the Romans "high courage and power, and a reputation for incivility from their valour in these struggles."[2] The subjugation of the Italian peninsula and the incorporation of defeated peoples such as Samnites and Etruscans into a comprehensive system of mutually supportive alliances provided the Romans with a massive reserve of manpower and resources. These alliances had proved their worth in defeating Pyrrhus: Plutarch (*Pyrrh.* 21) casts the downtrodden Hellenistic dynast as looking on in despair as he noticed that, after each defeat, "the army of the Romans, as if from a fountain gushing forth indoors, was easily and speedily filled up again." The king also noted that the Romans "did not lose courage in defeat . . . (instead) their wrath gave them all the more vigour and determination for the war." The outcome of the conflict with Pyrrhus was immensely significant in that the Romans proved the superiority of their alliances and the depth of their manpower reserves, factors that would underwrite Roman victory in future conflicts.

Roman aggression and martial valour was masked by an ancient, if increasingly disingenuous, desire to fight just and legal wars. Rome's relations with its neighbours were considered to be overseen by the Roman gods and were therefore tended by the rituals of a **college** of priests known as the *fetiales*, who were responsible for the ritual formulation of treaties and declaration of war. Tradition held that only aggression in self-defence was acceptable and that the *fetiales* would act as heralds or ambassadors, presenting Roman demands to a community or state held to have wronged the Roman people (this was, of course, a rudimentary form of diplomacy). If the offending community could offer no satisfaction within a stated period of time, war would be declared by a spear hurled into (now enemy) territory by one of the priests. In later history, when enemy territory was increasingly distant from the city of Rome, the ritual was undertaken in the city, in the precinct of the Temple of Bellona. Only if these procedures were properly followed could the war become a *bellum iustum*, a "just," divinely approved, and thus morally defensible conflict.[3]

Victory was shared by gods and humans. Legally declared and successfully concluded wars that resulted in at least 5,000 enemy deaths might earn its victorious general a **triumph**, in which he dressed in triumphal garb, painted his face purple, and paraded through the city, accompanied by his soldiers and displaying captives and booty to the admiring crowd. The destination of the procession was the Temple of Jupiter Optimus Maximus (whose icon the purple face of the triumphant general was meant to emulate) on the Capitoline Hill, where the general would undertake sacrifices in gratitude for divine support. Less glorious wars—those with fewer enemy deaths or concluded against enemies considered less worthy opponents

See Chapter 17, p. 393, for the representations of triumphs in art and architecture.

Compare Chapter 9, pp. 195–6, on sacrifice and see figure 9.1, no. 6, for the location of the Temple of Jupiter Optimus Maximus.

(such as slaves)—might earn an **ovation**, a more modest procession. That the degree of glory and divine pleasure was understood to be reflected in the body count of the enemy is a telling feature of the Roman attitude towards war and of Roman self-perception.

Invitations from beleaguered allies could also be a useful way to defend a war. Rome's initial drawn-out conflict with Carthage (264–241 BCE) began in much the same way as the war with Pyrrhus had, with pro-Roman "friends" asking for help. In this case, however, a poorly judged "friendship" with the Spanish city of Saguntum would pull the Romans into what is perhaps the defining event of the Republic—the war with Hannibal—the outcome of which would seal Roman supremacy in the western Mediterranean and serve notice to those in the East of Rome's growing power. Livy (21.1), whose magisterial history provides the narrative for the war, attributes its inception to a Carthaginian desire for revenge in the figure of Hannibal Barca. Deprived of Sicily as a result of the First Punic War, the Carthaginians tried to rebuild in Spain, an action initially tolerated by the Roman **senate**, which agreed that the River Ebro would be the demarcation between the two. The problem with this arrangement was the town of Saguntum, located south of the Ebro and in the Carthaginian sphere.

In the third century BCE, the Romans had developed the concept of **amicitia**, friendly relations with peoples outside their immediate scope of influence. *Amicitia* can best be understood as a form of association rather than an actual friendship. Like many relationships between Rome and its allies—for example, those in Italy, with whom the devastating Social War of the first century BCE would be fought over the inequality of their "alliance"—*amicitia* was certainly not a balanced partnership in any sense of the word but consistently favoured Roman interests over those of the other party.[4] Saguntum was one city that had concluded a treaty of *amicitia* with Rome, notably arranged after the Roman agreement with Carthage (Livy 21.2). But when Hannibal attacked it, the Romans dithered and the town was forced to surrender. A belated embassy of senators to Carthage and a demand for peace followed (by which the fiction of the *bellum iustum* might be satisfied), but it was rejected by the Carthaginian senate and the Second Punic War was declared in 218 BCE. According to Livy (21.1), this war was so convoluted in its frequent reversals of fortune that the Romans, who won, were nearly destroyed in the process. Indeed, it was the closest Rome would come to total defeat for nearly 800 years.

Deprived of a navy, the Carthaginians crossed into Italy by land over the Alps, a near-miraculous feat, especially with war elephants. Hannibal proved to be an exceptional battlefield commander, defeating the Romans in four engagements. In 218 BCE the Romans were beaten at the Ticinus River (in northern Italy) and then at the Trebia. Livy (21.53; compare Box 14.1) casts the blame on tensions between Roman **consuls**, a familiar theme in his narrative, in which youth and arrogance often triumph over wisdom

See Chapter 10, pp. 229–33 and 236, on consuls and dictators.

and caution with disastrous results. Worse was to come in 217 BCE, when the consul Flaminius, a disdainful populist, marched his army into an ambush at Lake Trasimene and the soldiers became trapped in thick fog between the lake and the hills. Those who tried to escape by swimming drowned under the weight of their armour. Flaminius was killed, and the Romans were saved only by the emergency appointment of a **dictator**, the famous Quintus Fabius Maximus (nicknamed "the Delayer" by his detractors). Yet Fabius's tactics of avoiding pitched battle, combined with the strength of Roman alliances—the source of power against Pyrrhus—allowed the Romans to battle a year later at Cannae. Here another populist consul, Varro, insisted on abandoning caution. In the rout that followed, Varro's consular colleague, Aemilius Paullus, was left dead on the battlefield, along with almost the entire army of 80,000. It was a disaster unequalled until Adrianople, nearly 600 years later.

Despite these victories, Hannibal did not attack Rome (why he did not press his advantage remains something of a mystery). The Romans entered a period of soul-searching and self-doubt, especially as some allies, notably Capua, deserted them. They tried public human sacrifice to appease the gods. But the senate remained strong, and the Roman people refused to give up, even when King Philip V of Macedon forged an alliance with Hannibal. The Romans also rebuilt. Capua was recaptured in 213 BCE, while the senate sold its silver and gold to raise new **legions**. By 209 BCE Tarentum, another fickle

Political History

Box 14.1: Rivalry among Colleagues and Military Disasters

Competition between aristocrats was an essential aspect of Roman politics, and the use of collegial offices in the republican *cursus honorum* underscored the spirit of rivalry that lay beneath the façade of a system ostensibly designed to control it. During the Second Punic War, the flaws of the Romans' use of two consuls were exposed, with catastrophic results similar to those that proved to be their undoing at Adrianople 600 years later. At each of the four main military confrontations—Ticinus, Trebia, Lake Trasimene, and Cannae—arguments between consuls (one of which was typically senatorial; the other, populist) hampered the Romans' ability to fight. For example, Livy (21.53) tells us that, before the battle at the Trebia (218 BCE), Sempronius virtually accused his co-consul, Scipio (father of Africanus), of cowardice. Yet Scipio had been wounded at the Ticinus engagement shortly beforehand, and Sempronius saw this weakness as an opportunity for military glory by pushing prematurely for a fight with Hannibal. In an invented speech, one of Livy's favourite literary devices, he has Sempronius evoke the honour of Rome's victorious soldiers in the First Punic War and the shame that they would feel to see their sons afraid to fight Hannibal. Sempronius's harangue worked, and he duly led the Romans to fight—and to defeat.

To some extent, Livy creates the tension between Sempronius and Scipio for literary purposes, but competition between politicians was an inescapable part of republican and imperial politics and played a significant role in driving conquest. The Republic collapsed amidst the desire of people such as Marius and Sulla to outdo each other, and young men such as Caesar looked for wars to bolster their reputations. Well before he dreamt of going to Gaul, Caesar had tired of his intended career as a **rhetor** and had raised a force to fight in the Mithridatic War.

Political competition continued to have deadly results under the Empire, producing instability and, sometimes, disaster. At Adrianople, a climate of jealousy emerged between Valens and Gratian that was almost a virtual repeat of Livy's scenarios of the Second Punic War. In all these cases, Roman politicians sought to make use of the opportunities for war to further their own goals. Many of Rome's wars were fought opportunistically, and this is a key point for understanding how the Romans conducted themselves with regard to their neighbours and, of course, to their perception of their own governmental responsibilities.

ally, was sacked and punished and the consul Claudius Marcellus was active in Sicily, where the famous mathematician Archimedes led the defence at Syracuse. In 212 BCE the general Cornelius Scipio and his brother Gnaeus were killed. The former's son, soon to be known as Scipio Africanus, took over in Spain. In the savage fighting there, Africanus (Livy's great hero) made his name and built his reputation.

In 207 BCE a Carthaginian army was overwhelmed in northern Italy, and Hannibal was forced to accept that his long campaign, which had come so close to success, was now facing a heavy defeat. Africanus became consul two years later and, circumventing the senate (which saw him as another young adventurer, like Varro), had himself assigned to the war in Africa, where he faced Hannibal in battle in 202 BCE. Defeated at Zama, Hannibal fled to the court of the Seleucid monarch Antiochus in Syria. Africanus had finished the war, and Rome—so nearly annihilated after Cannae—was finally victorious.

The Second Punic War is crucial for understanding how Rome subsequently conducted its foreign relations and how conflicts were changing Rome. With Carthage crushed, Rome was now dominant in the western Mediterranean. It had acquired vast landholdings, new allies, wealth, plunder, and slaves. Its power was noticed by the monarchs of the eastern Mediterranean—people such as Philip V, whose alliance with Hannibal now looked like poor judgment, and Antiochus, who sheltered the defeated Carthaginian commander. The conduct of the war also magnified a rising tension in republican politics. While the senate had remained the core of Roman resistance to Hannibal and had emerged from the war with immense prestige, it could not hope to always control the generals who used the climate of fear and the opportunities presented by conflict to their advantage. So it was that the success of Scipio Africanus also created a new spectre in Roman politics: a man who commanded the loyalty of his troops and who looked to overseas wars, not to the state, to make his name. The tension between ambitious men and the senate would reach its zenith with Marc Antony and Octavian (the future emperor Augustus), a rivalry that would destroy the Republic for good.

Roman Expansion in the Second Century BCE: Greed and Fear?

After the Second Punic War, the Romans expanded into the eastern Mediterranean, sacking Corinth and Carthage in 146 BCE. The question of whether such actions reflected a deliberate policy of expansion and an abandonment of the *bellum iustum* is difficult to answer. There is no real consensus amongst modern scholars on this matter, which has emerged as one of the classic problems of Roman history and a matter of ongoing debate. There are indications that the Romans occasionally conquered out of greed but also suggestions that they sometimes acted pre-emptively out of fear of being conquered.

Attempts to find a definitive answer to the question of whether the Romans were deliberately aiming to build an empire are compounded by the fact that the literary histories can be used to justify both the "greed" and the "fear" positions.[5] For example, Polybius notes that, on the eve of the First Punic War, fear of Carthaginian domination motivated Roman actions (see Box 14.2). Regarding the end of the Third Punic War, Polybius (37.1) refers to the idea that the Roman destruction reflected sound judgment,

Primary Source

Box 14.2: Polybius, 1.10.[1]

The Romans were long in doubt . . . but they yet saw that Carthaginian aggrandisement was not confined to Libya, but had embraced many districts in Spain as well; and that Carthage was, besides, mistress of all the islands in the Sardinian and Tyrrhenian seas: they were beginning, therefore, to be exceedingly anxious lest, if the Carthaginians became masters of Sicily also, they should find them very dangerous and formidable neighbours, surrounding them as they would on every side, and occupying a position which commanded all the coasts of Italy.

Note

1. Translated by Paton (1922).

commenting that "the removal of a perpetual menace, and the utter destruction of a city which had disputed the supremacy with [Rome], were the actions of sensible and far-sighted men." Even so, Polybius offers a different view by saying that wars with Pyrrhus and Hannibal provided the experience and desire for overseas conquest. He bluntly states that, after such conflicts, "it was perfectly natural that they not only gained the courage to strive for universal dominion, but (eventually) attained their aim" (Polyb. 1.63).

The militaristic nature of Roman society suggests that Polybius is not entirely wrong, but it is also hard to ignore the fact that the Romans were content to avoid the seizure of foreign territory for some time. For example, between 200 and 196 BCE, the Romans were invited to intervene in a dispute between Philip V and Antiochus on one side and two Roman allies, Pergamum and Rhodes, on the other. In 197 BCE Philip was defeated by a Roman expeditionary force, but the Romans avoided any territorial claims and the Roman commander, Flamininus, used the cliché of "freeing the Greeks" to show Roman support for the people of Greece in protecting them from Philip. Plutarch (*Flam.* 10) writes that the Greeks welcomed this proclamation with such a loud cheer that stunned birds fell from the sky. Clearly, "freeing the Greeks" was a disingenuous exercise, but it was also a telling insight into Roman plans: they did not want to occupy territory. At the same time, though, Greece became a protectorate, which only ensured more Roman intervention. Antiochus's interference in Greek affairs soon attracted another Roman army, and in 190 BCE the brother of Africanus, Scipio Asiaticus, won a famous victory at Magnesia.

Between 171 and 168 BCE the Romans found themselves back in Greece, fighting Perseus (son of Philip) in the Third Macedonian War. While the king of Pergamum, Eumenes, convinced the Romans to fight Perseus, Rome's African ally Massinissa claimed that Carthage was planning an alliance with the Macedonians. It was all too much for an exasperated senate, who ordered an expeditionary force to Macedonia, and Perseus was defeated at Pydna in 168 BCE. The historian Appian's (*Mac.* 9.11) verdict on the aftermath is revealing: the senate, he says, destroyed Perseus because of his ambition. Essentially, the Romans were unwilling to tolerate his power so close to their own.

After 148 BCE it seems that the Romans gradually gave up on a system that used intimidation and occasional displays of "invited" or justified force instead of occupation, although invitations could still be useful. As previously mentioned, Corinth and Carthage were sacked. Revealing his repugnance at the latter's recovery in the Second Punic War, Cato the Elder famously added the refrain that it should be eliminated to every speech he made in the senate (Plut. *Cat. Mai.* 26). A Roman force led by Scipio Aemilianus (the grandson of Aemilius Paullus) destroyed the city and enslaved or exiled its population. The result was a new province: Africa. Other examples include Macedonia, which was annexed after a brief rebellion, and Achaea, which became the property of the Roman people and was later formalized as part of the provincial system in 27 BCE.

Compare Chapter 5, p. 106, on the Aemilii Paulli and strategic adoption.

The End of the Republic: The Consequences of Conquest

Although the reasons for Rome's new-found interest in acquiring territory are unclear, it is evident that the set of deleterious social and economic consequences of such conquest came to a head in the last century of the Republic. In 133 BCE the king of Pergamum, a long-time Roman ally, died and left his kingdom to the Roman senate, who renamed his gift the province of Asia. Following this event, the Romans seemed content to take land from their neighbours in a more deliberate fashion. An appeal for help from the Greek city of Massilia resulted in the almost casual annexation of the territory surrounding it as Gallia Narbonensis, whose real estate provided a land route to Spain and thus a huge advantage to the Romans. More "invitations" followed, and the Roman senate took the opportunity to add Majorca, parts of the Balkans, Cilicia, and Cyrenaica to the empire. People were settled and roads were constructed, all the better to cement Roman control. The need to govern these possessions gave new opportunities to *publicani* and ambitious politicians, who found that provincial appointments held the prospect of accumulating fabulous wealth.

Compare Chapter 15, pp. 341–2, on the *publicani*.

That Roman conquest overseas caused disruption at home is amply demonstrated by the Gracchi's attempts to relieve the problems of the Italian peasants in the late second century BCE. During this time, the lives and livelihoods of this population may have traditionally been suspected of being threatened by long tours of duty abroad and

→ Compare Chapter 1, p. 17, for recent ideas on the plight of Italian peasants and Chapter 4, pp. 79 and 82–3, on slave-worked farms.

the development of *latifundia* ("corporate farms") worked by influxes of new slaves. Furthermore, grievances soon resulted in war at home too. The Social War reflected the Roman allies' belief that they were not being adequately compensated for providing a disproportionate share of troops to Rome's conquests. The war ended with Roman acquiescence to demands for a better division of the spoils and citizenship for a wide range of Italian communities. Finally, as ambitious men used the resources of Rome's young empire to further their own naked desire for power, Rome's political fabric changed and republican government was replaced by a monarchy. That this shift was based around Rome's foreign relations is an important point.

The notorious rivals of the early first century BCE, Marius and Sulla, each depended upon the glory to be won in foreign wars to build their reputations at home. Marius made his name fighting in North Africa and in Gaul; Sulla saw opportunities in the generation-long struggle with Mithridates, the king of Pontus (a region now in northern Turkey) between 89 and 63 BCE. The war with Mithridates dragged on for so long that it also provided a valuable proving ground for some of Marius and Sulla's successors in ambition, Pompey, Caesar, and Crassus. These men, later the members of the so-called First Triumvirate, favoured overseas warfare as a means to pursue their personal goals for power. Each would seek glory, power, and prestige in far-flung reaches, in rivalry not only with one another but also with the memory of Alexander the Great, whose exploits loomed large in their minds.

Pompey, who won his nickname "the Great" from success in war (but earlier had earned the less-flattering nickname "the teenage butcher"; see Val Max. 6.2.8) took on an unprecedented extra-governmental commission to fight pirates in the Mediterranean

→ Compare Chapter 3, p. 59, and Chapter 11, p. 244, on piracy.

in 67 BCE. Not long afterwards, Pompey delivered the final and crushing defeat to Mithridates, which won him yet more fame in Rome. Exceeding his orders, he used his celebrity to stabilize Rome's possessions in the Near East, bringing some of the remnants of the now-weak Seleucid dominion into the Roman provincial system and pushing the boundaries of Roman power as far as the Euphrates River. These actions had momentous consequences, for they not only massively enlarged Pompey's prestige, but they also eliminated much of the buffer between Rome and Parthia.

Crassus would engineer a war with Parthia a few years later in a bid to outstrip his fellow triumvirs in wealth and glory. Misunderstanding the Parthians and unused to their style of warfare, Crassus was soundly defeated at Carrhae in 55 BCE and was reportedly killed by having molten gold poured down his throat, a nasty reference to his lust for wealth (Cass. Dio 40.27). The defeat of Crassus produced a long-lived fear of the Iranian kingdom in the Roman psyche; not until the time of Marcus Aurelius and Lucius Verus would the Romans decisively overcome their old foe.

Caesar, for his part, had cast around for opportunities, seizing upon the chance to campaign in Gaul. His wars there, driven by unbridled ambition and a nervous jealousy of his triumviral colleagues, brought unparalleled misery for the Gallic people. (These days, Caesar's account of his actions in Gaul makes for uncomfortable reading.) But the deaths of thousands did not matter, for Caesar obtained the means to fortify his reputation in Rome, to the detriment of Crassus and Pompey. He even pushed as far as Britain in 55 BCE, purely for the sake of conquest.

With Crassus dead, Pompey and Caesar came to open blows. The war was played out in Greece (Pharsalus, 48 BCE) and North Africa (Utica and Thapsus, 46 BCE), new Roman territories that paid a heavy price for their leaders' ambition. Pompey was killed in Egypt, his head sent to his rival (App. *B Civ.* 2.85–6). Caesar, who had fathered a child with the Egyptian Queen Cleopatra, may have nurtured pretensions of eastern, Hellenistic kingship. His new ally Antony had reportedly tried to offer him a royal diadem at the Lupercalia festival in 44 BCE, but, sensing the lack of enthusiasm from the crowd, Caesar sensibly delayed (Plut. *Caes.* 61). Exactly one month later Caesar was dead—the Roman people were not yet ready for a king whose concept of power had more to do with Rome's conquered territories than Rome itself.

Antony and his enemy Octavian presided over the demise of the Republic. Octavian, a nephew of Caesar, used his connections to launch his career. Unlike Marius, Sulla, Pompey, and Caesar, he showed little interest in overseas adventures, preferring to remain close to Rome and the centre of political power. From here he emerged triumphant by demonizing Antony and his actions and associations with the East and exploiting disquiet at home over how polluting influences from the empire's overseas possessions might corrupt the state. Antony, like Caesar, had fallen in love with Cleopatra, and Octavian skilfully used Rome's historic suspicions of a despotic, servile, and effeminate East—the same prejudice that likely prevented Caesar from crowning himself in 44 BCE—to undermine Antony's position as a Roman noble.[6] Before long open war followed, and Antony and Cleopatra were defeated at Actium in 31 BCE. Committing suicide soon after, they left the "new" Roman empire under the dominion of one man (Octavian) with a complacent and impotent senate.

The transition from Republic to Empire was inextricably entwined with Rome's wars and foreign conquests. They provided the wealth necessary to fund the Roman military, and the former Hellenistic kingdoms and territories in the east, in particular, offered the impetus for ambitious and competitive Romans to fight for military and political glory. The spread of Roman dominion continued to provide the opportunities for popular men such as Marius, Caesar, and Octavian to subvert the senate and the *cursus honorum* to build powerful positions, based largely on the belief that the wealth of those conquests could be shared. Caesar's veterans were loyal to him not simply because he was successful but because they could share in the financial profits of his campaigns.

Pax Romana: New Enemies

In his *Moralia*, Plutarch (*Mor.* 207) noted that Augustus—the name taken by Octavian when he became Rome's first emperor—was astonished that Alexander the Great did not pay sufficient attention to safeguarding his realm. Such an opinion guided Augustus's approach to the massive territory that he controlled. Limited campaigns and a reorganization of Rome's fighting legions signalled a policy of consolidation. Any ideas of further exploration or conquest were curtailed by the loss of three legions under the command of Quinctilius Varus, together with their **auxiliaries**, in Germany in 9 CE. The loss of these legions, like the defeat of Crassus at the hands of the Parthians in 55 BCE, had a severe psychological impact on the Romans. At least attempts could be made to address the Parthian problem: a diplomatic coup saw the captured battle standards returned by the Parthians, an event celebrated with the commissioning of a famous statue, the *Augustus of Prima Porta* (now in the Vatican Museums; see Figure 14.1), and with a coin issue from 18 BCE that shows a kneeling Parthian soldier presenting the standards to Rome. Augustus, who understood well how to manipulate public opinion, managed to present this return as a foreign policy victory. Yet the geographic "limits" of the empire were set in the east with the Parthians, with buffer states such as Palmyra (under Roman influence), held in between. In the west, the Rhine and Danube rivers presented formidable natural barriers.

→ Compare Chapter 13, pp. 289–92 and 300, on soldiers and cultural integration.

Figure 14.1 *Augustus of Prima Porta.*
© Erin Babnik/Alamy

It is essential to point out at this stage that the Roman concept of borders was very different from our own. The edges of the Roman empire were not static demarcation lines, although wide rivers such as the Euphrates and Danube or heavily defended zones could certainly provide that impression. **Frontier** zones could also inhibit easy movement, especially of foreign armies, but most were places where the barbarians at the perimeters of the empire were able to interact with its economy, society, military forces, religion, and culture. Many non-Romans consequently gained wide experience of the imperial system by serving in its armed forces and adopting its customs and religions—a process that certainly worked in both directions.[7]

Where frontiers were restive the Romans tried to control them through punitive campaigns that projected military authority and with targeted diplomacy that identified high-ranking barbarians and sought to invest them with a stake in the stability of their homelands.[8] Such policies had important consequences for European history in particular, as they underwrote the later transformation of the Roman West into the early medieval kingdoms of Europe.

Between the death of Augustus in 14 CE and that of Marcus Aurelius in 180 CE, the Roman world enjoyed the so-called *pax Romana*, a period of relative peace and prosperity unmarred by any major catastrophe. The senate still advised, held some power, and played a role in Rome's foreign policy. Over time, however, it was increasingly the opinion of the emperor and his closest advisors that mattered. By the late Empire, Roman treaties had inevitably taken on an interpersonal, not interstate, flavour, and it was the emperor and his "friends"—the elite—who responded to and instigated diplomatic initiatives.[9]

Despite Augustus's admonition to his successor, Tiberius, to be content with the limits of the empire (Cass. Dio 56.33), expansion and wars continued. Few of the Julio-Claudian emperors heeded Augustus's advice. In 43 CE the emperor Claudius, perhaps trying to outdo Caesar, oversaw the invasion of Britain and its incorporation into the empire. Nero meddled in eastern affairs, and in 66 CE a revolt began amongst the Jews. Nero dispatched Vespasian, then a military officer, to deal with this problem. The rebellion that followed the demise of Nero, known conventionally as the Year of the Four Emperors, like the civil wars of the Republic, spanned the whole Mediterranean. Vespasian was the victor, backed by the rich resources of Egypt and Syria. When he assumed the imperial throne in 69 CE, he sent his son Titus to crush the remnants of the Jewish revolt, which made its last stand at a famous hilltop fortress called Masada. The garrison chose to commit suicide rather than surrender. The loot from the Temple in Jerusalem funded a significant building campaign in Rome, and the menorah, silver trumpets, and incense burners carried off by the victorious Romans are celebrated on the Arch of Titus in the Roman Forum.

Compare Chapter 13, p. 299, on architecture as military monuments and Chapter 17, p. 393, on the Arch of Titus.

The demise of the Flavian dynasty in 96 CE brought in five extremely successful emperors, but the end of their reigns witnessed a disturbing resurgence of the Germanic barbarians along the western frontiers of the empire. Nerva (who reigned from 96 to 98 CE) adopted Trajan, a successful army officer whose military experience and senatorial connections, modesty, and responsiveness to the needs of his soldiers made him an inspired choice for successor.[10] As noted at the beginning of this chapter, Trajan's desire for imperial expansion was influenced by Alexander's successes. Under Trajan's reign, the province of Dacia (modern Romania) was added to the empire following a punitive campaign against its king, Decebalus, who had made overtures to the Parthians. The wars there were celebrated on Trajan's Column, which was financed (like Trajan's new **Forum** and civic buildings) from the Dacian region's fabulous wealth of precious metal. Trajan also campaigned against the Parthians, adding new provinces of Armenia and Mesopotamia. More pragmatically, Trajan also annexed the kingdom of Nabataea in 106/107 CE, with its capital at Petra (now in Jordan). Rome now had control of the lucrative spice and incense trade, which had made immense wealth for the Nabataeans.

See Chapter 13, figure 13.3, and Chapter 17, figure 17.10, for images of Trajan's Column.

Under Trajan, the empire reached its largest territorial extent. But when Trajan died in 117 CE, Hadrian, who had wide experience of foreign wars, became emperor and immediately began a policy of consolidation. He withdrew from Mesopotamia and instituted a framework of barriers intended to control the movement of people and provide stability to frontier zones. The best known is Hadrian's Wall in northern Britain, but walls and barriers were also built in North Africa and parts of western Europe. Hadrian pursued a vicious campaign in Judea, known as the Bar Kochba War, sparked by his unpopular plans to rename the city of Jerusalem *Colonia Aelia Capitolina*. When Hadrian died, he left behind a smaller territory but one with relatively quiet frontier regions and a wary status quo with the Parthians.

Hadrian's successors, Antoninus Pius and Marcus Aurelius, oversaw the end of the *pax Romana*. Antoninus Pius may have sent an embassy to China during his reign,[11] but perhaps the most notable military event of this time was the construction of the Antonine Wall north of Hadrian's Wall, built as the Roman army campaigned in Scotland. This far-flung outpost of the Empire would not remain occupied beyond the end of the century. When Antoninus passed the Empire to his adoptive son and young protégé, Marcus Aurelius, in 161 CE, it might have been thought that the new incumbent—who experimented with co-rule by appointing his adoptive brother, Lucius Verus—faced an undemanding task. Yet the Empire found itself pressured on all sides simultaneously, exposing the essential fragility of such a large political entity and raising serious questions about its security.

Aurelius spent 17 of his 19 years as emperor fighting along the Rhine and Danube against a succession of Germanic tribal groups. In the east, Lucius Verus was assigned the war against the Parthians, whose aggressive King Vologeses IV threatened Roman interests with an invasion of Armenia and Syria. Verus possessed an immensely gifted team of subordinates, however, and his general, Avidius Cassius, achieved the sack of the Parthian capital of Seleucia-Ctesiphon in 164/165 CE. The Romans also captured the important trading city of **Dura-Europos** in Syria, situated in an imposing location on bluffs above the Euphrates (see figures 14.2 and 14.3). With the Parthians weakened, Mesopotamia became a protectorate under Roman influence and troops from Palmyra—a key Roman ally—were later stationed at Dura to watch the frontiers. **Frescoes** commemorating their assignment there were found during the dramatic rediscovery of Dura in the 1920s and 1930s.[12]

In 168 CE Lucius Verus returned in triumph, but both emperors faced a new threat on the Danube. These wars, which are not well understood, may have been caused by a migration of Germanic peoples. They were marked by a new savagery and made worse by a visitation of the bubonic plague, which Verus's troops brought home with them.

Compare Chapter 17, pp. 393–4, on artistic representation on Trajan's and Marcus Aurelius's Columns.

Marcus Aurelius died in 180 CE at Vindobona, after subduing his old nemesis, the Quadi tribe. During his reign, he erected a column celebrating his victory over the Germans in Europe. Superficially similar to Trajan's Column, with a winding scroll providing a visual record of the wars, a closer look reveals a disturbing distinction. Whereas Trajan's Column offers neat, well-sculpted images of an effortless conquest over barbarians, that of Aurelius shows pain, anguish, and a bloody contest narrowly won. Such was the new reality of Rome's relations with its neighbours.

Marcus Aurelius's experiences as emperor raised a vexing question that was to be asked again in the century to come. Aurelius and Verus had competent generals and were themselves successful. But if their foreign enemies pressed hard again and if these attacks were combined with other potential difficulties—weak government, civil war, military incompetence—would the empire be able to defend itself?

Figure 14.2   Dura's City Walls © Greg Fisher

The Third Century CE: A Changing Order

After Commodus, Marcus Aurelius's son and successor, died in 192 CE, a naked struggle for power followed. The eventual victor was Septimius Severus, from Leptis Magna, in Libya—Rome's first emperor of African origin. His accession, which reflected the growing importance of the provinces at the expense of Rome, also brought in a Syrian connection: his wife, Julia Domna, was from an important family at Emesa. Severus campaigned widely in the east, annexing one of Rome's last buffer states, the ancient kingdom of Osrhoene. He

Figure 14.3   Dura's New Citadel © Greg Fisher

also became one of the few emperors to campaign successfully against the Iranians, capturing Seleucia-Ctesiphon in 197 CE and extending Roman control to the key city of Nisibis.

Like Hadrian, Severus travelled extensively—he was on campaign in England when he died in 211 CE. He named his two sons, Geta and Caracalla, as co-emperors. Geta was quickly murdered, while Caracalla emulated his great hero, Alexander the Great, by embarking on a war in the east. He followed Alexander's route and, according to Cassius Dio (78.7), even equipped a Roman legion with Macedonian weapons but was murdered near the site of Crassus's defeat at Carrhae in 217 CE by one of his own men. Shortly thereafter, the Syrian faction of the Severan family assumed control first under the disastrous Elagabulus (218–222 CE) and then under the more stable Severus Alexander (222–235 CE).

During the reign of Severus Alexander, an important event that was to have drastic consequences for the stability of Rome's eastern frontiers occurred. In 224 CE a man with the royal name of Ardashir overthrew the Parthian Arsacid dynasty and established a new lineage: the Sasanian dynasty, as it was known, espoused a zealous and intolerant form of Zoroastrianism, an eastern religion. With a well-organized administration and highly effective army, the Sasanians posed a major threat to the security of the Roman East. Cassius Dio (79.3–4) attributed to the Sasanians the desire to reclaim the lost lands of the Achaemenid Empire, the great Persian realm taken by Alexander the Great. This motive is hard to establish, and it is not clear if Dio was reporting a Sasanian idea or what the Romans believed the Sasanians were thinking. But its perceived truth was a worrying development, for these lands had included much of Asia Minor, Syria, Palestine, and Egypt—all under Roman control. The Romans were able to campaign with some success against Ardashir; however, back in western Europe in 235 CE, Severus Alexander and his tempestuous mother, Julia Mamaea, were killed in a coup at the Rhine fortress of Moguntiacum.

Between 235 and 284 CE a series of pretenders, too many to record individually, made bids for imperial power. The period was marked by sustained and heavy pressure along all of Rome's frontiers, but Rome's ability to fight effectively was undermined by the relentless civil wars, economic collapse, and social problems that accompanied the military crisis. Notable during this period was the reign of Decius (248–251 CE), which saw a return of the plague and a catastrophic defeat on the Danube frontier, where Decius and his army stumbled into an ambush in a swamp. Decius's body was never found, and the elite of Rome's battle-hardened Danubian armies perished along with him and his son. In 253 CE two Germanic tribes, the Franks and Alamanni, crossed the Rhine and raided as far as Spain. Shortly afterwards the Goths (another Germanic people) invaded Greece and the western part of the empire, based in Gaul, attempted to secede.

The nadir came in 260 CE, when the emperor Valerian was captured at Edessa by Sasanian King Shapur I, "the Great." Weakened by illness, the Roman troops were defeated and marched into captivity, never to return. Later, lurid tales held that Valerian was flayed and his skin hung on the walls of one of Shapur's temples (Lactant. *De mort. pers.* 5). Shapur, one of Iran's most successful leaders, commemorated his victory on rock reliefs at Naqsh-i-Rustam in Iran and in an inscription known as the *Res Gestae Divi Saporis*.[13] After 260 CE, the pressure continued. The Palmyrenes, who had provided valuable assistance in the aftermath of Valerian's defeat, now rebelled under their queen, Zenobia. Roman forces were unable to resist, and many soldiers, despairing of their fortune, joined the opposite side. Zenobia, however, was crushed by a new emperor, Aurelian, who also defeated the breakaway "Gallic" Empire in the west and evacuated Dacia. But only with the accession of Diocletian in 284 CE did the tide start to turn towards renewed stability.

From Diocletian to Theodosius: Unity and Division

The accession of Diocletian marks the end of the so-called Third-Century Crisis. Diocletian understood the fundamental fact that the pressure exerted by Rome's enemies across its border regions required a new response from Roman government. One man was no longer sufficient, so he created the **tetrarchy** ("rule of four"), which consisted of two emperors and two deputies posted at strategic locations well suited for frontier war against the Germans in the west and the Sasanians in the east. A map of the key tetrarchic cities—Trier, Milan, Aquileia, Sirmium, Nicomedia, and Antioch—shows a line drawn through the most dangerous parts of the empire. North Africa is notably absent because there was no organized enemy there to pose a serious threat. Under Diocletian's tutelage, the breakaway Gallic Empire was finally restored to Roman control and a significant war in the east enabled his deputy, Galerius, to impose the Peace of Nisibis on the Sasanians in 298 CE.[14] This treaty placed Armenia, Iberia (modern Georgia), and parts of Mesopotamia under Roman control; it would stand until the disastrous defeat of Julian in 363 CE. Diocletian also oversaw the reorganization of the Roman army into smaller, more mobile units and undertook a comprehensive overhaul of provincial administration. Both reforms were intended, in part, to bring stability after three generations of crisis.

Diocletian and his colleague Maximian abdicated on 1 May 305 CE. In retirement, Diocletian contented himself with the cultivation of cabbages, free from the pressures of imperial office. He and Maximian hoped that the system they had inaugurated— whereby the two junior colleagues, Galerius and Constantius Chlorus, took over and created deputies of their own— would bring peace and stability. There was, however, a flaw in the system. In 306 CE Constantius Chlorus died in Britain (remarkably, of natural causes) with no designated successor. A series of contenders arose, with seven potential candidates vying for the imperial throne at one point. In the civil wars that followed, Constantius Chlorus's son Constantine emerged victorious in 324 CE.

Constantine built an incredibly complex imperial bureaucracy that rejected the tetrarchic system in favour of an absolute monarchy. He also oversaw the creation of a new officer corps of the army and is largely credited with fashioning a two-speed military system, with the elite mobile armies (*comitatenses*) and the less equipped frontier armies (*limitanei*).[15] He ended the persecution of Christians and invested significant effort in convening religious councils to determine orthodoxy. This focus on Christian belief was also significant in that Constantine fashioned a form of Christian imperial rule whereby the emperor was the viceroy of the supreme deity. Under the protection of a universal religion, the Roman Empire now possessed a powerful religious framework that had implications for its foreign policy, many of which lie outside the scope of this chapter. But with Christianity accepted, missionaries carried the new religion to the frontier areas—the Goths were famously Christianized during this period by the bishop Ulfilas. Constantine probably did not order conversion as state policy, but missionaries would later (under Justinian) be used as a conscious means of bringing frontier peoples into the political orbit of a Christian, Roman Empire and ensuring that they did not fall under the influence of Zoroastrian Iran.[16]

The fourth and fifth centuries CE witnessed the reversal of Roman gains in the east (by 363 CE) and the collapse of Roman authority in western Europe (a process well underway by the death of Theodosius in 395 CE). Roman woes in the west were due to several factors, including pressures from barbarians and the failure of Roman leadership. The early-medieval barbarian kingdoms that replaced Roman rule were themselves partly a product of Roman frontier policies, which supported powerful barbarian leaders in return for political submission, stability, and troops. This arrangement was loosely known as *foederati*, after *foedus* ("treaty"). Endowed with a stake in the Roman Empire, barbarian leaders could lead double lives. The fourth-century Mallobaudes, for example, was king of the Franks at the same time as he held a senior Roman military post (Amm. Marc. 31.10.6). It is no accident that Germanic leaders created kingdoms for themselves in a way that appropriated the forms of Roman government that they had experienced rather than rejecting them outright.[17]

In the late fourth century CE, apparently as a result of being attacked by a group known as the Huns, the Goths (who had long lived in and alongside the European frontier zones) petitioned the Romans for permission to enter the empire. Eventually, they were allowed to cross the Danube and settle in the Balkans. Mistreatment by rapacious Roman officials led to a humanitarian crisis, followed by a rebellion. Valens, emperor at the time, was determined to quash the revolt. Refusing to wait for his western colleague, Gratian, he brought the Goths to battle at Adrianople in 378 CE (see Box 14.3; compare Box 14.1). The result was a rout: Valens was killed on the battlefield, and his army was destroyed.

The Roman army never recovered from this battle's loss of experienced officers and non-commissioned officers. With Gratian dead in 382 CE and Theodosius, the last man to control the Empire by himself, dead 13 years later, a succession of young and feeble emperors came to the throne. All hope of a united Roman Empire vanished, and the territory was divided between east and west. As effective Roman authority and government waned in the fifth century CE, the net beneficiaries in the west were Rome's former foreign neighbours—the barbarians—who went on to establish successor states in Spain (Visigoths), Gaul (Franks), Britain (Saxons), and North Africa (Vandals). This was the era of Alaric, Attila the Hun, Stilicho, Aetius, and, in Britain, the events that would give rise to the legend of Arthur. Italy, the former heart of the empire, now became a successor state ruled by the Amal kings of the Ostrogoths, who created a fictional genealogy that connected them to Rome's own Trojan foundation myths.

Primary Source

Box 14.3: Ammianus Marcellinus, *History*, 31.12–13.[1]

Valens came to the vicinity of a suburb of Adrianople, where he impatiently waited for Gratian. There he received Richomeres, general of the household troops, sent in advance by Gratian with a letter, in which he said that he himself also would soon be there. Since the contents besought him to wait a while for the partner in his dangers, and not rashly to expose himself alone to serious perils, Valens called a council of various of his higher officers and considered what ought to be done. And while some . . . urged him to give battle at once, . . . others recommended that his imperial colleague be awaited, so that, strengthened by the addition of the Gallic army, he might the more easily crush the fiery over-confidence of the barbarians. However, the fatal insistence of the emperor prevailed, supported by the flattering opinion of some of his courtiers, who urged him to make all haste in order that Gratian might not have a share in the victory which (as they represented) was already all but won. . . . Certain it is that barely a third part of our army escaped. The annals record no such massacre of a battle except the one at Cannae.

Note

1. Translated by Rolfe (1939).

In the east, conflict between Rome and the Parthian Empire (and its successor, the Sassanid Empire) culminated at the end of the seventh century CE in a massive occupation by the Sasanians that lasted from 602 to 628 CE and spanned Egypt, Syria, Palestine, and large parts of Asia Minor. Constantinople itself was threatened but held out. Only a brilliant piece of generalship by the emperor Heraclius—largely lost to history—saved the Eastern Roman Empire from annihilation. But soon both the Romans and the Sasanians would be overwhelmed by groups of Arabs from northern Arabia who were espousing a new religion, Islam.[18] In the seventh century CE, the Eastern Empire was truncated to the Balkans and Asia Minor and conventionally became known as the Byzantine Empire. The Sasanians fared little better. Their dominions were eviscerated and quickly passed under control of the Muslims, who would go on to create first the Umayyad, and then the Abbasid, empire and permanently alter the course of history in the Near East.

Summary

Conquest of neighbours and frontier tensions defined the history of the Roman Republic and Empire. Military success was an important part of Roman civic and political life, and warfare provided a means for ambitious aristocrats to gain prestige and power. The wars with Pyrrhus and Carthage provided unprecedented opportunities for such fame, and the recovery from near annihilation in the Second Punic War provided the self-confidence and reputation for invincibility that led to the creation of an overseas empire. The question of whether the Romans followed a conscious program of imperialism has no easy answer, but it is clear that initial tentative overseas wars in Macedonia and Syria, where there was no acquisition of territory, eventually gave way to the outright occupation of places such as Cyrenaica, Majorca, Gaul, and Pergamum. Conquest affected the political and social fabric of the Republic, leading to a breakdown in senatorial government and the use of Rome's new empire as an arena for the ambitions of people such as Pompey, Caesar, and Octavian. When Octavian became the emperor Augustus, he followed a program of consolidation that was (if unintentionally) ignored by his successors.

Over time, Rome's principal foreign concerns were the Germanic barbarians in Europe and the Parthian and Sasanian kingdom in what is now Iran and Iraq, centred on its capital at Seleucia-Ctesiphon (near modern Baghdad). By the time of Marcus Aurelius's death in 180 CE, the Germanic tribes had become stronger. Along with unremitting civil war, these tribes exerted significant pressures throughout Europe during the third century CE. In part this was a consequence of Roman frontier policies, which identified key leaders and encouraged them to build strength through financial subsidy and recognition, with the hope that they would maintain the peace. By the time of Adrianople in 378 CE the Goths were not strangers to the Romans, but the outcome of this battle set the tone for the Western Empire. By the sixth century all the former Roman provinces had fallen under the control of Germanic barbarian kings. As successors to Roman authority, they all used Roman pretensions to power to legitimize themselves.

In the east, the Romans continued their uneasy relationship with the Sasanians, which was characterized by cautious diplomacy, trade links, occasional friendship, and savage bouts of war. With neither Empire strong enough to defeat the other, the two fought to a standstill, ending in the long invasion by the Sasanians in the early seventh century CE. In the end, the Arabs were the net beneficiaries of Rome's wars in the east and created a new empire out of the former Roman territories of Syria, Egypt, Palestine, Jordan, North Africa, and the territory of the former Sasanian Empire in Iran and Iraq.

Questions for Review and Discussion

1. Why are the Punic Wars so important in understanding subsequent forms of Roman conquest?

2. How did Roman conquest affect domestic matters in Rome?
3. Discuss whether expansion was a deliberate plan of the Romans or a consequence of protecting the state. What circumstances make it difficult to reach a definitive conclusion?
4. What signs indicated that the *pax Romana* was ending?
5. How would you characterize the relationship between Rome and its Germanic barbarian neighbours? Give evidence to support your answer.

Suggested Reading

Astin, A.E., M.W. Frederiksen, R.M. Ogilvie, and F.W. Walbank. 1989. *The Cambridge Ancient History, viii: Rome and the Mediterranean to 133 BC*. Cambridge: Cambridge University Press.

These internationally renowned experts present a succinct analysis of Rome's early expansion, including the Punic Wars and intervention in Greece.

Cameron, A., B. Ward-Perkins, and M. Whitby, eds. 2000. *The Cambridge Ancient History, xiv. Late Antiquity: Empire and Successors, AD 425-600*. Cambridge: Cambridge University Press.

This text is the best single-volume treatment of the different aspects of late antiquity.

Champion, C.B., ed. 2004. *Roman Imperialism: Readings and Sources*. Oxford: Blackwell.

Champion's work is a useful collection of primary and secondary source material.

Dignas, B. and W. Engelbert. 2007. *Rome and Persia in Late Antiquity: Neighbours and Rivals*. Cambridge: Cambridge University Press.

This work provides a comprehensive examination of the complex relationship between Rome and Iran (Persia) and includes discussion of a wide range of primary sources.

Fisher, G., ed. 2015. *Arabs and Empires before Islam*. Oxford: Oxford University Press.

This book represents the only full and up-to-date treatment of Rome's foreign policy towards Arabia from the Republic through the coming of Islam.

Hoyos, D., ed. 2011. *A Companion to the Punic Wars*. Malden, MA, and Oxford: Wiley-Blackwell.

This book is an up-to-date examination of the causes, actions, and consequences of the Punic campaigns.

Millar, F. 1995. *The Roman Near East: 31 BC–AD 337*. Cambridge, MA: Harvard University Press.

Millar examines the conquest of the Near East.

Potter, D.S. 2004. *The Roman Empire at Bay, AD 180–395*. London and New York: Routledge.

Potter's book provides an in-depth analysis of the events surrounding the end of the *pax Romana* and the

Third-Century Crisis, to the death of Theodosius in 395 CE.

Syme, R. 1939. *The Roman Revolution*. Oxford: Clarendon Press.

Syme's masterpiece on how Octavian destroyed Antony is still unsurpassed in its brilliance and control of the material it covers.

Whittaker, C.R. 1994. *Frontiers of the Roman Empire: A Social and Economic Study*. Baltimore: Johns Hopkins University Press.

This work places the function of imperial frontiers in context and is essential to any understanding of Roman frontier policies.

Notes

1   Cass. Dio 68.29, translated by Cary (1925).
2   Translations of Plutarch by Perrin (1920).
3   This procedure is outlined in detail in Billows (2008: 303–24); see also Yakobson (2009: 45–72).
4   Billows (2008: 320).
5   See, in detail, Champion (2004: 16–95).
6   The way Octavian achieved this is masterfully laid out in Syme (1939).
7   The framework for our understanding of how Roman frontiers functioned is neatly laid out in Whittaker (1994).
8   On this concept, see Heather (2001: 15–68).
9   See Mattern (1999: 1–23).
10   See Cass. Dio 68 on his character and Plin. *Pan.* 107 for an example of Trajan's attitude towards his soldiers.
11   Leslie and Gardiner (1996).
12   Goldman (1979).
13   See Maricq (1958: 245–60).
14   Blockley (1992: 5–8).
15   See Southern and Dixon (1996).
16   Constantine: Kulikowski (2006: 347–76); Justinian: van Rompay (2005: 239–66).
17   See Pohl (1997).
18   The history of the relationship between Rome, Iran, and the Arabs is explained in Fisher (2011).

15

The Economy

Matt Gibbs

In his philosophical treatise *On Duties* (*De officiis*), the statesman and orator Marcus Tullius Cicero offers his opinions on certain aspects of the late Republic's economy.[1] His scathing remarks about small-scale trade, manufacture, and the occupations that went alongside them likely reflect the views of a Roman elite that traditionally believed that the acquisition of land and agriculture was the most honourable way of investing and generating wealth. Upper-class disdain for certain occupations continued into the Empire, finding its way into Roman philosophical dialogues, court proceedings, and works of biography and history. But it is interesting to compare Cicero's depiction of the moral exemplar Marcus Cato with Plutarch's. When Cicero's (*Off.* 2.25) Cato is asked to identify the most profitable aspect of property ownership, he replies, "Raising livestock with great success."[2] The exchange continues:

> "And then?"
> "Raising livestock with some success."
> "After that?"
> "Raising livestock with little success."
> "And fourth?"
> "Raising crops."

Finally, Cato is asked about moneylending, to which he caustically retorts, "What about murder?" The conversation may never have happened, but the Roman aristocratic view is clear: agriculture and land ownership were suitable choices of investment for the upper echelons of Roman society.

Plutarch's (*Cat. Mai.* 21.5–7) portrayal of this same Cato, however, is quite different:

Having applied himself more intently to earning a living, he (Cato) believed that agriculture was more entertaining than profitable and invested his capital in things safe and sure: he bought ponds, hot springs, and districts given over to fullers, pitch works, land with natural pastures and woods, all of which brought him a great deal of money, and—as he would say—"could not be ruined by Jupiter." He also engaged in the most disreputable way of money-lending, namely on ships. This was his method: he required the borrowers to gather many partners, and when there were 50 partners and as many ships, he acquired one share in the company himself through an agent (his freedman Quintio) who sailed with the borrowers and worked with them. So he did not bear the entire risk himself but only a small part of it, and his profits were great.

If Plutarch's evidence has any substance, what does it say about Cato? Was he a hypocrite? Were his activities exceptional among the Roman aristocracy? Or was his method of investing and making money far more common than Roman literature, predominantly the work of the upper classes, suggests?

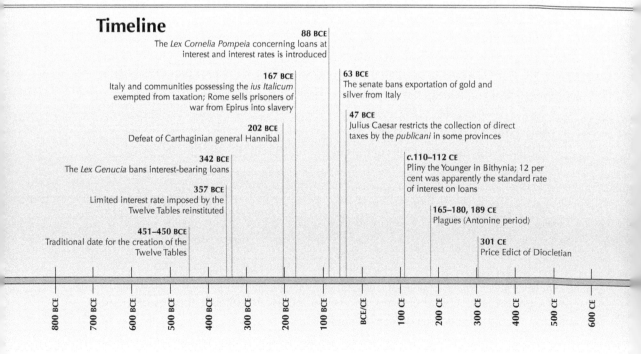

Timeline

88 BCE
The *Lex Cornelia Pompeia* concerning loans at interest and interest rates is introduced

167 BCE
Italy and communities possessing the *ius Italicum* exempted from taxation; Rome sells prisoners of war from Epirus into slavery

202 BCE
Defeat of Carthaginian general Hannibal

342 BCE
The *Lex Genucia* bans interest-bearing loans

357 BCE
Limited interest rate imposed by the Twelve Tables reinstituted

451–450 BCE
Traditional date for the creation of the Twelve Tables

63 BCE
The senate bans exportation of gold and silver from Italy

47 BCE
Julius Caesar restricts the collection of direct taxes by the *publicani* in some provinces

c.110–112 CE
Pliny the Younger in Bithynia; 12 per cent was apparently the standard rate of interest on loans

165–180, 189 CE
Plagues (Antonine period)

301 CE
Price Edict of Diocletian

800 BCE | 700 BCE | 600 BCE | 500 BCE | 400 BCE | 300 BCE | 200 BCE | 100 BCE | BCE/CE | 100 CE | 200 CE | 300 CE | 400 CE | 500 CE | 600 CE

Introduction

The Roman economy was inherently linked to almost all areas of Roman life. As such, it is an important focus of study in its own right and is often a critical factor in the investigation of Roman society and culture more generally. This chapter considers some of the key aspects of the Roman economy during the period 200 BCE–200 CE. It introduces the ongoing debate surrounding the interpretation of evidence and the use of theory, demography, agriculture and the ownership of land (including tenancy), moneylending, interest rates and taxation, and, finally, production and trade.

It is worth noting from the outset that the Roman economy was—like all pre-industrial societies—agrarian in nature. Nevertheless, agricultural surplus in the Roman world promoted a higher degree of specialization in trade and urbanization than had been achieved previously in the Mediterranean region and in parts of Europe. The Roman economy was also sophisticated in its modes of economic exchange, as it was extensively monetized and appears to have made use of coinage from an early date.[3] Coins arrived in Italy in the early sixth century BCE, in the hands of Greek colonists, and the Romans may have followed their example and created a basic monetary unit—the *as* (a pound of bronze)—by the end of the century.[4] As the empire grew, the conquests of southern and central Spain and Macedon in the second century BCE, the exploitation of the Asturian mines under Augustus, and the capture of further gold and silver resources during Trajan's Dacian campaigns all provided the large quantities of precious metal needed for the minting of coinage.[5]

In the broader historical context, the Roman period was the only time in history when the whole of the Mediterranean and much of Europe was contained within a single state, and a similar economic environment was not seen again until the Late Middle Ages. The Roman republican and imperial economy is therefore of interest beyond the scope of Roman studies, as it provides us with an opportunity to address far broader issues not only concerning other pre-industrial societies but also relating to economic competition, political developments, and historical socio-economic advances.

———— • ◆ • ————

Evidence and Theory

The evidence for the Roman economy is complicated and unevenly scattered across time and space. The fact that the realm of Roman influence was expanding over the long period of time under study here is one reason for this situation, while the nature of the evidence is another. Literary sources, typically written by upper-class Romans, tend to reflect the conservative opinions shared perhaps among only the Roman social elite. In addition, the literary evidence has little to say about the economy directly, and those pieces that do focus on economic aspects are problematic. For instance, Pliny the Elder's (*HN* 33.42–47) history of coinage and Tacitus's (*Ann.* 6.16) account of moneylending are perhaps unreliable because they describe events that predate the authors. But literary evidence nonetheless offers some striking events, facts, and inferences. Livy and Dionysius of Halicarnassus, for example, both record the mounting tensions between **patricians** and **plebeians** concerning land use, land ownership, and debt (see, for instance, Livy 2.23; Dion. Hal. *Ant. Rom.* 5.53, 63–64, 6.26–29). As seen at the outset of this chapter, literary evidence also gives us intriguingly contradictory information about the opinions and habits of the Roman elite regarding investment.

We do not, however, have to rely on the literary evidence alone. The ever-increasing amount of evidence from archaeology allows us to see the Roman economy in a new light, particularly in the area of trade. Though much of what was traded—agricultural produce, wood, textiles, and the products constructed from these materials—has often long since deteriorated, a good deal of the containers in which such commodities were transported survive. Ceramic vessels are plentiful in the archaeological record and are even discovered in shipwrecks.[6] These were typically used to store and transport the infamous Roman fish sauce (*garum*), olive oil, wine, spices, and a host of other perishable commodities to areas where they could be traded. Papyrological and epigraphical evidence is also critical. For example, the **Price Edict of Diocletian**, which set empire-wide prices for a vast range of commodities in the fourth century CE, and documentary materials from Egypt and from **Vindolanda** in northern Britain are suggestive of trade in such items at the edges of the empire.[7]

Despite the difficulties presented by the literary and archaeological evidence, modern scholars have tried to make sense of the Roman economy and to understand its intricacies and interrelated processes. For some time the study was dominated by a debate between the modernist and the primitivist (or substantivist and minimalist) approaches. The former was advanced by Michael Rostovtzeff, who, in *The Social and Economic History of the Roman Empire*, pictured the Roman economy (of the Empire in particular) as growing along modern lines. Both investors (who invested capital in productive industries) and workers (who specialized in specific wares) actively sought profits.[8] Moses Finley and his students championed the primitivist view, which developed in reaction to Rostovtzeff's modernist approach. In *The Ancient Economy*, Finley emphasized subsistence agriculture (essentially, farming to survive) and a lack of economic rationality.[9] This view also highlighted the role of communities as consumers rather than as centres of production, trade, and industry, the low status of trades- and craftspeople generally, and the lack of innovation in technology. Keith Hopkins, though influenced by Finley, offered a series of changes and checks to the primitivist view in several influential articles and chapters, arguing that agricultural production and cultivation increased during the central period (200 BCE–200 CE), as did the population (a relatively high proportion of which was apparently engaged in non-agrarian occupations) and **per capita production**. On the back of these changes, and with taxation possibly acting as a stimulus, trade and manufacture reached its zenith.[10]

Compare Chapter 1, pp. 8–9, ↩ on the contributions of Rostovtzeff, Finley, and Hopkins.

More recently, scholars have tended to embrace a more advanced and multi-faceted Roman economy, with some areas enjoying relatively sophisticated economic practices and others suffering from a distinct lack of progression. But the work of Finley, Rostovtzeff, and their proponents remains important. It revived interest in the Roman economy (and in ancient economies generally) and established a fundamental and largely accepted principle: the economy of the Roman world was by no means uniform. There were regional and structural differences between the provinces and between the eastern and western halves of the empire. In other words, the Roman economy was not a single, simple system managed by an all-embracing policy instituted by the Roman administration. On the contrary, the Roman economy was made up of several complex, interconnected, and integrated regional economies.[11] Therefore, scholars now typically deal with regional or provincial economies that were interconnected through transportation or societal networks and together formed a composite of what might be called the "Roman" economy.

Demography

As population is a determinant of economic performance, any discussion of the economy must consider demography; economies should perhaps be seen as responses to people's need for material goods and services.[12] As such, the ratio of people to the resources of the territory that they inhabit is an essential detail.[13] It is fair to say that the costs of maintaining political domination in the Mediterranean during the Republic and Empire were significant: for instance, most estimates of the average annual wage costs of the military prior to the pay increases implemented under Domitian (81–96 CE), including discharge bonuses, suggest a figure in excess of 400 million **sesterces**.[14] Moreover, the Romans undertook massive expenditure on road construction and public building. To offset these enormous costs, the government used an assortment of charges and revenues. The provincial populations were subject to an array of taxes in cash and in kind, most of which would have found their way into the imperial treasury in some form; however, Roman citizens were not directly taxed and citizen land was also exempt.

At the heart of the Roman economy, then, was the population of the empire. Of course, during the period under discussion, the population increased incrementally as Rome's imperial aspirations grew both figuratively and literally, especially during the late second and early first centuries BCE.[15] This, at least, is what **census** figures suggest: in 131 BCE, 318,823 adult Roman citizen males were recorded, while a little over a century later (in 28 BCE), the figure stood at 4,063,000.[16] These numbers, however, remain highly problematic, the latter particularly because we have no idea whether it refers to

Roman citizen adult males only or includes women and children.[17] The city of Rome itself appears to have increased in terms of population, from approximately 375,000 in 130 BCE to an estimated 750,000 to 1,000,000 (including slaves) by 28 BCE.[18] That said, population growth among Roman citizens alone was probably not responsible for the total increase in the Italian peninsula. Migration by non-citizens to Rome may well have played a role in the city's growth.[19]

For the Empire, we are hardly better served by the evidence. By 14 CE, at the end of Augustus's reign, modern estimates put the complete population (all men, women, and children) of the Roman empire at around 45.5 million.[20] By 164–165 CE, due to increases in the population of the western provinces (notably Africa, Gaul, and Spain) possibly resulting from largely peaceful conditions, this figure may well have reached between 60 and 70 million.[21] Of course, following the outbreak of the Antonine plague, the population decreased.[22] Contemporary accounts (for example, *P.Thmouis* 1.104.9–18); eye-witness reports from Aelius Aristides (*Or.* 48.38–44), Galen (19.15, 17–18), and Lucian (*Alex.* 36); and other, later literary sources (Amm. Marc. 23.6.24; Eutr. 8.12; Oros. 7.15.5; SHA *Marc.* 21.6–7) all attest to the pestilence and death in both rural and urban communities and to the famines that occurred in the plague's aftermath. The actual severity of the epidemic is still debated, however, in spite of Cassius Dio's (72.14.3–4) claim that the 189 CE plague in Rome was the worst that he had lived through. Nevertheless, modern estimates suggest that as much as 10 per cent of the overall population of the empire was lost to the devastation wrought by the plague. Such a change likely affected the economy, perhaps even significantly, and led to (or at least compounded) economic problems that were to arise in the next century.[23]

Land and Property

Under both the Republic and the Empire, the ownership of land (and, by extension, agriculture and agricultural production) was central to the Roman economy. Of course, Roman conquest and the creation of an empire carried significant implications for the economy, particularly regarding the newly acquired territory. This occupation and annexation meant an increase in population and a probable rise in land and property owners, a large number of whom were apt to be smallholders (almost certainly including army veterans), and in turn both provided a base from which provincial populations could be taxed. In fact, the massive expansion of Roman influence in the second century BCE, with extension over Italy, the Hellenistic East, and North Africa, often appears to have led to a change in traditional landholding patterns in the areas

See Chapter 14 , pp. 313–15, on Roman expansion in the second century BCE.

newly subjected to Roman control. The agrarian policy of the Roman state throughout the republican period generally promoted private ownership of land on an individual basis or through the creation of colonies. The transformation from Republic to Empire at the end of the first century BCE and during the beginning of the mid-first century CE saw similar changes in landholding in the west, alongside the expansion of "Roman" forms of agriculture.

Despite the socio-political changes that accompanied the shift from Republic to Empire, the position of land in the Roman consciousness remained unchanged. Throughout the Republic and Empire, land—particularly the agricultural and rural variety—was the primary form of investment and wealth, as well as the principal and relatively stable source of affluence in Roman society.[24] The place of land and agriculture in the Roman psyche is perhaps most clearly demonstrated in the tradition of agricultural manuals, written by the Roman aristocracy (for example, the works of Cato, Varro, and Columella). These manuals are works on the management of elite estates rather than on the more practical methods of farming.

Given that land ownership was the basis of socio-political influence, the distribution of land was very unequal, with the elite taking the lion's share. The Roman senator Pliny the Younger (*Ep.* 3.19) claimed in a letter to his friend Calvisius Rufus that the majority of his wealth was bound in property. But Pliny was certainly not alone: perhaps even the majority of senators and prominent members of the middle and upper **classes** of Roman society owed their affluence to similar landed investments.[25] In fact, these groups' share of agrarian land probably only increased over time as they bought more and more property throughout the Roman world.[26]

The extensive private landholdings of the Roman aristocracy, whether rural, urban, or a mixture of the two, were often made up of a collection of smaller, sometimes non-adjacent, holdings,[27] and could include areas in the owner's home territory or other provinces.[28] The accumulation of land in this way effectively acted as a form of risk management (contrast the cautionary tale of Lucius Tarius Rufus, told by Pliny the Elder [*HN* 18.37]). Diversification in the choice of crops, through individual choice, market value, or conditions of land, climate, and position, meant that a complete crop failure in a single year was unlikely, even if some areas were ruined.[29] And such failure was certainly a concern: in a letter to Julius Naso, Pliny the Younger (*Ep.* 4.6) complained that his Tuscan farms had been lashed by hail and that, although his Transpadane region was producing crops, the prices were low.

Tenancy also played an important part in land ownership and investment for landholders, particularly if owners were often away or lived in different communities, regions, or provinces and had to turn to alternative methods of managing their estates. This could, of course, be done in a number of ways. Tenants or slaves could be employed to manage the estate for the landowner, supervising a slave workforce provided by either the landlord or the tenants themselves. In some provinces, slave labour gave the landowners several options in ensuring the efficient running of their holdings. But there certainly were regional differences in management that were linked to disparities in culture and society. In Roman Egypt, for

example, where the demand for slave labour had not permeated the provincial subconscious-
ness as it had in other imperial provinces, slaves were predominately an urban presence, with
generally small numbers appearing in the domestic households of the towns and cities, and
were rare in the countryside.[30] As a result, some estates in Egypt during this period might
have functioned without slave labour but used several categories of free workers as full-time,
casual, or seasonal labourers instead.[31] On some estates in the empire, there were also tenants
who appear to have been of significant **status** and wealth (Plin. *Ep.* 6.3, 30).

Tenancy, in whatever form it took, did not necessarily mean that the tenant worked
without the landowner's supervision. Of course, tenant supervision of an estate required
less participation on the part of the landowner, but it also meant a loss in the overall profit.
The tenant operated independently and, as such, not only took responsibility for the
risks but also received the profits after the annual rent had been

→ Compare Chapter 4, p. 88,
on concerns over controlling
agricultural slaves and Chapter 5,
p. 109, on the *familia rustica*.

paid. A "slave-run" estate would certainly be more profitable
for the owner, but it had two notable disadvantages: the owner
assumed all responsibility for the risks involved and would
probably need to be involved in the close supervision of the estate in question. It appears
that, as a consequence, the greater the distance between an owner and his landholding,
the greater the chance that the land would be leased to tenants rather than run by slaves.

Naturally, tenancy depended on the situation of the landowner: wealthy landowners
with more interest in the land (and less in Roman politics) may have preferred to remain
close to their investments and use slaves, while rich senators may have chosen to use tenants
to manage their estates while they stayed in Rome. In several of his letters, Pliny the Younger
(for instance *Ep.* 3.19, 9.37) makes no secret about employing tenants. At the other end
of the economic scale we find Epimachos, a cultivator of a rather unassuming estate in the
Hermopolite **nome** in Egypt during the late first century CE. Some of the accounts of his farm
are preserved on papyri,[32] from which we learn that the leasing of land played a significant
role in his economic security. He made an income by leasing out his own property, sharing
the costs and risks with his tenants, and using this income to lease land himself, which he
then farmed.[33]

Of course, urban property could also be bought and leased to tenants.[34] "The incomes
from urban property are great, but the risks are far greater. If there were some remedy,
so that the houses of Rome would not burn so readily, I assure
you I would have given up my estates in the countryside and
purchased urban property," one Roman is reported to have said

→ Compare Chapter 5, pp. 109–11,
on *insulae* and rental space.

(Gell. *NA* 15.1). The apartment blocks (*insulae*) in Ostia—the city at the mouth of the
Tiber, situated around 30 kilometres west of Rome and described by Strabo as "the sea-
port of Rome" (3.2.6)—may well have represented attractive investments in this respect
for those willing to take the risk.[35] Despite Cicero's pronouncements that agriculture was
the most reputable area in which the upper classes of Roman society could earn money

(see Box 15.1), it seems possible that some of his wealth was based on the returns from urban property (see, for example, Cic. *Att.* 12.32, 16.1).[36]

Although the risks involved with propertied land in an urban context may have been more significant, urban property could bring a higher return than rural land. Moreover, in cases where urban properties were not providing enough revenue, there were ways in which unscrupulous individuals were still able to make a profit, notably by selling urban (and, in fact, rural) properties for demolition. The *senatus consultum de aedificiis non diruendis* ("decree of the **senate** regarding not demolishing buildings"; see Box 15.2) appears to have been an attempt to curb this practice,[37] and Strabo (5.3.7) may well be

Primary Source

Box 15.1 : Cicero, *On Duties*, 1.42.

Now, we learned generally these things about trades and occupations, which occupy free men, and which are sordid. First those occupations, which incur the hatred of men such as toll collectors and moneylenders, are condemned. On the other hand, the occupations of all hired men from whom labour and not skills are bought, are unbecoming and sordid; for in their case, that very wage itself is a pledge of their slavery. Also to be considered vulgar are those who buy from wholesale dealers and sell immediately, for they would make no profit unless they lied a great deal. And truly there is nothing more disgraceful than deception. All artisans too are engaged in sordid occupations, for no workshop can have anything noble about it. And the most shameful occupations are those which cater to our desires—"fishmongers, butchers, cooks, poulterers, and fishermen"—as Terence says. Add to these, if you like, perfumers, dancers, and the whole *ludus talarius*.[1] But those occupations which involve either greater intelligence or from which no small benefit is provided—like medicine, architecture, or the teaching of virtuous matters—these are appropriate for those whose social rank they suit. Trade, however, if it is small in scale, is to be considered sordid; but if it is large scale and well supplied, importing many things from all parts of the world, and distributing to many without deception, it is not to be wholly disparaged. In fact, it seems that it could be praised under the greatest law of respectability if one engaging in it, once satiated, or rather once he was satisfied that he had achieved his goals, then moved himself from the harbour into a country estate, as he had often moved from the deep sea into a harbour. For, of all the occupations from which profit is acquired, none is better than agriculture: none more profitable, none more delightful, none more fitting to a free man.

Note

1. Here Cicero may be alluding to the game of dice and gambling, to a type of performance involving dance that some regarded as licentious and undignified, or perhaps even to both.

Primary Source

Box 15.2: *CIL* 10.1401 = *ILS* 6043.[1]

In the consulship of Gnaeus Hosidius Geta and Lucius Vagellius (47 CE), September 22. Decree of the senate. Since the foresight of our excellent emperor has made provision also for the permanence of the buildings of our city and of all Italy . . . and since protection to public and private structures alike is fitting and appropriate to the approaching age, and since all ought to refrain from a most vicious kind of speculation and not bring about an appearance most incompatible with peace by the demolition of homes and villas; the senate decrees that if anyone purchases any building as a speculation, in order by tearing it down to obtain more than the price at which he purchased it, then he shall pay to the state treasury double the sum at which he bought the said property and the matter shall nonetheless be laid before the senate. And since a sale involving such evil precedent is no more admissible than such purchase, in order that sellers who knowingly and with malice aforethought sell contrary to this expressed will of the senate may also be restrained, the senate decrees that such sales shall be invalid.

Note

1. Adapted from the translation by Lewis and Reinhold (1990: 125–6, no. 33).

referring to it when he describes the demolition, continuous rebuilding, and repeated sales of property in Ostia.

Moneylending and Interest Rates

Pliny the Younger's (*Ep.* 3.19) words, "I am almost entirely bound up in estates, but I also loan money to some extent," certainly suggest that borrowing and lending money were activities known to the higher ranks of Roman society. Although land was the primary form of investment, the large fortunes of typical wealthy Romans might have consisted of a multitude of various speculations, such as land, livestock, cash, and precious objects.[38] Indeed, in Petronius's (37.8–9) novel, *Satyricon*, the fictional Trimalchio's fortune can be summarized as consisting of land, cash, and slaves, which apparently allowed him to be self-sufficient. But cash could not generate more capital unless it was invested or used in some way, such as lending it out in the form of interest-bearing loans.

Moneylending at interest won no moral approval (consider Cato's supposed pronouncement on the subject, given at the outset of this chapter) and was considered an activity that invited problems (see, for example, Tac. *Ann.* 6.16; Plut. *Mor.* 827F–828E).

Nonetheless, it seems that, although the elite might be snobbish about moneylending in theory, in reality these same wealthy individuals would not only lend money but also borrow it.[39] The difficulty of reconciling ideals with reality might result in some hypocrisy: the **consul** Gaius Rutilius Gallicus, himself a financier who dealt in loans, managed to find fault with the borrower Musonius (Plut. *Mor.* 830B).

The moral censure that moneylending earned may lead one to suspect that this activity was illegal. It was not, although the state appears to have occasionally taken an active role in the regulation of interest rates.[40] The laws of the **Twelve Tables** seem to have prohibited the lending of money at a rate higher than 100 per cent annually, or a monthly rate of 8.3 per cent (Tac. *Ann.* 6.16).[41] We also know that the limit fixed by the Twelve Tables was reinstituted in 357 BCE (Livy 7.16) and (unsurprisingly, given the exorbitant rate of interest) appears to have led to significant financial difficulties for poorer members of society. Ten years later, the rate was cut in half, and in 342 BCE a drastic attempt was made to deal with the problem: the *Lex Genucia* banned interest-bearing loans altogether (Livy 7.42). This ban, whether rescinded or ignored, did not last, and moneylending at interest continued. If Livy (35.7) is to be believed, the practice was again rife by the early second century BCE.[42] Although the developments are difficult to follow, attempts at regulating interest appear to have been made, and it is tempting to see the *Lex Iunia de feneratione* of 191 BCE as an effort to set a maximum rate of interest.[43]

Lending at interest was still causing problems in 89 BCE, however, when Aulus Sempronius Asellio tried to revive an old law that limited the practice (perhaps either the *Lex Genucia* or the *Lex Iunia*). His attempts were poorly received, and he was murdered by a group of moneylenders (App. *B Civ.* 1.54). A year later, the *Lex Cornelia Pompeia* may well have reinforced the sanction on interest-bearing loans (perhaps following the earlier *Lex Iunia*) and fixed a maximum rate at either 12 per cent or roughly 8.3 per cent annually (one-twelfth of the capital per year).[44] In 63 BCE the senate banned the exportation of gold and silver from Italy, perhaps in an attempt to contain interest rates (Cic. *Vat.* 12).[45] The evidence of Cicero's letters indicates that rates continued to fluctuate drastically in response to political upheavals in the late Republic, sometimes doubling in the space of two months. Although the senate attempted to impose some order by establishing an upper limit of 12 per cent annually in 51 BCE, some lenders paid no attention (Cic. *Att.* 1.12.1, 4.15.7, 5.21.13, 6.1.2; *Fam.* 5.6.2). However, this maximum soon became the typical rate for the rest of the republican period and into the **Principate**.[46]

Different rates nonetheless continue to appear based on the nature of the venture. In loans connected with maritime commerce, for example, rates were often very high due to the inherent risk of shipwreck and because a successful trip could yield a significant return.[47] But interest rates on loans attached to long-term enterprises tended to be lower. Most commonly, these investments were made in agricultural land and provided an income not only from the rents paid by tenant farmers but also from the sale of crops and livestock. Columella (*Rust.* 3.3.9–10) considers a return of 6 per cent typical for investments of this sort, and it seems that between 5 and 6 per cent was usual.

There were also some loans that were, in effect, free. Interest-free loans were to be found within the contexts of kinship and **patronage** and may have provided the lender

➔ Compare Chapter 3, p 66,
Chapter 4, p. 89, Chapter 7,
pp. 154–5, and Chapter 17,
pp. 384–5, on patronage.

with political advantage instead of monetary profit. These were loans literally for "political gain," made by politicians who reckoned that their financial gestures would advance their careers.[48] Furthermore, some interest-free loans could be made as acts of

euergetism towards civic communities. Such loans also functioned as displays of conspicuous generosity; however, they were not always without "interest." In 58 BCE works of art were transferred from borrowers in Sicyon to creditors in Rome, among whom was probably Cicero. His correspondence suggests that interest was compounded to the loan (Cic. *Att.* 1.13.1, 1.19.1, 2.1.10; Plin. *HN* 35.127).[49]

The Roman elite participated in this economic activity not only as lenders and creditors but also as borrowers and beneficiaries, on occasion even contracting loans to meet outstanding debts.[50] The members of the Roman upper class who invested money in this way—including well-placed individuals such as the **equestrian** Quintus Caecilius, uncle of Cicero's confidant, Titus Pomponius Atticus (Val. Max. 7.8.5; Sen. *Ep.* 118.2)—represented a class of creditors who could count on an income from finance as well as from the patrimonies at their disposal, which included land and property. Some of these men lent much more than others and therefore would have relied on the income derived from interest payments or defaulted land and possessions.

Alongside the image of the noble moneylenders from the narrow ranks of the Roman aristocracy stood the "professional" financiers.[51] It is plausible that these individuals appeared regularly at auctions, periodic markets (*nundinae*), and fairs throughout the Roman world.[52] Here they would provide the vendors, merchants, and traders with short-term credit, enabling the vendors and merchants to purchase goods without having the necessary funds with them and the traders to restock more quickly without having to wait for customers' payment. Although the actual activities and services of these financiers differed provincially and regionally (at least under the Empire),[53] their main financial functions appear to have involved the uniform practices of coinage testing and exchange, acceptance of deposited money, and the bestowal of credit in the form of interest-bearing loans, presumably at standard or above-standard rates.

Taxation

Taxes played an important role in the Roman economy: Cicero (*Leg. Man.* 17; compare *Dig.* 48.18.1.20) claimed that the revenues collected through taxation "were the sinews of the Republic." Tax revenues covered a variety of state expenses, ranging from provincial and civic administration to euergetism and military maintenance. The actual costs involved are impossible to calculate, but they must have been significant and likely grew as the empire expanded to include increasing numbers of provincial administrators, forces to provide **frontier** security, and recipients of state and imperial munificence. With expansion, however, the population subject to taxation also increased.

The Roman system of taxation was very different from the modern one. From 167 BCE until the civil wars after Julius Caesar's assassination, the Roman government did not subject its citizens to a regular poll tax (a charge imposed on each individual) or levy tax on "citizen land." This meant that the inhabitants of Italy, Roman colonies, and certain provincial cities and communities that possessed the "Italian right" (*ius Italicum*) were exempted from tax. After 167 BCE the term *tributum* denoted the direct taxes that were raised in the provinces in the form of a poll tax (*tributum capitis*) or land tax (*tributum soli*). During the Republic, the latter was usually a fixed sum—a *stipendium*—that provinces (such as Spain, Africa, and Gaul) paid annually. The republican *tributum soli* could also be represented as a tithe (*decuma*) on the grain or fruit harvest of the region or province, which was to be paid in kind.[54] The collection of this tax was leased to **publicani**, as was the case in Asia Minor (App. *B Civ.* 5.4.17–20). The *tributum capitis* seems to have first appeared in Africa in 146 BCE alongside the *tributum soli* (App. *Pun.* 135) but otherwise does not recur during the last century of the Republic.

The total tax revenue due on provinces (and communities) was typically expressed in terms of cash. But when the *tributum soli* was assessed and collected in kind, the Roman administration employed a fixed rate of exchange to calculate the "cash value" of the crops or products. This practice indicates that the Roman government could be flexible about payment (Tac. *Agr.* 19.4).[55] Moreover, it is clear that payment in kind was sometimes actively requested from some provinces (on Asia, for example, see App. *B Civ.* 5.1.4). This was particularly the case with those that grew a lot of grain, such as Egypt and Sicily (see, for example, P.Bour. 42; Cic. *Verr.* 2.3.73–74; Strabo 6.2.7; Aristid. *Or.* 26.12).[56]

During Augustus's reign, the system of taxation was overhauled significantly and was accompanied by an empire-wide census. Censuses were fundamental to the Roman imperial system of taxation. In Egypt, for instance, where the evidence for taxation is most prevalent, the census returns (which included household declarations of property) provided the data necessary for the calculation of the poll tax.[57] The *tributum capitis* and *tributum soli* thereafter became regular direct taxes on all provincial populations, although the actual assessments differed between them. In Egypt, the poll tax was levied on almost all adult males in the province who were between the ages of 14 and 62 or 65, while Roman and Alexandrian citizens, their slaves, some people who held official posts, and some categories of Egyptian priests were exempt.[58]

Indirect taxes (*vectigalia*) in the form of customs duties (*portoria*), taxes on slaves at auction, inheritance tax, and various other smaller imposts, multiplied considerably (see Tac. *Ann.* 1.78.2, 13.31.2; Cass. Dio 55.31.4). The *vectigalia* were likely easier to implement than the *tributum* direct taxes, and all the new taxes forced upon the populace in the early Empire were in the form of *vectigalia*,[59] from which even the population in Rome was sometimes not exempt (Suet. *Calig.* 40; *Vesp.* 23.3). *Vectigalia* could be significant. *Portoria*, for example, were exacted at ports, town gates, bridges, certain points on roads, provincial boundaries, and the frontiers of the empire.[60] Goods that travelled any distance within the empire could, theoretically, be subject to several *portoria* impositions. Rates of *portoria* were not uniform but could vary significantly between 2 per cent, as in Spain, and 5 per cent in the case of Sicily; duties on goods imported into and exported from Egypt appear to have been particularly heavy (Strabo 17.1.13).

The collection of this tax revenue was very important. Given the Roman administration's interest, it is hardly surprising to find numerous instances where the Roman army was involved in tax collection. Direct collection by the military, however, was occasional;[61] more often, soldiers were used to protect the tax collectors. In first-century CE Roman Egypt, for example, Nemesion, a collector of the poll tax in Philadelphia, employed soldiers (and others) as bodyguards.[62] In a letter to Trajan, Pliny the Younger (*Ep.* 10.27) notes that an imperial **freedman** on the staff of the **procurator** had asked for six soldiers in addition to those that he already had.[63] Collection typically fell to the *publicani*, private businessmen and contractors who paid for the right to collect specific taxes at auction and who acted in partnership with the state. These men were not simply tax collectors, however, and could be found managing a variety of state operations for which they had provided significant guarantees.

In the provinces outside Italy, the collection of the direct *tributum* taxes originally fell to the *publicani*. But during the late first century BCE, probably under Julius Caesar, the responsibility for the collection of *tributum* began to devolve to the civic authorities in individual communities. In 47 BCE Caesar restricted the ability of the *publicani* to collect these taxes in the cities of Asia and bestowed the responsibility upon the cities themselves (Cass. Dio 42.6; Plut. *Caes.* 48).[64] Generally, this process continued during the early first century CE, and it became normal practice for cities across the majority of the empire to collect the *tributum* taxes within their own territories.[65] Neither Augustus nor his successors introduced *publicani* to collect taxes in newly created provinces of the empire.

The direct and newly introduced taxes, however, continued to be collected by *publicani* until the middle of the second century CE and even later in some cases. But as the responsibility for collecting the majority of these taxes increasingly fell on civic authorities,[66] contracts would be auctioned off to the *publicani*, who would provide substantial security and then collect the tax for a percentage of the overall amount.[67] The emperors later created a kind of civil service, generally under the direction of imperial equestrian procurators, who controlled the collection of direct taxes—and, of course, the *publicani*— more closely. Later still, oversight of the collection of many taxes in addition to the direct ones fell to the procurators and their staff in some provinces.[68]

It is worth considering the practical systems of tax collection that developed at the community level. The Roman provincial administration of Egypt, for example, made use of liturgies.[69] These were positions of compulsory public duties, had a minimum property qualification—they were effectively based on the prospective holder's landed wealth—and covered a huge variety of service positions ranging from dike builders to bankers and tax collectors (see Box 15.3). Liturgical appointments were usually made by the village or city scribes (themselves liturgists). Where nominees were unable to perform

Primary Source

Box 15.3: *P.Petaus* 65 (186 CE).

To Apollonios, *strategos*[1] of the Herakleides division of the Arsinoite region, from Petaus, village scribe of Ptolemais Hormou and other villages. Maron son of Sabinus, Ischyrion son of Pasis, and Heron son of Hatres, the three collectors of money taxes of the village of Ptolemais Hormou, and Heron son of Herakleides, Herakleides son of Zoilos, Potamon son of Sokrates, Paaus son of Sokmas, Iustus son of Hermias, and Harpochration son of Potamon, likewise the six collectors of money taxes of the village of Syron, and Paesis son of Marres, Onnophris son of Petermouthis, Onnophris son of Pabois, and Horos son of Onnophris, likewise the four collectors of money taxes of the village of Kerkesoucha Orous, all 13 of these are now completing the allotted three-year term. To take their places, and with the consent and surety of those people in the villages and those farming in the areas around them who pledge mutual security according to custom, I nominate the following men who are of adequate wealth and suitable; their names are to be sent to the distinguished *epistrategos*[2] for selection by lot.

From Ptolemais Hormou, they are:

Petheus son of Ischyrion, whose mother is Thaubastis, owning property worth 700 drachmas.

Dios son of Papontos, whose mother is Thaubas, likewise 600 drachmas.

(The document continues with a list of a further 24 individuals, along with their respective property values [all between 600 and 800 drachmas], from the three villages. From these candidates, 13 would be chosen by lot.)

Notes

1. The chief local administrative official and governor of a nome.
2. An administrative official, above the *strategos*, responsible for several nomes.

their service, the scribes were either penalized financially, fulfilled the liturgy themselves, or found suitable replacements. If they failed (or absconded), the liturgist's community was held responsible by the state administration. Tax collectors were selected differently: for each position, two or three candidates were selected and their names were sent to a higher administrative official who selected the appointees by lot.[70]

The change and enforcement in the system of tax collection—making civic communities responsible for any deficits incurred in the tax revenue—provided the Roman government with a guarantee: they would receive the full value of the assessment because the communities were liable to make up any outstanding deficit from the collection.[71] Put simply, even if the assets of the individual taxpayers were insufficient to meet their tax obligations, the Roman government could look to the community and to those who had taken on the collection of these taxes (the *publicani* or the liturgists) to make up any shortfall.[72] As a result, those who had bid successfully for tax collection contracts or who had been assigned them as a liturgy often pleaded for release from the burden of this guarantee (for example, *P.Graux.* 2 = *Sel.Pap.* 2.281; *P.Mich.* 10.582). But the system could also be abused, not only by the *publicani* but also by the upper levels of the Roman provincial administration (see Box 15.4).

Production and Trade

The scale of production and trade in the Roman Republic and Empire, at least in terms of a pre-industrial society, were extraordinary and impressive, and it is certainly true that there were significant but gradual changes during the central period. Two of the most important changes were the geographical broadening of Rome's influence to establish a Mediterranean empire (marine archaeology demonstrates an acceleration of trade already from the second century BCE)[73] and the political change from a Republic torn by civil war to a relatively stable Empire. These factors supported a Mediterranean-wide emporium and created a demand for products that were both manufactured in and transported through the Roman provinces.

Places of production and manufacture were generally small. A variety of craftspeople and workshops were likely found in all kinds of rural and urban settlements, working not only for the needs of the community but also market sale. There were some notable exceptions, however, concerning textiles and pottery. The significant number of what appear to be much larger textile establishments at Timgad in North Africa and the presence of *fora vestiaria* (markets specializing in clothing) are suggestive of textile production that went far beyond the community's needs.[74] Moreover, the layout and size of workshops at Le Rozier (near La Graufesenque in southwest France) and Scoppieto (in Italy), where numerous potters would have worked beside one another, suggest production on a significant scale. It was these workshops, and perhaps others like them, that played a role in

Political History

Box 15.4: Oppressive Taxation and Rapacious Officials

The picture of the greedy Roman tax collector is certainly not uncommon. Documentary and literary evidence is littered with references to Roman officials and local administrators abusing their positions. The problem was largely one of Rome's own doing: when auctioning off contracts for tax collection, the state largely relied not only on the collectors' survival instincts but also on their profit motivation. The tax burden borne by the provincial populations, particularly under the Empire, could be oppressive without the added avarice of its collectors, and there are several examples of provincial governors (and even emperors) attempting to rein in their representatives at the local and provincial levels.

One of the most startling cases can be found during the reign of Tiberius (14–37 CE). Cassius Dio (57.10.5; compare Suet. *Tib.* 32.2) tells us that the emperor, who was notoriously careful with state expenditures, discovered that Aemilius Rectus—the provincial governor of Egypt—sent more money than had been requested. Evidently, Rectus was under the impression that an increase in provincial revenue would earn imperial favour. But Tiberius replied in a terse message: "I want my sheep shorn, not shaven" (Suetonius claims that, in a letter to several governors, Tiberius stated that "the good shepherd was to shear his flock of sheep, not skin it"). Tiberius's reproach apparently did not end there: Aemilius Rectus appears to have been in position for only a year or so, and he was likely recalled to Rome.

Of course, Aemilius Rectus would have done well to remember the example of Gaius Verres, the governor of Sicily between 73 and 71 BCE. After financially oppressing and exploiting the province, he was prosecuted by Cicero before the *praetor urbanus* Marcus Acilius Glabrio in the *quaestio de repetundis* (a court established to bring compensation for the illegal acquisition of money or property by Roman officials abroad) on charges of extortion in 70 BCE. Outfoxed by Cicero's tactics, Verres fled into exile before he had to meet Cicero in court again. Cicero published his orations for both *actiones* (court sessions), despite the fact that the second was never given in public (see Cicero's *Verrine Orations*).

Both occasions are startling in their demonstration not only of the political and economic power of provincial governors but also the senate's, and later the emperor's, awareness of the economic oppression of Rome's subjects.

the massive production and proliferation of the distinctive red pottery called *terra sigillata* (see Figure 15.1). In fact, the kilns at La Graufesenque were apparently able to accommodate 30,000 high-quality pots in a single firing.[75] There are also interesting allusions to trade and production on an even larger scale: some cities and towns may have had

Figure 15.1   Ceramic bowl, *terra sigillata*, Roman period in Complutum. © Carlos Mora/Alamy

quarters that were named after types of crafts, trades, or areas of production. In Egypt, for example, Arsinoe and Karanis had linen workshops' quarters (*P.Fay.* 59; *P.Tebt.* 2.321; *BGU* 15.2471; *SB* 6.9554 2c).

Agrarian production, however, was most common. In some areas much of it may well have been close to the level of subsistence (in effect, what people needed to survive), but there were certainly regional differences given the climactic variations between distant parts of the empire. Although regional specialization existed,[76] the basics of agricultural production were the so-called Mediterranean triad of grains, olives, and grapes (similar forms of crops and produce were either grown or transported even in non-Mediterranean regions of the empire). Cereal crops were likely the most widespread agricultural product. They offered a stable and low-risk venture for both subsistence and beyond, although it seems that they were not particularly lucrative. Olives and grapevines, however, became increasingly important commodities, leading to changes in both management and outlets for production. Such changes are often highlighted in the agricultural treatises of the Republic, most notably in those of Cato and Varro, and might reflect increases in demand. By the end of the Republic, Rome and Italy were, in part, supplied by olive oil and wine produced in Spain and in Africa.[77]

Animal husbandry also played a valuable role. Animals were not only an important source of food, but they also fulfilled secondary roles. Cattle were used for traction—pulling farm equipment, for example—and were valued for their hides, while sheep would be reared for their wool. Although it is very difficult to identify particular zones of husbandry, some general trends can be seen. For instance, in Italy sheep and goats are in greatest evidence, but pork production appears to have increased over time in both Italy and several other western provinces.[78] In northern provinces, particularly in Britain, cattle predominate, which may suggest a less intensive mode of production in favour of a more pastoral approach.[79]

The archaeological record illustrates both long- and short-distance trade, but not all movements of goods reflect this. Army supply, state intervention, transfers of agricultural produce between estates belonging to the same owner, and perhaps even gift exchange provide other explanations. Nevertheless, much of this evidence—wide-ranging in quantity, quality, and variety—also illustrates significant levels of private trade.

Trade depended almost entirely on the development of the transportation infrastructure, most notably the network of ports and harbours on the empire's coastlines and the system of roads that spread outward from Rome.[80] The state's concern was certainly concentrated on the construction of roads for the movement of troops and other military personnel, but trade was also encouraged and traders followed in the wake of the army. Furthermore, Roman investment in making river systems more navigable also enhanced the transport infrastructure. The cost of land transportation, which appears to have been higher than that of maritime or riverine passage, may well have determined the distribution of traded products. Nevertheless, despite the higher relative cost and the investment made in riverine transportation, goods were traded by land, particularly in regions that were not accessible by navigable waterways but where the demand for such products existed. The increasing network of high-quality roads (most in Italy) and the movement of goods along them was noted by ancient authors, who claim that vehicles—at least on Italian roads—could, and did, carry sizeable cargoes (Strabo 5.3.7; Varro, *Rust.* 1.16.6).[81]

Compare Chapter 16, pp. 361–3, on transport infrastructure.

Perhaps the most significant long-distance trade link was the trade in luxuries—including pepper, ivory, precious stones, Chinese silk, and perfumes—from the East and through India and Yemen. The ports of Egypt on the Red Sea, such as Myos Hormos and Berenike, played an important role in this trade, which continued through the first three centuries CE.[82] Evidence for cross-Arabian trade, particularly in aromatics, can be seen in outpost garrisons such as Hegra and in major cities in the region such as Petra.[83] The city of Palmyra also played an important role in overland and river trade in the region, as its location in an oasis where several routes intersected made the city a hub of commercial mediation. Palmyra offered merchants desert transportation, organized caravans that travelled into Mesopotamia, and provided merchants with access to its stalls in Mesopotamia and the Persian Gulf.[84]

Besides luxuries, a wide variety of commodities could be found moving throughout the provinces, including (but certainly not limited to) cereals, olive oil, wine, other perishable foods, slaves, metals, textiles, and pottery.[85] It is certainly true that local production for local consumption was important, but cities—particularly Rome—regularly imported many of the staples, such as wheat. Olive oil could also be produced locally, at least in the Mediterranean, but there were specific regions that were known for the production of this staple. Under the Romans, several regions (for example, Africa Proconsularis, Baetica, and Tripolitania) developed not only a clear specialization in the production of olive oil but also a significant capacity for its export.[86] From these regions, the oil was shipped in sizeable quantities to the northern provinces, where the army, Roman citizens, and subject populations likely formed a body of avid consumers.

Wine, which could be produced in most Roman provinces, and other foods (such as particular varieties of meat, fish, dairy, vegetables, and fruit) were transported both between cities and their hinterlands and between provinces. The trade of such comestibles is difficult to quantify to any real extent, but ancient authors do note the movement of such perishable goods. Strabo (4.4.3, 5.1.12; compare Polyb. 2.15.3) says that salted meat from Belgica was supplied to Rome and to most parts of Italy and claims that Rome was also supplied with Cisalpine pork, while one of Lucian's (*Nav.* 23) characters notes that he will have smoked fish from Spain. Wine, too, seems to have been transported over considerable distances, in spite of the fact that viticulture appears to have spread as far north as southern and eastern Britain and into Germany and even played an important role in the economy of southern Gaul.[87] In the first century BCE Italian merchants may have been actively trading wine for slaves in Gaul, at least if Diodorus Siculus (5.26.3) is to be believed, and the sheer quantities of Italian wine **amphorae** found on the riverbed of the Rhône are significant and suggestive of the flourishing trade in, and demand for, Italian wine (see Lucian *Nav.* 23).[88]

As we have already seen, the sale of slaves was taxed. Naturally, demand for this particular commodity continued throughout the period under discussion.[89] While it is difficult to judge the numbers in the slave markets with any accuracy, it would be fair to say that they could increase significantly when war was a con-

→ See Chapter 4, pp. 79–81 on slave markets.

tributing factor. Polybius (30.15) and Livy (45.34.5–6) speak of approximately 150,000 prisoners of war from Epirus being sold into slavery in 167 BCE, while Plutarch (*Caes.* 15) suggests that Caesar took at least a million Gauls captive, the majority presumably as slaves, during his Gallic campaigns in the mid-first century BCE. Josephus (*BJ* 6.420) claims that the suppression of the Jewish revolt of 66–70 CE led to the capture of 97,000 individuals. Slave sales and purchases probably happened in every Roman city, but two of the most active centres of the trade—apart from the city of Rome—appear to have been the island of Delos (until it was sacked in 69 BCE) and Ephesus, although many other towns and cities appear in the sources. For instance, the tax law of Palmyra (*IGRom* 3 1056 = *OGI* 629) highlights the import and export of slaves into and through the city and on into Syria.[90]

Expansion into the western Mediterranean and Europe gave the Romans access to a variety of precious metals. These resources were particularly novel for the Romans as Italy contained few of them.[91] Rome had originally been reliant on imports and indemnities from mines controlled by Carthage in the West and by the Hellenistic kingdoms in the East, but the defeat of Hannibal in 202 BCE and Perseus in 168 BCE paved the way for Roman exploitation of the mines near New Carthage in Spain and Macedon.[92] These provinces saw the significant development of mining and metal extraction and the organized exploitation of the bullion metal.[93] The mining operations were managed in a variety of ways: sometimes they were state operated, but more often they could be and were leased out to *publicani*.[94] The metals—in a variety of forms ranging from artifacts to simple ingots and coinage—could then be moved over short and long distances through sales, exchanges, imports, and exports.

Textiles were also traded. Like wine, they were likely produced in all provinces, but certain types from particular provinces were more highly valued and some might have been traded as luxuries. By the mid-first century CE, the province of Nearer Spain

(Hispania Citerior) was producing linen that, according to Pliny the Elder (*HN* 19.10), was "of the greatest lustre"; Egypt had become famous for its linen production, which was apparently in great demand in eastern trade, and, later, known for the cultivation of flax (Plin. *HN* 19.7, 13–14; SHA *Gall.* 6.4); and Apulian wool was the most highly esteemed (Plin. *HN* 8.190–1). The movement of textiles throughout the Roman world is also attested in the ancient sources, with Strabo (3.2.6, 4.4.3, 4.5.2, 5.1.12) noting that Belgica, Liguria, Turdetania in Baetica, the Insubrian area of northern Italy, and Patavium were all important sources of wool, while Pliny the Elder (*HN* 19.10) states that Zoëla flax—a form particularly suited for use in hunting-nets—was exported from Spain to Italy.

Pottery also plays an important role in the study of trade and the ancient economy, largely because it is the dominant surviving form of manufactured material, particularly as amphorae.[95] There certainly was a long-distance trade in the commodity originally stored in the pottery: consider once more the sheer quantities of Italian wine amphorae found on the riverbed of the Rhône, perhaps ranging above 100,000.[96] Moreover, *terra sigillata* was occasionally exported long distances. During the first century CE, the growing trade in red-slip ware from North Africa led to an ever-increasing supply that was used by the communities in and around the Mediterranean.

Summary

The Roman economy was perhaps one of the most advanced of all pre-industrial societies, although it remained primarily agrarian in nature. As Rome's territory increased, so did its population, which in turn led to several problems. The most concerning, perhaps, was the ever-increasing demand for land. Wherever and whenever possible, those who could afford to do so invested in land to varying degrees and with mixed results. Despite the risks associated with both rural and urban property, land remained the most sought-after form of investment. Tenancy played a significant role in the ownership of property, where workers, smallholders, and tenants would till the land not only for themselves but also for their employers and landlords.

The economy, however, offered several opportunities for those willing to take a risk. Moneylending and loans provided methods for a variety of individuals and financiers from several levels of society to borrow or lend money. The primary use of taxation was ostensibly to pay for various administrative and infrastructural enterprises of the Roman Republic and Empire, ranging from the military to acts of imperial beneficence; however, the system under the Empire became more complex and wide-ranging, with *vectigalia* levied on a staggering assortment of activities. Trade was also important and became ever more so as the empire expanded. Although the Roman administration's attitude to manufacture and trade was largely impartial, its interest in facilitating the movement of goods and services (for instance, for the supply of the Roman army) provided not only a framework upon which trade and production was cultivated but also indirect economic benefit for the state through *portoria* and other types of taxation. A huge variety of goods, ranging from grain to luxury items, were manufactured and traded, and some were transported over long distances.

In sum, the Roman economy was not a stagnant, monolithic, simple structure. It was a diverse, multi-faceted system borne by the Romans' aspirations for imperial expansion and control.

Questions for Review and Discussion

1. Was the Roman economy based on subsistence farming or did trade play a significant role? Provide examples to support your answer.
2. Using two different forms of evidence, consider how we can obtain data for the Roman economy.
3. What was the most important form of economic investment for the Romans? Why was it more significant than other types?
4. How did the Roman elite use, manage, and keep their wealth?
5. How advanced were trade and the economy in the Roman Republic and Empire? Were these aspects stagnant or constantly in flux? Give evidence to support your answers.

Suggested Reading

Andreau, J. 1999. *Banking and Business in the Roman World*. Cambridge: Cambridge University Press.

This volume considers the financial life of the Roman elite, bankers, and the interests of the state in business and banking between the fourth century BCE and the end of the third century CE. Andreau illustrates the extent to which profit and initiative predominated over more traditional Roman values.

Bowman, A.K., and A.I. Wilson, eds. 2009. *Quantifying the Roman Economy: Methods and Problems*. Oxford: Oxford University Press.

Using documentary evidence and archaeology, the chapters in this volume focus on the performance of the economy during the Roman Empire. The volume analyzes Rome's domination of the Mediterranean and Europe and how the Romans created the conditions for the integration of agriculture, commerce, production, and trade.

Duncan-Jones, R. 1990. *Structure and Scale in the Roman Economy*. Cambridge: Cambridge University Press.

Duncan-Jones offers a series of studies falling into five distinct categories—time and distance, demography, agrarian patterns, urbanization, and taxation—that explore some of the most important aspects of the Roman economy and considers not only how they were connected but also how they interacted.

Harris, W.V., ed. 2008. *The Monetary Systems of the Greeks and Romans*. Oxford: Oxford University Press.

The chapters in this volume consider monetization, credit, coinage, the demand for credit and coinage, and the nature of money during the Republic and Empire.

Mattingly, D.J., and J. Salmon, eds. 2001. *Economies beyond Agriculture in the Classical World*. London and New York: Routledge.

The relevant chapters in this book (by Woolf, Mattingly et al., Aubert, Maxfield, Adams, Delaine, Wilson, and Drinkwater) challenge the traditional view that the predominantly agricultural economy of Rome was underdeveloped. They demonstrate that the exploitation of natural resources, production, transport, and the building trade all made significant contributions to the Roman economy.

Morley, N. 1996. *Metropolis and Hinterland: The City of Rome and the Italian Economy,*
200 BC–AD 200. Cambridge: Cambridge University Press.

Morley considers the growth of Rome, the effects of its imperial aspirations, and its demands of consumption on the Roman economy.

Parkins, H., and C. Smith, eds. 1998. *Trade, Traders and the Ancient City*. London and New York: Routledge.

The chapters in this volume consider the relationship between the nature of exchange, commerce, and the cities of the ancient world while examining the role that trade played in both Greek and Roman economies.

Scheidel, W., and S. von Reden, eds. 2002. *The Ancient Economy*. Edinburgh: Edinburgh University Press.

This text contains chapters from interdisciplinary perspectives on a variety of subjects, ranging from olive production to taxes, trade, and rents, and their place in the Roman economy.

Scheidel, W., I. Morris, and R. Saller, eds. 2007. *The Cambridge Economic History of the Greco-Roman World*. Cambridge: Cambridge University Press.

Certain chapters in this volume—by Morel, Harris, Kehoe, Morley, Jongman, and Lo Cascio—not only provide expansive overviews of the Roman economy from early Republic to Empire but also examine the role of production, distribution, consumption, and state interest. Some of the chapters also consider specific provinces and areas of the empire, notably the eastern Mediterranean and western provinces (Alcock and Leveau, respectively), Egypt (Rathbone), and the Roman frontier zones (Cherry).

Notes

1   I would like to thank Georgy Kantor for reading and commenting on a draft of this chapter.
2   All translations are mine unless otherwise noted.
3   On Roman coinage and its history, see Hollander (2008: 112–36); Lo Cascio (2008: 160–73); Harris (2008: 174–207); Reden (2010); Katsari (2011); and Metcalf (2012).
4   See Hollander (2007: 15, n. 8).
5   Earlier, the Romans were reliant on imports and indemnities from the Hellenistic kingdoms and Carthage. See Howgego (1992: 4–7).
6   Wilson and Robinson (2011: 1–13); Parker (1992).
7   For Egypt, see Rathbone (2007a: 709–12) and Gibbs (2012); for Vindolanda, see Bowman (1998).
8   See Rostovtzeff (1957).
9   See Finley (1999).
10   See Hopkins (1980: 101–25; 1995/96: 41–75) and bibliographies therein.
11   On this, see Fulford (1987) and Woolf (1992). On the degree of connectivity between these regions and its uncertainty, see Horden and Purcell (2000).
12   Scheidel (2007a: 38); Nicolet (1992: 600).
13   Nicolet (1992: 600).
14   Hopkins (1980: 124–5); MacMullen (1984a). See Rathbone (1996: 310), however, for problems with such estimates.
15   Harris (2007: 516); Roselaar (2010: 196). On the "low count" theory, the number of citizens increased, but a slight decline in population is possible if manumissions and grants of citizenship are detracted. See de

Ligt (2004) and Scheidel (2004). According to the "high count" theory, the growth was very significant. See Lo Cascio and Malanima (2005) and Kron (2005).
16   Liv. Per. 59; RG 8.2. All of the extant census figures can be found in Brunt (1971: 13–14) and Nicolet (1992: 603).
17   A point well made by Harris (2007: 516).
18   See, for instance, Brunt (1971: 384). For a further bibliography, see Roselaar (2010: 181, n. 124).
19   Roselaar (2010: 199).
20   See Frier (2000: 812, Table 5).
21   Frier (2000: 813–14, Table 6); Scheidel (2007a: 47).
22   See Duncan-Jones (1996: 108–36).
23   Frier (2000: 816).
24   Duncan-Jones (1990: 126); Garnsey and Saller (1987: 64); Jones (1974: 125); Rostovtzeff (1957: 17).
25   Garnsey and Saller (1987: 64); Duncan-Jones (1982: 19).
26   Kehoe (2006: 298).
27   Duncan-Jones (1990: 126).
28   Garnsey (2000: 696).
29   Kehoe (1992: 110–12).
30   Lewis (1999: 57–9); Bowman (1996a: 138); Bagnall (2005: 195).
31   Mattingly (2006: 288). The third-century CE estate of Aurelius Appianus, in Theadelphia in the Arsinoite nome of Egypt, is a case in point (Rathbone 1991: 88–211).
32   P.Lond. 1.131 and 1.131 R = SB 8.9699. For translations, see Johnson (1936: 177–207, nos. 104–05).
33   Kehoe (1992: 63–4).
34   Garnsey (1998: 68).
35   Ibid.: 69; Meiggs (1973: 237).

36   For Cicero's landholdings, see Shatzman (1975: 403–09).

37   Marzano (2007: 79–80).

38   Andreau (2000: 769).

39   Ibid.

40   See Bresson and Hollander (forthcoming) for a detailed consideration of Roman interest rates.

41   Andreau (1999: 91); Zehnacker (1980: 353–62).

42   See also Livy 32.27, 35.41.

43   Astin (1978: 319–23) but see also Barlow (1978: 59–60), who argues that Lex Iunia de feneratione may have abolished interest altogether.

44   Andreau (1999: 92).

45   See also Cic. Flac. 67.

46   For examples, see Shelton (1998: no. 173); P.Oxy. 55.3798.22, 44.3198.11; and Plin. Ep. 9.28, 10.54.

47   Andreau (1999: 54–6); Rathbone (2003: 197–229); Jones (2006: 180–6)

48   Andreau (1999: 144–5).

49   Ibid.: 143.

50   See, for instance, Plin. Ep. 3.19.8–9. The loan here was possibly taken under more advantageous terms (Kehoe [1997: 46]).

51   See, for instance, the Suplicii, who were bankers in Puteoli (Jones [2006]; D'Arms [1981: 121–48]).

52   One of Pliny the Younger's (Ep. 8.2.1) letters, however, may suggest that they appeared at only the larger rural markets and in towns.

53   Andreau (2000: 772).

54   The decuma was one-tenth of the grain harvest or one-fifth of the fruit harvest.

55   Rathbone (1996: 314; 1989: 173–4).

56   Bagnall (1985: 292); Wallace (1938: 47).

57   Bagnall and Frier (1994: 26–30); Capponi (2005: 83–96).

58   Capponi (2005: 138–41). Compare the Roman province of Syria where, at least by the early third century CE, males were liable from the ages of 14 to 65 and females from 12 to 65 (Dig. 50.15.3).

59   Rathbone (1996: 314–5).

60   Duncan-Jones (1990: 195).

61   The example of the praetorian guard collecting taxes under Caligula is perhaps a case in point (Suet. Calig. 40).

62   Nemesion was not the only tax collector who used military support. See, for example, P.Tebt. 2.391 and Hanson (1989: 435–6, n. 26).

63   On the role of the army and taxation, see Davies (1974: 327); Alston (1995: 79–81); and Pollard (2000: 100–04).

64   Brunt (1990: 388–93).

65   Sharp (1999: 215–16); Brunt (1990: 388).

66   See, for instance, the Monumentum Ephesenum and the Flavian Lex municipalis: Lo Cascio (2003: 249–65); Sharp (1999: 226); Bowman (1996b: 362); Tacitus, Ann. 13.50; and Cottier et al. (2008).

67   Sharp (1999: 216); Brunt (1981: 169).

68   Brunt (1990: 355–6).

69   Lewis (1999: 177–83); Capponi (2005: 65–81).

70   See Lewis (1997: 65–79; 1999: 179–80).

71   Brunt (1981: 169).

72   Bowman (1996b: 362).

73   Harris (2007: 532).

74   Wilson (2001: 285).

75   Peacock (1982: 114–28).

76   See, for instance, Roselaar (2010: 166–72) on regional specialization in Italy during the Republic.

77   See Nicolet (1992: 613–15) for further discussion of the changes in the late Republic.

78   King (2001: 212–20).

79   Wilson (2008b: 174); MacKinnon (2004).

80   See Chapter 16 of this volume.

81   See also Sartre (2000: 658) for Syria and Adams (2007: 22–6, 30–3, 36–42) for Egypt.

82   See Gibbs (2012) for further bibliography, with the addition of Young (2001).

83   Sartre (2000: 659); Alcock (2007: 689–90).

84   Sartre (2000: 661).

85   For a more detailed investigation into the traded items listed here, as well as trade generally during the Empire, see Harris (2000: 710–40, esp. 716–29).

86   Mattingly (1988: 33–56; 1995: 223–6).

87   See Brun and Laubenheimer (2001: 1–260).

88   Tchernia (1983: 87–104).

89   See Harris (2011: 57–109); Bradley (2011: 241–64); Morley (2011: 265–86); Scheidel (2011: 287–310).

90   See Matthews (1984: 157–80); Gawlikowski (1988: 163–72).

91   Nicolet (1992: 624–6).

92   See also Howgego (1992: 4).

93   Wilson (2008b: 176); Howgego (1992: 7, n. 52).

94   See Hirt (2010: 107–356) on the various forms of management of these mining operations.

95   Peacock and Williams (1986); Peña (2007).

96   Tchernia (1983: 87–104).

16

Roman Technology and Engineering

Milorad Nikolic

Vitruvius's *De architectura* (*On Architecture*) is the only surviving piece of Roman literature that is specifically devoted to architecture. Active in the second half of the first century BCE, Vitruvius took part in the Roman construction boom under the emperor Augustus, to whom he dedicated his book of collected knowledge. In the following excerpt, he discusses the required skills of an engineer:

> The skill set of an engineer consists of familiarity with a number of disciplines and education in a variety of fields. His judgment puts to the test all work executed in the other fields of technology. This set of skills is the combined result of practice and theory. . . . Those who are thoroughly trained in both, equipped with a comprehensive tool set, execute a proposed plan with expertise and in a timely fashion. . . . Such a person must be educated in the liberal arts, skilled with a pencil, trained in land surveying, well versed in history, have diligently studied philosophy, appreciate music, should have some understanding of medicine, be familiar with legal argumentation, and have knowledge of astronomy and celestial mechanics. (Vitr. *De arch*. 1.1–3)[1]

Vitruvius's catalogue of qualities strikes us as strange since these fields of study are largely absent from engineering programs in modern universities. To be sure, the qualities he lists represent an ideal situation. It is hardly plausible to assume that every individual engaged in engineering could possess all those skills. His precepts show, nonetheless, a fundamental feature of technology in the ancient world: the human being was the measure of all things.

Timeline

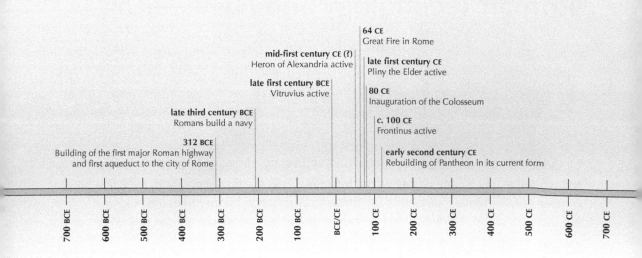

Introduction

Modern engineers develop technology based on the investigation and application of scientific and mathematical principles. In the Roman period, the situation was quite different. In fact, the study and explanation of natural phenomena was a gentleman's occupation. These individuals, whom we call natural philosophers, employed reason rather than experiment in their study of the natural world. Notable Roman natural philosophers were Lucretius (first century BCE) and Seneca the Younger (early first century CE). The practical application and technical mastery of physical principles were left to skilled craftspeople, who derived their expertise from personal experience and probably from technical manuals that must have been in circulation among professionals in the same field.[2]

The inconsistent survival of technical installations and implements is a challenge for modern scholars. Tools and devices made from perishable organic materials (wood, leather), corroding metals (iron, copper), or metals that are easily reused and recycled for other purposes (lead, bronze, copper) rarely appear in the archaeological record. Only a few written sources that deal specifically with applied technologies and physical principles have survived. Most evidence is, therefore, archaeological or incidental from non-technical literary works. For example, the only literary reference to a water-driven reciprocating marble saw comes from a poem about the serenity of life along the Moselle River, written by Ausonius in the fourth century CE. Modern commentators have often written about a certain degree of technological stagnation during the Roman period, especially if compared to the medieval era. More recent scholarship, however, argues that such an assessment is incorrect and merely a result of the difference in the survival of evidence from the two periods. As more and more information from the Roman period comes to light, its technological development appears less and less static.

Another difference between ancient technology and modern engineering is the sense of immediacy. Sources of motive energy were, with a few significant exceptions, human or animal. The strength of hands and feet was directed or magnified by the pulley, lever, and inclined plane, but there was no possibility of accelerating locomotion on land beyond the speed of horses, donkeys, oxen, or camels. Moreover, Roman technology was purposeful and pragmatic. Its goal was to solve specific problems and respond to precise and immediate needs, not to earn money by its widespread dissemination and sale.

The greatest Roman achievement probably lay in what we today would term civil engineering (building construction and transport infrastructure). Through their excellent organization and administration and virtually inexhaustible resources (human and financial), the Romans developed these technologies on a scale unprecedented in Europe. This chapter shows how Roman territorial and cultural expansion was facilitated by applying technology and building infrastructure and vice versa. A full impression of Roman society and the interaction between Romans and newly incorporated peoples is impossible without the consideration of Roman technology, as it not only marked the ancient physical landscape but also impacted many

Compare Chapter 3, pp. 57–8, on ◂╌
Roman technological achievement
and its impact on societies.

aspects of the daily lives of those who made up that society. The chapter also raises a few pertinent research questions in the history of ancient technology.

———— • • ————

Terminology and Transfer of Knowledge

Modern students of ancient technology must beware of anachronisms in vocabulary. For want of a better word, we call those people who were occupied with the design, construction, and operation of mechanical devices in antiquity engineers. Some of these could convert muscle, water, or wind power into useful work. We must understand, however, that the Romans did not possess technologically viable engines in the modern sense of the word, that is, devices that convert chemical energy from fossil fuels into kinetic energy for use in industrial-sized technical applications. It is therefore worthwhile to look at terminology, as it will help explain the nature and the origins of Roman technological achievement.

The English language owes much of its basic technical vocabulary directly to Greek and Latin. The word *technology* is ultimately derived from the Greek word *tekhnē* ("skill," or "craft"). The closest Latin equivalent, *ars*, is the root of the word *artifex* ("artificer; a professional workman, craftsman, or artisan"). *Artifex* and *faber* ("a worker in wood, stone, or metal") perhaps come closest to the meaning of the modern English word *engineer*, itself derived from the Latin *ingenium* ("skill"; "cleverness"; "talent"). A person who is *ingeniosus* is "full of intellect" and "superior in mind." The word is also related to the Latin verb *ingignere* ("to beget"). Another term that Roman authors use to denote a person responsible for the design and construction of buildings and mechanical contrivances, **architectus**, is derived from the Greek *arkhitektōn* ("chief artificer"). The word can be translated, depending on context, as both "architect" and "engineer." The word *machine* is derived from the Latin **machina**, which is related to the Greek *mēkhanē* (compare *mechanics*), meaning an artificial device for performing a task.

It is no coincidence that many of these terms are ultimately of non-Latin origin. This brief glimpse at vocabulary demonstrates a key feature of Roman technology: the willingness to adopt technological achievements from other cultures and to apply them skilfully to Roman needs. The Roman state, and wealthy individuals within it, often used its almost limitless financial and human resources to enhance existing technologies and structures on an extraordinary scale. For example, Roman water supply and drainage systems were adopted from the Etruscans;[3] the first construction of a significant naval fleet was accomplished by using know-how from allies of non-Roman extraction;[4] and certain aspects of building construction and geometry were adopted from the Greeks.[5]

Before this chapter explores a few technologies in more detail, it is necessary to outline the transfer of written technical information in antiquity, currently a very active field of study. Research focuses on the following three questions: To what extent and in what form was technical expertise exchanged? What role did the few technical texts that survive from Greek and Roman antiquity play in the overall scheme of technical development? Is it possible to use categories from modern engineering and science to describe ideas from ancient technology and **natural philosophy**? We will examine the first two questions here.

It is possible that the trade secrets of ancient engineers were jealously guarded, which would explain the rarity of surviving written material. Although there is no direct evidence for this kind of protectionism in the Roman period, such practices were common among master masons in the fifteenth century CE[6]. The ability to convey water over long distances, for example, is important not only from a practical aspect but also in terms of popular esteem and, consequently, power. Whoever commanded the skill, whether it was the person in charge of design and construction or the one paying for the project, had access to a source of prestige.

Compare Chapter 3, pp. 56–8, on ← infrastructures built as benefactions by the elite.

That said, the storage and exchange of information are essential for large-scale engineering projects. The civil-engineering achievements in the Roman world could not

Compare Chapter 12, p. 274, ← and Chapter 17, pp. 390–1, on the Colosseum.

have succeeded without written transmission of information and technical drawings. For example, neither the **aqueducts** nor the **Colosseum** could have been built without knowledge being passed to subsequent generations of craftspeople and engineers. It is likewise inconceivable that trial and error was the guiding principle behind these structures. They can only be a result of the accumulated knowledge that generations of specialists stored in technical manuals. John Peter Oleson writes: "The relatively high level of basic literacy in the Roman empire . . . may well have fostered the spread of some craft techniques and innovations in popular written form," that is, in subliterary technical manuals.[7]

Only a very small number of ancient literary sources that specifically deal with technology have survived. Among these, Vitruvius, Heron of Alexandria, Pliny the Elder, and Frontinus have received particular attention in modern scholarship. A brief survey of these authors and their surviving texts provides some information about engineers' theoretical knowledge. Of Vitruvius's life only a few details are known. He was born probably about 80 or 70 BCE. Textual references to Octavian (the future emperor Augustus) and to existing buildings in Rome indicate that his *De architectura* was written in the 20s BCE. Books 1 through 7 of this treatise deal with architecture proper, such as the layout of public and residential buildings and the construction methods of floors and walls. Book 8 treats water-supply systems, while books 9 and 10 are concerned with engineering topics such as clocks and various kinds of machines. Louis Callebat has suggested that these three parts were written at different times and that Book 8, whose topic lies mid-way between architecture and engineering, was added last.[8]

Not much is known about the life of Heron of Alexandria either. In one of his works, he discusses a method for determining the distance between Rome and Alexandria by timing the same lunar eclipse at both places. The only lunar eclipse that was visible from these two locations in five centuries occurred in 62 CE, which places Heron's life in the first century CE.[9] This versatile author wrote about mathematics, physics, surveying, pneumatics, and mechanics. He drew his information from earlier writers, most notably Ktesibios, a Greek inventor and mathematician who flourished in Alexandria in the third century BCE.[10] Heron describes not only practical devices such as surveying instruments and gearing mechanisms but also gadgets, so-called *automata*, that appear impractical from a modern point of view. They were perhaps objects used to demonstrate mechanical principles, working models that may or may not have also been built on a larger scale. One of Heron's (*Pneum.* 1.50) small-scale models, a rotating sphere with two angled nozzles propelled by steam, effectively anticipates the invention of the steam turbine. Other inventions automatically open temple doors, refill wine cups, or make mechanical birds sing. The surviving descriptions of Heron's *automata* contain copies of line drawings that show how these devices function.

Heron's work illustrates ancient engineers' qualitative awareness of the laws that govern the physical world around them. Although his *automata* are often described as toys with no practical application, such an assessment ignores their potential applicability. This blinkered thinking about technological innovation is not unique: the thirteenth-century CE scientist Roger Bacon, for example, described gunpowder in firecrackers as a toy.[11] Heron's *automata* certainly show a qualitative understanding of many mechanical principles, such as thermal expansion of gases and the principle of communicating tubes. Without calculus at the disposal of the ancients, however, these principles could not be expressed in mathematical terms.

Pliny the Elder was born in 23 CE and was a successful military commander and administrator. His only surviving written work is the *Natural History* (*Historia naturalis*), completed in 77 CE.[12] "By reading through about 2,000 volumes . . . 20,000 facts worthy of attention obtained from 100 authors," Pliny (*HN* pref. 17) draws together information on the natural world as it pertains to humans. He treats topics as diverse as astronomy, anatomy, zoology, botany, medicine, and mineralogy. Pliny's work, however, is frequently anecdotal. The credibility of his information varies widely, depending on the sources he used. Pliny died near Stabiae in 79 CE, during the eruption of Mount Vesuvius.

→ Compare Introduction, pp. xxiv–xxvii, on the eruption of Mount Vesuvius and Pliny the Elder's death.

→ Compare Chapter 10, pp. 229–31, on the consulship and provincial governors.

Born around 35 CE, Frontinus too had a successful career in politics and the military. He was elected to the chief Roman magistracy of **consul** three times and spent three or four years in Britain as provincial governor. In 97 CE, about six years before the end of his life, Frontinus was appointed *curator aquarum*—head civil servant in charge of the urban waterworks of the city of Rome. In this function Frontinus wrote his treatise on the aqueducts of the city. As he states, he did so both for his own benefit and for that of his successors (Frontin. *Aq.* 1.2). The text takes stock of his equipment and workforce, pointing out technical, financial, and administrative details of the system and giving an overview of the history of Roman water supply. Recent scholarship has pointed out the political dimension of the treatise and argues that it was not intended to be primarily a technical handbook.[13] Frontinus's work is a precise, albeit incomplete, source of information on the water supply system of the city of Rome in the late first century CE. The text, however, contains no information about matters beyond the city.

Technology Assimilated

Rome grew from a humble city-state to a large territorial entity within a relatively short time. It was natural that, as their reach extended further and further, the Romans became familiar with different cultures and their skills and technologies. Exchange of expertise and ideas happened inevitably through intercultural contact and through travelling traders and craftspeople. This exchange created a cultural feedback loop as new technologies enabled further expansion that, in turn, led to the introduction of yet more ideas and technologies.

See Chapter 14 on Roman expansion.

Compare Chapter 15, pp. 344–9, on trade and traders.

Compare Chapter 7, pp. 144–53, Chapter 12, pp. 268–70, and Chapter 17, pp. 381–3, on the influence of Greek cultural forms.

As the Roman territory included more geographical areas that were different from central Italy, it was only natural that the Romans employed the local traditional technologies and skills to modify the environment according to their own needs. The propagation of this technological movement occurred, broadly speaking, from east to west. The Romans were introduced to the millennia-old cultures of Greece, Egypt, and Mesopotamia, adopted and adapted their technical know-how, and applied it to promote the development of cities in the largely non-urbanized societies in the west and north (Gaul, Spain, Germany, Britain). The urbanization of these geographical areas is one of the most lasting consequences of Roman technical and administrative influence, as many modern cities in Northern and Western Europe were originally founded by the Romans.

Streets and Bridges

Roads were a significant factor in Roman territorial expansion and control. In fact, the Roman road network was so well laid out that, in many instances, modern European highways follow the ancient Roman roads. Its primary purpose was the fast and efficient movement of infantry, but the Roman public road network that spanned some 120,000 kilometres throughout the empire[14] was, of course, also used by civilian travellers. Traders made use of these roads as well, but land transport was generally slow and expensive, so most goods were transported by ship. Furthermore, the axles and frames of **chariots** and carts usually had no springs, so clattering along on a road paved with stone slabs would have been a tooth-rattling experience even over short distances.

The first major Roman road was the Via Appia, or Appian Way. Named after Appius Claudius Caecus, during whose censorship it was constructed, the road was built in 312 BCE between Rome and Capua (196 kilometres) to expedite the deployment of legionaries to central Italy. As Rome got involved in military affairs in the Hellenistic kingdoms of the eastern Mediterranean in the second half of the third century BCE, it was extended to reach the port town of Brindisi (for a total length of 569 kilometres). During subsequent centuries well-developed roads were built in all Roman provinces, from Britain to Africa and from Spain to Mesopotamia. With regular rest stations and milestones showing the distance to major points along the route,[15] the Roman highways had all the amenities that make long-distance travel as convenient as possible. In that respect, the roads were symbols of Roman technical skill and, especially in newly conquered regions, metaphors for Roman culture as a whole: stable, durable, and convenient. They were also a reminder that, should the need arise, the army had a means of access to any particular area.[16]

As they were originally meant to be used by soldiers marching on foot, Roman roads were—at least in theory—supposed to meet a number of conditions. They had to offer stable footing throughout the year in most varied weather, avoid excessively steep gradients, be as straight as possible to represent the shortest possible distance between two places, and be sufficiently durable to survive extreme climate conditions and prolonged use with a minimum of maintenance. Given the diverse climatic and topographical conditions in the varied regions of the empire, there is no typical construction method for a Roman road. Usually a trench or bed was excavated and its edges lined with upright stones that formed the curb.

In the absence of any written evidence, dating the construction, improvement, and completion of roads is very difficult. It can be said, though, that the earliest roads had a simple gravel surface. By the late Republic, important or well-used stretches of major roads were frequently paved with polygonal stone slabs resting on a layered bed of sand, coarse gravel, and fine gravel. (The Latin term for this stratified arrangement, *via strata*, is the origin of the English word *street*.) The surface usually had a slight camber to allow rainwater to run off to the sides. In situations where roads were cut into bedrock, the need for stratified layers did not arise. Roads that were built in marshy conditions could be supported by a wooden framework consisting of parallel beams fixed in place by wooden stakes with transversal poles on which the road surface proper was laid.[17] Road widths could also vary significantly depending on the local topographic conditions, difficulty of construction, access to labour and material, and the importance of the individual road.[18] Generally, the major highways were wide enough that two wagons could easily fit side by side. Jean-Pierre Adam gives a select list of road widths in Roman Italy that range from 2.4 to 7.5 metres.[19]

Bridges were another important part of the road network. Engineers of the Roman army could build temporary (or collapsible) bridges and pontoon bridges. An example, built across the Danube on campaign in 104 CE, is depicted on Trajan's Column. The earliest structures were made of wood, but Roman mastery of arch construction enabled architects to design stone bridges so durable that some of them remained in use for centuries. Bridges across rivers represent a particular engineering challenge because the construction of piers in running water requires special provisions to prevent the obliteration of the underwater foundations. If the river was prone to significant seasonal fluctuations, it was sometimes possible—in the summer months—to divert the entire course of the river temporarily during the construction of the pier foundations. Alternatively, waterproof cofferdams made of wooden planks could be lowered into the river and the water bailed out with some type of water-lifting device. Workers could then excavate the riverbed until they reached bedrock, at which point construction of the foundations could begin. Shapes and material of bridge foundations and piers varied depending on the local availability of building material, strength and depth of the river, height and width of the bridge's arches, and the designers' faith in the firmness of the underground. Generally, the piers consisted of stone masonry or **concrete** faced with stones to prevent erosion by the flowing water.

Broad structures submerged in running water obstruct the flow and have to contend with very strong forces, so bridge piers were generally prow-shaped and narrow. In general, it was desirable to build bridges with as few piers as possible. Where the current was deemed too strong, the piers could be perforated in the direction of the flow to create less obstruction. In some cases, additional works were placed in the water upstream from the piers to provide some protection against continuous pressure and erosion. Whenever feasible, the preferred method of construction was to cross the river with only one arch and place the piers on dry land on either side, well away from the flowing water. The limiting factor was the width of the arch.

The Romans were comfortable building arches in excess of 30 metres in diameter. For example, the bridge of Narni, built during Augustus's reign, had an arch 32 metres wide. However, this size was not always practical in bridge construction. A true arch is always the shape of a semi-circle; therefore, the height of the bridge always grows proportionally with the width of the single arch. A true arch of 30 metres diameter requires a height of 15 metres, which means that, depending on the elevation of the river banks, the bridge could potentially require very steep ramps on either side or significant embankments for users to reach the apex. If these ramps became too steep, heavy wheeled vehicles could not use the bridge, as the draught animals would be unable to drag the heavy load up the ramp or slow the vehicle down the ramp on the opposite side. Bridge construction was therefore a compromise between the number of piers to be built in the water and the height of the bridge apex and the gradient of the required ramps. The Romans also built bridges with segmental arches that allowed broad spans with low rise. The Alconétar Bridge in Spain, dating from the second century CE, is one of the few surviving examples of this type.

Water Transport

The Mediterranean Sea has always provided a natural mode of transport for its surrounding communities. Sea transport was much less expensive than land transport in antiquity. A cargo ship could carry many times the load of an ox cart, and draught animals, unlike ships, needed to be watered and fed. On the other hand, seafaring on the Mediterranean Sea could be treacherous. Literary and archaeological evidence of shipwrecks is abundant. Seafaring

Compare Chapter 15, pp. 344–9, on the transport of goods.

was usually limited to the summer months (April to October) to avoid winter storms. Moreover, navigation was very difficult in the absence of the magnetic compass. Mariners navigated by prominent landmarks and the sun during the daytime and by the stars during the night. In good weather conditions, much of the land and islands in the area were visible.[20] In the winter months, however, inclement weather and reduced visibility made navigation generally impossible.

Beyond the obvious advantage of being able to navigate by landmarks, staying within sight of land was expedient for a number of reasons. There was no great need for provisions as the crew could make landfall during the night and have access to shelter, food, and water—a necessity for warships, whose narrow hulls usually did not have sufficient room for such items. In the event of a wreck, salvation was relatively close. These advantages notwithstanding, the proximity of land also had a number of drawbacks: the rocks and cliffs of the jagged coastline of certain places, such as southern Turkey or the eastern Adriatic Sea, increased the risk of shipwrecks, and the coves and inlets of the same stretches of coast were ideal hideouts for pirates. Piracy often disrupted maritime trade during the late Republic, to the extent that, in 67 BCE, Pompey was given extraordinary powers and the authority to requisition as many ships and resources needed to suppress it.

In contrast to the Greeks, the Romans were never avid seafarers. The topography of Italy is not fragmented like that of Greece. The Italian peninsula is long and narrow, with only the Apennine Mountains forming a ridge that runs lengthwise roughly down the centre. Consequently, communication over land was relatively easy. Moreover, due to relatively large plains along the Tyrrhenian and the Adriatic seas, agricultural land was not as limited in Italy as it was in Greece. The Romans, then, did not contribute much to naval technology, but they did use and adapt the maritime knowledge of other cultures.

Serious Roman involvement in seafaring began in 264 BCE, when Rome was drawn into a military conflict with Carthage (which had a long naval tradition) over territory in Sicily. In order to expel the Carthaginian garrisons from the island, the Romans had to take to the sea. The Roman **senate**, therefore, decided to build a fleet of 120 warships. The historian Polybius (1.20) reports the unlikely story that the inexperienced Roman carpenters used a Carthaginian vessel that had previously run aground as their template. It is more likely that the Romans requisitioned the services of shipbuilders from the Greek city-states in southern Italy that had their own navies (see Box 16.1).[21]

→ Compare Chapter 14, pp. 310–11, on the First Punic War.

Part of ancient marine fighting strategy was the ramming of enemy vessels with a metal-covered beak-shaped forward extension of the keel, which could incapacitate the enemy by penetrating their hull below the water line. The Romans were clearly uncomfortable with this type of warfare, which was new to them. Being accomplished warriors on land, they simply transferred their preferred type of warfare onto the ships. They equipped their new vessels with bridges, the so-called *corvus* ("raven"), that could be dropped onto

Political History

Box 16.1: Roman Shipbuilding

In his *History*, Polybius (1.20) relates the story of how, during the First Punic War (264–241 BCE), the Romans used a wrecked Carthaginian ship as a template for the construction of their own navy:

> For when the Romans first took in hand the sending over of troops to Messene (in Sicily), not only did they not have decked ships, but no large vessels at all, not even a single galley. They made use of quinqueremes and triremes from Tarentum and Locris, and even from Elea and Neapolis, on which they audaciously carried men across. At this time, the Carthaginians had put to sea against them in the Strait of Messina. One of their decked ships, in their eagerness, ran aground. The wreck thus fell into the hands of the Romans, who used it as a template on which they modelled the construction of their entire fleet. Had it not been for this accident, it is clear that, due to their inexperience, they would not have been able to carry out their plans.

Although this particular story is likely false, the Romans did adopt unfamiliar foreign technologies for their own benefit in other cases.

the decks of enemy ships. Polybius (1.22) describes the device: a long metal pike projecting downward at the far end of the bridge would lodge itself firmly into the wood, thereby making escape for the enemy ship impossible, providing a stable anchor for the bridge, and allowing legionaries to board the enemy vessel. In this way the Romans turned naval combat from ramming manoeuvres into infantry battles. After some resounding victories, but also some serious setbacks that required repeated rebuilding of their entire fleet, the Romans established naval supremacy over the Carthaginians and won the First Punic War.

This episode exemplifies the inventiveness and perseverance that was so much a hallmark of Roman culture and especially of Roman technological achievement. As the Republic drew to a close, numerous cultures with long seafaring traditions—most notably, the many Greek states and kingdoms along the north shore of the Mediterranean Sea—had firmly become part of Roman culture. The Roman state could, therefore, draw on a large pool of maritime experience as the distinction between Roman and foreign in those territories faded away. With the Romans gradually becoming masters of the Mediterranean shoreline in the first century BCE, their military naval activity was reduced to policing activities against pirates.

A second area of maritime expertise acquired by the Romans involved merchant vessels. During the Republic, the population of the city of Rome grew too large to be supplied with foodstuffs from the surrounding countryside alone. Sicily and, during the early Empire, Egypt became the breadbasket of Rome. Goods such as olive oil and wine also came from other provinces, including Spain. Other shipments consisted of glass, artwork, or ingots of raw metal (such as copper) from all over the Mediterranean region and from as far away as the Red Sea and India via Egypt and the Levant. The shipments arrived at Puteoli (modern Pozzuoli), the ancient port of Naples, and were then loaded onto smaller craft and brought up the coast to the Tiber River and to Rome. The emperor Claudius remedied this awkward route by building a substantial harbour at Ostia, a city at the mouth of the Tiber and some 25 kilometres west of Rome. Ostia grew into such a vital commercial hub that its harbour facilities had to be expanded under Trajan. From Ostia the goods were towed on barges upriver to Rome.

→ Compare Chapter 15, pp. 347–9, on sea transport.

It is a widespread misconception that all ancient sea routes hugged the coast.[22] The situation is quite complex and depends on origin and destination, prevailing winds, and water currents. It was not unusual for cargo ships to take a direct route across open water. Unlike warships, cargo vessels had smaller crews and relatively broad hulls and were built for maximum loading capacity, which meant that they had room for sailors' provisions and did not need to make landfall. Sailing on a direct course was especially common for the ship convoys that transported grain, the lifeblood of the population's food supply, from Alexandria to Rome. Efficient loading and unloading of these vital goods called for special harbour installations that required the use of concrete, a building material that the Romans utilized with unprecedented mastery.

Concrete

Concrete was invented in the late third century BCE. The development of this material, which could be shaped into any desirable form and (once hardened) was as durable as stone, revolutionized building construction and hard landscape architecture. Its use in Roman buildings disproves the general, erroneous idea that the Romans were not technological innovators. Walls were built with a core of mortar mixed with an aggregate of small stones, called **opus caementicium**. The type of wall facing can serve as a broad indicator of the construction date, although different techniques no doubt existed simultaneously and were, in part, a matter of personal taste. Wall facing was initially made of irregularly shaped stone blocks. The uneven appearance of the surface pattern led to the Latin term **opus incertum**. An example of such construction is the Sanctuary of Jupiter Anxur in Terracina, Italy, dated to the first century BCE. During the late Republic, square blocks of regular size were used in a pattern that was reminiscent of a diagonal net covering, giving this new type the label **opus reticulatum**.

The advantage of the regular facing was an increase in construction speed. Due to the fact that all stones were the same shape and size, it was no longer necessary to look for suitably shaped ones to fill a particular spot. During the early Empire a facing of fired brick, called **opus testaceum**, became common, speeding up the construction process and further reducing cost. These walls consisted of a shell of two parallel brick walls, with the space between them filled with mortared rubble. Skilled craftsmen no longer had to chip stones into regular shapes. Instead, bricks could be easily shaped from clay and fired in mass production by unskilled workers.

The mastery of concrete construction enabled the Romans to build structures with unparalleled efficiency and to design interior space in innovative shapes. Examples of this innovation are the "octagonal room" in Nero's **Domus Aurea**, with its clever use of curved walls and light shafts, as well as the final form of the **Pantheon** as rebuilt under Hadrian (see Figure 16.1). The construction of utilitarian structures also benefited greatly from this building material. The **Porticus Aemilia**, a storage facility on the banks of the Tiber River in Rome, was built from concrete in the second century BCE. At a length of 487 metres and a width of 60 metres, it consisted of rows of individual, interconnected, and barrel-vaulted storerooms that formed one big space. This modular construction allowed the use of identical form-work for each part and reduced the requirement for skilled labour to a minimum.

Compare Chapter 17, pp. 385, 390, and 392, on the Porticus Aemilia, the Domus Aurea, and the Pantheon.

Figure 16.1   The cupola of the Pantheon, showing oculus. © ISTOCK/fotoVoyager

The ability to set and harden under water is probably the most important quality of Roman concrete, as it allowed the efficient construction of harbour installations not just at Ostia but all over the Mediterranean.[23] Vitruvius (*De arch.* 2.6.1) reveals that the special ingredient that gives Roman concrete this quality is ***pozzolana***, a volcanic ash from the region of Puteoli. The mortar, consisting of a mixture of *pozzolana*, lime, water, and aggregate, forms the basis of these important testaments of Roman technological skill.

Water Supply

Water supply systems, like roads, served a double function in the Romans' cultural world. On the one hand, they were vital pieces of the technological infrastructure of cities. On the other hand, they brought and promoted Roman culture, showcasing Roman dominance and cultural superiority. Their psychological and metaphorical effect must have been particularly strong in western provinces, where the Romans brought their lifestyle to groups that had no previous experience with such extensive urban amenities. But even in the eastern Roman provinces (that is, in former Hellenistic kingdoms), where urbanism and all its technical features had already existed prior to the arrival of the Romans, the scale of such installations reached unprecedented levels. During the late first and second centuries CE in particular—a period characterized by relative political stability—the Romans could afford to build widely visible and exposed water supply structures without fear of sabotage by foreign invaders.

Aqueducts brought water to a number of different delivery points, such as public fountains, wealthy private households, and most important the Roman bathhouses (especially the imperial ***thermae***).[24] In all ancient aqueducts, water was transported by gravity, a form of energy that is free, universal, and continuous and requires no fuel, attention, supervision, or rest. These water-supply systems therefore operated continuously and generally without any shut-off mechanisms. Bronze taps and stopcocks were used occasionally, mostly for controlling water flow in smaller distribution lines.[25]

If an aqueduct required repairs, the water could be diverted into a temporary conduit or allowed to overflow at a convenient and safe point upstream from the repair site. Settling tanks and inspection shafts for regular maintenance were standard features of aqueducts because the build-up of calcium deposits on the conduit walls (*sinter*) required regular cleaning, usually by workers who entered the aqueduct channels and chipped away at it with hand tools. The traces of surviving aqueducts suggest that these structures consisted mostly of spectacular bridges, arcades, and tunnels. In fact, some 90 per cent of aqueducts from the Roman period ran at or below ground level.[26]

The construction of the aqueducts that supplied the city of Rome with water began in 312 BCE, during the censorship of Appius Claudius, the same man who was responsible for building the Via Appia. The Romans had originally made use of water from the Tiber, wells, and springs, but this water had become insufficient for an increasing urban population. The first Roman aqueduct, the Aqua Appia, was built as an underground vaulted channel that brought water from a source 16 kilometres east of Rome. In 272 BCE the Aqua Anio Vetus was built to satisfy the city's ever-growing water needs. Construction of the Aqua Marcia began in 144 BCE, and the Aqua Tepula was built approximately 18 years later, its channel running to a large extent on top of the Aqua Marcia. The Aqua Julia, the Aqua Virgo, and the Aqua Alsietina were added between 33 and 2 BCE. In about 52 CE the emperor Claudius finished two more aqueducts, the Aqua Claudia and the Aqua Anio Novus, construction of which had started under Claudius's predecessor Caligula. Finally, the Aqua Traiana (109 CE) and the Aqua Alexandrina (226 CE) brought the number of aqueducts supplying imperial Rome to 11.

In the Augustan period, cities in the Roman provinces also began to enjoy the benefits of the long-distance delivery of fresh water. Cities in Germany, France, and Spain, such as Cologne, Nîmes, Lyon, and Segovia, profited from this new technology that was initially introduced to supply the areas' Roman garrisons and veteran colonies with water for bathing.

Compare Chapter 13, pp. 296–7, on Roman garrisons.

Ultimately, the technology served as a vehicle for adaptation of local populations to the urbanized Roman lifestyle. The expansion of the water-supply system shows that the Romans were as open to sharing and disseminating technologies as they were to adopting and adapting them from other cultures.

Imperial Roman aqueducts could have a total length of 90 kilometres or more (Aqua Marcia: 91 kilometres; Cologne: 95 kilometres; Carthage: 132 kilometres). The aqueduct supplying the Roman city of Nemausus (modern Nîmes) is famous for the **Pont du Gard**, which stands approximately 48 metres high across the Gard River and is the highest surviving aqueduct bridge from the Roman period. This aqueduct is also remarkable for its very shallow slope of 34 centimetres per kilometre, averaged over the entire 50-kilometre-long channel, and a minimum of only 7 centimetres per kilometre just downstream of the Pont du Gard.[27]

The width of an aqueduct's water channel was usually somewhat less than a metre, and its height had to be sufficient for a maintenance worker to enter, inspect the conduit surface, and do any necessary repairs. The channels were usually covered, either by stone slabs or by a barrel vault. As only the lower cross-section of the channel came in contact with water, the surface of the bottom portion (floor and walls) was lined with special waterproof plaster, the so-called **opus signinum**, which contained crushed ceramics as additional aggregate.[28]

Once the water arrived in a city, it was necessary to distribute it to the consumers. For that purpose it was collected in a primary distribution basin (**castellum divisorium**), two of which have survived at the sites of Nîmes and **Pompeii** and remain in relatively good condition. Both surviving examples have one open-channel inflow from the aqueduct and a number of outflow pipes (13 at Nîmes; 3 at Pompeii) that distributed water to different regions of the city, their flow most likely controlled by a system of sluice gates.[29] The cleverly designed distribution system probably consisted of lead pipes that brought the water to secondary delivery points. At Pompeii, these were water towers, approximately six metres high and originally equipped with a small lead tank on top.[30] As access to running water at home was costly and something only wealthy people could generally afford, large numbers of public fountains in Roman cities ensured that no one needed to walk far to fetch fresh water. According to Frontinus, the city of Rome had a total of 591 public fountains.[31] Running water was also sometimes available on the lower floors of multi-storey apartment buildings. Archaeological evidence for such arrangements survives at, for example, Pompeii, **Herculaneum**, and Ostia.[32]

As we have seen, the reasons for the construction of aqueducts in the Roman period were chiefly to supply water to bath buildings and to create expressions of Roman cultural achievement. Water brought to the city by aqueduct was, of course, also used for drinking and other purposes, but it is important to note that wells and domestic cisterns continued to play an important role throughout antiquity and that some places, such as Roman London, never had an aqueduct at all.[33]

When the Roman Empire came under increasing pressure from Gothic tribes in the fourth and fifth centuries CE, many aqueducts gradually fell out of use because the administration responsible for their upkeep diminished. Aqueducts that were easily accessible were welcome targets for sabotage by hostile armies, as was the case during the siege of Rome in 537/538 CE. Alternatively, many fell out of use through neglect and disrepair. Some, however, were maintained: portions of the Aqua Virgo, for example, are used to bring water to the Trevi Fountain to this day.[34]

Instruments

The planning and construction of roads and aqueducts over hundreds of kilometres required not only large numbers of construction workers and adequate material but also (and especially) planners skilled in geometry and the use of surveying instruments capable of measuring distances and angles in the horizontal and the vertical planes. Geometry had, of course, long been familiar to astronomers and builders in the ancient Near East and Egypt. Via the Greeks it became a field of expertise to the Romans as well. Heron of Alexandria and Vitruvius both describe a variety of instruments for determining right angles, horizontal levels, and even a device whose function approximates that of a modern theodolite (**dioptra**).[35] An excellent example of surviving technical literature is the so-called *Corpus Agrimensorum Romanorum*, an early medieval copy of a Roman text on land surveying.[36]

The simplest implements are those that measure vertical or horizontal lines. The former was achieved by means of a plumb bob, a simple weight suspended on a string. The latter was achieved by means of the **chorobatēs** ("land walker"), described by Vitruvius as a long wooden beam with a central lengthwise groove that was filled with water in order to establish a true horizontal line. The beam was some six metres long and stood on two legs whose length could be adjusted by wedges.[37]

Heron of Alexandria describes the *dioptra* as an instrument that consisted of a horizontal circular disc resting on a stationary central pole. A sight was mounted on the disc and could be rotated 360 degrees to measure angles in the horizontal plane. The disc itself could be inclined on the pole in order to measure vertical angles. As the Romans did not have magnifying lenses, these instruments had no scopes in the modern sense but merely a slit with or without crosshairs. The distance over which an engineer could survey in one go was, therefore, limited to the strength of his unaided vision.

A very simple implement for measuring right angles in the horizontal plane was the **groma**. This instrument consisted of a horizontal wooden cross that could rotate about its centre on a horizontal arm that, in turn, was mounted at the top of a vertical pole. Plumb bobs at the ends of the cross ensured that the lines of sight were straight. This instrument satisfied most of the basic requirements of Roman builders: the laying out of straight lines and right angles.[38]

With the exception of the *groma*, there are no surviving examples of these instruments in the archaeological record and it is impossible to guess to what extent each was in use. By virtue of its simplicity and relatively small size, it is plausible to assume, though, that the *groma* was widely used. The *chorobatēs* appears cumbersome, but it is also simple enough that it may have been in widespread use. The *dioptra*, in contrast, requires a very elaborate manufacturing process and must have been very expensive. Whether it was actually hauled through the countryside by donkeys and used in the field is uncertain but by no means impossible.[39]

Sources of Energy

The prosperity and persistence of Roman culture (as with any successful pre-industrial culture) is all the more remarkable because it was based largely on sources of energy that, in modern terms, would be considered renewable: human and animal power, water power, passive solar energy, biomass (such as wood), wind energy, and gravitational energy. Mechanization of production processes was relatively limited, and the use of hand tools was normal. Where the strength of the worker was insufficient, it could be amplified by employing additional manpower, animals, levers and gears, wedges, screws, block and tackle, or a combination of these options (see Box 16.2).

Process heat (for activities such as cooking and smelting) and space heat (for areas such as homes and baths) were generated by burning wood, charcoal, chaff, or residue from olive oil production, such as the pits or discarded flesh of the olives (*amurca*). Large amounts of biomass were consumed for these purposes, which was a contributing factor to the deforestation of the Mediterranean region. An ingenious method of space heating

Primary Source

Box 16.2

In the remains of Roman bakeries, most notably at the sites of Pompeii and Ostia, large grain mills have been found that were driven by animals.[1] These mills consisted of a stationary cone-shaped bottom stone (*meta*) and a hollow, hourglass-shaped rotating upper stone (*catillus*). The grain was poured into the top of the *catillus* and, as the latter was turned, came out as flour at its bottom rim. The *catillus* was driven by animals (usually mules or donkeys) yoked to one or two radially attached beams. This device was hence known as *mola asinaria*, or "donkey mill." Vitruvius (*De arch.* 10.5) writes that grain mills could also be driven by water power (*mola aquaria*). In his arrangement, a transmission of meshing cogwheels transforms the rotation of a vertical water wheel into the horizontal rotation of the millstone.

Remains of the donkey mills at Pompeii. © John Oleson

Note

1. Wilson (2008a: 406).

for the hot rooms in the *thermae* was the passive use of solar radiation. The outside walls of the hot rooms were semicircular in shape and featured large window fronts facing the southwest in order to capture and retain solar heat during the early afternoon, the warmest time of the day.

The energy of the wind was almost exclusively harnessed for sail ships. The Romans never used wind to drive, for example, grain mills, but literary evidence from Heron of Alexandria indicates that small wind rotors may have been employed to operate pipe organs.[40] Water in long-distance conduits moved exclusively by gravity. While piston pumps for water did exist, they were not used in supply lines or urban distribution systems but for small-volume lifting needs such as bilge pumps or fire extinguishers.

Levers and screws were used for wine and olive presses (*torcula*). Tread wheels and block and tackle were used in cranes for constructing buildings. A relief carving on the **Tomb of the Haterii**, from the reign of Domitian, shows in great detail a construction crane in operation. This crane consists of an A-frame that can swivel both vertically and horizontally. From its apex is suspended a block-and-tackle arrangement that allows the lifting of heavy weights. The lifting mechanism is driven by men walking in a large tread wheel at the base of the crane and turning a drum, around which the lifting rope is wrapped.

The People behind the Works

The Tomb of the Haterii, built by a family of successful contractors who must have struck it rich in the Flavian dynasty's building boom, is an excellent example of the type of evidence that survives regarding the people behind the works. The human factor of Roman technology is currently a very active field of research. Ancient authors, who were generally from a higher social class, did not concern themselves with those who, in their eyes, did disdainful work (a view called the banausic prejudice). In contrast to the Greek period, names of architects, engineers, and craftspeople from the Roman period were only rarely transmitted. Nero's architect Celer, the Flavian architect Rabirius, and Trajan's architect Apollodorus of Damascus are notable rare exceptions. It is, therefore, ironic that the practitioners who were so important to Vitruvius (see the beginning of this chapter) appear faceless and name-less. However, this anonymity is not true in all cases. Builders such as the Haterii expressed their professional pride on their tombs. The tomb of Eurysaces the Baker, from the late first century CE and located in front of the Porta Maggiore in Rome, is another expression of a successful craftsperson's pride. Mosaics and reliefs with implements of various trades, such as knives or carpenters' tools, abound in the archaeological record.[41] Those who advertise pride in trade were often **freedmen** who do not appear to have bought into the elite, freeborn contempt for manual labour.

Compare Chapter 3, p. 62, on expressions of professional pride on Roman tombstones.

Despite these examples, in many instances we have no particular information about the management of large-scale projects, such as how the workload was divided, how the decision-making process worked, or what the chain of command was.[42] Of the Roman aqueducts, we know from Frontinus that the administrators of the waterworks had a gang of state-owned slaves at their disposal for repairs and maintenance.[43] We do not know, however, who exactly built the aqueducts and roads. From the spotty evidence supplied by inscriptions, a variegated picture emerges. Private contractors were involved, some-times employing slave labour or free waged labourers.[44] The army could also be involved, sometimes with legionaries doing part of the work. More frequently, army specialists were employed for particular tasks, such as surveying. Each project was unique, and there appears to have been no standard procedure for implementation or organization (see Box 16.3 for a glimpse of Roman project management).

Primary Source

Box 16.3: Pliny the Younger, *Letters*, 10.37 and 10.38.

Gaius Plinius to the Emperor Trajan

My Lord, the people of Nicomedia have spent 3,318,000 sesterces on an aqueduct that was never finished and has been abandoned and, in the meantime, torn down again. For a second one, another 200,000 sesterces have been allocated. After this one, too, has been abandoned, and so much money has been wasted, yet more expense is necessary if they are to have a water supply. I myself have visited the source, from which very clean water could be delivered on arcades, as originally attempted, so that the higher parts of the city, too, would be supplied. A very few arches are still standing. Some could be rebuilt from stone blocks taken from the earlier structure. The remainder, I think, should be made of brick, as it is easier and cheaper. First, however, it is necessary that you send an engineer (*aquilex*; literally, "water collector") or an architect (*architectus*), so that the previous events do not repeat themselves. I assure you of this one thing, that the usefulness and beauty of the work will be worthy of your reign.

Trajan to Pliny

It is vital that Nicomedia gets a water supply system. I trust, indeed, that you will take care of this matter with the necessary attention, but, for Heaven's sake, you have to find out whose fault it is that the people of Nicomedia have lost so much money to this point. Perhaps somebody has profited from starting and abandoning these aqueducts. Let me know what you find out.

Summary

Backed by vast financial resources and manpower, the Romans were skilled at adapting and refining technologies from the cultures with which they established close contact. During the late Republic and early Empire, the exchange of goods and ideas in an expanding territory with a centralizing administration, language, and currency allowed for an unprecedented dissemination of technical know-how. To suit their needs of coping with a broad range of technical problems and environmental conditions, the Romans adapted existing technologies from other cultures and brought them to maturity in large-scale contexts.

But the Romans were also innovators. Major technological achievements were possible through the efficiency of the Roman civil and military administration. This successful administration was instrumental in technological advancement, which served as a tool for Roman territorial expansion. For example, Roman roads were initially built to serve the needs of the military but were also used for trade, travel, and communication.

Roman water supply systems and the associated baths played an important role in the acculturation of non-Roman cultures to Roman life, particularly in the western part of the empire. New cities and growing populations, moreover, required technological innovation in water supply, sewage disposal, transport and storage of goods, and construction of residential high-rise buildings.

In architecture the Romans demonstrated extraordinary skill in the construction of arches, modular buildings, and domes. The Porticus Aemilia and Pantheon point to another area of Roman mastery: concrete. The Romans invented concrete that hardened under water, allowing the construction of harbour installations throughout the Mediterranean, the crucial infrastructure of the Roman economy.

Roman technological progress was certainly not characterized by stagnation, despite a general contempt for manual labour by some upper-class authors. Skilled craftspeople and engineers were vital for the functioning of Roman civilization. While only a minute number of written documents detailing these activities have survived, professional pride and financial success is evident in inscriptions and commemorative relief sculpture.

Questions for Review and Discussion

1. What types of sources regarding ancient technology are available to modern scholars? What are their respective advantages and drawbacks?
2. How did roads aid in Roman territorial expansion?
3. How did concrete change construction in Rome?
4. Discuss how the Roman aqueducts played both a utilitarian and a more abstract cultural role in antiquity.
5. Is it fair to say that the Romans merely stole other cultures' technological achievements? Why or why not?

Suggested Reading

Adam, J.-P. 1994. *Roman Building*. New York: Routledge.

This volume explores the technical aspects of Roman architecture and looks at materials and techniques employed in the construction of private and public buildings, civil engineering works, and urban infrastructure. An abundance of illustrations makes this work very approachable.

Cuomo, S. 2007. *Technology and Culture in Greek and Roman Antiquity*. Cambridge: Cambridge University Press.

Cuomo focuses on the human aspect of ancient technology, particularly the interaction of technicians and technologies and the social perceptions of both. Individual chapters consist of focused case studies ranging chronologically from classical Athens to late antiquity.

Hirt, A.M. 2010. *Imperial Mines and Quarries in the Roman World*. Oxford: Oxford University Press.

This work is an extremely detailed investigation of the administrative mechanisms involved in mining and quarrying in the Roman period. It is a good model for the collection and interpretation of evidence.

Hodge, A.T. 2002. *Roman Aqueducts and Water Supply*, 2nd edn. London: Duckworth.

Hodge's approachable and comprehensive book is the standard work on Roman hydraulic systems. The author makes complicated technical features accessible to laypersons, covering not only aqueducts but also large-scale works such as dams, sewage systems, and bath buildings.

Humphrey, J.W., J.P. Oleson, and A.N. Sherwood, eds. 1998. *Greek and Roman Technology: A Sourcebook*. New York: Routledge.

This unique book is a topical collection of passages from ancient Greek and Roman "technical" authors, incidental mentions of technology, and select papyri and epigraphic evidence. The volume, which sets the context for the

ancient passages with brief commentaries, is indispensable for quickly finding relevant literary evidence for a broad range of technologies.

Landels, J.G. 2000. *Engineering in the Ancient World*, rev. edn. Berkeley: University of California Press.

A quick and easy read about a select range of technologies, this book can be an introduction to the field.

Oleson, J.P., ed. 2008. *The Oxford Handbook of Engineering and Technology in the Classical World*. Oxford: Oxford University Press.

This volume must be considered the new standard work on ancient technology. Topical chapters written by eminent scholars explore technologies from the Greek and Roman period in great depth. Thorough bibliographies make this work an excellent starting point for more detailed studies.

Pitassi, M. 2009. *The Navies of Rome*. Woodbridge, UK: Boydell Press.

Pitassi offers a descriptive, chronological summary of the development of the Roman navy, its makeup, technical aspects, and role in politics.

Taylor, R. 2003. *Roman Builders*. Cambridge: Cambridge University Press.

This book is a study of the architectural process from the initial design stage to the final decoration and surface finishing. Different from Adam's *Roman Building*, which focuses on techniques and methods, Taylor's text explores and follows the procedures of construction and illustrates the subsequent steps with examples from a variety of buildings.

Wikander, Ö., ed. 2000. *Handbook of Ancient Water Technology*. Leiden, The Netherlands: Brill.

Wikander's *Handbook* is a monumental edited work on "everything" that pertains to ancient hydraulic technology from the Bronze Age to late antiquity. Divided into topical chapters, it is a comprehensive starting point for students who want to explore the development of aspects of ancient water technology through time and space.

Notes

1 All translations are mine unless otherwise indicated.
2 Oleson (2004).
3 Hodge (2002: 45–7).
4 Pitassi (2009: 46). Compare the unlikely story recorded by Polybius (1.20–21) of how the Romans built their fleet.
5 Note the examples throughout Lewis (2001).
6 Gimpel (1976: 141).
7 Oleson (2004: 66).
8 Callebat (1973: ix).
9 Neugebauer (1938: 22); Drachmann (1948: 76–7); Keyser (1988: 220); Landels (2000: 201).
10 Schmidt (1899: ix); Usher (1954: 98); Drachmann (1976: 2).
11 Rice and Grafton (1994: 11).
12 Feder (1998: 348).
13 DeLaine (1996); Saastamoinen (2000); Del Chicca (2004); Rodgers (2004).
14 Quilici (2008: 551).
15 A Roman measure of distance, *mille passus*, representing a double stride of a walking person, is the origin of the English word *mile*.
16 Kissel (2002: 147).
17 White (1984: 95).
18 According to Siculus Flaccus, a Roman land surveyor of uncertain date, Roman roads had a hierarchy of use, much as modern roads do. *Viae publicae* were the equivalent of major highways; *viae militares* were roads of strategic significance; *actus* were minor provincial highways; and *privatae* were private roads built and maintained by private landowners. See Adam (1994: 277).
19 Adam (1994: 279).
20 Horden and Purcell (2000: 127).
21 Casson (1991: 14); Pitassi (2009: 46).
22 Simonsen (2003: 259).
23 Oleson (1988); Oleson et al. (2004, 2006).
24 Hodge (2002: 6).
25 Ibid.: 322; Jansen (1996: 47).
26 Hodge (2000: 57).
27 Hodge (2002: 200).
28 Pliny *HN* 35.46; Lancaster (2008: 261).
29 Hodge (2002: 261).
30 Larsen (1982: 41).
31 Frontin. *Aq.* 2.78.
32 Hodge (2002: 306).
33 Ibid.: 5
34 Ibid.: 389, n. 8.
35 Heron *Dioptra*; Vitr. *De arch.* 8.5.1.
36 Lewis (2001: 3).
37 Vitr. *De arch.* 8.5.1.
38 Lewis (2001: 120).
39 Hodge (2002: 200, 202).
40 Heron *Pneum.* 1.43.
41 Cuomo (2007: 77).
42 See, for example, Leveau (1991: 155).
43 Frontin. *Aq.* 2.98, 2.99, 2.100, 2.116.
44 Hirt (2010) deals with these organizational aspects for Roman imperial mines and quarries

17

Art and Architecture

Beth Munro

An interesting contrast exists between the high value that Romans placed on owning art and commissioning architecture and their relatively low estimation of artists and builders. Cicero (*Off.* 1.42), for example, does not include such occupations among those appropriate to men of high status. He does allow, however, that architecture can be considered an honourable profession for those of suitable social rank because it requires knowledge (*prudentia*). In general, we know very little about artists and architects of the ancient Roman world, but authors of this period tell us a good deal about famous Greek artists from the Classical and Hellenistic periods.[1] This bias in the ancient literature may have adversely affected modern studies of Roman art and architecture by implicitly encouraging the idea that ancient Greek works were superior to Roman creations. But Roman literary sources are not to be trusted on this subject. Indeed, we now recognize that Roman decorative objects and buildings were some of the finest ever produced and the most technically advanced for the time.

Ironically, part of the way we perceive the quality of Roman art and architecture is by understanding how objects and buildings were made, that is, by understanding the work of the artist. Unfinished carvings, piles of reused materials, quarries, and workshop remains can reveal the skills and resources required to produce the material world of the Romans. While it is crucial to understand what objects and buildings meant to those who used them and how they functioned in society more generally, they can also tell us about resources, the construction industry, and the economics of production.

Introduction

The study of Roman art and architecture predominantly relies on material evidence, such as the remains of buildings and objects recovered by modern archaeologists or

Timeline

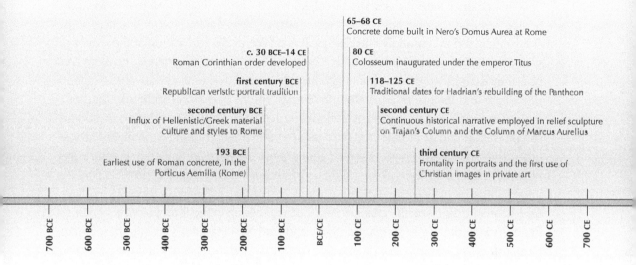

65–68 CE
Concrete dome built in Nero's Domus Aurea at Rome

c. 30 BCE–14 CE
Roman Corinthian order developed

80 CE
Colosseum inaugurated under the emperor Titus

first century BCE
Republican veristic portrait tradition

118–125 CE
Traditional dates for Hadrian's rebuilding of the Pantheon

second century BCE
Influx of Hellenistic/Greek material culture and styles to Rome

second century CE
Continuous historical narrative employed in relief sculpture on Trajan's Column and the Column of Marcus Aurelius

193 BCE
Earliest use of Roman concrete, in the Porticus Aemilia (Rome)

third century CE
Frontality in portraits and the first use of Christian images in private art

700 BCE | 600 BCE | 500 BCE | 400 BCE | 300 BCE | 200 BCE | 100 BCE | BCE/CE | 100 CE | 200 CE | 300 CE | 400 CE | 500 CE | 600 CE | 700 CE

early modern collectors. It is important to recognize, however, that only very little material evidence from the Roman world has survived. Given that whole categories of material, such as wood and textiles, are rarely preserved, our focus tends to be on buildings and their decoration; objects made of stone, plaster, or ceramic; and, to a lesser extent, objects made of metal or glass. Our understanding of Roman art and architecture has also been limited by the habits of collectors in the Renaissance period and onwards. The first excavations at Pompeii, for example, ignored most of what was not made of marble.[2] It is therefore critical to acknowledge that our understanding of Roman art and architecture is, and always will be, limited.

Roman art and architecture as objects of study belong to the larger evidentiary category of material culture, which can be defined as objects and structures created to facilitate the activities, reflect the preferences, and perpetuate the habits of a given community or population. Traditional approaches to understanding Roman material culture have tended to concentrate on describing and categorizing the forms and styles of objects and buildings. Over the past 30 years, however, scholars have also been studying how, why, and by whom objects and buildings were made. This focus has shed light on the natural resources, the skills and organization of the workforce, and the overall economy of the Roman world. In addition, the fact that Roman emperors commissioned much of the material culture means that we can also often understand art and architecture as being politically motivated. For example, the dissemination of the emperor's image through various media (statues, busts, coins) and reminders of the far-reaching Roman influence in a variety of architectural genres (arches, temples, fora) were crucial for establishing and maintaining control over Roman territory.

This chapter introduces a sample of Roman art and architecture that marks particular trends and innovations. The selected works are integrated into thematic discussions organized in a broadly chronological way. We begin by looking at the extent to which the Romans were influenced by Greek and indigenous Italic material culture and how they established their own identity through innovations such as the veristic style in portraiture and the use of concrete in buildings. The next section examines Augustus's influence on art and architecture, including a return to youthful depiction in portrait sculpture, the import of coloured marbles, and the creation of the Roman Corinthian order. The chapter also considers how various emperors were portrayed in sculpture and how they created symbols of their dominance through major building projects, including the imperial palaces, the Colosseum, and the Pantheon. Finally, it deals with private art and architecture and the changes to artistic expression in the third to fourth centuries CE, especially the use of *spolia*, frontality, and Christian imagery. Overall, these topics demonstrate the diversity of Roman material culture and the process of artistic creation as an indicator of the skills, tastes, and wealth distribution in the Roman world.

———— • ◆ • ————

Defining *Romanness*

The Romans developed many essential aspects of their culture—the political system, legal code, and religious offices—during the republican period. The structures of social hierarchy and the concept of Roman citizenship were also more clearly defined. At the same time, the Romans developed their own distinct artistic and architectural styles and techniques, initially by adopting, adapting, and combining non-Roman traditions.

The first cultures that directly influenced the Romans were the other indigenous populations of Italy, such as the Etruscans. For example, Etruscan blackware pottery (*bucchero*) was found in sixth-century BCE burials in Rome, which indicates trade between the two groups. It is also believed that the Temple of Jupiter Optimus Maximus on the Capitoline Hill was directly influenced by Etruscan temple architecture. As the most important temple throughout Rome's history, it was rebuilt many times, and little archaeological evidence of the first-phase temple has been recovered.[3] It may, however, have closely resembled an Etruscan temple, as it was built on a high rectangular podium that could be accessed only by a set of stairs on one of the short sides. The temple was fronted by a porch with wooden columns that supported a wooden roof decorated with terracotta

→ See Chapter 9, p. 212, on the destruction and rebuilding of the Temple of Jupiter Optimus Maximus on the Capitoline Hill and Figure 9.1, number 6, for its location.

statues that probably resembled the so-called Apollo of Veii. The overall design of early Italic temples became the standard for Roman temples, with a few noteworthy exceptions, such as the Temple of Venus and Roma in the Roman Forum.

The Greeks were long-term trading partners with the Italic peoples. Greek red-figure pottery found at Etruscan tomb sites, such as the Euphronious Krater (515 BCE), testifies to such contact. Beginning in the eighth century BCE, numerous Greek trading posts and colonies were established in southern Italy and Sicily. Greek material culture was therefore well known on the Italian peninsula even before the founding of Rome. After Roman military victories in mainland Greece in the second century BCE, there was a dramatic increase in the import of Greek styles and materials. This influx was a result of a combination of factors: peaceful, neighbourly contact between the cultures, the migration of Greek artists to Rome (both as slaves and free people), and the looting of local works of art by the Roman army. Plundering conquered enemies was normal practice in ancient warfare as it increased the wealth of the state and showed Roman dominance over the newly conquered territory (see, for example, Box 17.1, which describes the triumphal procession of Lucius Aemilius Paullus and his

See Chapter 5, p. 106, on Lucius ← Aemilius Paullus; Chapter 4, p. 78, and Chapter 14, p. 314–15, on the Macedonian War and its human spoils; and Chapter 7, pp. 144–53, and Chapter 12, pp. 268–70, on Greek cultural influence in Rome.

army after the defeat of the king of Macedon in 168 BCE). Physical objects were thus incorporated into public and private Roman art collections, and the artistic styles and subject matter of subjected populations became fashionable in Italy.

A survey of the wall paintings and mosaics in **Pompeii** demonstrates this latter point. The second-century BCE Alexander Mosaic from the House of the Faun, which depicts Alexander the Great in battle with the Persian King Darius III, is thought to be a copy of a 300 BCE wall painting from Greece. The mosaic, which originally adorned the floor of

Primary Source

Box 17.1: Plutarch, *Life of Aemilius Paullus*, 32.2.[1]

Every temple was open and filled with garlands and incense, while numerous servitors and lictors restrained the thronging and scurrying crowds and kept the streets open and clear. The triumph was spread out over three days. The first day barely sufficed for the exhibition of the captured statues, paintings, and colossal figures, which were carried on two hundred and fifty chariots.

Note

1. Translated by Perrin (1918).

an entertaining room in a large urban house and is now on display in the Archaeological Museum in Naples, contains an estimated 2 to 5 million cut stone pieces (*tesserae*). It is clearly the work of skilled craftsmen: the mosaic accurately captures the movement of the figures and shadow and light and gives a good sense of perspective. Alexander was obviously still a popular figure in the second century BCE, although it is unclear whether this popularity was due to his legendary character or the fact that his depiction would have presented an expression of the owner's cultural capital—the demonstration of a cultured background and Greek education.

The desire to demonstrate knowledge of Greek culture can also be seen in Pompeii in the first-century CE Macellum, the town's main food market, which displayed wall paintings of single scenes from Greek myths (see Figure 17.1). The Macellum was an unusual spot for such images, as they usually appeared in upper-class domestic settings. However, in the market they would not have been seen by the elite but by their slaves and members of the middle and lower **classes**. These mythological scenes may therefore have been popular among these groups or (as has been suggested) intended to provide cultural or moral guidance.[4]

Greek influence also penetrated temple architecture during the late Republic. Not only did the Romans import white marble from Greece as a building material, but temples built in Rome in the second and first centuries BCE also used Greek rather than Italic **orders**. For example, the **pseudo-peripteral** Temple of Portunus, built around 100 BCE in the meat market (Forum Boarium), is set on a typically Italic high podium, but its decorative elements

Figure 17.1   Mythological wall paintings from the Macellum, Pompeii, *c.* 65 CE. Left: Io and Argus. From the west wall of the Macellum, Pompeii (VII 9, 4-12). Pompeii, Italy, Alinari / Art Resource, NY. Right: Deutsches Archäologisches Institut Rom, Neg. 80.1565

belong to the Ionic order. (Ionic columns replace the Tuscan columns that would be expected on a temple of traditional Italic design. The features of the various orders are shown in Figure 17.2.) Another example is the Round Temple, likewise located in the Forum Boarium (see Figure 17.3). This temple has 18 Corinthian columns made originally of imported

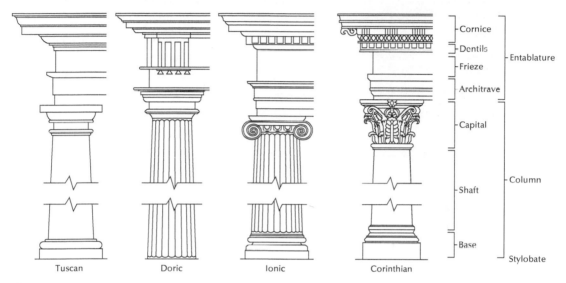

Figure 17.2 Column Orders.

white Greek marble and arranged around a low, circular podium. The import of Greek marble to Rome was a display not only of wealth among the Roman elite but also of admiration for Greek materials and techniques.[5]

During this same period, we also begin to see some uniquely Roman innovations in areas such as portrait sculpture. Unlike the majority of classical Greek sculpture, which depicts idealized versions of people and gods, individuals in the late republican period are portrayed in a realistic manner (Figure 17.4 provides an example). This style, called **verism**, shows individual characteristics while also

Figure 17.3 Round Temple in the Forum Boarium, Rome, mid-second century BCE. © Beth Munro

Figure 17.4   Portrait bust of a man, from Palestrina, Italy, first century BCE. © PRISMA ARCHIVO/Alamy

➔ Compare Chapter 3, p. 65; Chapter 4, p. 89; Chapter 7, pp. 154–5; and Chapter 10, p. 237, on patronage.

utilizing stock traits of advanced age, including sagging chins, creases in the cheeks, baggy eyes, and lines on the forehead. These pronounced facial features do not necessarily reflect the actual age of the subjects (which is generally unknown; some may have been middle-aged, while others were undoubtedly older) but link them with the traditional ideal of an austere, experienced Roman man.

Two art historical theories attempt to explain the development of the veristic style. The first argues that it developed in response to the increased societal emphasis on family ancestry. Pliny the Elder (*HN* 35.6–7) tells us that wax masks of ancestors (*imagines*), intended to look like the deceased, formed part of funeral processions. Permanent marble or bronze sculptures were then created in the style of these masks to demonstrate the family resemblance between the deceased and their living family members.[6] A good example of this practice is the so-called *Togatus Barberini*, or *Man with His Ancestors* (shown in Figure 3.1, p. 54). The second argument holds that the portrayal of individuals with aged faces was not an attempt to create a link with ancestors but to symbolize the client–patron relationship that developed during the republican period.[7] Elite males often had a clientele of ex-slaves and lower-class individuals with whom they conducted business; elite *patroni* could, for example, finance the endeavours of their clients and use them as agents in business deals. In return, clients supported their patrons in political arenas and showed their respect for them with gifts. Depicting patrons in the veristic style may have symbolized their elevated social status. Whatever the reason, the use of verism during the Republic is a distinctive element of Roman art and sets Roman statues apart from those imported from the newly conquered territories in the Greek East.

The major innovation in Roman building construction during the Republic was **concrete**, a hardened mix of a lime-based mortar (lime powder and water), *pozzolana* (a volcanic ash from the environs of Mount Vesuvius), and aggregate (small stones, broken pottery, shells, sand, etc.). Prior to the second century BCE, the majority of construction was done in stone masonry, sometimes bonded in mortar. Roman concrete had the distinct advantage of being able to set underwater, thus enabling the construction of harbours and **aqueducts**. Roman concrete was also very stable and durable and, as such, ideal for curved features, which were difficult to execute in worked stone. With the

➔ See Chapter 16, pp. 366–8, on concrete and harbours, and pp. 368–70, on aqueducts.

advent of concrete there was an increase in the use of arches and vaulting (the extension or rotation of an arch to create an arched ceiling), not only as passageways and decorative features but also in the substructures of larger building complexes where series of vaults created platforms and terraced hillsides.

The earliest known use of extensive concrete vaulting is the **Porticus Aemilia** in Rome, which dates to 193 BCE. This storage hall, located on the banks of the Tiber, conforms to the rising slope of the riverbank by a series of platforms linked by stairs and roofed by a sequence of concrete vaults. This use of concrete for vaulting and terracing is also visible in the remains of the late-second-century BCE Sanctuary of Fortuna at Praeneste (modern Palestrina, Italy), where several platforms lead up to a temple on a steep hill (see Figure 17.5). The increasing use of concrete led the Romans away from traditional Greek designs and allowed them to experiment with architectural spaces. It also demonstrates a desire to use locally sourced materials (lime and *pozzolana*) for construction, as doing so was cheaper and faster than importing quarried stone blocks.

Augustan Rome: Image of an Empire

Under Augustus, art and architecture changed from the eclectic mix wrought by Greek and Italic influences into something confidently Roman. As the pacifier of civil war, Augustus was keen to promote a singular, strong, peaceful image of the Roman state and an image

Figure 17.5   Digital reconstruction of the Sanctuary of Fortuna, Praeneste (Palestrina, Italy), first century BCE.

of himself as its supporter and protector. During his reign, art and architecture became carriers of propaganda, subtly and explicitly promoting imperial policy and authority. One of the main ways of achieving this promotion was the dissemination of the emperor's image in sculpture and coinage. Breaking with the tradition of verism, Augustus was portrayed as a young man throughout his reign. Initially, this depiction was perhaps due to his actual youthfulness (he was 36 years old when he effectively became emperor), but the youthful image of Augustus later became a symbol of the timelessness of Roman power. He was shown in different political and religious roles, such as **pontifex maximus** and military commander (consider, for example, the statue called the *Augustus of Prima Porta*, shown in Figure 14.1, p. 318). In all his statues, however, his facial features and hair are nearly identical, ensuring that he was always recognizable. A particular feature of these works is the parting of his hair over the forehead. Augustus's wife Livia was also portrayed as a young adult and with distinctive facial features that make her easily identifiable (see Figure 17.6). Livia's portraits show her with large almond-shaped eyes that contrast with her small mouth. Part of her hair is gathered into a central node at the top of her forehead, with the rest parted down the middle and set in a bun at the back of her head.

Imperial family portraiture likewise appears in public monuments of the period. The best-known example is the **Ara Pacis** ("Altar of Peace"; see Figure 17.7). Relief panels showing members of the imperial family, including children, point to the family unit as a key element of Augustus's ideology of a peaceful and strong Roman state that, after the devastation of civil war, was once again enjoying prosperity.[8] Children, as real and symbolic representatives of fecundity and regeneration, were central to the emperor's program:

Figure 17.6   Portrait of Livia, early first century CE. © The Bridgeman Art Library Limited/Alamy

Augustan legislation famously concerned itself with the encouragement of marriage and the production of legitimate children. The first depiction of children as children (rather than as little adults) in sculpture appears on the side of the Ara Pacis and not only reinforces Augustus's legislation but also demonstrates the expertise of the artist in portraying the human form realistically. Children appear in the mythological/symbolic panels on the front and back of the altar as well. The so-called Tellus panel (whose interpretation has been much debated) pictures two infants thought to represent fertility, and the Romulus panel pictures the mythological founder of Rome as a boy with his adoptive father, Faustulus, and the god Mars.

The location of the Ara Pacis in the **Campus Martius** ("Field of Mars") is likewise a symbol for the end of the civil war. The altar takes up a prominent position in a site that had been used for gatherings of the Roman military during the Republic. As a monument, it is a masterpiece of political and religious symbolism. A giant sundial with a 22-metre-high Egyptian monolithic obelisk as a pointer complemented the Augustan restructuring of the Campus Martius, further symbolizing Roman domination over its new territories. Hauled to Rome from Egypt, the obelisk was an appropriate reminder of Augustus's momentous victory over Marc Antony and Cleopatra in 31 BCE. The monument was

Compare Chapter 5, pp. 104–06, ◄ and Chapter 8, pp. 172–3 and 184–6, on Augustan legislation.

undoubtedly intended to astound not only because of its mathematical precision but also because of the engineering feat that was required to transport the obelisk from Egypt by land and sea. Recognition of this challenge would have further supported the imperial message of domination and control of the natural world (see Box 17.2).

In the centre of Rome, Augustus developed a new forum laden with symbolic imagery. The layout and location of the Forum of Augustus directly adjacent to the Forum of Julius Caesar (to the side of the Roman Forum) represent the connection between Augustus and his adoptive father, Julius Caesar. The Temple of Mars Ultor ("Mars the Avenger") stood at its north end as a permanent reminder of the fulfillment of Augustus's filial duty to his assassinated father: Augustus had vowed to build this temple should he defeat Brutus and Cassius, two of the conspirators in Caesar's murder. Statues of the legendary founders of Rome and ancestors of the Julian clan, Aeneas and Romulus, adorned the Forum of Augustus, as did statues of the *summi viri* ("the greatest men") of the Republic that was dead in all but Augustan rhetoric and symbolism.

Figure 17.7   Procession of the imperial family, Ara Pacis, Rome, 13–9 BCE. © Stefano Politi Markovina/Alamy

Primary Source

Box 17.2 : Augustus, *The Deeds of the Divine Augustus*, 27–8.[1]

I added Egypt to the empire of the Roman people . . . I recovered all the provinces beyond the Adriatic Sea towards the east, together with Cyrene, the greater part of them being occupied by kings. I previously recovered Sicily and Sardinia which had been taken in the slave war. I founded colonies of soldiers in Africa, Sicily, Macedonia, both Spanish provinces, Achaea, Asia, Syria, Gallia Narbonensis and Pisidia. Italy too has twenty-eight colonies founded by my authority, which were densely populated in my lifetime.

Note

1. Translated by Brunt and Moore (1967).

The Forum of Augustus also represented Augustus's influence over the Roman state. Like the Forum of Julius Caesar, it was rectangular and defined by porticoes around an open space. This structured design was very similar to many of the fora built in the provincial cities during the late Republic and early Empire, such as at Pompeii, and reflects the Roman fondness for orthogonal city planning (the development of urban spaces along a grid system) that can be observed outside of Rome. The long history of the city of Rome, as well as its location among hills, made this type of planning difficult. Nevertheless, Augustus was the first to make substantial changes to the city. He divided it into 14 administrative regions, developed the Campus Martius, built the Forum of Augustus, and restored many temples. Augustus also emphasized resources that were harnessed in Italy, namely Luna marble (now known as Carrara marble). This white marble from northern Italy was used instead of Greek marble for, among other things, column capitals and exterior facing such as that of the concrete podium of the Temple of Mars Ultor. The interior of the Forum of Augustus combined Luna marble with coloured marbles from North Africa to emphasize the resources on Italian soil and those in newly acquired territories overseas.

The creation of the Roman Corinthian order also helped to promote a confident image of Rome. Although an adaption of the Greek Corinthian, the Roman form was surely understood as an advancement beyond the Greek architectural orders. Prior to the late first century BCE, the Corinthian capital had been used only with features of the Ionic or Doric orders. On the Temple of Peace (Concord) at Paestum, for example, built around 100 BCE, an Italic version of the Corinthian capital was combined with a Doric **architrave** and **frieze** and an Ionic **cornice**. But this practice changed when the

Corinthian capital was refined and combined with its own, better proportioned **entablature**, which included the introduction of **modillions** to the bottom of the cornice. It was not so much that the Corinthian became standardized but that the architrave, frieze, and cornice were adjusted to create an order that was distinct from the Doric and the Ionic.[9] The Temple of Mars Ultor displays a good example of the Roman Corinthian order in its adapted state (see Figure 17.8). With this architectural change occurring at approximately the same time as Augustus's reign and the rebuilding of the city of Rome, the Corinthian order became *the* Roman order and was widely used on temples and other buildings for centuries.

Fine, high-status household items, including glass jars and silver drinking vessels, form another category of material evidence from the early imperial period. The Portland Vase (see Figure 17.9) and Boscoreale Cups are excellent examples of these types of luxury objects, which are generally decorated with mythological or historical scenes. The Portland Vase, a cameo glass vessel depicting a mythological or allegorical scene of love and marriage, dates to between 5 and 25 CE and was made using the "dip overlay" method. This three-part manufacturing process involved the dipping of partially cooled blue glass into molten white glass, blowing the vessel, and then carving the cooled, hardened white layer to reveal a decorative scene. The process was not only time consuming, but the fine carving also required great skill.

Figure 17.8   The Temple of Mars Ultor, Rome, late first century BCE. Photo by Andrea Samoil

Figure 17.9 The Portland Vase, cameo glass, 5–25 CE. © The Bridgeman Art Library Limited/Alamy

The silver Boscoreale Cups depict Augustus and Tiberius (his successor) in a variety of scenes. One cup shows two images, one of Augustus on military campaign and another of him interacting with gods. The latter image suggests that this cup was probably made after Augustus's death, as it was uncommon during the early Empire to depict a living ruler and gods together (gods and the emperor appear together on the Ara Pacis, but they are depicted in separate panels). The second Boscoreale Cup shows the emperor Tiberius riding a triumphal **chariot** and making a sacrifice to Jupiter in front of a temple. This image may refer to the **triumphs** celebrated by Tiberius after his victory over the Germans in 7 BCE or the Illyrians in 12 CE. As on the Ara Pacis, we begin to see the depiction of what may have been historical events in concert with allegorical scenes. This combination of genres likewise conveys the imperial message of piety, peace, and prosperity.

Imperial Dynasties and Dominance

After the death of Augustus, the influence of the emperor continued to dominate public art and architecture, as it was through these media that emperors were able to demonstrate (sometimes simultaneously) their domination of and piety towards the imperial community. Some emperors, however, allowed their power to foster megalomania, an attitude that was also reflected in the urban topography. Nero, for example, built an enormous palace for himself, the so-called **Domus Aurea** ("Golden House"), after the Great Fire of 64 CE had consumed much of Rome's privately owned residential area.

Compare Chapter 12, p. 274, and Chapter 16, p. 367, on the Domus Aurea.

The entire complex may have covered up to 1.2 square kilometres of prime real estate, taking up parts of the Caelian, Palatine, and Esquiline hills. Much of the structure has been lost, but a section containing residential rooms around a large garden was preserved under the Baths of Trajan. The main room of this part contains one of the earliest concrete domes. Nero's architects used concrete to create a self-supporting dome in the centre of this entertaining suite. Although the execution presented challenges (for example, the architects had to connect the walls built on an octagonal floor plan with the circular ceiling—a less than ideal situation), the dome's construction had great significance for the future of Roman architecture. Ideologically and physically, the palace displayed the emperor's dominance over the city of Rome, which is why the palace was demolished shortly after Nero's death in 68 CE to create space for public building projects (see Box 17.3).

The most significant of these ventures was the **Colosseum**, or, as it is more correctly known, the Flavian Amphitheatre (see Figure 12.2, p. 274). Initiated by Vespasian, the first

Political History

Box 17.3: Nero and the Great Fire of 64 CE

In 64 CE a fire began in the shops outside the **Circus Maximus**, near the base of Rome's Palatine and Caelian hills. At the time, the Circus was largely constructed of wood, and little of that area of the city was built to withstand such a strong fire (Tac. *Ann*. 15.38–40). The fire spread quickly and caused devastation in most regions of the city over a period of five days. Not only did the wind carry the flames, but looters also intentionally spread fires to raid empty houses (Cass. Dio 62.17). The impression given by the ancient authors is one of chaos and destruction.

The emperor Nero was out of Rome during this time, and Tacitus (*Ann*. 15.38) goes so far as to suggest that he ordered the fire to be started. Indeed, Nero's response to the Great Fire was highly inappropriate, though not altogether unexpected; Suetonius (*Ner*. 1) writes that Nero "so far degenerated from the noble qualities of his ancestors, that he retained only their vices; as if those alone had been transmitted to him by his descent."[1] In the ashes of the city, Nero constructed his Domus Aurea and, in doing so, effectively took land away from the people for his own private use. This action can be contrasted with the construction projects of Augustus, who stated explicitly that he built on private land only (*RG* 21).

Note

1. Translated by Reed and Thompson (1889).

emperor of the Flavian dynasty, and inaugurated by his son Titus in 80 CE, the structure was intended to provide the populace with a large entertainment venue. The architecture of the Colosseum illustrates Roman expertise with concrete and vaulted construction. The exterior appears as a series of arches on three levels and a fourth level of solid wall with intermittent rectangular openings. A complex series of vaulted passageways underneath carried the seating and access staircases for the spectators, who could walk

See Chapter 3, p. 60, and Chapter 12, p. 282, on seating at public entertainment.

through 80 arched entrances. The **amphitheatre** had an estimated seating capacity of 55,000. This seating was arranged according to social standing and class, with the bottom rows (*ima cavea*) reserved for public officials and the aristocracy, the middle section (*media cavea*) for less wealthy citizens, and the top seats (*summa cavea*) for the poorest in society.

The imperial residence on the Palatine Hill, its traditional site since Augustus, was also expanded and renovated under the Flavians. Like Nero's Domus Aurea, the intent of this palace was to provide a luxurious home for the emperor in Rome. However, unlike the Domus Aurea, the new imperial palace begun by Vespasian was limited to the

Palatine. New archaeological research on the area indicates that construction of the palace was not completed until the reign of Trajan or Hadrian, some 20 to 30 years later (and there was further expansion under the Severans).[10] The northwest side of the complex, which had been finished by Domitian, continued to develop the use of curves and vaulting for opulent private and entertaining spaces.

The design of curved structures built of concrete reached an apex with the reconstruction of the **Pantheon**, a temple originally built in the Augustan period by Marcus Agrippa but completely rebuilt under Trajan and Hadrian.[11] As its name suggests, the Pantheon was dedicated to "all the gods," and the round shape it took in its Hadrianic restoration emphasized its cosmic connection. Further demonstrating Roman expertise in the use of concrete and the understanding of the principles of mechanics, the design and construction of the Pantheon reveal several interesting features. For example, a traditional, rectangular temple porch was joined to a cylindrical structure, and a last-minute decision must have been made to lower the porch's entablature and pediment to accommodate shorter-than-expected granite columns imported from Egypt. However, the most impressive aspect of the building is how the architects achieved the self-supporting hemispherical dome, which measures 21.6 metres tall and 43.2 metres across. Certain "tricks" were used to manage this feat. First, the aggregate in the concrete is heavier in the lower section of the dome and lighter at the top. Second, the thickness of the dome tapers towards the top to reduce the weight of the dome even further. Third, a circular opening was left in the centre of the dome. Called an *oculus* ("eye"), this opening again reduces weight, but it also allows light and air into the otherwise windowless structure (see Figure 16.1, p. 367).

By the time the Pantheon was constructed in its current form, Roman architecture had matured into its own confident style. The reliance on concrete as a locally available, cost-effective, quick, and stable building material allowed Roman architects to explore the curved form and new ways of presenting spaces. One only has to look at any number of imperial buildings from the second and third centuries CE to see this creativity and innovation at work. The Baths of Caracalla and Baths of Diocletian, for example, are particularly noteworthy for their vast vaulted bathing halls constructed in brick-faced concrete.

New perspectives appear in relief sculpture as well. The Arch of Titus, located on the eastern side of the Roman Forum, is the first monument to display the use of **spatial illusionism** confidently. The two panels facing each other on the inside of the triumphal arch show soldiers parading plunder taken from the Jewish temple in Jerusalem and Titus riding in a chariot in a triumphal procession, respectively. In the middle of each panel, the figures

See Chapter 14, pp. 319, on the Jewish revolt.

protrude from the visual plane in deeper relief and then recede into the plane as the procession exits in the direction of the Forum. This three-dimensional effect creates the illusion of movement as the observer passing under the arch becomes a virtual participant in the triumphal procession, enveloped by the activity on both panels.

Roman relief sculpture developed further during the second century CE, depicting a continuous historical narrative for the first time. Trajan's Column, the centrepiece in the Forum of Trajan, records the activities of the Roman army during the Dacian Wars (see Figure 17.10). The narrative, which incorporates over 2,500 figures in 55 individual scenes, begins at the bottom of the 38-metre-tall column and spirals to the top. Trajan is portrayed 60 times to enable those viewing the column from different angles to recognize him. In these various depictions, Trajan oversees all typical activities of an army on campaign: he addresses his troops, checks engineering works, welcomes ambassadors, leads troops into battle, receives captives, and makes sacrifices. Interestingly for a monument meant to commemorate a series of wars, scenes of battle are few and far between. The lack of battle scenes and the focus on engineering works, religious sacrifice, and general military presence reinforce the idea that war is a horrible but necessary prerequisite for Roman peace and prosperity.

See Chapter 13, pp. 290–91 and ← 299–300, on Trajan's column as a military monument.

See Chapter 14, pp. 320–21, on ← the campaigns of Trajan and Marcus Aurelius.

The use of continuous narrative on a commemorative column reappears on the Column of Marcus Aurelius, which stands in its original location in the Campus Martius of Rome. Like Trajan's Column, this structure also commemorates military activities, specifically the campaigns against the Marcomanni and Quadi that took place in the 170s CE. Artistically, however, the Column of Marcus Aurelius differs from Trajan's Column both in technique and subject portrayal. The figures are sculpted in high relief—they almost come out of the backing stone—and depict violent battles between the Romans and their Germanic adversaries (of the 116 scenes spiralling the column, 36 depict battle). The emperor appears in similar scenes as Trajan, addressing the troops, leading them into battle, and receiving captives. The emotive nature of the Roman troops and their captives may be a reflection of the nature of the battles themselves. Trajan's Dacian Wars were aimed at expanding the empire whereas, in the wars against the Marcomanni and Quadi, Rome was on the defensive from invading enemies. In this light, the Column of Marcus Aurelius appears to emphasize the horrors of war because the conflict was initiated by the enemy.

Portrait sculpture also changed in style, artistic technique, and ideology. During the Flavian period, artists had begun using drills to create the portraits of women. Figure 17.11 shows a marble bust commonly referred to as the Flavian Woman, who is depicted with deep-set curls in her

Figure 17.10   Detail of Trajan's Column, Rome, 112 CE. © Hemis/Alamy

Figure 17.11   Portrait bust of Vibia Matidia, first century CE. © De Agostini Picture Library / G. Dagli Orti / The Bridgeman Art Library / Alamy

luxurious hairpiece. By Hadrian's time, the drill was also used to sculpt male hair and beards. Hadrian was the first to bring about a significant change in the image of the emperor. For the first time since the Hellenistic period, rulers were portrayed with a full beard and voluminous, curly hair. Hadrian was portrayed with a beard probably as a result of his interest in Greek philosophy and culture (philosophers were often portrayed in this way in Greek sculpture). From the mid-second century CE on, eyes were rendered with more structure as well. The border of the iris was incised, and the pupils were drilled rather than just painted on as they had been previously. The use of incised lines meant that the gaze of the portrait subject could be more clearly defined.

In addition to the publicly visible images of the emperor that were disseminated throughout the empire, privately commissioned art also adorned the imperial residences. One of the best-known and best-preserved imperial residences is Hadrian's Villa at Tivoli, approximately 30 kilometres east of Rome. Sprawled over one square kilometre, the complex contained over 30 individual buildings, including two bath complexes, the so-called Maritime Theatre (of unknown function), dining rooms, reception halls, service quarters, and numerous peristyle courtyards. The villa was presumably used by the emperor as a retreat but, given its vast plan, it was also a place to meet and entertain senators, members of the imperial administration, extended family, and other guests.

The decoration and materials used to construct Hadrian's Villa point to the wealth and expanse of the empire in the second century CE. For instance, marble was imported from Greece and North Africa, likely at great expense. Floor decoration, as in many elite houses, consisted of mosaics and **opus sectile** panels in geometric patterns. The walls were painted in geometric **frescoes** or covered in marble **veneer**. Numerous marble sculptures have been recovered from the villa, many of which are copies of famous Hellenistic statues depicting mythological figures and exotic animals. Another collection of statues portrays members of the imperial family as well as Antinous, Hadrian's young male lover, who famously drowned in the Nile. One statue discovered at Hadrian's Villa shows Antinous as a pharaoh in Egyptian clothing and is thought to commemorate his death. The well-preserved art of Hadrian's Villa gives us a good indication of the emperor's wealth, personal tastes, and interests in Hellenistic art.

Hadrian's Villa is also significant architecturally. It displays mastery of well-known Greek and Roman styles and building techniques while demonstrating a proclivity to experiment with established models, particularly the curved form that had been growing in popularity since the early Empire. Hadrian's admiration of ancient Greece also dictated the style of many of the buildings in his villa, such as the Poikile, a large peristyle courtyard named after the famous Stoa Poikile in ancient Athens. The two bath buildings and the Serapeum, so called because it was thought to be a shrine for the worship of the Egyptian god Serapis, had domed ceilings (see Figure 17.12). The segmented half-dome of the Serapeum, which opens out onto the so-called Canopus, an oblong pool surrounded by a colonnade with statues, was possibly designed by Hadrian. The famous architect Apollodorus of Damascus, who designed the Forum and Markets of Trajan in Rome, criticized Hadrian's drawings of architectural "pumpkins."[12] Not knowing exactly what this term refers to, scholars have suggested that these "pumpkins" might have been alternate concepts for the dome (like we see at the Serapaeum) or the concave and convex forms in the floor plan of the villa's Piazza D'Oro. Regardless of whether or not these features were ever anything more than drawings done by Hadrian in his youth, the architecture of his villa demonstrates his active interest in the field.

Responses to Economic and Social Change

Roman art and architecture were not only for the emperors. "Ordinary" people also had the ability to commission, buy, or create art and architecture on a variety of scales. Some had the means to build large houses and fill them with art on a near-imperial level, while others may have had one or two pieces of art displayed in a modest home. Indeed, we can

Figure 17.12   Serapaeum at Hadrian's Villa, Tivoli, 125–128 CE. © AEP/Alamy

observe great diversity in the quality and style of art and architecture across the Roman empire. While individual wealth and social standing affected the ability to own large houses or precious art, external social and economic factors dictated the styles and pace of the production of material culture.

Good examples of this dynamic can be found in the architectural design and function of villas throughout the provinces. In the Roman context, a villa was a large piece of real estate generally located in the countryside and usually dedicated to agricultural production (see Box 17.4). The different landscapes throughout the empire meant, however, that the type of agricultural production varied by region. In the hilly areas of the Mediterranean, olive oil and wine were major agricultural products. Presses, tanks, and storage jars for these items survive in the archaeological record. Animal farming and grain production often supplemented these activities. In coastal regions, the remains of open-air fish tanks indicate commercial fish farming. The proximity to Rome and the efficiency of product distribution usually dictated the size of the villa. In the early Empire, the largest villas were on the Italian peninsula (for example, Settefinestre in Tuscany). As the empire expanded and the provinces became important centres in their own right, villas such as Fishbourne in England and Montmaurin in southern Gaul became notable.

Villas generally had two main architectural components: the *pars rustica*, which held the agricultural production facilities (stables, workshops, presses, storage areas, yards); and

→ See Chapter 5, p. 110, on the urban atrium-style house.

the *pars urbana*, the residential rooms (dining rooms, baths, bedrooms, offices, libraries). Architecturally, villas often resemble large versions of the urban house, with residential rooms in three wings around one or more closed courtyards and agricultural production facilities in the fourth wing or placed around a separate, productive courtyard. An architectural survey of

Primary Source

Box 17.4: Vitruvius, *On Architecture*, 6.6.1–2.[1]

First of all the orientations of sites should be examined with respect to their healthiness . . . and villas should be located accordingly. Their dimensions should be appropriate to the size of the farm and the quantity of produce . . . The baths too should be connected to the kitchen, for in this way washing facilities for the farmworkers will not be far away. The oil-press should also be next to the kitchen since in this way it will be well placed to deal with the olive harvest.

Note

1. Translated by Schofield (2006).

villas throughout the empire demonstrates that the scale of production affected the size of the villa, at least in the earlier periods of the Empire.[13] In Britain, villas such as the Rockborne in Hampshire often consisted of only two or three wings around an open courtyard. One wing was normally used for agricultural production, while the other two contained a bath complex and residential space. Bathing suites in these villas were also smaller, with fewer rooms in smaller spaces than at villas in France and Spain. These differences demonstrate the adaptability of architecture to suit different geographic or economic requirements.

The availability of resources in different areas is evident in the materials used to build public and private structures in the province of Spain during the Empire. Villas such as Sao Cucufate (in modern Portugal) were built of a combination of bricks and local granite. This example, from the fringes of the empire, contrasts with the ubiquitous use of local limestone in Italy's villas. Similarly, the columns of the basilica at Baelo Claudia (in modern Spain) consist of local limestone, undoubtedly from the mountains inland of the settlement (see Figure 17.13). The builders of the Roman imperial fora, however, had access to imported marble, thanks to the wealth of the emperor. The difference between provincial cities such as this one and Rome is further highlighted by the use of stucco to make the columns at Baelo Claudia look like they were carved of marble. This practice was used throughout the empire when architects wanted to make structures appear more costly but did not have the money or ability to acquire actual marble columns. Such inventiveness again demonstrates builders' adaptability to local resources, scale, and needs.

Figure 17.13   Remains of the basilica at Baelo Claudia, Spain, early first century CE. © Beth Munro

Figure 17.14   Detail of the exterior wall of the church of Saint-Just of Valcabrère, France, eleventh century CE. © Beth Munro

From the chaotic third century CE onwards, *spolia* (reused decorative elements from earlier structures) became an increasingly common feature of building construction. There is evidence that marble was being reused in Pompeii even in the early first century CE, but it becomes very noticeable only in later periods. For example, decorative panels from Hadrianic structures were reused to decorate the Arch of Constantine. There are three possible reasons for this apparent thrift: Constantine may have wanted to associate himself with successful emperors of the past; he may have wanted to give the people a sign of his austerity; or marble may have become increasingly expensive or difficult to obtain. Reuse and recycling in art and architecture are also common in less high-profile contexts from the end of antiquity to the Middle Ages. **Amphorae**, for example, were reused to construct parts of the Circus of Maxentius in Rome. In the fourth century CE, stones that contain inscription fragments were used as paving in a house at the Crypta Balbi in Rome and in the southern Italian villa at Faragola. Fragments of Roman marble sarcophagi and inscriptions from nearby sites were also frequently found in the walls of medieval churches, such as at Saint-Just of Valcabrère, located one kilometre from the Roman settlement of Lugdunum Convenarum (Saint-Bertrand-de-Comminges, France; see Figure 17.14).

Figure 17.15   *Opus sectile* panel of Junius Bassus, Rome, early-to mid-fourth century CE. © Alamy

The economic and political instability of the later Empire is also reflected in the art of the third and fourth centuries CE, particularly in sculpture. Famous examples are the two sculptures of the tetrarchs, one in Venice and the other in the Vatican. The **tetrarchy** was a system of shared rule, instituted by Diocletian after the political turmoil of the third century CE, that saw 26 emperors over a 50-year period. In this system, a pair of emperors worked in the eastern half of the empire while another worked in the western half. Each pair consisted of a junior ("Caesar") and a senior ("Augustus") emperor. These offices and the concept of shared power are reflected in the fascinating iconography of the tetrarchs. They are pictured in nearly identical pairs, embracing each other. Any attempt to render personal facial features has disappeared; instead, the subjects have the large eyes characteristic in sculpture of this period and look directly outwards.

See Chapter 2, pp. 42–3, and ← Chapter 14, p. 323, on the tetrarchy.

This frontal gaze became an artistic convention in the mid-third century CE and continued into the Byzantine period. An excellent example is the *opus sectile* panel of Junius Bassus, in which Bassus gazes at the viewer, his large eyes emphasizing his frontal pose (see Figure 17.15). Arguably an unnatural position, this **frontality** reflects the intensity and urgency of a period of economic and political turmoil. It is also thought that it allows the viewer to engage more directly with the figures. This exchange of gaze becomes particularly relevant with the spreading and eventual formalization of Christianity as the Empire's main religion.

One final development of third- and fourth-century CE art is the introduction and growing prominence of Christian scenes. These pieces appeared initially in private contexts during a time when Christianity was still a forbidden religion in Rome. Images of Christ and of biblical scenes, however, appear in the catacombs in Rome from the third century CE onwards. Eventually, these images became more publicly visible and appear, for example, on sarcophagi. The sarcophagus of Junius Bassus is decorated with vignettes from Genesis, including a central panel showing Adam and Eve. Christian representations also eventually appeared in house decoration. The most famous example is probably in **Dura-Europos** in Syria, where the wall paintings in a house built around 235 CE are the earliest known images of Christ in a domestic setting. Another domestic example is the floor mosaic at Hinton St. Mary in Britain, which features the head of Christ as the central panel. The introduction of such Christian images into funerary and domestic art demonstrates a major social and religious change across the Roman empire. Whether people worshipped the Christian God in their homes just as

See Chapter 9, pp. 209–10, ← on domestic religion.

they had worshipped pagan deities in domestic settings is not clear in all cases. But these Christian images are one of the ways in which art informs us about the timing and nature of fundamental social change.

Summary

Over six centuries, Roman art and architecture developed in style and content, from the collecting and imitating habits of the Republic to a self-assured and dominant material presence across the empire. Yet, at the same time, certain motifs and designs run throughout

the Roman period. For example, the affection for depicting Greek mythology in wall painting and mosaic does not go out of style until the fifth century CE.[14] Under Hadrian, we see
a great resurgence of Greek-influenced architectural design and replication of Hellenistic
art, much as the Romans had experienced in the Republic. Furthermore, we can observe
that the portrayal of individuals during the Empire experienced cycles of realism and
idealism to support various propaganda programs. The great diversity of media and styles
of Roman art and architecture is also significant in its own right. In imperial works, this
variety was controlled by the policy or personal tastes of the emperor. In private works, it
was more often dictated by personal levels of wealth, taste, and utility.

The changes in material culture, while sometimes dictated by the imperial message,
are at other times responses to cultural or economic changes. These factors are best studied
through the analysis of the production processes in quarries, workshops, and homes. Our
modern understanding of Roman art and architecture is also continually changing with
new archaeological discoveries and the reassessment of known buildings and objects. The
material culture of the Romans is now interpreted not only as a representation of society's
taste and cultural knowledge but also as a source of information about the Roman economy.

Questions for Review and Discussion

1. How was Roman material culture influenced by that of the Etruscans and Greeks?
2. Why was age an important feature in portraiture? What social or political gain was
    to be achieved by being portrayed as young or old?
3. Why is the dome important to Roman architecture?
4. How is the art of the middle and lower classes different from imperial art?
5. How did the resources in Italy and the provinces affect Roman art and architecture?

Suggested Reading

Elsner, J. 1998. *Imperial Rome and Christian Triumph: The Art of the Roman Empire AD 100–450*. Oxford: Oxford University Press.
    For a thematic approach on the transformation of art from the high Empire to late antiquity, this book offers an accessible but stimulating discussion of issues such as third-century CE frontality.

Kleiner, F. 2007. *A History of Roman Art*. Boston: Cengage.
    This volume provides a good overall introduction to Roman art and architecture. It historically contextualizes selected works well and has excellent photographs and digital reconstructions to illustrate written descriptions.

MacDonald, W. 1982. *The Architecture of the Roman Empire, I and II*. New Haven, CT: Yale University Press.

MacDonald's two volumes provide the best introduction to the major architectural projects of the emperors. In particular, the second volume thematically approaches common architectural features, such as the arch and portico.

Stamper, J.W. 2005. *The Architecture of Roman Temples: The Republic to the Middle Empire*. New York: Cambridge University Press.

This book provides a chronological investigation of the design and construction of Roman temples and clearly addresses the architectural heritage of the Greek and Etruscan traditions.

Stewart, P. 2008. *The Social History of Roman Art*. Cambridge: Cambridge University Press.

While providing another good introduction to significant works of art, this book also introduces ideas on how to think critically about art and how to place it in the social contexts of ancient Rome.

Wilson-Jones, M. 2000. *Principles of Roman Architecture* New Haven, CT: Yale University Press.

This volume is an essential companion for students of Roman architecture. It should be consulted after gaining a basic knowledge of building types, however, as it provides more in-depth discussions of architectural theory and construction techniques.

Notes

1   See, for example, Paus. 3.17.6.
2   Cooley (2003: 68).
3   Ridley (2005).
4   Barringer (1994: 164–6).
5   This attitude of Greek cultural superiority is clearly expressed by the Roman architect Vitruvius in his treatise *De architectura*. In Book 1.1, he refers to Greek mathematics and philosophy as guiding principles for the Roman architect.
6   Kleiner (2007: 54).
7   Tanner (2000: 31).
8   Wallace-Hadrill (1993: 66–8).
9   Wilson-Jones (2000: 1–16, 135–58) provides an excellent summary of the Greek orders, some problems with their use, and how the Roman Corinthian order was developed.
10   Wulf-Rheidt and Sojc (2009: 268–79).
11   Hetland (2007) summarizes the latest evidence and debate about the dating of the reconstruction of the Pantheon, argued by some to have begun under the emperor Trajan.
12   Cass. Dio 69.4.1–5.
13   See Marzano (2007) for a detailed discussion of this relationship in central Italy.
14   Dunbabin (2008).

Conclusion

The chapters of this volume have looked beyond the lives, works, successes, and failures of the "great men" of Roman history to investigate ancient Roman society by asking who else was present, what they were doing, and what their lives were like. However, the task of summarizing Roman society to provide a conclusion is confounding because Roman society was no monolithic entity. It was an exceptionally diverse culture marked by extreme social and massive economic inequalities. Indeed, it is clear that the casual way in which members of Roman society are commonly referred to as "the Romans," a convention also adopted in this book, is somewhat misleading. By conjuring an image of toga-clad people who blanketed the Mediterranean region and Europe with bath buildings and Latin, turning everything and everyone they encountered "Roman," the term implies a uniformity that did not exist.

What common ground does exist, then, between the chapters of a volume that demonstrates the complexity and heterogeneity of Roman society? It is, surely, that every chapter of this book has described how all components of Roman society valued difference over uniformity or equality. The preceding chapters have, in short, examined how law, social attitudes, education, religious practices, political institutions, military activities, economic habits, literary and artistic accomplishments, and technological feats promoted the perpetuation of social difference. For example, the experience of slaves as human property contrasted sharply with the ideals that invested freedom and citizenship with value, a situation vividly seen in the context of justice: access to, and the experience of, Roman justice reflected social value. The hierarchical structure of the household prescribed different standards of behaviour for its various members; ideals of physical form and sexual behaviour stressed differences between males and females; and seating at spectacles organized social and economic inequalities into a tidy visual display.

Snobbish attitudes about sources of wealth ensured that, even when economic parity was achieved, social parity was not. Civic religion supported the uneven distribution of political power, while non-civic religion allowed for the cultivation of individual identity. Education provided a means by which individuals might invest themselves with social value, and literary pursuits and artistic forms functioned as avenues for self-definition and self-differentiation. The successes of the Roman army, itself a stratified organization of individuals, resulted in the creation of an empire of different communities that received different treatment, while engineering projects advertised the difference between life before and during Roman rule.

Taken separately, the chapters illustrate the variety within Roman society. But when considered in conjunction with each other, they equally demonstrate the elasticity of social behaviour and real experience within established hierarchies of difference. For example, bonds of affection could surmount social status, making slaves cherished members of the family. Foreign adoptions that distressed political authorities, such as rhetoric, drama, and religious cults, might appear (like the depiction of the cult of Mater Magna on a Pompeian wall) as benign objects of popular enjoyment and reverence. The imposition of Roman rule on conquered communities resulted in political subjection and taxation, as well as an opportunity for intermarriage with Roman soldiers and social mobility. Behaviours that were officially censured as being unsuitable to Roman males or citizens were often engaged in by those very people, even those in positions of recognized authority. Elite disdain for manual labour did not prevent those whose success derived from such work from taking pride in their accomplishments. These are but a few examples of the tensions between the desire to maintain social difference and the need to preserve social cohesion, of the inconsistencies between social ideals and lived realities, and of the complicated relationships between social stereotypes and actual experiences. It is surely these contradictions that made Roman society vital and dynamic.

Investigations into Roman society often shatter our assumptions and our expectations. However, it is this disillusionment that makes such explorations fascinating and relevant. The aim of this collection has been to introduce the elemental institutions and concepts of Roman society and culture so that readers may pursue more complex studies of ancient Rome with sensitivity and curiosity. Such efforts cannot fail to reward those who undertake them.

Epilogue

Roman Themes in Modern Society and Popular Culture

Although we have reached the end of this volume, we cannot "conclude" Roman society and culture for the simple reason that, in many ways, they both live on in the present. Due to the simple fact that ancient Rome is still relevant, these last few pages look beyond the classics curriculum to suggest ways that readers may apply their knowledge of the period more generally and immediately to identify the influence of Rome in their daily lives. As chapters 7, 16, and 17 demonstrated, Roman culture has directly and indirectly shaped our intellectual and physical landscapes. At a minimum, the Roman world brought us both Vergil's writings and concrete, that is, foundational literature in the study of the humanities and foundational material for the buildings in which the discipline is pursued. Some elements of the Roman republican government are recognizable ancestors of some current systems, including the Electoral College system in the United States.

It is not merely Rome's legacies, however, that give Roman society contemporary relevance. This civilization also provides an interesting point of comparison with modern issues, such as concern over the nature and influence of entertainment, the benefits and difficulties of religious multiculturalism, the problems involved in sending armed forces to police distant communities and diverse cultural or ethnic groups, decisions about taxation and government expenditure, and the role of private benefaction in the provision of community services. Conversely, Roman society can function as a useful contrast to our own society and help us think more productively about our own social values regarding, for example, education, social categories, human rights, sexual identity, and gender roles.

But there is another place where ancient Rome has particular contemporary relevance: popular culture. Pop culture is neither the only nor the most important place to engage with Rome, but it is worthy of discussion for two reasons. First, pop culture is quite possibly the place where people most often actively engage with Roman society, as

Rome looms large in everything from movies and television programs to novels, comics, video games, and Internet memes. Second, social history and popular culture have several interesting points of contact. As the first chapter of this volume stressed, historians write history in response to the present and, in some sense, create the past from the present. Producers of culture, popular and otherwise, often create the present by making selections from the past and adapting them to current concerns. In this light, pop culture can be understood as a corollary of history. Yet it is also a living form of our own social history since it reflects, perpetuates, and perhaps even shapes our social values.

The critical questions are, then, why do we keep mining Roman society for our own entertainment? How do we present Romans? What do our use and presentation of Romans say about us? Our purpose is not to answer these questions since readers, as consumers and producers of contemporary pop culture, are well positioned to do that for themselves. Instead, our purpose is to discuss one major problem (the degree to which historicity should be sacrificed for entertainment) and one major interpretive approach (understanding the use of antiquity in pop culture to reflect contemporary values and anxieties) that bear on the process of answering them.

Let us begin with the tense relationship between history and entertainment. Should productions that are first and foremost meant to amuse us be held to some standard of historical accuracy? It is difficult to answer this question definitively, much less to determine a generalized degree of acceptable accuracy, because pop culture embraces a vast array of different media, and each type can be used for many purposes. For example, are cartoons to be held to a different standard than novels? Should a political cartoon be held to a different level than *Garfield*? As the foregoing chapters illustrated, our knowledge of the "reality" of antiquity is hardly watertight. Is "accuracy" possible to achieve, even if it were made a priority?

The problem becomes still more complicated when we consider that some instances of Rome in pop culture depend upon historical inaccuracy to achieve their purpose. By way of example, we can consider the different ways that misrepresentations of Roman history and culture are used to make jokes in an Internet meme and in a *Far Side* cartoon. A cheezburger.com parody showing Cesare Maccari's nineteenth-century painting of the Roman would-be revolutionary Catiline shunned by the other members of the senate includes the caption "Flatulus knew he overdid the deviled eggs."[1] Here, the open abuse of history makes the meme funny. Although it is perhaps funnier to those who recognize the historical event that Maccari portrays, the audience does not need to know the details of the Catilinarian conspiracy to appreciate the incongruity of the sombre scene and the explanation offered for it (bad smells). However, the joke in the *Far Side* cartoon shown in Figure E.1 depends upon the audience's lack of knowledge of antiquity. Knowing that *vomitoria* were simply entrances to seating at theatres and amphitheatres reduces the amusement factor to a simple pun.

As these two examples suggest, historical accuracy is sometimes a killjoy that can be

THE FAR SIDE® By GARY LARSON

"Well, I'm an assistant regurgitation engineer...but I should make senior RE next year."

In ancient Rome, it was tough for the guys who worked in the vomitoriums to get dates.

Figure E.1

ignored with little harm. In other situations, the question of the appropriate balance of pedantry and historical licence for popular enjoyment is more pressing. It is an issue that arises particularly in reference to long, narrative presentations of Roman history and society, such as novels, television shows, and movies. Here, success often depends upon concealing the line between history and fiction, and the current tendency of novelists and television and film producers to consult academics and of academics to employ popular cultural productions in the classroom blurs the line yet further. But even when they work together, problems can ensue. On a movie set, for example, historians and Hollywood producers have different, often incompatible priorities. The former are concerned with authenticity, as rooted in the detail and containment of the plot within the realm of historical probability. The latter are concerned with fulfilling the modern audience's expectations of entertainment because fulfilled expectations ensure audience enjoyment and consequent success at the box office. As a result, the two sides are often unable to satisfy each other.

To illustrate the cross purposes at which historical consultants and movie producers might find themselves, consider an anecdote told by Kathleen Coleman, eminent Harvard historian and consultant on the movie *Gladiator*: "One message from the production office said: 'Kathy, we need to get a piece of evidence which proves that women gladiators had sharpened razor blades attached to their nipples. Could you have it by lunchtime?'"[2] We can see that, although the producers were to some extent concerned with the accuracy of their presentation (they wanted proof for the use of razor blades on the nipples of female gladiators), their desire for proof was just a matter of dotting the i's and crossing the t's: it had never occurred to them that Roman gladiatorial history might not have been as they wished to present it. Indeed, Coleman could not produce a piece of evidence proving that women gladiators had sharpened razor blades attached to their nipples—not even had she been given until after lunchtime to do so—because no such evidence exists. The production office's assumption reflects the tendency of many pop culture productions to prescribe society and history more than they describe it, that is, to present what we think *should* have been there. Why do we think razor-bladed nipples should have been there? Not because the Romans wanted to see them (they did not) but seemingly because *we* want to see them without having to admit ownership to the desire. We can enjoy the spectacle and blame the Romans.

In the end, no gladiatorial nipples sported razor blades in *Gladiator*. Even so, Coleman famously requested that her name be removed from the credits, possibly because of too many similar instances in which her advice was not heeded. She muses that "maybe there is a residual notion in the film industry that the hiring of a consultant is in itself sufficient to give a film a veneer of respectability."[3] Admittedly, the popular interest that Hollywood can generate is beneficial for the field of history. Nevertheless, in a collection of scholarly essays about *Gladiator*, Coleman poses the question that haunts professional historians: "Will generations to come persist in believing that the cinematic fiction is what 'really happened'? If so—and this is the really worrying question, especially on the lips of those whose bank balances are swelled by the takings at the box office—does it matter?"[4]

Few members of a blockbuster movie's audience are likely to think that they are watching a documentary, but simply knowing that not everything is "real" helps little in the identification of what is and is not historically accurate. Common sense cannot sift history from fiction, since historical societies often confound our ideas of what is normal. The beginnings of chapters 4 and 13, which deal with HBO's *Rome* and Ridley Scott's *Gladiator*, respectively, demonstrate this point. Audiences might have been surprised to discover that Hollywood intervened not in the placement of a slave in the same room as two people having sex but in the presentation of the Roman army as a well-oiled machine composed of identical components.

Does it matter if pop culture dictates general understanding of ancient history and society? If it does, what is the remedy? If it does not, are we comfortable with it dictating popular understanding of all points in history and any society, or are there some eras and locations that should be off limits? How do we decide? The problems surrounding historical accuracy in pop culture are chronic and intractable, but the implications of not considering them at all could have serious consequences for our collective concept of the past.

However, if we are able to distance ourselves from concerns over historical accuracy in pop culture, the opportunity for a different sort of historical inquiry presents itself: we can consider *how* we use concepts of Rome and ideas about Romans for entertainment. From this standpoint, historical accuracy or inaccuracy is immaterial. The starting point instead is the recognition that pop culture is our fabrication—everything in it is primarily a figment of our creation, not a documentary resurrection of historical figures or events. The question is, then, what characteristics do we impute to Romans and Roman society in our creations and to what effect or purpose?[5] This sort of examination can tell us a great deal, not about real ancient Romans but about ourselves since we are the creators and audience of these entertaining "Romans" upon whom we impose our social values, cultural tastes, political dispositions, or moral ideals (or their opposites). Such inquiries find a home in the field of reception studies, where investigations of pop cultural representations of antiquity are gaining momentum.[6] Reception studies more generally examine the use of the past in the present, considering what is and is not borrowed and how selections are adapted, manipulated, or given a new context to infuse a contemporary cultural form with literary or artistic meaning or to make social commentary.[7]

What have we made the Romans do for us? We have frequently cast them as embodiments of abhorrent thinking or behaviour that provide satisfying contrasts with our mainstream social values. Those who study Rome in the cinema, for example, have often identified the political nemeses and social anxieties of contemporary audiences dressed up in togas and cuirasses. Indeed, in the early to mid-twentieth century, at the very time that academics were emulating ancient Greek and Roman statesmen and intellectuals, Hollywood was casting Romans as the bad guys—self-indulgent, greedy, immoral, and cruel—and the downtrodden of Roman society (slaves, Christians) as the heroes. For American audiences, whose national identity is bound up in the rejection of monarchy, the Roman Empire could be used to make implicit statements about the undesirability of undemocratic political systems. As Martin Winkler points out, "since the silent era, Hollywood has seen the Roman [E]mpire as an ancient parallel to modern military or totalitarian empires in general."[8]

Moreover, Romans have often been invested with distasteful imperiousness by the application of characteristics that recall more recent imperial pasts. For instance, a good deal of attention has been devoted to the use of accents and the mental knee-jerk response that they could be expected to elicit. Gideon Nisbet notes that "whip-cracking Romans have been delivering clipped British RP [received pronunciation, or standard British pronunciation] to oppressed, all-American Christians since Cecil B. de Mille invented the convention in his thirties epics."[9] The British accent of the Hollywood Roman was an audible reference to the fraught history between imperial Britain and the fledgling American colonies. As such, American audiences could know immediately that they were watching the struggle between an arrogant imperial power and honest and determined men who would throw off its yoke.

Besides political anxieties and sympathies, issues playing out in the audience's moral sphere, such as sexual promiscuity versus "family values" or women's roles in a changing world, are also represented in pop culture. On the screen, these themes come out in the qualities given to the characters: their actions and attitudes function as a code for the audience to decipher according to their socially inculcated expectations of "good" and "bad" or "right" and "wrong." In the 1960 production of *Spartacus*, for example, the Roman general Crassus makes sexual advances towards his male slave by opining that eating oysters and eating snails are, morally speaking, pretty much the same thing. This reference to bisexuality could be depended upon to prompt a negative response, as even audience members who were open to bisexuality as a sexual orientation would know that, given the social climate of the times, the trait was not meant to be admirable.

At least they would have if the scene had not been cut from the final release. As William Fitzgerald observes, implicit homoeroticism is a common feature of "toga movies," but overt bisexuality was too uncomfortable a trait to entertain in the 1960s, even in a Roman villain.[10] But Crassus's character is otherwise sculpted negatively, largely (as Jeffrey Tatum has argued) by presenting him as the antithesis of Spartacus, who is presented as a paragon of moral virtue. Crassus is rich, powerful, and power hungry while Spartacus is a slave whose aspiration is simple and honourable: to live like a man, not like an animal. Crassus is profligate and a sexual predator whereas Spartacus is self-controlled (indeed, a virgin) and respectful of the woman who will become his wife and only lover. In short, Spartacus represents American ideals, but Crassus is "an exponent of tyranny decked out in vices so ostentatious that they could not fail to disgust middle-class American audiences."[11]

More recently, popular depictions of the Romans have become less categorically negative and have sometimes even drifted towards the positive. This shift is a function of changing economic times, political realities, and social norms. Perhaps the power, wealth, and parties—all the things the Romans have gained a Hollywood reputation for—are not so bad after all.[12] The evolution of entertainment media has surely also played a role in presenting Romans as the good guys (and the consequent recasting of the non-Roman former heroes). Television and the Internet allow more frequent access to pop cultural productions, which are often irreverent or satirical plays on established cinematic genres. Put otherwise, we no longer simply revisit the Romans for entertainment but revisit our revisitations, and the differences between them mark the changes in our social, political, or moral disposition.[13]

Consider, for example, the 2005 Pepsi commercial (whose status as an element of pop culture is assured by its presence on YouTube) that consists of a slightly adapted clip from *Spartacus*. In the original scene, the victorious Roman commander imperiously demands to know which of the defeated slaves is Spartacus, to which they all respond, "I'm Spartacus!" in a show of mutual loyalty. In the commercial, the Roman would like to identify Spartacus in order to return a misplaced can of Pepsi. The same response becomes a competition to get a consumer product that rightfully belongs to someone else. This inversion is matched by another: the only person not consumed by greed (for Pepsi), at least at first, is the Roman. In the end, Spartacus is the big loser, robbed of his Pepsi by his brethren and his captors. Consumerism has won out over communism, a comfortable message in 2005 but quite different from the one the scene sent in 1960.

These examples are now part of our own history, and thanks to the global financial crises since 2005, our present circumstances have changed again. So too, perhaps, will our Romans. Let us consider one final, more recent example, this time as involved members of the audience. Based on the novel by Suzanne Collins, the film *The Hunger Games* (2012) takes place in Panem, a futuristic nation where poverty-stricken peripheral districts must send children, selected by lottery to be tributes, to the wealthy central city (Capitol), where they will fight to the death as a form of entertainment. Given the social and economic climate into which it was released—around the time when concerns over the widening gap between the (few) rich and the (ever-growing) poor prompted the

Occupy and the We Are the 99 Percent movements—we may be inclined to interpret this movie as a comment on our present and, perhaps, as a reflection of current anxiety about our future.

Now let us consider how the Romans figure in this interpretation, what force they lend, and the many questions this presence should raise for us as the audience. In *The Hunger Games*, we have shadows of Romans: the name of the nation is taken directly from the phrase *panem et circenses* ("bread and circuses"); the games are reminiscent of gladiatorial combat; and the relationship between the wealthy, consumer Capitol and the outlying districts it has bled dry is suggestive of the Roman taxation of the provinces. Perhaps, then, the movie does not ask "Is this where we're going?" but, rather more ominously, "Is this where we're going *again*?" The spectre of history repeating itself moves what otherwise seems to be an impossible fiction to the realm of possible reality.

If one of the purposes of pop culture is to make us think about our social and political choices, this movie is successful. But is the goal realized by feeding on poor popular understanding of the very thing that we are supposed to fear, by brandishing what amounts to a bogeyman? Consider, for example, one reviewer's assessment: "*The Hunger Games* is really one huge allusion to the Roman Empire."[14] The implication is that the major features of the movie's premise are also the main characteristics of Roman society. No one could deny that games, taxes, and a generally unempathetic elite are elements that could justifiably be applied to Roman society, but the suggestion that they encapsulate it is tantamount to saying that Canadian society can be fully understood by invoking hockey, medicare, and polite citizens or that American society can be captured by citing football, federal military budgets, and Republicans.

Is the perceived allusion in such films a reference to the Roman society of history or to the much flatter Roman society of Hollywood, which may pass for historical in popular understanding? Furthermore, even if we are comfortable with Hollywood rendering historical societies into two-dimensional caricatures for movies set in the past, are we still comfortable when these distortions could shape the way that we imagine our future and thereby influence our actions in the present? Or would pedantic insistence on a more nuanced use of history neuter effective social commentary? If we agree to banish historical concerns here, do we do so only because we agree with *The Hunger Games*' basic message that gross social and economic inequality is bad? What if a caricature of Roman society were used to promote a message with which we disagree? Surely we cannot hold different productions to different standards of historical licence based solely upon our approval or disapproval of the results.

We may now come back to Flatulus, the *vomitoria*, the would-be razor-bladed nipples of *Gladiator*, Romans with British accents, sexually charged food, and Pepsi-drinking Roman slaves with renewed respect for the problems they pose. In isolation, each is a frivolous example of the misrepresentation of history for current purposes, yet together they are part of larger, difficult, but important questions about the use and the very purpose of history in the present. Whatever answers we formulate to these questions, it is undeniable that Rome is still relevant: it is part of the way we understand our past, think about our present, and imagine our future. The relationship between how it was and how we make it out to be is complicated, and the avenues of inquiry are intricate. The investigation, however, bestows one of the major benefits common to all disciplines within the humanities: we not only become better, savvier, and more critical consumers and producers of our own culture but also more aware of our own prejudices and hypocrisies and of the influence that social forces and media have on our perception of the world.

Notes

1 See http://cheezburger.com/4299203584.

2 Winner (2005). The points made in this paragraph are heavily dependent upon Coleman (2004).

3 Coleman (2004: 48). Note that she does not explicitly give this thought as the reason why she did not want her name attached to *Gladiator*.

4 Ibid.: 50.

5 Joshel, Malamud, and McGuire (2001: 2); Pomeroy (2008: 29).

6 Lowe and Shahabudin (2009) present a collection of essays on a whole range of popular media and presentations that involve antiquity. See also Wyke (1997); Joshel, Malamud, and McGuire (2001); Winkler (2004, 2007); Pomeroy (2008); and Kovacs and Marshall (2011).

7 For a sense of the purpose and range of reception studies and the classics, see Hardwick (2003) and the essays in Hardwick and Stray (2008). Note that reception scholars often recognize that the present has investigative potential for the past as well, as modern use of past cultural forms may be a means to ask questions that might otherwise never have been considered.

8 Winkler (2001: 51).

9 Nisbet (2008: 130).

10 Fitzgerald (2001: 38).

11 Tatum (2007: 142).

12 Joshel, Malamud, and McGuire (2001: 11):
    It is possible to discern a shift in the direction away from the self-satisfied 1950s statement, "We are not the Romans," and the related anxious question, "Have we become the Romans of [E]mpire?" to a more confident imperative, "Be like the Romans!" In some of the most recent popular representations of imperial Rome, moralism is elided in an invitation to join a city of limitless power and fabulous parties.

13 See Futrell (2001) for the political ideologies that had been attached to various tellings of the Spartacus tale on the big screen.

14 Slager (2012).

Appendix:
Resources for Students

---•---

Primary Sources

Sourcebooks

Sourcebooks on ancient Rome compile important evidence on specific topics and explain the significance of each excerpt. As such, they are invaluable tools for both students and professional academics and are an excellent place to start research. The ancient sources tend to be largely literary and inscriptional, although images of material evidence are sometimes also included. A selection of sourcebooks that are useful for the study of Roman society and that feature English translations is listed below.

Some sourcebooks deal with Roman society and history generally, illuminating these subjects under a variety of headings. The following titles are of this type:

Cherry, D., ed. 2001. *The Roman World: A Sourcebook*. Malden, MA: Blackwell.

Dillon, M., and L. Garland, eds. 2005. *Ancient Rome*. London and New York: Routledge.

Lewis, N., and M. Reinhold, eds. 1990. *Roman Civilization: Selected Readings*, 3rd edn. New York: Columbia University Press. (This book has two volumes, subtitled *The Republic and The Augustan Age* and *The Empire*, respectively.)

Lomas, K., ed. 1996. *Roman Italy, 338 BC–AD 200*. London and New York: Routledge.

Parkin, T., and A. Pomeroy, eds. 2007. *Roman Social History*. London and New York: Routledge.

Shelton, J., ed. 1998. *As the Romans Did: A Sourcebook in Roman Social History*, 2nd edn. Oxford: Oxford University Press.

Other sourcebooks, such as the following, focus on more specific subjects:

Campbell, B., ed. 1994. *The Roman Army, 31 BC–AD 337*. London and New York: Routledge.

Futrell, A., ed. 2006. *The Roman Games*. Malden, MA: Blackwell.

Gardner, J., and T. Wiedemann, eds. 1991. *The Roman Household*. London and New York: Routledge.

Hope, V., ed. 2007. *Death in Ancient Rome*. London and New York: Routledge.

Hubbard, T., ed. 2003. *Homosexuality in Greece and Rome: A Sourcebook of Basic Documents*. Berkeley: University of California Press.

Humphrey, J., J.P. Oleson, and A. Sherwood, eds. 1997. *Greek and Roman Technology*. London and New York: Routledge.

Johnson, M., and T. Ryan, eds. 2005. *Sexuality in Greek and Roman Literature and Society*. London and New York: Routledge.

Joyal, M., J. Yardley, and I. McDougall, eds. 2009. *Greek and Roman Education*. London and New York: Routledge.

Lefkowitz, M., and M. Fant, eds. 2005. *Women's Life in Greece and Rome: A Source Book in Translation*, 3rd edn. Baltimore: Johns Hopkins University Press.

Levick, B., ed. 2000. *The Government of the Roman Empire: A Sourcebook*, 2nd edn. London and New York: Routledge.

Mahoney, A., ed. 2001. *Roman Sports and Spectacles*. Newburyport, MA: Focus.

Pollitt, J.J. 1983. *The Art of Rome c. 753 B.C.–A.D. 337: Sources and Documents*. Cambridge: Cambridge University Press.

Sage, M., ed. 2008. *The Republican Roman Army*. London and New York: Routledge.

Warrior, V., ed. 2002. *Roman Religion: A Sourcebook*. Newburyport, MA: Focus.

Wiedemann, T., ed. 1981. *Greek and Roman Slavery*. London and New York: Routledge.

These sourcebooks consider particular places, persons, and times:

Bagnall, R., and R. Cribiore. 2006. *Women's Letters from Ancient Egypt 300 BC–AD 800*. Ann Arbor: University of Michigan Press. (Although this book is perhaps not technically a sourcebook, it gathers, translates, and explains a fascinating corpus of ancient letters.)

Cooley, A., and M. Cooley, eds. 2004. *Pompeii*. London and New York: Routledge.

Evans Grubbs, J., ed. 2002. *Women and the Law in the Roman Empire: A Sourcebook on Marriage, Divorce and Widowhood*. London and New York: Routledge.

Hejduk, J., ed. 2008. *Clodia: A Sourcebook*. Norman: University of Oklahoma Press.

Ireland, S., ed. 2008. *Roman Britain*, 3rd edn. London and New York: Routledge.

Jones, P., ed. 2006. *Cleopatra: A Sourcebook*. Norman: University of Oklahoma Press.

Kraemer, R., ed. 2004. *Women's Religions in the Greco-Roman World: A Sourcebook*. New York: Oxford University Press.

Lee, A.D., ed. 2000. *Pagans and Christians in Late Antiquity*. London and New York: Routledge.

Mellor, R., ed. 2006. *Augustus and the Creation of the Roman Empire: A Brief History with Documents*. Boston and New York: Bedford/St. Martins.

Ogden, D., ed. 2009. *Magic, Witchcraft, and Ghosts in the Greek and Roman Worlds: A Sourcebook*, 2nd edn. Oxford: Oxford University Press.

Rowlandson, J., ed. 1998. *Women and Society in Greek and Roman Egypt: A Sourcebook*. Cambridge: Cambridge University Press.

Translations

The drawback of sourcebooks is that they provide textual evidence only as excerpts. It is often desirable to consider an excerpt in its broader original context or to read a work of ancient literature in its entirety. In such cases, dependable translations of the ancient texts are required. Ideally, though, students of Roman antiquity will endeavour to acquire a solid grasp of Latin and ancient Greek in order to be able to read the primary literature in the original language, as translations can differ significantly depending on a translator's interpretation. Tone, puns, and wordplay in the original language are often impossible to render in English, and such vital nuances are lost to those who must rely entirely on translations.

While high-quality English translations of ancient literature are available from well-known publishers such as Penguin and the Oxford World Classics series, the most valuable translations for the student of classical antiquity is the Loeb Classical Library series, published by Harvard University Press. This series uses green binding to denote Greek works and red binding for Latin. Another feature is that the original text is printed on the left pages, with the English appearing on the right. Perhaps more important, and unlike some translations that target a more general readership, these volumes also include the ancient book, chapter, and section divisions or line numbers, critical information for citing and locating passages in ancient literature. Loeb translations are common holdings in university libraries.

Other translations are available online. Produced and overseen by Tufts University, the Perseus Digital Library (www.perseus.tufts.edu/hopper) provides translations of canonical works of Classical literature. *Lacus Curtius* (http://penelope.uchicago.edu/Thayer/E/Roman/home.html), created and maintained by Bill Thayer, also provides translations of most works important to the study of Roman history, in addition to a collection of other resources for the student of ancient Rome. Translations of the Vindolanda tablets are also available online (http://vindolanda.csad.ox.ac.uk).

Databases of Artistic and Archaeological Material

In addition to translations of ancient literature, the Perseus Digital Library also includes a database of Greek and Roman artistic, architectural, and numismatic evidence that can be searched under a number of different headings (for example, region, period, or context). VROMA (www.vroma.org) includes an image archive, while *Pompeian Households: An On-line Companion* (by P. Allison, 2004; http://www.stoa.org/projects/ph/index.html) provides information on 30 Pompeian houses, including floor plans and photographs.

Secondary Sources
Dictionaries and Encyclopedias

Pride of place must be given to the indispensable *Oxford Classical Dictionary* (Oxford University Press, 2012), edited by Simon Hornblower, Antony Spawforth, and Esther Eidinow. The current, fourth edition should be consulted over previous editions. This weighty volume, a regular holding in every university library, contains brief explanations of most terms and concepts of importance to ancient society and provides skeletal bibliography.

The second edition of the Cambridge Ancient History (CAH) series, published by Cambridge University Press between 1970 and 2005, also deserves special mention. The CAH consists of 14 volumes (some of them in two parts), each dealing with a specific time period and including extended discussions of topics germane to that timeframe, such as legal or religious issues. The bibliography of each volume is also extensive. Volumes 7 through 14 will be of interest to students of Rome.

In December 2012, Blackwell released a print and online encyclopedia of the ancient world featuring contributions by specialists and edited by eminent scholars. Access to the site will require a subscription that may be taken by university libraries (see www. encyclopediaancienthistory.com for more information).

Atlases and Topographical Dictionaries

Atlases of the Roman empire (and its constituent parts) and reference tools for the topography of the city of Rome can also be very useful. Maps of varying quality can be readily found online, but the following books are worth consulting:

> Cornell, T., and J. Matthews. 1982. *Atlas of the Roman World*. New York: Facts on File.
> Talbert, R. 2000. *Barrington Atlas of the Greek and Roman World*. Princeton, NJ: Princeton University Press.

Reference works on Roman topography must include Samuel Platner and Thomas Ashby's magisterial lexicon, despite its relative age. Ernest Nash and Lawrence Richardson provide more recent treatments, but all of these have been superseded by Eva Margareta Steinby's books:

Nash, E. 1961. *Pictorial Dictionary of Ancient Rome*. 2 vols. London: A. Zwemmer.

Platner, S., and T. Ashby. 1929. *A Topographical Lexicon of Ancient Rome*. London: Oxford University Press.

Richardson, L., Jr. 1992. *A New Topographical Dictionary of Ancient Rome*. Baltimore: Johns Hopkins University Press.

Steinby, E., ed. 1993–1999. *Lexicon Topographicum Urbis Romae*. 6 vols. Rome: Quasar.

Omnes Viae (www.omnesviae.org) is a website that superimposes the Peutinger Table Map (*Tabula Peutingeriana*), a medieval copy of a map of the Roman empire from the late third century CE, onto Google Earth. *Lacus Curtius* provides scans of some detailed maps of the Roman world. This same website features an (as yet incomplete) electronic version of Platner and Ashby's work, which is also available on the Perseus Digital Library. 'ORBIS (http://orbis.stanford.edu/#) is a geospacial network model of the Roman world created by Walter Scheidel and Elijah Meeks. It allows users to determine routes, cost, and time of travel in antiquity.

Introductions

Recent years have seen a lively industry in "companions" and "handbooks." Generally of very high quality, these works are collections of essays on particular topics written by leaders in their fields and edited by established academics. The essays usually provide brief but sensitive introductions to the topics at hand, including an assessment of the state of current scholarship and scholarly thought on the subject and important bibliography.

Most prolific of these collections is the Blackwell Companions to the Ancient World series, which currently has 58 "companions" in print. Volumes focus on particular authors (for example, Victoria Emma Pagán's *A Companion to Tacitus*, 2011), institutions (Paul Erdkamp's *A Companion to the Roman Army*, 2007), social practices (Jörg Rüpke's *A Companion to Roman Religion*, 2007), social relationships (Beryl Rawson's *A Companion to Families in the Greek and Roman Worlds*, 2010), or cultural, political, and historical eras (Nathan Rosenstein and Robert Morstein-Marx's *A Companion to the Roman Republic*, 2006, and David S. Potter's *A Companion to the Roman Empire*, 2006).

Oxford University Press currently has 14 titles in its Handbooks in Classics and Ancient History series. The most generally useful for students of Roman society are probably Alessandro Barchiesi and Walter Scheidel's *The Oxford Handbook of Roman Studies* (2010) and Michael Peachin's *The Oxford Handbook of Social Relations in the Roman World* (2011).

Similarly, the Cambridge Companion series, published by Cambridge University Press, includes a number of books relevant to the topics of this volume. Titles are as varied as A.J. Woodman's *The Cambridge Companion to Tacitus* (2010), Harriet I. Flower's *The Cambridge Companion to the Roman Republic* (2004), and Karl Galinsky's *The Cambridge Companion to the Age of Augustus* (2005).

The Key Themes in Ancient History series, another collection published by Cambridge University Press, also provides clear, brief introductions to issues in ancient society—domestic space, food, trade, money, religion, slavery, art in its social context, public order—written by leaders in their fields. At present, the series features 26 titles (some of which are specific to either Greek or Roman antiquity, while others cover both).

Although more than a decade old, Routledge's Approaching the Ancient World series still provides some very useful and comprehensible introductions to the ancient historians' and classicists' use of ancient evidence, theories, and models. Notable titles are David S. Potter's *Literary Texts and the Roman Historian* (1999); William R. Biers's *Art, Artefacts and Chronology in Classical Archaeology* (1992); C.J. Howgego's *Ancient History from Coins* (1995); John Bodel's *Epigraphic Evidence: Ancient History from Inscriptions* (2001); and Roger S. Bagnall's *Reading Papyri, Writing Ancient History* (1995). Finally, Neville Morley's *Theories, Models and Concepts in Ancient History* (2004) offers an articulate introduction to various theoretical approaches.

Bibliographic Databases

The most comprehensive and generally available bibliographic database for classicists is *L'Année philologique*. Formerly published annually in an ever-thickening physical volume, this publication listed every book, article, and book review published that year in the field of classical studies, dividing them according to topic. It is now available electronically (www.annee-philologique.com/) and is searchable by topic, keyword, modern author, or ancient author.

Access to either format of *L'Année philologique* requires a subscription (which university libraries often hold); however, other databases are readily available to anyone with an Internet connection. These include Diotima (www.stoa.org/diotima/biblio.shtml), TOCS-IN (http://projects.chass.utoronto.ca/amphoras/tocs.html), and—for those who can read German—Gnomon www.gnomon.ku-eichstaett.de/Gnomon/Gnomon.html).

Glossary

ad digitum An action by an official referee in a gladiatorial contest (see **gladiator**), in which he interrupts the fight by stepping between the two opponents and raising his finger.

aedile A magistracy that involved maintaining the physical infrastructure of the city and overseeing the mounting of games. As such, serving as an aedile could help one win a higher magistracy, even though the office was outside of the *cursus honorum*. Two **plebeian** aediles and two curule aediles were elected annually.

aerarium militare The Roman military treasury.

aetiological elegy Poetry that is written in elegiac metre and explores the origin of things.

agones Dramatic competitions of Greek origin.

amicitia Literally, "friendship"; a term that often refers to a political alliance between two parties, either individuals or Rome and another community. In the latter case, the relationship was often unequal, with Rome being the greater power.

amphitheatre An elliptical theatre lined with banks of seating on all sides, creating an oval floor (the *arena*) where activities and performances took place.

amphora (**amphorae**, pl) A storage vessel used to hold a variety of products, ranging from olive oil to wine. Typically made from ceramic, amphorae were durable and strong. Made in different sizes, they are distinguished by their opposing handles, wide bodies, and tapering bases.

apotropaic Having a protective quality, particularly against unseen but malignant forces such as envy, the Evil Eye, and demons.

aqueduct Gravity-fed, Roman long-distance water-supply system consisting generally of covered water channels made of stone or **concrete**.

Ara Pacis "Altar of (Augustan) Peace." This structure is particularly famous for its sculptures, which visually present key themes of the Augustan program. The Ara Pacis was dedicated in 9 BCE in the **Campus Martius**.

architectus A Latin word that is the origin of the English *architect* but can also be translated as "engineer." The Latin term is derived from the Greek *arkhitektōn*, which means "chief artificer."

architrave A horizontal, sometimes decorated, row of lintels resting on columns; the lowest part of a structure's **entablature**.

Arval Brothers A priestly **college** responsible for the cult of the goddess Dea Dia. At the beginning of each year, this college—like other priests—also undertook vows (*vota*) regarding the safety of the Roman people and the imperial family.

Atellanae fabulae An early form of vulgar comedy—named after the Campanian town of Atella—that featured stock characters and was performed on stage.

athletic contest A competition of traditional Greek athletics, promoted by Augustus.

augur (*augures*, pl) A priest whose main responsibility was the observation and interpretation of signs (*auspicia*) sent by the Roman gods. The **college** of augurs was also responsible for the "inauguration" (assuring divine approval) of places, priests, and magistrates.

auriga A Roman chariot racer.

auspicium (*auspicia*, pl) A sign from the gods in the form of a significant activity of birds or four-footed animals, a celestial event (such as lightning), or an unusual natural occurrence. Such signs could be either self-offering or solicited. Members of the **college** of *augures* were responsible for the observance of *auspicia* and their interpretation, though magistrates with *imperium* also had the ability to seek and receive *auspicia*.

auxiliaries Light infantry and cavalry military troops generally consisting of non-Roman citizens who served alongside the **legions**.

bellum iustum "Just war"; a war imagined to be defensive and that was undertaken with divine approval. Romans traditionally embraced the ideal of just war, and priests known as *fetiales* oversaw the rituals associated with its declaration.

boxers Fist-fighting athletes wearing gloves weighted with pieces of iron and sometimes fitted with spikes around the knuckles. Boxing competitions probably featured prizes for the winners.

brigandage The act and use of violence to maraud, rob, or raid on land or sea; an illegal act that was a recourse for escaped slaves and established criminals.

Campus Martius "Field of Mars"; an area of originally open, publicly owned ground in the city of Rome where, in early Rome, the army mustered and citizens' assemblies were held. From the late Republic onwards, the Campus Martius was the site of an increasing number of building projects.

canabae Settled communities close to military bases, made up of local women with whom soldiers had formed relationships, as well as their children and veterans.

Capitoline Triad The term used to refer to Jupiter, Juno, and Minerva, who received joint worship in Rome and in some Roman colonies. The cult of these three deities, which was among the most ancient and traditional, was established in Rome on the Capitoline Hill.

castellum divisorium End point of a Roman aqueduct, usually located at the highest point of a city, from where the water was distributed to secondary distribution points. Two examples survive in good condition: one at **Pompeii** and one at Nîmes.

cataphracts Heavily armed cavalrymen who, along with their horses, were usually covered in armour. They emerged in the first century BCE in ranks of Rome's enemies, particularly those from the steppes of central Asia and other parts of the East. The Romans employed units of cataphracts beginning in the second century CE.

censor An elected official whose duties included updating the citizenship list, distributing new citizens among the voting tribes, and, on occasion, behaving as a moral watchdog over the lives of Roman citizens. Two censors were elected from the number of former **consuls** every 5 years for 18-month terms.

census Traditionally beginning during the reign of Servius Tullius, a register of adult male citizens that was carried out in Rome and that provided a record for those eligible for military service, taxation, and voting rights. Property details and occupations were also included. The practice lapsed during the late Republic but was revived and extended to the provinces under Augustus.

chariot A horse-drawn two-wheeled vehicle used primarily for racing by the Romans. The most typical set-up was the *quadriga*, which usually had four horses abreast.

chorobatēs A Greek term meaning "land-walker"; a surveying instrument consisting of a wooden beam with a central length-wise groove filled with water, used to establish a true horizontal line. The beam was some six metres long and stood on two legs whose length could be adjusted by means of wedges.

cinaedus (*cinaedi*, pl) A male who was perceived as effeminate and who might be suspected of engaging in homosexual activity as the passive partner.

Circus Maximus The first and largest track for **chariot** races in Rome. At a length of more than 600 metres, it could hold more than 150,000 spectators.

class A division of society according to wealth.

cognitio (*cognitiones*, pl) A judicial inquiry held by emperors, provincial governors, and various kinds of magistrates. *Cognitiones* could hear both criminal and civil cases.

college A collective of individuals. Roman priests belonged to colleges (*collegia* or *sodalitates*) according to their particular focus and function. Each priest was generally considered to have the same religious authority as his fellow college members; however, the pre-eminent position of *pontifex maximus* was an exception.

Colosseum The largest **amphitheatre** in Rome. Its official name was the Flavian Amphitheatre, so-called because it was built under Vespasian and inaugurated by Titus.

comedy A poetic genre that took the form of a dramatic script with humorous content and that was generally intended for performance. Roman comedy featured stock characters and was influenced by both Atellan farce (a native Italian comedic form) and Greek New Comedy.

comitia centuriata The "Centuriate Assembly"; one of the popular voting assemblies, in which the population—divided into 193 "centuries" according to their wealth—elected individuals to high public office and ratified motions put before them by the magistrates and **senate**. The Centuriate Assembly lost some importance to the Tribal Assembly (*comitia tributa*) over the course of the Republic.

comitia tributa The "Tribal Assembly"; a popular voting assembly in which the population was divided into 35 tribes. Tribal affiliation had originally been determined by geography, but this connection loosened over the course of Roman history. The Tribal Assembly came to gain importance at the expense of the Centuriate Assembly (*comitia centuriata*) during the Republic.

concilium plebis tributum The "Plebeian Assembly"; a popular voting assembly traditionally dated to 494/493 BCE and whose membership included only **plebeians**. This assembly elected its own magistrates—10 **tribunes** and 2 **aediles**—to protect plebeian interests. Its decisions were called *plebiscita* ("plebiscites").

concordia "Harmony"; an ideal of Roman marriage. The term might suggest genuine affection or merely an absence of discord.

concrete Known in Latin as *opus caementicium*, a building material made of unslaked lime, *pozzolana* (volcanic ash), and an aggregate of rubble. Mixed with water, it is initially malleable and hardens to the consistency of stone within a few weeks.

concubinage A sexual relationship between a man and a woman in which the intent to marry was absent. Concubinage could range from a temporary liaison to a long-term quasi-marital relationship. The partners were sometimes of disparate **status** (for example, freeborn men and **freedwomen**; see *ingenuus* and *libertus*).

constructivism The theory that a person's sexual identity is the result of social influences, including a society's norms and values (contrast **essentialism**).

consul A member of the highest regular magistracy (the consulship), an office invested with the powers that had originally belonged to the king (see *imperium*). Two consuls were elected annually, and each had veto power over the other.

controversiae Oratorical exercises in which the declaimer argued one side of a fictitious legal case.

contubernium (*contubernia*, pl) A quasi-marital relationship involving two people (often slaves) without the legal capacity to contract legal marriage (*conubium*).

conubium The ability to enter into a legal marriage and thereby have legitimate offspring. This power was generally granted by

citizenship, minimum age (12 for girls, 14 for boys), and a sufficient degree of genetic separation from the prospective spouse.

conventus By the late Republic (and throughout the imperial period), a term used to refer to governors' annual inspection tours of their provinces. Governors' activities during the *conventus* included the hearing of court cases.

cornice The top part of an **entablature**, sometimes heavily decorated and usually projecting outward beyond the **architrave** and the **frieze** in order to deflect rainwater runoff away from the building's foundation.

corvus "Raven"; a device that, during the First Punic War, allowed the Romans to turn naval battles into infantry engagements. The *corvus* consisted of a long metal pike projecting downward at the far end of a ship's drawbridge attached to the mast foot. The pike would lodge itself firmly into the wood of the enemy ship's deck, making escape for the enemy impossible, providing a stable anchor for the bridge, and allowing legionaries (see **legion**) to board the enemy vessel.

cursus honorum The "sequence of offices"; the regular, legally approved order in which magistracies might be held in Roman government (in ascending order, **quaestor**, **praetor**, and **consul**). After 180 BCE, minimum ages were established for the holding of each office.

damnati Convicted criminals.

damnatio ad bestias The sentencing of criminals to be publicly devoured by wild animals.

damnatio memoriae The official erasure of the memory of a deceased individual who had been declared an enemy of the state.

This process often involved destroying images, removing the person's name from public inscriptions, and, if an emperor, annulling his acts.

decimation A punishment sometimes inflicted upon Roman soldiers by their own commanders when a whole unit displayed cowardice or had deserted its post. One of every ten soldiers was selected by lot to be beaten to death by his comrades; the remainder were given rations of barley instead of wheat and were denied the protection of the camp.

decurion The last of the top three economic divisions (after **senatorials** and **equestrians**). As the wealthiest men of the empire's local communities, decurions held local magistracies and sat on town councils. The minimum wealth required to qualify as a decurion varied from place to place.

delator (*delatores*, pl) An informer who would provide incriminating information or bring prosecutions against others for personal gain.

deracination The uprooting of an individual from his or her family and surroundings to a new, unfamiliar location. This term often describes the experience of the newly enslaved in Roman society.

determinism versus voluntarism debate With reference to sexual orientation, a debate concerning whether an individual's sexual preference is predetermined and unchangeable or a matter of choice.

dictator An individual appointed in times of emergency and invested with almost limitless power by the state (see also *imperium*). A dictator, who was aided by a *magister equitum* ("master of the horse"), should hold the position for only six months.

didactic Poetry that has (or pretends to have) an instructional quality.

Di Manes Variously interpreted as "spirits of the dead" or "gods of the underworld" (categories that might not be mutually exclusive). The *Di Manes* are regularly mentioned on Roman epitaphs as the entities to whom the dead person is entrusted.

dioptra A surveying instrument that is similar in function to a modern engineer's level or a theodolite but without magnifying lenses in the scope.

domus The "family" (and the physical house in which it lived), including relatives who were not all under the legal power of the same *paterfamilias*. Contrast *familia*.

Domus Aurea Nero's "Golden House"; a palace that Nero built in the city of Rome after the Great Fire of 64 CE had destroyed large parts of the residential districts in the city centre. The Golden House, whose name derives from its lavish wall decorations, was revolutionary in its creative use of **concrete** to create odd-shaped rooms and domed ceilings.

drama Theatrical performance of plays, either tragedies or comedies.

Dura-Europos A city on the Euphrates River captured by the Romans during the second century CE, sacked by the Sasanid Persians in the 250s CE, and abandoned thereafter. The city is significant for the wealth of its remains, particularly as they pertain to the military.

entablature The horizontal superstructure that rests on the columns of classical buildings. The entablature consists of individual bands (usually an **architrave**, **frieze**, and **cornice**) of different widths and breadths and, depending on the architectural **order**, different types of decoration.

epic A long poem written in hexametric verse that deals with lofty and/or large-scale subjects, such as warfare, heroic adventure, or history.

epigrammatist An author of brief and usually satirical poems of varied content and some witty punch lines.

eques (*equites*, pl) See **equestrian**.

equestrian Originally, a term applied to a member of the cavalry in the early Roman army. The word came to refer more casually to male citizens (but not **freedmen**) whose property was worth 400,000 **sesterces**.

essentialism In the context of ancient sexuality, the belief that any given human is innately heterosexual or homosexual in orientation and that this "essential" behaviour is uninfluenced by social values or norms (contrast **constructivism**).

euergetism A form of beneficence whereby the emperor or other wealthy individuals would give gifts—ranging from money and buildings to spectacles and games—to communities. The practice can be seen as a combination of socio-economic display, patriotism, and (on occasion) political favour.

familia The free and servile members of a Roman household who were under the legal power of the *paterfamilias*.

fasces Literally, "bundle"; specifically, the bundle of rods with a protruding axe head carried by the attendants (**lictors**) of curule magistrates, governors, military commanders with *imperium*, and, perhaps curiously, Vestal Virgins.

fetiales Priests who ritually enacted Rome's treaties with other communities and declarations of war. In the latter case, the ritual actions of the *fetiales* ensured the Roman gods' approval of the pursuit of armed conflict, rendering it a "just war" (**bellum iustum**).

flagitatio The demand for redress (typically concerning misappropriated property) through shouting in a public place, often in front of the house of the offender. The idea was that the offender would be shamed into providing some form of recompense.

forum (**fora**, pl) A complex of buildings and other architectural features in an urban setting that hosts a variety of political, judicial, economic, religious, educational, and social activities. Small centres often had just one forum, but the city of Rome had many (of which the Forum Romanum was the oldest), each serving different primary purposes.

freedman/freedwoman/freedperson See *libertus/a*.

fresco A painting technique in which pigment is applied to wet plaster.

frieze The central, sometimes decorated, horizontal band of a building's **entablature**.

frontality An artistic convention that developed in the later Roman Empire and depicted prominent figures in two-dimensional art directly from the front.

frontiers The boundaries of the area under Roman control, which was often inhabited by Roman soldiers and a mixture of Roman and non-Roman civilians from neighbouring or more distant regions.

fugitivus/a (*fugitivi/ae*, pl) A runaway slave. Running away was considered a "defect" that had to be declared at the point of sale, and slaves with a past history of absconding might be branded on the face or made to wear a collar.

gender identity Identification of oneself as male or female through observation of the socially accepted behaviours associated with either gender.

gladiators Semi-free professional fighters who competed with each other in numerous different styles of fighting and weaponry.

gnōmai See *sententiae*.

grammaticus A paid teacher who taught literature to students with rudimentary literacy skills in order to improve their reading, writing, and oratorical abilities.

groma A simple surveying instrument used to lay out straight lines and right angles.

gymnasium A Greek-style open exercise area that, in the Roman period, was frequently attached to a bath building. In Greece, the function of gymnasia included educational aspects, which led to the areas developing into secondary schools by the Hellenistic period. Gymnasia retained this mixed function in the Roman cities of the Greek East, while in the West the focus was on exercise facilities.

haruspex (*haruspices*, pl) A ritual expert skilled in interpreting the appearance of a sacrificial animal's internal organs. These organs were interpreted to determine whether the gods deemed the sacrifice acceptable or, in specific circumstances, to ascertain the means of resolving a situation of divine dissatisfaction. This knowledge was originally considered to be an Etruscan specialization. A select group of Etruscan *haruspices* was sometimes also consulted by the senate to interpret and suggest ritual remedies for *prodigia*, signs of divine displeasure. Compare **(quin)decimviri sacris faciundis**.

Herculaneum A town on the Bay of Naples that, like **Pompeii**, was destroyed by the eruption of Mount Vesuvius in 79 CE. Thanks to the remarkable preservation of its buildings beneath the volcanic debris, it has proven to be a valuable source of information about Roman art and architecture.

honestior (*honestiores*, pl) One of the terms that came to describe Roman citizen society by at least the second century CE. As members of the **senatorial**, **equestrian**, or decurial (see **decurion**) orders, *honestiores* enjoyed greater access to the machinery of justice and lighter punishment for crimes than their poorer counterparts, the **humiliores**.

humilior (*humiliores*, pl) By the second century CE, a term often used in law to describe a citizen who was not of the top three economic classes (see *honestior*). *Humiliores* were less able to gain access to the system of justice and were subject to harsher punishments for crimes than *honestiores*.

imperium "The right to command"; the legal power invested in **praetors**, **consuls**, **dictators**, and eventually emperors (a word which, like *empire*, derives from *imperium*).

infamia Literally, "bad reputation"; the diminution of an individual's legal privileges (but not the removal of **status**) as a result of engaging in disreputable professions or being convicted of performing disreputable acts.

ingenuus/a (***ingenui/ae***, pl) A freeborn person. Freeborn Roman citizens experienced the greatest legal privileges and the fewest legal disabilities.

interrex Literally, "between kings." An *interrex* was appointed for a period of five days to oversee the election of new **consuls**, if the consuls for the year had died and therefore could not conduct the elections.

iugerum (***iugera***, pl) A Roman unit used for measuring an area of land. One *iugerum* is equivalent to an area of land measuring 240 x 120 Roman feet (or 28,800 square Roman feet).

ius Italicum The privilege granted to communities in the Roman provinces concerning their land. Legally, this land was treated as if it were in Italy; in effect, the land and its inhabitants were free from direct taxation.

ius occidendi Given to fathers by the emperor Augustus, the right to kill an adulterous daughter, but only if she were caught in the very act in her father's house or that of her husband and if her father killed her lover at the same time.

lanista The owner and manager of a troupe of **gladiators**.

lares familiares The gods specific to a *familia* that were worshipped at a shrine or in a cult-niche (so-called *lararium*) in the house and by the household, particularly its servile members.

latifundium (***latifundia***, pl) An expansive farm worked in large part by slaves. In Italy the development of *latifundia* in the

second century BCE has traditionally been identified as resulting from Rome's overseas wars (which provided Italy with agricultural slaves) and coming at the expense of small, peasant-worked farms. This scenario has been questioned, in part because archaeological evidence does not appear to support it.

legion The largest unit of the Roman army, ideally consisting of roughly 5,000 heavily armed men who were Roman citizens.

lex (***leges***, pl) "Law." Laws were regularly identified by the name(s) of the magistrate(s) who passed them. For example, the *Lex Hortensia* was passed by Quintus Hortensius and the *Lex Valeria Horatia* by Lucius Valerius and Marcus Horatius. Laws might also be identified with an adjective describing their subject, such as *lex agraria* ("law on agricultural land") or *lex annalis* ("law on years"), or with a genitive of description (see **lex pugnandi**).

lex pugnandi Literally, "law of fighting"; a written body of rules that governed gladiatorial contests (see **gladiator**).

libertus/a (***liberti/ae***, pl) An ex-slave or **freedperson**. Freedpersons, though often granted citizenship upon **manumission**, continued to owe their former masters (***patroni***) deference (***obsequium***) and a certain number of days of free labour each year (***operae***). Additionally, *liberti* were unable to hold public office and, although they might meet the minimum property requirement, would never be considered **equestrians**.

lictor The attendant of curule magistrates, commanders with **imperium**, and Vestal Virgins. Lictors cleared paths for their officials and carried their symbols of office (***fasces***).

ludi Public games offered by the state as civic celebrations.

ludi circenses Games including **chariot** races in the **Circus Maximus**.

ludi magister A paid teacher who taught students the basics of reading and writing.

Ludi Saeculares A religious festival with sacrifices and dramatic performances to celebrate the transition from one *saeculum* (the arbitrarily fixed longest possible time of a human life, traditionally 100 years) to the next.

ludi scaenici Games that included dramatic performances.

Ludus Magnus A large gladiatorial school attached to the **Colosseum** in Rome.

lyric Poetry that explores personal feelings and emotions. Originally (in Greek) sung to the accompaniment of a lyre, such poems were probably recited in the Roman period.

machina Latin origin of the English word *machine*. The Latin term is related to the Greek *mēkhanē* (compare the English *mechanics*), which refers to an artificial device for performing a task.

manumission The process of freeing a slave from servitude. A manumitted slave was often granted citizenship (with some restrictions) but also became the freedperson (*libertus/a*) of his or her ex-master (*patronus*).

marriage *cum manu* A form of marriage in early Rome in which a bride became part of her husband's *familia*, that is, subject to the legal power of her husband or his *paterfamilias* (if he were still living). Contrast **marriage *sine manu***.

marriage *sine manu* The form of marriage most common by the second century BCE, in which a bride remained a member of her natal *familia* and under the legal power of her natal *paterfamilias* rather than her husband's. Contrast **marriage *cum manu***.

materfamilias (*matresfamilias*, pl) The wife of the *paterfamilias*; a term of respect used to refer to a matron in legal sources.

military diploma A document, usually inscribed in bronze, certifying honourable discharge from the Roman army and, in the case of a non-Roman citizen, the acquisition of Roman citizenship after discharge.

mime A popular form of theatrical performance that tended towards vulgar themes.

missio The release of a defeated **gladiator** from a fight.

modillions Horizontal stone elements projecting in regular intervals from the wall of a building immediately underneath the **cornice**. Modillions could be heavily decorated and probably mimicked the projecting wooden cantilevers that used to hold up roofs in wood structures.

munus (*munera*, pl) In the context of spectacle, a privately sponsored game or games that featured combat between **gladiators** especially.

natural philosophy The attempt by individuals, usually upper-class males, to explain natural phenomena, such as earthquakes or climate, purely by reason. Natural philosophy succeeded natural mythology and preceded natural science, although there is significant chronological overlap.

nature versus nurture debate With reference to sexuality, a debate concerning

whether sexual orientation is biologically determined or a function of social
influences.

neoteroi "The modern ones"; a term perhaps coined by Cicero and used by modern scholars to refer to first-century BCE
poets whose works reflect the influence of
Hellenistic poetry.

nexum Debt bondage, in which borrowers pledged themselves or, more precisely,
their labour (or its fruits) to their creditors
as collateral on a loan. *Nexum* was abolished at some point in the fourth century
BCE.

nobilis (*nobiles*, pl) "Well-known one"; a
term indicating that a person had consular
ancestry.

nome An administrative division in the
province of Egypt.

novus homo (*novi homines*, pl) "New
man." In the Republic, this term referred
to an **equestrian** who was the first person
in his family to gain an elected magistracy,
particularly the consulship (see **consul**).
New men tended to suffer the disdain of
members of the senate whose families had
long enjoyed **senatorial** status.

nutrix (*nutrices*, pl) A female in charge of
an infant's care but who is not the infant's
mother. Children of all economic **classes**
and social **statuses** might be entrusted to
nurses, who were often paid professionals
or the freed dependents (see *libertus/a*) of
a wealthy family.

obsequium Deference and respect owed
(and required by law) by **freedpersons** to
their ex-masters, their patrons (*patroni*).

opera (*operae*, pl) "Labour" or "service";
the work that **freedpersons** owed to their
ex-masters, their patrons (*patroni*), on an
annual basis. The amount and nature of
this service would have been agreed upon
prior to **manumission**.

opus caementicium See **concrete**.

opus incertum The irregular facing of
concrete walls. To make the surface more
durable and aesthetically pleasing, walls of
mortared rubble were faced with irregularly shaped stones.

opus reticulatum The facing of **concrete**
walls in which the stones were all the same
size, making the wall look as if it were covered by diagonal netting. Compare *opus
incertum*.

opus sectile An art form very similar to
mosaics but one that uses larger, specially
cut pieces instead of small, uniformly
shaped ones to define major parts of the
motif.

opus signinum Mortar that contains
crushed ceramics to waterproof **aqueducts**.

opus testaceum A wall facing consisting
of fired bricks, a method that significantly
reduced cost and sped up the construction
process. Compare *opus reticulatum*.

order Architectural style in classical
building construction, characterized by
specific column shapes and decorations as
well as individual structural and decorative
elements of the facade. Not to be confused
with *ordo*.

ordo A word often used by the Romans
to point to a segment or echelon of the
citizenry, which can be variously translated
as "rank," "class," "station," or "condition."

ovation A celebratory procession to honour a victorious general, though a smaller

celebration than a **triumph**. An ovation might be awarded to a general whose victory was considered less glorious than one that would deserve a triumph. Factors in the decision could include the number of enemy dead or the worthiness of the enemy.

paedagogus (*paedagogi*, pl) A male slave responsible for providing early instruction to the young free children in his charge.

panegyric A formal public speech delivered in praise of a person.

Pantheon The ultimate demonstration of Roman skill in **concrete** construction. The Pantheon is a Hadrianic rebuilding of an originally Augustan temple dedicated to all the gods. In its current form, its body consists of a circular concrete drum 48 metres in diameter by 24 metres in height and is covered by a hemispherical concrete dome.

pantomime A solo performance representing themes through dance rather than voice.

pastoral Poetry that is set in the countryside and emphasizes the idyllic life of herdsmen, especially in contrast with hectic urban lifestyle.

paterfamilias (*patresfamilias*, pl) The eldest living male member of the household, who had legal power (*patria potestas*) over and responsibility for those legally defined as his property (children, grandchildren, slaves, and, if in a **marriage** *cum manu*, his wife).

patria potestas The legal power of the *paterfamilias* over those within his *familia*, including the theoretical right to kill them or to compel a child to divorce. In reality, these powers were rarely exerted.

patrician A member of one of the landed, hereditary aristocratic families of Rome. According to tradition, patricians were the descendants of the senators (the *patres*) selected by Romulus. In early Rome, patricians enjoyed a monopoly over magistracies and priesthoods. Contrast **plebeian**.

patronage A social relationship marked by mutual responsibilities and expected etiquettes that existed between social unequals, most often **freedpersons** and their ex-masters (*patroni*). It might also exist (perhaps on a more ephemeral basis) between the freeborn poor and their wealthy counterparts.

patronus (*patroni*, pl) "Patron"; often one's ex-master or social superior in a relationship of **patronage**.

per capita production A measurement of the amount of goods and services (for instance, labour) produced or provided by each person equally.

Piazza Navona A modern square in the **Campus Martius** of Rome that preserves the elongated shape of a stadium built under Domitian's reign for Greek-style **athletic contests**.

Pisonian conspiracy A 65 CE conspiracy to assassinate Nero, led by Gaius Calpurnius Piso. The plot was betrayed, and the conspirators were forced to commit suicide.

plebeian Originally any Roman citizen who was not a **patrician** (a member of one of the early aristocratic families) but eventually any citizen who did not have **senatorial**, **equestrian**, or decurial wealth (see **decurion**).

plebiscitum (*plebiscita*, pl) A decision of the Plebeian Assembly (*concilium plebis tributum*), which was binding on both **patricians** and **plebeians** after 449 BCE. This regulation was modified or reaffirmed in 339 BCE and received its final modifications or reaffirmation in 287 BCE.

plebs See **plebeian**.

pomerium The sacred boundary of the city of Rome, within which the army could not muster except in exceptional circumstances, such as the celebration of a **triumph**. Those invested with the command of an army could therefore not cross the *pomerium* to enter the city without the proper religious ceremonies. The boundary was expanded a few times as Rome grew.

Pompeii A Roman town on the Bay of Naples that was destroyed and buried in the eruption of Mount Vesuvius in 79 CE. Under official excavation in large parts since the eighteenth century, the city's remains are a major source of information for life during the early Roman Empire. Compare **Herculaneum**.

Pont du Gard The highest surviving Roman **aqueduct** bridge (48 metres) that brought a water channel across the river Gardon to the Roman city of *Nemausus* (modern Nîmes) in France.

pontifex (*pontifices*, pl) A "pontiff." The **college** of pontiffs was responsible for the correct observance of ritual activities and other matters (such as burial) that were considered to be of concern to the gods. See *sacra publica populi Romani*.

pontifex maximus "Highest pontiff", the leading member of the **college** of *pontifices*, the most prominent and influential of the four major colleges of Roman priests. Selected by popular vote to serve for life, the *pontifex maximus* became increasingly influential in Roman society and politics,

as he also acted as the spokesman for the *pontifices* in the **senate**. Beginning with Augustus, the position was held by the reigning emperor but did not carry supreme religious or theological authority.

Porticus Aemilia A storage facility on the banks of the Tiber River in Rome, built from **concrete** in the second century BCE. At a length of 487 metres and a width of 60 metres, it consisted of rows of individual interconnected, barrel-vaulted storerooms that formed one large space.

pozzolana A volcanic ash from the region of Puteoli, near Naples. Mortar consisting of a mixture of *pozzolana*, lime, water, and aggregate formed the basis of Roman **concrete**.

praefectus urbi In imperial times, the magistrate in charge of maintaining order and public safety in the city of Rome. He was in charge of the urban cohorts, units of soldiers who were permanently stationed in the city as a sort of police force. The *praefectus urbi* was generally selected from the ranks of former **consuls**.

praetor Upon the expulsion of the monarchy, a magistrate who held the power of the former king. Two praetors—the title would soon change to **consul**—were elected annually. The praetorship was reintroduced as a **patrician** office in 367 BCE, when **plebeians** became eligible to hold the consulship (they could hold the praetorship after 337 BCE). The office of praetor, a sort of junior consulship, was the second office on the *cursus honorum*. See also *imperium*.

praetorian guard A select group of soldiers who were responsible for the protection of generals in the Republic and, during the Empire, of the emperors. The praetorian guards had shorter terms of service and higher salaries than soldiers enrolled in the **legions**.

Price Edict of Diocletian An edict promulgated by the emperor Diocletian in 301 CE, which fixed maximum prices for commodities, transportation costs, and wages for the entire Roman empire.

princeps A term with republican connotations and precedent in Pompey the Great, chosen by Augustus to reflect his constitutional position as "leading citizen," or "first man of the state." It was not an official title and was not granted by the **senate**, but it was assumed by emperors at their accession.

Principate A modern term designating the Roman Empire from the beginning of the reign of Augustus (the first *princeps*) to the third century (the so-called third-century crisis).

procurator An official, agent, or representative of the Roman government. Under the Empire, the title was used for those employed by the emperor in the civil administration (normally **equestrians**, but **freedmen** are known). There were several types of procurator, ranging from Praesidial procurators, who governed minor provinces (but only Egypt and Mesopotamia by the end of the second century CE), to those who administered imperial estates and those who supervised the collection of both direct and indirect taxes in both senatorial and imperial provinces.

prodigium (*prodigia*, pl) An unusual natural occurrence deemed by the **senate** to be a sign from the gods. *Prodigia* were often understood to signal divine displeasure and therefore needed to be expiated. Rituals of expiation were prescribed by the (*quin*)*decimviri sacris faciundis* or the *haruspices*.

pseudo-peripteral The use of engaged columns around three sides of a building (typically a Roman temple with a rectangular floor plan), making it appear to be surrounded by a single row of free-standing columns.

publicani Groups of private businessmen and contractors who, in the absence of a civil service during the Republic and early Empire, bought contracts from the Roman administration to handle civic duties, such as those involving tax collection, army supplies, and public works and services. From the second century CE onwards, the *publicani* were replaced by individuals either bidding for contracts or pressed into service by the Roman administration.

pulvinar A cushioned seat of particular honour. This term was used to refer to the imperial box at spectacle venues, such as those held in the **Circus Maximus**.

quaestio (*quaestiones*, pl) A special tribunal of inquiry and, later, a permanent jury court established to try criminal activity.

quaestor A magistrate who was primarily in charge of state finances. The quaestorship was an annually elected office that was lowest on the *cursus honorum*. Upon holding this office, one generally gained entry to the **senate**.

(*quin*)*decimviri sacris faciundis* The "Ten (later, Fifteen) Men for the Performance of Sacred Rites," sometimes represented as the *X(V)viri sacris faciundis*. This **college** of priests interpreted the **Sibylline Books** when the gods' displeasure had been made manifest (for instance, through *prodigia*) to determine how it might be averted with ritual. They were also responsible for overseeing the cult of foreign deities adopted into the

Roman pantheon as a consequence of the interpretation of the Sibylline Books.

religio "(Form of) worship." Although it is the origin of the English word *religion*, *religio* was not used by the Romans to indicate a specific set of practices or beliefs. Beginning in the late Republic, the term came to indicate a speaker's or author's approval for the practices or beliefs he or she was describing. *Religio* therefore suggested that the practices were "correct," "Roman," "traditional," and "divinely approved." Contrast *superstitio*.

rhetor (*rhetores*, pl) A paid teacher who instructed students in advanced oratorical studies through training exercises (*suasoriae* and *controversiae*), often over the course of several years.

sacramentum A military oath sworn by soldiers to their commander-in-chief during the Republic and to the emperor and the Roman state during the Empire.

sacra publica populi Romani The ritual activities undertaken by Rome's civic priests and magistrates for the continued welfare of the Roman political community. These included prayers, sacrifices, vows (*vota*), dedications, festivals, games, and the maintenance of civic cults.

senate A council that was originally convened to advise the kings of Rome but became an advisory board for the **consuls** and, ultimately, a body of almost supreme influence in the Republic. Membership (which in the Republic varied between 300 and 1,000 depending on the period and perhaps reached 2,000 in the late Empire) came to be extended to those who had been **quaestor**, the lowest office on the *cursus honorum*.

senatorial In the Republic, the rank granted to an **equestrian** who had gained entry to the **senate** through holding an elected magistracy. Under the Empire, when minimum property requirements had increased from an equestrian fortune (400,000 **sesterces**) to 1,000,000 sesterces, the designation became hereditary.

senatus consultum ultimum "The final decree of the senate" (often abbreviated to *SCU*); a device, first used in 121 BCE, in which the **senate** authorized the **consul**(s) to protect the state from the seditious behaviour of other magistrates or the people, using any means necessary.

sententiae Pithy sayings that expounded sentiments accepted to be general truths and considered suitable reading and copying material for beginning students. Also called *gnōmai*.

sesterce A Roman monetary unit and coin.

sex An individual's biological status as male or female, or the sexual act. Contrast **sexuality**.

sexuality The sexual knowledge, beliefs, attitudes, values, and behaviours of individuals, influenced by ethical, spiritual, cultural, and moral concerns. Contrast **sex**.

sexual orientation A characteristic determined by the preferred gender of one's sexual partners.

Sibylline Books Collections of prophetic Greek verses that were officially recognized as containing information necessary to preserve good relations between the Roman community and its gods. The books were to be interpreted only by the (*quin*)*decimviri sacris faciundis* and were housed in the Temple of Jupiter Optimus Maximus on the Capitoline Hill in the Republic; Augustus, a *quindecimvir* himself, moved them to the Temple of Apollo next to his house on the Palatine Hill.

sine missione "Without release"; a gladiatorial fight that did not permit the release of either participant. These fights were banned by Augustus at the beginning of the imperial period.

socius (**socii**, pl) "Ally"; a term used to refer to a community that formed a military alliance with Rome during the conquest of Italy. Although technically independent, such communities were in fact subjects of Rome and were required to contribute troops to fight alongside the Roman legions.

spatial illusionism The illusion of three-dimensional space in a two-dimensional medium, such as relief carving. This illusion can be achieved through differential depth of carving, foreshortening of projecting limbs, or by painting in different shades.

spolia Decorative elements from earlier structures removed and reused on a new structure. *Spolia* could be used to save money or to associate visually the new structure with the earlier one.

stataria Slave markets; the places where slaves would be brought and sold. These most commonly existed in port towns and in major centres (such as the city of Rome) and have often been identified through inscriptional evidence.

status A person's legal standing; a description of the legal privileges and protections any given person did or did not enjoy. Although the English word *status* derives from the Latin term, the latter does not also mean social esteem. This concept, both familiar and important to the Romans, was represented in Latin by different words, such as *existimatio*.

stuprum "Sexual misconduct." Under Augustus, this term generally came to be more closely defined as sex with any marriageable citizen woman to whom one was not married or with freeborn boys. *Stuprum* did not apply to sex with prostitutes.

suasoriae Oratorical exercises aimed at persuading the audience to the speaker's point of view. Speeches centred on dilemmas presented to historical or mythological figures: speakers would choose to urge one course of action over another.

summa rudis The chief referee in a gladiatorial fight.

superstitio A term indicating disapproval of a set of practices or beliefs. *Superstitio* therefore often had the flavour of "excessive," "superstitious," and "useless" and, beginning in the late Republic, was employed by elite writers to describe the "vapid" ritual activities of foreigners. Contrast **religio**.

tetrarchy The "rule of four"; a system of imperial leadership instituted by Diocletian in 293 CE, in which rule was undertaken by two emperors (*Augusti*) and two deputies (*Caesares*, who would eventually succeed to the throne) who were all stationed in different, strategic areas of the empire. The system was effectively removed by 324 CE, when Constantine declared himself sole emperor.

theatre A semi-circular open-air building for dramatic performances. In Roman construction, the seating for the audience is a semi-circle around the "orchestra," itself a semi-circle whose straight base line is formed by the stage building (*scaenae frons*).

thermae Lavishly decorated large-scale Roman public bath buildings from the imperial period, consisting of the baths proper and generally including large outdoor areas for exercise and other amenities, such as libraries, lecture rooms, and food outlets.

Tomb of the Haterii The tomb of a family of successful building contractors from the period of Domitian. The lavish decoration on this tomb shows in detail a Roman construction site, including a crane and its function.

tragedy A poetic genre that took the form of a dramatic script dealing with human suffering or with individuals who face choices between painful options. Roman tragedies tended to take their subject matter from mythology or history.

tribune An elected official whose role was, ideally, to protect the plebeian population. Ten tribunes were elected annually by the Plebeian Assembly (*concilium plebis tribunum*). Although one had to be a **plebeian** to be eligible for the tribunate, those who held it were generally of the economic elite. In the late Republic, this office became means for ambitious men to further their own agendas.

triumph The procession of a victorious Roman general through the city of Rome from the triumphal gate (*porta triumphalis*) to the Temple of Jupiter Optimus Maximus on the Capitoline Hill. The procession often included the general's army, the spoils of war, captives, freed prisoners of war, and animals for sacrifice.

triumvir A member of a three-man board—*triumviri* or *tresviri* (a "triumvirate")—that appeared in Roman public life. A triumvir was typically elected by the Roman people; however, the so-called First Triumvirate (made up of Caesar, Pompey,

and Crassus) is an exception and was never described as a triumvirate in antiquity. There were, in fact, many different kinds of *triumviri*, whose responsibilities ranged from the administrative to the financial and the religious.

Twelve Tables The archaic Roman law code dating to the mid-fifth century BCE. The Twelve Tables were traditionally seen as the foundation for the later development of Roman law.

venalicia See *stataria*.

venalicius (*venalicii*, pl) A slave trader, who was often responsible for sourcing slaves as well (for example, by picking up foundling children).

venationes Beast hunts mounted as a form of entertainment.

veneer A thin layer of a valuable or valuable-looking material applied to the surface of a cheaper, more workable material, giving the impression that the piece or structure is made of the more expensive substance. For example, marble veneer on a concrete structure implies that it is solid marble.

verism A Roman sculptural style in which (in contrast to idealized treatments) subjects were depicted with their own idiosyncratic characteristics and standard physical signs of advancing age.

verna (*vernae*, pl) A "home-born slave"; a child born to a woman in servitude. *Vernae* were often considered to be more docile and more trustworthy than slaves who had been reduced to the condition by capture in war, though suspicion generally remained.

vexillations A detachment of the Roman army dispatched to supplement other military units, primarily in times of war.

vici Subdivisions of *canabae*.

vigiles Men who were part of a para-military body, originally introduced by Augustus, that fought both crime and fires. The ranks of the *vigiles* included officials responsible for arrest, interrogation, and incarceration of suspected criminals.

vilicus (m)/*vilica* (f) A country estate manager and his wife, respectively, both of whom were slaves but who were responsible for the running of the estate and overseeing its servile labour force in their master's absence.

Vindolanda A Roman **auxiliary** fort in northern England, not far from Hadrian's Wall and best known for its surviving wooden tablets that document life amongst the soldiery, their dependants, and civilians on the frontier.

votum (*vota*, pl) "Vow"; a promise made to the gods to perform certain sacrifices or other rituals should the gods prove themselves propitious for defined undertakings or preserve the continued welfare of individuals, the Roman community, or its leaders for a stated period of time.

Works Cited

Adam, J.-P. 1994. *Roman Building*. London and New York: Routledge.

Adams, C.E.P. 2007. *Land Transport in Roman Egypt: A Study of Economics and Administration in a Roman Province*. Oxford: Oxford University Press.

Adams, J.N. 1982. *The Latin Sexual Vocabulary*. Baltimore: John Hopkins University Press.

Alcock, S.E. 1993. Graecia Capta: *The Landscapes of Roman Greece*. Cambridge: Cambridge University Press.

———. 2007. "The Eastern Mediterranean." In *The Cambridge Economic History of the Greco-Roman World*, edited by W. Scheidel, I. Morris, and R. Saller, 671–97. Cambridge: Cambridge University Press.

Alföldy, G. 1988. *The Social History of Rome*. Translated by D. Braund and F. Pollock. Baltimore: Johns Hopkins University Press.

Allison, P. 2004. *Pompeian Households: An Analysis of the Material Culture*. Los Angeles: Cotsen Institute of Archaeology Press.

———. 2006. "Mapping for Gender: Interpreting Artefact Distribution inside 1st–2nd Century A.D. Forts in Roman Germany." *Archaeological Dialogues* 13 (1): 1–20.

Alston, R. 1995. *Soldier and Society in Roman Egypt*. London and New York: Routledge.

Andreau, J. 1999. *Banking and Business in the Roman World*. Cambridge: Cambridge University Press.

———. 2000. "Commerce and Finance." In *The High Empire, A.D. 70–192*, 2nd edn, edited by A.K. Bowman, P. Garnsey, and D. Rathbone, 769–86. The Cambridge Ancient History, vol. 11. Cambridge: Cambridge University Press.

Astin, A.E. 1978. *Cato the Censor*. Oxford: Oxford University Press.

Aubert, J.-J. 2002. "A Double-Standard in Roman Criminal Law? The Death Penalty and Social Structure in Late Republican and Early Imperial Rome." In Speculum Iuris: *Roman Law as a Reflection of Social and Economic Life in Antiquity*, edited by J.-J. Aubert and B. Sirks, 94–133. Ann Arbor: University of Michigan Press.

Babbitt, F.C. trans. 1927. *Plutarch: Moralia*, vol. 1. Loeb Classical Library 197. Cambridge, MA: Harvard University Press.

Bablitz, L. 2007. *Actors and Audience in the Roman Courtroom*. London and New York: Routledge.

Badian, E. 1982. "Review: Figuring out Roman Slavery." *Journal of Roman Studies* 72: 164–9.

Bagnall, R.S. 1977. "Army and Police in Roman Upper Egypt." *Journal of the American Research Center in Egypt* 14: 67–86.

———. 1985. "Agricultural Productivity and Taxation in Late Roman Egypt." *Transactions of the American Philological Association* 115: 289–308.

———. 1995. *Reading Papyri, Writing Ancient History*. London and New York: Routledge.

———. 2005. "Evidence and Models for the Economy of Roman Egypt." In *The Ancient Economy: Evidence and Models*, edited by J. Manning and I. Morris, 187–204. Stanford, CA: Stanford University Press.

———, and B.W. Frier. 1994. *The Demography of Roman Egypt*. Cambridge: Cambridge University Press.

Baldwin, B., trans. 1983. *The Philogelos or Laughter-Lover: An Ancient Jokebook Translated*. Amsterdam: J.C. Gieben.

Barlow, C.T. 1978. "Bankers, Moneylenders and Interest Rates in the Roman Republic." PhD diss., University of North Carolina.

Barringer, J. 1994. "The Mythological Paintings in the Macellum at Pompeii." *Classical Antiquity* 13 (2): 149–66.

Barrow, R. 1949. *The Romans*. Harmondsworth, UK: Penguin.

Basore, J.W., trans. 1928. *Seneca: Moral Essays*, vol. 1. Loeb Classical Library 214. Cambridge, MA: Harvard University Press.

———, trans. 1932. *Seneca: Moral Essays*, vol. 2. Loeb Classical Library 254. Cambridge, MA: Harvard University Press.

Beard, M. 1998. "Documenting Roman Religion." In *La mémoire perdue 2: Recherches sur l'administration romaine*, edited by C. Moatti, 75–101. Rome: École Française de Rome.

———. 2008. *The Fires of Vesuvius: Pompeii Lost and Found*. Cambridge, MA: Belknap Press.

———, and J.A. North, eds. 1990. *Pagan Priests: Religion and Power in the Ancient World*. Ithaca, NY: Cornell University Press.

———, ———, and S. Price, eds. 1998. *Religions of Rome*. 2 vols. Cambridge: Cambridge University Press.

Beaugrand-Champagne, D. 2004. *Procès de Marie-Josèphe-Angélique*. Montreal: Libre Expression.

Bell, S., and T. Ramsby, eds. 2012. *Free at Last! The Impact of Freed Slaves on the Roman Empire*. London: Bristol Classical Press.

Bendlin, A. 2012. "Sacrifice, Roman." In *Encyclopedia of Ancient History*, edited by R. Bagnall, K. Brodersen, C. Champion, A. Erskine, and S. Huebner, 6002–05. Oxford: Wiley-Blackwell.

———. 2013. "The Urban Sacred Landscape." In *A Companion to Ancient Rome*, edited by P. Erdkamp, 461–77. Cambridge: Cambridge University Press.

Bergmann, B. 1999. "Introduction: The Art of Ancient Spectacle." In *The Art of Ancient Spectacle*, edited by B. Bergmann and C. Kondoleon, 9–35. New Haven, CT: Yale University Press.

———. 2012. "Housing and Households: The Roman World." In *Classical Archaeology*, 2nd edn, edited by S.E. Alcock and R. Osborne, 228–48. Oxford: Wiley-Blackwell.

Biers, W.R. 1992. *Art, Artefacts and Chronology in Classical Archaeology*. London and New York: Routledge.

Billows, R. 2008. "International Relations." In *The Cambridge History of Greek and Roman Warfare*, vol. 1, edited by P. Sabin, H. van Wees, and M. Whitby, 303–24. Cambridge: Cambridge University Press.

Bishop, M.C., and J.C.N. Coulston. 2005. *Roman Military Equipment from the Punic Wars to the Fall of Rome*. Oxford: Oxbow Books.

Blockley, R.C. 1992. *East Roman Foreign Policy: Formation and Conduct from Diocletian to Anastasius*. ARCA, Classical and Medieval Texts, Papers and Monographs 30. Leeds, UK: Francis Cairns.

Bloomer, W.M. 1997. "Schooling in Persona: Imagination and Subordination in Roman Education." *Classical Antiquity* 16: 57–78.

Bodel, J. 2008. "Cicero's Minerva, *Penates*, and the Mother of the *Lares*: An Outline of Roman Domestic Religion." In *Household and Family Religion in Antiquity*, edited by J.P. Bodel and S.M. Olyan, 248–75. Oxford: Wiley-Blackwell.

———, ed. 2001. *Epigraphic Evidence: Ancient History from Inscriptions*. London and New York: Routledge.

Bonner, S.F. 1977. *Education in Ancient Rome: From the Elder Cato to the Younger Pliny*. London: Methuen.

Booth, A.D. 1979. "The Schooling of Slaves in First-Century Rome." *Transactions of the American Philological Association* 109: 11–19.

Bosworth, B. 1999. "Augustus, the *Res Gestae*, and Hellenistic Theories of Apotheosis." *Journal of Roman Studies* 89: 1–18.

Bowman, A.K. 1996a. *Egypt after the Pharaohs, 332 BC–AD 642: From Alexander to the Arab Conquest*, 2nd edn. London: British Museum Press.

———. 1996b. "Provincial Administration and Taxation." In *The Augustan Empire, 43 B.C.–A.D. 69*, 2nd edn, edited by A.K. Bowman, E. Champlin, and A. Lintott, 344–70. The Cambridge Ancient History, vol. 10. Cambridge: Cambridge University Press.

———. 1998. *Life and Letters on the Roman Frontier: Vindolanda and its People*. London and New York: Routledge.

Bradley, K.R. 1987. *Slaves and Masters in the Roman Empire: A Study in Social Control*. Oxford: Oxford University Press.

———. 1991. *Discovering the Roman Family*. Oxford: Oxford University Press.

———. 1992. "'The Regular, Daily Traffic in Slaves': Roman History and Contemporary History." *The Classical Journal* 87 (2): 125–38.

———. 1994. *Slavery and Society at Rome*. Cambridge: Cambridge University Press.

———. 1998. "The Sentimental Education of the Roman Child: The Role of Pet-Keeping." *Latomus* 57 (3): 523–57.

———. 2011. "Slavery in the Roman Republic." In *The Ancient Mediterranean World*, edited by K. Bradley and P. Cartledge, 241–64. The Cambridge World History of Slavery, vol. 1. Cambridge: Cambridge University Press.

———. 2012. *Apuleius and Antonine Rome: Historical Essays*, edited by M. George. Toronto: University of Toronto Press.

Brélaz, C. 2005. *La sécurité publique en Asie Mineure sous le Principat (Ier-IIIème s. ap. J.-C.)*. Basel, Switzerland: Schwabe.

Bresson, A., and D.B. Hollander. Forthcoming. "Interest Rates, from Greece to Rome: Deflation and Inflation." In *The Oxford Handbook of Economies in the Classical World*, edited by A. Bresson, E. Lo Cascio, and F. Velde. Oxford: Oxford University Press.

Brown, P. 1988. "Arnaldo Dante Momigliano 1908–1987." *Proceedings of the British Academy* 74: 405–42.

Brun, J.-P., and F. Laubenheimer. 2001. "La viticulture en Gaule." *Gallia* 58: 1–260.

Brunt, P.A. 1971. *Italian Manpower 225 B.C.–A.D. 14*. Oxford: Clarendon Press.

———. 1981. "The Revenues of Rome." *Journal of Roman Studies* 71: 161–72.

———. 1982. "A Marxist View of Roman History." *Journal of Roman Studies* 72: 158–63.

———. 1990. *Roman Imperial Themes*. Oxford: Clarendon Press.

————, and J.M. Moore, eds. and trans. 1967. Res Gestae Divi Augusti: *The Achievements of the Divine Augustus*. Oxford: Oxford University Press.

Burke, P. 2005. *History and Social Theory*, 2nd edn. Ithaca, NY: Cornell University Press.

Burton, G.P. 1975. "Proconsuls, Assizes and the Administration of Justice under the Empire." *Journal of Roman Studies* 65: 92–106.

Callebat, L. 1973. *Vitruve, de l'architecture, livre VIII*. Association Guillaume Budé. Paris: Belles Lettres.

Cameron, A. 2011. *The Last Pagans of Rome*. Oxford: Oxford University Press.

Campbell, B. 1984. *The Emperor and the Roman Army 31 BC–AD 235*. Oxford: Clarendon Press.

Capponi, L. 2005. *Augustan Egypt: The Creation of a Roman Province*. London and New York: Routledge.

Carcopino, J. 2003. *Daily Life in Ancient Rome*, 2nd edn. Translated by E.O. Lorimer. New Haven, CT, and London: Yale University Press.

Carter, M. 2003. "Gladiatorial Ranking and the *SC de Pretiis Gladiatorum Minuendis* (*CIL* II 6278 = *ILS* 5163)." *Phoenix* 57: 83–114.

————. 2006/07. "Gladiatorial Combat: The Rules of Engagement." *The Classical Journal* 102 (2): 97–113.

Cary, E. 1925. *Dio Cassius: Roman History*, vol. 8, bks 61–70. Loeb Classical Library 176. Cambridge, MA: Harvard University Press.

Casson, L. 1991. *The Ancient Mariners*, 2nd edn. Princeton, NJ: Princeton University Press.

Champion, C.B., ed. 2004. *Roman Imperialism: Readings and Sources*. Oxford: Blackwell.

Clark, A.J. 2007. *Divine Qualities: Cult and Community in Republican Rome*. Oxford: Oxford University Press.

Clarke, J. 1998. *Looking at Lovemaking: Constructions of Sexuality in Roman Art 100 BC–AD 250*. Berkeley: University of California Press.

————. 2003. *Roman Sex 100 BC–AD 250*. New York: Harry N. Abrams.

————. 2007. *Looking at Laughter: Humor, Power, and Transgression in Roman Visual Culture 100 BC–AD 250*. Berkeley: University of California Press.

Cohoon, J.W., trans. 1939. *Dio Chrysostom: Discourses 12–30*. Loeb Classical Library 339. Cambridge, MA: Harvard University Press.

Coleman, K. 1990. "Fatal Charades: Roman Executions Staged as Mythological Enactments." *Journal of Roman Studies* 80: 44–73.

————. 2004. "The Pedant Goes to Hollywood: The Role of the Academic Consultant." In *Gladiator: Film and History*, edited by M. Winkler, 45–52. Oxford: Blackwell.

Cooley, A. 2003. *Pompeii*. London: Duckworth.

————, and M. Cooley. 2004. *Pompeii: A Sourcebook*. London and New York: Routledge.

Cooper, A. 2006. *The Hanging of Angelique: The Untold Story of Canadian Slavery and the Burning of Old Montréal*. Toronto: Harper Perennial.

Corbeill, A. 2001. "Education in the Roman Republic: Creating Traditions." In *Education in Greek and Roman Antiquity*, edited by Y.L. Too, 261–87. Leiden, The Netherlands: Brill.

Corcoran, T.H. 1971. *Seneca: Natural Questions*, vol. 1 books 1–3. Loeb Classical Library 450. Cambridge, MA: Harvard University Press.

Cornell, T.J. 1995. *The Beginnings of Rome: Italy and Rome from the Bronze Age to the Punic Wars (c. 1000–264 BC)*. London and New York: Routledge.

Costa, C.D.N., trans. 2005. *Lucian: Selected Dialogues*. Oxford: Oxford University Press.

Cottier, M., M.H. Crawford, C.V. Crowther, J.-L. Ferrary, B.M. Levick, O. Salomies, and M. Wörrle. 2008. *The Customs Law of Asia*. Oxford: Oxford University Press.

Coulston, J.C.N. 2000. "'Armed and Belted Men': The Soldiery in Imperial Rome." In *Ancient Rome: The Archaeology of the Eternal City*, edited by J.C.N. Coulston and H. Dodge, 76–118. Oxford: Oxford School of Archaeology.

Crawford, M., ed. 1996. *Roman Statutes*, 2 vols. Bulletin of the Institute of Classical Studies Supplement 64. London: Institute of Classical Studies.

Cribiore, R. 1996. *Writing, Teachers, and Students in Graeco-Roman Egypt*. Atlanta: Scholars Press.

————. 2001. *Gymnastics of the Mind: Greek Education in Hellenistic and Roman Egypt*. Princeton, NJ: Princeton University Press.

Cuomo, S. 2007. *Technology and Culture in Greek and Roman Antiquity*. Cambridge: Cambridge University Press.

Dal Lago, E., and C. Katsari, eds. 2008. *Slave Systems: Ancient and Modern*. Cambridge: Cambridge University Press.

D'Arms, J. 1981. *Commerce and Social Standing in Ancient Rome*. Cambridge, MA: Harvard University Press.

Davies, R.W. 1974. "The Daily Life of the Roman Soldier under the Principate." *Aufstieg und Niedergang der römischen Welt* 2 (1): 299–338.

DeFelice, J. 2007. "Inns and Taverns." In *The World of Pompeii*, edited by J. Dobbins and P. Foss, 474–86. London and New York: Routledge.

DeLaine, J. 1996. "'De aquis suis'?: The 'commentarius' of Frontinus." In *Les littératures techniques dans l'Antiquité romaine*, edited by C. Nicolet,

117–45. Entretiens sur l'Antiquité classique, 42. Vandoeuvres-Genève: Fondation Hardt.

Del Chicca, F., ed. 2004. *Sextus Julius Frontinus: De aquae ductu urbis Romae*. Rome: Herder.

De Ligt, L. 2004. "Poverty and Demography: The Case of the Gracchan Land Reforms." *Mnemosyne* 57 (6): 725–57.

Dill, S. 1904. *Roman Society from Nero to Marcus Aurelius*. London: MacMillan.

Dixon, S. 1992. *The Roman Family*. Baltimore: Johns Hopkins University Press.

Dolansky, F. 2008. "*Togam virilem sumere*: Coming of Age in the Roman World." In *Roman Dress and the Fabrics of Roman Culture*, edited by J. Edmondson and A. Keith, 47–70. Toronto: University of Toronto Press.

———. 2011. "Reconsidering the Matronalia and Women's Rites." *Classical World* 104 (2): 191–209.

Donovan, K. 1995. "Slaves and Their Owners in Ile Royale, 1713–1760." *Acadiensis* 26 (1): 3–32.

Drachmann, A.G. 1948. *Ktesibios, Philon, and Heron: A Study in Ancient Pneumatics*. Acta Historica Scientiarum Naturalium et Medicinalium 4. Copenhagen: Munksgaard.

———. 1976. "Ktesibios' Waterclock and Heron's Adjustable Siphon." *Centaurus* 20 (1): 1–10.

Dunbabin, K.M.D. 1978. *The Mosaics of Roman North Africa*. New York: Oxford University Press.

———. 2008. "Domestic Dionysos? Telete in Mosaics from Zeugma and the Late Roman Near East." *Journal of Roman Archaeology* 21: 193–224.

Duncan-Jones, R. 1982. *The Economy of the Roman Empire*. Cambridge: Cambridge University Press.

———. 1990. *Structure and Scale in the Roman Economy*. Cambridge: Cambridge University Press.

———. 1996. 'The Impact of the Antonine Plague.' *Journal of Roman Archaeology* 9: 108-36. Durry, M. 1938. *Les cohortes prétoriennes*. Paris: de Boccard.

Eck, W. 2011. "Prosopography." In *The Oxford Handbook of Roman Studies*, edited by A. Barchiesi and W. Scheidel, 146–59. Oxford: Oxford University Press.

Edmondson, J. 1996. "Dynamic Arenas: Gladiatorial Presentations in the City of Rome and the Construction of Roman Society during the Early Empire." In *Roman Theater and Society*, edited by W.J. Slater, 69–112. Ann Arbor: University of Michigan Press.

———. 2008. "Public Dress and Social Control in Late Republican and Early Imperial Rome." In *Roman Dress and the Fabrics of Roman Culture*, edited by J. Edmondson and A. Keith, 21–46. Toronto: Toronto University Press.

Edwards, C. 1993. *The Politics of Immorality in Ancient Rome*. Cambridge: Cambridge University Press.

Ellis, S.P. 2000. *Roman Housing*. London: Duckworth.

Engels, Donald. 1980. "The Problem of Female Infanticide in the Greco-Roman World." *Classical Philology* 75 (2): 112–20.

Fantham, E. 2006. *Julia Augusti: The Emperor's Daughter*. London and New York: Routledge.

Feder, L. 1998. *The Handbook of Classical Literature*. New York: Da Capo Press.

Feeney, D. 1998. *Literature and Religion at Rome: Cultures, Contexts, and Beliefs*. Cambridge: Cambridge University Press.

———. 2005. "The Beginnings of a Literature in Latin." *Journal of Roman Studies* 95: 226–40.

Finley, M. 1980. *Ancient Slavery and Modern Ideology*. Harmondsworth, UK: Penguin.

———. 1999. *The Ancient Economy*. Berkeley: University of California Press.

Fisher, G. 2011. *Between Empires: Arabs, Romans, and Sasanians in Late Antiquity*. Oxford: Oxford University Press.

Fitzgerald, W. 2001. "Oppositions, Anxieties, and Ambiguities." In *Imperial Projections: Ancient Rome in Modern Popular Culture*, edited by S. Joshel, M. Malamud, and D. McGuire Jr, 23–49. Baltimore: Johns Hopkins University Press.

Flemming, R. 2008. "Festus and Women's Role in Roman Religion." In *Verrius, Festus and Paul*, edited by F. Glinister and C. Wood, 87–108. *Bulletin of the Institute of Classical Studies* Supplement 93. London: Institute of Classical Studies.

Flower, H. 1996. *Ancestor Masks and Aristocratic Power in Roman Culture*. Oxford: Clarendon Press.

Forbes, C.A. 1955. "The Education and Training of Slaves in Antiquity." *Transactions of the American Philological Association* 86: 321–60.

Fowler, W. 1909. *Social Life at Rome*. New York: MacMillan.

Frier, B.W. 2000. "Demography." In *The High Empire, A.D. 70–192*, 2nd edn, edited by A.K. Bowman, P. Garnsey, and D. Rathbone, 787–816. The Cambridge Ancient History, vol. 11. Cambridge: Cambridge University Press.

———, and T. McGinn. 2003. *Casebook on Roman Family Law*. Oxford: Oxford University Press.

Fuhrmann, C.J. 2012. *Policing the Roman Empire: Soldiers, Administration, and Public Order*. Oxford and New York: Oxford University Press.

Fulford, M. 1987. "Economic Interdependence among Urban Communities of the Roman Mediterranean." *World Archaeology* 19 (1): 58–75.

Futrell, A. 2001. "Seeing Red: Spartacus as Domestic

Economist." In *Imperial Projections: Ancient Rome in Modern Popular Culture*, edited by S. Joshel, M. Malamud, and D. McGuire Jr, 77–118. Baltimore: Johns Hopkins University Press.

Gager, J. 1992. *Curse Tablets and Binding Spells from the Ancient World*. Oxford: Oxford University Press.

Gaimster, D. 2000. "Sex and Sensibility at the British Museum." *History Today* 50 (9): 10–15. www.historytoday.com/david-gaimster/sex-and-sensibility-british-museum.

Galinsky, K. 2011. "The Cult of the Emperor: Unifier or Divider?" In *Rome and Religion: A Cross-Disciplinary Dialogue on the Imperial Cult*, edited by J. Brodd and J.L. Reed, 1–22. *Writings from the Greco-Roman World* Supplement Series 5. Atlanta: Society of Biblical Literature.

Gardner, J.F. 1986. "Proof of Status in the Roman World." *Bulletin of the Institute of Classical Studies* 33 (1): 1–14.

———. 1993. *Being a Roman Citizen*. London and New York: Routledge.

———, and T. Wiedemann, eds. 1991. *The Roman Household: A Sourcebook*. London and New York: Routledge.

Garnsey, P. 1970. *Social Status and Legal Privilege in the Roman Empire*. Oxford: Clarendon Press.

———. 1996. *Ideas of Slavery from Aristotle to Augustine*. Cambridge: Cambridge University Press.

———. 1998. *Cities, Peasants and Food in Classical Antiquity: Essays in Social and Economic History*. Cambridge: Cambridge University Press.

———. 2000. "The Land." In *The High Empire, A.D. 70–192*, 2nd edn, edited by A.K. Bowman, P. Garnsey, and D. Rathbone, 679–709. The Cambridge Ancient History, vol. 11. Cambridge: Cambridge University Press.

———, and R. Saller. 1987. *The Roman Empire: Economy, Society and Culture*. Berkeley: University of California Press.

Gawlikowski, M. 1988. "Le commerce de Palmyre sur terre et sur eau." In *L'Arabie et ses mers bordières*, edited by J.-F. Salles, 163–72. Lyon, France: GS-Maison de l'Orient.

George, M. 2002. "Slave Disguise in Ancient Rome." *Slavery and Abolition* 23 (2): 41–54.

———. 2007. "The Lives of Slaves." In *The World of Pompeii*, edited by J. Dobbins and P. Foss, 538–49. London and New York: Routledge.

———. 2008. "The 'Dark Side' of the Toga." In *Roman Dress and the Fabrics of Roman Culture*, edited by J. Edmondson and A. Keith, 94–112. Toronto: Toronto University Press.

Gibbs, M. 2012. "Manufacture, Trade, and the Economy," in *The Oxford Handbook of Roman*

Egypt, edited by C. Riggs, 38–55. Oxford: Oxford University Press.

Gibson, R., ed. 2003. *Ovid Ars Amatoria Book 3*, Cambridge: Cambridge University Press.

Gilliver, K. 2007. "Display in Roman Warfare: The Appearance of Armies and Individuals on the Battlefield." *War in History* 14 (1): 1–21.

Gimpel, J. 1976. *The Medieval Machine*. Harmondsworth, UK: Penguin.

Glancy, J.A. 2010. "Christian Slavery in Late Antiquity." In *Human Bondage in the Cultural Contact Zone: Transdisciplinary Perspectives on Slavery and Its Discourses*, edited by R. Hörmann and G. Mackenthun, 63–79. Münster, Germany: Waxmann Verlag GmbH.

Goldberg, S. 1998. "Plautus on the Palatine." *Journal of Roman Studies* 88: 1–20.

Golden, M. 1992. "The Uses of Cross-Cultural Comparison in Ancient Social History." *Classical Views* 36: 309–31.

———. 2011. "Afterword: The Future of the Ancient Greek Family." In *Families in the Greco-Roman World*, edited by R. Laurence and A. Strömberg, 177–90. London and New York: Continuum International Publishing Group.

Goldman, B., ed. 1979. *The Discovery of Dura-Europos*. New Haven, CT: Yale University Press.

Goldsworthy, A. 1996. *The Roman Army at War 100 BC–AD 200*. Oxford: Clarendon Press.

Goold, G.P., F.W. Cornish, J.P. Postgate, and J.W. Mackail, eds. and trans. 1913. *Catullus. Tibullus. Pervigilium Veneris*. Loeb Classical Library 6. Cambridge, MA: Harvard University Press.

Gordon, R. 2008. "*Superstitio*, Superstition and Religious Repression in the Late Roman Republic and Principate (100 BCE–300 CE)." In *The Religion of Fools? Superstition Past and Present*, edited by S.A. Smith and A. Knight, 72–94. *Past & Present* Supplement 3. Oxford: Oxford University Press.

Green, P., trans. 1982. *Ovid: The Erotic Poems*. London: Penguin.

Greene, E. 2011. "Women and Families in the Auxiliary Military Communities of the Roman West in the First and Second Centuries AD." PhD diss., University of North Carolina.

Gruen, E. 1990. *Studies in Greek Culture and Roman Policy*. Leiden, The Netherlands: Brill.

Grünewald, T. 2004. *Bandits in the Roman Empire: Myth and Reality*. Translated by J. Drinkwater. London and New York: Routledge.

Hales, S. 2003. *The Roman House and Social Identity*. Cambridge: Cambridge University Press.

Handford, S.A., trans. 1954. *Fables of Aesop*. London: Penguin.

Hanson, A.E. 1989. "Village Officials at Philadelphia: A Model of Romanization in the Julio-Claudian Period." In *Egitto e storia antica dall'ellenismo all'età araba*, edited by L. Criscuolo and G. Geraci, 429–40. Bologna, Italy: CLUEB.

Hanson, J.A., trans. 1989. *Apuleius: Metamorphoses (The Golden Ass)*, vol. 2, books 7–11. Loeb Classical Library 453. Cambridge, MA: Harvard University Press.

Hardwick, L. 2003. *Reception Studies*. Greece and Rome New Surveys in the Classics 33. Oxford: Oxford University Press.

———, and C. Stray, eds. 2008. *A Companion to Classical Receptions*. Oxford: Wiley-Blackwell.

Harries, J. 2007. *Law and Crime in the Roman World*. Cambridge: Cambridge University Press.

Harrill, J.A. 1995. *The Manumission of Slaves in Early Christianity*. Tübingen, Germany: Mohr Siebeck.

Harris, W.V. 1980. "Towards a Study of the Roman Slave Trade." In *The Seaborne Commerce of Ancient Rome*, edited by J.H. D'Arms and E.C. Kopff, 117–40. Ann Arbor: University of Michigan Press.

———. 1988. "On the Applicability of the Concept of Class in Roman History." In *Forms of Control and Subordination in Antiquity*, edited by T. Yuge and M. Doi, 598–610. Leiden, The Netherlands: Brill.

———. 1994. "Child-Exposure in the Roman Empire." *Journal of Roman Studies* 84: 1–22.

———. 1999. "Demography, Geography, and the Sources of Roman Slaves." *Journal of Roman Studies* 89: 62–75.

———. 2000. "Trade." In *The High Empire, A.D. 70–192*, 2nd edn, edited by A.K. Bowman, P. Garnsey, and D. Rathbone, 710–40. The Cambridge Ancient History, vol. 11. Cambridge: Cambridge University Press.

———. 2007. "The Late Republic." In *The Cambridge Economic History of the Greco-Roman World*, edited by W. Scheidel, I. Morris, and R. Saller, 511–42. Cambridge: Cambridge University Press.

———. 2008. "The Nature of Roman Money." In *The Monetary Systems of the Greeks and Romans*, edited by W.V. Harris, 174–207. Oxford: Oxford University Press.

———. 2011. *Rome's Imperial Economy: Twelve Essays*. Oxford: Oxford University Press.

Hauken, T. 1998. *Petition and Response: An Epigraphic Study of Petitions to Roman Emperors, 181–249*. Bergen, Norway: Norwegian Institute at Athens.

Heather, P. 2001. "The Late Roman Art of Client-Management: Imperial Defence in the Fourth-Century West." In *The Transformation of Frontiers: From Late Antiquity to the Carolingians*, edited by W. Pohl, I. Wood, and H. Reimitz, 15–68. Leiden, The Netherlands: Brill.

Helmbold, W.C., trans. 1939. Reproduced by permission of the publishers and the Trustees of the Loeb Classical Library from *Plutarch: Moralia*, Loeb Classical Library Volume VI, translated by W.C. Helmbold, 1939, page 447, Cambridge Mass.: Harvard University Press 1939 by the President and Fellows of Harvard College. Loeb Classical Library ® is a registered trademark of the President and Fellows of Harvard College.

Hemelrijk, E. 1999. Matrona Docta: *Educated Women in the Roman Elite from Cornelia to Julia Domna*. London and New York: Routledge.

Henrichs, A. 2008. "What is a Greek Priest?" In *Practitioners of the Divine: Greek Priests and Religious Officials from Homer to Heliodorus*, edited by B. Dignas and K. Trampedach, 1–14. Washington, DC: Center for Hellenic Studies.

Hetland, L. 2007. "Dating the Pantheon." *Journal of Roman Archaeology* 20: 95–112.

Hinds, S. 2004. "Petrarch, Cicero, Virgil: Virtual Community in *Familiares* 24,4." *Materiali e discussioni per l'analisi dei testi classici* 52: 157–75.

Hirt, A.M. 2010. *Imperial Mines and Quarries in the Roman World: Organizational Aspects, 27 BC–AD 235*. Oxford: Oxford University Press.

Hodge, A.T. 2000. "Aqueducts." In *Handbook of Ancient Water Technology*, edited by Ö. Wikander, 39–66. Leiden, The Netherlands: Brill.

———. 2002. *Roman Aqueducts and Water Supply*, 2nd edn. London: Duckworth.

Hollander, D.B. 2007. *Money in the Late Roman Republic*. Leiden, The Netherlands: Brill.

———. 2008. "Demand for Money in the Late Roman Republic." In *The Monetary Systems of the Greeks and Romans*, edited by W.V. Harris, 112–36. Oxford: Oxford University Press.

Homoth-Kuhs, C. 2005. *Phylakes und Phylakon-Steuer im griechisch-römischen Ägypten: Ein Beitrag zur Geschichte des antiken Sicherheitswesens*. APF Beiheft 17. Munich and Leipzig, Germany: Saur.

Hope, V. 2000. "Status and Identity in the Roman World." In *Experiencing Rome: Culture, Identity and Power in the Roman Empire*, edited by J. Huskinson, 125–52. London and New York: Routledge.

———. 2003. "Trophies and Tombstones: Commemorating the Roman Soldier." *World Archaeology* 35 (1): 79–97.

———. 2007. *Death in Ancient Rome: A Sourcebook*. London and New York: Routledge.

Hopkins, K. 1978. *Conquerors and Slaves* (Sociological Studies in Roman History 1). Cambridge: Cambridge University Press. Reprinted with the permission of Cambridge University Press.

Hopkins, K. 1978. "Review: Rules of Evidence." *Journal of Roman Studies* 68: 180, 182. Reprinted with the permission of Cambridge University Press.

———. 1980. "Taxes and Trades in the Roman Empire." *Journal of Roman Studies* 70: 101–25.

———. 1995/96 'Rome, Taxes, Rent and Trade.' *Kodai: Journal of Ancient History* 6/7: 41-75.

———, and G. Burton. 1983a. "Political Succession in the Late Republic." In *Death and Renewal*, by K. Hopkins, 31–119. Sociological Studies in Roman History 2. Cambridge: Cambridge University Press.

——— and ———. 1983b. "Ambition and Withdrawal: The Senatorial Aristocracy under the Emperors." In *Death and Renewal*, by K. Hopkins, 120–200. Sociological Studies in Roman History 2. Cambridge: Cambridge University Press.

Horden, P., and N. Purcell. 2000. *The Corrupting Sea: A Study of Mediterranean History*. Oxford: Blackwell.

Hornblower, S., A. Spawforth, and E. Eidinow, eds. 2012. *The Oxford Classical Dictionary*, 4th edn. Oxford: Oxford University Press, 2012.

Horsfall, N. 1993. "Empty Shelves on the Palatine." *Greece & Rome* 40 (1): 58–67.

Howgego, C. 1992. "The Supply and Use of Money in the Roman World 200 BC to AD 200." *Journal of Roman Studies* 82: 1–31.

———. 1995. *Ancient History from Coins*. London and New York: Routledge.

Hubbard, T. ed. 2003. *Homosexuality in Greece and Rome: A Sourcebook of Basic Documents*. Berkeley: University of California Press.

Isaac, B. 1992. *The Limits of Empire: The Roman Army in the East*. Oxford: Oxford University Press.

Jackson, J., trans. 1937. Reproduced by permission of the publishers and the Trustees of the Loeb Classical Library from *Tacitus: Annals Books*, 13–16. translated by J. Jackson, 1937 pages 42–45, Cambridge Mass.: Harvard University Press 1939 by the President and Fellows of Harvard College. Loeb Classical Library ® is a registered trademark of the President and Fellows of Harvard College.

James, S. 2002. "Writing the Legions: The Development and Future of Roman Military Studies in Britain." *Archaeological Journal* 159: 1–58.

———. 2004. *The Excavations at Dura-Europos Conducted by Yale University and the French Academy of Inscriptions and Letters, 1928 to 1937. Final Report VII. The Arms and Armour and Other Military Equipment*. London: British Museum Press.

———. 2006. "Engendering Change in Our Understanding of the Structure of Roman Military Communities." *Archaeological Dialogues* 13 (1): 31–6.

Jansen, G. 1996. "Die Verteilung des Leitungswassers in den Häusern Pompejis." In *Cura Aquarum in Campania*, edited by N. de Haan and G. Jansen, 47–50. Leuven, Belgium: Peeters.

Jeppesen-Wigelsworth, A. 2010. "The Portrayal of Roman Wives in Literature and Inscriptions." PhD thesis, University of Calgary, http://hdl.handle.net/1880/47797.

———. Forthcoming. "*Amici* and *Coniuges* in Cicero's Letters: Atticus and Terentia." *Latomus*.

Johns, C. 1982. *Sex or Symbol: Erotic Images of Greece and Rome*. London: British Museum Publications.

Johnson, A.C. 1936. *Roman Egypt to the Reign of Diocletian*. An Economic Survey of Ancient Rome, edited by T. Frank, vol. 2. Baltimore: Johns Hopkins University Press.

Johnson, W.A. 2011. "Teaching the Children How to Read: The Syllabary." *The Classical Journal* 106 (4): 445–63.

Jones, A.H.M. 1974. *The Roman Economy: Studies in Ancient Economic and Administrative History*. Oxford: Blackwell.

Jones, D. 2006. *The Bankers of Puteoli: Finance, Trade and Industry in the Roman World*. Stroud, UK: Tempus.

Joshel, S. 2010. *Slavery in the Roman World*. Cambridge: Cambridge University Press.

———, M. Malamud, and D. McGuire Jr, eds. 2001. *Imperial Projections: Ancient Rome in Modern Popular Culture*. Baltimore: Johns Hopkins University Press.

Joyal, M., I. McDougall, and J.C. Yardley, eds. 2009. *Greek and Roman Education. A Sourcebook*. London and New York: Routledge.

Kaster, R., trans. and ed. 1995. *De grammaticis et rhetoribus. C. Suetonius Tranquillus*. Oxford: Clarendon Press.

Katsari, C. 2011. *The Roman Monetary System: The Eastern Provinces from the First to the Third Century AD*. Cambridge: Cambridge University Press.

Kehoe, D.P. 1992. *Management and Investment on Estates in Roman Egypt during the Early Empire*. Bonn, Germany: Habelt.

———. 1997. *Investment, Profit, and Tenancy: The Jurists and the Roman Agrarian Economy*. Ann Arbor: University of Michigan Press.

———. 2006. "Landlords and Tenants." In *A Companion to the Roman Empire*, edited by D.S. Potter, 298–311. Oxford: Wiley-Blackwell.

Kelly, B. 2007. "Riot Control and Imperial Ideology in the Roman Empire." *Phoenix* 61 (1–2): 150–76.

———. 2011. *Petitions, Litigation, and Social Control in Roman Egypt*. Oxford: Oxford University Press.

———. 2013. "Policing and Security." In *The Cambridge Companion to Ancient Rome*, edited by P. Erdkamp. Cambridge: Cambridge University Press, 410–24.

Kendrick, W. 1987. *The Secret Museum: Pornography in Modern Culture*. New York and Toronto: Viking.

Kennedy, D. 1992. "'Augustan' and 'Anti-Augustan': Reflections on Terms of Reference." In *Roman Poetry and Propaganda in the Age of Augustus*, edited by A. Powell, 26–58. London: Bristol Classical Press.

Keyser, P. 1988. "Suetonius 'Nero' 41.2 and the Date of Heron Mechanicus of Alexandria." *Classical Philology* 83 (3): 218–20.

King, A.C. 2001. "The Romanization of Diet in the Western Empire: Comparative Archaeological Studies." In *Italy and the West: Comparative Issues in Romanization*, edited by S. Keay and N. Terrenato, 210–23. Oxford: Oxbow.

King, C. 2003. "The Organization of Roman Religious Beliefs." *Classical Antiquity* 22 (2): 275–312.

Kissel, T. 2002. "*Veluti naturae ipsius dominus.*" *Antike Welt* 33 (2): 143–52.

Kitto, H. 1951. *The Greeks*. Harmondsworth, UK: Penguin.

Kleijwegt, M. 1991. *Ancient Youth: The Ambiguity of Youth and the Absence of Adolescence in Greco-Roman Society*. Amsterdam: Gieben.

Kleiner, F.S. 2007. *A History of Roman Art*. Boston: Cengage.

Kovacs, G., and C. Marshall, eds. 2011. *Classics and Comics*. Oxford: Oxford University Press.

Kron, G. 2005. "The Augustan Census Figures and the Population of Italy." *Athenaeum* 92: 441–95.

Kulikowski, M. 2006. "Constantine and the Northern Barbarians." In *The Cambridge Companion to the Age of Constantine*, edited by N. Lenski, 347–76. Cambridge: Cambridge University Press.

Laes, C. 2011. *Children in the Roman Empire: Outsiders Within*. Cambridge: Cambridge University Press.

Lampe, P. 2003. *From Paul to Valentinus: Christians at Rome in the First Two Centuries*. Minneapolis: Fortress Press.

Lancaster, L. 2008. "Roman Engineering and Construction." In *The Oxford Handbook of Engineering and Technology in the Classical World*, edited by J.P. Oleson, 256–84. Oxford: Oxford University Press.

Landels, J.G. 2000. *Engineering in the Ancient World*. Berkeley: University of California Press.

Larsen, J.D. 1982. "The Water Towers in Pompeii." *Analecta Romana Instituti Danici* 11: 41–67.

Last, H. 1953. "Obituary: Professor M.I. Rostovtzeff." *Journal of Roman Studies* 43: 133–4.

Lattimore, R. 1962. *Themes in Greek and Latin Epitaphs*. Urbana: University of Illinois Press.

Law Commission of Canada, ed. 2004. *What is Crime?* Vancouver: University of British Columbia Press.

Lazer, E. 2009. *Resurrecting Pompeii*. London and New York: Routledge.

Le Bohec, Y. 2000. *The Imperial Roman Army*. London and New York: Routledge.

Ledger, S. 1997. *The New Woman: Fiction and Feminism at the* fin de siècle. Manchester: Manchester University Press.

Lendon, J.E. 2005. *Soldiers and Ghosts: A History of Battle in Classical Antiquity*. New Haven, CT: Yale University Press.

Leslie, D., and K. Gardiner. 1996. *The Roman Empire in Chinese Sources*. Rome: Bardi.

Leveau, P. 1991. "Research on Roman Aqueducts in the Past Ten Years." In *Future Currents in Aqueduct Studies*, edited by A.T. Hodge, 149–62. London: Duckworth.

Lewis, M. 2001. *Surveying Instruments of Greece and Rome*. Cambridge: Cambridge University Press.

Lewis, N. 1997. *The Compulsory Public Services of Roman Egypt*, 2nd edn. Florence: Edizioni Gonnelli.

———. 1999. *Life in Egypt under Roman Rule*. Durham, NC: American Society of Papyrologists.

———, and M. Reinhold. 1990. From *Roman Civilization: Selected Readings*, vol. 2, 3rd edn. By N. Lewis Lewis and M. Reinhold. Copyright © 1990. Columbia University Press. Reprinted with permission of the publisher.

Lintott, A. 1993. *Imperium Romanum: Politics and Administration*. London and New York: Routledge.

———. 1999a. *The Constitution of the Roman Republic*. Oxford: Oxford University Press.

———. 1999b. *Violence in Republican Rome*, 2nd edn. Oxford: Oxford University Press.

———. Forthcoming. "Crime and Punishment." In *The Cambridge Companion to Roman Law*, edited by D. Johnston. Cambridge: Cambridge University Press.

Lo Cascio, E. 2003. "Appaltatori delle imposte e amministrazione finanziaria imperiale." In *Tâches publiques et entreprise privée dans le monde romain*, edited J.J. Aubert, 249–65. Recueil de Travaux publiés par la Faculté des Lettres et Sciences humaines 52. Geneva: Droz.

———. 2008. "The Function of Gold Coinage in the Monetary Economy of the Roman Empire."

In *The Monetary Systems of the Greeks and Romans*, edited by W.V. Harris, 160–73. Oxford: Oxford University Press.

————, and P. Malanima. 2005. "Cycles and Stability: Italian Population before the Demographic Transition (225 B.C.–A.D. 1900)." *Rivista di storia economica* 21 (3): 5–40.

Lowe, D., and K. Shahabudin, eds. 2009. *Classics for All: Reworking Antiquity in Mass Culture*. Newcastle upon Tyne, UK: Cambridge Scholars Publishing.

Lutz, C. 1947. "Musonius Rufus: The Roman Socrates." *Yale Classical Studies* 10: 3–147.

McGinn, T. 1998. *Prostitution, Sexuality, and the Law in Ancient Rome*. Oxford and New York: Oxford University Press.

McKeown, N. 2007. *The Invention of Ancient Slavery?* London: Duckworth.

MacKinnon, M. 2004. *Animal Production and Consumption in Roman Italy: Integrating the Zooarchaeological and Textual Evidence. Journal of Roman Archaeology* Supplementary Series 54. Portsmouth, RI: *Journal of Roman Archaeology*.

MacMullen, R. 1974. *Roman Social Relations 50 BC to AD 284*. New Haven, CT, and London: Yale University Press.

————. 1984a. "The Roman Emperor's Army Costs." *Latomus* 43: 571–80.

————. 1984b. "The Legion as Society." *Historia* 33: 440–56.

Mantle, I. 2002. "The Roles of Children in Roman Religion." *Greece & Rome* 49 (1): 85–106.

Maricq, A. 1958. "*Res Gestae Divi Saporis*." *Syria* 35: 245–60.

Markschies, C. 1999. *Between Two Worlds: Structures of Earliest Christianity*. London: SCM Press.

Marzano, A. 2007. *Roman Villas in Central Italy: A Social and Economic History*. Columbia Studies in the Classical Tradition 30. Leiden, The Netherlands: Brill.

Mattern, P. 1999. *Rome and the Enemy: Imperial Strategy in the Principate*. Berkeley: University of California Press.

Matthews, J.F. 1984. "The Tax Law of Palmyra: Evidence for Economic History in a City of the Roman East." *Journal of Roman Studies* 74: 157–80.

Mattingly, D.J. 1988. "Oil for Export: A Comparative Study of Roman Olive Oil Production in Libya, Spain and Tunisia." *Journal of Roman Archaeology* 1: 33–56.

————. 1995. *Tripolitania*. London: Batsford.

————. 2006. "The Imperial Economy." In *A Companion to the Roman Empire*, edited by D.S. Potter, 283–97. Oxford: Wiley-Blackwell.

————. 2011. *Imperialism, Power, and Identity*. Princeton, NJ: Princeton University Press.

Meiggs, R. 1973. *Roman Ostia*, 2nd edn. Oxford: Clarendon Press.

Melchior, A. 2011. "Caesar in Vietnam: Did Roman Soldiers Suffer From Post-Traumatic Stress Disorder?" *Greece & Rome* 58 (2): 209–23.

Mellor, R. 1992. "The Local Character of Roman Imperial Religion." *Athenaeum* 80 (2): 385–400.

Ménard, H. 2000. "Le vol dans les tablettes de la Bretagne romaine (*Britannia*)." *Revue historique de droit français et étranger* 78 (2): 289–99.

Mennen, I. 2011. *Power and Status in the Roman Empire, AD 193–284*. Impact of Empire 12. Leiden, The Netherlands: Brill.

Metcalf, W.E., ed. 2012. *The Oxford Handbook of Greek and Roman Coinage*. Oxford: Oxford University Press.

Milnor, K. 2011. "Women." In *The Oxford Handbook of Roman Studies*, edited by A. Barchiesi and W. Scheidel, 815–26. Oxford: Oxford University Press.

Mohler, S.L. 1940. "Slave Education in the Roman Empire." *Transactions of the American Philological Association* 71: 262–80.

Mommsen, T., P. Krueger, and A. Watson, eds. 1985. *The Digest of Justinian*, vol. 1. Philadelphia: University of Pennsylvania Press.

Morgan, T. 1998. *Literate Education in the Hellenistic and Roman Worlds*. Cambridge: Cambridge University Press.

————. 2007. *Popular Morality in the Early Roman Empire*. Cambridge: Cambridge University Press.

Morley, N. 2006. "Social Structures and Demography." In *A Companion to the Roman Republic*, edited by N. Rosenstein and R. Morstein-Marx, 299–323. Oxford: Wiley-Blackwell.

————. 2011. "Slavery under the Principate." In *The Ancient Mediterranean World*, edited by K. Bradley and P. Cartledge, 265–86. The Cambridge World History of Slavery, vol. 1. Cambridge: Cambridge University Press.

Mouritsen, H. 1999. "Electoral Campaigning in Pompeii: A Reconsideration." *Athenaeum* 87 (2): 515–23.

————. 2004. "Freedmen and Freeborn in the Necropolis of Imperial Ostia." *Zeitschrift für Papyrologie und Epigraphik* 150: 281–304.

————. 2005. "Freedmen and Decurions: Epitaphs and Social History in Imperial Italy." *Journal of Roman Studies* 95: 38–63.

————. 2011. *The Freedman in the Roman World*. Cambridge: Cambridge University Press.

Neugebauer, O. 1938. "Über eine Methode zur Distanzbestimmung Alexandria Rom bei Heron." *Kgl. Danske Videnskabernes Selskab, Historisk-filosofiske Meddelelser* 26 (2): 3–26.

Nicolet, C. 1980. *The World of the Citizen in Republican Rome*. Translated by P.S. Falla. Berkeley: University of California Press.

————. 1992. "Economy and Society, 133–43 B.C.," in *The Last Age of the Roman Republic, 146–43 B.C.*, 2nd edn, edited by J.A. Crook, A. Lintott, and E. Rawson, 599–643. The Cambridge Ancient History, vol. 11. Cambridge: Cambridge University Press.

Nippel, W. 1995. *Public Order in Ancient Rome*. Cambridge: Cambridge University Press.

Nisbet, G. 2008. *Ancient Greece in Film and Popular Culture*: Updated Second Edition. Exeter, UK: Bristol Phoenix Press.

North, J.A. 1976. "Conservatism and Change in Roman Religion." *Papers of the British School at Rome* 44: 1–12.

————. 1998. "The Books of the *Pontifices*." In *La mémoire perdue 2: Recherches sur l'administration romaine*, edited by C. Moatti, 45–63. Rome: École Française de Rome.

————. 2000. *Roman Religion*. Greece and Rome New Surveys in the Classics 30. Oxford: Oxford University Press for the Classical Association.

Oates, J.F., R.S. Bagnall, S.J. Clarkson, A.A. O'Brien, J.D. Sosin, T.G. Wilfon, and K.A. Worp, eds. 2011. *Checklist of Editions of Greek, Latin, Demotic and Coptic Papyri, Ostraca and Tablets*. Last modified 1 June 2011. http://library.duke.edu/rubenstein/scriptorium/papyrus/texts/clist.html.

Oleson, J.P. 1988. "The Technology of Roman Harbours." *International Journal of Nautical Archaeology* 17 (2): 147–57.

————. 2004. "Well-Pumps for Dummies: Was there a Roman Tradition of Popular, Sub-Literary Engineering Manuals?" In *Problemi di macchinismo in ambito romano*, edited by F. Minonzio, 65–86. Como, Italy: Commune di Como.

————, L. Bottalico, C. Brandon, R. Cucitore, E. Gotti, and R.L. Hohlfelder. 2006. "Reproducing a Roman Maritime Structure with Vitruvian Pozzolanic Concrete." *Journal of Roman Archaeology* 19: 29–52.

————, C. Brandon, S.M. Cramer, R. Cucitore, E. Gotti, and R.L. Hohlfelder. 2004. "The ROMACONS Project: A Contribution to the Historical and Engineering Analysis of Hydraulic Concrete in Roman Maritime Structures." *International Journal of Nautical Archaeology* 33 (2): 199–229.

Olson, K. 2008. *Dress and the Roman Woman: Self-Presentation and Society*. London and New York: Routledge.

Orlin, E.M. 1997. *Temples, Religion, and Politics in the Roman Republic*. Leiden, The Netherlands: Brill.

————. 2010. *Foreign Cults in Rome: Creating a Roman Empire*. Oxford: Oxford University Press.

Ortiz, D.R. 1993. "Creating Controversy: Essentialism and Constructivism and the Politics of Gay Identity." *Virginia Law Review* 79 (7): 1833–57.

Packer, J.E. 1971. *The Insulae of Imperial Ostia*. Memoirs of the American Academy in Rome 31. Rome: American Academy in Rome.

————. 2010. "Pompey's Theater and Tiberius' Temple of Concord: A Late Republican Primer for an Early Imperial Patron." In *The Emperor and Rome: Space, Representation, and Ritual*, edited by B.C. Ewald and C.F. Noreña, 135–67. Yale Classical Studies, vol. 35. New York: Cambridge University Press.

Parker, A.J. 1992. *Ancient Shipwrecks of the Mediterranean and Roman Provinces*. BAR International Series 580. Oxford: Tempus Reparatum.

Paton, W.R. 1922. *Polybius: The Histories*, vol. 1, bks 1–2. Loeb Classical Library 128. Cambridge, MA: Harvard University Press.

Patterson, O. 1982. *Slavery and Social Death: A Comparative Study*. Cambridge, MA: Harvard University Press.

Peachin, M., ed. 2011. *The Oxford Handbook of Social Relations in the Roman World*. Oxford: Oxford University Press.

Peacock, D.P.S. 1982. *Pottery in the Roman World: An Ethnoarchaeological Approach*. London: Longman.

————, and D.F. Williams. 1986. *Amphorae and the Roman Economy: An Introductory Guide*. London: Longman.

Peña, J.T. 2007. *Roman Pottery in the Archaeological Record*. Cambridge: Cambridge University Press.

Perrin, B., trans. 1916. *Plutarch: Lives*, vol. 4. Loeb Classical Library 80. Cambridge, MA: Harvard University Press.

————, trans. 1918. *Plutarch's Lives*, vol. 9. Loeb Classical Library 98. Cambridge, MA: Harvard University Press.

————, trans. 1920. *Plutarch: Lives,* vol. 9. Loeb Classical Library 101. Cambridge, MA: Harvard University Press.

Petersen, L.H. 2009. "'Clothes Make the Man': Dressing the Roman Freedman Body." In *Bodies and Boundaries in Graeco-Roman Antiquity*, edited by T. Fögen and M.M. Lee, 181–214. Berlin and New York: Walter de Gruyter.

Phang, S. 2001. *The Marriage of Roman Soldiers (13 BC–AD 235)*. Leiden, The Netherlands: Brill.

————. 2008. *Roman Military Service*. Cambridge: Cambridge University Press.

Pitassi, M. 2009. *The Navies of Rome*. Woodbridge: Boydell Press.

Pohl, W., ed. 1997. *Kingdoms of the Empire: The Integration of Barbarians in Late Antiquity*. Leiden, The Netherlands: Brill.

Pollard, N. 2000. *Soldiers, Cities, and Civilians in Roman Syria*. Ann Arbor: University of Michigan Press.

Pomeroy, A. 2008. *Then It was Destroyed by the Volcano: The Ancient World in Film and on Television*. London: Duckworth.

Potter, D. 1996. "Performance, Power, and Justice in the High Empire." In *Roman Theater and Society*, edited by W.J. Slater, 129–59. Ann Arbor: University of Michigan Press.

———. 1999. *Literary Texts and the Roman Historian*. London and New York: Routledge.

Prescendi, F. 2010. "Children and the Transmission of Religious Knowledge." In *Children, Memory, and Family Identity in Roman Culture*, edited by V. Dasen and T. Späth, 73–94. Oxford: Oxford University Press.

Quilici, G. 2008. "Land Transport, Part 1: Roads and Bridges." In *Handbook of Engineering and Technology in the Classical World*, edited by J.P. Oleson, 551–79. Oxford: Oxford University Press.

Rabinowitz, N.S., and L. Auanger, eds. 2002. *Among Women: From the Homoerotic to the Homosocial in the Ancient World*. Austin: University of Texas Press.

Radice, B., trans. 1963. Approximately 248 words (p.36) from *The Letters of the Younger Pliny* translated with an introduction by Betty Radice (Penguin Classics 1963, Reprinted 1969). Copyright © Betty Radice, 1963, 1969.

Rankov, B. 2007. "Military Forces." In *Rome from the Late Republic to the Late Empire*, edited by P. Sabin, H. Van Wees, and M. Whitby, 30–75. The Cambridge History of Greek and Roman Warfare, vol. 2. Cambridge: Cambridge University Press.

Rathbone, D.W. 1991. *Economic Rationalism and Rural Society in Third-Century A.D. Egypt: The Heroninos Archive and the Appianus Estate*. Cambridge: Cambridge University Press.

———. 1996. "The Imperial Finances." In *The Augustan Empire, 43 B.C.–A.D. 69*, 2nd edn, edited by A.K. Bowman, E. Champlin, and A. Lintott, 309–23. The Cambridge Ancient History, vol. 10. Cambridge: Cambridge University Press.

———. 2003. "The Financing of Maritime Commerce in the Roman Empire, I–II AD." In *Credito e moneta nel mondo romano. Atti degli Incontri capresi di storia dell'economia antica (Capri 12–14 ottobre 2000)*, edited by E. Lo Cascio, 197–229. Bari, Italy: Edipuglia.

———. 2007a. "Roman Egypt." In *The Cambridge Economic History of the Greco-Roman World*, edited by W. Scheidel, I. Morris, and R. Saller, 698–719. Cambridge: Cambridge University Press.

———. 2007b. "Warfare and the State (A): The Economics of War." In *Rome from the Late Republic to the Late Empire*, edited by P. Sabin, H. Van Wees, and M. Whitby, 158–76. The Cambridge History of Greek and Roman Warfare, vol. 2. Cambridge: Cambridge University Press.

Rawson, B. 2003. *Children and Childhood in Roman Italy*. Oxford: Oxford University Press.

———, ed. 2011. *A Companion to Families in the Greek and Roman Worlds*. Oxford: Wiley-Blackwell.

Rawson, E. 1991. *Roman Culture and Society: Collected Papers*. Oxford: Clarendon Press.

Reden, S. von. 2010. *Money in Classical Antiquity*. Cambridge: Cambridge University Press.

Reed, J.E., and A. Thompson, trans. 1889. *Suetonius: The Lives of the Twelve Caesars; An English Translation, Augmented with the Biographies of Contemporary Statesmen, Orators, Poets, and Other Associates*. Philadelphia: Gebbie & Co.

Reinhold, M. 1971. "Usurpation of Status and Status Symbols in the Roman Empire." *Historia* 20 (2–3): 275–302.

Rice, E.F., and A. Grafton. 1994. *The Foundations of Early Modern Europe, 1460–1559*, 2nd edn. New York: Norton.

Ridley, R. 2005. "Unbridgeable Gaps: The Capitoline Temple at Rome." *Bullettino della Commissione Archeologica Comunale di Roma* 106: 83–104.

Riggsby, A.M. 1997. "'Public' and 'Private' in Roman Culture: The Case of the *cubiculum*." *Journal of Roman Archaeology* 10: 36–56.

———. 1999. *Crime and Community in Ciceronean Rome*. Austin, TX: University of Texas Press.

Ripat, P. 2006a. "Roman Omens, Roman Audiences, and Roman History." *Greece & Rome* 53 (2): 155–74.

———. 2006b. "The Language of Oracular Inquiry in Roman Egypt." *Phoenix* 60 (3–4): 304–28.

Rives, J.B. 2007. *Religion in the Roman Empire*. Oxford: Blackwell.

———. 2011. "Magic in Roman Law: The Reconstruction of a Crime." In *The Religious History of the Roman Empire: Pagans, Jews, and Christians*, edited by J.A. North and S. Price, 71–108. Oxford: Oxford University Press.

Robert, L. 1940. *Les gladiateurs dans l'Orient grec*. Paris: E. Champion.

Robinson, O.F. 1995. *The Criminal Law of Ancient Rome*. Baltimore: The Johns Hopkins University Press.

Rodgers, R.H. 2004. *Frontinus: De aquaeductu urbis romae*. Cambridge: Cambridge University Press.

Rolfe, J.C. 1939. *Ammianus Marcellinus: History*, vol. 3, bks 27–31, *Excerpta Valesiana*. Loeb Classical Library 331. Cambridge, MA: Harvard University Press.

Roller, M. 2011. "Culture-Based Approaches." In *The Oxford Handbook of Roman Studies*, edited by A. Barchiesi and W. Scheidel, 234–49. Oxford: Oxford University Press.

Roselaar, S.T. 2010. *Public Land in the Roman Republic: A Social and Economic History of Ager Publicus in Italy, 396–89 BC*. Oxford: Oxford University Press.

Rosenstein, N. 2004. *Rome at War: Farms, Families, and Death in the Middle Republic*. Chapel Hill: North Carolina University Press.

Rostovtzeff, M. 1957. *The Social and Economic History of the Roman Empire*. Oxford: Clarendon Press.

Roth, J. 1994. "The Size and Organization of the Roman Imperial Legion." *Historia* 43: 346–62.

Rüpke, J. 2008. Fasti Sacerdotum: *A Prosopography of Pagan, Jewish, and Christian Religious Officials in the City of Rome, 300 BC to AD 499*. Oxford: Oxford University Press.

Russell, D.A., trans. 2002.Reproduced by permission of the publishers and the Trustees of the Loeb Classical Library from *Quintillan: Volume I*, Loeb Classical Library, Volume 124, edited and translated by Donald A. Russell, 2002, by the President and Fellows of Harvard College. Loeb Classical Library ® is a registered trademark of the President and Fellows of Harvard College. Cambridge, MA: Harvard University Press.

Rutledge, S.H. 2001. *Imperial Inquisitions: Prosecutors and Informants from Tiberius to Domitian*. London and New York: Routledge.

Saastamoinen, A. 2000. "The Literary Character of Frontinus' De aquaeductu." In *Technology, Ideology, Water: From Frontinus to the Renaissance and Beyond*, edited by C. Bruun and A. Saastamoinen, 15–40. Rome: Acta Instituti Romani Finlandiae.

Sablayrolles, R. 1996. *Libertinus miles: Les cohortes de vigiles*. Rome: École française de Rome.

Saller, R. 1980. "Anecdotes as Historical Evidence for the Principate." *Greece & Rome* 27 (1): 69–83.

———. 1984. "*Familia, Domus* and the Roman Conception of the Family." *Phoenix* 38 (4): 336–55.

———. 1994. *Patriarchy, Property, and Death in the Roman Family*. Cambridge: Cambridge University Press.

———. 1999. "*Pater Familias, Mater Familias,* and the Gendered Semantics of the Roman Household." *Classical Philology* 94 (2): 182–97.

———. 2003. "Women, Slaves, and the Economy of the Roman Household." In *Early Christian Families in Context: An Interdisciplinary Dialogue*, edited by D. Balch and C. Osiek, 185–204. Grand Rapids, MI: William B. Eerdmans Publishing Company.

Sandwell, I. 2005. "Outlawing Magic or Outlawing Religion? Libanius and the Theodosian Code as Evidence for Legislation against Pagan Practices in the Fourth Century AD." In *Understanding the Spread of Christianity in the First Four Centuries*, edited by W.V. Harris, 87–123. Leiden, The Netherlands: Brill.

Santangelo, F. 2011. "*Pax deorum* and Pontiffs." In *Priests and State in the Roman World*, edited by J.H. Richardson and F. Santangelo, 161–86. Stuttgart, Germany: Franz Steiner.

Sartre, M. 2000. "Syria and Arabia." In *The High Empire, A.D. 70–192*, 2nd edn, edited by A.K. Bowman, P. Garnsey, and D. Rathbone, 635–63. The Cambridge Ancient History, vol. 11. Cambridge: Cambridge University Press.

Scheid, J. 2003. *An Introduction to Roman Religion*. Edinburgh: Edinburgh University Press.

Scheidel, W. 1995. "The Most Silent Women of Greece and Rome: Rural Labour and Women's Life in the Ancient World (I)." *Greece & Rome* 42 (2): 202–17.

———. 1996a. "The Most Silent Women of Greece and Rome: Rural Labour and Women's Life in the Ancient World (II)." *Greece & Rome* 43 (1): 1–10.

———. 1996b. "The Demography of the Roman Imperial Army." In *Measuring Sex, Age and Death in the Roman Empire*, edited by W. Scheidel, 95–138. *Journal of Roman Archaeology* Supplementary Series 21. Portsmouth, RI: *Journal of Roman Archaeology*.

———. 1997. 'Quantifying the Sources of Slaves in the Early Roman Empire.' *Journal of Roman Studies* 87: 156–69.

———. 2001a. "Progress and Problems in Roman Demography." In *Debating Roman Demography*, edited by W. Scheidel, 1–81. Leiden, The Netherlands: Brill.

———. 2001b. "Roman Age Structure: Evidence and Model." *Journal of Roman Studies* 2001: 1–26.

———. 2004. "Human Mobility in Roman Italy I: The Free Population." *Journal of Roman Studies* 94: 1–26.

———. 2005. "Human Mobility in Roman Italy II: The Slave Population." *Journal of Roman Studies* 95: 64–79.

———. 2007a. "Demography." In *The Cambridge Economic History of the Greco-Roman World*, edited by W. Scheidel, I. Morris, and R. Saller, 38–112. Cambridge: Cambridge University Press.

————. 2007b. "Roman Funerary Commemoration and the Age at First Marriage." *Classical Philology* 102 (4): 389–402.

————. 2011. "The Roman Slave Supply." In *The Ancient Mediterranean World*, edited by K. Bradley and P. Cartledge, 287–310. The Cambridge World History of Slavery, vol. 1. Cambridge: Cambridge University Press.

Schmidt, W. 1899. *Herons von Alexandria Druckwerke und Automatentheater*, vol. 1. Leipzig, Germany: Teubner.

Schofield, R., trans. 2006. *Vitruvius: On Architecture*. London: Penguin.

Schultz, C.E. 2006. *Women's Religious Activity in the Roman Republic*. Chapel Hill: University of North Carolina Press.

Scott Ryberg, I. 1955. *Rites of the State Religion in Roman Art*. Memoirs of the American Academy in Rome 22. Rome: American Academy in Rome.

Scullard, H.H. 1981. *Festivals and Ceremonies of the Roman Republic*. Ithaca, NY: Cornell University Press.

Shackleton Bailey, D.R., trans. 1993. Reproduced by permission of the publishers and the Trustees of the Loeb Classical Library from *Martial: Epigrams*, 3 vols. 1993, pages 109, 171, 177, Cambridge MA.: Harvard University Press 1939 by the President and Fellows of Harvard College. Loeb Classical Library ® is a registered trademark of the President and Fellows of Harvard College.

————, ed. and trans. 1999. Reproduced by permission of the publishers and the Trustees of the Loeb Classical Library from *Letter to Atticus*, 4 vols., pages 25–27, Cambridge Mass.: Harvard University Press 1999 by the President and Fellows of Harvard College. Loeb Classical Library ® is a registered trademark of the President and Fellows of Harvard College.

Sharp, M. 1999. "Shearing Sheep: Rome and the Collection of Taxes in Egypt, 30 BC–AD 200." In *Lokale Autonomie und römische Ordnungsmacht in den kaiserzeitlichen Provinzen vom 1. bis 3. Jahrhundert*, edited by W. Eck, 213–42. Munich: Oldenbourg.

Shatzman, I. 1975. *Senatorial Wealth and Roman Politics*. Brussels: Latomus.

Shaw, B. 1982. "Social Sciences and Ancient History." *Helios* 9 (2): 17–57.

————. 1984. "Bandits in the Roman Empire." *Past & Present* 105 (1): 3–52.

————. 1992. "Under Russian Eyes." *Journal of Roman Studies* 82: 216–28.

————. 2001. "Raising and Killing Children: Two Roman Myths." *Mnemosyne* 54 (1): 31–77.

Shelton, J., ed. 1998. *As the Romans Did: A Sourcebook in Roman Social History*, 2nd edn. Oxford: Oxford University Press.

Sherwin-White, A.N. 1980. *The Roman Citizenship*, 2nd edn. Oxford: Clarendon Press.

Shumka, L. 1993. "Children and Toys in the Roman World: A Contribution to the History of the Roman Family." MA thesis, University of Victoria.

Sigismund Nielsen, H. 1996. "The Physical Context of Roman Epitaphs and the Structure of the Roman Family." *Analecta Romana Instituti Danici* 23: 35–60.

————. 2001. "The Value of Epithets in Pagan and Christian Epitaphs from Rome." In *Childhood, Class and Kin in the Roman World*, edited by Susanne Dixon, 165–177. London and New York: Routledge.

————. 2007. "Children for Profit and Pleasure." In *Age and Aging in the Roman Empire*, edited by M. Harlow and R. Laurence, 37–54. *Journal of Roman Archaeology* Supplementary Series 65. Portsmouth, RI: *Journal of Roman Archaeology*.

Simonsen, K. 2003. "Winter Sailing." *Mouseion* 3 (3): 259–68.

Slager, C. 2012. *The Mad Reviewer*. 10 March. http://carrieslager.wordpress.com/2012/03/10/the-hunger-games-and-ancient-rome.

Snell, D.C. 2011. "Slavery in the Ancient Near East." In *The Ancient Mediterranean World*, edited by K. Bradley and P. Cartledge, 4–21. The Cambridge World History, vol. 1. Cambridge: Cambridge University Press.

Southern, P., and Dixon, K. 1996. *The Late Roman Army*. London and New York: Routledge.

Stallibrass, S., and R. Thomas. 2008. *Feeding the Roman Army: The Archaeology of Production and Supply in NW Europe*. Oxford: Oxbow Books.

Ste. Croix, G.E.M. de. 2006. *Christian Persecution, Martyrdom, and Orthodoxy*. Oxford: Oxford University Press.

Stewart, P. 2008. *The Social History of Roman Art*. Cambridge: Cambridge University Press.

Storey, G.R. 2004. "The Meaning of 'Insula' in Roman Residential Terminology." *Memoirs of the American Academy in Rome* 49: 47–84.

Syme, R. 1939. *The Roman Revolution*. Oxford: Clarendon Press.

Tanner, J. 2000. "Portraits, Power, and Patronage in the Late Roman Republic." *Journal of Roman Studies* 90: 18–50.

Tatum, W.J. 2007. "The Character of Marcus Licinius Crassus." In *Spartacus: Film and History*, edited by M. Winkler, 128–43. Oxford: Blackwell.

Tcherikover, V.A., A. Fuks, and M. Stern, eds. 1964. *Corpus Papyrorum Judaicarum*, vol. 3. Cambridge, MA: Harvard University Press.

Tchernia, A. 1983. "Italian Wine in Gaul at the End of the Republic." In *Trade in the Ancient Economy*, edited by P. Garnsey, K. Hopkins, and C.R. Whittaker, 87–104. Berkeley: University of California Press.

Tomlin, R.S.O. 1988. "The Curse Tablets." In *The Temple of Sulis Minerva at Bath*, vol. 2, edited by B. Cunliffe, 59–277. Oxford: Oxbow.

Toner, J. 2009. *Popular Culture in Ancient Rome*. Cambridge: Polity.

Toynbee, J.M.C. 1971. *Death and Burial in the Roman World*. Ithaca, NY: Cornell University Press.

Treggiari, S. 1975. "Roman Social History: Recent Interpretations." *Histoire Sociale/Social History* 8: 149–64.

———. 1991. *Roman Marriage: Iusti Coniuges From the Time of Cicero to the Time of Ulpian*. Oxford: Clarendon Press.

———. 2002. *Roman Social History*. London and New York: Routledge.

Trudel, M. 1960. *L'Esclavage au Canada français: Histoire et conditions de l'esclavage*. Ste Foy: Presses de l'Université Laval.

Trümper, M. 2009. *Graeco-Roman Slave Markets: Fact or Fiction?* Oxford: Oxbow.

Turcan, R. 1988. *Religion romaine*. Vol. 1, *Les dieux*. Vol. 2, *Le culte*. Iconography of Religions 17: Greece and Rome 1. Leiden, The Netherlands: Brill.

Usher, A.P. 1954. *A History of Mechanical Inventions*. Cambridge: Dover.

Usher, S., trans. 1985. *Dionysius of Halicarnassus: Critical Essays*, vol. 2. Loeb Classical Library 466. Cambridge, MA: Harvard University Press.

van Rompay, L. 2005. "Society and Community in the Christian East." In *The Cambridge Companion to the Age of Justinian*, edited by M. Maas, 239–66. Cambridge: Cambridge University Press.

Várhelyi, Z. 2010. *The Religion of Senators in the Roman Empire: Power and the Beyond*. Cambridge: Cambridge University Press.

Varone, A. 2002. Erotica Pompeiana: *Love Inscriptions on the Walls of Pompeii*. Translated by Ria P. Berg, with revisions by D. Harwood and R. Ling. Rome: L'Erma di Bretschneider.

Versluys, M. 2002. Aegyptiaca Romana: *Nilotic Scenes and the Roman Views of Egypt*. Leiden, The Netherlands: Brill.

Versnel, H.S. 2010. "Prayers for Justice, East and West: New Finds and Publications since 1990." In *Magical Practice in the Latin West*, edited by R. Gordon and F.M. Simón, 275–354. Religions in the Graeco-Roman World 168. Leiden, The Netherlands: Brill.

Ville, Georges. 1981. *La gladiature en occident des origines à la mort de Domitien*. Rome: École Française de Rome.

Vuolanto, V. 2003. "Selling a Freeborn Child: Rhetoric and Social Realities in the Late Roman World." *Ancient Society* 33: 169–207.

Wahl, J. 2010. "Slavery in the United States." http://eh.net/encyclopedia/article/wahl.slavery.us.

Wallace, S.L. 1938. *Taxation in Egypt from Augustus to Diocletian*. Princeton, NJ: Princeton University Press.

Wallace-Hadrill, A. 1993. *Augustan Rome*. London: Bristol Classical Press.

———. 1994. *Houses and Society in Pompeii and Herculaneum*. Princeton, NJ: Princeton University Press.

———. 2003. "*Domus* and *Insulae* in Rome: Families and Housefuls." In *Early Christian Families in Context: An Interdisciplinary Dialogue*, edited by D. Balch and C. Osiek, 3–18. Grand Rapids, MI: William B. Eerdmans Publishing Company.

Watson, G.R. 1969. *The Roman Soldier*. Ithaca, NY: Cornell University Press.

Weaver, P. 1972. Familia Caesaris: *A Social Study of the Emperor's Freedmen and Slaves*. Cambridge: Cambridge University Press.

Welch, K. 2007. *The Roman Amphitheatre From its Origins to the Colosseum*. Cambridge: Cambridge University Press.

White, K.D. 1984. *Greek and Roman Technology*. Ithaca, NY: Cornell University Press.

White, P. 1993. *Promised Verse: Poets in the Society of Augustan Rome*. Cambridge, MA: Harvard University Press.

Whittaker, C.R. 1994. *Frontiers of the Roman Empire: A Social and Economic Study*. Baltimore: Johns Hopkins University Press.

———. 1997. "Moses Finley, 1912–1986." *Proceedings of the British Academy* 94: 459–72.

Wiedemann, T. 1981. *Greek and Roman Slavery*. London and New York: Routledge.

———. 1989. *Adults and Children in the Roman Empire*. London and New York: Routledge.

———. 1992. *Emperors and Gladiators*. London and New York: Routledge.

Williams, C. 2010. *Roman Homosexuality: Ideologies of Masculinity in Classical Antiquity*, 2nd edn. Oxford: Oxford University Press.

Wilson, A. 2001. "Timgad and Textile Production." In *Economies beyond Agriculture in the Classical World*, edited by D.J. Mattingly and J. Salmon, 271–96. London and New York: Routledge.

———. 2008a. "Large-Scale Manufacturing, Standardization, and Trade." In *The Oxford*

Handbook of Engineering and Technology in the Classical World, edited by J.P. Oleson, 393–417. Oxford: Oxford University Press.

——. 2008b. "Economy and Trade." In *Roman Europe*, edited by E. Bispham, 170–202. Oxford: Oxford University Press.

——, and D. Robinson. 2011. "Introduction: Maritime Archaeology and the Ancient Economy." In *Maritime Archaeology and Ancient Trade in the Mediterranean*, edited by D. Robinson and A. Wilson, 1–13. Oxford: Oxford Centre for Maritime Archaeology.

Wilson-Jones, M. 2000. *Principles of Roman Architecture*. New Haven, CT: Yale University Press.

Winkler, M., ed. 2001. "The Roman Empire in the American Cinema after 1945." In *Imperial Projections: Ancient Rome in Modern Popular Culture*, edited by S. Joshel, M. Malamud, and D. McGuire Jr, 50–76. Baltimore: Johns Hopkins University Press.

——, ed. 2004. *Gladiator: Film and History*. Oxford: Blackwell.

——, ed. 2007. *Spartacus: Film and History*. Oxford: Blackwell.

Winks, R. 1971. *The Blacks in Canada: A History*. Montreal: McGill-Queens University Press.

Winner, D. 2005. "A Blow to the Temples." *Financial Times* 28 Jan.

Woolf, G. 1992. "Imperialism, Empire and the Integration of the Roman Economy." *World Archaeology* 23 (3): 283–93.

——. 1998. *Becoming Roman: The Origins of Provincial Civilization in Gaul*. Cambridge: Cambridge University Press.

Wright, F.A., trans. 1933. *Jerome: Select Letters*. Loeb Classical Library 262. Cambridge, MA: Harvard University Press.

Wulf Rheidt, U., and N. Sojc. 2009. "Evoluzione strutturale del Palatino sud-orientale in epoca flavia (Domus Augustana, Domus Severiana, stadio)." In *Divus Vespasianus. Il bimillenario dei Flavi*, edited by F. Coarelli, 268–79. Naples: Electa.

Wyke, M. 1997. *Projecting the Past: Ancient Rome, Cinema and History*. London and New York: Routledge.

Yakobson, A. 2009. "Public Opinion, Foreign Policy, and 'Just War' in the Late Republic." In *Diplomats and Diplomacy in the Roman World*, edited by C. Eilers, 45–72. Leiden, The Netherlands: Brill.

Young, G.K. 2001. *Rome's Eastern Trade: International Commerce and Imperial Policy, 31 BC–AD 305*. London and New York: Routledge.

Zanker, P. 1998. *Pompeii: Public and Private Life*. Translated by D.L. Schneider. Cambridge, MA: Harvard University Press.

Zarmakoupi, M., ed. 2010. *The Villa of the Papyri at Herculaneum: Archaeology, Reception, and Digital Reconstruction*. Sozomena: Studies in the Recovery of Ancient Texts, edited on behalf of the Herculaneum Society, 1. Berlin: Walter de Gruyter.

Zehnacker, H. 1980. "*Uncarium fenus* (Tacitus, *Annales*, VI, 16)." In *Mélanges de literature et d'épigraphie latines, d'histoire ancienne et d'archéologie: hommage à la mémoire de Pierre Wuilleumier*, 353–62. Paris: Belles Lettres.

Index

———◦———

Page numbers in *italics* indicate illustrations.

Achaea, 27, 315
Adam, Jean-Pierre, 362
ad digitum ("to the finger"), 276–77, 419
adoption, 106
Adrianople, 311, 312, 324, 326
adultery, 104, 172–73, 185; Augustus's laws, 105–6, 184
aediles, 26, 61, 227, 228–29, 251, 266, 419
Aemilius Paullus Macedonicus, Lucius, 106, 311
Aeneas, 25, 152
aerarium militare (military treasury), 294, 419
Aesculapius, cult of, 207
Aesop, 66
Africa, 315
aggregate, 366, 368, 369, 384
agones, 265, 269, 270, 419
agriculture, 346; women and, 17
Agrippa, Marcus, 33, 34, 392; Attica (wife), 128; Gaius (son), 34; Lucius (son), 34
Alconétar Bridge, 363
Alexander, Severus, 42, 322; Julia Mamaea (wife), 322
Alexander the Great, 156, 307, 318
alimenta, 38
alphabet, learning the, 121, 122
American South: slave-owning society, 74
amicitia ("friendship"), 154, 310–11, 419
Ammianus Marcellinus: *History*, 325
amphitheatre, 61, 273, 391, 419
amphorae, 348, 349, 398, 419
anachronism, 15
Andronicus, Livius, 146, 147
Angélique, Marie-Joseph, 86–87
animal husbandry, 346
Annales d'histoire économique et sociale, 3
Annales School, 3
L'Année épigraphique, 199, 278
Antinous (Hadrian's lover), 394
Antioch, 323
Antiochus, 313
Antonine plague, 73, 76, 330, 334
Antonine Wall, 39, 320
Antoninus Pius, 39, 320
Antonius, Marcus. *See* Marc Antony
Apollodorus of Damascus, 373, 395
apotropaic images and objects, 173–74, 178, 419
Appian, 79, 315

appointments, 237
apprenticeship, 129, 134; *tirocinium fori* ("recruitment to the forum"), 128
Apuleius: *Metamorphoses*, or *The Golden Ass*, 88, 146, 301
aqueducts, 359, 368–69, 419; decline in use, 370; length and width, 369; maintenance, 368; origins, 368–69
Aquileia, 323
Arabia, 38
Arabs, 325, 326
Ara Pacis ("Altar of Peace"), 386–87, *387*, 419
archaeological evidence, xxix, 19, 332
archaeology, xxix
arches, 363
Archimedes, 312
architecture, 375, 378, 382–83; in Augustan period, 385–90; Greek influence on, 382–83; orders, 382–83, 388–89; material evidence of, 378, *379*; responses to economic and social change, 395–99; study of, 378–80; timeline of, *379*; villas, 396–97; *see also specific buildings*
architectus, 358, 419
architrave, 388, 419
Arch of Constantine, 398
Arch of Titus, 319, 392
Archpoet, 146
Ardashir, 322
Aristodemus of Nysa, 122
Armenia, 38, 39, 40, 319, 320, 323
Arminius, 34
army, 29, 286, 304, 403; under Augustus, 33–34; auxiliaries, 287, 289–92, 294, 297, 303, 318, 420; bases, *297*, 298; civilians and, 300–302; class divisions in, 49; composition of, 287–94; under Constantine, 323; construction of marching camps, 297; under Diocletian, 323; as *distinct society*, 303; film depictions, 285–86, 288; heterogeneity of, 293–94; legions, 31, 287–89, 294, 303, 426; logistics and communication, 296; negative perceptions of, 303; praetorian guard, 41, 251, 252, 287, 292–93, 430–31; professionalization, 294–95; recruitment standards, 294; resources for, 297; response time, 297; size of, 220; society and, 300–303; soldiers' discipline, 298; successes of,

299, 326; timeline, 286; training, 294, 296; urban
cohorts, 251–52; women and families and, 301–2
ars, 358
art, 378; in Augustan period, 385–90; depiction of
Christian scenes, 399; economic and social change
and, 395–99; frontality, 399, 424; Greek influence,
400; material evidence of, 378, 379; mosaics
and wall paintings, *209*, 210, 373, 381–82,
382; portrait sculpture, 383–84, 386, 393–94;
representations of sexuality, 166; study of, 378–80;
timeline of, 379
artifacts, collections of sexually explicit, 167–69
artifex, 358
artistic evidence. *See* iconographic evidence
artists: attitudes towards, 378
Arval Brothers, 419; protocol of, 191–94, 196, 197;
protocol for sacrifice, 195–96, 198; vows of, 194–
95, 201, 204, 212
Asellio, Aulus Sempronius, 339
Asia (Roman province), 28, 315
Assyria, 38, 39
Atellanae fabulae, 268, 419
athletes: attitudes towards, 270–71
athletic contest (*athletarum certamen*), 270, 420
atlases, 416–17
Attalus III of Pergamum, 28
Atticus, 121, 122, 124
augur(es), 197, 201, 420, 201
Augustan period, 25; art and architecture in, 385–90;
religion in, 200
Augusti, 42–43
Augustine, 126, 146; *Confessions*, 126
Augustus (Octavian), 25, 32–33, 33–34, 58, 124,
145, 151, 194, 236, 238, 289, 318; adultery laws
of, 105–6, 172–73, 184; citizenship reforms,
54; conflict with Marc Antony, 317; *The Deeds of
the Divine Augustus*, 35, 388; descendents of, 35;
efforts to define social strata, 60; establishment of
praetorian guard, 292; foreign relations of, 318;
Livia (wife), 35, 101, 386; military forces and,
33–34, 251, 252, 294; as *pontifex maximus*, 203;
purges of the senate, 59; religion and, 33; religious
offices held by, 201; statues and depictions of, 386;
succession after, 34–35; system of taxation under,
341; *tribunicia potestas* ("tribunician power"),
235–36; writers and, 156–57
Augustus of Prima Porta, *318*, 318, 386
Aurelian, 323
auriga (charioteer), 272, 420
Ausonius, 357
auspicium (*auspicia*), 201–2, 420

Bacchus, cult of, 205, 211, 248
Bacon, Roger, 360

Badian, Ernst, 12
Baelo Claudia, basilica at, 397, *397*
bakeries, 372
Balkans, 315
banausic principle, 373
barbarians, 308, 324, 326
Bar Kokhba War, 39, 320
Barrow, R.H., 6; *The Romans*, 5
Bassianus (Caracalla), son of Severus, 41–42
Bassus, Junius: sarcophagus of, 399
battles, 298; Battle of Actium, 33, 145, 317; Battle of
Cannae, 299, 312; Battle of Pydna, 27; Battle of
Teutoburg Forest, 34; Battle of Ticinus, 312; Battle
of Zama, 27
behaviour, appropriate, 64; citizenship and, 79;
marriage and, 103
bellum iustum ("just war"), 309–10, 311, 313, 420
Bloch, Marc, 3
Bloomer, W. Martin, 131
Boscoreale Cups, 389–90
boxers, 270, 420
boys: abandonment of, 104; age of marriage, 98;
education of, 119, 120, 121, 122, 124, 126, 128,
129, 134, 135; sexual relations with, 183, 185;
teachers and, 133
Bradley, K., 121; "'The Regular, Daily Traffic in Slaves':
Roman History and Contemporary History, 11
bridges, 362–63
brigandage, 242–43, 244, 252, 253, 256, 420
Britain, 41
British Museum: *secretum* ("secret museum"), 168
brothels, xxx, xxxii, 178, 302
Brundt, Peter, 14
Brutus, Marcus Junius, 15, 23, 32
builders: attitudes towards, 378
buildings, 380; for *ludi*, 266–68; concrete and, 384–
85; for slaves, 81; *see also* architecture
Bulla (brigand), 241–42, 243, 253
Bulwer-Lytton, Edward: *The Last Days of Pompeii*, xxix
burglaries, 256
burials, 94–95
Byzantine Empire, 238, 325

Cabinet of Obscene Objects (Reserved Cabinet), 167
Caecilius, Quintus, 340
Caecus, Appius Claudius, 230, 361, 368
Caesar, Julius. *See* Julius Caesar
Caesar, Lucius Aelius, 39
Caesares, 42–43
Caligula (Gaius Julius Caesar), 31, 35–36, 89–90,
295, 302
Callebat, Louis, 359
Callimachus, 144, 145; *Aetia*, 144
Callistratus, 250

Campus Martius, 128, 212, 266, 270, 386, 420; sundial and obelisk at, 387

canabae, 300, 420

capite censi ("counted by head"), 220

Capitolia, 270

Capitoline Hill, 191, 212, 380

Capitoline Triad, 196, 234, 279, 420

Capua, 311

Caracalla, 50, 321–22

Carcopino, Jérôme, 6–7; *Daily Life in Ancient Rome*, 4

Carthage, 270; conflict with Rome, 27, 310, 311, 326, 364; sack of, 313, 315

cartoons, 405–6

Cassius, Avidius, 40, 320

Cassius Longinus, Gaius, 32, 84

Cassius Dio, 41, 241–42, 264, 281, 293, 303, 307, 322, 345

castellum divisorium (primary distribution basin), 369, 420

Catallus, 58–59, 143–44, 145, 257; *Poems*, 183, 257

cataphracts, 291, 306n19, 420

Cato the Elder, 124, 132–33, 315

Cato the Younger, 99–100

Celer (architect), 373

censors, 26, 59, 221, 222, 223, 227–28, 234, 420

census, 33, 76, 333, 421

Centuriate Assembly. *See comitia centuriata* (Centuriate Assembly)

centuries, 219–20

Ceres, 200, 234, 266

Commentarii Fratrum Arvalium qui supersunt, 192–93

chariots and chariot racing, 265, 271, 271–72, 361, 421

children: abandonment of, 79–80; depictions of, 386; education of, 118, 120–34; exposure, 104, 106; fathers' right to kill adult, 104; legitimate versus illegitimate, 98; mortality, 80, 106; responsibilities to *familia*, 106–7; slave childminders' influence over, 133; of slaves, 79; work performed by, 107

chorobatēs ("land walker"), 370–71, 421

Christianity, 73, 88, 146, 198, 253, 288; in art, 399; Constantine and, 43, 323–24; missionaries, 324

Cicero, 32, 128, 149, 181, 199, 227, 233, 270, 281, 340, 345; on agriculture, 336; as augur, 202; career of, 150–51; children of, 121; death of, 151; on education, 122, 132; on influence of Greek literary practices, 149–50; on libraries and visiting scholars, 121; Marcus (son), 122, 124; oratorical attack on Marc Antony, 16; on oratory, 120; on professions, 378; Quintus (brother) marriage to Pomponia, 101, 102; Quintus (son), 124; on religious officials, 200; on taxation, 340; Terentia (wife), 100, 101; Tullio (daughter), 104, 122. Works: *In Defence of Sextus Roscius of America*, 250; *Letters to Atticus*, 102; *On Duties (De officiis)*,

98, 329–30, 337; *On the Nature of the Gods*, 232; *Philippics*, 151; *Republic*, 221

Cilicia, 28, 315

cinaedus (cinaedi), 173, 182, 186, 421

Circus Maximus, 265, 266, 271, 391, 421

citizenship, Roman, 29, 50, 51, 55; appropriate behaviour and, 59; Augustus's reforms, 54; granted to allies, 222–23; impact on lifestyle, 61; social mobility and, 58; veterans and, 291–92

Clarke, John R., 173, 177, 178

class, 48, 49–50, 67, 421; changes over time, 52–57; education and, 119; importance of, 61–65; land ownership and, 335; timeline of, 47; *see also* status

classis, 49

Claudius, 35, 36, 295, 319

Cleopatra, Queen of Egypt, 32, 317

clientes, 65, 154

Clodius Albinus, 41

cognitio (cognitiones) ("inquiry"), 248, 249, 421

coins, xxx–xxxi; commemorating Caesar's assassination, 15–16; introduction of, 331

Coleman, Kathleen, 406, 407

colleges, priestly, 191, 200–201, 421

Colosseum, 36, 265, 273–74, 274, 359, 390–91, 421

Columella, 79, 83, 87, 340

Column of Marcus Aurelius, 393

comitia centuriata (Centuriate Assembly), 49–50, 220, 222, 224, 421; classes of, 221

comitia curia (Curial Assembly), 224–25

comitia tributa (Tribal Assembly), 221–23, 224, 421; new citizens and, 222–23

Commodus, 40, 41, 293, 321

concepts: lack of consistent definitions of, 13–14

concilium plebis tributum (Tribal Assembly of Plebians), 53, 223–24, 229, 235, 421–22, 434

concordia, 101, 422

concrete, 363, 366–68, 375, 384–85, 404, 422; ability to set underwater, 368, 384

concubinage, 102–3, 422

conquest, 307–9, 403; consequences of, 315–17; end of Republic and, 315–17; to end of Second Punic War, 309–13; impact of, 308; importance of, 307, 325–26; *pax Romana* and, 318–21; in second century BCE, 313–15; in third century CE, 321–25; timeline of, 308; *see also* expansion

Constantine, 25, 43, 80, 308, 323–24

Constantine XI Palaeologus, 238

Constantinople, 308, 325

Constantius, 42, 43

Constantius Chlorus, 323

Constitutio Antoniniana, 42

construction: concrete and, 366–68; human factor, 373; *see also* architecture

constructivism, 169–70, 422

consuls, 26, 53, 83, 226, 227, 229–31, 232, 233, 311, 422, 430; authority and duties of, 229–30; *consules ordinarii*, 229; *consul suffectus*, 230; legal benefits of, 105; length of term, 231; *pro consule*, 231
controversiae, 422
contubernium (*contubernia*), 85, 103, 422
conubium, 76–77, 98, 422
conventus ("tours of inspection"), 248, 422
Corbeill, Anthony, 131
Corinth, 28; sack of, 313, 315
Cornelian Laws (*leges Corneliae*), 247
Cornelii family, 106
cornice, 388, 422
Corpus Inscriptionum Latinarum, 61, 199, 208, 269, 273, 280
Corpus Inscriptionum Semiticarum, 207
corvus, 364, 422
Cotta, 288
courts, 246, 248–49, 258; abuses of, 248–49; quality of justice of, 249
craftspeople, 332, 344, 356, 359, 373, 375
cranes, 372–73
Crassus, Marcus Licinius, 31, 124, 316
Cribiore, Raffaella, 121, 123, 133
crime, 243–48; community defence, 256–58; definition of, 246; delicts (*delicta*), 247–48, 258; documentary sources of, 245–46; as intellectual or cultural category, 246–48; of political nature, 246; prevention, 255–56; rates of, 244–45; reports of, 244; self-defence, 256; as social phenomenon, 243–46, 258; of theft, 247; Twelve Tables and, 77–78, 230–31, 246, 256, 434; types of, 243–44
cross-cultural comparisons, 14–15
crucifixion, 249, 250
cult niches: in houses, 209–10
cultural exchange: study of, 10–11
cultural studies, 3
culture: defining Roman, 380–85; Greek, 144–45, 147–49, 149–50, 153, 160, 380–81, 382–83, 400
curiae, 223, 224, 225
cursing, 189–90, 211–13
cursus honorum ("sequence of offices"), 30, 228, 312, 422
Cybele, 147, 148
Cyrenaica, 315, 326
Cyrene, 28

Dacia, 38, 319
damnati (convicted criminals), 274, 275, 422
damnatio ad bestias (convicts devoured by wild beasts), 275, 422
damnatio memoriae, 38, 40, 422–23
Danube frontier, 40
Das Archiv des Petaus, 343

databases: of artistic and archaeological material, 416; bibliographic, 418
Decebalus (king of Dacia), 319
decemviri, 230
decimation, 298, 423
Decius, 234, 322
decurions, 52, 423
defixiones, 189, 190, 212
deities, 196; communication with, 195; in daily life, 205–6; in domestic settings, 209–10, 210–11; guardian, 210; in Rome, 209; success of Rome and, 197; triad (Ceres, Liber, and Libera), 224, 234; *see also specific deities*
delator (*delatores*), 172, 249, 423
Delos, island of, 80, 348
demography, 333–34
demons, 173
Demosthenes, 151
Dentatus, Manius Curius, 231
deracination, 82, 423
determinism versus voluntarism debate, 170, 423
dictators, 227, 236, 311, 423
dictionaries, 416; topographical, 416–17
Digest, 108, 288
Digest of Justinian, 74
Dill, Samuel: *Roman Society from Nero to Marcus Aurelius*, 4
Di Manes, 207–8, 208–9, 423
Dio Chrysostom, 122
Diocletian, 42, 323
Diodorus Siculus, 348
Dionysius, Marcus Pomponius, 124
Dionysius of Halicarnassus, 23, 77, 123, 332
dioptra (theodolite), 370, 371, 423
divinization, 196
divorce, 99, 100, 101–2, 172, 185
dominate, 45n2
Domitian, 37, 38, 158, 192, 212, 234, 270, 333, 392
Domus Aurea ("Golden House"), 274, 367, 390, 391, 423
domus ("family"), 97, 423
Dover, Kenneth: *Greek Homosexuality*, 168
drama, 5, 148, 268, 423; competitions (*agones*), 269
Drusus, Nero, 34
Dura-Europos, 40, 320, 399, 423; city walls, 321; new citadel, 321

Eastern Empire, 238, 325; *see also* Byzantine Empire
economy, Roman, 331, 349–50; agrarian nature of, 331; Cicero on, 329–30; demography and, 333–34; evidence of, 331–32; land and property, 334–38; modernist versus primitivist perspective, 332–33; moneylending and interest rates, 338–40; papyrological evidence, 332; Plutarch on, 330;

production and trade, 344–49; study of, 332–33; taxation, 340–44; timeline of, 330

education, 118–19, 403; apprenticeship, 129; class and status and, 128, 129, 132, 134; copying exercises, 123; early, 120–24, 134; *enkyklios paideai* ("common/general education"), 132; ethical and moral dimensions of, 130–35; evidence of, 119–20; *grammaticē*, 124–26, 131, 134; handwriting, 122; learning the alphabet, 121, 122; *liberalia studia* ("liberal studies"), 132; literature and, 142; military training, 128; open-air, 122; parental involvement in, 132–33; play and, 121; *progymnasmata*, 127; reading, 123; replication of social system, 131–32; rhetoric, 126–29, 131, 142; of slaves, 123–24; sources for investigating, 134; syllabic sets, 122–23; timeline of, 118; use of maxims and sayings, 123, 130–31

Egypt, xxx, 34; papyrological evidence from, xxxii; textiles from, 349

Elagabalus, 42, 322

elected officials. *See magistrates*

Electoral College (in US), 404

emperors, 33, 238; centrality to literature, 157–58; divine protection and, 212; image in art and architecture, 379–80, 386, 394; literature and, 156–57; material culture and, 379, 390, 400; Roman army and, 295; support for buildings sacred buildings, 199–200; in third century CE, 321–23; worship of, 196–97

empire: expansion of, 147–48, 313–15, 319, 334–35; use of term, xxvi

Empire: foreign relations, 308, 309; land ownership under, 335; shift to, 25; split between east and west, 324–25; transition to, 317, 335; use of term, xxvi, 45n2

Encolpus, Marcus Antonius: tombstone of, 209

encyclopedias, 416

energy: process heat, 371–72; sources of, 357, 371–73; wind, 372

engineering: civil, 357; human factor, 373; knowledge transfer, 358–59; terminology, 357–58; timeline of, 356

engineers, 357–58; derivation of term, 358; prejudice against, 373; skills of, 355

entablature, 388, 423–24

entertainment: history and, 405–7; importance of, 264–65; political importance of, 279–83; public, 265–79, 283; seating at, 60, 282, 391; sources for information about, 264; timeline of, 264; *see also ludi*; *munus (munera)*

epic, 143, 424; Homeric, 131, 152

Epicurus, 150

epigram, 158

epigrammatists, 143, 424

epigraphic evidence, xxxi–xxxii, 19, 94, 332

Epirota, Quinus Caecilius, 124

epitaphs, 94–95, 97–98; dedications to gods, 207–9

equestrians, 34, 52, 53, 54–55, 57, 198, 282, 340, 424

equites, 219, 220, 225

erotic art, 166; destruction of, 166–67; interest in, 168

essentialism, 169, 424

Etruscans, 25–26, 358, 380

euergetism, 340, 424

Euphronious Krater, 381

Eurysaces the Baker, tomb of, 373

evidence, ancient, xxvii–xxxiii; archaeological, xxvii, xxix, 19, 332; of class and status, 49; epigraphic, xxvii, xxxi–xxxii, 19, 94, 332; iconographic (art historical), xxvii, xxix–xxx, 19; literary, xxvii–xxix, 4–5, 7–8, 19, 332; numismatic, xxvii, xxx–xxxi, 19; papyrological, xxvii, xxxii, xxxiii n22, 19

Evil Eye, 173

executions, 249–50, 275

expansion, 27–28, 315; economic impact of, 334–35; invitations from allies and neighbours, 315; new technologies and, 361; under *pax Romana*, 319; in second century BCE, 313–15; trade and, 344; under Trajan, 319; *see also* conquest

expurgation, 167–68, 186

familia, 97, 98, 424

families, 112; versus households, 96–97; slave, 108; *see also* household

fasces, 228, 424

Febvre, Lucien, 3

Festus, 201

fetiales, 309–10, 424

Figulus, Gaius Marcius, 231

Finley, Moses, 4, 9, 11–12, 332, 333; *The Ancient Economy*, 332

Fiorelli, Giuseppe: catalogue of "Pornographic Collection", 167

First Triumvirate, 31, 316

Fitzgerald, William, 409

five good emperors, period of the, 38

Flaccus, Aulus Clodius, 269

flagitatio, 257, 424

flamen dialis, 99; wife of the, 200

Flamininus, Titus Quinctius, 27, 311, 314

Flavian Amphitheatre. *See* Colosseum

Flavian period, 36–37, 158, 319; portrait sculpture in, 393–94

Flavian Woman, 393–94

Flavius Basilius, 231

foederati, 324

food: trade in, 347–48; over sea routes, 365–66

fora vestiaria (clothing markets), 344

Forbes, Christopher, 129

foreign relations: *amicitia* ("friendship"), 310–11; in early and middle Republic periods, 309–13; to end of Second Punic War, 309–13; oversight of the gods, 309–10; *pax Romana*, 318–21; role of *fetiales* in, 309–10; in second century BCE, 313–15; in third century CE, 321–25

forum (fora), 424; Forum, 26, 59, 258, 273; Forum of Augustus, 387, 388; Forum of Julius Caesar, 387, 388; Forum of Trajan, 393

Foucault, Michel: *Histoire de la sexualité*, 168–69

fountains, public, 370

Fowler, W. Warde, 1–2, 6; *Social Life at Rome in the Age of Cicero*, 4

Francesco I, 167

Francheville, François Poulin de, 86

freedman/freedwoman/freedperson. *See libertus(a)*

frescoes, 177, 320, 394, 424

friezes, 388, 424

frontiers, 39, 80, 289, 318, 320, 326, 424

Frontinus, 360, 370

fugituvus/a (fugitivi/ae), 74, 425

funerary commemorations, 94–95, 129, 108; of children, 103

Gabinetto Segreto, 167

Gaius (legal writer), 50, 256

Gaius Verres, 345

Galba, Servius Sulpicius, 36, 249

Galen (doctor), 130

Galerius, 42, 323

Gallia Narbonensis, 315

Gallic Empire, 323

Gallic Wars, 31, 317

Gallicus, Gaius Rutilius, 339

games: annual public, 198; Greek, 269; *see also ludi; munus (munera)*

gender identity, 171, 179, 184, 186, 425

gender roles: constructivist views of, 170

geometry, 370

Germanic tribes, 40, 295, 308, 319, 320, 322, 326; leaders, 324

Germanicus (son of Tiberius), 34, 35, 213

girls: abandonment of, 104; age of marriage, 98, 105, 128; education of, 119, 120, 122, 123, 124, 128–29, 132, 134; sexual misconduct and, 184; *see also* women

Gladiator (film), 285, 288, 406, 407

gladiatorial combats, 273, 274, 276–79; fights to the death, 277–79; officials of, 277; people consulted over, 281–82; rules of, 276–77, 279

gladiators, 40, 59, 270, 276, 425; classifications of, 276; expense of, 278, 279; ranking of, 276; training of, 276; weapons, 276; wounding and killing in combat, 277–79

Gladstone, William, 6

gods. *See* deities

Goths, 322, 324, 326

government, 26, 218–19, 239; criticisms of, 217–18; in early Republic, 26; people's participation in, 236–37; in Republic and early Empire, 217–39; timeline of, 218; voting assemblies, 219–25

Gracchus, Gaius Sempronius, 29, 223, 226; reforms of, 17, 28, 315–16

Gracchus, Tiberius Sempronius, 17, 223, 226, 231, 232, 234, 235; land reforms of, 28

graffiti, xxxi, xxxii, 164, 179, 181

grammaticus (grammaticē), 124–26, 131, 134, 425; areas of study, 126; ethical focus of, 131

Gratian, 324

Greece: athletic games of, 270; conflict with, 27; drama, 268; foreign relations with, 314; influence of culture, 144–45, 147–49, 149–50, 153, 160, 380–81, 382–83, 400; study of history of, 5

groma, 371, 425

gymnasium, 269, 425

Hadrian, 38–39, 63, 320, 394, 400; Roman army and, 295

Hadrian's Villa, 394–95; Poikile, 395; Serapaeum, 395, 395; statues in, 394

Hadrian's Wall, 39, 41, 320

Hamilton, William, Sir, 168

Hannibal, 27, 310, 311, 313

Harris, William, 81

haruspex (haruspices), 196, 201, 202, 203, 425

heating, 371–72

Hemelrijk, Emily, 124

Heraclius, 325

Herculaneum, 167, 255, 370, 425; remains of houses in, 109; Temple of Mater Magna, 205

Herennia, Psyche, 85

Heron of Alexandria, 359–60, 370, 371, 372

highways, 361–62

historia, 18

historical periods: Augustan, 25, 200, 385–90; early imperial, 236–37; early Republic, 26; late Republic period, 17, 28–33, 144–45, 150–52, 159, 236–37, 295; middle Republic, 27–28; Principate, 25, 33, 45n2, 246, 289, 339, 431

history: balanced with entertainment, 405–7; dating periods of, 25; popular culture and, 404–11; new approaches to, 7–11; study of, 18–19; timeline of Roman, 24; traditional approaches to, 4–7

Homer, 126, 131, 152

homosexuality: constructivist views of, 170; debates over causes of, 170; essentialist views of, 169; female, 183–84

honestior (honestiores), 52, 55, 67, 249, 425

Hopkins, Keith, 9, 12, 58, 332; *Conquerors and Slaves: Sociological Studies in Roman History*, 10; "Review: Rules of Evidence", 13

Horace, 58, 144, 148; *Epistle* 2.1 (*Epistle to Augustus*), 156–57; *Odes*, 145, 153

Horatius, Marcus, 224, 230

Hortensius, Quintus, 99–100

household, Roman: complexity of, 112; versus family, 96–97; investigation of, 95–96; physical structures of, 109–12; timeline of, 96

household members and relationships, 98–108; parents and children, 103–7; slaves and freedpersons, 107–8; wives and marriage, 98–103

House of Sallust, 110, 111

House of the Faun, 381–82

House of the Prince of Naples, 110

House of Vettii, xxx, 164, 178

houses, 109–12; atrium/peristyle, 109, *110*, 110–12; crime prevention and, 255–56; cubicula in, 110, 111, 177; libraries and visiting scholars in, 121; public and private spaces in, 110; sexual scenes in, 177–78; sleeping habits in, 111–12, 113; usage of rooms of, 113

Housman, A.E., 168

humilior (*humiliores*), 52, 55, 59, 67, 425

Hunger Games, The (film), 409–10

Huns, 324

Iberia, 323

iconographic (art historical) evidence, xxvii, xxix–xxx, 19

Ides of March, 32

Inscriptiones Latinae Selectae, 295

imperial cult, 55, 197, 200, 216n9, 279

imperialism, 6, 78, 139, 160, 191, 326; culture and literature and, 147–48

imperial residences, 394; privately commissioned art in, 394–95

imperium, 201, 227, 425

infamia ("evil reputation"), 172, 282–83, 425–26

ingenuus/a (*ingenui/ae*), 50, 89, 426

inscriptions: as evidence, xxxi–xxxii; tombstone, 94–95, 97–98

instruments (engineering), 370–71

interest rates, 339–40

interrex ("between kings"), 230, 426

introductions, 417–18

Isis, cult of, 203, 210, 212

Islam, 325

Isthmian Games, 27

iugerum (*iugera*), 28, 426

iuniores ("juniors"), 220

ius Italicum ("Italian right"), 330, 341, 426

ius occidendi, 172, 426

jargon, 13–14

Jerome, 121, 122, 146

Jewish revolt, 319

jokes, 46–47

Josephus: *The Jewish War*, 296

Julian calendar, 32

Julianus, Marcus Didus Severus, 41

Julio-Claudians, 35–36, 319

Julius Caesar, 32, 59, 64, 185, 228, 229, 236, 312, 316, 317; conflict with Pompey, 317; death of, 15, 32, 317; *Gallic Wars*, 298, 299; invasion of Italy, 31–32; as *pontifex maximus*, 201; in power in Rome and Italy, 31–32; religious offices of, 201; writings of, 149

Juno, 191, 196, 210, 279, 420

Jupiter, 196, 198, 201, 205, 210, 279, 280

Jupiter Optimus Maximus, 191, 192, 212, 270

justice system, 402; courts, 248–49; crowd justice, 257–58; payment of damages, 247; punishments, 78, 88, 249–50; quality of, 249; self-help, 255–58; status and access to, 55, 60–61; timeline of, 242; *see also* crime; *leges* (*lex*)

Juvenal, 159, 183; on entertainment, 283; scorn for spectacle, 263, 264; seventh *Satire*, 133–34; sixth *Satire*, 6; on women, 6–7, 132

kinaidos, 181–82

Kitto, H.D.F.: on Athenian women, 5–6; *The Greeks*, 5

Ktesibios, 359

land ownership, 334–35, 349; diversification in, 335; Gracchan reforms to, 17, 28, 315–16; tenancy, 335–37; unequal distribution of, 335; urban property, 336–38

lanista (owner/manager of a troupe of gladiators), 276, 426

lares familiares, 210, 426

Last, Hugh, 8, 11

latifundium (*latifundia*), 79, 316, 426

laudatio Turiae, 7

Laughter-Lover, The (*Philogelos*), 46

law, Roman, 5, 242, 243; slavery and, 74; *see also* crime; *leges* (*lex*); justice system

Lendon, Ted, 298

Lepidus, Marcus Aemilius, 32, 151, 236

Levant, 300

levels and screws, 372–73

lex (*leges*), 426; *leges Corneliae*, 247; *Lex Aelia Sentia*, 90; *lex annalis* ("law on years"), 228; *Lex Aquilia*, 76; *Lex Cornelia Pompeia*, 339; *Lex Domitia*, 200; *Lex Fucia Caninia*, 90; *Lex Genucia*, 339; *Lex Hortensia*, 26; *Lex Iunia de feneratione*, 339; *Lex Julia*, 29; *Lex Julia de adulteriis*, 172; *Lex Licinia Sextia*, 26, 229, 230–31, 235; *Lex Poetelia Papiria*,

77; *Lex Publilia*, 223; *lex pugnandi*, 277, 426; *Lex Roscia*, 60; *Lex Scantinia*, 183; *Lex Titia*, 236; *Lex Valeria Horatia*, 223; *Lex Villia*, 228; Twelve Tables, 77–78, 230–31, 246, 256, 339, 434

libertus/a (*liberti/ae*) (freedmen/freedwomen/ freedpersons), 10, 36, 48, 50, 51–52, 58, 89, 105, 131, 426; importance of advertising status, 63; legal standing of, 89, 90; marriage, 102–3; obligations of, 89–90; prejudices against, 58–59; rights of, 61; in Roman households, 107–8; social mobility of, 57; status of, 55

lictors, 228, 426

limes, 39, 40, 41

literacy, 123, 359

literary evidence, xxvii–xxix, 4–5, 7–8, 13–14, 19, 332

literature, xxvii–xxix, 19; adoption of foreign cultural practices and, 146–47; authors from other regions of Italy, 147; beginning of, 144, 146; chronology, 144–46; comedy, xxvii, 148, 149, 268, 421; debate over place of, 141–42; defining, 140–44; drama, 148; early Roman, 144; education and, 142; elite and, 153–58; on emperors, 156–57; end of Latin, 146; endurance of, 143–44; errors in manuscript copying, xxviii–xxix; expansion and, 147–48; Flavian period, 158; genres of, xxvii, 142–43; Golden Age (Augustan), 145–46, 152–53, 155 56, 159; Greek literary culture and, 144–45, 147–49, 149–50, 153, 160; historians' relationship with, 12–14; history and mythology in, 143; importance of, 139; influence on later literature, 153; in late Republic period, 144–45, 150–52, 159; as leisure, 140, 141, 142; narratives of cultural decline, 158–60, 160–61; Neronian period, 157–58; patronage and, 154–55, 158; philosophy and history in, 159–60; Pliny the Younger on, 140–42; pro- versus anti-Augustan, 155–56; representation and social reality, 154–55; Silver Age (early imperial period), 145–46, 159–60; spirit of play in, 149; study of, 125–26, 131; terminology in, 154; Tiberian period, 157; timeline of, 140; use of term, 142, 160; verse satire, 149, 166

liturgies, 343–44

Livia (wife of Augustus), 35, 101, 386

Livy, 77, 146, 217, 218, 224, 270, 271, 310, 332, 348; on Augustus, 156; on end of Monarchy, 23. Works: *On Architecture*, 145; *From the Foundation of the City (Ab urbe condita)*, 152–53

loans, 338–40

Lucan, 158; *Civil War*, 143, 159

Lucian of Samosata, 129; *The Dream (Somnium)*, 117–18

Lucilius, 149

Lucius Verus, 39, 40, 320

Lucretia, 23

Lucretius, 150, 356; *De Rerum Natura (On the Nature of Things)*, 150

ludi (games), 148, 265–66, 266–72, 427; athletic events, 270–71; *circenses*, 266, 427; cost of, 279; performances of, 268; principal, 266; *scaenici*, 266, 267, 268, 427; temporary structures for, 266–68

ludi magister, 122, 133, 427

Ludi Megalenses ("Megalesian Games"), 147

Ludi Romani ("Roman Games"), 146, 270, 271

Ludi Saeculares, 268, 427

Ludus Magnus, 274

luxuries, trade in, 347

Macedonia, 27, 315, 326

machina, 358, 427

machine: derivation of term, 358

Macrinus, 42

Maecenas, 33, 155, 156

Magerius, mosaic of, 279–82

magic, 213

magistrates, 227–36; annually elected, 228–33; curule, 201, 227 28; with *imperium*, 227, 228; judicial powers of, 248; minimum ages of, 228; other, 234–36; tribunes, 234; "new men", 229–31; *see also* aediles; censors; consuls; praetors; quaestors

manumission, 16, 51, 54, 74, 78, 89–90, 426, 427; as control mechanism, 90, 91; legal status and, 89; restrictions on, 90; in Roman households, 107–8; *see also* slavery; slaves

marble, 379, 380, 383, 388, 394, 397

Marc Antony, 58, 32, 145, 151, 236, 294; Cicero's oratorical attacks on, 16; conflict with Octavian, 313, 317; relationship with Cleopatra, 32–33

Marcella, Minicia, 128–29

Marcellus, Claudius, 34, 231, 312

Marcomannic Wars, 40

Marcus Aurelius, 39–40, 320–21

Marius, Gaius, 29, 53, 231, 233, 294, 316

marriage, 98; affection in, 100, 101; age of, 98; Augustus's laws of, 105–6; *concordia* and, 101, 422; *conubium*, 76–77, 98, 422; *cum manu*, 99, 427; forms of, 99; lack of intent to be married, 102–3; legitimate versus illegitimate, 102; nature of relationship, 100–101; political jockeying and, 99–100; property ownership and, 100, 112; *sine manu*, 99, 100, 427; women's experience of, 100

Martial, 122, 124, 143, 155, 158, 176, 179, 182, *Epigrams*, 157, 158, 180, 181, 184

Massilia, 315

masters of the horse, 227

materfamilias (*matresfamilias*), 97, 114n3, 427

material culture, 379–80; artifacts, xxix–xxx; continuous historical narrative in, 393; fine

household items, 389–90; Greek, 380–81; reflection of economic and social change, 395–99; relief sculpture, 392–93; *see also* architecture; art
Mater Magna, cult of, 204, 205, 207
Maximian, 42, 323
maxims and sayings, 123, 127, 130–31
Maximus, Quintus Fabius ("the Delayer"), 311
Mediterranean Sea, 39, 296, 363–64, 365
Melissus (slave), 61–62
men: ideal body type, 177; as religious officials, 200
merchant vessels, 365–66
Mesopotamia, 38, 39, 319, 320, 323
Messalla, Marcus Valerius, 202
metals: trade in, 348
military. *See* army
military diploma, 291–92, 427; text of, 291, *292*
Millar, Fergus: *The Emperor in the Roman World*, 12; Hopkins on, 13
mills, grain, 372
Milo, Titus Annius, 31
mime, 268, 427
Minerva, 196
mining, 348
missio ("release"), 277, 427
Mithras, cult of, 203
Mithridates, king of Pontus, 316
Mithridatic War, 29, 316
modillions, 389, 427
Monarchy: expulsion of, 23–24, 25, 26; use of term, xxvi
moneylending, 332, 338–39, 340, 349; elite and, 339, 340
morals: education and, 130–34
Morgan, Teresa, 131
mosaics, 373, 381–82
Mount Vesuvius, xxvii, xxxi, xxxii, 37, 165, 209, 360, 384; date of eruption, xxviii–xxix
munus (*munera*), 265, 266, 272–79, 427; *see also ludi*
Museum Herculanense: *secretum* ("secret museum"), 167

Nabataea, 319
Nabis, king of Sparta, 217, 218, 219
names: freedpersons and, 107–8; legal standing and, 50, 51
Narcissus, 64–65
natural philosophy (science), 150, 356, 358, 427
nature versus nurture debate, 170, 427–28
navigation, marine, 364
Nearer Spain: textiles from, 348
neoteroi, 428
Nero, 35, 36, 157–8, 274, 295, 319, 390; Great Fire and, 391; performances of, 269–70, 283
Neronia, 269–70
Nerva, Marcus Cocceius, 38

New France: slaves in, 75
nexum (debt bondage), 47, 59, 77, 428
Nicomedia, 204, 323, 374
Nielsen, Hanne Sigismund, 102
Niger Pescennius, 41
Nisbet, Gideon, 408
Nobilior, Marcus Fulvius, 270
nobilis (*nobiles*), 53, 428
nome, 336, 428
novus homo (*novi homines*) ("new man"), 53, 150, 231–33, 428
Numa (second king of Rome), 197
numismatics, xxx–xxxi, 19
nutrix (*nutrices*), 120, 428

Obscene Publications Act (UK), 168
obsequium, 51, 89, 426, 428
occupations: engineers, 355, 357–58, 373; physicians, 129, 130; of slaves, 129–30, 133
Octavian. *See* Augustus
Oleson, John Peter, 359
olive oil: trade in, 347
opera (*operae*), 51, 89–90, 107, 426, 428
optimates ("best men"), 28, 235
opus caementicium, 366; *see also* concrete
opus incertum, 366, 428
opus reticulatum, 366, 428
opus sectile, 394, *398*, 428
opus signinum, 369, 428
opus testaceum, 367, 428
oracles, 147
oratory: decline of, 158–59
orders, 428; Italic and Ionic, 382–83; Roman Corinthian, 388–89
ordo, 52, 428
Ostia, 255, 336, 366, 368, 370
Ostrogoths, 324
Otho, 36
ovation, 310, 428–29
Ovid, 85; exile of, 139, 157. Works: *Art of Love* (*Ars Amatoria*), 139, 157, 175–76, 177; *Fasti*, 145; *Medea*, 145; *Metamorphoses*, 143, 144, 146; *Poems of Sorrow* (*Tristia*), 157; *Propertius*, 145
Oxyrhynchus Papyrus, 301

paedagogus (*paedagogi*), 120, 429
Palaemon, Quintus Remmius, 133
Palatine Hill, 37, 147, 152, 271, 391–92
Palatine Library, 152
Palmyra, 347, 348
Palmyrenes: rebellion of, 322–23
panegyric, 145, 156, 429
Pantheon, 39, *367*, 367, 375, 392, 429
pantomime, 268–69, 429

Papio-Poppaean law, 105
papyrological evidence, xxxii, xxxiii n22, 19
paraphylakes, 254, 255; relief depicting, *254*
parents: education of children and, 118, 132–33;
    hierarchy of duty and, 103
Parthians, 40, 318, 319, 325; conflict with, 320
paterfamilias (*patresfamilias*), 95, 131, 172, 429;
    authority of, 97, 99, 104, 115n23
patria potestas, 97, 104, 429
patricians, 26, 52–53, 223, 229, 235, 332, 429
patronage, 10, 65–66, 154–55, 222, 237, 270, 340, 429
patronus (*patroni*), 65, 89–90, 107, 154, 237, 426,
    429; depicting, 384
Paulinus, Decmus Theodorus, 231
Paullus, Lucius Aemilius, 78, 234
Paulus, 90
pax deorum ("peace of the gods"), 194
pax Romana, 318–21
Peace of Nisibis, 323
Peachin, Michael, 4
Pedanius Secundus, 83, 84
pederasty, 182–83
Peina (slave girl), 89
Pepsi commercial, 409
Pergamum, king of, 315
Pericles: on women, 5, 6
Perseus Digital Library, 417
Perseus (son of Philip), 314, 315
Persius, 153–54, 159; *Satires*, 154
Pertinax, Publius Helvius, 40–41
Petrarch, 146
Petronius, 158; *Satyricon*, 159, 182, 301, 338
pets, 121
phallus, 173–74; as apotropaic object, 173–74, 186
Philip V, 311, 313, 314
Philocalus, Furius, 122, 133
philosophy: study of, 132
physicians, 129, 130
Piazza Navona, 270, 429
piers, 363
pilleus, 60
pirates, 59, 244
Pisonian conspiracy, 157–58, 429
plague, 334
Plancus, Lucius Minutius, 234
Plato, 149
Plautius Silvanus, 244
Plautus, 146, 149, 256–57
play: early education and, 121
Plebian Assembly. *See concilium plebis tributum*
    (Tribal Assembly of Plebians)
plebians, 26, 33, 52–53, 219, 225, 332, 429; voting
    assembly of, 223–24
plebiscitum (*plebiscita*), 26, 53, 223, 429–30

Pliny the Elder, 332, 349, 360, 384; death in
    Pompeii, xxvii–xxviii
Pliny the Younger, 47, 64, 85, 140–42, 159–60,
    204, 237, 256, 342; Calpurnia (wife), 101;
    correspondence with Trajan, 38; on dining
    etiquette, 63; on land ownership, 335, 336; on
    moneylending, 338. Works: *Epistulae* (*Letters*),
    140–42, 158, 272, 374; letter to Tacitus,
    xxvii–xxviii; *Panegyric*, 38
Plotina (wife of Trajan), 39
Plutarch, 79–80, 120, 129, 130, 132, 309, 314, 348;
    study of, 126. Works: *Cato Maior*, 330; *How the
    Young Man Should Study Poetry*, 126; *Life of Aemilius
    Paullus*, 381; *Life of Sulla*, 30; *Moralia*, 87, 318
Michigan Papyri, 245
poetry, xxvii, 150; aetiological elegy, 145, 419;
    comedy, xxvii, 148, 149, 268, 421; didactic, 145,
    423; epic, 5, 145, 148, 150, 153; genres of, 145;
    Hellenistic (Greek), 144–45, 148, 154; lyric, 145,
    153, 427; panegyric, 145, 156; pastoral, 145, 153,
    429; study of, 125, 131; tragedy, xxvii, 131, 145,
    148; *see also* literature
poets, 144–45; Augustan cohort, 145; *neoteroi*, 145;
    relationship with political class, 154–55
policing officials, 250–55, 258; activities of, 253–55;
    evidence on Egyptian papyri, 254–55; outside Rome,
    252–53; in Rome, 250–52; soldiers as, 300–301
political office, 61; games and, 281; popularity and,
    53–54; religious office and, 200–201, 213
political system. *See* government
Polybius, 148, 217, 298, 313–14, 348; *History*, 365
Polynices, Marcus Aurelius, 272, 273, 283
polytheism, 205, 211
pomerium, 232, 430
Pompeii, 61, 167, 430; as ancient evidence, xxvii;
    excavation of, xxix; Macellum, 382; procession
    scene in Via dell'Abbondanza, 205, *206*; remains
    of houses in, 109, 110; *spolia* in, 398, veterans in,
    301; wall paintings and mosaics from, 381–82,
    water distribution in, 369, 370
Pompey the Great, 128, 228, 316; conflict with
    Caesar, 317; Pompeia (daughter), 122, 126; theatre
    of, 266
Pomponia (wife of Quintus), 101
Pont de Gard, 369, 430
pontifex (*pontices*), 194, 201, 430
pontifex maximus, 28, 203, 236, 386, 430; Augustus
    as, 33, 238; Caesar as, 32, 201; Marcus Aurelius
    as, 39
popular assembly, 26
popular culture, 404–5; historical accuracy in, 405–8;
    influence of Roman culture in, 409–10; Romans
    depicted in, 408–9
populares ("populists"), 28, 235

population: of Roman Empire, 333–34
Porcia (daughter of Cato the Younger), 99–100
pornography: concern with, 168; labelling art as, 166
Porticus Aemilia, 367, 375, 385, 430
Portland Vase, 389–90, *390*
ports: trade and, 347
Potitus Lucius Valerius, 230
pottery and ceramics: Greek, 381; trade in, 349
pozzolana, 368, 384, 422, 430
praefectus urbi, 40, 83, 430
praetor peregrinus ("foreign Praetor"), 229
praetors, 26, 227, 229, 230, 233, 430
praetor urbanus ("urban praetor"), 229
Priapus, wall painting of, *164*
Price Edict of Diocletian, 332, 431
priesthoods, 26, 201–3, 236; archives, 194; colleges,
    191, 200–201, 421; auspication and, 201–2
priests, 203; conflicts between magisterial and priestly
    roles, 202–3; knowledge of, 203; not full-time role,
    202–3; religious authority of, 202
primary sources, xxvii, xxxiii n1; databases of artistic
    and archaeological material, 416; sourcebooks,
    413–15; translations, 415
primus inter pares ("first among equals"), 33
princeps, 33, 45n2, 145, 431
Principate period, 25, 33, 45n2, 246, 289, 339, 431
procurators, 34, 431
prodigium (*prodigia*), 202, 431
production, 349; agrarian, 346; places of, 344–46;
    per capita, 333, 429; pottery and ceramics, 344–
    45; textiles, 344
programmata, xxxi
Propertius, 152, 209
pro praetor ("with the authority of a praetor"), 229
Prosenes, Marcus Aurelius, 211; sarcophagus of, 208
prostitutes, 105, 174, 183; soldiers and, 302
provinces: administration of, 56; class and status in,
    55–57, 58; Roman and local identities/culture in,
    57; study of, 10–11; taxation, 333, 341
pseudo-peripteral, 382, 431
Ptolemy VIII of Egypt, 28
publica iudicia ("public courts"), 248
publicani, 31, 315, 341, 342, 431
public works, 333
Publius Quinctilius Varus, 34
Pulcher, Appius Claudius, 202
Pulcher, Publius Clodius, 31
pulvinar (imperial box), 271, 431
Punic Wars, 27; First, 27, 229, 310–11, 365; Second
    (Hannibalic War), 27, 312, 313, 315, 326; Third,
    27, 313
punishments, 78, 88, 249–50; *see also* justice system
Pylades of Cilicia, 268
Pyrrhus of Epirus, king, 309, 326

quaestio (*quaestiones*), 248, 251, 431
quaestio de adulteriis, 172
quaestiones perpetuae ("permanent jury courts"), 247,
    248
quaestor, 26, 225, 228, 233, 431
(quin)decimviri sacris faciundis, 201–2, 204, 431–32
Quintilian, 120, 121, 122, 123, 125, 126, 130, 183;
    The Orator's Education (*Institutio Oratoria*), 120,
    125; on teachers, 133

rape, 185–86
reception studies, 408
Rectus, Aemilius, 345
relief sculpture, 373, 392–93
religio, 211, 432
religion, 191; Augustus and, 33; civic, 191, 197–203,
    204, 403; civic versus non-civic, 206, 213–14;
    diversity at Rome, 206–7, 211, 212, 213; domestic
    worship, 209–11, 213; foreign, 206–7; individual
    preference and, 211; local and regional nature of,
    204–5; officials, 200–201; processions, 205; *religio*
    versus *superstitio*, 211; ritual communication, 195;
    ritual practice versus belief, 194–95; at Rome,
    204–13; sacrifice, 195–96; timeline of, 190
remarriage, 101, 102
Renaissance, writers of the, 146
Republic: demise of, 33; end of, 315–17; institution
    of, 23, 25; land ownership under, 334; use of term,
    xxvi
Res Gestae Divi Sapris, 322
rhetoric, 126–29, 131, 142; study in Latin versus
    Greek, 127; use of sayings and maxims, 127
rhetor (*rhetores*), 126, 432
roads, 361–62, 374
Romanization, 11, 56–57
Roman Military Diplomas, 291
Rome, 25, 308; under Augustus, 34, 388; Flavian
    building program, 36, 37; "great drain" (*cloaca
    maxima*), 26; Great Fire of 64 CE, 390, 391;
    kingship of early, 25–26; map of sacred
    topography, *192*; population of, 334
Rome (television series), 72, 298, 407
Romulus, 25, 52, 156, 197, 271
Romulus Augustulus, 238
Rostovtzeff, Michael, 4, 333; *The Social and Economic
    History of the Roman Empire*, 8–9, 332
Rufus, Caninius, 140, 141
Rufus, Musonius, 132

sacramentum (legion's oath), 288, 432
sacra publica populi Romani, 197, 432
sacrifice, 195–96; civic religion and, 198
Saguntum, 27, 310, 311
Saint-Just of Valabrère, 398, *398*

Saller, Richard, 11, 14, 107
Sallust, 53, 59, 151–52, 153, 160; *The War with Jugurtha*, 233
Salus Augusti or Augusta, 196
Salus Publica (goddess), 196, 197
Sanctuary of Fortuna, 385, *385*
Sanctuary of Jupiter Anxur, 366
Sasanian dynasty, 322, 325, 326
Sassanid Empire, 308, 309, 325
Saturnalia, 65
Saturninus, Lucius Antonius, 37
Scaevola, Quintus Mucius, 128
Scheidel, Walter, 17, 81
scholarship, debates: anachronism, 15; concepts and jargon, 13–14; cross-cultural comparisons, 14–15; theoretical approaches, 14
school, 121–22, *125*; *see also* education
Scipio Nascia, Publius Cornelius, 27, 226, 231, 312, 313
Scipio Nascia, Publius, 28
Scipio, Gnaeus, 312
Scipio Aemilianus, Cornelius, 148, 315
Scipio Asiaticus, Lucius Cornelius, 314
Scribonia Attice: tomb of, *95*, 95
seafaring, 364–66; marine warfare, 364–65; merchant vessels, 365–66
secondary sources, xxvii, xxxiii n1, 416–18; atlases and topographical dictionaries, 416–17; bibliographic databases, 418; dictionaries and encyclopedias, 416; introductions, 417–18
Second Triumvirate, 32
Seleucia-Ctesiphon, 326
Seleucid, 316
Sejanus, Lucius Aelius, 35
senate, 26, 33, 52, 54, 225–27, 238, 319, 432; authority of, 226–27; at Constantinople, 238; decision-making by, 223, 226–27; imperial, 227; interest rates and, 339; origins of, 225; Punic wars and, 313
senatorial order, 52, 54–55, 105, 282, 303, 432; crimes involving, 246; ejection from senate, 59; struggle with *populares*, 28
senators, 59–60, 225–27, 237–38
senatus consultum de aedificiis non diruendis ("decree of the senate regarding not demolishing buildings"), 337–38
senatus consultum ultimum ("final decree of the senate"), 29, 31, 226, 432
Senatus Populusque Romanus (SPQR), 33
Seneca, 132, 133, 158, 159, 180–81, 257–58, 275; Helvia (mother), 132; Novatilla (daughter), 132
Seneca the Younger, 356
seniores ("elders"), 220, 221
sententiae, 123, 142, 432

"Servian constitution", 219–21
Servius Tullius, 77, 219
sesterces, 52, 432
Seutonius, 34
Severans: period of the, 40–42
Severus, Septimus Lucius, 41, 63–64, 78, 281, 293, 321; campaigns of, 321–22; Geta (son), 41–42, 321; Julia Domna (wife), 41, 321
sex, 432; use of term, 169
Sextius, Lucius, 231
sexual categories, 171
sexuality, 18, 164–65, 432; artistic representation of, xxx, 166; biological constant, 170–71; constructivist views of, 169–70; depicted in film, 408–9; essentialist views of, 169; female, 174–77; female homosexuality, 183–84; law and, 184–86; literary sources, 165–67; oral sex, 179, 186; passive-sexual labels as abuse, 181–82; pederasty, 182–83; penetration and status, 180–81; penetrative model of, 171; phallocentric, 171, 181; pleasure and, 165; Roman attitudes towards, xxx; same-sex couplings, 179–81, 186; stereotypes of male, 181–82; timeline of, 165; use of term, 169
sexual orientation, 169, 171
sexual roles: gender and social status and, 171
sexual scenes, 177–78, 186; private houses, 177–78; public places, 178
sexual standards, 166
Shapur I, Sasanian king, 322
ships and shipbuilding, 364–65, 372
shrines, domestic, 209–10
Sibylline Books, 202, 204, 207, 432–33
Sicily, 27
sine missione ("without release"), 277, 433
slave markets, 80–81, 348
slave-owning society, 74
slavery, 6, 72–91; evidence of experience of, xxix, 82–83, 85; intensification of, 78; invocation of, 15–16; in provinces, 56; qualitative approach to, 75, 76, 90; quantitative approach to, 74–75, 75–76, 90; self-enslavement, 81; success at Rome, 88–90; timeline of, 73
slaves, 65, 402; abandoned children as, 79–80; in American South, 85; apprenticeship for, 129; as both *persona* and *res*, 76–77; as chattel, 75, 76; children of, 79; crime prevention and, 256; cross-cultural analysis of experience of, 85–86; debt, 75, 77; economic value of work by, 107; education of, 123–24, 134; estimates of number of, 75–76; facilities for, 81; family units of, 108; gaps in evidence of experience of, 90; home-born (*vernae*), 64, 79, 103, 107, 434; importation of, 80–81; inducements for good behaviour, 89; job specialization, 83–84; legal

standing of, 51; management of landholdings and, 335–36; mechanisms of control, 88–90, 90–91; mistreatment of, 84–85, 87; in New France, 86; occupations of, 129–30, 133; pendants of, 88–89; personal relationships of, 85; population in Rome, 78; quarters for, 111–12; rape and, 186; rebellion and resistance, 87; roles on *latifundia*, 79; in Roman households, 107–8; runaway (*fugitivi/ ae*), 74, 88–89, 425; social mobility of, 57; society with, 74–75; sources of, 77–81, 90; status and, 48–49; status of, 55; tasks of, 83–84, 88; trade in, 348; yearly demand for, 81; *see also* manumission

Smirat: mosaic of *venatio* held in, 279–81, *281*, 282

social disparity, 47, 52, 55, 402–3; omnipresence of, 66–67; visual and behavioural distinctions, 59–60

social history, 2–3, 9; classicists and, 4; debates and problems, 11–15; development of, 3–4; study of, 19; Trevelyan's definition of, 15

social mobility, 47, 57–59, 66; acceptance of, 58–59; advertising acquisition of higher status, 63–64; demotion, 59; importance of advertising, 63–64; of slaves, 57

social stratification: patronage and, 65–66; persistence of, 65–67; seating at public entertainments, 60; social success and, 66; social ties and, 65

Social War, 29, 222, 301, 311, 316

society, Roman, 2–3; use of term, xxvi

socius (*socii*), 27, 433

soldiers, 304; appearance of, 306n25; crimes by, 301; effect of warfare on, 299; families of, 302, 306n44; loyalty to commanders, 29; policing duties of, 252–53, 255, 300–301; as tax collectors, 342; *see also* army

sourcebooks, 413–15; translations of, 415

sources: abbreviations, xvii–xxiv; historians' relationship with, 12–14; *see also* primary sources; secondary sources

Spartacus, 31, 87

Spartacus (film), 408–9

spatial illusionism, 392, 433

spolia, 398, 433

Spurius Furius, 229

stataria, 80, 433

stationarii ("post-holders"), 252–53

statues, 394

status, 18, 26, 47, 48, 50–52, 67, 79, 119, 433; access to justice and, 60–61; adopting visual markers of higher, 62–63; changes over time, 52–57; courts and, 249; desire for improved, 61–62; education and, 119; etiquette errors, 64–65; importance of, 61–65; land ownership and, 335; as legal standing, 50, 51–52; marriage and, 102; provinces and, 55–57, 58; sexuality and, 171, 180–81; slaves and, 48–49, 57; as social prestige,

50; stereotypes and, 62; timeline of, 47; treatment of individuals and, 62, 64

Ste. Croix. Geoffrey de: *The Class Struggle in the Ancient Greek World from the Archaic Age to the Arab Conquests*, 14

Strabo, Gnaeus Pompeius, 29, 30–31; death of, 31–32

streets, 361–62; derivation of term, 362

stuprum ("sexual misconduct"), 184–86, 433

suasoriae, 127, 433

Suburban Baths, 178, 179

Suetonius, 78, 96, 126, 133, 212, 277; *On Teachers of Grammar and Rhetoric* (*De grammaticis et rhetoribus*), 125, 133

Sulla, Lucius Cornelius, 29–30, 228, 247, 288, 316

summa rudis ("chief stick"), 277, 433

superstitio, 211, 433

Syria, 40, 41, 320, 326

Tacitus, 36, 84, 112, 142, 160, 244, 264, 266, 332, 391; *Agricola*, 217; *Annals*, 23, 267; *Dialogus de oratoribus* ("Dialogues on Oratory"), 159

Tarentum, 311–12

Tarpeian Rock, 78

Tarquinius Priscus, 270

Tarquinius Superbus, 23

Tatum, Jeffrey, 409

Taurus, Statilius, 33, 273

taxation, 340–44, 349; Augustus and, 33; community responsibility for deficits, 344; *decuma* (tithe), 341; *ius Italicum* ("Italian right"), 330, 341, 426; *portoria* (customs duties), 341, 342, 350; *stipendium*, 341; *tributum*, 341; use of revenues, 340–41; *vectigalia* ("indirect taxes"), 341–42

tax collection, 342–44; liturgies, 343–44; officials, 345

teachers: criticisms of, 133–34; influence of, 135; misconduct of, 133, 183; *see also* education

technology: artifacts of, 356–57; literary evidence of, 357, 359; derivation of term, 358; maritime, 364–65; from other cultures, 358, 361, 374; terminology, 357–58; timeline of, 356; transfer of knowledge, 358–59

Tellus panel, 386

temples, 198–200; design of, 380–81; Tempe of Bellona, 310; Temple of Apollo, 152, 200; Temple of Diana Planciana, 199; Temple of Jupiter Optimus Maximus, 380–81; Temple of Jupiter Tonans, 200; Temple of Mars Ultor, 387, 388, *389*, 389; Temple of Peace, Paestum, 388; Temple of Portunus, 382; Temple of Tellus, 199; Temple of Venus and Roma, 39

Terence, 146, 149

Terentia (wife of Cicero), 100, 101

tetrarchy ("rule of four"), 42, 146, 323, 398–99, 433; junior ("Caesar"), 42, 399; sculptures of, 398–99; senior ("Augustus"), 42, 399
textiles: trade in, 348–49
Theatre of Pompey, 148, 200
theatres, 54, 148, 254, 264, 265, 266, 433
theatrical performances: competitive, 269–70; Greek influence on, 268; for *ludi*, 268
Theocritus: *Idylls*, 153
Theodosian Code, 80
Theodosius, 324
theory, 14
thermae, 368, 372, 433–34
Third-Century Crisis, 323
Third Macedonian War, 78, 314–15
Thucydides, 152
Tiberius, 34, 35, 157, 227, 238, 244, 319, 345; Vipsania Agrippina (wife), 101
time, 143
tirocinium fori ("recruitment to the forum"), 128
Titus, 37, 390
togas, 59–60, 61
Togatus Barberini, or *Man with His Ancestors*, 53, 54, 384
Tomb of the Haterii, 372, 373, 434
tombstone: free born and freedpersons sharing, 114n5; inscriptions, 97–98, 107
torture: used in courts, 249
toys, 121
trade, 349–50; expansion of empire and, 344; long distance, 346, 347; in luxuries, 347; in metals, 348; other commodities, 347; in pottery and ceramics, 349; in slaves, 348; in textiles, 348–49; transportation and, 346–47; transportation by sea, 365–66; wine and food, 347–48
tradespeople, 373; *see also* craftpersons
tragedy, xxvii, 131, 145, 148, 434; Greek, 268
Trajan (Traianus), 38, 204, 275, 288, 291, 307, 319–20; Roman army and, 295
Trajan's Column, 38, 290, *300*, 319, 362, *393*, 393
translations: of sourcebooks, 415
transport, water (sea), 363–66
Treggiari, Susan, 103
tresviri capitales, 251
Trevelyan, G.M., 15
tria nomina, 50
tribes, 221–23
tribunes, 26, 53, 223, 234–36, 434; consular, 233; with consular power, 230
triumph, 31, 310, 390, 429, 430, 434
triumvirs, 31, 434
Triumvirs for the Restoration of the State (*Triumviri Rei Publicae Constituendae*), 32
tutors, 99, 121, 122; of *grammaticē*, 124; *see also grammaticus*

Vindolanda: the Latin Writing Tablets, 254, 303
Twelve Tables, 77–78, 230–31, 246, 256, 434; moneylending and, 339
Tyrannio, 124

Urso: games at, 279, 280

Valens, 324
Valerian, 322
Valerius, Lucius, 224
Varius: Thyestes, 145
Varro, 79, 311
Varus, Quinctilius, 318
Vedius Pollio, 64
Vegetius, 288
Velleius Paterculus, 128
venalicius (venalicii), 81, 82, 434
venationes, 274–75, 279–81, 434
veneer, 394, 434
Vergil, 404; on Augustus, 156. Works: *Aeneid*, 145, 152; *Eclogues*, 145, 153; *Georgics*, 145
verism, 383–84, 434; art historical theories of, 384
verna (vernae), 64, 79, 103, 107, 434
Verrius Flaccus, 124
Vespasian, 36–37, 197, 203, 319, 390; divinization of, 196; as *pontifex maximus*, 203
Vestal Virgins, 200
veterans: remuneration for, 289, 294
vexillations, 297, 434–35
Via Appia (Appian Way), 38, 361–62
Vibia Matidia, portrait bust of, *394*
vici, 300, 302, 435
vigiles, 251, 252, 435
vilicus/vilica, 83, 435
Villa of the Papyri, xxxii
villas, 396–97
Vindex, Julius, 36
Vindolanda, 253, 302, 332, 435
Vitellius, 36
Vitruvius, 110, 359, 370, 372; *On Architecture (De architectura)*, 109, 355, 359, 396
Vologeses IV, King, 320
voting assemblies, 219–25, 239; *comita centuriata* (Centuriate Assembly), 49–50, 220, 221, 222, 224, 421; *comita curia* (Curial Assembly), 224–25; *comita tributa* (Tribal Assembly), 221–23, 224, 421; *concilium plebis tributum* (Tribal Assembly of Plebians), 53, 223–24, 224, 229, 235, 421–22, 434; "Servian constitution", 219–21
voting rights, 61, 89
votum (vota), 435; of Arval Brothers, 192–93; of consuls, 191

Wallace Hadrill, Andrew, 110

wall paintings, 373, 381–82; of domestic sacrificial scene, *209*, 210; from Marcellum, Pompeii, *382*

walls: construction of, 366, 367

warfare, 296–99; aftermath, 299; battles, 298; *bellum iustum* ("just war"), 309–10, 311, 313, 420; civil war, 293, 295; marine, 364–65; in middle Republic, 27–28; overseas, 315, 316; political rivalry and, 312; preparing for, 296–98; processions and honours for, 310; slavery and, 78–79

water supply, 358, 360, 368–70, 372, 375; distribution in cities, 369–70; in provinces, 369

wealth, 47, 48, 67; military service and, 219–20; political power and, 220–21; status and, 53

weapons, 33, 322; of auxiliaries, 290; of gladiators, 276; of legions, 288

Weber, Max, 9

Wiedemann, Thomas, 275

Williams, C., 164, 181

wine: trade in, 347, 348

Winkler, Martin, 408

wives, 98–103; education of, 128–29; household duties, 100; legal authority of, 99; retention of rights of, 99; ties to own *paterfamilias*, 99, 100

women, 1–2, 6–7, 16; adultery and, 172–73; education of, 132; experience of marriage, 100; in Greek society, 5–6; heterogeneity of experiences of, 18; ideal body type, 176–77; maxims about, 131; "new", 1–2, 6–7; as religious functionaries, 200; sexuality and, 174–77; soldiers and, 302

Year of the Four Emperors, 36, 319

Zenobia, 322–23